MW01028825

THE MACARTHUR NEW TESTAMENT COMMENTARY

2 CORINTHIANS

John MacArthur

MOODY PUBLISHERS/CHICAGO

All Scripture quotations, unless otherwise indicated, are taken from the *New American Standard Bible®*, Copyright © The Lockman Foundation 1960, 1962, 1963, 1968, 1971, 1972, 1973, 1975, 1977, 1995. Used by permission.

Scripture quotations marked NKJV are taken from the *New King James Version.* Copyright © 1982 by Thomas Nelson, Inc. Used by permission. All rights reserved.

Scripture quotations marked NIV are taken from the *Holy Bible, New International Version®*. NIV.® Copyright © 1973, 1978, 1984 by International Bible Society. Used by permission of Zondervan Publishing House. All rights reserved.

Scripture quotations marked KJV are taken from the King James Version.

Cover Design: Smart Guys design

Library of Congress Cataloging-in-Publication Data

MacArthur, John
    2 Corinthians / John MacArthur
       p. cm. — (the MacArthur New Testament commentary)
    Includes bibliographical references and index.
    ISBN-13: 978-0-8024-0865-5
     1. Bible. N. T. Corinthians, 2nd—Commentaries. I. Title: Second Corinthians. II. Title.

BS2675.53.M23 2003
227'.3077—dc22

2003016632

There are many joys in my ministry—
among the highest is the cherished partnership with other men who,
by their sacrifice and devotion to God's truth,
have served in long faithfulness in the same direction.
Such a man is David Cotnoir who has lead the ministry of
Grace to You Canada for nearly two decades.
To him I dedicate this volume with deep gratitude.

Contents

Preface

It continues to be a rewarding, divine communion for me to preach expositionally through the New Testament. My goal is always to have deep fellowship with the Lord in the understanding of His Word and out of that experience to explain to His people what a passage means. In the words of Nehemiah 8:8, I strive "to give the sense" of it so they may truly hear God speak and, in so doing, may respond to Him.

Obviously, God's people need to understand Him, which demands knowing His Word of Truth (2 Tim. 2:15) and allowing that Word to dwell in them richly (Col. 3:16). The dominant thrust of my ministry, therefore, is to help make God's living Word alive to His people. It is a refreshing adventure.

This New Testament commentary series reflects this objective of explaining and applying Scripture. Some commentaries are primarily linguistic, others are mostly theological, and some are mainly homiletical. This one is basically explanatory, or expository. It is not linguistically technical but deals with linguistics when that seems helpful to proper interpretation. It is not theologically expansive but focuses on the major doctrines in each text and how they relate to the whole of Scripture. It is not primarily homiletical, although each unit of thought is generally treated as one chapter, with a clear outline and logical flow of thought.

Most truths are illustrated and applied with other Scripture. After establishing the context of a passage, I have tried to follow closely the writer's development and reasoning.

My prayer is that each reader will fully understand what the Holy Spirit is saying through this part of His Word, so that His revelation may lodge in the mind of believers and bring greater obedience and faithfulness—to the glory of our great God.

Introduction to 2 Corinthians

Second Corinthians is the most personally revealing of all Paul's epistles. At the same time, it is perhaps the least familiar of all his inspired writings, often overlooked both by individual believers and preachers alike. The neglect of this magnificent epistle is an immense loss to the church, however, for it has much to offer. No one in ministry should be ignorant of the riches of these insights. A church should not ordain anyone who has not read this epistle and commentaries on this treatise.

In 2 Corinthians Paul's godly character shines through as he interacts with the most troubled of his congregations. Its thirteen chapters reveal his humility; he described himself as a lowly clay pot (4:7), stressed his human weakness and inadequacy (3:5; 11:30; 12:5, 9–10), and was reluctant to defend himself when attacked (11:1, 16–17, 21; 12:11). Second Corinthians also reveals Paul's passionate concern for his flock, both for their spiritual growth (3:18; 7:1), and for their spiritual safety (11:2–4, 29). His declaration, "For we do not preach ourselves but Christ Jesus as Lord, and ourselves as your bond-servants for Jesus' sake" (4:5) sums up his selfless concern for them.

An effective, God-honoring minister must be spiritually sound, as Paul was. He was "not like many," who were guilty of "peddling the word of God, but as from sincerity, but as from God, [he spoke] in Christ in the sight of God" (2:17). The apostle would not think of "walking in craftiness or adulterating the word of God" (4:2).

Faithful, uncompromising preachers of the truth can expect a hostile reaction from the world, which will hate them like it hated Jesus (John 7:7; 15:19). No preacher in the history of the church has faced such intense persecution as did Paul, and in this letter he models how to handle suffering in the ministry (2 Cor. 1:4–10; 4:7–12; 6:4–10; 11:23–33).

Much of Paul's suffering in connection with the Corinthian church came from the savage attacks launched against him by a group of false apostles. Those charlatans had deceived some of the Corinthians into believing that Paul was weak, ineffective, and not a true apostle. The major theme of this epistle is Paul's defense of his integrity and his apostleship against those attacks (1:12–13; 2:17; 3:5; 4:2, 5; 5:9–10; 6:3–4, 11; 7:2; 8:20–21; 10:7; 11:5–6, 30; 12:11–12; 13:5–6).

Though it is an intensely intimate look at Paul, 2 Corinthians nonetheless contains rich theological truth. Here the new covenant receives its most complete exposition outside of Hebrews (3:6–18). In 2 Corinthians 5:1–11 Paul presents important teaching on what happens to believers when they die. Verses 14–21 of that same chapter discuss the doctrine of reconciliation, culminating in the fifteen Greek words of 5:21. They provide the most concise, yet profound summary of the substitutionary atonement of Jesus Christ to be found anywhere in Scripture. Similarly, 8:9 is a brief Christological gem of immense value.

Second Corinthians also has much to teach regarding the practical aspects of living the Christian life. In 6:14–7:1 Paul discusses the principle of separating from unbelievers. Chapters 8 and 9 provide the most detailed teaching on giving in the New Testament; chapter 11 gives instruction on how to distinguish true servants of God from false teachers (vv. 7–15, 20); and chapter 12 reveals how God uses suffering in the lives of His children (vv. 5–10). The epistle closes with a look at several important elements of the sanctification process (12:20–13:14).

THE CITY OF CORINTH

Few cities in the ancient world were blessed with as favorable a geographic location as Corinth was. The city was strategically located on the narrow isthmus connecting the mainland of Greece with the Peloponnesus, the large, leaf-shaped peninsula that makes up the southernmost part of Greece. (Since the completion of a canal across the isthmus in the late nineteenth century, the Peloponnesus is now technically an island.) Corinth thus controlled the trade route between the northern and southern parts of Greece. In addition, travelers going to and from Italy from northern Greece and Asia Minor embarked and disembarked from Corinth's port towns, Cenchrea on the southeastern side of the isthmus, and Lechaeum on the northwestern side. Since the isthmus was narrow (less than four miles wide at its narrowest; the road connecting Cenchrea and Lechaeum was about ten miles long), many ship's captains elected to unload their cargo at one of the two port cities and have it and their ship (if it was small enough) hauled across the isthmus to the other city, where they would reload their cargo and set sail again. They thus avoided a long and dangerous sea voyage around the southern tip of the Peloponnesus.

Corinth in Paul's day was a large and prosperous commercial city, one of the leading cities in Greece. It owed its prosperity not only to the trade that flowed through it, but to several other factors as well. Corinth hosted the biennial Isthmian Games, which drew large crowds to the city. It also had the coveted status of a Roman colony and was the capital of the Roman province of Achaia (which is why the city's unbelieving Jews were able to bring Paul before the Roman governor, Gallio; Acts 18:12–17). Corinthian brass and pottery wares were famous throughout the Roman world.

But Corinth also had its dark side. A sizeable percentage of its population consisted of slaves, and it was a center of the slave trade. Corinth was such an immoral city that its name became a byword for sexual vice; the verb "to Corinthianize" meant to commit sexual immorality, and "Corinthian girl" became a slang term for a prostitute.

Throughout its long history, Corinth had been one of the most influential of the Greek city-states, at times rivaling Athens in importance. But a major turning point in the city's history came in 146 B.C. when the invading Romans destroyed it and killed or sold into slavery all its inhabitants. The site lay in ruins for about a century, until Julius Caesar rebuilt it and resettled it, largely with freed slaves from all over the Roman world. Many cultured Greeks were aghast and scorned the new city's lower class population. Its status as a busy seaport and its booming economy drew large numbers of immigrants, adding to the ethnic melting pot of Corinth's population. The transient nature of much of that population contributed to the city's loose morals. Pfeiffer and Vos note that "much of the population was mobile (sailors, businessmen, government officials, *et al.*) and was therefore cut off from the inhibitions of a settled society" (*The Wycliffe Historical Geography of Bible Lands* [Chicago: Moody, 1967], 481).

It was to this wealthy, diverse, important, and immoral city that the apostle Paul came on his second missionary journey.

THE CHURCH AT CORINTH

Arriving in Corinth from Athens (Acts 18:1), Paul met Aquila and Priscilla, the husband and wife who became two of his closest associates (cf. Acts 18:18; Rom. 16:3; 1 Cor. 16:19; 2 Tim. 4:19). The pair had recently left Rome when Emperor Claudius ordered all Jews to leave the imperial city (Acts 18:2). Since they were tentmakers like himself, Paul lived and worked with them (v. 3).

As was his custom, the apostle began his evangelistic work in Corinth in the city's Jewish synagogue. Silas and Timothy, newly arrived from Macedonia, assisted him in the work (v. 5). As so often was the case, most of the Jews rejected the gospel and became hostile, causing the apostle to leave the synagogue for the house of "Titius Justus, a wor-shiper of God [i.e., a Gentile who had shown interest in Israel's God]" (v. 7). The unbelieving Jews' antagonism intensified when "Crispus, the leader of the synagogue, believed in the Lord with all his household," along with many others (v. 8). Hoping to capitalize on the inexperience of the new proconsul (governor) Gallio, the Jews hauled Paul before him, charging the apostle with worshiping God contrary to Jewish law (vv. 12–13). Gallio, however, refused to intervene in what he perceived as an internal dispute within Judaism and dismissed the charges against Paul (vv. 14–16). After staying "many days longer" (v. 18), the apostle left Corinth.

THE OCCASION OF SECOND CORINTHIANS

After his departure from Corinth, disturbing news reached Paul about problems that had arisen in the Corinthian church. In response, he wrote a noncanonical letter (not extant) in which he confronted those issues (1 Cor. 5:9). While ministering in Ephesus on his third missionary journey, Paul heard of still more trouble at Corinth (1 Cor. 1:11; 16:17). In addition, the Corinthians wrote him a letter seeking clarification on some issues (1 Cor. 7:1). Paul's response was to write them the letter known as 1 Corinthians. Since the apostle could not leave the work in Ephesus (1 Cor. 16:8), he sent Timothy (possibly bearing 1 Corinthians) to Corinth.

While 1 Corinthians apparently resolved some of the problems in Corinth, a new and potentially more dangerous threat soon arose. False teachers, claiming to be apostles sent by the Jerusalem church, arrived in Corinth and soon wooed many of the congregation away from their loyalty to Paul and the truth. (See the discussion of their identity in chapter 26 of this volume.). When Paul heard about this threat (possibly from Timothy), he left Ephesus and went to Corinth.

The visit (the "sorrowful," or "painful" visit; cf. 2 Cor. 2:1) did not go well, reaching its lowest ebb when someone (possibly one of the false apostles) defied Paul and openly insulted him (2:5–8, 10; 7:12). To his immense sorrow, the Corinthians did not take action against the offender. Paul returned to Ephesus, wrote a strongly worded letter (which also has not been preserved) known as the "severe letter" (see 2:4), and sent it to Corinth with Titus (7:5–16).

Leaving Ephesus, Paul went to Troas, where he hoped to meet Titus. Though there was an open door for ministry there, Paul's concern over the situation at Corinth prevented him from taking full advantage of it (2:12–13). Restless, unable to wait any longer for Titus, Paul went on to Macedonia where he at long last met him. Titus's news that most of the Corinthians had repented and reaffirmed their loyalty to Paul (7:7) brought great joy and relief to the apostle.

But he was wise enough to know that although the situation at Corinth had improved dramatically, the church was not out of danger yet. The false apostles were still there, and a minority of the Corinthians remained confused or loyal to them. As he prepared for his upcoming visit to Corinth (12:14; 13:1), Paul wrote 2 Corinthians from Macedonia (possibly from Philippi, as some ancient manuscripts indicate). In it he vigorously defended his apostleship against the false teachers' attacks, gave instruction regarding the collection for the poor believers at Jerusalem, and confronted the false apostles and their followers head-on.

THE AUTHOR OF 2 CORINTHIANS

That Paul wrote this epistle, as it twice claims (1:1; 10:1), is almost universally accepted, even by critical scholars who deny that Paul wrote other New Testament books attributed to him. It is impossible to imagine a motive for someone to forge such an emotional and highly personal letter. The letter's Pauline vocabulary, similarities to 1 Corinthians, and correlation with the evidence from Acts also prove Paul's authorship.

The external evidence also confirms that Paul wrote this letter. The church father Polycarp quoted from it early in the second century, while later in that century it was included in the Muratorian Canon. Clement of Alexandria, Iranaeus, and Tertullian also quote from 2 Corinthians.

THE UNITY OF 2 CORINTHIANS

While the authorship of 2 Corinthians has not been questioned, its unity has been the subject of much debate. In particular some scholars, without any reason other than their bent to discredit the integrity of Scripture, deny the book's unity. Noting the abrupt change in tone between chapters 1–9 and 10–13, they argue that they were originally two separate letters that somehow became fused into the letter now known as 2 Corinthians.

At the outset it must be stated that such theories are entirely subjective, based on supposed internal evidence within the book itself. R. C. H. Lenski writes,

> One fact in regard to Second Corinthians must be strongly emphasized at the very beginning: all, literally all textual evidence proves this letter a unit. No abbreviated text has ever been discovered that might raise a question on this score, and no text that showed an omission or omissions has ever been found. This fact alone stands as a bulwark against the hypotheses of our day. (*The Interpretation of Saint Paul's First and Second Epistles to the Corinthians* [Minneapolis: Augsburg, 1963], 795)

Further, there is no evidence from early translations of the Bible, or from the writings of the church fathers that 2 Corinthians ever existed as two or more separate letters. There is also no evidence as to who compiled those hypothetical letters into 2 Corinthians, when they did it, or why they did it, only conjecture on the part of the critics. What happened to the conclusion of the first letter and the introduction to the second to allow the two to be joined is also unknown; Donald Guthrie remarks, "It must have been extremely fortunate that the two depleted fragments happened to join together or were skillfully manipulated to make a single epistle with at least the appearance of a whole, enough at any rate to elude suspicion until the eighteenth century" (*New Testament Introduction* [Revised Ed.; Downer Grove, Ill.: InterVarsity, 1990], 451). The critics also often fail to take into account the physical difficulty involved in editing the scrolls on which ancient letters were written (for a discussion of this point, see David E. Garland, *2 Corinthians*, The New American Commentary [Nashville: Broadman & Holman, 1999], 38–39).

Some propose that chapters 10–13 are the severe letter mentioned in 2:4, and hence were written before chapters 1–9. This theory, however, faces major difficulties, in addition to the lack of textual evidence already noted.

First, the absence of any reference to the false apostles in chapters 1–9 is puzzling if the Corinthians had already received chapters 10–13. Even if they had rejected the false apostles before Paul wrote chapters 1–9, he surely would have commended them for doing so. Yet, chapters 1–9 do not mention the conflict between Paul and the false teachers, only the single individual who defied him (2:5–11; 7:12).

Second, chapters 10–13 are silent regarding that individual. Yet, the severe letter was written to deal with the Corinthians' refusal to discipline him (2:4–9). If chapters 10–13 constitute the severe letter, how could they fail to refer to the offense that prompted its writing?

Third, Paul described the severe letter as one written "out of much affliction and anguish of heart . . . with many tears" (2:4). That description does not seem to fit the contents of chapters 10–13, with Paul's biting irony and stern rebukes of the false teachers and their followers. Why would he regret (cf. 7:8) having so forcefully defended his apostleship, or relating his human weakness that proved God empowered his ministry?

Fourth, in 12:18 Paul spoke of Titus's trip to Corinth in connection with the collection (cf. 8:6, 16–24) as having already taken place. Since, as noted above, he brought the severe letter to Corinth on that trip, chapters 10–13 obviously cannot be the severe letter; Titus could not have delivered a letter describing his bringing of that letter as having already happened.

Finally, Paul sent the severe letter to avoid visiting Corinth (2:1–4), but he wrote chapters 10–13 to prepare for an upcoming visit (12:14; 13:1).

Others, acknowledging those difficulties, argue that chapters 10–13 were a separate letter, but one that was written after chapters 1–9. Once again, it must be noted that there is no evidence that chapters 10–13 ever circulated separately from chapters 1–9. A variation of that view is that before Paul sent chapters 1–9, he received word of further troubles in Corinth. He then wrote chapters 10–13 and sent the entire letter. Paul's busy life of ministering, traveling, and working to support himself may possibly have prevented him from writing 2 Corinthians at one sitting. Yet nowhere in chapters 10–13 does he mention receiving new information from Corinth.

The difference in tone between the two sections of the epistle must not be overstated. In chapters 1–9 Paul defended himself (e.g., 1:17; 4:2; 5:12–13), and rebuked the false teachers (e.g., 2:17); while in chapters 10–13 he expressed his love and concern for the Corinthians (11:11; 12:14–15; 13:9). When the plan of the epistle is taken into account, the reason for Paul's change in tone is perfectly understandable. Chapters 1–9 are addressed to the majority (cf. 2:6), who repented because of the severe letter; chapters 10–13 to the unrepentant minority, who still clung to the false apostles (the "some" in 10:2 who still regarded Paul as if he "walked according to the flesh").

DATE AND PLACE OF WRITING

The date of Paul's ministry in Corinth can be determined with reasonable accuracy because of his trial before the Roman proconsul Gallio. According to an inscription found in Delphi, Gallio most likely assumed office in July, A.D. 51. Paul's trial before him probably took place shortly after Gallio took office, toward the end of the apostle's ministry in Corinth (cf. Acts 18:18). Leaving Corinth, Paul went to Palestine via Ephesus (Acts 18:22). He returned to Ephesus on his third missionary journey (Acts 19:1), where he ministered for about two and a half years (Acts 19:8, 10). Paul wrote 1 Corinthians toward the end of his stay in Ephesus (1 Cor. 16:8), most likely late in A.D. 55. Paul planned to leave Ephesus after the Feast of Pentecost (1 Cor. 16:8), most likely in the spring of A.D. 56. He went to Macedonia from where, as noted above, he wrote 2 Corinthians later that year.

OUTLINE

I. Apostolic Ministry (1:1–7:16)
    A. The Minister's Greeting (1:1–11)
    B. The Minister's Plans (1:12–2:13)
        1. Concerning travel (1:12–2:4)
        2. Concerning the offender (2:5–11)
        3. Concerning Titus (2:12–13)
    C. The Ministry's Nature (2:14–7:16)
        1. Its triumph (2:14–17)
        2. Its commendation (3:1–5)
        3. Its basis (3:6–18)
        4. Its theme (4:1–7)
        5. Its trials (4:8–18)
        6. Its motivation (5:1–10)
        7. Its message (5:11–21)
        8. Its conduct (6:1–10)
        9. Its exhortation (6:11–7:16)

II. Apostolic Collection (8:1–9:15)
    A. The Pattern of Giving (8:1–9)
        1. The Macedonians (8:1–7)
        2. The Lord Jesus Christ (8:8–9)
    B. The Purpose of Giving (8:10–15)
    C. The Procedure of Giving (8:16–9:5)
    D. The Promise of Giving (9:6–15)

III. Apostolic Vindication (10:1–13:14)
   A. Paul's Authority (10:1–18)
   B. Paul's Conduct (11:1–15)
   C. Paul's Suffering (11:16–33)
   D. Paul's Credentials (12:1–13)
   E. Paul's Unselfishness (12:14–19)
   F. Paul's Exhortations (12:20–13:14)

Comfort in Trouble
(2 Corinthians 1:1–11)

1

Paul, an apostle of Christ Jesus by the will of God, and Timothy our brother, to the church of God which is at Corinth with all the saints who are throughout Achaia: Grace to you and peace from God our Father and the Lord Jesus Christ. Blessed be the God and Father of our Lord Jesus Christ, the Father of mercies and God of all comfort, who comforts us in all our affliction so that we will be able to comfort those who are in any affliction with the comfort with which we ourselves are comforted by God. For just as the sufferings of Christ are ours in abundance, so also our comfort is abundant through Christ. But if we are afflicted, it is for your comfort and salvation; or if we are comforted, it is for your comfort, which is effective in the patient enduring of the same sufferings which we also suffer; and our hope for you is firmly grounded, knowing that as you are sharers of our sufferings, so also you are sharers of our comfort. For we do not want you to be unaware, brethren, of our affliction which came to us in Asia, that we were burdened excessively, beyond our strength, so that we despaired even of life; indeed, we had the sentence of death within ourselves so that we would not trust in ourselves, but in God who raises the dead; who delivered us from so great a

peril of death, and will deliver us, He on whom we have set our hope. And He will yet deliver us, you also joining in helping us through your prayers, so that thanks may be given by many persons on our behalf for the favor bestowed on us through the prayers of many. (1:1–11)

Trouble is an inescapable reality in this fallen, evil world. Eliphaz, one of Job's would-be counselors, declared, "Man is born for trouble, as sparks fly upward" (Job 5:7). With that sentiment Job, certainly no stranger to trouble, agreed: "Man, who is born of woman, is short-lived and full of turmoil" (Job 14:1). Jeremiah, the weeping prophet, lamented, "Why did I ever come forth from the womb to look on trouble and sorrow, so that my days have been spent in shame?" (Jer. 20:18). That life is filled with trouble, sorrow, pain, disappointment, disillusionment, and despair is the testimony of the rest of Scripture.

Adding to the pain of trouble is the disturbing reality that God sometimes seems distant and unconcerned. Job cried out despondently, "Why do You hide Your face and consider me Your enemy?" (Job 13:24). The psalmist asked pensively, "Why do You stand afar off, O Lord? Why do You hide Yourself in times of trouble?" (Ps. 10:1). Speaking for Israel, the sons of Korah asked God, "Why do You hide Your face and forget our affliction and our oppression?" (Ps. 44:24). The prophet Isaiah affirmed, "Truly, You are a God who hides Himself, O God of Israel, Savior!" (Isa. 45:15). Even David, "a man after [God's] own heart" (1 Sam. 13:14; cf. Acts 13:22) and "the sweet psalmist of Israel" (2 Sam. 23:1), had moments of doubt and discouragement. In Psalm 13:1 he asked despairingly, "How long, O Lord? Will You forget me forever? How long will You hide Your face from me?" while in Psalm 22:1 he expressed his anguish in words echoed by the Lord Jesus Christ on the cross: "My God, my God, why have You forsaken me?" (cf. Matt. 27:46).

Many people today question why bad things happen to good people. But Scripture rejects the underlying assumption that people are truly good. The apostle Paul declared, "There is none righteous, not even one" (Rom. 3:10; cf. Pss. 14:1–3; 53:1–3) because "all have sinned and fall short of the glory of God" (Rom. 3:23; cf. 1 Kings 8:46; Ps. 143:2; Prov. 20:9; Eccles. 7:20; Jer. 17:9). Consequently, because "God is a just judge, [He] is angry with the wicked every day" (Ps. 7:11 NKJV). Bad things happen to all people because they are sinners who live in a fallen, sin-cursed world.

Because believers are redeemed sinners who live in a fallen world, bad things even happen to them. In fact, God allows those things to happen for several important reasons.

First, God allows bad things to happen to His people to test the validity of their faith. According to Proverbs 17:3, "The Lord tests hearts."

Second Chronicles 32:31 says, "God left [Hezekiah] alone only to test him, that He might know all that was in his heart." Centuries earlier Moses told Israel, "The Lord your God has led you in the wilderness these forty years, that He might humble you, testing you, to know what was in your heart, whether you would keep His commandments or not" (Deut. 8:2). Peter wrote,

> In this [salvation] you greatly rejoice, even though now for a little while, if necessary, you have been distressed by various trials, so that the proof of your faith, being more precious than gold which is perishable, even though tested by fire, may be found to result in praise and glory and honor at the revelation of Jesus Christ. (1 Peter 1:6–7)

Those tests are not for God's sake, because the omniscient God knows every person's heart. Instead, they reveal to those tested whether their faith is real. No trial, no matter how severe, can destroy genuine saving faith, because the saved "one ... endures to the end" (Matt. 24:13).

Job, the most faithful man of his time, went through almost inconceivable suffering. He lost his wealth, all of his children were killed, and he was stricken with a painful, debilitating disease. Worse, those closest to him turned against him; his wife foolishly urged him to "curse God and die!" (Job 2:9), while his friends' inept counsel finally drove him to exclaim in exasperation, "Sorry comforters are you all. ... How then will you vainly comfort me, for your answers remain full of falsehood?" (Job 16:2; 21:34). Most disconcerting of all, though Job knew of no major sin in his life, God seemed to be his implacable enemy. In Job 19:6–11, he cried out in despair and confusion,

> Know then that God has wronged me and has closed His net around me. Behold, I cry, "Violence!" but I get no answer; I shout for help, but there is no justice. He has walled up my way so that I cannot pass, and He has put darkness on my paths. He has stripped my honor from me and removed the crown from my head. He breaks me down on every side, and I am gone; and He has uprooted my hope like a tree. He has also kindled His anger against me and considered me as His enemy.

Desperately seeking sympathy from his friends, Job pleaded with them, "Pity me, pity me, O you my friends, for the hand of God has struck me" (Job 19:21).

Yet despite his misery, suffering, and despair caused by Satan's violent assaults (cf. Job 1:6–12; 2:1–7), Job's faith in God remained intact. In Job 13:15 he confidently declared, "Though He slay me, I will hope in Him." Confronted by God's glorious, majestic holiness, Job expressed genuine repentance for having doubted Him:

I know that You can do all things, and that no purpose of Yours can be thwarted. "Who is this that hides counsel without knowledge?" Therefore I have declared that which I did not understand, things too wonderful for me, which I did not know. "Hear, now, and I will speak; I will ask You, and You instruct me." I have heard of You by the hearing of the ear; but now my eye sees You; therefore I retract, and I repent in dust and ashes. (Job 42:2–6)

The prophet Habakkuk also faced a dilemma that tested his faith. Distressed by the rampant sin in Israel, he cried out to God,

How long, O Lord, will I call for help, and You will not hear? I cry out to You, "Violence!" Yet You do not save. Why do You make me see iniquity, and cause me to look on wickedness? Yes, destruction and violence are before me; strife exists and contention arises. Therefore the law is ignored and justice is never upheld. For the wicked surround the righteous; therefore justice comes out perverted. (Hab. 1:2–4)

To his dismay, God's answer was the opposite of what he had hoped for. Instead of bringing a spiritual revival in Israel, God was going to bring devastating judgment on the nation. Even more perplexing, He chose to use a godless, pagan nation as the instrument of that judgment:

Look among the nations! Observe! Be astonished! Wonder! Because I am doing something in your days—you would not believe if you were told. For behold, I am raising up the Chaldeans, that fierce and impetuous people who march throughout the earth to seize dwelling places which are not theirs. They are dreaded and feared; their justice and authority originate with themselves. Their horses are swifter than leopards and keener than wolves in the evening. Their horsemen come galloping, their horsemen come from afar; they fly like an eagle swooping down to devour. All of them come for violence. Their horde of faces moves forward. They collect captives like sand. They mock at kings and rulers are a laughing matter to them. They laugh at every fortress and heap up rubble to capture it. Then they will sweep through like the wind and pass on. But they will be held guilty, they whose strength is their god. (Hab. 1:5–11)

Yet despite his confusion over a worse nation being the instrument of Israel's judgment, Habakkuk's faith endured. Though the dilemma did not change, he expressed his continued trust in God's faithfulness, justice, and holiness:

Are You not from everlasting, O Lord, my God, my Holy One? We will not die. You, O Lord, have appointed them to judge; and You, O Rock, have established them to correct. Your eyes are too pure to approve evil, and You can not look on wickedness with favor. Why do You look with favor on those who deal treacherously? Why are You silent when the wicked swallow up those more righteous than they? (Hab. 1:12–13)

Those whose faith is genuine will pass the tests God allows in their lives, bringing them assurance, confidence, and hope.

Second, God allows bad things to happen to His people to wean them from the world. Trials strip away the worldly resources that believers trust in, leaving them completely dependent on divine resources. Before He fed the five thousand "Jesus, lifting up His eyes and seeing that a large crowd was coming to Him, said to Philip, 'Where are we to buy bread, so that these may eat?'"(John 6:5). Philip and the other disciples immediately took inventory, and the results were not promising: "Philip answered Him, 'Two hundred denarii worth of bread is not sufficient for them, for every- one to receive a little.' One of His disciples, Andrew, Simon Peter's brother, said to Him, 'There is a lad here who has five barley loaves and two fish, but what are these for so many people?'"(John 6:7–9). But Philip and the others missed the point: "This He was saying to test him, for He Himself knew what He was intending to do" (John 6:6). Jesus used this incident to show the disciples the futility of trusting in human resources.

Third, God allows bad things to happen to His people to call them to their heavenly hope. To the Romans Paul wrote, "We also exult in our tribulations, knowing that tribulation brings about perseverance; and perseverance, proven character; and proven character, hope; and hope does not disappoint" (Rom. 5:3–5). Those who hope for heaven will never be disappointed in this life, and suffering is the first step in produc- ing that hope. Paul expressed his heavenly hope when he wrote to the Corinthians, "Momentary, light affliction is producing for us an eternal weight of glory far beyond all comparison, while we look not at the things which are seen, but at the things which are not seen; for the things which are seen are temporal, but the things which are not seen are eter- nal" (2 Cor. 4:17–18). The greater the burden of trials that believers bear in this life, the sweeter their hope of heaven becomes.

Fourth, God allows bad things to happen to His people to reveal to them what they really love. Those who seek the proven character that suffering produces (Rom. 5:3–4), and to be fellow sufferers with the Lord Jesus Christ (cf. Acts 5:41; 1 Peter 4:13), will gladly endure trials. But those who focus on worldly things will react with anger and despair when tri- als strip them away.

The way Abraham faced the severe trial involving his son Isaac revealed his love for God. Genesis 22:1–2 says, "God tested Abraham, and said to him, 'Abraham!' And he said, 'Here I am.' He said, 'Take now your son, your only son, whom you love, Isaac, and go to the land of Moriah, and offer him there as a burnt offering on one of the mountains of which I will tell you.'" Abraham must have been shocked at this seemingly incomprehensible command. Isaac was the son he had longed for for decades. Then, when Abraham was old and his wife past her child-bearing years, the unbelievable announcement came that they were to have a son (Gen. 18:10, 14). So incredible was the news that their long-cherished hopes were to be realized that both Abraham (Gen. 17:17) and Sarah (Gen. 18:12) initially greeted it with laughter. Further, Isaac was the son of the covenant, through whom Abraham's descendants were to come (Gen. 17:19; 21:12; Rom. 9:7).

All of God's promises and Abraham's hopes were bound up in Isaac. Yet when God commanded him to slay Isaac as a sacrifice, Abraham was ready to obey. God stopped him, then spared Isaac and provided another sacrifice. Abraham's willingness proved that he loved God above all else, even more than his own son. And he also believed in God's promise that through Isaac the nation would come—he believed that if he killed him, God would raise Isaac from the dead (Heb. 11:17–19).

Fifth, God allows bad things to happen to His people to teach them obedience. The psalmist acknowledged, "Before I was afflicted I went astray, but now I keep Your word. . . . It is good for me that I was afflicted, that I may learn Your statutes" (Ps. 119:67, 71). The painful sting of affliction reminds believers that sin has consequences. God uses trials to bring believers to obedience and holiness, as the writer of Hebrews reveals:

> You have forgotten the exhortation which is addressed to you as sons, "My son, do not regard lightly the discipline of the Lord, nor faint when you are reproved by Him; for those whom the Lord loves He disciplines, and He scourges every son whom He receives." It is for discipline that you endure; God deals with you as with sons; for what son is there whom his father does not discipline? But if you are without discipline, of which all have become partakers, then you are illegitimate children and not sons. Furthermore, we had earthly fathers to discipline us, and we respected them; shall we not much rather be subject to the Father of spirits, and live? For they disciplined us for a short time as seemed best to them, but He disciplines us for our good, so that we may share His holiness. All discipline for the moment seems not to be joyful, but sorrowful; yet to those who have been trained by it, afterwards it yields the peaceful fruit of righteousness. (Heb. 12:5–11)

Sixth, God allows bad things to happen to His people so He can reveal His compassion to them. Believers' suffering allows Him the opportunity to display His loving-kindness, which, David declared, is better than anything else in life: "Because Your lovingkindness is better than life, my lips will praise You" (Ps. 63:3). Believers never know God more intimately than when He comforts them in their suffering. Isaiah exults, "Shout for joy, O heavens! And rejoice, O earth! Break forth into joyful shouting, O mountains! For the Lord has comforted His people and will have compassion on His afflicted" (Isa. 49:13; cf. 51:12; 52:9; 66:13). This revelation of God's compassion enhances worship.

Seventh, God allows bad things to happen to His people to strengthen them for greater usefulness. The more they are tested and refined by trials, the more effective their service will be. "Consider it all joy, my brethren," wrote James, "when you encounter various trials, knowing that the testing of your faith produces endurance. And let endurance have its perfect result, so that you may be perfect and complete, lacking in nothing" (James 1:2–4).

Finally, God allows bad things to happen to His people to enable them to comfort others in their trials. Jesus said to Peter, "Simon, Simon, behold, Satan has demanded permission to sift you like wheat; but I have prayed for you, that your faith may not fail; and you, when once you have turned again, strengthen your brothers" (Luke 22:31–32). After enduring his own trial and experiencing God's comfort, Peter would be able to help others. As we will learn later in this chapter, Paul's opening emphasis to the Corinthians is that God "comforts us in all our affliction so that we will be able to comfort those who are in any affliction with the comfort with which we ourselves are comforted by God" (1:4).

As was customary in ancient letters, the epistle begins with the name of the sender, **Paul.** As he did in eight of his other epistles, he declared himself to be **an apostle of Christ Jesus** (cf. Rom. 1:1; 1 Cor. 1:1; Gal. 1:1; Eph. 1:1; Col. 1:1; 1 Tim. 1:1; 2 Tim. 1:1; Titus 1:1). Since false teachers invariably challenged his apostolic credentials, Paul states that he was not self-appointed, but an apostle **by the will of God** (cf. 1 Cor. 1:1; Eph. 1:1; Col. 1:1; 2 Tim. 1:1). Although he was not one of the Twelve, Paul was personally chosen to be an apostle by the Lord Jesus Christ (Acts 26:15–18; 1 Cor. 15:7–10). As an apostle, the truths he wrote to the Corinthians are the inspired words of the living God. Thus, the false teachers' attack on his credibility was also an attack on God's divinely revealed truth.

Timothy was not an apostle but Paul's beloved **brother** in Christ. He was a native of Lystra, a city in Asia Minor (modern Turkey). His mother and grandmother were devout Jewish believers (2 Tim. 1:5), but his father was a pagan Greek (Acts 16:1). After joining Paul on the apostle's second missionary journey, Timothy became his protégé and cherished son in the faith. Paul wrote two inspired epistles to him, and he is mentioned in eight others, six of them in the salutation.

Timothy was such a faithful reproduction of Paul that the apostle confidently sent him as his representative to the churches in Macedonia (Acts 19:22), Philippi (Phil. 2:19–24), Thessalonica (1 Thess. 3:2), and Ephesus (1 Tim. 1:3). The Corinthians also knew him; he was there when the Corinthian church was founded (Acts 18:5) and later served as Paul's personal emissary to that congregation (1 Cor. 4:17; 16:10).

As was his custom, Paul extended his greetings **to the church of God which is at Corinth.** They were a community of believers that belonged to God, since "He purchased [them] with His own blood" (Acts 20:28). Paul did not identify **the saints who are throughout Achaia** to whom he also extended his greetings. There was, however, a church at Cenchrea (Rom. 16:1), a city about eight miles away that served as Corinth's port. As he did in the salutations of all his letters, Paul wished the Corinthians God's **grace and** the divine **peace** that is one of its benefits. Both come only **from God our Father and the Lord Jesus Christ.**

As noted in the introduction to this volume, the major theme in this epistle is Paul's defense of his apostleship against the many and varied attacks of the false teachers at Corinth. In this opening section of 2 Corinthians, Paul defended himself against the false charge that his trials were God's punishment for his sin and unfaithfulness. The apostle made the point that God was comforting him in his suffering, not chastening him. In so doing, he penned what is undoubtedly the most significant passage on comfort anywhere in Scripture. In it Paul describes the person, promise, purpose, parameters, power, perpetuity, and participation of comfort.

The Person of Comfort

Blessed be the God and Father of our Lord Jesus Christ, the Father of mercies and God of all comfort, (1:3)

After the salutation Paul began the body of his epistle with the affirmation that God is to be **blessed.** *Eulogētos* (**blessed**) is the root of the English word "eulogy" and literally means, "to speak well of." The Old Testament frequently refers to God as the "the God of Abraham, Isaac, and Jacob" (e.g., Ex. 3:6, 15, 16; 4:5; 1 Kings 18:36; 1 Chron. 29:18; 2 Chron. 30:6). But the New Testament identifies Him as **the God and Father of our Lord Jesus Christ** (cf. 2 Cor. 11:31; Rom. 15:6; Eph. 1:3, 17; 1 Peter 1:3), since "God, after He spoke long ago to the fathers in the prophets in many portions and in many ways, in these last days has spoken to us in His Son, whom He appointed heir of all things, through whom also He made the world" (Heb. 1:1–2).

Unlike Abraham, Isaac, Jacob, and the Old Testament prophets, **Jesus Christ** is the same essence as the Father; "He is the radiance of His glory and the exact representation of His nature" (Heb. 1:3). Jesus shocked and outraged the Jewish authorities by boldly declaring, "I and the Father are one" (John 10:30). To His equally obtuse disciples Jesus stated plainly, "He who has seen Me has seen the Father" (John 14:9). Paul wrote to the Philippians that Jesus "existed in the form of God" (Phil. 2:6), and to the Colossians, "He is the image of the invisible God" (Col. 1:15) and, "In Him all the fullness of Deity dwells in bodily form" (Col. 2:9). The New Testament teaching that Jesus is God in human flesh is the central truth of the gospel (cf. John 1:1; 5:17–18; 8:58; 20:28; Rom. 9:5; Titus 2:13; Heb. 1:8; 2 Peter 1:1; 1 John 5:20), and those who reject it cannot be saved (John 8:24).

Some may wonder why, since they are fully equal, the Father is referred to as **the God . . . of our Lord Jesus Christ** (cf. Mark 15:34; John 20:17). In His deity Jesus is fully equal to the Father, but in His humanity He submitted to Him. Paul's statement reflects Jesus' submission to the Father during the Incarnation (cf. John 14:28), when He voluntarily gave up the independent use of His divine attributes (Phil. 2:6–7; cf. Matt. 24:36).

The title **Lord Jesus Christ** summarizes all of His redemptive work. **Lord** describes His sovereign deity; **Jesus** (the Greek equivalent of the Hebrew name Yeshua; "God saves") describes His saving death and resurrection; **Christ** ("anointed one") describes Him as the King who will defeat God's enemies and rule over the redeemed earth and the eternal state.

Paul further described God using two Old Testament titles. He is **the Father of mercies** to those who seek Him. Faced with a choice of punishments, David said to Gad, "Let us now fall into the hand of the Lord for His mercies are great" (2 Sam. 24:14). In Psalm 86:15 he wrote, "But You, O Lord, are a God merciful and gracious, slow to anger and abundant in lovingkindness and truth." "The Lord is compassionate and gracious," he added in Psalm 103:8, "slow to anger and abounding in lovingkindness." Later in that same psalm David further praised God's mercy, compassion, and lovingkindness: "Just as a father has compassion on his children, so the Lord has compassion on those who fear Him. . . . The lovingkindness of the Lord is from everlasting to everlasting on those who fear Him" (vv. 13, 17). The prophet Micah described God's mercy and compassion in forgiving sins:

> Who is a God like You, who pardons iniquity and passes over the rebellious act of the remnant of His possession? He does not retain His anger forever, because He delights in unchanging love. He will again

have compassion on us; He will tread our iniquities under foot. Yes, You will cast all their sins into the depths of the sea. (Mic. 7:18–19)

The New Testament also reveals God's mercy. Zechariah, the father of John the Baptist, spoke of "the tender mercy of our God, with which the Sunrise from on high will visit us" (Luke 1:78). To the Romans Paul wrote, "Therefore I urge you, brethren, by the mercies of God, to present your bodies a living and holy sacrifice, acceptable to God, which is your spiritual service of worship" (Rom. 12:1). Later in that epistle he declared that "the Gentiles [would] glorify God for His mercy (Rom. 15:9). In Ephesians 2:4 he described God as "being rich in mercy." It was "His great mercy [that] has caused us to be born again to a living hope through the resurrection of Jesus Christ from the dead" (1 Peter 1:3).

The Old Testament also reveals God to be the **God of all comfort.** In Isaiah God said of suffering Israel, "'Comfort, O comfort My people,' says your God" (Isa. 40:1). In Isaiah 49:13 the prophet exulted, "Shout for joy, O heavens! And rejoice, O earth! Break forth into joyful shouting, O mountains! For the Lord has comforted His people and will have compassion on His afflicted." "Indeed," he confidently asserts, "the Lord will comfort Zion; He will comfort all her waste places. And her wilderness He will make like Eden, and her desert like the garden of the Lord; joy and gladness will be found in her, thanksgiving and sound of a melody" (Isa. 51:3; cf. 52:9; 66:13).

In the New Testament Jesus promised, "Blessed are those who mourn, for they shall be comforted" (Matt. 5:4). To the Thessalonians Paul wrote, "Now may our Lord Jesus Christ Himself and God our Father, who has loved us and given us eternal comfort and good hope by grace, comfort and strengthen your hearts in every good work and word" (2 Thess. 2:16–17).

Paul had experienced much pain, suffering, and heartbreak, particularly because of the false teachers at Corinth. They slandered his character to discredit him in the minds of the people and, even more painful to the apostle, sought to deceive the Corinthian church with lies about the gospel. But in God's merciful comforting of him he received the strength he needed to carry on. For that Paul was deeply grateful and blessed God.

THE PROMISE OF COMFORT

who comforts us in all our affliction (1:4*a*)

God comforts His people not only because He is by nature a merciful comforter but also because He has promised to comfort them.

The Lord is a "friend [who] loves at all times" (Prov. 17:17); "a friend who sticks closer than a brother" (Prov. 18:24), who promised, "I will never desert you, nor will I ever forsake you" (Heb. 13:5; cf. Deut. 31:6, 8; Ps. 37:28; Isa. 41:10).

The apostle Paul knew this blessed truth not only by divine revelation but also from his experience. Later in this epistle he wrote, "But God, who comforts the depressed, comforted us by the coming of Titus" (2 Cor. 7:6). In Romans 8:31–39 he wrote,

> What then shall we say to these things? If God is for us, who is against us? He who did not spare His own Son, but delivered Him over for us all, how will He not also with Him freely give us all things? Who will bring a charge against God's elect? God is the one who justifies; who is the one who condemns? Christ Jesus is He who died, yes, rather who was raised, who is at the right hand of God, who also intercedes for us. Who will separate us from the love of Christ? Will tribulation, or distress, or persecution, or famine, or nakedness, or peril, or sword? Just as it is written, "For your sake we are being put to death all day long; we were considered as sheep to be slaughtered." But in all these things we overwhelmingly conquer through Him who loved us. For I am convinced that neither death, nor life, nor angels, nor principalities, nor things present, nor things to come, nor powers, nor height, nor depth, nor any other created thing, will be able to separate us from the love of God, which is in Christ Jesus our Lord.

Having paid the ultimate price to redeem believers, the death of His Son, God will be with them to love, strengthen, protect, and comfort them in every extremity. Paul previously had reminded the Corinthians, "No temptation has overtaken you but such as is common to man; and God is faithful, who will not allow you to be tempted beyond what you are able, but with the temptation will provide the way of escape also, so that you will be able to endure it" (1 Cor. 10:13). To the Philippians he wrote, "He who began a good work in you will perfect it until the day of Christ Jesus" (Phil. 1:6). It is God's sovereign plan to be with His children and comfort them.

Affliction translates the Greek word *thlipsis*, which literally means, "pressure." Throughout **all** the stress, persecution, and trials he experienced in his turbulent life, Paul experienced God's comforting, strengthening presence. The apostle's life was thus an amazing juxtaposition of **affliction** and comfort, a seeming paradox he expressed later in this letter:

> But we have this treasure in earthen vessels, so that the surpassing greatness of the power will be of God and not from ourselves; we are

afflicted in every way, but not crushed; perplexed, but not despairing; persecuted, but not forsaken; struck down, but not destroyed; always carrying about in the body the dying of Jesus, so that the life of Jesus also may be manifested in our body. For we who live are constantly being delivered over to death for Jesus' sake, so that the life of Jesus also may be manifested in our mortal flesh. (4:7–11)

Because God constantly comforted and protected him, Paul was indestructible until the time came in God's sovereign plan for him to die. Though his enemies repeatedly tried to kill him (cf. Acts 9:23; 14:19; 20:3; 21:30–31; 23:12–13), they were unsuccessful, because "there is no wisdom and no understanding and no counsel against the Lord" (Prov. 21:30). The promise to all believers is that God will faithfully sustain and strengthen them as long as they are obedient to His will, until His appointed time to bring them to Himself.

The Purpose of Comfort

so that we will be able to comfort those who are in any affliction with the comfort with which we ourselves are comforted by God. . . . But if we are afflicted, it is for your comfort and salvation; or if we are comforted, it is for your comfort, which is effective in the patient enduring of the same sufferings which we also suffer; and our hope for you is firmly grounded, knowing that as you are sharers of our sufferings, so also you are sharers of our comfort. (1:4*b*, 6–7)

Paul viewed God's comforting of him not only as an end in itself to express His care and fulfill His promise but also as the means to an end. Suffering believers receive God's comfort **so that** they **will be able to comfort those who are in any affliction.** Believers receive comfort as a trust or stewardship to be passed on to others. This purpose of comfort is to equip the comforted to be comforters.

God had used Paul to confront, challenge, and convict the Corinthians. As noted in the introduction to this volume, 2 Corinthians is the fourth letter Paul wrote to them; in addition to 1 Corinthians, the apostle wrote them two noninspired letters. In those letters Paul rebuked them for their sin. Now, having confronted them, he was able to comfort them with the **comfort with which** he had been **comforted by God.** Paul viewed himself as a conduit through which God's comfort could flow to the Corinthians—a conduit widened by all the suffering he had endured. Those who experience the most suffering will receive the most comfort. And those who receive the most comfort are thereby most richly equipped to comfort others.

An incident in Peter's life illustrates that truth. Knowing that he would soon face a severe trial (his denial of Christ), Jesus said to him in Luke 22:31–32, "Simon, Simon, behold, Satan has demanded permission to sift you like wheat; but I have prayed for you, that your faith may not fail; and you, when once you have turned again, strengthen your brothers." Having received divine comfort in his trial, Peter would then be able to draw from that to comfort and strengthen others.

Paul reminded the Corinthians that believers **are comforted by God,** who alone is the source of true comfort. As noted earlier, Paul wrote later in this epistle that it is God "who comforts the depressed" (2 Cor. 7:6). The early church experienced "the comfort of the Holy Spirit" (Acts 9:31). Paul reminded the Thessalonians that it is "God our Father who has loved us and given us eternal comfort and good hope by grace" (2 Thess. 2:16). Comfort based on human wisdom is short-lived, because it does not address the deep issues of the heart. The only true source of hope and strength is God's supernatural, transcendent comfort that comes by the Spirit and the Scriptures.

In the course of godly living and ministry, it is inevitable that believers will be **afflicted.** Paul warned Timothy that "all who desire to live godly in Christ Jesus will be persecuted" (2 Tim. 3:12). But in God's providence, even the apostle's suffering brought **comfort and salvation** to the Corinthians. Paul could have been referring to the time of their salvation, when he suffered much to bring them the gospel (cf. Acts 18:1–17). But more likely the apostle referred not to their justification but to his ongoing involvement in their sanctification. Perhaps no other church caused Paul more pain and grief than the Corinthian assembly. Even after the apostle had invested at least eighteen precious months of his life ministering in Corinth, the church remained divisive, worldly, and rebellious. But God comforted Paul in his affliction, enabling him to bet ter comfort the very people who had caused part of his suffering.

Not all the Corinthians, of course, were suffering for their sins. Some were, like Paul, suffering for righteousness' sake. The apostle was able to extend to them **comfort, which** was **effective in** strengthening them for **the patient enduring of the same sufferings which** he and Timothy **also suffered.** And in the mutuality of ministry in the body of Christ, they were then enabled to comfort Paul. Believers are in a partnership with each other and must never view their suffering in isolation. When they suffer for Christ, God comforts them and equips them to comfort others.

Because righteous suffering for Christ is a mark of true believers (2 Tim. 3:12), Paul was able to say confidently to the faithful believers in

Corinth, **Our hope for you is firmly grounded, knowing that as you
are sharers of our sufferings, so also you are sharers of our comfort.** They demonstrated the reality of their faith by their willingness to
share Paul's and Timothy's **sufferings** for the gospel. Because of their
faithful endurance, they **also** were **sharers of** the same **comfort** with
which God comforted Paul and Timothy.

THE PARAMETERS OF COMFORT

**For just as the sufferings of Christ are ours in abundance, so also
our comfort is abundant through Christ.** (1:5)

Though God is the God of comfort who comforts His children,
there is an important condition for receiving that comfort. God does not
promise comfort to those who suffer for their unrepentant sin, but to
those who suffer for Christ. Those who experience **the sufferings of
Christ . . . in abundance** will find that God's **comfort is abundant
through Christ.** Thus, God's promised comfort extends as far as believers' suffering is for the sake of Christ.

Peter stated the conditions for receiving God's comfort in 1 Peter
4:12–16:

> Beloved, do not be surprised at the fiery ordeal among you, which
> comes upon you for your testing, as though some strange thing were
> happening to you; but to the degree that you share the sufferings of
> Christ, keep on rejoicing, so that also at the revelation of His glory you
> may rejoice with exultation. If you are reviled for the name of Christ,
> you are blessed, because the Spirit of glory and of God rests on you.
> Make sure that none of you suffers as a murderer, or thief, or evildoer, or
> a troublesome meddler; but if anyone suffers as a Christian, he is not to
> be ashamed, but is to glorify God in this name.

Believers will receive comfort in this life and rewards in eternity "to the
degree that [they] share the sufferings of Christ." When they "are reviled
for the name of Christ, [they] are blessed, because the Spirit of glory and
of God" will strengthen and comfort them. But then Peter cautions, "Make
sure that none of you suffers as a murderer, or thief, or evildoer, or a troublesome meddler," since the promise of divine comfort does not extend
to such people. Sinning Christians can expect God's chastening instead
of His comfort (cf. Heb. 12:5–11).

Paul counted it a privilege to share the **sufferings of Christ.** He
wrote later in this epistle that

we are afflicted in every way, but not crushed; perplexed, but not despairing; persecuted, but not forsaken; struck down, but not destroyed; always carrying about in the body the dying of Jesus, so that the life of Jesus also may be manifested in our body. For we who live are constantly being delivered over to death for Jesus' sake, so that the life of Jesus also may be manifested in our mortal flesh. So death works in us, but life in you. (4:8–12)

He reminded the Galatians, "I bear on my body the brand-marks of Jesus" (Gal. 6:17). To the Colossians he wrote, "I rejoice in my sufferings for your sake, and in my flesh I do my share on behalf of His body, which is the church, in filling up what is lacking in Christ's afflictions" (Col. 1:24). In Philippians 3:10 he expressed his longing to "know [Christ] and the power of His resurrection and the fellowship of His sufferings, being conformed to His death" (cf. Rom. 8:17). That believers will suffer for Christ is a constant New Testament theme (cf. Matt. 10:22; Luke 14:27; John 15:18–20; Acts 5:41).

THE POWER OF COMFORT

For we do not want you to be unaware, brethren, of our affliction which came to us in Asia, that we were burdened excessively, beyond our strength, so that we despaired even of life; indeed, we had the sentence of death within ourselves so that we would not trust in ourselves, but in God who raises the dead; who delivered us from so great a peril of death, (1:8–10*a*)

To show the Corinthians the power of God's comfort, Paul reminded them of a serious, life-threatening situation from which God had delivered him. The apostle used the phrase **we do not want you to be unaware** or its equivalent six times in his epistles (cf. Rom. 1:13; 11:25; 1 Cor. 10:1; 12:1; 1 Thess. 4:13). It expressed his great concern that his readers not have inadequate information.

The situation that produced the **affliction which came to** Paul **in** the province of **Asia** is unknown. It may have involved Paul's being beaten (cf. 2 Cor. 11:23–25), imprisoned (cf. 11:23), or both. Since he gave them no details, the incident must have been well-known to the Corinthians. But though they were aware of the situation, they did not know its severity or how God had worked in it. It had evidently happened recently, after Paul wrote 1 Corinthians, since he did not mention it in that letter. Since it happened in **Asia,** before he came to Macedonia (2:13), it likely took place in Ephesus, the chief city of **Asia.** In 1 Corinthians 16:9,

Paul wrote to the Corinthians that he planned to remain in Ephesus, "for a wide door for effective service has opened to me, and there are many adversaries." Possibly, one or more of those adversaries had come close to taking the apostle's life.

So severe was the trial, Paul wrote, **that we were burdened excessively.** He was unbearably crushed to the point of depression by something **beyond** even his formidable **strength** to endure. The situation was so serious that Paul **despaired even of life.** The Greek word translated **despaired** literally means "no passage," "no way out," or "no exit." Paul saw no escape from the desperate situation that threatened his **life. Indeed,** he added, **we had the sentence of death within ourselves.** *Apokrima* (**sentence**) appears only here in the New Testament. It refers to an official judgment, a legal decision, or resolution. In his own mind, Paul had passed the **sentence of death** on himself; he believed he would die for the gospel's sake. He wrote to Timothy shortly before his execution, "I am already being poured out as a drink offering, and the time of my departure has come" (2 Tim. 4:6). But unlike the situation he refers to here, that future realization caused Paul no despair, because he knew his work was done (2 Tim. 4:7–8).

God had a purpose for allowing Paul's suffering: to teach him **not** to **trust in** himself. God took him to the extremity from which no human resources could deliver him because, as He said to Paul later in this epistle, "My grace is sufficient for you, for power is perfected in weakness" (2 Cor. 12:9). Only the **God who raises the dead** had the power to deliver Paul from his ordeal; man's extremity is God's opportunity. Thus, God's power alone comforted Paul and **delivered** him **from** his **great peril of death.**

THE PERPETUITY OF COMFORT

and will deliver us, He on whom we have set our hope. And He will yet deliver us, (1:10*b*)

Paul was confident that God not only had delivered him in the past but also would **deliver** him in the future. Because God is faithful, He is always ready to comfort and deliver His children. In Lamentations 3:21–23 Jeremiah wrote, "This I recall to my mind, therefore I have hope. The Lord's lovingkindnesses indeed never cease, for His compassions never fail. They are new every morning; great is Your faithfulness." As Paul's life drew to a close, he confidently described God's faithful comforting of him:

At my first defense no one supported me, but all deserted me; may it not be counted against them. But the Lord stood with me and strengthened me, so that through me the proclamation might be fully accomplished, and that all the Gentiles might hear; and I was rescued out of the lion's mouth. The Lord will rescue me from every evil deed, and will bring me safely to His heavenly kingdom; to Him be the glory forever and ever. Amen. (2 Tim. 4:16–18)

Paul knew that God would bring him safely through every circumstance until it was time for him to enter the Lord's presence. Peter wrote of the same reality in 2 Peter 2:9: "The Lord knows how to rescue the godly from temptation, and to keep the unrighteous under punishment for the day of judgment." The constancy of God's comfort led Paul to describe Him as **He on whom we have set our hope** (cf. Ps. 71:5; Rom. 15:13; 1 Tim. 1:1). The more believers suffer and experience God's comfort, the stronger their **hope** in Him grows (Rom. 5:3–5).

THE PARTICIPATION OF COMFORT

you also joining in helping us through your prayers, so that thanks may be given by many persons on our behalf for the favor bestowed on us through the prayers of many. (1:11)

As noted in the previous point, the apostle was confident that God would continue to comfort him in the future. But he urged the Corinthians to participate in that gracious work of God by **joining in helping** him **through** their **prayers.** Paul understood, as did James, that "the effective prayer of a righteous man can accomplish much" (James 5:16). Therefore he viewed the prayers of the saints as crucial to his ministry. He implored the believers at Rome, "Now I urge you, brethren, by our Lord Jesus Christ and by the love of the Spirit, to strive together with me in your prayers to God for me" (Rom. 15:30). To the Ephesians he wrote, "With all prayer and petition pray at all times in the Spirit, and with this in view, be on the alert with all perseverance and petition for all the saints, and pray on my behalf, that utterance may be given to me in the opening of my mouth, to make known with boldness the mystery of the gospel" (Eph. 6:18–19; cf. Col. 4:3; 2 Thess. 3:1). He wrote confidently to the Philippians, "I know that this will turn out for my deliverance through your prayers and the provision of the Spirit of Jesus Christ" (Phil. 1:19; cf. Philem. 22). In 1 Thessalonians 5:25 he said simply, "Brethren, pray for us." Paul understood the balance between God's sovereign purpose and believers' responsibility.

In prayer, human impotence casts itself at the feet of divine omnipotence. When God's people intercede for each other, His power and sovereign purposes are realized. Thus, the purpose of prayer is not to manipulate God but to exalt His power and submit to His will. When God answered the Corinthians' prayers for Paul, **thanks** would **be given by many persons on** the apostle's **behalf for the favor bestowed on** him **through the prayers of many.** Prayer, like everything else in a Christian's life, is to glorify God (cf. 1 Cor. 10:31).

Katharina von Schlegel's magnificent hymn "Be Still, My Soul" expresses the confident hope of every believer in God's comfort:

> Be still my soul: the Lord is on thy side;
>   Bear patiently the cross of grief or pain.
> Leave to thy God to order and provide;
>   In ev'ry change He faithful will remain.
> Be still, my soul: thy best, thy heavenly Friend
>   Thro' thorny ways leads to a joyful end.
>
> Be still, my soul: thy God doth undertake
>   To guide the future as He has the past.
> Thy hope, thy confidence let nothing shake;
>   All now mysterious shall be bright at last.
> Be still, my soul: the waves and winds still know
>   His voice who ruled them while He dwelt below.
>
> Be still, my soul: the hour is hastening on
>   When we shall be forever with the Lord,
> When disappointment, grief, and fear are gone,
>   Sorrow forgot, love's purest joys restored.
> Be still, my soul: when change and tears are past,
>   All safe and blessed we shall meet at last.

The Soul's Warning System (2 Corinthians 1:12–14)

2

For our proud confidence is this: the testimony of our conscience, that in holiness and godly sincerity, not in fleshly wisdom but in the grace of God, we have conducted ourselves in the world, and especially toward you. For we write nothing else to you than what you read and understand, and I hope you will understand until the end; just as you also partially did understand us, that we are your reason to be proud as you also are ours, in the day of our Lord Jesus. (1:12–14)

On the night of November 27, 1983, Avianca Flight 011, en route from Paris to Bogotá via Madrid, approached Madrid's Barajas airport. The weather was good, and there were no mechanical problems with the 747 jet. The crew was experienced; the pilot had more than 20,000 hours of flying time and had made this same approach twenty-five times before. Yet, with its flaps extended and its landing gear down, the jumbo jet smashed into a series of low hills about seven miles short of the runway. The plane cartwheeled, broke into pieces, and came to rest upside down. Tragically, 181 of the 192 people on board lost their lives. Investigators determined that a series of errors by the crew caused the crash. The crew misunderstood the reality of their location. They thought they knew the truth about the plane's position, but they did not. Shockingly, the final and fatal error came when the pilot, so sure he knew where he was heading, ignored the computerized voice of the plane's GPWS (Ground Proximity Warning System), which repeatedly warned him, "Pull up! Pull up! Pull up!" The cockpit recorder had his strange reply to the warning. He said, "Shut up, gringo" and switched off the warning device. The next moment, he was dead with the rest of the victims.

That tragic story is a compelling illustration of the way people often ignore the truth of their life's direction and the warning messages from their consciences. The conscience is a warning system, placed by God into the very framework of the human soul. Like physical pain, which warns of damage to the body, the conscience warns of damage to the soul. It reacts to the proximity of sin, warning the soul to "Pull up!" before it suffers the terrible consequences of sin.

But today's culture aggressively and systematically tries to silence the conscience. People have been taught to ignore any and all guilt feelings conscience produces, viewing them as harmful to their self-esteem. They believe their problems stem not from their sin but from external factors beyond their control. Sin and guilt are viewed as psychological issues, not moral and spiritual ones. Thus, people imagine that their guilt feelings are erroneous and harmful attacks on their self-esteem. But the voice of conscience cannot be safely rejected; those who attempt to do so face spiritual ruin (cf. 1 Tim. 1:19; 4:2; Titus 1:15).

The conscience is the soul reflecting on itself; both the Greek word *suneidēsis* (**conscience**) and the English word "conscience" have the idea of knowing oneself. According to Romans 2:14, even those without God's written law have an innate moral sense of right and wrong: "For when Gentiles who do not have the Law do instinctively the things of the Law, these, not having the Law, are a law to themselves." The conscience either affirms right behavior or condemns sinful behavior.

The conscience, however, is not infallible. It is neither the voice of God, nor His moral law, as Colin G. Kruse helpfully observes:

> The conscience is not to be equated with the voice of God or even the moral law, rather it is a human faculty which adjudicates upon human action by the light of the highest standard a person perceives.
>
> Seeing that all of human nature has been affected by sin, both a person's perception of the standard of action required and the function of the conscience itself (as a constituent part of human nature) are also affected by sin. For this reason conscience can never be accorded the position of ultimate judge of one's behavior. It is possible that the conscience may excuse one for that which God will not excuse, and conversely it is equally possible that conscience may condemn a person

for that which God allows. The final judgment therefore belongs only to God (cf. 1 Cor. 4:2–5). Nevertheless, to reject the voice of conscience is to court spiritual disaster (cf. 1 Tim. 1:19). We cannot reject the voice of conscience with impunity, but we can modify the highest standard to which it relates by gaining for ourselves a greater understanding of the truth. (*The Second Epistle of Paul to the Corinthians*, The Tyndale New Testament Commentaries [Grand Rapids: Eerdmans, 1995], 70–71)

Since the conscience holds people to their highest perceived standard, believers need to set that standard to the highest level by submitting to all of God's Word. As they continually fill their minds with the truths of Scripture, believers clarify God's perfect law. Their consciences will then call them to live according to that law.

The conscience functions like a skylight, not like a lamp; it does not produce its own light, but merely lets moral light in. Because of that, the Bible teaches the importance of keeping a clear or good conscience. "The goal of our instruction," Paul wrote to Timothy, "is love from a pure heart and a good conscience and a sincere faith" (1 Tim. 1:5). A few verses later Paul stressed the importance of "keeping faith and a good conscience, which," he warned, "some have rejected and suffered shipwreck in regard to their faith" (v. 19). A necessary qualification for deacons is that they hold "to the mystery of the faith with a clear conscience" (1 Tim. 3:9). Peter commanded believers to "keep a good conscience so that in the thing in which you are slandered, those who revile your good behavior in Christ will be put to shame" (1 Peter 3:16). Both Paul (Acts 23:1; 2 Tim. 1:3) and the writer of Hebrews (Heb. 13:18) testified that they had maintained good consciences.

At salvation, God cleanses the conscience from its lifelong accumulation of guilt, shame, and self-contempt. The writer of Hebrews wrote that "the blood of Christ, who through the eternal Spirit offered Himself without blemish to God, [will] cleanse [the] conscience from dead works to serve the living God" (Heb. 9:14). As a result, believers have their "hearts sprinkled clean from an evil conscience" (Heb. 10:22). The cleansed conscience no longer accuses because of past sins, which are pardoned (Pss. 32:5; 103:12; Prov. 28:13; Mic. 7:18–19; Col. 1:14; 2:13–14; 1 John 1:9) through the blood of Christ (Eph. 1:7; 1 John 1:7; Rev. 1:5).

Believers must guard the purity of their cleansed consciences, winning the battle for holiness on the inside where conscience works. Paul gained victory at that point, so that he declared to the Sanhedrin, "I have lived my life with a perfectly good conscience before God up to this day" (Acts 23:1), and to the Roman governor Felix, "I also do my best to maintain always a blameless conscience both before God and before men" (Acts 24:16). He wrote to Timothy, "I thank God, whom I serve with a clear conscience" (2 Tim. 1:3). He reminded his young protégé that "the goal of our instruction is love from a pure heart and a good conscience and a sincere faith" (1 Tim. 1:5) and exhorted him to keep "a good conscience, which some have rejected and suffered shipwreck in regard to their faith" (1 Tim. 1:19). As noted above, Paul instructed that deacons must hold "to the mystery of the faith with a clear conscience" (1 Tim. 3:9). Christians must also be careful not to cause other believers to violate their consciences (1 Cor. 8:7–13; 10:24–29).

Paul wrote 2 Corinthians to defend himself against the assaults of the false apostles at Corinth (2 Cor. 11:13). Those lying deceivers sought to discredit him, undermine his authority, and then replace the truth of God with their satanic lies. They attacked his integrity, falsely accusing him of not being honest and sincere in his dealings with the Corinthians. The false apostles also portrayed Paul as a manipulator, scheming to defraud the Corinthians and to promote his personal agenda. In short, according to the false apostles, Paul's motives were corrupt, his words untrustworthy, and his actions devious.

As he answered those outrageous lies, Paul's primary concern was not to defend himself but protect the people from the deceivers. He knew that before they could peddle their demon doctrines to the Corinthians, the false apostles first had to destroy the Corinthians' trust in Paul. Thus, their savage personal attack on Paul was merely the prelude to an all-out assault on divine truth.

In his defense, Paul did not call on friends to verify his spiritual integrity; rather, he appealed to the highest human court: his own conscience. The apostle's **proud confidence** was in **the testimony** (witness, evidence) **of** his **conscience.** Paul frequently used *kauchēsis* (**proud confidence**), the related noun *kauchēma,* and the verb *kauchaomai* in this letter—twenty-nine of their fifty-nine uses in the New Testament are in 2 Corinthians. Negatively, *kauchēsis* describes unwarranted boasting in one's achievements and merits (cf. Rom. 3:27; James 4:16). It can also be used, however, of legitimate confidence in what God is doing in one's life (cf. 2 Cor. 7:4, 14; 8:24; 11:10; Rom. 15:17; 1 Cor. 15:31), as it is here. Boasting in the Lord and what He accomplishes in His people is proper; in fact, God Himself delights in such boasting:

> Thus says the Lord, "Let not a wise man boast of his wisdom, and let not the mighty man boast of his might, let not a rich man boast of his riches; but let him who boasts boast of this, that he understands and knows Me, that I am the Lord who exercises lovingkindness, justice and righteousness on earth; for I delight in these things," declares the Lord. (Jer. 9:23–24; cf. 1 Cor. 1:31; 2 Cor. 10:17).

In proving his integrity, Paul's clear conscience was a source of peace, comfort, and joy to him. Others might falsely accuse him of heinous sins, but Paul's conscience did not accuse him. It exonerated him of their charges and protected him from false guilt.

The false apostles had launched a three-pronged attack on Paul's credibility. On the moral level, they accused him of secretly being a wicked sinner, justly suffering all the time because of the chastening of God. On the relational level, they accused him of being insincere, deceptive, and manipulative. They charged that he was not what he appeared to be on the surface; that in reality, he was using the Corinthians for his own selfish purposes. On the theological level, they charged that Paul misrepresented God's Word and was a liar and a false teacher. What hurt Paul more than those baseless, slanderous lies was the sad fact that many in the Corinthian congregation believed them.

In this passage Paul appealed to the supreme human court, his fully informed conscience, to overturn the false verdicts of Satan's messengers. His conscience exonerated him of moral, relational, and theological wrongdoing.

PAUL'S CONSCIENCE
EXONERATED HIM OF MORAL WRONGDOING

that in holiness and godly sincerity, not in fleshly wisdom but in the grace of God, we have conducted ourselves in the world, and especially toward you. (1:12b)

The first false charge was that Paul's suffering was God's chastening for his sin. But Paul's conscience affirmed that his conduct had been **in holiness and godly sincerity.** Later in this epistle, Paul responded in detail to their lies about his character, noting that he was careful to give

> no cause for offense in anything, so that the ministry will not be discredited, but in everything commending ourselves as servants of God, in much endurance, in afflictions, in hardships, in distresses, in beatings, in imprisonments, in tumults, in labors, in sleeplessness, in hunger, in purity, in knowledge, in patience, in kindness, in the Holy Spirit, in genuine love, in the word of truth, in the power of God; by the weapons of righteousness for the right hand and the left, by glory and dishonor, by evil report and good report; regarded as deceivers and yet true; as unknown yet well-known, as dying yet behold, we live; as punished yet not put to death, as sorrowful yet always rejoicing, as poor yet making many rich, as having nothing yet possessing all things. (6:3–10)

Paul's life was above reproach. The false apostles' allegations were nothing more than slanderous lies, and his conscience testified to that.

Holiness is from *hagiotēs*, a word that describes moral purity or pure motives. (Some English versions, reflecting a reading with less support in the Greek manuscripts, read "simplicity" instead of **holiness.**) The writer of Hebrews used *hagiotēs* in Hebrews 12:10 to describe the holiness of God. Paul's **holiness,** confirmed in his own mind, contrasts sharply with the immorality and corruption of which he was wrongly accused.

Sincerity translates the Greek word *eilikrineia,* a compound word made up of *eilē* ("sunlight") and *krinō* ("to judge"). It pictures something held up to the light of the sun for inspection. In Paul's day, unscrupulous potters would fill the cracks in their pots with wax before selling them. Careful buyers would hold the pots up to the sun, by which light the wax-filled cracks would be clearly visible.

Paul's **sincerity** flowed from his **holiness** and purity of life. He characterized it as **godly** because God was its object and its source. In 1 Corinthians 15:10 Paul acknowledged that God's grace was the source of his spiritual power: "By the grace of God I am what I am, and His grace toward me did not prove vain; but I labored even more than all of them, yet not I, but the grace of God with me." To the Colossians he wrote, "For this purpose also I labor, striving according to His power, which mightily works within me" (Col. 1:29; cf. Eph. 1:19; Phil. 1:6; 2:12–13). Paul was a sincere man, a man of integrity. His life would stand up to the closest scrutiny; there were no skeletons in his closet.

Lest anyone think that Paul achieved **holiness and godly sincerity** by his own efforts, he added that they came **not in fleshly wisdom but in the grace of God.** They did not stem from Paul's wisdom or his insights into religion and spirituality. **Fleshly wisdom** cannot produce **holiness and godly sincerity,** because it is nothing more than the manifestation of sinful man's rebellion against God. It consists of the fallible insights of the sin-darkened heart apart from God's revelation in Jesus Christ and in Scripture. In 1 Corinthians 3:19 Paul described it as "the wisdom of this world [that] is foolishness before God. For it is written, 'He is the one who catches the wise in their craftiness'" (cf. 1 Cor. 1:20–21; 2:5–8). Such humanistic rationalism cannot produce spiritual growth, which comes only by **the grace of God.**

As further proof of his integrity, Paul declared that he had **conducted** himself properly throughout **the world.** There was no place where he had ministered from which a legitimate accusation against him could come. At all places and at all times, he had consistently lived a life above reproach.

Paul's integrity and godliness should have been **especially** evident to the Corinthians. They had observed him firsthand during the eighteen months that he ministered in their city (Acts 18:11). The shining purity of his life was set against the dark, ugly backdrop of Corinth's immorality. Corinth was corrupt, even by the pagan standards of that day, as R. C. H. Lenski notes:

> Corinth was a wicked city even as larger cities of the empire went at this period. The very term "Corinthian" came to mean a profligate. *Korinthiazomai*, "to Corinthianize," meant to practice whoredom; *Korinthiastēs* = a whoremonger; *Korinthia korē* (girl) = a courtesan. (*The Interpretation of the Acts of the Apostles* [Minneapolis: Augsburg, 1961], 744)

There was nothing in Paul's life or conduct that would have confirmed any such accusation against him.

Paul's conscience exonerated him of the false charges leveled against his personal life. Yet his clear conscience did not mean that he was without sin. In 1 Corinthians 4:4 Paul wrote, "For I am conscious of nothing against myself, yet I am not by this acquitted; but the one who examines me is the Lord." Though conscience is the highest human court, it is not infallible. Sin is so deceitful that believers sometimes sin without their conscience being aware of it. Thus, they must constantly examine themselves in light of Scripture, allowing God to be the final judge. Like David, they must constantly pray, "Search me, O God, and know my heart; try me and know my anxious thoughts; and see if there be any hurtful way in me, and lead me in the everlasting way" (Ps. 139:23–24).

PAUL'S CONSCIENCE
EXONERATED HIM OF RELATIONAL WRONGDOING

For we write nothing else to you than what you read and understand, and I hope you will understand until the end; just as you also partially did understand us, (1:13–14a)

This simple statement offers the powerful testimony of Paul's conscience regarding the second allegation against him. Not only was Paul innocent of moral wrongdoing; he also was not guilty of relational wrongdoing. He had defrauded no one; he had used no one for his own selfish ends; he had deceived and manipulated no one. Later in this letter he pleaded with the Corinthians, "Make room for us in your hearts; we wronged no one, we corrupted no one, we took advantage of no one" (7:2), while in 11:9 he reminded them, "When I was present with you and was in need, I was not a burden to anyone; for when the brethren came from Macedonia they fully supplied my need, and in everything I kept myself from being a burden to you, and will continue to do so."

Nor did Paul **write** his letters to the Corinthians with a hidden agenda; he wrote **nothing else to** them other **than what** they could **read and understand.** There was no deception involved; Paul wrote what he meant, and meant what he wrote. His letters were clear, straightforward, consistent, genuine, transparent, and without ambiguity. Both **read** and **understand** are compound forms of the verb *ginōskō* (to know), forming a play on words in the Greek. Philip E. Hughes notes, "The play on words *anaginōskete . . . epiginōskete,* cannot successfully be reproduced in English. *Anaginōskete* refers to what they read in his letters and *epiginōskete* to what they know through personal contact with him. They are being assured that the two are in complete harmony" (*The Second Epistle to the Corinthians,* The New International Commentary on the New Testament [Grand Rapids: Eerdmans, 1992], 27, n. 3).

Until the end translates *telos,* which in this context means "completely," or "fully." Paul wanted the Corinthians to understand him completely, **just as** they **also partially did understand** him. He wanted them to gain an ever-deeper understanding of God's Word, and of himself and his motives. Then they would trust Paul and would not be swayed by the lies of the false apostles.

Paul's conscience once again exonerated him from the false charges against him. Later in this epistle Paul wrote, "For they say, 'His letters are weighty and strong, but his personal presence is unimpressive and his speech contemptible.' Let such a person consider this, that what we are in word by letters when absent, such persons we are also in deed when present" (10:10–11). What Paul wrote in his letters was perfectly consistent with who he was in person.

PAUL'S CONSCIENCE
EXONERATED HIM OF THEOLOGICAL WRONGDOING

that we are your reason to be proud as you also are ours, in the day of our Lord Jesus. (1:14*b*)

The last and most serious charge against Paul was that he was a false teacher. The false apostles alleged that he was guilty of spiritual wrongdoing because he taught errant theology. Like the two previous charges, Paul replied to this charge throughout this letter. In 2:17 he wrote, "For we are not like many, peddling the word of God, but as from sincerity, but as from God, we speak in Christ in the sight of God." In 4:2 he reminded the Corinthians, "We have renounced the things hidden because of shame, not walking in craftiness or adulterating the word of God, but by the manifestation of truth commending ourselves to every man's conscience in the sight of God," while in 13:8 he insisted, "For we can do nothing against the truth, but only for the truth."

Paul was no spiritual con man, no huckster twisting the truth of God for his own ends, as the Corinthians well knew. They should not have been ashamed of Paul because he allegedly mishandled and twisted God's Word. Instead, he should have been their **reason to be proud,** as they were his. They should have boasted in the Lord about how God had so mightily used Paul, both in Corinth and elsewhere. The Corinthians should have been so **proud** of Paul that they eagerly looked forward to **the day of our Lord Jesus,** when they will embrace him in eternal and perfect fellowship. Paul looked forward to that day, when the presence of those to whom he had ministered would bring him great joy. To the Thessalonians he wrote, "For who is our hope or joy or crown of exultation? Is it not even you, in the presence of our Lord Jesus at His coming? For you are our glory and joy" (1 Thess. 2:19–20).

The day of our Lord Jesus is not the Day of the Lord, the time of God's fierce and final judgment on the sinful world (cf. Isa. 13:6–22; Joel 1:15; 2:11; Acts 2:20; 1 Thess. 5:2–4; 2 Thess. 1:10, "that day"; 2 Peter 3:10). Instead, **the day** referred to here is the time when glorified believers will appear before the **Lord Jesus,** when their salvation will be completed and made perfect (1 Cor. 1:8; 3:10–15; 4:5; 2 Cor. 5:10; Phil. 1:10; 2:16). Paul was able to look forward to **the day of our Lord Jesus** with great joy. He did not fear the false accusations against him, because his conscience verified that he had not perverted divine truth, and he would gladly stand before his Lord with no fear.

Paul was able to endure difficulties of all sorts—physical abuse, false accusations, disappointments, defections—with absolute contentment because his conscience did not accuse him. How can believers enjoy a clear conscience like Paul did?

First, by learning God's word. In Psalm 37:30–31 David wrote, "The mouth of the righteous utters wisdom, and his tongue speaks justice. The law of his God is in his heart; his steps do not slip."

Second, by meditating on God's Word. In Psalm 119:11 the psalmist wrote, "Your word I have treasured in my heart, that I may not sin against You."

Third, by continual watchfulness and prayer. In Matthew 26:41 Jesus warned, "Keep watching and praying that you may not enter into temptation; the spirit is willing, but the flesh is weak."

Fourth, by avoiding spiritual pride. Paul cautioned the Corinthians, "Therefore let him who thinks he stands take heed that he does not fall" (1 Cor. 10:12).

Fifth, by recognizing the seriousness of sin. It was sin that caused the death of the Lord Jesus Christ (Rom. 4:25).

Sixth, by purposing not to sin. In Psalm 119:106 the psalmist resolved, "I have sworn and I will confirm it, that I will keep Your righteous ordinances."

Seventh, by resisting the first hint of temptation. James 1:14–15 graphically shows the rapid progression from temptation to sinful act: "Each one is tempted when he is carried away and enticed by his own lust. Then when lust has conceived, it gives birth to sin; and when sin is accomplished, it brings forth death."

Finally, by instantly confessing and repenting of sin. "If we confess our sins," John wrote, "He is faithful and righteous to forgive us our sins and to cleanse us from all unrighteousness" (1 John 1:9).

Those who heed Solomon's charge, "Watch over your heart with all diligence, for from it flow the springs of life" (Prov. 4:23) will, as did Paul, enjoy the encouraging blessedness of a clear conscience.

Portrait of a Godly Pastor
(2 Corinthians 1:15–2:4)

3

In this confidence I intended at first to come to you, so that you might twice receive a blessing; that is, to pass your way into Macedonia, and again from Macedonia to come to you, and by you to be helped on my journey to Judea. Therefore, I was not vacillating when I intended to do this, was I? Or what I purpose, do I purpose according to the flesh, so that with me there will be yes, yes and no, no at the same time? But as God is faithful, our word to you is not yes and no. For the Son of God, Christ Jesus, who was preached among you by us—by me and Silvanus and Timothy—was not yes and no, but is yes in Him. For as many as are the promises of God, in Him they are yes; therefore also through Him is our Amen to the glory of God through us. Now He who establishes us with you in Christ and anointed us is God, who also sealed us and gave us the Spirit in our hearts as a pledge. But I call God as witness to my soul, that to spare you I came no more to Corinth. Not that we lord it over your faith, but are workers with you for your joy; for in your faith you are standing firm. But I determined this for my own sake, that I would not come to you in sorrow again. For if I cause you sorrow, who then makes me glad but the one whom I made sorrowful? This is the

very thing I wrote you, so that when I came, I would not have sorrow from those who ought to make me rejoice; having confidence in you all that my joy would be the joy of you all. For out of much affliction and anguish of heart I wrote to you with many tears; not so that you would be made sorrowful, but that you might know the love which I have especially for you. (1:15–2:4)

Our society often judges people by what they do, not by their character. For sports heroes, movie stars, businessmen, or politicians, it is performance, not principle, that counts. Sadly, that pragmatic outlook has even infiltrated the church. Pastors, for example, are too often evaluated by the outward trappings of success—the size of their congregations, their success as fund-raisers, the extent of their radio or TV ministries, how well their books sell, or their influence in the public arena. But such external criteria (by which many false teachers and cult leaders could be judged successful) do not impress God. Unlike "man [who] looks at the outward appearance, . . . the Lord looks at the heart" (1 Sam. 16:7). The seventeenth-century Puritan John Owen said pointedly, "A minister may fill his pews, his communion roll, the mouths of the public, but what that minister is on his knees in secret before God Almighty, that he is and no more" (cited in I. D. E. Thomas, *A Puritan Golden Treasury* [Edinburgh: Banner of Truth, 1977], 192). The noble nineteenth-century Scottish pastor Robert Murray McCheyne reminded a fellow pastor, "It is not great talents God blesses so much as great likeness to Jesus" (Andrew A. Bonar, *Memoirs of McCheyne* [Reprint; Chicago: Moody, 1978], 95). It is not what a man *does* that makes him a noble and useful pastor, but what he *is*.

The apostle Paul had all the external marks of success. He was the greatest missionary the world has ever known, used by God to initially spread the gospel and plant churches throughout the Roman world. God also inspired him to write thirteen New Testament books, nine of them to those churches. The many congregations he founded held him in the highest regard as their spiritual father and teacher (1 Cor. 4:15). He lived a life that was observably above reproach, as his conscience testified (Acts 23:1; 24:16; 2 Tim. 1:3). Yet he knew that the true measure of a man of God is not his external success or reputation but God's evaluation of his heart. In 1 Corinthians 4:4–5 he wrote,

> For I am conscious of nothing against myself, yet I am not by this acquitted; but the one who examines me is the Lord. Therefore do not go on passing judgment before the time, but wait until the Lord comes who will both bring to light the things hidden in the darkness and disclose the motives of men's hearts; and then each man's praise will come to him from God.

    As he wrote this letter, Paul, as so often in his ministry, was being mercilessly attacked. Because God so mightily used him, he was a prime target of Satan's attacks. This attack, however, deeply disturbed him because it came from his beloved Corinthian church—a church Paul had given at least eighteen months of his life to birth. The attack from the church came in the form of sin, mutiny, and misrepresentation, led by some self-appointed false teachers who sought to discredit Paul and destroy his reputation in the eyes of the Corinthian congregation. After the people lost confidence in Paul, they hoped to replace him as the authoritative teachers. They would then have the platform they needed to teach their demonic doctrines. To accomplish that evil goal, they attacked Paul's apostleship, character, and ministry on every conceivable level.

    Second Corinthians is Paul's defense of his genuineness and spiritual integrity against the false apostles' slanderous attacks. In 1:12–14, he gave a general defense of his personal righteousness, appealing to the highest court in the human realm, his own conscience. As noted in the previous chapter of this volume, the apostle's conscience exonerated him of all the false charges leveled against him. His personal life, relationships with others, and ministry were all above reproach. After that general response, Paul replied in 1:15–2:4 to the specific charge that he was not trustworthy. The false apostles claimed that Paul did not always speak the truth, but was unfaithful, fickle, and vacillating. They supported that trumped-up charge with the flimsiest, most trivial evidence: a change in Paul's travel plans.

    Instead of merely explaining why he made that change in plans, Paul dealt with the deeper issue of his integrity and truthfulness. Rather than engage in a battle of details, of specific charges and counter-charges, he elevated the discussion to the motives and attitudes of his heart. By so doing, he provided a priceless look at a noble man of God. As this text unfolds, it reveals seven attitudes that were the benchmarks of his spiritual character: loyalty, honesty, reliability, authenticity, sensitivity, purity, and love.

LOYALTY

In this confidence I intended at first to come to you, so that you might twice receive a blessing; that is, to pass your way into Macedonia, and again from Macedonia to come to you, and by you to be helped on my journey to Judea. (1:15–16)

    The only reason Paul planned to visit the Corinthians in the first place was his loyalty to them. It was **in** the **confidence** expressed in verse 14, that the Corinthians would be as loyal to him as he was to them, that Paul had **intended at first to come to** them. Despite the rebellion against him in the Corinthian congregation, Paul believed the majority was still loyal to him. In 1 Corinthians 16:5–6, Paul wrote that he intended to leave Ephesus, minister in Macedonia, then come to spend the winter (when travel was difficult) with the believers in Corinth. After writing 1 Corinthians, Paul decided to change his plan and also make a visit to Corinth before going to Macedonia **so that** the Corinthians might **twice receive** the **blessing** (*charis;* "grace," "favor," "benefit") of fellowship with him before *and* after his Macedonian trip. According to this revised travel plan, Paul would **pass** through Corinth on his way **into Macedonia, and again** on his way back **from Macedonia.** The Corinthians would then help him **on** his **journey to Judea.** Adding a second visit to Corinth was further evidence of Paul's love and loyalty to the believers there.

However, as he will later explain (cf. 1:23–2:1), the apostle had to cancel the first visit and revert to his original plan of visiting Corinth only after ministering in Macedonia. Paul's enemies pounced on this minor change in travel plans and accused him of untrustworthiness and fickleness. They ridiculously, but apparently with some success, argued that if Paul's statements about his travel plans were untrustworthy, why should the Corinthians believe his theological statements?

But Paul was not fickle. His circumstances changed but not his heart attitude. Here Paul affirms that he is loyal to his flock. He would always do whatever he could for their spiritual benefit, as the Corinthians had ample evidence to prove.

HONESTY

Therefore, I was not vacillating when I intended to do this, was I? Or what I purpose, do I purpose according to the flesh, so that with me there will be yes, yes and no, no at the same time? But as God is faithful, our word to you is not yes and no. (1:17–18)

Not content with impugning his loyalty, Paul's accusers also questioned his honesty. Paul was likely quoting one of their accusations when he denied that he was guilty of **vacillating** in what he had said he **intended to do.** The apostle found it incredible that anyone would construe a change in travel plans as evidence of a dishonest character. Certainly the Corinthians were not slighted by Paul's change in plans; the two visits became instead one long visit (cf. 1 Cor. 16:6–7).

The words *mēti ara* in Paul's first question introduce a question that calls for an indignant, negative answer. Paul said in effect, "Was I vacillating when I intended to do this? No way!" He was no shifty opportunist; no shallow, fickle, frivolous liar. Nor did he **purpose according to the flesh.** Paul did not make plans in purely human fashion. He did not seek to please himself, to make decisions to suit his own selfish interests. He did not talk out of both sides of his mouth; his words were not **yes, yes and no, no at the same time.** After closely observing Paul's life during his more than eighteen months in their city, the Corinthians had plenty of reason to affirm that he was an honest man.

To support his claim to honesty, Paul emphatically declared, **But as God is faithful, our word to you is not yes and no.** He may have been taking an oath, boldly calling God as faithful witness to his truthfulness (cf. v. 23; 11:10, 31; Rom. 1:9; 9:1; Gal. 1:20; Phil. 1:8; 1 Thess. 2:5, 10). Jesus did not forbid all taking of oaths in Matthew 5:33–37, only deceptive ones meant to misrepresent true intention for the sake of some personal gain. During His trial before the Sanhedrin, Jesus even allowed Himself to be placed under oath by the high priest (Matt. 26:63–64). Paul's point is that God is truthful, and he, as God's representative, is also truthful. No matter how his plans changed, Paul remained both loyal and honest.

RELIABILITY

For the Son of God, Christ Jesus, who was preached among you by us—by me and Silvanus and Timothy—was not yes and no, but is yes in Him. For as many as are the promises of God, in Him they are yes; therefore also through Him is our Amen to the glory of God through us. (1:19–20)

Throughout the history of the church, heretics have always assaulted the nature of Christ, and the false apostles at Corinth appear to be no exception in their effort to diminish Him. Having slanderously accused Paul of being untrustworthy because of his change in travel plans, they also alleged that his teaching on the Lord Jesus was untrustworthy. Responding to their attack on his Lord, Paul emphasized Christ's nature as the God-man by using the full, rich title **the Son of God, Christ Jesus.**

Paul was not the only one who preached the truths of **the Son of God** to the Corinthians; **Silvanus and Timothy** had preached the message to them. **Silvanus** (Silas) was a prominent leader in the Jerusalem church. The Jerusalem Council entrusted him to carry its decision to the church at Antioch (Acts 15:22). He later became Paul's companion on the apostle's second missionary journey, replacing Barnabas (Acts 15:39–40). **Timothy** was Paul's beloved son in the faith. As the son of a Jewish Christian mother and a pagan Gentile father (Acts 16:1), he was uniquely qualified to minister alongside the apostle. Both **Silvanus and Timothy** had ministered with Paul at Corinth (Acts 18:5). Their preaching was not untrustworthy, it **was not yes and no, but** was a firm, unwavering, resounding **yes** to God's truth in Jesus Christ.

Then Paul sums up the glory of Christ by reminding the Corinthians that **as many as are the promises of God, in Him they are yes.** All of God's salvation **promises**—of blessing, peace, joy, goodness, fellowship, forgiveness, strength, and hope of eternal life—**are yes,** meaning they all come true, in Christ. They are all made possible by His person and work. After His resurrection, Jesus told His disciples, "All things which are written about Me in the Law of Moses and the Prophets and the Psalms must be fulfilled" (Luke 24:44). In 1 Corinthians 1:30 Paul declared that "Christ Jesus . . . became to us wisdom from God, and righteousness and sanctification, and redemption." To the Colossians he wrote, "For it was the Father's good pleasure for all the fullness to dwell in Him. . . . For in Him all the fullness of Deity dwells in bodily form" (Col. 1:19; 2:9). It was the realization of "the surpassing value of knowing Christ Jesus [as his] Lord" that made Paul willing to suffer "the loss of all things, and count them but rubbish so that [he might] gain Christ" (Phil. 3:8).

Then Paul drove home the point of his argument by reminding the Corinthians, **Therefore also through Him is our Amen to the glory of God through us. Amen** is a solemn affirmation of the truthfulness of a statement (cf. Rom. 1:25; 9:5; 11:36; 15:33; 16:27; Gal. 1:5; Eph. 3:21; Phil. 4:20; 1 Tim. 1:17; 6:16; 2 Tim. 4:18; Heb. 13:21; 1 Peter 4:11; 5:11; 2 Peter 3:18; Jude 25; Rev. 1:6; 7:12). When Paul, Silas, and Timothy preached the gospel, it was all about Christ, who by His glorious work brings to pass all salvation realities. The Corinthians probably even had joined in saying **Amen to the glory of God.** The congregation had affirmed that the preachers reliably spoke God's truth about Christ when they believed the gospel message Paul and his companions preached, and it transformed their lives. How utterly absurd, Paul argued, to accept and experience the gospel message as reliable, but consider those who preached it unreliable. How ridiculous to trust Paul's word about eternal things, but not about mundane things like travel plans.

The apostle who was exacting in communicating the true gospel of Christ was also exacting in the lesser matters of life. God did not choose an unstable, unreliable apostle to preach His truth.

Now He who establishes us with you in Christ and anointed us is God, who also sealed us and gave us the Spirit in our hearts as a pledge. (1:21–22)

As important as they were, Paul's ultimate claim to integrity and authenticity as God's messenger and Christ's apostle was not his loyalty, honesty, reliability, or any other personal feature; it was what God had done in his life. Paul described four glorious works that God had done in his life with the four verbs **establishes, anointed, sealed,** and **gave.** The phrase **with you** and the fourfold repetition of **us** indicates Paul's confidence that the Corinthians also experienced those divine works, as do all believers.

First, God **establishes** believers **in Christ** at salvation. This is the work of saving grace that puts believers into union with Him (cf. 5:17; Rom. 8:1; 16:11–13; 1 Cor. 1:30; 3:1; 7:22; Gal. 2:20; Eph. 5:8; Col. 1:2, 28; 4:7) and with each other. Paul's authenticity was inextricably linked with that of the Corinthians, and to deny it was to deny the reality of their own spiritual life. Because they were fellow members of the body of Christ, by attacking Paul's authenticity, the Corinthians ripped the fabric of the church's spiritual unity. Since Paul was their spiritual father (1 Cor. 4:15), to deny his authenticity was, figuratively, to saw off the branch on which they were sitting.

Second, God **anointed** believers. To anoint someone is to commission them for service (cf. Ex. 28:41; Num. 3:3; 1 Sam. 15:1; 16:1–13; 2 Sam. 2:4; 1 Kings 1:39; 5:1; 19:16; Ps. 89:20). The verb *chriō* (**anointed**) appears four other times in the New Testament, each time in a passage referring to Christ (Luke 4:18; Acts 4:27; 10:38; Heb. 1:9). The related noun *chrisma* describes the anointing all believers have when they receive from Christ the Holy Spirit (cf. 1 Cor. 12:13), who guides, empowers, and teaches them (1 John 2:20, 27).

Third, God **sealed** believers. *Sphragizō* (**sealed**) refers to stamping an identifying mark on something (cf. Matt. 27:66; John 3:33; 6:27; Rom. 15:28; Rev. 7:3–4). Here, as in Ephesians 1:13, 4:30, and 2 Timothy 2:19, it refers to believers', stamped as God's, receiving the indwelling Holy Spirit (Rom. 8:9), whose presence identifies them as God's true and eternal possession, whom He will protect and keep.

Fourth, God **gave** believers **the Spirit in** their **hearts as a pledge.** The indwelling Holy Spirit is not only the anointing and seal but also the down payment or guarantee of believers' eternal inheritance (cf. 1 Peter 1:4), the first installment of future glory. Later in this epistle Paul wrote, "Now He who prepared us for this very purpose [believers' eternal existence in heaven; cf. vv. 2, 4] is God, who gave to us the Spirit as a pledge" (2 Cor. 5:5). To the Ephesians he wrote, "In Him, you also, after listening to the message of truth, the gospel of your salvation—having also believed, you were sealed in Him with the Holy Spirit of promise, who is given as a pledge of our inheritance, with a view to the redemption of God's own possession, to the praise of His glory" (Eph. 1:13–14).

God set both Paul and all believers on the unshakable and eternal promise of salvation in Christ. God has guaranteed that promise of eternal inheritance through the indwelling Holy Spirit. How foolish it was, in light of Paul's preaching those glorious, eternal divine realities, to question his legitimacy as an apostle because of a minor change in his travel plans!

SENSITIVITY

But I call God as witness to my soul, that to spare you I came no more to Corinth. Not that we lord it over your faith, but are workers with you for your joy; for in your faith you are standing firm. But I determined this for my own sake, that I would not come to you in sorrow again. (1:23–2:1)

Only after defending his integrity by affirming his loyalty, honesty, reliability, and authenticity did Paul finally explain why he changed his travel plans. And he prefaced his explanation with the solemn oath **I call God as witness to my soul.** The apostle appealed to God to verify the truth of what he was about to write and to judge him if he were lying.

It was **to spare** the Corinthians the rod of discipline (cf. 13:2, 10; 1 Cor. 4:21) that Paul **came no more to Corinth.** He mercifully wanted to give them time to correct the problems he wrote of in 1 Corinthians. Also, some at Corinth were guilty of being led into mutiny (the mutiny that prompted Paul to write the "severe letter" referred to in 2 Cor. 2:4) against him by the false teachers who had come to the church, and he wanted to give them time to repent. The apostle was also hoping for a good report from Titus about the Corinthians' repenting and rejecting the false apostles in favor of him before visiting them. That report, a positive one as Paul hoped, is described in 7:6ff. The apostle displayed great patience and sensitivity toward the Corinthians. He knew that, as Augustine wrote, "As severity is ready to punish the faults which it may discover, so charity is reluctant to discover the faults which it must punish" (cited in Philip E. Hughes, *The Second Epistle to the Corinthians,* The New International Commentary on the New Testament [Grand Rapids: Eerdmans, 1992], 47).

Ever sensitive to avoid provoking unnecessary conflict, Paul quickly added the very positive disclaimer, **Not that we lord it over your faith, but are workers with you for your joy.** Paul never abused his apostolic authority to gain prestige or power, or to further his own selfish aims. His goal, even in disciplining the unruly Corinthians, was the **joy** that holiness would bring them.

Paul was confident that **in** their **faith** (their salvation) the Corinthians were **standing firm** (cf. Rom. 5:2; 1 Cor. 15:1; Gal. 5:1; Phil. 1:27). He claimed no authority over their **faith,** which was a private matter between them and God. Saving faith is a personal matter between the believer and the Lord. No one but the Lord has authority over that relationship. Salvation is an individual matter and does not come through a hierarchical ecclesiastical organization.

Paul was **determined** not only for their sake but also **for** his **own sake, that** he **would not come to** the Corinthians **in sorrow again.** The apostle was referring to a painful visit he had earlier made to Corinth. Learning of the false prophets' arrival, Paul left Ephesus and hurried to Corinth to deal with the situation. The visit was not a success; in fact, someone (possibly one of the false apostles) openly insulted Paul (cf. 2 Cor. 2:5–8, 10; 7:12), and the Corinthians did not defend him. It was that painful visit that had prompted Paul to write the "severe letter" he referred to in 2:4. By giving the Corinthians time to repent, Paul hoped to avoid another painful encounter with them. Thus, his change in travel plans was not motivated by fickleness and unreliability, as the false teachers claimed, but by Paul's sensitivity toward his beloved church.

PURITY

For if I cause you sorrow, who then makes me glad but the one whom I made sorrowful? This is the very thing I wrote you, so that when I came, I would not have sorrow from those who ought to make me rejoice; having confidence in you all that my joy would be the joy of you all. (2:2-3)

Paul's sensitivity and patience with the Corinthians did not mean that he was unwilling to discipline them if they did not repent. His zeal for the purity of the church made him willing to **cause** them **sorrow** if necessary. If he did, the only thing that would make him **glad** would be the repentance of those **whom** he **made sorrowful.** It was his concern for purity in the Corinthian church that prompted the letters he **wrote** them (cf. 2:9; 7:8). Paul, of course, hoped they would repent, **so that when** he **came** to Corinth he **would not have sorrow from those**

who ought to make him **rejoice.** But, unlike many in the evangelical church today, Paul did not place church unity above truth and holiness. He was willing to confront unrepentant sin, even at the cost of his own joy.

Paul hoped the sinful issues he confronted in his letters would be settled before he again visited Corinth, and he had **confidence** that they would be. Then his **joy would be the joy of** them **all;** they could not have mutual joy as long as the Corinthians continued in sin. Paul's expression of **confidence** in the Corinthians was also meant to encourage the majority of the congregation, who looked to him as their revered spiritual leader. That his **confidence** was not misplaced became evident when Titus returned from Corinth with news that the majority had repented (7:6–16.).

Sensitivity and the desire to avoid unnecessary confrontation must always be balanced with a commitment to the purity of the church. (For further discussion of this matter, see the discussion of 12:19–13:3 in chapters 33–36 of this volume.)

LOVE

For out of much affliction and anguish of heart I wrote to you with many tears; not so that you would be made sorrowful, but that you might know the love which I have especially for you. (2:4)

It took real love, not sentimentalism, for Paul to confront the Corinthians' sin. Writing 1 Corinthians and especially the "severe letter" caused him much **affliction and anguish of heart** and **many tears.** Nothing is more painful for a pastor than confronting sin in his beloved congregation. But Paul's goal in writing was **not so that** they **would be made sorrowful, but that** the Corinthians **might know the love which** he had **especially for** them. He took no pleasure in their sorrow but desired that it would bring them to repentance (cf. 7:10) and joy. The apostle exemplified the truth of Proverbs 27:6: "Faithful are the wounds of a friend."

The lying teachers were dead wrong about Paul. He was not an untrustworthy deceiver, and to take a trivial issue and attempt to use it to discredit his ministry was reprehensible. As he examined his heart honestly before God, Paul found loyalty, honesty, reliability, authenticity, sensitivity, purity, and love—the traits that mark all godly pastors.

The Blessings of Forgiveness
(2 Corinthians 2:5–11)

4

But if any has caused sorrow, he has caused sorrow not to me, but in some degree—in order not to say too much—to all of you. Sufficient for such a one is this punishment which was inflicted by the majority, so that on the contrary you should rather forgive and comfort him, otherwise such a one might be overwhelmed by excessive sorrow. Wherefore I urge you to reaffirm your love for him. For to this end also I wrote, so that I might put you to the test, whether you are obedient in all things. But one whom you forgive anything, I forgive also; for indeed what I have forgiven, if I have forgiven anything, I did it for your sakes in the presence of Christ, so that no advantage would be taken of us by Satan, for we are not ignorant of his schemes. (2:5–11)

We live in a culture that views forgiveness not as a virtue, but as a sign of weakness. Our heroes are the vengeful, who challenge their enemies to give them an opportunity to strike; those who proudly see themselves as their enemies' "worst nightmare." Some even argue that forgiveness is unhealthy. Self-help books boldly assert that people should cultivate self-esteem and blame others for causing their problems. The victim mentality reigns supreme, and as a result of these and other perspectives, vengeance and retaliation are exalted, not the noble and Christlike virtues of forgiveness and restoration.

But the price of refusing to forgive is high. Unforgiveness produces hatred, bitterness, animosity, anger, and retribution. It not only clogs up the arteries but also the courts with thousands of vengeful lawsuits. Refusing to forgive imprisons people in their past. Unforgiving people keep their pain alive by constantly picking at the open wound and keeping it from healing. Bitterness takes root in their hearts and defiles them (Heb. 12:15). Anger rages out of control and negative emotions run unchecked. Life is filled with turmoil and strife instead of joy and peace.

On the other hand, forgiveness frees people from the past. It is liberating, exhilarating, and healthy. Forgiveness relieves tension, brings peace and joy, and restores relationships. In addition to its personal and societal benefits, there are at least ten biblical reasons for forgiving others.

First, believers are never more like God than when they forgive. God is "a God of forgiveness" (Neh. 9:17), "a forgiving God" (Ps. 99:8), to whom "belong compassion and forgiveness" (Dan. 9:9). The prophet Micah asked rhetorically, "Who is a God like You, who pardons iniquity and passes over the rebellious act of the remnant of His possession?" (Mic. 7:18). The parable of the prodigal son aptly illustrates God's forgiveness (Luke 15:11–32). Like the father in the parable, who watched for his wayward son and ran to meet him, God eagerly forgives repentant sinners. God's forgiveness means that He will not hold believers' sins against them as requiring punishment (cf. Isa. 43:25; 44:22; Jer. 31:34); He has cast them behind His back (Isa. 38:17) and buried them in the depths of the sea (Mic. 7:19). Believers are never more like God than when they eagerly and passionately forgive. In Matthew 5:44–45 Jesus said, "But I say to you, love your enemies and pray for those who persecute you, so that you may be sons of your Father who is in heaven; for He causes His sun to rise on the evil and the good, and sends rain on the righteous and the unrighteous."

Second, the sixth commandment, "You shall not murder" (Ex. 20:13), does not just forbid murder but also anger, malice, lack of forgiveness, and desire for revenge. In Matthew 5:21–22 Jesus declared,

> You have heard that the ancients were told, "You shall not commit murder" and "Whoever commits murder shall be liable to the court." But I say to you that everyone who is angry with his brother shall be guilty before the court; and whoever says to his brother, "You good-for-nothing," shall be guilty before the supreme court; and whoever says, "You fool," shall be guilty enough to go into the fiery hell.

The apostle John added, "Everyone who hates his brother is a murderer" (1 John 3:15). Those who refuse to forgive others but are bitter, hateful, and full of animosity are guilty of violating the sixth commandment.

Third, whoever offends another person offends God more, because all sin is ultimately against Him. David committed adultery with Bathsheba and murdered her husband Uriah. Yet he acknowledged to God in Psalm 51:4, "Against You, You only, I have sinned and done what is evil in Your sight" (cf. 2 Sam. 12:9). Any wrong done against believers is insignificant compared to the wrong done to God. How then can they refuse to forgive?

Fourth, those who have been forgiven of great sin against God must forgive the lesser sin of others against them. At salvation, God forgives believers' staggering, unpayable debt of sin because of Christ's substitutionary death on their behalf. For them to refuse to forgive other people is utterly unthinkable. Jesus graphically illustrated that incongruity in a parable recorded in Matthew 18:21–35. A king's servant (probably a regional governor who embezzled tax revenue) owed him ten thousand talents—a vast sum that the servant could never have repaid. The king felt compassion for him and released him from his debt. But inexplicably, unbelievably, the servant refused to forgive his fellow servant who owed him a small amount of money.

The point of the illustration is simple. God freely forgives believers' massive debt to His holiness—a debt they could never repay even if they spent eternity in hell. Therefore they must readily forgive the sins by which others offend them. To refuse to do so is reprehensible, insensitive ingratitude that makes a mockery of God's forgiveness of them.

Fifth, believers who refuse to forgive forfeit the blessing of fellowship with other Christians. In the Lord's parable, it was the unforgiving servant's outraged fellow servants who reported him to his lord (Matt. 18:31), an act symbolizing church discipline. Those who refuse to forgive can cause rifts in the church fellowship and destroy its unity. They must be brought before the Lord for chastening, and if impenitent are thereby alienated from the church fellowship. Like Hymenaeus and Alexander (1 Tim. 1:20) and the incestuous man at Corinth (1 Cor. 5:5), they are delivered to Satan and forfeit the blessings of associating with God's people.

Sixth, failing to forgive results in divine chastening. In addition to their separation from the church fellowship, God brings suffering into the lives of those who refuse to repent. God reacts with holy anger against unforgiving believers and chastens them (Matt. 18:32–34). His goal is to bring them to repentance, so they will willingly pay what they owe (v. 34); in other words, be willing to forgive others. Otherwise, "Judgment will be merciless to one who has shown no mercy" (James 2:13).

Seventh, God will not forgive believers who refuse to forgive others. Jesus stated this truth plainly in the Sermon on the Mount: "For if you forgive others for their transgressions, your heavenly Father will also forgive you. But if you do not forgive others, then your Father will not forgive your transgressions" (Matt. 6:14–15). The Lord was not, of course, referring to the eternal forgiveness of justification (Acts 10:43; Rom. 3:23–24; Col. 1:14; 2:13; Eph. 1:7; 4:32; Titus 2:14; Heb. 7:25; 1 Peter 2:24) but to the temporal forgiveness of sanctification. Believers who fail to forgive others do not cease to be God's children, but they will face their heavenly Father's chastening. They will not forfeit their eternal blessings in heaven, but they will forfeit their temporal blessings in this life.

Eighth, failing to forgive others renders believers unfit to worship. In the familiar words of the Lord Jesus Christ in Matthew 5:23–24, "Therefore if you are presenting your offering at the altar, and there remember that your brother has something against you, leave your offering there before the altar and go; first be reconciled to your brother, and then come and present your offering." God does not want the hypocritical worship of those who refuse to forgive others. Reconciliation must precede worship.

Ninth, to refuse to forgive is to usurp God's authority. It is to set oneself up as a higher court, with higher standards, than God. Paul forbad such arrogant pride in Romans 12:19: "Never take your own revenge, beloved, but leave room for the wrath of God, for it is written, 'Vengeance is Mine, I will repay,' says the Lord" (cf. Prov. 24:29). Only God can righteously deal with sin, since He alone is omniscient, just, and always acts in perfect holiness.

Finally, offenses against believers must be recognized and embraced as the trials that mature them. Jesus commanded believers who face criticism, injustice, and mistreatment, "Love your enemies and pray for those who persecute you, so that you may be sons of your Father who is in heaven; for He causes His sun to rise on the evil and the good, and sends rain on the righteous and the unrighteous" (Matt. 5:44–45). A proper response of forgiveness leads to spiritual maturity (James 1:2–4).

The perfect model of forgiveness is the Lord Jesus Christ, who while on the cross prayed for His tormentors, "Father, forgive them; for they do not know what they are doing" (Luke 23:34). Peter called on believers to follow the Lord's example in 1 Peter 2:19–23:

> For this finds favor, if for the sake of conscience toward God a person bears up under sorrows when suffering unjustly. For what credit is there if, when you sin and are harshly treated, you endure it with patience? But if when you do what is right and suffer for it you patiently endure it, this finds favor with God. For you have been called for this purpose,

since Christ also suffered for you, leaving you an example for you to follow in His steps, who committed no sin, nor was any deceit found in His mouth; and while being reviled, He did not revile in return; while suffering, He uttered no threats, but kept entrusting Himself to Him who judges righteously.

The apostle Paul understood the importance of forgiveness. In this passage he urged the Corinthians to forgive one of their number. This individual (his identity hidden by the terms "any" in verse 5 and "such a one" in verse 6) had apparently verbally and publicly assaulted Paul during the apostle's "painful visit" to Corinth (see 2:1). Following Paul's instructions, the Corinthian church disciplined the sinning member and put him out of the fellowship. He had since repented, and now not only did Paul forgive him, but he also instructed the Corinthians to do so too. From this passage seven motives emerge that enrich the New Testament teaching on forgiveness. Believers are to forgive to deflect pride, show mercy, restore joy, affirm love, prove obedience, restore fellowship, and thwart Satan.

To Deflect Pride

But if any has caused sorrow, he has caused sorrow not to me, but in some degree—in order not to say too much—to all of you. (2:5)

The clause **if any has caused sorrow** assumes the condition to be true. Paul acknowledged the reality of the offense and its impact on the church.

One of the chief causes of an unforgiving heart is pride. A prideful reaction to an offense can run the gamut from wallowing in self-pity to violent retaliation, and everything in between. But there was no place in Paul's heart for self-glory, self-protection, self-pity, a wounded ego, or retaliation. Paul acknowledged that the offender who assaulted him had **caused sorrow,** but he refused to take it personally (cf. 12:10). By refusing to make an issue out of his personal injury, the apostle intended to soften the animosity toward the repentant offender. The church would deal with him apart from any consideration of Paul.

The members of the "Paul party" at Corinth (1 Cor. 1:12; 3:4) were deeply offended when Paul was publicly insulted. They perhaps felt that the sinning individual needed more discipline and penance before being restored to fellowship. Paul, however, defused the situation by insisting that the offender had not really **caused sorrow** to him. He was not bitterly resentful, nor did he seek vengeance on the one who had insulted him. He dismissed the grief and embarrassment the individual had caused him and urged the church to deal with him objectively. They had no right to carry out a vendetta on the apostle's behalf.

Paul humbly rose above the offense and forgave the offender, refusing to see himself as a victim or to carry a grudge against the one who offended him. There was no place in Paul's mind for pride or bitter resentment, because how people judged him was inconsequential. As he wrote in 1 Corinthians: "To me it is a very small thing that I may be examined by you, or by any human court; in fact, I do not even examine myself. For I am conscious of nothing against myself, yet I am not by this acquitted; but the one who examines me is the Lord" (1 Cor. 4:3–4).

Though he was not concerned about the offense as it related to him, Paul was concerned about its ramifications in the Corinthian congregation. The man's offense did cause the Corinthians some **sorrow,** since he had caused strife in the congregation. While acknowledging to the Corinthians that the offender had **caused sorrow . . . to all of** them, Paul added two disclaimers to minimize the impact of the offense. The sorrow was limited in extent; it had only affected the Corinthian church **in some degree.** Paul also did not want **to say too much** about the offense; he did not want to exaggerate it. Instead, he downplayed the incident and cautioned the Corinthians not to blow it up out of proportion. The man had repented; the incident was closed; and it was time to move on.

Paul had nothing but love and forgiveness in his heart toward the person who had wronged him. He was not about to let that individual steal his joy, impair his usefulness, or become the dominating issue in the Corinthian church. Paul exemplified the forgiveness Jesus commanded. Responding to Peter's question, "'Lord, how often shall my brother sin against me and I forgive him? Up to seven times?' (Matt. 18:21) Jesus said to him, 'I do not say to you, up to seven times, but up to seventy times seven'" (v. 22).

Joseph is an Old Testament example of a man who forgave self-lessly like Paul did. Motivated by jealousy, his brothers sold him into slavery in Egypt. But God providentially cared for him, eventually elevating him to the position of prime minister of Egypt. When a famine forced his brothers to seek food in Egypt, Joseph revealed himself to them. Genesis 45:1–15 records that dramatic encounter:

> Then Joseph could not control himself before all those who stood by him, and he cried, "Have everyone go out from me." So there was no man with him when Joseph made himself known to his brothers. He wept so loudly that the Egyptians heard it, and the household of Pharaoh heard of it. Then Joseph said to his brothers, "I am Joseph! Is

my father still alive?" But his brothers could not answer him, for they were dismayed at his presence. Then Joseph said to his brothers, "Please come closer to me." And they came closer. And he said, "I am your brother Joseph, whom you sold into Egypt. Now do not be grieved or angry with yourselves, because you sold me here, for God sent me before you to preserve life. For the famine has been in the land these two years, and there are still five years in which there will be neither plowing nor harvesting. God sent me before you to preserve for you a remnant in the earth, and to keep you alive by a great deliverance. Now, therefore, it was not you who sent me here, but God; and He has made me a father to Pharaoh and lord of all his household and ruler over all the land of Egypt. Hurry and go up to my father, and say to him, 'Thus says your son Joseph, "God has made me lord of all Egypt; come down to me, do not delay. You shall live in the land of Goshen, and you shall be near me, you and your children and your children's children and your flocks and your herds and all that you have. There I will also provide for you, for there are still five years of famine to come, and you and your household and all that you have would be impoverished."' Behold, your eyes see, and the eyes of my brother Benjamin see, that it is my mouth which is speaking to you. Now you must tell my father of all my splendor in Egypt, and all that you have seen; and you must hurry and bring my father down here." Then he fell on his brother Benjamin's neck and wept, and Benjamin wept on his neck. He kissed all his brothers and wept on them, and afterward his brothers talked with him.

Despite their harsh treatment of him, Joseph was not bitter toward his brothers. Instead, he freely forgave them and comforted them with the truth that God had used their treachery for His own purposes. After Jacob's death, Joseph's brothers once again feared that he would take vengeance against them:

When Joseph's brothers saw that their father was dead, they said, "What if Joseph bears a grudge against us and pays us back in full for all the wrong which we did to him!" So they sent a message to Joseph, saying, "Your father charged before he died, saying, 'Thus you shall say to Joseph, "Please forgive, I beg you, the transgression of your brothers and their sin, for they did you wrong."' And now, please forgive the transgression of the servants of the God of your father." And Joseph wept when they spoke to him. Then his brothers also came and fell down before him and said, "Behold, we are your servants." But Joseph said to them, "Do not be afraid, for am I in God's place? As for you, you meant evil against me, but God meant it for good in order to bring about this present result, to preserve many people alive. So therefore, do not be afraid; I will provide for you and your little ones." So he comforted them and spoke kindly to them. (Gen. 50:15–21)

Forgiveness breaks the bitter chains of pride, self-pity, and vengeance that lead to despair, alienation, broken relationships, and loss of joy.

To Show Mercy

Sufficient for such a one is this punishment which was inflicted by the majority, (2:6)

The **punishment** that had already been **inflicted** on the sinning individual by the church was **sufficient.** He had suffered enough, and it was time to show him mercy and restore him to fellowship. *Epitimia* (**punishment**) appears only here in the New Testament. Both its use in extrabiblical Greek writings and the context of this passage suggest *epitimia* refers to an official disciplinary act **by the majority:** excommunication or disfellowshipping. The New Testament teaches that the church is to discipline sinning believers. Jesus outlined that process in Matthew 18:15–18:

> If your brother sins, go and show him his fault in private; if he listens to you, you have won your brother. But if he does not listen to you, take one or two more with you, so that by the mouth of two or three witnesses every fact may be confirmed. If he refuses to listen to them, tell it to the church; and if he refuses to listen even to the church, let him be to you as a Gentile and a tax collector. Truly I say to you, whatever you bind on earth shall have been bound in heaven; and whatever you loose on earth shall have been loosed in heaven.

Paul had earlier dealt with another sinning member of the Corinthian congregation:

> In the name of our Lord Jesus, when you are assembled, and I with you in spirit, with the power of our Lord Jesus, I have decided to deliver such a one to Satan for the destruction of his flesh, so that his spirit may be saved in the day of the Lord Jesus. . . . But actually, I wrote to you not to associate with any so-called brother if he is an immoral person, or covetous, or an idolater, or a reviler, or a drunkard, or a swindler—not even to eat with such a one. (1 Cor. 5:4–5, 11)

To the Thessalonians Paul wrote,

> Now we command you, brethren, in the name of our Lord Jesus Christ, that you keep away from every brother who leads an unruly life and not according to the tradition which you received from us. . . . If anyone does not obey our instruction in this letter, take special note of that

person and do not associate with him, so that he will be put to shame. Yet do not regard him as an enemy, but admonish him as a brother. (2 Thess. 3:6, 14–15)

The Corinthian congregation had officially acted and put the sinning individual out of the church. Apparently that discipline had had its desired effect, and the man had repented. It was time to forgive and restore him. In Galatians 6:1 Paul commanded, "Brethren, even if anyone is caught in any trespass, you who are spiritual, restore such a one in a spirit of gentleness; each one looking to yourself, so that you too will not be tempted." He exhorted the Ephesians, "Be kind to one another, tenderhearted, forgiving each other, just as God in Christ also has forgiven you" (Eph. 4:32). In Colossians 3:13 he wrote that believers are to be characterized by "bearing with one another, and forgiving each other, whoever has a complaint against anyone."

Believers are never more like God than when they show forgiving mercy to a repentant sinner.

To Restore Joy

so that on the contrary you should rather forgive and comfort him, otherwise such a one might be overwhelmed by excessive sorrow. (2:7)

Mournfully confessing his tragic sin with Bathsheba, David acknowledged the sad reality that sin steals joy. In Psalm 51 he begged God, "Restore to me the joy of Your salvation" (v. 12), and, "Deliver me from bloodguiltiness, O God, the God of my salvation; then my tongue will joyfully sing of Your righteousness" (v. 14). Confession and repentance restores the joy that God desires all Christians to have (John 15:11; 16:24; 17:13; 2 John 12; cf. Gal. 5:22).

Some of the Corinthians believed that the individual who had insulted Paul needed to suffer further before being restored. But Paul disagreed, and insisted **that on the contrary** the Corinthians **should rather forgive and comfort him.** His pain had brought him to repentance, and now it was time to restore his joy. The church cannot set arbitrary limits on grace and mercy; it cannot reject a truly penitent individual, no matter how serious the sin was.

For the Corinthians not to **forgive** the repentant person would be sin and steal their joy. It would, in fact, bring God's chastening on them (cf. Matt. 6:14–15; 18:35). Unforgiveness would also render them unfit for worship (Matt. 5:23–24).

Positively, the Corinthian congregation needed to **comfort him.** **Comfort** translates the familiar New Testament word *parakaleō*, which means, "to come alongside," "to strengthen," or "to encourage." The Corinthians were to "restore such a one in a spirit of gentleness" (Gal. 6:1); to come alongside him, lift him up, and help him to walk in obedience. Paul feared that **otherwise such a one might be overwhelmed by excessive sorrow,** not only the sorrow of his punishment, but also the sorrow caused by the Corinthians' continued rejection of him. *Katapinō* (**overwhelmed**) is variously translated in the New Testament as "swallow" (2 Cor. 5:4; Matt. 23:24; 1 Cor. 15:54), "drown" (Heb. 11:29); and "devour" (1 Peter 5:8). God does not want believers be totally consumed by the grief caused by their sin. Later in this epistle Paul wrote, "The sorrow that is according to the will of God produces a repentance without regret, leading to salvation" (2 Cor. 7:10). After sorrow has done its convicting work, it is to be replaced by joy.

To Affirm Love

Wherefore I urge you to reaffirm your love for him. (2:8)

Paul's desire to see the repentant individual joyful, rather than sorrowful, caused him to **urge** the Corinthians **to reaffirm** their **love for him.** In its only other New Testament appearance, *kuroō* (**reaffirm**) speaks of formally ratifying a covenant (Gal. 3:15). The Corinthians had officially and publicly disciplined the offender (v. 6). Now they needed to conclude the matter by publicly and lovingly restoring him to the fellowship. By so doing they would display their collective as well as individual affection for him.

Agapē (**love**) is the **love** of choice, of will, of humble service to others. It is the **love** not of sentimental feelings but of action (cf. 1 Cor. 13:4–7). **Love** is essential in the life of the church. On the night before His death Jesus said, "A new commandment I give to you, that you love one another, even as I have loved you, that you also love one another. By this all men will know that you are My disciples, if you have love for one another" (John 13:34–35). Paul commanded the Ephesians, "Be imitators of God, as beloved children; and walk in love, just as Christ also loved you and gave Himself up for us, an offering and a sacrifice to God as a fragrant aroma" (Eph. 5:1–2).

At its core, unforgiveness is a lack of love. Forgiveness, on the other hand, fulfills the royal law of love (cf. James 2:8). Forgiving love is a precious jewel, a rich treasure in the life of the church. Without it, churches are torn, split, and fragmented. Churches that faithfully practice church discipline must also forgive penitent sinners. The greatest demonstration of love, both by individual believers and the church collectively, is forgiving others.

TO PROVE OBEDIENCE

For to this end also I wrote, so that I might put you to the test, whether you are obedient in all things. (2:9)

As already noted, forgiveness reflects some of the most noble Christian virtues, including humility, mercy, joy, and love. But even if it did not, forgiveness would still be the right thing to do, because God requires it. One reason Paul **wrote** the severe letter between 1 and 2 Corinthians (2:4) was **so that** he **might put** the Corinthians **to the test** and see **whether** they would be **obedient in all things.** Whether they were willing to forgive would be a real **test** of whether the Corinthians' hearts were right before God. As even a cursory glance at human history shows, fallen man does not readily forgive. Repeated wars, longtime feuds, centuries of deadly retaliation between racial and religious groups, and personal vengeance have marred human history since the Fall. Sinful, prideful humanity sees forgiveness as weakness and vengeance as strength. The Corinthians had proven themselves **obedient** by disciplining the offender. Forgiving him and receiving him back into the fellowship would also be proof of their obedience. Jesus commanded, "If your brother sins, rebuke him; and if he repents, forgive him" (Luke 17:3). By disciplining the sinning member, the Corinthians had obeyed the first part of that admonition; by fully forgiving him, they would obey the latter.

God has always tested His people to reveal what is in their hearts. In Exodus 16:4 "the Lord said to Moses, 'Behold, I will rain bread from heaven for you; and the people shall go out and gather a day's portion every day, that I may test them, whether or not they will walk in My instruction.'" Moses admonished Israel to

> remember all the way which the Lord your God has led you in the wilderness these forty years, that He might humble you, testing you, to know what was in your heart, whether you would keep His commandments or not. . . . In the wilderness He fed you manna which your fathers did not know, that He might humble you and that He might test you, to do good for you in the end. (Deut. 8:2, 16)

In Deuteronomy 13:3 he added, "You shall not listen to the words of that prophet or that dreamer of dreams; for the Lord your God is testing you to find out if you love the Lord your God with all your heart and with all your soul."

Paul put the Corinthian church to the test to see if they would both discipline and forgive. Unlike most churches today, the Corinthian church passed both tests. They did the hard work of confronting sin; they also obeyed Paul's command to graciously forgive and restore the sinning individual. Later in this epistle Paul wrote,

> So although I wrote to you, it was not for the sake of the offender nor for the sake of the one offended, but that your earnestness on our behalf might be made known to you in the sight of God. For this reason we have been comforted. And besides our comfort, we rejoiced even much more for the joy of Titus, because his spirit has been refreshed by you all. For if in anything I have boasted to him about you, I was not put to shame; but as we spoke all things to you in truth, so also our boasting before Titus proved to be the truth. His affection abounds all the more toward you, as he remembers the obedience of you all, how you received him with fear and trembling. (7:12–15)

As Titus discovered and reported to Paul, the Corinthians had obeyed the apostle and forgiven the offender. Out of the chaos and confusion of their turbulent past had come an obedient church.

TO RESTORE FELLOWSHIP

But one whom you forgive anything, I forgive also; for indeed what I have forgiven, if I have forgiven anything, I did it for your sakes in the presence of Christ, (2:10)

Paul's agreement with the majority's decision to **forgive** the offender demonstrated his humility. He did not agree with the "Paul party" who wanted the individual to suffer more. **Indeed,** Paul had already **forgiven** him **if,** he added, **I have forgiven anything.** Once again, the apostle downplayed the offense against him. His primary concern was for the fellowship to be restored and for there to be unity in the Corinthian church. Thus, he forgave the individual primarily for the Corinthians' **sakes.**

Paul lived his whole life **in the presence of Christ,** aware that the Lord knew his every thought, word, and deed. Later in this chapter he reminded the Corinthians that he spoke "in Christ in the sight of God" (2:17). In 4:2 he wrote that he commended himself "to every man's conscience in the sight of God" (cf. 7:12; 12:19). To Timothy he wrote, "I solemnly charge you in the presence of God and of Christ Jesus, who is to judge the living and the dead, and by His appearing and His kingdom: preach the word; be ready in season and out of season; reprove, rebuke, exhort, with great patience and instruction" (2 Tim. 4:1–2). Paul eagerly forgave the one who had offended him because Christ, in whose presence he constantly lived, had fully forgiven him.

Forgiveness is crucial to maintaining unity in the church fellowship. Without it discord, disharmony, bitterness, and vengeance can destroy unity.

To Thwart Satan

so that no advantage would be taken of us by Satan, for we are not ignorant of his schemes. (2:11)

Satan's goal for the church is the opposite of God's. God wants a humble, merciful, joyful, loving, obedient fellowship; Satan wants one where sin reigns supreme. If sin is confronted, Satan wants it done so in a harsh, graceless, merciless manner. Both failing to deal with sin and failing to forgive repentant sinners can destroy a church. Paul stressed that the Corinthians must forgive and restore the repentant individual **so that no advantage would be taken of** them **by Satan.** An unforgiving spirit plays right into the devil's hands and gives him the leverage he needs to split a church apart.

Believers dare not be **ignorant of** Satan's **schemes** but must "stand firm against the schemes of the devil" (Eph. 6:11) and "not give the devil an opportunity" (Eph. 4:27). Two vitally important ways of doing that are dealing with sin and forgiving sinners.

Forgiveness affects the one who forgives (2 Cor. 2:5), the one forgiven (2:6–8), and the entire church (2:9–11). The hard work of disciplining sinners and restoring those who repent is a true test of a church's love for the Lord.

Restoring the Disheartened Pastor's Joy
(2 Corinthians 2:12–17)

5

Now when I came to Troas for the gospel of Christ and when a door was opened for me in the Lord, I had no rest for my spirit, not finding Titus my brother; but taking my leave of them, I went on to Macedonia. But thanks be to God, who always leads us in triumph in Christ, and manifests through us the sweet aroma of the knowledge of Him in every place. For we are a fragrance of Christ to God among those who are being saved and among those who are perishing; to the one an aroma from death to death, to the other an aroma from life to life. And who is adequate for these things? For we are not like many, peddling the word of God, but as from sincerity, but as from God, we speak in Christ in the sight of God. (2:12–17)

The call to the ministry is an invitation to unparalleled blessing and unequalled privilege. But at the same time, it is an invitation to discouragement, difficulty, sorrow, pain, and despair. Every pastor, no matter how richly blessed his ministry may be, knows those dark times when he is disheartened and downcast. No less a man of God than Charles Spurgeon wrote,

Fits of depression come over the most of us. Usually cheerful as we may be, we must at intervals be cast down. The strong are not always vigorous, the wise not always ready, the brave not always courageous, and the joyous not always happy. There may be here and there men of iron, to whom wear and tear work no perceptible detriment, but surely the rust frets even these; and as for ordinary men, the Lord knows, and makes them to know, that they are but dust.
("The Minister's Fainting Fits," in *Lectures to My Students,* First Series [Reprint; Grand Rapids: Baker, 1980], 167)

Some pastors become so disheartened that they leave the ministry, as the following letter reveals:

My dear Jim: I am through. Yesterday I handed in my resignation, to take effect at once, and this morning I began to work for the _____ Land Company. I shall not return to the pastorate. I think I can see into your heart as you read these words and behold not a little disappointment, if not disgust. I don't blame you at all, I'm somewhat disgusted with myself. Do you recall the days in the seminary when we talked of the future and painted pictures of what we were to do for the kingdom of God? We saw the boundless need for an unselfish Christian service, and longed to be out among men doing our part toward the world's redemption. I shall never forget that last talk on the night before our graduation. You were to go to the foreign field and I to the First Church, of _____. We had brave dreams of usefulness, and you have realized them. As I look back across twenty-five years I can see some lives that I have helped, and some things which I have been permitted to do that are worthwhile; but, sitting here tonight, I am more than half convinced that God never intended me to be a minister. If He did, I am not big enough and brave enough to pay the price. Even if it leads you to write me down as a coward, I'm going to tell you why I've quit. . . .

In these years I have found not a few earnest, unselfish, consecrated Christians. I do not believe that I am specially morbid or unfair in my estimate. So far as I know my own heart, I am not bitter. But through all these years a conviction has been growing within me that the average church member cares precious little about the kingdom of God and its advancement, or the welfare of his fellow men. He is a Christian in order that he may save his soul from hell, and for no other reason. He does as little as he can, lives as indifferently as he dares. If he thought he could gain heaven without even lifting his finger for others, he would jump at the chance. Never have I known more than a small minority of any church which I have served to be really interested in and unselfishly devoted to God's work. It took my whole time to pull and push and urge and persuade the reluctant members of my church to undertake a little something for their fellow men. They took a covenant to be faithful in attendance upon the services of the church, and not one out of ten ever thought of attending prayer meeting. A large percentage seldom attended church in the morning, and a pitifully small number in the evening. It didn't seem to mean anything to them that they had dedicated themselves to the service of Christ.

I am tired; tired of being the only one in the church from whom real sacrifice is expected; tired of straining and tugging to get Christian people to live like Christians; tired of planning work for my people and then being compelled to do it myself or see it left undone; tired of dodging my creditors when I would not need to if I had what is due me; tired of the affrighting vision of penniless old age. I am not leaving Christ. I love Him. I shall still try to serve Him.

Judge me leniently, old friend. I can't bear to lose your friendship.

Yours as of old, William.
(cited in A. T. Robertson, *The Glory of the Ministry* [New York: Revell, 1911], 24–27)

Like William, the apostle Paul was no stranger to discouragement. But unlike William, Paul persevered in his ministry until the end of his life (2 Tim. 4:7). After listing the physical suffering he had endured in his ministry he wrote, "Apart from such external things, there is the daily pressure on me of concern for all the churches. Who is weak without my being weak? Who is led into sin without my intense concern?" (2 Cor. 11:28–29). It was the Corinthian church above all others that caused Paul deep, disheartening disappointment. They had broken his heart by their immaturity, shallowness, sin, indifference, disaffection toward him, and even outright rebellion against his apostolic authority. Paul's first inspired letter to the Corinthians is a sad litany of sin, selfishness, disorderliness, worldliness, and just about every other kind of spiritual disaster. The Corinthians, dragging into the church their former sinful patterns, tolerated the grossest form of sexual perversion, a man committing incest with his father's wife (1 Cor. 5:1–8). They fought each other, and hauled each other into court (1 Cor. 6:1–8). They were confused about marriage and singleness (1 Cor. 7). They abused their freedom in Christ and were arrogant about it (1 Cor. 8:1). Sin and selfishness stained their celebration of the Lord's Supper (1 Cor. 11:17–34). So twisted had their understanding of spiritual gifts become that when someone in their assembly cursed Jesus Christ in an unknown language, they thought it was the work of the Holy Spirit (1 Cor. 12:3). In addition, some false apostles had recently arrived in Corinth telling lies about Paul and assaulting his character. In order to capture the church with their heresy, they sought to destroy the apostle's credibility, and then replace him as the authoritative teachers in the Corinthian congregation. It broke Paul's heart that some of the Corinthians were being deceived by them.

But in spite of all their problems Paul loved the Corinthians deeply and had invested at least eighteen months of his life ministering to them (Acts 18:11). The apostle's intense love for them gave the Corinthians the potential to hurt him deeply—and they did (2 Cor. 12:15). His last visit to Corinth had been intensely painful (2:1), and Paul's pain, grief, and discouragement are evident in this passage. Adding to it was the fact that things also were not going well in Ephesus, where he had recently ministered, and from where he wrote 1 Corinthians. His preaching had touched off a riot that could have cost him his life (Acts 19:23–41). He had also, as noted in chapter 1 of this volume, undergone a severe trial there, so that he was "burdened excessively, beyond [his] strength, so that [he] despaired even of life; indeed, [he] had the sentence of death within [himself]" (2 Cor. 1:8–9). Not surprisingly, in light of all Paul was going through, there is an element of pathos and grief in 2 Corinthians.

The present text may be divided into two sections: Paul's discouragement over the Corinthians and his encouragement because of Christ.

PAUL'S DISCOURAGEMENT

Now when I came to Troas for the gospel of Christ and when a door was opened for me in the Lord, I had no rest for my spirit, not finding Titus my brother; but taking my leave of them, I went on to Macedonia. (2:12–13)

After leaving Ephesus, Paul **came to Troas. Troas** was a seaport on the Aegean Sea in western Asia Minor, located in the province of Mysia near the mouth of the Dardanelles. It was about ten miles from the famous city of Troy, for which it was named. **Troas** was founded in 300 B.C., and Emperor Augustus had granted it the coveted status of a Roman colony.

The serious riot in Ephesus (Acts 19:23–41), sparked by Paul's fearless preaching of the gospel, may have prompted the apostle's departure for **Troas.** But more important, Paul hoped to meet Titus there. Paul had sent him to Corinth to find out how the church there had responded to 1 Corinthians and, especially, to the "severe letter" (see 2 Cor. 2:3–4). Anxiously awaiting Titus's report, Paul feared the worst, and his heart was heavy with concern. The apostle knew that Titus would pass through **Troas** on his way back to Ephesus from Corinth. Unable to wait any longer, Paul went there hoping to meet him and get his report sooner.

Paul had passed through **Troas** before, on his second missionary journey (Acts 16:8–11). On that visit, however, the apostle apparently did not found a church. When Paul visited **Troas** on his way back from Macedonia and Corinth, there was a church there (Acts 20:6–12). Therefore, it seems likely that he founded the church at **Troas** on this visit. While waiting for Titus, Paul, as he did whenever he had the opportunity, preached the **gospel of Christ.** His mission in going to **Troas** included evangelization, not merely meeting Titus.

Paul's statement that **a door was opened for** him **in the Lord** further confirms that the apostle preached in **Troas** while waiting for Titus. How else could he have known that the **Lord** had **opened** a **door** there for him unless he had been given the opportunity to preach and had positive responses? The apostle commonly used that phrase to describe ministry opportunities. In 1 Corinthians 16:8–9, Paul spoke of an open door at Ephesus: "But I will remain in Ephesus until Pentecost; for a wide door for effective service has opened to me, and there are many adversaries." Returning to their home church at Antioch after the first missionary journey, Paul and Barnabas "began to report all things that God had done with them and how He had opened a door of faith to the Gentiles" (Acts 14:27). Paul urged the Colossians to pray "at the same time for us as well, that God will open up to us a door for the word, so that we may speak forth the mystery of Christ" (Col. 4:3).

The **door** that **was opened** at **Troas** represented a divinely prepared opportunity, the kind Paul longed for and prayed for. But he was so overwrought and burdened by the situation at Corinth that he found it difficult to focus on the opportunity; he **had no rest for** his **spirit.** The turmoil and discontent of his heart were debilitating and threatened to close the **door** that **was opened for** ministry at **Troas.** His intense concern for the Corinthian church raised troubling questions in his mind. Would they affirm their love for him? Or would they follow the false apostles? Would they deal with the specific issues he had rebuked them for: divisions, strife, incest, marriage, singleness, divorce, the role of women, idolatry, spiritual pride, the abuse of the Lord's Supper, misuse of spiritual gifts? Paul's heart ached because he did not know the answer to those questions, and as a result he had no freedom to minister. Until he heard from Titus, the apostle feared the worst. He was so burdened by the situation at Corinth that he lost interest in the open **door** of ministry at **Troas. Not finding Titus** in **Troas,** Paul **went on to Macedonia.** He could wait no longer; he had to find Titus to hear about the response of the Corinthians. So he headed for the province of **Macedonia,** bordering the northwest shore of the Aegean Sea, north of Achaia.

This was a dark hour in the apostle's life. He loved the Corinthians so much that his heart was torn apart by concern for them, to the point that he was actually depressed (2 Cor. 7:5–6). But Paul did not quit. He was "afflicted in every way, but not crushed; perplexed, but not despairing" (4:8). He was discouraged but not defeated, and he still held on to hope for a good report when he met Titus. Until then he was dealing with serious fears. Relief came when he focused on his Lord.

PAUL'S ENCOURAGEMENT

But thanks be to God, who always leads us in triumph in Christ, and manifests through us the sweet aroma of the knowledge of Him in every place. For we are a fragrance of Christ to God among those who are being saved and among those who are perishing; to the one an aroma from death to death, to the other an aroma from life to life. And who is adequate for these things? For we are not like many, peddling the word of God, but as from sincerity, but as from God, we speak in Christ in the sight of God. (2:14–17)

Verse 14 marks an abrupt change in Paul's attitude and he launches into **thanks . . . to God,** the reason for which is not readily apparent in the text. It is true that he finally met Titus in Macedonia (7:5–7) and received a generally encouraging report about the situation in Corinth. That report certainly brought Paul some much-needed relief. Yet it was not the key factor in Paul's joy and encouragement, or he would have mentioned it in this passage. Instead, he delayed mentioning it until chapter 7. And Paul knew there was still a recalcitrant minority in the Corinthian church that was hostile to him. The false apostles were still there, as was the baleful influence of the wretchedly sinful city of Corinth. The apostle was also wise enough to know that, having proved fickle once, the Corinthians could turn on him again. In any case, Paul obviously did not consider all the problems at Corinth to be resolved, or else he would not subsequently have written the lengthy epistle of 2 Corinthians.

But Paul did not look to his circumstances for comfort, joy, and encouragement, but to the "Father of mercies and God of all comfort" (1:3). The cure for his discouragement was a thankful heart. Paul took his focus off his difficulties and put it onto his God.

The apostle used as a backdrop for verses 14–17 an important event in the Roman world, the Triumph. William Barclay describes it:

> In [Paul's] mind is the picture of a Roman Triumph and of Christ as a universal conqueror. The highest honor which could be given to a

victorious Roman general was a Triumph. To attain it he must satisfy certain conditions. He must have been the actual commander-in-chief in the field. The campaign must have been completely finished, the region pacified and the victorious troops brought home. Five thousand of the enemy at least must have fallen in one engagement. A positive extension of territory must have been gained, and not merely a disaster retrieved or an attack repelled. And the victory must have been won over a foreign foe and not in a civil war.

In a Triumph the procession of the victorious general marched through the streets of Rome to the Capitol in the following order. First came the state officials and the senate. Then came the trumpeters. Then were carried the spoils taken from the conquered land. For instance, when Titus conquered Jerusalem, the seven-branched candlestick, the golden table of the shew-bread and the golden trumpets were carried through the streets of Rome. Then came pictures of the conquered land and models of conquered citadels and ships. There followed the white bull for the sacrifice which would be made. Then there walked the captive princes, leaders and generals in chains, shortly to be flung into prison and in all probability almost immediately to be executed. Then came the lictors bearing their rods, followed by the musicians with their lyres; then the priests swinging their censers with the sweet-smelling incense burning in them. After that came the general himself. He stood in a chariot drawn by four horses. He was clad in a purple tunic embroidered with golden palm leaves, and over it a purple toga marked out with golden stars. In his hand he held an ivory sceptre with the Roman eagle at its top, and over his head a slave held the crown of Jupiter. After him rode his family; and finally came the army wearing all their decorations and shouting *Io triumphe!* their cry of triumph. As the procession moved through the streets, all decorated and garlanded, amid the cheering crowds, it made a tremendous day which might happen only once in a lifetime.

That is the picture that is in Paul's mind. He sees Christ marching in triumph throughout the world, and himself in that conquering train. It is a triumph which, Paul is certain, nothing can stop.

(*The Letters to the Corinthians*, rev. ed. [Louisville: Westminster, 1975], 183–84. Italics in original.)

That joyous picture is in sharp contrast with the discouragement Paul expressed in verses 12 and 13. He figuratively went from the pit of despair to the exhilaration of marching in a triumphal parade.

In verses 14–17, Paul lists five privileges in which he was spiritually triumphant: the privilege of being led by a sovereign God, the privilege of promised victory in Christ, the privilege of influence for Christ, the privilege of pleasing God in Christ, and the privilege of power in Christ.

PAUL WAS THANKFUL FOR THE PRIVILEGE OF BEING LED BY A SOVEREIGN GOD

But thanks be to God, who always leads us (2:14a)

Recognizing the Lord's sovereign leading is foundational to a pastor's (or any believer's) joy, and it is the undergirding strength of his ministry. Paul's confident hope was that **God . . . always leads** believers, through every circumstance of life. No matter what trials or persecutions he endured in Corinth, Ephesus, or anywhere else he ministered, Paul rejoiced that God was in control.

The apostle never lost his sense of wonder at the privilege of belonging to the ranks of the sovereign Lord, of marching behind the Commander in Chief in His Triumph. To Timothy he wrote,

> I thank Christ Jesus our Lord, who has strengthened me, because He considered me faithful, putting me into service, even though I was formerly a blasphemer and a persecutor and a violent aggressor. Yet I was shown mercy because I acted ignorantly in unbelief; and the grace of our Lord was more than abundant, with the faith and love which are found in Christ Jesus. It is a trustworthy statement, deserving full acceptance, that Christ Jesus came into the world to save sinners, among whom I am foremost of all. Yet for this reason I found mercy, so that in me as the foremost, Jesus Christ might demonstrate His perfect patience as an example for those who would believe in Him for eternal life. (1 Tim. 1:12–16)

Contemplating the marvelous privilege of being led by God instead of fretting over his circumstances contributed to turning Paul's discouragement into joy.

PAUL WAS THANKFUL FOR THE PRIVILEGE OF PROMISED VICTORY IN CHRIST

in triumph in Christ, (2:14b)

In keeping with the imagery of the Roman Triumph, Paul proclaimed that God leads believers **in triumph in Christ.** They follow the all-conquering Commander in the victory parade, sharing in the triumph of His decisive victory over sin, death, and hell. In Matthew 16:18 Jesus spoke of His ultimate victory over Satan and the forces of hell: "I will build My church; and the gates of Hades will not overpower it." His followers share in His victory, as Paul declared in Romans 16:20: "The God of peace will soon crush Satan under your feet." The writer of Hebrews also spoke of that victory: "Since then the children share in flesh and blood, He Himself likewise also partook of the same, so that through death He might render powerless him who had the power of death, that is, the devil" (Heb. 2:14). In 1 John 3:8 the apostle John wrote, "The Son of God appeared for this purpose, to destroy the works of the devil." Christ won that victory on the cross: "When He had disarmed the rulers and authorities, He made a public display of them, having triumphed over them through Him" (Col. 2:15). As Paul wrote to the Romans, "In all these things we overwhelmingly conquer through Him who loved us" (Rom. 8:37). Believers are not only coconquerors with Christ, but also "heirs of God and fellow heirs with Christ" (Rom. 8:17; cf. Gal. 3:29; Eph. 3:6; Titus 3:7; James 2:5). They follow behind their Commander in the Triumph, bringing the spoils of war—the souls of men and women "rescued . . . from the domain of darkness, and transferred . . . to the kingdom of His beloved Son" (Col. 1:13; cf. Rom. 8:18–25, 28–30).

Though they may suffer setbacks and discouragement, believers' ultimate triumph is certain. They will march victoriously in the Lord Jesus Christ's Triumph on that glorious day when the heavenly choir cries out, "The kingdom of the world has become the kingdom of our Lord and of His Christ; and He will reign forever and ever" (Rev. 11:15). Believers will forever reign with Him (2 Tim. 2:12; 1 Peter 1:3–5).

PAUL WAS THANKFUL FOR THE PRIVILEGE OF HAVING INFLUENCE FOR CHRIST

and manifests through us the sweet aroma of the knowledge of Him in every place. (2:14c)

The **sweet aroma** of the Triumph arose from the incense-filled censers carried by the priests in the parade and from the garlands of flowers that were thrown into the streets. The fragrance speaks of influence; Paul's point is that God, in wonderful condescending grace and mercy, **manifests through** believers **the sweet aroma of the knowledge of** Christ **in every place.** He uses human preachers to give off the **sweet aroma** of the gospel, to influence people with the saving **knowledge** of Christ. To the Romans Paul wrote, "How then will they call on Him in whom they have not believed? How will they believe in Him whom they have not heard? And how will they hear without a preacher? How will they preach unless they are sent? Just as it is written, 'How beautiful are the feet of those who bring good news of good things'!" (Rom. 10:14–15).

It is not that believers deserve such a high privilege of being influences for the eternal gospel. Paul was keenly aware of his unworthiness for such service to God. In 1 Corinthians 15:9 he wrote, "For I am the least of the apostles, and not fit to be called an apostle, because I persecuted the church of God." To the Ephesians he added, "I was made a minister, according to the gift of God's grace which was given to me according to the working of His power. To me, the very least of all saints, this grace was given, to preach to the Gentiles the unfathomable riches of Christ" (Eph. 3:7–8). As previously noted, he expressed to Timothy his wonder that Christ chose him, a persecutor of the church, to preach the gospel:

> I thank Christ Jesus our Lord, who has strengthened me, because He considered me faithful, putting me into service, even though I was formerly a blasphemer and a persecutor and a violent aggressor. Yet I was shown mercy because I acted ignorantly in unbelief; and the grace of our Lord was more than abundant, with the faith and love which are found in Christ Jesus. It is a trustworthy statement, deserving full acceptance, that Christ Jesus came into the world to save sinners, among whom I am foremost of all. Yet for this reason I found mercy, so that in me as the foremost, Jesus Christ might demonstrate His perfect patience as an example for those who would believe in Him for eternal life. (1 Tim. 1:12–16)

No preacher should take lightly his inestimable privilege of proclaiming the saving **knowledge** of the Lord Jesus Christ. Whether or not preachers are successful, achieve popularity, or fulfill their ambitions is immaterial. The satisfaction of having an eternal influence for Jesus Christ should be sufficient. The issue is not results, but privilege. The disheartened preacher is disheartened because he focuses on circumstances; the joyful preacher is joyful because he focuses on the eternal worth of his service to God. The disheartened preacher considers his difficulties; the joyful preacher considers his privilege.

PAUL WAS THANKFUL FOR THE PRIVILEGE OF PLEASING GOD IN CHRIST

For we are a fragrance of Christ to God among those who are being saved and among those who are perishing; to the one an aroma from death to death, to the other an aroma from life to life. (2:15–16a)

In the Triumph, the emperor seated on his great throne at the capitol smelled the fragrant aroma of the incense when it reached him at the end of the parade. Paul likens the preacher's ministry to **a fragrance of Christ to God.** Although a preacher proclaims the gospel to men, it is in reality God who is his audience. His faithful gospel ministry causes the sweet aroma of the knowledge of Christ to be manifest to people, but the **fragrance** of that gospel ministry ascends to the very throne of **God.**

Pleasing God was the consuming passion of Paul's heart. Later in this epistle he wrote, "Therefore also we have as our ambition, whether at home or absent, to be pleasing to Him" (5:9). In Galatians 1:10 he asked pointedly, "For am I now seeking the favor of men, or of God? Or am I striving to please men? If I were still trying to please men, I would not be a bond-servant of Christ." He admonished the Ephesians to try "to learn what is pleasing to the Lord" (Eph. 5:10) and the Colossians to "walk in a manner worthy of the Lord, to please Him in all respects" (Col. 1:10). Paul declared to the Thessalonians, "Just as we have been approved by God to be entrusted with the gospel, so we speak, not as pleasing men, but God who examines our hearts" (1 Thess. 2:4) and exhorted them, "Finally then, brethren, we request and exhort you in the Lord Jesus, that as you received from us instruction as to how you ought to walk and please God (just as you actually do walk), that you excel still more" (1 Thess. 4:1). What matters is not the preacher's popularity or the size of his church. It is that he pleases God by his faithful proclamation of the gospel.

While it always pleased God, the **fragrance of Christ** from Paul's preaching had a twofold effect on the people who heard it. To **those who are being saved,** the **fragrance** of apostolic preaching was **an aroma from life to life.** These are the elect and redeemed people of God, who are headed for full and final glorification. On the other hand, the same message was to **those who are perishing**—those unbelieving sinners destined for eternal damnation—**an aroma from death to death.** In the Roman Triumph, both the victors, who were to be honored, and the vanquished, who were to be executed, smelled the aroma from the priests' censers. To the former, it symbolized their victory; to the latter, their impending deaths. Christ Himself has the same dual effect on people, as Peter noted in 1 Peter 2:6–8:

> For this is contained in Scripture: "Behold, I lay in Zion a choice stone, a precious corner stone, and he who believes in Him will not be disappointed." This precious value, then, is for you who believe; but for those who disbelieve, "The stone which the builders rejected, this became the very corner stone," and, "A stone of stumbling and a rock of offense"; for they stumble because they are disobedient to the word, and to this doom they were also appointed.

It pleases God to express His mercy when He redeems repentant sinners. And though He has no pleasure in the death and damnation of those who reject the gospel (Ezek. 18:23, 32; 33:11; 1 Tim. 2:4; 2 Peter 3:9), He is nevertheless pleased by the expression of His justice. When God's Word is faithfully preached, it will accomplish His purpose: "So shall My word be which goes forth from My mouth; it shall not return to Me empty, without accomplishing what I desire, and without succeeding in the matter for which I sent it" (Isa. 55:11).

PAUL WAS THANKFUL FOR THE PRIVILEGE OF POWER IN CHRIST

And who is adequate for these things? For we are not like many, peddling the word of God, but as from sincerity, but as from God, we speak in Christ in the sight of God. (2:16*b*–17)

No one **is adequate** with his human ability to render appropriate service to almighty God. Human resources are insufficient to influence people for eternity. Paul repeatedly acknowledged his inadequacy to carry out divine ministry. In 3:5 he declared, "Not that we are adequate in ourselves to consider anything as coming from ourselves, but our adequacy is from God." Because he had learned the secret of spiritual power, the apostle could write, "Therefore I am well content with weaknesses, with insults, with distresses, with persecutions, with difficulties, for Christ's sake; for when I am weak, then I am strong" (12:10), because, "By the grace of God I am what I am" (1 Cor. 15:10). To the Colossians he wrote, "For this purpose also I labor, striving according to His power, which mightily works within me" (Col. 1:29). Paul was totally dependent on God's power and enabling grace (cf. Eph. 1:18–20; 3:7, 20; Phil. 2:13).

The **many** false teachers who lack true spiritual power and operate in their own inadequacy resort to **peddling the word of God. Peddling** is from the verb *kapēleuō;* which is derived from the noun *kapēlos*. A *kapēlos* was a huckster, a con artist or street hawker who cleverly deceived unwary buyers into purchasing a cheap imitation of the real thing. Paul had in mind especially the false apostles at Corinth, who peddled a corrupt mixture of divine truth and Jewish legalism to the Corinthians.

But, unlike those spiritual con men, Paul, in **sincerity,** spoke **in** the power of **Christ in the sight of God.** Since he recognized his own inadequacy and depended entirely on God's power to energize his ministry, the apostle had no need to resort to corrupting the Word to influence people. Paul "did not . . . preach the gospel . . . in cleverness of speech" (1 Cor. 1:17), but in the power of Christ. *Eilikrineia* (**sincerity**) comes from *eilē* ("sunlight") and *krinō* ("to judge"). It pictures something held up to the light of the sun for inspection. Paul's pure life and unadulterated message would stand up to the closest scrutiny. Any man can proclaim a whittled-down false gospel, but those who preach the true gospel can do so only by means of divine power.

Paul found his way out of the gloom of discouragement by focusing on his privileges instead of his problems. The contemplation of those privileges—of being associated with the King of Kings in His Triumph, of influencing people for eternity, of pleasing God, and of having His power undergirding his ministry—healed his broken heart and restored his joy.

The Competent Minister
(2 Corinthians 3:1–6)

6

Are we beginning to commend ourselves again? Or do we need, as some, letters of commendation to you or from you? You are our letter, written in our hearts, known and read by all men; being manifested that you are a letter of Christ, cared for by us, written not with ink but with the Spirit of the living God, not on tablets of stone but on tablets of human hearts. Such confidence we have through Christ toward God. Not that we are adequate in ourselves to consider anything as coming from ourselves, but our adequacy is from God, who also made us adequate as servants of a new covenant, not of the letter but of the Spirit; for the letter kills, but the Spirit gives life. (3:1–6)

The pastoral ministry, more than any other profession, demands the best, the most spiritually qualified, and the most skilled men. The standards are high for many reasons: because the spiritual dimension of life is more important than the physical; because serving God is more demanding than serving anyone else; because His kingdom and glory are at stake; and because His servants face a more stringent evaluation of their service (Heb. 13:17; James 3:1).

So daunting is the challenge of the ministry that Paul asked rhetorically, "Who is adequate for these things?" (2 Cor. 2:16). Who is competent to take on the monumental and eternally significant duty of preaching the Word of God and leading the people of God? In this passage, he answers that question: "Our adequacy is from God, who also made us adequate" (3:5–6). Only those whom God calls into ministry, gifts, and empowers are adequate; self-made ministers are inadequate and incompetent. Paul was a competent minister because God appointed him to preach the gospel. In Acts 26:16 he related how God had said to him, "For this purpose I have appeared to you, to appoint you a minister." To the Ephesians he wrote, "I was made a minister, according to the gift of God's grace which was given to me according to the working of His power" (Eph. 3:7). In the first chapter of Colossians Paul twice declared, "I was made a minister" (vv. 23, 25). Writing to Timothy he said, "I thank Christ Jesus our Lord, who has strengthened me, because He considered me faithful, putting me into service. . . . I was appointed a preacher and an apostle (I am telling the truth, I am not lying) as a teacher of the Gentiles in faith and truth. . . . I was appointed a preacher and an apostle and a teacher" (1 Tim. 1:12; 2:7; 2 Tim. 1:11).

Paul addressed this issue because his own competency as a minister was under relentless attack by the false apostles who had come to Corinth. Painfully, all through 2 Corinthians, Paul had to defend himself against the lies his enemies told about him. The false apostles sought to discredit him so they could usurp his place as the authoritative teacher and then teach their damning, demonic lies to the Corinthians. To accomplish that goal, they not only viciously attacked Paul's character but also challenged his competency as a minister.

As he replied to their scurrilous attacks, the apostle found himself in a delicate position. He was aware that no matter what he said in his defense, the false apostles would twist it around and accuse him of pride, egotism, and self-commendation. Nothing would have been further from the truth; Paul was not interested in mounting a self-serving defense designed to protect his prestige and reputation. Yet the apostle knew that it was crucial that he defend himself, because he was the apostolic channel through which God's truth flowed to the Corinthians. If they succeeded in discrediting him, the false apostles would block the pipeline through which divine truth flowed to the church.

As he defended his spiritual adequacy, Paul revealed five marks of a competent minister of Jesus Christ—all of which he exemplified. A competent and effective minister has an established reputation for godliness, has been used in transforming lives, has confidence in his calling, has humble dependence on God's power, and has a new covenant message.

AN EFFECTIVE MINISTER
HAS AN ESTABLISHED REPUTATION FOR GODLINESS

Are we beginning to commend ourselves again? Or do we need, as some, letters of commendation to you or from you? (3:1)

A useful and spiritually influential minister does not need to **commend** himself or depend on the secondhand testimony of others, because his virtuous, godly life is well-known. To defuse any allegation that he was commending himself, Paul made no overt claims in his own defense. Instead, he gently rebuked the Corinthians by asking them two questions, both of which demand a negative answer.

Paul began by asking, **Are we beginning to commend ourselves again?** The apostle used the editorial **we,** because it is a less threatening, humbler, more gentle approach than using the singular "I." What may have prompted Paul's question were accusations from the false apostles that he was in fact commending himself in a selfish, proud manner. They may have pointed to the occasions in 1 Corinthians when Paul asserted his apostolic authority (cf. 1 Cor. 4:15–16; 11:1; 14:18; 15:10). But in a letter filled with rebuke and correction, Paul's appeals to his authority were necessary for the sake of the truth of God. In no way was the apostle motivated by self-exaltation—a truth he reiterates throughout 2 Corinthians. In 5:12 he declared, "We are not again commending ourselves to you but are giving you an occasion to be proud of us, so that you will have an answer for those who take pride in appearance and not in heart," while in 10:12 he added, "For we are not bold to class or compare ourselves with some of those who commend themselves; but when they measure themselves by themselves and compare themselves with themselves, they are without understanding." In 10:18 Paul stated plainly that "it is not he who commends himself that is approved, but he whom the Lord commends."

Paul's disclaimers indicate that what he wrote was not designed to elevate himself in people's thinking; it was simply to state the truth so as to protect the legitimacy of his ministry. Even his bold affirmation of a clear conscience, "For our proud confidence is this: the testimony of our conscience, that in holiness and godly sincerity, not in fleshly wisdom but in the grace of God, we have conducted ourselves in the world, and especially toward you" (1:12) was not a braggart's claim of self-vindication. In 1 Corinthians 4:4–5 he wrote,

> For I am conscious of nothing against myself, yet I am not by this acquitted; but the one who examines me is the Lord. Therefore do not go on passing judgment before the time, but wait until the Lord comes

who will both bring to light the things hidden in the darkness and disclose the motives of men's hearts; and then each man's praise will
come to him from God.

Paul knew that the only commendation that means anything is the one
that comes from God, not from others, nor even one's own conscience.

Though he was a humble man, Paul was fully aware of his vital
importance to the church as both a preacher of the gospel supernaturally
given to him by God (Gal. 1:11–12) and an inspired writer of biblical revelation. Therefore, it was necessary for him to defend himself so that God's
truth would not be hindered. The sorrow and frustration of his heart over
their fickleness came through when he wrote, **Are we beginning to
commend ourselves again?** He was not trying to prompt the Corinthians to commend him, but to make them evaluate their attitude. One
meaning of *sunistanō* (**commend**) is "to introduce." After all they had
gone through together, did Paul really need to reintroduce himself to the
Corinthians? Did they not know him well enough by now? Was it really
necessary for Paul to start all over again and prove to them what kind of
man he was? After all the time they had known him, after he had ministered among them for at least eighteen months (Acts 18:11), how could
they believe the false apostles' lies about him? Surely they knew him better than that after all the teaching, preaching, fellowship, prayers, love,
and tears they had personally experienced with him.

Paul drove home his point by asking a second question demanding a negative answer, **Or do we need, as some, letters of commendation to you or from you?** In their attempt to discredit Paul, the false
teachers claimed that he lacked the proper official **letters of commendation.** Such **letters** were commonly used in the ancient world to introduce people to those who did not know them (cf. Neh. 2:7; Acts 9:2;
18:27; 22:5; Rom. 16:1; 1 Cor. 16:3). When the false apostles arrived in
Corinth, they likely produced deceptive **letters of commendation,** possibly purporting to have come from the Jerusalem church (cf. Acts 15:24).
They used those letters to help them gain acceptance by the Corinthians.

Not only did the false apostles present **letters of commendation to** the Corinthians, but they also sought them **from** the Corinthians.
Because they were unregenerate, the false apostles' lives were corrupt.
Therefore, they could not remain long in one location before being
unmasked. But before they moved on, they sought **letters of commendation** from those whom they had deceived. They then used those **letters** to enhance their credibility with their next victims.

But Paul was not like the false apostles. He needed no **letters of
commendation** to prove his credibility to the Corinthians; they had firsthand knowledge of his virtuous, godly, sincere life and powerful preach-

ing. For the Corinthians to demand **letters of commendation** from Paul was ludicrous. That they could be so foolish and deceived as to doubt what they knew was true about the beloved apostle was tragic. Paul's blameless life and effective ministry was his letter of commendation.

AN EFFECTIVE MINISTER
HAS BEEN USED IN TRANSFORMING LIVES

You are our letter, written in our hearts, known and read by all men; being manifested that you are a letter of Christ, cared for by us, written not with ink but with the Spirit of the living God, not on tablets of stone but on tablets of human hearts. (3:2–3)

Paul's authenticity was evident not only from his blameless life but also from his impact on the lives of the Corinthians. As noted above, the false apostles relied on letters of commendation to gain acceptance. But Paul's **letter** was far superior to those of the false apostles—it was the Corinthians themselves. God had used Paul to write that letter in the debauched, vile city of Corinth. The only testimonial the apostle needed to verify the divine source of his labor—apart from the obvious virtue of his life—was the reality that the Corinthians had been saved and were being sanctified through the truth he preached and taught.

Unlike the false apostles' letters of recommendation, Paul did not carry his in his pocket or luggage; it was **written in** his **heart.** The apostle's language conveyed the great affection that he had for the Corinthians (cf. 6:11–13). Because they were precious to him, he and those who served with him carried them in their **hearts** all the time. As he wrote later in this epistle, "You are in our hearts to die together and to live together" (7:3).

Paul's letter of commendation was not private correspondence, hidden in hearts and therefore readable by only a few; it was **known and read by all men.** All who witnessed the transformed lives of the Corinthians had read it; it was continually being **manifested** or made conspicuous. C. K. Barrett writes, "The existence of the Corinthian Christians in Christ is a communication from Christ to the world, a manifestation of His purpose for humanity; this communication, incidentally, has the effect of commending Paul as a trustworthy bearer of the word of Christ" (*The Second Epistle to the Corinthians,* Black's New Testament Commentary [Peabody, Mass.: Hendrickson, 1997], 108).

The Corinthians were **a living letter of Christ,** because it is He alone who saves and sanctifies, through the preaching of His Word by faithful men like Paul. This introduces an essential and wondrous truth—

that when a preacher proclaims divine revelation accurately, it is Christ speaking through him. Referring to believers yet to come through all the centuries of the church, Jesus said, "They will hear My voice" (John 10:16). In verse 27 He repeated that truth, saying, "My sheep hear My voice." How have all the sheep heard His voice? When the preacher accurately proclaims the Word of God, it is not only the mind of Christ (1 Cor. 2:16) but also the very voice of the Lord of the church to His sheep.

Paul said saving faith always "comes from hearing, and hearing by the word of Christ" (Rom. 10:17), and people cannot hear without a preacher (v. 14). It is then God's plan to bring the voice of the Great Shepherd to His sheep by the means of faithful preachers. When Paul spoke, or any other preacher accurately handling the Word of Truth speaks, Christ has spoken—so that the results of the truth working are really a **letter** written by Christ. The apostle would never claim to be the author of that divine spiritual **letter** because he did not want his enemies to charge him with exalting himself. But **Christ** used Paul to minister to the Corinthians, and thus they actually did commend his ministry. The phrase **cared for by us** (from *diakoneō;* "to minister," or "to serve") alludes to Paul's role as Christ's preacher; it was through his gospel proclamation that the **letter** came to be written. In the apostle's analogy, Christ wrote the **letter,** and Paul delivered it through his ministry to the Corinthians.

Unlike the false apostles' letters, Paul's was **written not with ink but with the Spirit of the living God.** Human words written in ink are silent; they just sit fading on a page. Anyone can write a dead letter with ink, but only Christ, through the supernatural power of **the Spirit of the living God,** can write a living letter. Paul's letter (the Corinthians' transformed lives) was written by the supernatural power of the divine Spirit. That provided irrefutable proof that the apostle was a true servant of Jesus Christ. In 1 Corinthians 2:4–5 Paul wrote, "My message and my preaching were not in persuasive words of wisdom, but in demonstration of the Spirit and of power, so that your faith would not rest on the wisdom of men, but on the power of God," and he reminded the Thessalonians, "Our gospel did not come to you in word only, but also in power and in the Holy Spirit" (1 Thess. 1:5). "For this reason we also constantly thank God that when you received the word of God which you heard from us, you accepted it not as the word of men, but for what it really is, the word of God, which also performs its work in you who believe" (1 Thess. 2:13). Paul proclaimed the word of Christ, and the Spirit of God transformed the Corinthians. In the words of Peter,

> For you have been born again not of seed which is perishable but imperishable, that is, through the living and enduring word of God. For, "All flesh is like grass, and all its glory like the flower of grass. The grass

withers, and the flower falls off, but the word of the Lord endures forever." And this is the word which was preached to you. (1 Peter 1:23–25)

The result of such preaching by Christ through Paul was a living letter, known and read by all. Paul needed no further authentication of his ministry.

By way of further contrast, Paul notes that his letter of commendation was **not** written **on tablets of stone but on tablets of human hearts.** With this statement the apostle directly confronted the false apostles, who preached a false gospel that mixed Christianity with circumcision, old covenant ceremony, and legalism. The **tablets of stone** were those on which God supernaturally inscribed the Ten Commandments (Ex. 31:18; 32:15–16). But the miracle of Sinai cannot match the miracle of salvation. At Corinth, God had written not on **tablets of stone,** but on **human hearts.** In both cases God inscribed the same law; His standards of morality do not change. Some wrongly assume that because believers are under the new covenant they no longer have to keep God's law. But that is not true. Being under the new covenant does not excuse believers from keeping the Law; it frees them and by the Spirit enables them to keep it. The Law written on the **tablets of stone** at Sinai was external; it confronted people with their inability to obey perfectly the holy, righteous, and good requirements of God and thus condemned them. But in the new covenant, God writes His law on the **hearts** of those He redeems. The power of the indwelling Holy Spirit enables them to keep that law, and the righteousness of Jesus Christ, imputed to them by grace, covers all their violations of it.

The Old Testament prophets revealed that God would write His law on **human hearts.** Jeremiah recorded God's gracious new covenant promise: "'But this is the covenant which I will make with the house of Israel after those days,' declares the Lord, 'I will put My law within them and on their heart I will write it; and I will be their God, and they shall be My people'" (Jer. 31:33). Similarly Ezekiel wrote, "I shall give them one heart, and put a new spirit within them. And I shall take the heart of stone out of their flesh and give them a heart of flesh, that they may walk in My statutes and keep My ordinances and do them. Then they will be My people, and I shall be their God" (Ezek. 11:19–20; cf. 36:26–27).

The false apostles at Corinth were clinging to the external Law written on **tablets of stone,** advocating salvation by works, rituals, and ceremonies. This, as always, is a damning message because no one can be perfect enough to keep the whole Law:

> For as many as are of the works of the Law are under a curse; for it is written, "Cursed is everyone who does not abide by all things written in the book of the law, to perform them." Now that no one is justified by

the Law before God is evident; for, "The righteous man shall live by faith." However, the Law is not of faith; on the contrary, "He who practices them shall live by them." Christ redeemed us from the curse of the Law, having become a curse for us—for it is written, "Cursed is everyone who hangs on a tree." (Gal. 3:10–13)

Paul's rebuke of the Galatians applied equally to the Corinthians:

I do not nullify the grace of God, for if righteousness comes through the Law, then Christ died needlessly. . . . Are you so foolish? Having begun by the Spirit, are you now being perfected by the flesh? . . . You have been severed from Christ, you who are seeking to be justified by law; you have fallen from grace. (Gal. 2:21; 3:3; 5:4)

The false apostles, like all legalists throughout history, denied the continuity between the Law written on **tablets of stone** and that written on **tablets of human hearts.** (Ironically, so do their opposite numbers, the antinomians, who argue that salvation by grace abrogates believers' obligation to the Law.) But God's law written on **human hearts** does not nullify His Law written on **tablets of stone.** The Ten Commandments concisely summarize all of God's moral law. Responding to a scribe's question as to which was the greatest commandment in the Law, Jesus said, " 'You shall love the Lord your God with all your heart, and with all your soul, and with all your mind, and with all your strength.' The second is this, 'You shall love your neighbor as yourself' " (Mark 12:30–31). Jesus' answer summed up the two sections of the Ten Commandments: love for God, and love for man. Thus there is no discontinuity between the external Law written on stone and the internal one written on the heart. Both instruct believers to avoid offending God and other people. But the Law written on stone cannot save sinners because they shatter it. Salvation brings a new heart that loves the Law and longs to keep it (Ps. 119:97) and provides forgiveness for every failure.

Paul needed no letter of commendation written with pen and ink. The transformed lives of the Corinthians, and the reality that God's law was written on their hearts, proved his authenticity.

AN EFFECTIVE MINISTER
HAS CONFIDENCE IN HIS CALLING

Such confidence we have through Christ toward God. (3:4)

Paul's defense of his ministry was not designed to relieve any nagging self-doubt on his part. The apostle never questioned that God had called him to the ministry. That resolute **confidence** gave him the courage and boldness necessary for a very difficult ministry. No obstacle, persecution, or discouragement could make Paul question his calling. His confidence also narrowed his focus and gave him a single-minded, unswerving devotion to the ministry God had called him to. In 1 Corinthians 9:16 the apostle wrote,"For if I preach the gospel, I have nothing to boast of, for I am under compulsion; for woe is me if I do not preach the gospel." Later in 2 Corinthians Paul likened himself to a clay pot containing the priceless treasure of divine truth (4:7). Then in 4:8–11 he listed the trials of the ministry:

> We are afflicted in every way, but not crushed; perplexed, but not despairing; persecuted, but not forsaken; struck down, but not destroyed; always carrying about in the body the dying of Jesus, so that the life of Jesus also may be manifested in our body. For we who live are constantly being delivered over to death for Jesus' sake, so that the life of Jesus also may be manifested in our mortal flesh.

But none of that diverted him from carrying out his duty:"But having the same spirit of faith, according to what is written, 'I believed, therefore I spoke,' we also believe, therefore we also speak" (4:13). Concerning his calling to the ministry, Paul had a one-track mind. There were no alternatives or compromises for him. God spoke, Paul believed, and unflinchingly he spoke. Though Paul saw himself as nothing more than a clay pot, the fact that God had called him to the ministry gave him resolute **confidence.**

The other apostles also ministered with the same high level of resolve that Paul possessed. As the hostile Sanhedrin "observed the confidence of Peter and John and understood that they were uneducated and untrained men, they were amazed, and began to recognize them as having been with Jesus" (Acts 4:13). Facing the threat of persecution the apostles refused to back down, praying instead, "Now, Lord, take note of their threats, and grant that Your bond-servants may speak Your word with all confidence" (Acts 4:29).

Paul's **confidence** was not brash, arrogant trust in his own abilities. It was not self-confidence but confidence **through Christ toward God.** To the Romans he wrote, "For I will not presume to speak of anything except what Christ has accomplished through me, resulting in the obedience of the Gentiles by word and deed" (Rom. 15:18). In 1 Corinthians he acknowledged, "By the grace of God I am what I am, and His grace toward me did not prove vain; but I labored even more than all of them, yet not I, but the grace of God with me" (1 Cor. 15:10). In Ephesians 3:7 he affirmed, "I was made a minister, according to the gift of God's grace which was given to me according to the working of His power." Paul accomplished his ministry not by his own abilities or talents, but **through** the power of **Christ** working in him.

The false apostles, in contrast, were self-confident and arrogant, trusting fully in their own cleverness. But they were in reality man-pleasing, insincere corrupters of the Word of God (cf. 2 Cor. 2:17). On the other hand, the goal of Paul's ministry was, **through** the power of **Christ,** to please **God.** His Lord was both the source of the apostle's ministry and its ultimate goal.

AN EFFECTIVE MINISTER
HAS HUMBLE DEPENDENCE ON GOD'S POWER

Not that we are adequate in ourselves to consider anything as coming from ourselves, but our adequacy is from God, who also made us adequate (3:5–6*a*)

As noted in the previous point, Paul was confident, bold, coura-geous, and resolute in his ministry. Lest anyone misunderstand him, he hastened to add the disclaimer, **Not that we are adequate in our-selves.** In his own strength and wisdom, he could accomplish nothing (cf. 1 Cor. 1:18; 2:5). Later in this epistle Paul wrote, "I am well content with weaknesses, with insults, with distresses, with persecutions, with dif-ficulties, for Christ's sake; for when I am weak, then I am strong" (2 Cor. 12:10). His own inadequacy and lack of human resources allowed Paul to be a channel through which divine power flowed.

God does not look for the mighty and the noble according to human standards when He chooses men for the ministry (cf. 1 Cor. 1:26). "It is not great talents God blesses," the godly Scottish pastor Robert Mur-ray McCheyne reminded a young minister, "so much as great likeness to Jesus. A holy minister is an awful weapon in the hand of God" (Andrew A. Bonar, *Memoirs of McCheyne* [Chicago: Moody, 1978], 95). Though Paul had a brilliant and highly trained mind (Acts 26:24), he did not depend on it. Nor did the apostle rely on his oratorical skills (cf. Acts 14:12) to persuade people (1 Cor. 2:4). Paul did not rely on his natural abilities to carry out his ministry, but instead ministered "in demonstration of the Spirit and of power" (1 Cor. 2:4; cf. 1 Cor. 4:20; 1 Thess. 1:5).

So little trust did Paul place in his human abilities that he made the remarkable confession that he was unwilling **to consider anything as coming from** himself. **Consider** is from *logizomai,* which means "to reason," "to calculate," or "to credit to one's account." Apart from God's power and wisdom, Paul was not adequate to rightly assess or judge his ministry. Nor did he concoct his own plans but instead followed God's leading (cf. Acts 16:6–10). He did not trust in anything **coming from** himself; on his own he was useless and powerless. Paul served humbly, in the Spirit's power, fully acknowledging that his **adequacy** was **from God, who** alone was able to make him effective.

AN EFFECTIVE MINISTER
HAS A NEW COVENANT MESSAGE

as servants of a new covenant, not of the letter but of the Spirit; for the letter kills, but the Spirit gives life. (3:6*b*)

Paul's discussion of the qualities of a competent minister now turns from the messenger to his message; from the character of his ministry to its content.

The false apostles at Corinth were likely Judaizers or a closely related sect who had mingled in some popular philosophical fascinations from the culture. The Judaizers followed Paul throughout his ministry like a relentless plague. They were false teachers who basically at the core affirmed that salvation was through faith in Christ plus keeping the Mosaic Law (including its ceremonial aspects). They adopted whatever elements of their victims' ideologies would give them a hearing, then sought to negate the gospel of grace and impose Jewish customs on Gentile believers. They were actually hucksters, guilty of "peddling the word of God" (2:17) to achieve their ends.

True ministers, however, are **servants of a new covenant.** They do not mingle the old (the Mosaic covenant of law) and the **new covenant,** because the **new covenant** alone saves. The wonderful reality of the new covenant is that no one has to come to God via external Judaism. Nor are Gentiles second-class citizens in God's kingdom, but are "fellow heirs and fellow members of the body, and fellow partakers of the promise in Christ Jesus through the gospel" (Eph. 3:6), "no longer strangers and aliens, but . . . fellow citizens with the saints, and [members] of God's household" (Eph. 2:19). The revolutionary concept that Gentiles were spiritually equal with Jews shocked both believing and unbelieving Jews (cf. Acts 11:2–3).

To understand the glory and grace of the new covenant requires a brief review of the biblical covenants. There were two covenants that have no relation to salvation, the Noahic (Gen. 9:16) and the priestly (Num. 25:10–13). They expressed God's promises never to destroy the world by water again and always to provide a priesthood for His people.

Two covenants related to salvation: the Abrahamic (Gen. 17:7; 18:10–19) and the Davidic (2 Sam. 7:12–16; 23:5). In the Abrahamic covenant, God promised Abraham a people, land, blessing, and, ultimately, the Messiah. In the Davidic covenant, God promised David a greater son than Solomon, who would be King over the glorious earthly kingdom of God and bring salvation and blessing to Israel and the world. The question is how those promises are to be received; Jews throughout history have waited for their fulfillment. In the Mosaic covenant (Ex. 24:7–8) God said that all covenant blessing in His kingdom is for the righteous— and the standard is perfect obedience to His law. But no one can keep that standard! So how are people to be saved, blessed, and enter the glorious kingdom? The new covenant has the answer. It alone provides the conditions for blessing, salvation, and eternal life (Jer. 31:31–34; Ezek. 16:60; 37:26; Heb. 8:6–13). Anyone ever saved—from Adam to the last person saved before the destruction of the present heaven and earth—is saved on new covenant terms. Though not officially ratified until the death of Jesus Christ, whose sacrifice as the substitute for sinners paid in full the penalty of all the sins of all who would ever believe, the new covenant has always been in operation. Salvation comes to those who realize they are violators of God's law, hopeless and unable to obey— they cry for grace, mercy, and a new heart (cf. Luke 18:13).

So the heart of the **new covenant** and the gospel message is the Cross. Recounting the words of the Lord Jesus Christ at the Last Supper, Paul wrote, "In the same way He took the cup also after supper, saying, 'This cup is the new covenant in My blood; do this, as often as you drink it, in remembrance of Me'" (1 Cor. 11:25). The **new covenant,** unlike the old covenant, was not ratified by the blood of bulls and goats but by the blood of Christ:

> But when Christ appeared as a high priest of the good things to come, He entered through the greater and more perfect tabernacle, not made with hands, that is to say, not of this creation; and not through the blood of goats and calves, but through His own blood, He entered the holy place once for all, having obtained eternal redemption. For if the blood of goats and bulls and the ashes of a heifer sprinkling those who have been defiled sanctify for the cleansing of the flesh, how much more will the blood of Christ, who through the eternal Spirit offered Himself without blemish to God, cleanse your conscience from dead works to serve the living God? For this reason He is the mediator of a new covenant, so that, since a death has taken place for the redemption of the transgressions that were committed under the first covenant, those who have been called may receive the promise of the eternal inheritance. (Heb. 9:11–15)

The competent minister, then, does not preach salvation by legalism, ritual, or ceremony—the "things which are a mere shadow of what is to come; but the substance belongs to Christ" (Col. 2:17). He preaches Christ crucified for believers' sins (1 Cor. 1:23), risen for their justification (Rom. 4:25), and ever living to make intercession for them (Heb. 7:25). Entrance to God's kingdom comes through faith in Christ alone (John 1:12; 3:18, 36; 14:6; Acts 4:12; 16:31; Rom. 3:21–22; 10:9). That is the message of the new covenant preacher; therefore Paul wrote, "For I determined to know nothing among you except Jesus Christ, and Him crucified" (1 Cor. 2:2).

As a minister of the new covenant Paul was a servant **not of the letter but of the Spirit.** The contrast between the **letter** and the **Spirit** further distinguishes the new covenant from the old covenant. Mere external adherence to the **letter** of the Law will not result in salvation. Though "the Law is holy, and the commandment is holy and righteous and good" (Rom. 7:12), nevertheless "by the works of the Law no flesh will be justified in His sight" (Rom. 3:20), because "a man is justified by faith apart from works of the Law" (Rom. 3:28; cf. Gal. 2:16). Salvation comes only through the "washing of regeneration and renewing by the Holy Spirit" (Titus 3:5; cf. John 3:5; Rom. 8:2; 1 Cor. 6:11; 2 Thess. 2:13).

The writer of Hebrews highlights the contrast between the external **letter** of the old covenant and the internal reality of the new covenant:

> "Behold, days are coming, says the Lord, when I will effect a new covenant with the house of Israel and with the house of Judah; not like the covenant which I made with their fathers on the day when I took them by the hand to lead them out of the land of Egypt; for they did not continue in My covenant, and I did not care for them, says the Lord. For this is the covenant that I will make with the house of Israel after those days, says the Lord: I will put My laws into their minds, and I will write them on their hearts. And I will be their God, and they shall be My people. And they shall not teach everyone his fellow citizen, and everyone his brother, saying, 'Know the Lord,' for all will know Me, from the least to the greatest of them. For I will be merciful to their iniquities, and I will remember their sins no more." When He said, "A new covenant," He has made the first obsolete. But whatever is becoming obsolete and growing old is ready to disappear. (Heb. 8:8–13)

The difference between the old Mosaic, Sinaitic covenant and the new covenant is not a difference in moral standards. God's moral law does not change, because it is grounded in His immutable holiness. But under the old covenant, the law was external, consisting of written commands; in the new covenant, it is internal, written on the heart by the Holy Spirit.

The letter kills in two ways. First, it **kills** through the living death of grief, frustration, unfulfillment, guilt, and shame that results from people's inability to keep the Law. Paul wrote, "I was once alive apart from the Law; but when the commandment came, sin became alive and I died; and this commandment, which was to result in life, proved to result in death for me; for sin, taking an opportunity through the commandment, deceived me and through it killed me" (Rom. 7:9–11). Second, **the letter kills** through eternal death (damnation in hell), the penalty for not keeping it. "For as many as are of the works of the Law are under a curse," wrote Paul, "for it is written, 'Cursed is everyone who does not abide by all things written in the book of the law, to perform them' " (Gal. 3:10).

But under the new covenant, **the Spirit gives life.** In Jeremiah 31:33 God said, "I will put My law within them and on their heart I will write it; and I will be their God, and they shall be My people." The **Spirit** enables new covenant believers to fulfill God's law, so that they may say with the psalmist, "O how I love Your law! It is my meditation all the day" (Ps. 119:97; cf. vv. 113, 163, 165).

That does not mean that believers before the death of Christ lived in constant frustration, guilt, and remorse, never knowing the joy and peace of obedience. In Psalm 119:165 the psalmist wrote, "Those who love Your law have great peace, and nothing causes them to stumble" (cf. Ps. 19:7–11). In Psalm 32:1–2 David extolled the blessedness of forgiveness: "How blessed is he whose transgression is forgiven, whose sin is covered! How blessed is the man to whom the Lord does not impute iniquity, and in whose spirit there is no deceit!" They had been saved on new covenant terms—repentance, grace, and faith (cf. Isa. 55:1–2, 6–7). They were regenerated by God and thus were able to love and keep God's law because the Holy Spirit was operative in their lives (see the disussion in chapter 7 of this volume). The point is that the **letter kills** those who seek salvation through keeping the law whether they lived in Old Testament times or today! No one in any age could be saved by keeping the Law, since "whoever keeps the whole Law and yet stumbles in one point, he has become guilty of all" (James 2:10). The Law was never intended to be a means to salvation but rather to be "our tutor to lead us to Christ, so that we may be justified by faith" (Gal. 3:24). Therefore a true minister of Jesus Christ proclaims the new covenant message of the gospel, which alone "is the power of God for salvation to everyone who believes" (Rom. 1:16).

Who is adequate for such a ministry? To whom does God entrust the inestimable privilege of proclaiming transforming new covenant truth? To godly, effective, confident, humble, dependent men who preach the unadulterated truth of the gospel. From where does their adequacy come? "All Scripture is inspired by God and profitable for teaching, for reproof, for correction, for training in righteousness; so that the man of God may be adequate, equipped for every good work" (2 Tim. 3:16–17).

Amazingly, God's infallible Word preached by fallible men gifted and taught by the Holy Spirit, rightly dividing Scripture and clearly proclaiming it, is the means God has chosen for the spread of the saving new covenant gospel. People cannot hear it without a preacher (Rom. 10:14). Even the saved could not understand the Scripture without a man to guide them (cf. Acts 8:30–31).

The Glory of the New Covenant— Part 1: It Gives Life, Produces Righteousness, and Is Permanent (2 Corinthians 3:6–11)

7

who also made us adequate as servants of a new covenant, not of the letter but of the Spirit; for the letter kills, but the Spirit gives life. But if the ministry of death, in letters engraved on stones, came with glory, so that the sons of Israel could not look intently at the face of Moses because of the glory of his face, fading as it was, how will the ministry of the Spirit fail to be even more with glory? For if the ministry of condemnation has glory, much more docs the ministry of righteousness abound in glory. For indeed what had glory, in this case has no glory because of the glory that surpasses it. For if that which fades away was with glory, much more that which remains is in glory. (3:6–11)

As it has since apostolic times, ritual, ceremonial, sacramental Christianity poses a serious threat to the authentic, biblical gospel. In such false systems, the religious institution becomes a surrogate Christ, displacing the true Christ. People connect only to the institution through mechanical works rather than to the living Jesus Christ through faith. External ceremonies take the place of internal worship. The sacraments become *means* of grace instead of *symbols* of grace. Ministers become exalted intermediaries between the people and God, performing the rituals supposedly necessary for salvation, instead of humble servants who bring grace to save, sanctify, and equip the saints for the work of the ministry (Eph. 4:12). The Reformers' protest of this dead legalism ignited the quest to recover the pure New Testament gospel after centuries of ceremonialism and the Protestant Reformation flamed. The church today must also be on its guard against the relentlessly deadly heresy of ceremonialism.

To Paul's great sorrow, the church at Corinth had been infiltrated by the devastating plague of ceremonialism. Self-styled "apostles" (in reality, legalistic heretics) sought to bring the Corinthians under the crushing yoke of bondage to the Law (cf. Acts 15:10; Gal. 5:1). They taught that being circumcised, observing Sabbaths, new moons, festivals, and the Old Testament dietary regulations were necessary for salvation. In essence, they argued that Gentiles must first become Jewish proselytes before they could be saved and enter God's kingdom.

In contrast to those false teachers, who were ministers of the old covenant (claiming the Mosaic covenant has saving efficacy), Paul was a minister of the new covenant. As noted in the previous chapter of this volume, an adequate, spiritually effective minister preaches the new covenant gospel. But because Paul preached that liberating message, the false apostles at Corinth, who opposed the new covenant gospel message, savagely attacked him. As he defended his integrity and his ministry, Paul gave a rich, if brief, overview of the new covenant.

That the apostle should have had to defend himself to the Corinthians grieved him deeply. He had poured his life into the Corinthian church during the year and a half to nearly two years he had ministered there (Acts 18:11) teaching and shepherding them. Because of his intimate relationship with the Corinthians, 2 Corinthians is the most personal of Paul's inspired letters, the one in which he is the most transparent. For example, he wrote plaintively, "Our mouth has spoken freely to you, O Corinthians, our heart is opened wide. You are not restrained by us, but you are restrained in your own affections. Now in a like exchange—I speak as to children—open wide to us also" (2 Cor. 6:11–13).

The pain and anguish of his heart as he wrote this epistle flowed from Paul's deep affection for the Corinthians. In 12:14 he described them as his children, then wrote "I will most gladly spend and be expended for your souls. If I love you more, am I to be loved less?" (v. 15). In 1 Corinthians 4:14–15 he explained his motive for rebuking the Corinthians: "I do not write these things to shame you, but to admonish you as my beloved children. For if you were to have countless tutors in Christ, yet you would not have many fathers, for in Christ Jesus I became your father through the gospel."

There were many other issues besides the situation at Corinth that brought pain and suffering into Paul's life. In 2 Corinthians 4:8–10 he spoke of being "afflicted in every way, but not crushed; perplexed, but not despairing; persecuted, but not forsaken; struck down, but not destroyed; always carrying about in the body the dying of Jesus, so that the life of Jesus also may be manifested in our body." Later he wrote of enduring "afflictions, . . . hardships, . . . distresses, . . . beatings, . . . imprisonments, . . . tumults, . . . labors, . . . sleeplessness, [and] hunger" (6:4–5). When he visited Macedonia he was "afflicted on every side: conflicts without, fears within" (7:5). In 11:23–29 Paul summarized his sufferings for the cause of Christ—sufferings none of the false apostles could match:

> Are they servants of Christ?—I speak as if insane—I more so; in far more labors, in far more imprisonments, beaten times without number, often in danger of death. Five times I received from the Jews thirty-nine lashes. Three times I was beaten with rods, once I was stoned, three times I was shipwrecked, a night and a day I have spent in the deep. I have been on frequent journeys, in dangers from rivers, dangers from robbers, dangers from my countrymen, dangers from the Gentiles, dangers in the city, dangers in the wilderness, dangers on the sea, dangers among false brethren; I have been in labor and hardship, through many sleepless nights, in hunger and thirst, often without food, in cold and exposure. Apart from such external things, there is the daily pressure on me of concern for all the churches. Who is weak without my being weak? Who is led into sin without my intense concern?

But of all the churches under his care, Paul appears most anxious for the Corinthians. They had been blessed with much; "in everything [they] were enriched in Him, in all speech and all knowledge, even as the testimony concerning Christ was confirmed in [them], so that [they were] not lacking in any gift" (1 Cor. 1:5–7). As noted above, they had the unequaled privilege of having had the unique apostle as their pastor for nearly two years. Yet despite their rich blessings, the Corinthians were in turmoil. They had a hard time putting off their old life. Their congregation was split into quarreling factions (1 Cor. 1:11–12). They were so spiritually immature that Paul addressed them as if they were "infants in Christ" (1 Cor. 3:1). They tolerated gross sexual perversion that would have made a pagan blush, and instead of mourning over that sin, they were arrogant (1 Cor. 5:1–2). The Corinthians aired their dirty laundry in public before pagan judges instead of settling their disputes among themselves (1 Cor. 6:1–8). They perverted their freedom in Christ into a justification for practicing sexual immorality (1 Cor. 6:12–20)—even to the point of consorting with prostitutes (1 Cor. 6:16). At the opposite extreme, some argued for total sexual abstinence—even in marriage (7:1–5). Flaunting their liberty to eat meat sacrificed to idols, the stronger believers rode roughshod over the consciences of the weaker ones (1

Cor. 8:1–13; cf. 10:23–32). Women abandoned their God-designed role and joined the feminist movement of their day (1 Cor. 11:1–16; 14:34–35). The Corinthians conducted themselves at the Lord's Supper as if it were a pagan feast: Some gorged themselves while others went hungry and, shockingly, some even got drunk (1 Cor. 11:17–34). So perverted had their practice of spiritual gifts become that Paul had to spend three chapters straightening them out (1 Cor. 12–14). Amazingly, when someone in an ecstatic frenzy cursed Jesus, the Corinthians believed that he was speaking under the Holy Spirit's control (12:3). As a result of their prideful misuse of spiritual gifts, their worship services were chaotic (1 Cor. 14:26–33). Falling prey to the prevailing Greek philosophy of the day, the Corinthians even wavered on the key doctrine of the Resurrection (1 Cor. 15).

Now, on top of all that, many of the Corinthians had embraced the false apostles, falling for their slanderous lies about Paul's character and ministry. The apostle was heartbroken over the devastating influx of ceremonialism into the Corinthian church and the consequent abandoning of the truth by some. Of all the pain in his life this was the most intense—to see the defection of his beloved Corinthian church into sacramentalism, ceremonialism, and ritualism. A. T. Robertson writes,

> If Paul is able to look on the bright side of the preacher's life, he knows what the dark side is. There is plenty of cloud in his life to set off the light. Indeed, when Paul is driven to boast of his work in comparison with that of the Judaizers at Corinth it is the catalogue of his trials which he counts. He has his "prisons," his "stripes," his "shipwreck," his "perils" of various kinds, his "watchings often," his "hunger and thirst." "If I must needs glory, I will glory of the things that concern my weakness." But just now Paul cannot glory even in his weakness. He cannot glory in anything. He is a broken man, broken in spirit and in body. (*The Glory of the Ministry* [New York: Revell, 1911], 31–32)

What must have been especially galling to Paul is that the Corinthians knew better. They had been saved under Paul's new covenant ministry —a salvation they celebrated every time they partook of the Lord's Supper (1 Cor. 11:24–25). They understood that the sacrifice of Jesus Christ permanently and fully atoned for sin, thus rendering the sacrifices of the old covenant obsolete (cf. Heb. 10:12). They knew that the old covenant saved no one; it merely showed people how sinful they were and made them desperate for grace and mercy from God. Then it pointed sinners to the Savior. That after all of Paul's teaching to the contrary they could follow those who confused the truth of salvation is astonishing; and yet as history and the present proves, it is not unusual (cf. Gal. 3:1–7).

Second Corinthians 3:6–18 is a condensed summary of the new covenant distinctives, the most complete exposition of which is found in the book of Hebrews. As Paul does in this passage, the writer of Hebrews makes clear the superiority of the new covenant. The new covenant has always been a better covenant than the Mosaic Law because it has a better mediator, Jesus Christ (Heb. 8:6). A mediator acts as an intermediary between two parties in a dispute (cf. Gal. 3:20). The mediators of the old covenant, Israel's prophets, priests, and Moses (cf. Ex. 20:19; Deut. 5:5; Gal. 3:19), could not adequately represent both God and men, since they were mere men. But as the God-man, Jesus can perfectly represent men to God and God to men. Therefore Paul declares that there is "one mediator also between God and men, the man Christ Jesus" (1 Tim. 2:5). New covenant believers have direct access to God through Jesus Christ alone, "for through Him we . . . have our access in one Spirit to the Father" (Eph. 2:18). There is no need for priests, the saints, or Mary to intercede with God on believers' behalf.

The new covenant is also superior to the old because it has better promises, the most significant of which is the promise of complete forgiveness and permanent cleansing from all sin. Jeremiah records God's new covenant promise, "I will forgive their iniquity, and their sin I will remember no more" (Jer. 31:34). The old covenant could not provide cleansing from sin, "for it is impossible for the blood of bulls and goats to take away sins" (Heb. 10:4). Forgiveness of sin comes only through the blood of Christ. The writer of Hebrews declares, "we have been sanctified through the offering of the body of Jesus Christ once for all. . . . He [Christ], having offered one sacrifice for sins for all time, sat down at the right hand of God" (Heb. 10:10, 12; cf. 7:27; 9:12; Matt. 26:28).

Hebrews 8:8–12 describes seven characteristics of the new covenant.

First, the new covenant comes from God. In Hebrews 8:8 God declares, "I will effect a new covenant." Its terms are based on His sovereign plan and purpose.

Second, the new covenant is different from the old covenant. It is not an upgrade but something entirely new. The Greek word translated "new" in Hebrews 8:8 is *kainos*, which means new in the sense of different, not new in the sense of subsequence in time.

Third, the new covenant is made "with the house of Israel and with the house of Judah" (Heb. 8:8), but that does not mean, of course, that Gentiles are excluded from it, because "it is those who are of faith who are sons of Abraham. . . . And if you belong to Christ, then you are Abraham's descendants, heirs according to promise" (Gal. 3:7, 29). Gentiles enter into the blessings of the new covenant through faith in Jesus Christ. The Law given to Moses has always been applied to Gentiles, even those who never heard Moses, and violation of it will bring eternal judgment. So also new covenant forgiveness has always been offered to Gentiles who have sought grace and forgiveness from God.

Fourth, the new covenant is gracious, not legalistic. In Hebrews 8:9 God said the new covenant is "not like the covenant which I made with their fathers on the day when I took them by the hand to lead them out of the land of Egypt; for they did not continue in My covenant, and I did not care for them." Israel's disobedience did not abrogate the old covenant but caused the nation to forfeit its promised blessings. Though under the new covenant God, as a loving Father, chastens His disobedient children (Heb. 12:5–11), they will never forfeit its blessing of forgiveness of sin (Jer. 31:34).

Fifth, the new covenant is internal, unlike the old covenant, which was written on tablets of stone (2 Cor. 3:7; cf. Ex. 31:18). Hebrews 8:10 records God's promise under the new covenant to "put [His] laws into [His people's] minds, and [to] write them on their hearts."

Sixth, the new covenant is personal. It will finally be fulfilled to Israel (Rom. 9:26–27), but only when the Jews repent and believe the gospel. Salvation comes only to individuals. The Jews, one day in the future, on new covenant terms through faith in Jesus Christ (Zech. 12:10), "all will know [the Lord], from the least to the greatest" (Heb. 8:11).

Seventh, the new covenant brings complete forgiveness. As noted above, that is something the old covenant could not provide (Heb. 10:4). It is the blood of Jesus Christ that provides the forgiveness of sin promised under the new covenant (Matt. 26:28; cf. Heb. 9:14–15).

In addition to the list given by the author of Hebrews, Paul in this passage reveals eight distinctive qualities of the new covenant: It gives life, produces righteousness, is permanent, brings hope, is clear, is Christ centered, is energized by the Spirit, and is transforming.

The New Covenant Gives Life

who also made us adequate as servants of a new covenant, not of the letter but of the Spirit; for the letter kills, but the Spirit gives life. (3:6)

As noted in the previous chapter Paul, in contrast to the false apostles at Corinth, was a servant of the **new covenant.** The old covenant was a "ministry of death" (3:7) and a "ministry of condemnation" (3:9). In contrast, the **new covenant** is **not of the letter but of the Spirit** and brings eternal **life.**

Most of the Jewish people of Paul's day had succumbed to misrepresentation of God's purpose in giving the Law. They had been taught by their religious leaders that it was a way of salvation—a purpose for which God had never intended the Law (Rom. 3:20). On the contrary, "The Law came in so that the transgression would increase" (Rom. 5:20; cf. Gal. 3:19). The Law revealed to people their utter inability to live according to God's holy standard, and thus their need for a Redeemer (Gal. 3:24). That does not mean that there is anything wrong with the Law (Rom. 7:7); on the contrary, it is "holy and righteous and good" (Rom. 7:12). The problem lies not in the Law but in sinners' inability to keep it.

The zealous Pharisee Saul of Tarsus was shocked to realize that the Law he had so rigidly observed brought him not life, but death: "I was once alive apart from the Law; but when the commandment came, sin became alive and I died; and this commandment, which was to result in life, proved to result in death for me; for sin, taking an opportunity through the commandment, deceived me and through it killed me" (Rom. 7:9–11).

The Law kills in three ways. First, it kills by killing joy, peace, and hope, and replacing them with the frustration, sorrow, hopelessness, and guilt that come from one's inability to obey it. Second, sinners' inability to keep the Law perpetrates spiritual death (Gal. 3:10; cf. Rom. 6:23). Finally, the violated Law becomes the basis of eternal condemnation, actually killing those who seek to be saved by keeping it. Instead of recognizing their inability to keep the Law and allowing that to drive them to Christ, they follow the dead works of sacramentalism, rituals, and ceremonies. They are like the Jews of whom Paul wrote: "Not knowing about God's righteousness and seeking to establish their own, they did not subject themselves to the righteousness of God" (Rom. 10:3). Having distorted the Law's true purpose, the legalist is left with the mere **letter** of the Law—its external requirements apart from its true spiritual purpose. Legalists are like those Jews "who though having the letter of the Law and circumcision [were] transgressor[s] of the Law. For he is not a Jew who is one outwardly, nor is circumcision that which is outward in the flesh" (Rom. 2:27–28).

But Scripture declares of **new covenant** believers, "The law of the Spirit of life in Christ Jesus has set [them] free from the law of sin and of death" (Rom. 8:2). They are thus freed to "serve in newness of the Spirit and not in oldness of the letter" (Rom. 7:6). Realizing one is a sinner under condemnation by the Law should produce repentance and a cry to God for mercy. The publican in Luke 18 is the classic example. Under the burden of his sin and violation of God's law he pleaded, "'God, be merciful to me, the sinner!'" and went home justified. The Pharisee who saw his law-keeping as the means of his salvation was not justified but condemned (Luke 18:9–14).

THE NEW COVENANT PRODUCES RIGHTEOUSNESS

But if the ministry of death, in letters engraved on stones, came with glory, so that the sons of Israel could not look intently at the face of Moses because of the glory of his face . . . how will the ministry of the Spirit fail to be even more with glory? For if the ministry of condemnation has glory, much more does the ministry of righteousness abound in glory. (3:7a, 8–9)

The phrase **but if** could be better translated "since." Paul's Jewish opponents often accused him of opposing God's law (Acts 21:28), but that was not the case. The Ten Commandments, the moral summary of God's holy law, were written **in letters engraved on stones** by God Himself (Ex. 32:15–16). Because of that, Paul affirmed that the Law was imbued **with** God's **glory;** that is, perfectly reflecting His righteous person.

But unlike his legalistic opponents, Paul saw the old covenant of the Law in its proper perspective—as a **ministry of death.** The Law saves no one; it only drives people to see their need for a Savior. In fact, it is the greatest mass murderer in history. The Law will inevitably condemn all those who do not come to saving faith in Jesus Christ to eternal punishment in hell.

The Law condemns sinners by defining the standard of divine righteousness. In Romans 7:7 Paul wrote, "What shall we say then? Is the Law sin? May it never be! On the contrary, I would not have come to know sin except through the Law; for I would not have known about coveting if the Law had not said, 'You shall not covet'" (cf. Rom. 3:20; 5:13, 20). The depraved human mind cannot truly understand sinful behavior until confronted with God's holy law.

The Law also condemns sinners by exacerbating sin. "Sin," Paul lamented, "taking opportunity through the commandment, produced in me coveting of every kind; for apart from the Law sin is dead" (Rom. 7:8). The natural tendency of sinful, fallen human nature is to rebel against God's law by doing the very things it forbids. Thus the Law actually produces more sin in the lives of the unredeemed. John Bunyan illustrated that truth in a dramatic scene from *Pilgrim's Progress:*

> Then [Interpreter] took [Christian] by the hand, and led him into a very large parlour that was full of dust, because it was never swept; the which, after he had reviewed a little while, the Interpreter called for a man to sweep. Now, when he began to sweep, the dust began so abundantly to fly about that Christian had almost therewith been choked. Then said the Interpreter to a damsel that stood by, "Bring hither the

water, and sprinkle the room"; the which, when she had done, it was swept and cleansed with pleasure.

Chr.   Then said Christian, "What means this?"

Inter.   The Interpreter answered, "This parlour is the heart of a man that was never sanctified by the sweet grace of the gospel: the dust is his original sin and inward corruptions, that have defiled the whole man. He that began to sweep at first is the law; but she that brought water, and did sprinkle it, is the gospel. Now, whereas thou sawest that, so soon as the first began to sweep, the dust did so fly about, that the room by him could not be cleansed, but that thou wast almost choked therewith: this is to show thee that the law, instead of cleansing the heart, by its working, from sin, doth revive, put strength into, and increase it in the soul, even as it doth discover and forbid it; for it doth not give the power to subdue (Rom. 5:20; 7:9; 1 Cor. 15:56). (Reprint, Grand Rapids: Zondervan, 1976], 33–34)

When face-to-face with his sinfulness revealed by the Law, Paul saw himself as in a mirror and recognized that he was spiritually dead: "I was once alive apart from the Law; but when the commandment came, sin became alive and I died; and this commandment, which was to result in life, proved to result in death for me; for sin, taking an opportunity through the commandment, deceived me and through it killed me" (Rom. 7:9–11). He realized that he was a helpless, doomed sinner headed for eternal destruction in hell. Once again, however, the apostle stressed that there was nothing wrong with God's law: "For we know that the Law is spiritual, but I am of flesh, sold into bondage to sin" (Rom. 7:14). "Is the Law then contrary to the promises of God?" he wrote to the Galatians. "May it never be! For if a law had been given which was able to impart life, then righteousness would indeed have been based on law" (Gal. 3:21). The Law was never intended to be a means of salvation. The Law provides no grace, mercy, or forgiveness. It has no power to enable the sinner to be righteous. Its purpose was to reveal God's holy, pure standard and drive exposed sinners to the Savior (Gal. 3:24; Heb. 4:12–13). But to those who rely on it for salvation the Law has a **ministry of death.**

To illustrate the Law's glory, Paul turned to a familiar event in Israel's history—Moses' receiving the Law on Mount Sinai. After he had been in the presence of God's Shekinah glory, **the sons of Israel could not look intently at the face of Moses because of the glory of his face.** Exodus 34:29 reads, "It came about when Moses was coming down from Mount Sinai (and the two tablets of the testimony were in Moses' hand as he was coming down from the mountain), that Moses did not know that the skin of his face shone because of his speaking with Him."

So intense was the light of God's glory reflected in Moses' face that "when Aaron and all the sons of Israel saw Moses, behold, the skin of his face shone, and they were afraid to come near him" (v. 30). After Moses reassured them, "the sons of Israel came near, and he commanded them to do everything that the Lord had spoken to him on Mount Sinai" (v. 32). After that, Moses wore a veil after coming from the presence of God (vv. 33–35). Paul's point is that the Law's glory was evident to all who saw Moses' face after he came down from the mountain.

But if the old covenant had a certain fading glory **how,** Paul asked, **will the ministry of the Spirit** (the new covenant) **fail to be even more with glory?** The Law written on stone in the old covenant, which produced death and condemnation, had the glory of God in it because it revealed His glorious nature as holy and just. The new covenant reveals God's glory in a full manner because it not only reveals His holy nature, justice, wrath, and judgment (as did the old covenant), but it also manifests His compassion, mercy, grace, and forgiveness (cf. Ex. 33:19). And by the new covenant, the **Spirit** gives life and righteousness: "The law of the Spirit of life in Christ Jesus [sets believers] free from the law of sin and of death" (Rom. 8:2). The old covenant commands righteousness; the new covenant confers it. The old covenant made people hearers of the truth; the new covenant enables them to be doers of the truth.

Old Testament saints were not saved by keeping the Law, but being broken over their inability to keep it, they came to God as penitents, hungering and thirsting for righteousness and mourning over their sin (cf. Matt. 5:2–7). God then mercifully and graciously forgave their sins based on what Christ would accomplish in the future by His substitutionary death (cf. 2 Cor. 5:21). Having been saved by grace through faith, the Old Testament saints found the moral law a source of blessing and joy. They could then exult with the psalmist, "O how I love Your law! It is my meditation all the day" (Ps. 119:97; cf. 119:113, 163, 165). The Law then became to them "more desirable than gold, yes, than much fine gold; sweeter also than honey and the drippings of the honeycomb" (Ps. 19:10; cf. 119:103). It was not their attitude to the Law that saved them; rather, salvation changed their attitude to the Law, and they repented and in faith sought God's gracious forgiveness.

But apart from salvation in Christ, the old covenant remained a **ministry of condemnation,** of judgment, and, ultimately, of damnation. It brought people to the bar of God's judgment but provided no means of satisfying His justice except for eternal punishment in hell. Yet despite its shortcomings, the old covenant did have **glory,** because it reflected God's nature as holy. And if even the old covenant had a certain **glory,** how **much more does the ministry of righteousness** (a descriptive name for the new covenant) **abound in glory** by revealing God's nature as loving and gracious. The new covenant far surpasses the old covenant because it provides what the old covenant could not—**righteousness:** "But now," under the new covenant, "apart from the Law the righteousness of God has been manifested . . . even the righteousness of God through faith in Jesus Christ for all those who believe" (Rom. 3:21–22). In the new covenant, God imputes the righteousness of Christ to believers (2 Cor. 5:21), wrapping them in a "robe of righteousness" (Isa. 61:10).

Paul's own spiritual odyssey illustrates the superiority of the new covenant to the old covenant. His old covenant credentials were impeccable: He was "circumcised the eighth day, of the nation of Israel, of the tribe of Benjamin, a Hebrew of Hebrews; as to the Law, a Pharisee; as to zeal, a persecutor of the church; as to the righteousness which is in the Law, found blameless" (Phil. 3:5–6). He led an outwardly blameless life of rigid conformity to the old covenant rituals and regulations. In fact, Paul was a rising star in first-century Judaism; he was "advancing in Judaism beyond many of [his] contemporaries among [his] countrymen, being more extremely zealous for [his] ancestral traditions" (Gal. 1:14).

But after his dramatic, life-changing encounter with the risen Christ on the road to Damascus, Paul's perspective changed radically. All his old covenant achievements, of which he had been so proud, he "counted as loss for the sake of Christ" (Phil. 3:7). He despised them as "rubbish [excrement] so that [he might] gain Christ" (v. 8). He no longer counted on a "righteousness of [his] own derived from the Law, but that which is through faith in Christ, the righteousness which comes from God on the basis of faith" (v. 9). The new covenant both reveals and by grace provides the righteousness unattainable under the old covenant.

THE NEW COVENANT IS PERMANENT

fading as it was . . . For indeed what had glory, in this case has no glory because of the glory that surpasses it. For if that which fades away was with glory, much more that which remains is in glory. (7*b*, 10–11)

The reflected glory in Moses' face, **fading as it was,** symbolized the impermanence of the old covenant. Like the glory on Moses' face, the old covenant was never intended to be permanent. Its glory (cf. v. 7) was a fading, passing glory. It was not the solution to the plight of sinners, since it could not save them. The old covenant prescribed what men were to do but could not enable them to do it. It provided a basis for damnation, but not salvation; for condemnation, but not for justification;

for moral culpability, but not for moral purity.

That the old covenant was not the final revelation of God's redemptive purpose is clear even in the Old Testament. Speaking through Jeremiah, God promised a new covenant (Jer. 31:31–34). Commenting on the implications of that, the writer of Hebrews noted, "When He said, 'A new covenant,' He has made the first obsolete. But whatever is becoming obsolete and growing old is ready to disappear" (Heb. 8:13). Anyone who read the Old Testament should have realized that the old covenant was not intended to be permanent.

On the other hand, the new covenant is permanent. Paul wrote, **For indeed what had glory** (the old covenant), **in this case has no glory because of the glory** (of the new covenant) **that surpasses it. For if that which fades away** (the old covenant) **was with glory, much more that which remains** (the new covenant) **is in glory.** The old covenant, as noted above, **had glory.** But so superior is the new covenant that it is as if the old covenant had **no glory because of the glory that surpasses it.** The old covenant **fades away** when its function is complete, when it has produced conviction and repentance, but the new covenant **remains** permanently and will never be superseded or supplemented. The gospel message of salvation by grace through faith is God's final word to man. Jesus Christ's sacrificial death on the cross has "obtained eternal redemption" for His people (Heb. 9:12), making Him "the mediator of a new covenant" (v. 15). So comprehensive and final is Christ's death that it paid the price for the sins of the old covenant saints: "Since a death has taken place for the redemption of the transgressions that were committed under the first covenant, those who have been called may receive the promise of the eternal inheritance" (v. 15; cf. Rom. 3:24–25). To His completed work nothing may be added. Any attempt to return to the external ritual and ceremony of the old covenant brings not blessing, but a curse (Gal. 3:10; James 2:10).

The Glory of the New Covenant— Part 2: It Brings Hope, and Is Clear, Christ Centered, Energized by the Spirit, and Transforming (2 Corinthians 3:12–18)

8

Therefore having such a hope, we use great boldness in our speech, and are not like Moses, who used to put a veil over his face so that the sons of Israel would not look intently at the end of what was fading away. But their minds were hardened; for until this very day at the reading of the old covenant the same veil remains unlifted, because it is removed in Christ. But to this day whenever Moses is read, a veil lies over their heart; but whenever a person turns to the Lord, the veil is taken away. Now the Lord is the Spirit, and where the Spirit of the Lord is, there is liberty. But we all, with unveiled face, beholding as in a mirror the glory of the Lord, are being transformed into the same image from glory to glory, just as from the Lord, the Spirit. (3:12–18)

Throughout redemptive history Satan has sought to confuse the issue of salvation and make it a matter of human effort. One of his most devious and effective schemes has always been to offer an external, ceremonial, sacramental religious substitute for the true gospel of grace through faith. Such false religions do not provide salvation but damn people by deluding them into thinking that because they are religious, all is well between them and God. In Paul's world that satanic, ritualistic counterfeit religion took the form of Jewish legalism, which was advocated within the church by the Judaizers. That heretical group rejected the truth that the new covenant fully provided the means of salvation, making the old covenant obsolete (Heb. 8:13). They argued that Gentiles must first become Jewish proselytes before they could be saved. To that end they advocated observing the rituals and ceremonies of the old covenant. But to cling to the shadow of the old covenant when the reality of the new covenant had arrived was foolish (cf. Heb. 10:1).

The Judaizers aggressively propagated their misrepresentation of the purpose for the old covenant. As we have seen, no one in any age has ever been saved by keeping the Law or by performing ceremonies and rituals. Salvation has always been by grace through faith. "The Law," Paul wrote to the Galatians, "has become our tutor to lead us to Christ, so that we may be justified by faith" (Gal. 3:24). The writer of Hebrews devoted an entire chapter to demonstrating that the noble men and women of God in the Old Testament were saved by faith, not by keeping the Law. They form a "cloud of witnesses" (Heb. 12:1) testifying to the spiritual benefit of living by faith. The writer began by reminding his readers that the Old Testament saints obtained right standing before God by their faith: "For by it the men of old gained approval" (Heb. 11:2). Then, after listing a representative sampling of the Old Testament heroes of faith (Heb. 11:4–38), the writer repeated his assertion that "all these . . . gained approval through their faith" (v. 39), thus bracketing the list of Old Testament heroes with a statement extolling faith.

Yet despite their strong faith and exemplary lives, those Old Testament heroes of faith incredibly "did not receive what was promised, because God had provided something better for us, so that apart from us they would not be made perfect" (Heb. 11:39–40). Even those at the pinnacle of Old Testament redemptive history could not "be made perfect" (i.e., saved; cf. Heb. 7:11, 19; 9:9; 10:1, 14; 12:23) by the old covenant. Apart from the new covenant, the "something better" God provided for us, there would be no salvation. Had there never been a new covenant, the Old Testament believers would never have been saved, because the old covenant could not redeem them. Forgiveness of sin comes only through the atoning sacrifice of the Lord Jesus Christ. The sacrificial death of the Lord Jesus Christ was savingly efficacious and applied to those under the old covenant (Rom. 3:24–25; Heb. 9:14–15).

Proclaiming and defending the new covenant gospel is a high priority for every man of God. It was the task Paul faced at Corinth, where false teachers had infiltrated the church. Claiming to be apostles, they proclaimed that the rituals and ceremonies of the old covenant were prerequisites for salvation. To boost their own credibility with the Corinthians, the false apostles attacked Paul's integrity and the credibility of his ministry. As part of his response to the false teachers' attacks, Paul demonstrated the superiority of the new covenant over the old covenant. In 2 Corinthians 3:6–18 he lists eight qualities of the new covenant: It gives life, produces righteousness, is permanent, brings hope, is clear, Christ–centered, energized by the Spirit, and transforming. The previous chapter of this volume considered the first three of those qualities: The new covenant gives life, produces righteousness, and is permanent. This chapter looks at the last five: The new covenant brings hope, is clear, Christ–centered, energized by the Spirit, and transforming.

THE NEW COVENANT BRINGS HOPE

Therefore having such a hope, we use great boldness in our speech, (3:12)

Though Old Testament believers rightly had **hope** in God's mercy (Job 13:15; Pss. 31:24; 33:18, 22; 38:15; 39:7; 42:5, 11; 43:5; 62:5; 71:5, 14; 119:49, 166; 130:5, 7; 131:3; 146:5; Jer. 29:11; 31:17; Lam. 3:24), that **hope** was not based on the old covenant. The old covenant, with its endless sacrifices, provided no **hope** of forgiveness for sin (cf. Heb. 10:4). In contrast, **hope** came in the new covenant, which provides forgiveness of sin and complete redemption, because Jesus "through His own blood ... obtained eternal redemption" (Heb. 9:12). "Therefore He is able also to save forever those who draw near to God through Him, since He always lives to make intercession for them" (Heb. 7:25). The **hope** of the Old Testament saints was based on the new covenant (cf. Heb. 11:24–26; 1 Peter 1:10–12).

Hope is the confident belief that God will fulfill all the promises of His new covenant. Many of those have already been fulfilled; yet great and glorious as the new covenant is, the heart of it has not yet been fully manifested. The new covenant was ratified at the Cross, though its benefits have always been appropriated by faith, but the fullness of its **hope** will not be experienced until believers' future glorification. It is then that they will receive their glorified bodies and be freed not only from sin's penalty, but also from its presence (Rom. 8:16–17, 23–25, 29–30; Gal. 5:5; Phil. 3:20–21; 2 Peter 1:4; 1 John 3:2).

Paul expressed new covenant **hope** in his benediction for the Romans: "Now may the God of hope fill you with all joy and peace in believing, so that you will abound in hope by the power of the Holy Spirit" (Rom. 15:13). He prayed for the Ephesians that the "eyes of [their hearts] may be enlightened, so that [they would] know what is the hope of His calling, what are the riches of the glory of His inheritance in the saints"

(Eph. 1:18). Later in that epistle he reminded them, "There is one body and one Spirit, just as also you were called in one hope of your calling" (Eph. 4:4). He described to the Colossians "the hope laid up for you in heaven, of which you previously heard in the word of truth, the gospel" (Col. 1:5; cf. vv. 23, 27). The apostle urged the Thessalonians to "put on . . . as a helmet, the hope of salvation" (1 Thess. 5:8). The writer of Hebrews declared that

> God, desiring even more to show to the heirs of the promise the unchangeableness of His purpose, interposed with an oath, so that by two unchangeable things in which it is impossible for God to lie, we who have taken refuge would have strong encouragement to take hold of the hope set before us. This hope we have as an anchor of the soul, a hope both sure and steadfast and one which enters within the veil. (Heb. 6:17–19)

He also wrote of "a better hope, through which we draw near to God" (Heb. 7:19). Peter wrote, "Blessed be the God and Father of our Lord Jesus Christ, who according to His great mercy has caused us to be born again to a living hope through the resurrection of Jesus Christ from the dead" (1 Peter 1:3), then exhorted his readers, "Fix your hope completely on the grace to be brought to you at the revelation of Jesus Christ. . . . Your faith and hope are in God" (vv. 13, 21).

So sure, well established, and irrevocable is the hope provided by the new covenant that those who preach it confidently **use great boldness in** their **speech.** They fearlessly and unhesitatingly proclaim the gospel message. *Parrēsia* (**boldness**) describes courageous, confident, outspoken proclamation of the gospel, without reluctance or wavering no matter how severe the opposition. Paul unhesitatingly preached the liberating message of the new covenant, even though it enraged his Jewish opponents, who clung fiercely to the old.

The New Covenant Is Clear

and are not like Moses, who used to put a veil over his face so that the sons of Israel would not look intently at the end of what was fading away. But their minds were hardened; for until this very day at the reading of the old covenant the same veil remains unlifted, (3:13–14*a*)

The bold new covenant preachers were **not like Moses, who used to put a veil over his face** after being in God's presence:

> When Moses had finished speaking with them, he put a veil over his face. But whenever Moses went in before the Lord to speak with Him, he would take off the veil until he came out; and whenever he came out and spoke to the sons of Israel what he had been commanded, the sons of Israel would see the face of Moses, that the skin of Moses' face shone. So Moses would replace the veil over his face until he went in to speak with Him. (Ex. 34:33–35)

Moses veiled himself to hide from the frightened Israelites the blazing glory that shone forth from his face (Ex. 34:30). Though the glory of the old covenant was designed to fade in the face of the more glorious new covenant, it was nevertheless a devastating, brilliant, blinding glory. As Moses had been unable to see the glory of God because it would have destroyed him (Ex. 33:20), so the partial glory on Moses' face was too much for the people to look on.

Moses' veiling of his face was **so that the sons of Israel would not look intently at** what Paul calls **the end of what was fading away.** That expression symbolizes the shadowy, veiled, diminishing nature of the glorious Mosaic covenant. It was replete with types, pictures, symbols, and mystery. It could never be fully understood without the new covenant, connected to the person and work of the coming Messiah. Even the inspired writers of the Old Testament did not fully understand everything that they wrote (1 Peter 1:10–12). A parallel for new covenant believers is the book of Revelation; only those alive in the end times will fully understand its symbolism.

In contrast, the new covenant reveals the mysteries of God that were obscure in the old covenant. A mystery in the New Testament describes a truth formerly hidden but now revealed. It is a privilege of new covenant believers to understand those mysteries. In Matthew 13:11 Jesus told His disciples, "To you it has been granted to know the mysteries of the kingdom of heaven." The New Testament reveals many mysteries that were not made clear in the Old Testament, including the partial and temporary hardening of Israel (Rom. 11:25); the gospel message of salvation (Rom. 16:25; 1 Cor. 2:7; Eph. 6:19; Col. 4:3; 1 Tim. 3:16); the teaching of the new covenant in general (1 Cor. 4:1; 1 Tim. 3:9); the Rapture of the church (1 Cor. 15:51); the unity of Jews and Gentiles in the church (Eph. 3:3–4, 9); the union of Christ and the church (Eph. 5:32; Col. 1:26–27); the truth that Jesus is God incarnate (Col. 2:2–3, 9); and the full revelation of lawlessness in the end times (2 Thess. 2:7). The new covenant makes clear truth that was vague and obscure in the old covenant.

Then Paul gave the reason that the Israelites did not **look intently** so as to comprehend the veiled and fading glory of the old covenant. It was not Moses' fault, or the fault of the old covenant, but because **their minds were hardened. Hardened** is a form of the verb *pōroō*, which could also be translated "stubborn." Israel failed to grasp the glory of the old covenant because of stubborn, hard-hearted unbelief. The writer of Hebrews warned his unbelieving Jewish readers not to follow their forefathers' example:

> Do not harden your hearts as when they provoked Me, as in the day of trial in the wilderness. . . . While it is said, "Today if you hear His voice, do not harden your hearts, as when they provoked Me." . . . He again fixes a certain day, "Today," saying through David after so long a time just as has been said before, "Today if you hear His voice, do not harden your hearts." (Heb. 3:8, 15; 4:7)

Throughout their history the Jewish people (with a few exceptions such as Zacharias and Elizabeth [Luke 1:5–6], Simeon [Luke 2:25], Anna [Luke 2:36], and others of the believing remnant [cf. Rom. 11:5]) "stiffened their necks so as not to heed [God's] words" (Jer. 19:15; cf. 7:26; 17:23; Deut. 10:16; 2 Kings 17:14; 2 Chron. 30:8; Neh. 9:29). Stephen summed up Israel's tragic past when he confronted the Jewish leaders of his day: "You men who are stiff-necked and uncircumcised in heart and ears are always resisting the Holy Spirit; you are doing just as your fathers did" (Acts 7:51). Sadly, Paul noted that **until this very day at the reading of the old covenant** (such as when it was read in the synagogue service; cf. Luke 4:17–21) **the same veil remains unlifted.** The **old covenant** remained obscured, its purpose misunderstood. People wrongly thought that they could be saved by keeping it. By lowering its moral requirements they achieved an external, superficial righteousness. But by doing so they rendered the Law's purpose of revealing their sin and helplessness ineffective. Since they did not realize they were lost, they saw no need for a Savior. The veil of ignorance obscures the true purpose of the old covenant to the hardened heart. That, in turn, made them ignorant of their need for the new covenant.

Jesus declared such ignorance to be inexcusable: "You search the Scriptures because you think that in them you have eternal life; it is these that bear witness of Me. . . . For if you believed Moses, you would believe Me, for he wrote about Me" (John 5:39, 46). Even the disciples displayed this kind of ignorance, prompting Jesus to rebuke two of them on the road to Emmaus for being "foolish men and slow of heart to believe in all that the prophets have spoken!" (Luke 24:25). The writer of Hebrews sternly warns of the danger of rejecting the new covenant:

> Anyone who has set aside the Law of Moses dies without mercy on the testimony of two or three witnesses. How much severer punishment do

you think he will deserve who has trampled under foot the Son of God, and has regarded as unclean the blood of the covenant by which he was sanctified, and has insulted the Spirit of grace? For we know Him who said, "Vengeance is Mine, I will repay." And again, "The Lord will judge His people." It is a terrifying thing to fall into the hands of the living God. (Heb. 10:28–31)

Even Moses grieved over the hard-hearted blindness of his people. In Exodus 32:32 he pleaded with God, "But now, if You will, forgive their sin—and if not, please blot me out from Your book which You have written!" So intense was his concern that he was willing to sacrifice himself on their behalf. Paul echoed that same attitude in the New Testament: "For I could wish that I myself were accursed, separated from Christ for the sake of my brethren, my kinsmen according to the flesh, who are Israelites" (Rom. 9:3–4).

A true understanding of the old covenant would have prepared them for the removal of the veil that kept (and still keeps) people from understanding the clear revelation of the new covenant.

THE NEW COVENANT IS CHRIST–CENTERED

because it is removed in Christ. But to this day whenever Moses is read, a veil lies over their heart; but whenever a person turns to the Lord, the veil is taken away. . . . But we all, with unveiled face, beholding as in a mirror the glory of the Lord, (3:14b–16, 18a)

The veil that obscured the old covenant is only **removed in Christ,** and the revelation of the old covenant in the Old Testament is mystery apart from Him. But Christ has come and ratified the new covenant by His death. Therefore, for those who come to faith in Him, spiritual perception is no longer impaired and everything becomes clear. It deeply saddened Paul's heart to have to write concerning the Jewish people that **to this day whenever Moses is read** (as part of the Sabbath worship; cf. Acts 13:27; 15:21), **a veil lies over their heart.** Even though the new covenant had come to make them clear, they did not understand the true meaning of the Old Testament Scriptures—an ignorance that, ironically, led to their fulfilling the Old Testament predictions that Messiah would suffer: "For those who live in Jerusalem, and their rulers, recognizing neither [Christ] nor the utterances of the prophets which are read every Sabbath, fulfilled these by condemning Him" (Acts 13:27).

The **veil** of a hardened **heart** made them think they could save themselves, causing them, therefore, to miss the meaning of both covenants. In their arrogant pride, they sought to establish their own righteousness by good works, keeping the Law (at least externally; cf. Luke 18:21), and performing the appropriate ceremonies. But the broken and contrite heart that God accepts (Ps. 51:17; Isa. 57:15; 66:2; Matt. 5:3; Luke 18:11–14) is one that is penitent, meek, mourns over sin, hungers and thirsts for righteousness, and pleads for mercy and forgiveness. Paul again made the point that the problem was not with the old covenant but with the heart. Those who are unwilling to be broken over their sin, confess it, and repent of it will never experience the new covenant's blessings.

It is only when **a person turns to the Lord** (cf. Isa. 45:22) that **the veil is taken away.** The blessings of the new covenant come only by God's grace through faith in the Lord Jesus Christ. All the mists that veiled the truth in the old covenant are then blown away like fog before a high wind. In 2 Corinthians 4:6 Paul describes this experience using the metaphor of turning on a light: "For God, who said, 'Light shall shine out of darkness,' is the One who has shone in our hearts to give the Light of the knowledge of the glory of God in the face of Christ."

Paul borrowed the image of salvation as a **veil** being **taken away** from Moses' unveiling himself in God's presence: "Whenever Moses went in before the Lord to speak with Him, he would take off the veil until he came out" (Ex. 34:34). Moses removed his veil because he wanted a direct vision of God's glory. So it is with sinners who turn to God through Jesus Christ. The **veil is taken away** and they have a clear vision of the glory of God reflected in the face of Jesus Christ. (For Paul's description of how the veil was removed in his own life, see Acts 22:3–16; Phil. 3:4–12.) Philip E. Hughes writes,

> Further light is thrown on this passage when we consider what took place on the occasion of the transfiguration of Christ. On that mountain height Moses and Elijah appeared with Christ, but it was *Christ alone* who was transfigured with heavenly radiance before the eyes of Peter, James, and John. It was *His* face that shone as the sun and *His* garments that became white and dazzling. It was of *Him alone* that the voice from the cloud said, "This is My beloved Son, in whom I am well pleased; hear ye Him." And thereafter the disciples saw no one, *save Jesus only.* It is He who abides. The glory in which Moses and Elijah appeared was not their own but Christ's glory—the glory which He had had with the Father before the world was (Jn. 17:5). Just as in the wilderness the glory which shone from Moses' face was the reflected glory of Yahweh, so too on the mount of transfiguration the glory with which he was surrounded was the glory of the same Yahweh. Christ's alone is the full, the abiding, the evangelical glory. To turn to Him is to turn to the Light of the world. To follow Him is not to walk in darkness, but to have the light of life

(Jn. 8:12). (*The Second Epistle to the Corinthians,* The New International Commentary on the New Testament [Grand Rapids: Eerdmans, 1992], 114–115. Italics in original.)

The inclusive phrase **we all** includes all new covenant believers. In the old covenant analogy, only Moses saw God with an unveiled face. But in the new covenant every Christian can **with unveiled face** behold **the glory of the Lord** revealed in Jesus Christ (cf. Matt. 17:1–2; John 1:14; Col. 1:15; Heb. 1:3; 2 Peter 1:17–18). Believers gaze at Christ's glory as if looking **in a mirror,** an illustration that speaks of a close, intimate look. Mirrors in ancient times were not made of glass, but of polished metal. They provided a clear but less than perfect reflection—an apt analogy of the new covenant, where believers see Christ clearly, but not as clearly as they will in the future (1 Cor. 13:12; cf. 1 John 3:2).

THE NEW COVENANT IS ENERGIZED BY THE SPIRIT

Now the Lord is the Spirit, and where the Spirit of the Lord is, there is liberty. (3:17)

There was nothing in the old covenant to energize obedience. The Law was a jailer, locking up sinners and condemning them to death and hell. But the new covenant liberates through the power of "the Spirit [who] gives life" (3:6).

Paul's declaration that **the Lord is the Spirit** strongly affirms the deity of the Holy Spirit (cf. Acts 5:3–4). The same God who gave the old covenant gave the new covenant. The same God who gave the Law is the God who brings salvation under the new covenant. The almighty Yahweh of the Old Testament is the same God who grants **liberty** in the new covenant from the futile attempts to earn salvation by keeping the Law. It is **the Spirit of the Lord** who brings the **liberty** of salvation to repentant sinners of any age—liberty from bondage to the Law (Rom. 7:1–6), Satan (Heb. 2:14–15), fear (Rom. 8:15), sin (Rom. 6:2, 7, 14), and death (Rom. 8:2).

There has been much confusion about the Holy Spirit's ministry in the Old Testament. Some believe that His ministry in some economies or dispensations was different than in others. But there is a consistency in the Spirit's ministry throughout redemptive history. The Holy Spirit's ministry in the Old Testament can be summarized in four categories.

The first ministry of the Holy Spirit in the Old Testament was creation. Genesis 1:2 records that "the earth was formless and void, and darkness was over the surface of the deep, and the Spirit of God was moving (lit. "hovering") over the surface of the waters." In Psalm 104:30 the psalmist wrote of the Holy Spirit's role in creation, "You send forth Your Spirit, they are created; and You renew the face of the ground." Isaiah asked rhetorically,

> Who has measured the waters in the hollow of His hand, and marked off the heavens by the span, and calculated the dust of the earth by the measure, and weighed the mountains in a balance and the hills in a pair of scales? Who has directed the Spirit of the Lord, or as His counselor has informed Him? (Isa. 40:12–13)

The Spirit of God was involved in the creation not only of the physical world, but also of man: "The Spirit of God has made me, and the breath of the Almighty gives me life" (Job 33:4).

The second ministry of the Holy Spirit in the Old Testament was empowerment. The Old Testament frequently records that the Spirit of the Lord came upon various individuals (and that He departed from the rebellious King Saul; 1 Sam. 16:14). That, of course, was not referring to the normal relationship of the Holy Spirit to Old Testament believers; all true children of God must have the Holy Spirit (cf. Rom. 8:9), because the divine life imparted in regeneration is not humanly sustainable. The Old Testament references to the Holy Spirit coming upon people describe the Spirit's empowering specific people to perform special tasks. Four categories of people received the Spirit's special empowering: judges (Othniel [Judg. 3:9–10], Gideon [Judg. 6:34], Jephthah [Judg. 11:29], Samson [Judg. 14:6, 19; 15:14; cf. 13:25]); craftsmen (Bezalel [Ex. 31:2–3; 35:30–31], Oholiab [Ex. 31:6; 35:34] and others [Ex. 36:1], Hiram [1 Kings 7:13–14]); prophets (Balaam [Num. 24:2], Amasai [1 Chron. 12:18], Jahaziel [2 Chron. 20:14], Zechariah the son of Jehoiada [2 Chron. 24:20], Ezekiel [Ezek. 11:5]); and civic leaders (Moses [Num. 11:17], the seventy elders of Israel [Num. 11:25–26], Joshua [Num. 27:18], Saul [1 Sam. 10:6, 10; 11:6; cf. 1 Sam. 16:14], David [1 Sam. 16:13; cf. Ps. 51:11]).

The third ministry of the Holy Spirit in the Old Testament was revelation. He is the divine Author of the Old Testament Scriptures. Zechariah 7:12 laments concerning rebellious Israel, "They made their hearts like flint so that they could not hear the law and the words which the Lord of hosts had sent by His Spirit through the former prophets; therefore great wrath came from the Lord of hosts" (cf. Neh. 9:30). The Old Testament was written by "men moved by the Holy Spirit [who] spoke from God" (2 Peter 1:21).

The fourth and most significant ministry of the Holy Spirit in the Old Testament was regeneration. Some maintain that regeneration or the new birth is foreign to the Old Testament. But the evidence clearly shows that Old Testament believers were regenerated. The convicting work of the Spirit, which precedes regeneration (cf. John 16:8), is not restricted to the New Testament. In Genesis 6:3 "the Lord said, 'My Spirit shall not strive with man forever, because he also is flesh; nevertheless his days shall be one hundred and twenty years.'" The Spirit of God striving with sinful hearts to bring conviction of sin is not unique to the New Testament.

Further, total depravity has defined the human condition since the Fall. In fact, Paul's classic description of total depravity in Romans 3:10–18 comes entirely from the Old Testament. There is no clearer statement of total depravity anywhere in Scripture than the one found in Jeremiah 17:9: "The heart is more deceitful than all else and is desperately sick; who can understand it?" Since fallen, totally depraved people are incapable of saving themselves, no one in any age could be saved apart from the regenerating work of the Holy Spirit.

How could a totally depraved person exclaim, "O how I love Your law!" (Ps. 119:97, 113, 163) apart from regeneration? How could Noah be "a righteous man, blameless in his time" (Gen. 6:9) if he were unregenerate? How can the New Testament hold up Abraham as a model of faith (Rom. 4:1–16; Gal. 3:6–9) unless he was regenerated by the Holy Spirit? How could the Old Testament say that "David did what was right in the sight of the Lord, and [did not turn] aside from anything that He commanded him all the days of his life, except in the case of Uriah the Hittite" (1 Kings 15:5; cf. 3:14; 11:4, 33) if he were not regenerate? How could the Old Testament figures listed in Hebrews 11 have lived such exemplary lives of faith if the Holy Spirit had not regenerated them? The transformed lives of the Old Testament saints testify to their having been regenerated by the Holy Spirit.

Jesus' conversation with the noted Jewish teacher Nicodemus offers convincing proof that Old Testament believers experienced regeneration. The conversation took place before the ratification of the new covenant with Jesus' death (Luke 22:20). Yet Jesus declared to Nicodemus, "Truly, truly, I say to you, unless one is born again he cannot see the kingdom of God. . . . Unless one is born of water and the Spirit he cannot enter into the kingdom of God" (John 3:3, 5). Thus Old Testament conversion involved being "born again," and being "born of water (cf. the new covenant text of Ezek. 36:24–27) and the Spirit." Salvation in any age has always been through the regenerating work of the Holy Spirit.

The difference between the Holy Spirit's ministry under the old and new covenants is one of degree. Jesus implied that when He told His disciples, "I will ask the Father, and He will give you another Helper, that He may be with you forever; that is the Spirit of truth, whom the world cannot receive, because it does not see Him or know Him, but you know Him because He abides with you and will be in you" (John 14:16–17). As old covenant believers, the disciples already possessed the Holy Spirit, as Jesus' statement, "He abides with you" indicates. Yet there was a fullness of the Spirit's presence and ministry in their lives that awaited the ratification of the new covenant. Then, Jesus declared to them, the Spirit "will be in you." He also spoke of that coming fullness in John 7:37–39:

> Now on the last day, the great day of the feast, Jesus stood and cried out, saying, "If anyone is thirsty, let him come to Me and drink. He who believes in Me, as the Scripture said, 'From his innermost being will flow rivers of living water.'" But this He spoke of the Spirit, whom those who believed in Him were to receive; for the Spirit was not yet given, because Jesus was not yet glorified.

There is a degree to which new covenant believers experience the power and the enabling of the Spirit that goes beyond that of old covenant believers. In addition, the Spirit unites believers into one body in the church (1 Cor. 12:13). But the essential work of the Holy Spirit in salvation was the same in the old covenant as in the new.

THE NEW COVENANT IS TRANSFORMING

are being transformed into the same image from glory to glory, just as from the Lord, the Spirit. (3:18*b*)

When the veil is removed in Christ, believers receive "the Light of the knowledge of the glory of God in the face of Christ" (4:6) and are **transformed into the same image from glory to glory.** The phrase **are being transformed** translates a present passive participle of the verb *metamorphoō* and refers to believers' progressive sanctification. The Christian life is a continual process of growing into the **image** of the Lord Jesus Christ, ascending **from** one level of **glory** to another.

Believers' transformation into the likeness of Christ was a frequent theme in Paul's writings. In Romans 12:2 he admonished, "Do not be conformed to this world, but be transformed by the renewing of your mind." He reminded the Colossians that they had "put on the new self who is being renewed to a true knowledge according to the image of the One who created him" (Col. 3:10), while in Galatians 4:19 he wrote, "My children, with whom I am again in labor until Christ is formed in you." Most personally, he wrote that the "one thing" he did was run "toward the goal for the prize of the upward call of God in Christ Jesus" (Phil. 3:13–14). The prize to which believers are called is to be like Christ (1 John 3:2). That is also the goal in this life—to be like the Lord. The process of being transformed into the **image** of Jesus Christ will culminate in believers' glorification, when Christ "will transform the body of [their] humble state into conformity with the body of His glory, by the exertion of the power that He has even to subject all things to Himself" (Phil. 3:21; cf. 1 Cor. 15:49, 51–53).

Ceremonial, sacramental religion offers nothing to new covenant believers. It does not provide justification, has no power to sanctify, and will not lead to glorification. The Christian life does not consist in rituals but in a relationship to Jesus Christ; not in ceremonies but in "the simplicity and purity of devotion to Christ" (2 Cor. 11:3). As believers single-mindedly focus on the Scriptures, they will see God's glory reflected in the face of Jesus and be transformed into His image by the powerful internal work of the **Lord, the Spirit** (cf. Eph. 3:16). Verse 18 will be further discussed in the next chapter.

Looking at the Face of Jesus
(2 Corinthians 3:18–4:6)

9

But we all, with unveiled face, beholding as in a mirror the glory of the Lord, are being transformed into the same image from glory to glory, just as from the Lord, the Spirit. Therefore, since we have this ministry, as we received mercy, we do not lose heart, but we have renounced the things hidden because of shame, not walking in craftiness or adulterating the word of God, but by the manifestation of truth commending ourselves to every man's conscience in the sight of God. And even if our gospel is veiled, it is veiled to those who are perishing, in whose case the god of this world has blinded the minds of the unbelieving so that they might not see the light of the gospel of the glory of Christ, who is the image of God. For we do not preach ourselves but Christ Jesus as Lord, and ourselves as your bond-servants for Jesus' sake. For God, who said, "Light shall shine out of darkness," is the One who has shone in our hearts to give the Light of the knowledge of the glory of God in the face of Christ. (3:18–4:6)

Life in this fallen, evil world is a struggle. In the picturesque language of the book of Job, "Man is born for trouble, as sparks fly upward" (Job 5:7). The Christian life is no exception; in fact, the more devoted a believer is to Jesus Christ, the more difficult life seems to get. The Lord Jesus Christ warned His own, "In the world you have tribulation" (John 16:33). Paul and Barnabas preached the sobering truth that "through many tribulations we must enter the kingdom of God" (Acts 14:22). Paul reminded Timothy that "all who desire to live godly in Christ Jesus will be persecuted" (2 Tim. 3:12).

But in the same verse in which He warned them of the trials they would endure, the Lord comforted His disciples by telling them, "Take courage; I have overcome the world" (John 16:33). He also promised to send the Holy Spirit to be their Helper (John 14:16, 26; 15:26; 16:7). The writer of Hebrews records God's promise, "I will never desert you, nor will I ever forsake you" (Heb. 13:5). Through the psalmist God declared to His people, "Call upon Me in the day of trouble; I shall rescue you, and you will honor Me" (Ps. 50:15). He promises His children that in their deepest weakness they will find His greatest strength (2 Cor. 12:9–10).

How do believers experience triumph in the midst of trouble? How do they appropriate God's promised help in tribulation? The answer lies in the truth that brackets this passage: by gazing at the glory of God revealed in the face of Jesus Christ in the mirror of Scripture (3:18; 4:6). Nowhere is God's glory more clearly manifest than in the person of His Son. Therefore, the only way to successfully live the Christian life is by "beholding . . . the glory of the Lord" (v. 18) or by "fixing our eyes on Jesus, the author and perfecter of faith, who for the joy set before Him endured the cross, despising the shame, and has sat down at the right hand of the throne of God" (Heb. 12:2).

For Paul, focusing on Christ was not only a vital theological truth but also a vital practical principle. As he penned 2 Corinthians, Paul faced the most difficult circumstances of his ministerial experience. It is helpful to read these extended passages together to see the depth of his struggle reflected throughout the epistle: "just as the sufferings of Christ are ours in abundance" (2 Cor. 1:5); "but if we are afflicted, it is for your comfort and salvation" (1:6);

> For we do not want you to be unaware, brethren, of our affliction which came to us in Asia, that we were burdened excessively, beyond our strength, so that we despaired even of life; indeed, we had the sentence of death within ourselves so that we would not trust in ourselves, but in God who raises the dead; who delivered us from so great a peril of death, and will deliver us, He on whom we have set our hope. And He will yet deliver us. (1:8–10)

"For out of much affliction and anguish of heart I wrote to you with many tears" (2:4); "I had no rest for my spirit" (2:13);

We are afflicted in every way, but not crushed; perplexed, but not despairing; persecuted, but not forsaken; struck down, but not destroyed; always carrying about in the body the dying of Jesus, so that the life of Jesus also may be manifested in our body. For we who live are constantly being delivered over to death for Jesus' sake, so that the life of Jesus also may be manifested in our mortal flesh. So death works in us, but life in you. (4:8–12)

"Therefore we do not lose heart, but though our outer man is decaying, yet our inner man is being renewed day by day. For momentary, light affliction is producing for us an eternal weight of glory far beyond all comparison" (4:16–17);

But in everything commending ourselves as servants of God, in much endurance, in afflictions, in hardships, in distresses, in beatings, in imprisonments, in tumults, in labors, in sleeplessness, in hunger, in purity, in knowledge, in patience, in kindness, in the Holy Spirit, in genuine love, in the word of truth, in the power of God; by the weapons of righteousness for the right hand and the left, by glory and dishonor, by evil report and good report; regarded as deceivers and yet true; as unknown yet well-known, as dying yet behold, we live; as punished yet not put to death, as sorrowful yet always rejoicing, as poor yet making many rich, as having nothing yet possessing all things. (6:4–10)

"For even when we came into Macedonia our flesh had no rest, but we were afflicted on every side: conflicts without, fears within. But God, who comforts the depressed, comforted us by the coming of Titus" (7:5–6);

Are they servants of Christ?—I speak as if insane—I more so; in far more labors, in far more imprisonments, beaten times without number, often in danger of death. Five times I received from the Jews thirty-nine lashes. Three times I was beaten with rods, once I was stoned, three times I was shipwrecked, a night and a day I have spent in the deep. I have been on frequent journeys, in dangers from rivers, dangers from robbers, dangers from my countrymen, dangers from the Gentiles, dangers in the city, dangers in the wilderness, dangers on the sea, dangers among false brethren; I have been in labor and hardship, through many sleepless nights, in hunger and thirst, often without food, in cold and exposure. Apart from such external things, there is the daily pressure on me of concern for all the churches. (11:23–28)

Because of the surpassing greatness of the revelations, for this reason, to keep me from exalting myself, there was given me a thorn in the flesh, a messenger of Satan to torment me—to keep me from exalting myself! Concerning this I implored the Lord three times that it might leave me. And He has said to me, "My grace is sufficient for you, for power is perfected in weakness." Most gladly, therefore, I will rather boast about my weaknesses, so that the power of Christ may dwell in me. Therefore I am well content with weaknesses, with insults, with distresses, with persecutions, with difficulties, for Christ's sake; for when I am weak, then I am strong. (12:7–10)

As the last reference indicates, Paul's suffering had overwhelmed even his formidable human strength. Not the least of his trials was the assassination of his character at Corinth and the defection of many in the church there to follow false apostles. But Paul's trials did not destroy his faith or cause him to leave the ministry. He expressed his grave concern over the situation at Corinth in 2 Corinthians 11:3: "But I am afraid that, as the serpent deceived Eve by his craftiness, your minds will be led astray from the simplicity and purity of devotion to Christ." Yet that expression of concern and sorrow also contains the essence of living the Christian life. Christianity is nothing more or less than devotion to Jesus Christ. Paul was able to cope with the trials he faced in life because he kept his mind on his Lord.

In fact, Paul's Christian life began with a vision of God's glory revealed in Jesus Christ. That dramatic encounter on the road to Damascus forever shattered his proud, legalistic, pharisaical self-confidence (cf. Phil. 3:4–6). When he saw God's blazing glory revealed in the face of Jesus, he transferred all the legalism that had been in his spiritual gain column to the loss column (Phil. 3:7–8).

The remarkable reality of the new covenant is that every believer can see God's glory revealed in Jesus Christ. That was a privilege not granted to even the most noble of the Old Testament saints, "because God had provided something better for us, so that apart from us they would not be made perfect" (Heb. 11:40). The veil that partially obscured God's glory in the old covenant was not removed until "God [who] spoke long ago to the fathers in the prophets in many portions and in many ways, in these last days [spoke] to us in His Son . . . [who] is the radiance of His glory" (Heb. 1:1–3).

It is important to establish that when Scripture speaks of looking into the face of Jesus it is not speaking of a subjective, mystical experience. Donald S. Whitney writes,

> The essence of mysticism is the attempt to experience God unmediated, that is, without means. This is the belief that apart from any external assistance, you enter *directly* into an experience of the presence of God. . . . The problem is, as spiritual as this may sound, the Bible never commands us to do this or ever describes such an experience. (*Ten Questions to Diagnose Your Spiritual Health* [Colorado Springs, Colo.: NavPress, 2001], 60. Italics in original.)

Thus, when Paul speaks of looking into the face of Jesus, he has in mind an objective, historical look at the person of Christ revealed in the Bible. The apostle Peter confirms the superiority of Scripture over experiences in 2 Peter 1:19. Though he had a remarkable vision of Christ's glory at the Transfiguration, Peter regarded Scripture as a more reliable source of knowledge, describing it as "the prophetic word made more sure" (lit., "the more sure prophetic word").

Looking at the face of Jesus as revealed in Scripture provides new covenant believers with strength, joy, and hope to face all of life's trials. Those come from an understanding of God, who is most clearly revealed in Jesus Christ. In this passage Paul gives an eightfold description of looking into the face of Jesus. It is a clarifying look, a transforming look, a strengthening look, a purifying look, a truth-loving look, a privileged look, a humbling look, and a sovereignly granted look.

A CLARIFYING LOOK

But we all, with unveiled face, beholding as in a mirror the glory of the Lord, (3:18*a*)

While the creation reveals certain truths about God (Rom. 1:20), those truths are insufficient to save. A saving knowledge of God comes only through Jesus Christ (cf. John 14:6; Acts 4:12; Rom. 1:16). Unlike old covenant believers, every new covenant believer can gaze into the face of Christ **with** an **unveiled face. We all,** writes Paul, have the privilege of **beholding** in His face **as in a mirror the glory of the Lord.** Since in Christ "all the fullness of Deity dwells in bodily form" (Col. 2:9), believers see in His person and works what God is like. He manifested the mercy (Matt. 9:36; 14:14; 15:32; 20:34; Mark 1:41; 5:19; Luke 7:13), wisdom (John 7:46; cf. Matt. 7:29; Luke 4:22), power (Matt. 13:54; 14:2; Luke 4:36), and sovereign authority (Matt. 9:6; John 17:2) of God. Never is God more clearly revealed than in the face of Jesus Christ; "God . . . in these last days has spoken to us in His Son. . . . And He is the radiance of His glory and the exact representation of His nature" (Heb. 1:1–3).

All three aspects of salvation—justification, sanctification, and glorification—involve looking to Jesus. Believers' new life in Christ begins when they look into His face and embrace Him as Lord and Savior. But just as they look to Him for justification, so also must they look to Him for sanctification, which involves "fixing our eyes on Jesus, the author and perfecter of faith" (Heb. 12:2) and discerning the mind of Christ from Scripture (1 Cor. 2:16), because "the one who says he abides in Him ought himself to walk in the same manner as He walked" (1 John 2:6).

Ultimately, at glorification Christ "will transform the body of our humble state into conformity with the body of His glory, by the exertion of the power that He has even to subject all things to Himself" (Phil. 3:21).

There is no reason for believers to be defeated by the difficulties of life if they have a proper understanding of God. And those who fail to understand God are not looking into the face of Christ. The better believers know Christ, the better they know God since seeing Him is seeing the Father (John 14:9); the better they know God the better equipped they are to handle life's trials and difficulties. Suffering merely weakens dependence on self so that the power of God can be manifest in them (cf. 2 Cor. 12:9).

A Transforming Look

are being transformed into the same image from glory to glory, just as from the Lord, the Spirit. (3:18*b*)

As believers look at the glory of God in the face of Christ, they **are** constantly **being transformed into the same image from glory to glory.** They progress to ever-higher levels of **glory;** in other words, they move ever closer to the likeness of Jesus Christ. As noted in the previous chapter of this volume, Paul taught in Philippians 3:12–14 that the goal of the Christian life is to become like Christ:

> Not that I have already obtained it or have already become perfect, but I press on so that I may lay hold of that for which also I was laid hold of by Christ Jesus. Brethren, I do not regard myself as having laid hold of it yet; but one thing I do: forgetting what lies behind and reaching forward to what lies ahead, I press on toward the goal for the prize of the upward call of God in Christ Jesus.

To the Galatians he wrote, "My children, with whom I am again in labor until Christ is formed in you" (Gal. 4:19). The early believers were called "Christians" (lit., "of the party of Christ") at Antioch because of their Christlikeness (Acts 11:26). The measure of spiritual maturity is "the measure of the stature which belongs to the fullness of Christ" (Eph. 4:13), because God's ultimate goal in salvation is that believers "become conformed to the image of His Son" (Rom. 8:29).

That goal is accomplished in believers' lives as they gaze steadily into the face of Jesus Christ revealed in Scripture. When they do so, **the Lord, the Spirit** changes them into Christ's image.

A Strengthening Look

Therefore, since we have this ministry, as we received mercy, we do not lose heart, (4:1)

Therefore points back to Paul's discussion of the new covenant in 3:6–18. Strength to endure trials comes from the unveiled look into the face of Christ made possible under the new covenant. That look was also the source of strength for Paul's new covenant **ministry.** The apostle used the plural **we** as a humbler way of referring to himself. By so doing, he softened the personal nature of his defense of himself and his ministry (cf. the discussion of 3:1 in chapter 6 of this volume). The phrase **we have this ministry** emphasizes Paul's humble acknowledgment that God had graciously granted him the privilege of being a new covenant minister (cf. 5:18; Acts 20:24; 26:16; Rom. 15:15–16; 1 Cor. 4:1–3; Eph. 3:7–8; Col. 1:23, 25; 1 Tim. 1:12; 2:7; 2 Tim. 1:11). Paul's call to the **ministry** was based solely on God's **mercy.** God's **mercy** is His withholding of the judgment that sinners deserve, temporarily in the case of the unsaved to give opportunity for repentance and faith, and permanently in the case of the redeemed. In this context God's **mercy** means that instead of condemning Paul because he was a "blasphemer and a persecutor and a violent aggressor" (1 Tim. 1:13), God showed him **mercy** by "putting [him] into service" (v. 12).

As he kept his eyes on Jesus, Paul was strengthened and did **not lose heart.** *Engkakeō* (**lose heart**) means to give in to fear, lose courage, or behave like a coward. Despite his suffering and the savage attacks on him by the false apostles, Paul had not surrendered. His courage came from confident knowledge of the God of glory, whom he had perceived in the face of Jesus Christ. God's sovereign mercy saved him, made him a minister, and strengthened him to do the work of the ministry.

A Purifying Look

but we have renounced the things hidden because of shame, not walking in craftiness (4:2a)

From the moment he first saw the glory of Christ at his dramatic conversion, Paul certainly **renounced** his former **hidden** life of **shame.** He despised his sin and cried out for deliverance from it: "Wretched man that I am! Who will set me free from the body of this death?" (Rom. 7:24). His Christian life was from the outset a life of purity, as he pursued holiness.

When people see the glory of God revealed in the face of Jesus Christ and are born again, when they understand who God is, what His holy law demands, and the provision of salvation in Jesus Christ, they renounce and turn from their sin and devote themselves to the pursuit of godliness. A repentance that does not involve turning from sin is foreign to Scripture. (For a discussion of the biblical view of repentance, see John MacArthur, *The Gospel According to Jesus,* rev. ed. [Grand Rapids: Zondervan, 1994], and *The Gospel According to the Apostles* [Nashville: Word, 2000].)

The adversative conjunction *alla* (**but**) could be translated "on the contrary," or "on the other hand." It indicates a contrast between Paul and the false apostles at Corinth. The **things hidden because of shame** could be the very **things** they were accusing him of. **But** in reality it was the false apostles, not Paul, who were guilty of them. It was they who had a secret life of **shame** and who brought a hidden agenda to Corinth. Paul once had a **hidden,** secret life of **shame** before his conversion (cf. Phil. 3:4–6). He was like his fellow Pharisees, whom Jesus scathingly denounced in Matthew 23:27: "Woe to you, scribes and Pharisees, hypocrites! For you are like whitewashed tombs which on the outside appear beautiful, but inside they are full of dead men's bones and all uncleanness." Like them, Paul could not help but be filthy on the inside, because legalism cannot restrain the flesh, and a false salvation transforms no one.

Aischunē (**shame**) describes disgraceful, dishonorable deeds that produce embarrassment and humiliation. Such a dark, hidden, hypocritical lifestyle had characterized Paul before his conversion. But that secret life of sin died when he met Jesus Christ. He became "a new creature; the old things [in his life] passed away; behold, new things [came]" (2 Cor. 5:17). That does not mean, of course, that Paul never again sinned, but that when he did sin he confessed it and turned away from it. Though he felt the plague of indwelling sin (Rom. 7:14–23), he no longer had a sinful, secret life that he willfully clung to. Like Paul, believers must shun the shameful deeds that once characterized them. When they attempt to creep back into their lives, they must defeat them through prayer and the Word.

There is, however, another way to interpret this statement. The context being new covenant ministry and the fruitful proclamation of the Word, Paul may be saying that he rejected any and all personal feelings of shame about the offensive gospel (cf. 1 Cor. 1:18, 23–25). It was foolishness to Greeks and a stumbling block to Jews, and therefore universally rejected. Though it thus brought shame upon anyone who proclaimed it, Paul refused to hide its truth (Rom. 1:16–17).

Further contrasting himself with the false apostles, Paul declared that he was **not** guilty of **walking in craftiness.** *Panourgia* (**craftiness**) refers to trickery (Luke 20:23) and deceit (2 Cor. 11:3; Eph. 4:14). Someone who practiced *panourgia* was unscrupulous, willing to do anything to achieve his goals. In a plain testimony to their own corruption, the false apostles had accused Paul of being (like they were secretly) a manipulator, of seeking money, power, and influence. None of that, however, was true. Paul was no deceiver; he had no hidden agenda. He was nothing more than what he appeared to be: a bold, fearless preacher of the new covenant gospel message. His approach was simple, plain, and straightforward, as he stated in 1 Corinthians 2:1–2: "And when I came to you, brethren, I did not come with superiority of speech or of wisdom, proclaiming to you the testimony of God. For I determined to know nothing among you except Jesus Christ, and Him crucified." The apostle rejected the idea, prevalent in the pagan religions of his day, of a deep, hidden, secret knowledge available only to the initiated. He also rejected efforts to remove the perceived shameful features of the gospel and thus deceive people (cf. 2 Cor. 2:17).

It was in part because of his plain, clear approach to the ministry that the false teachers attacked Paul. They preferred a subtler, more veiled approach, one more appealing, palatable, and less offensive to unbelievers. Plain preachers like Paul are offensive because they preach the straightforward, unvarnished truth, whether or not it brings shame on them. This was Paul's attitude when he wrote, "For even if I boast somewhat further about our authority, which the Lord gave for building you up and not for destroying you, I will not be put to shame, for I do not wish to seem as if I would terrify you by my letters" (2 Cor. 10:8–9). He was never ashamed of the gospel; he never hid its truth or used trickery that adulterated it. The false teachers did not want to offend people; they wanted to make money from them. They also wanted an element of mystery in their message. As the ones initiated to the mysteries, that would boost both their own prestige and impress their followers.

The false apostles were, in effect, first-century marketing experts. They viewed the gospel as a product and themselves as salesmen. Part of selling the product (the gospel) was veiling its truth and sprucing it up by adding some mystery and magic. By tweaking the message, repackaging it to make it more popular and trendy, they hoped to better appeal to first-century consumers. They would then succeed in making converts (and money). Paul's straightforward, powerful presentation of the pure unadulterated gospel (cf. Rom. 1:16) frustrated and threatened them. It also exposed their secret lives of shame. It is no wonder, then, that they bitterly opposed Paul.

The difference between Paul and the false apostles was that he had looked to Christ for salvation and they had not. No one can truly look into the face of Jesus and be a deceiver. No one can truly look into the face of Jesus and continue to cultivate a shameful, secret life of sin, because "everyone who has this hope fixed on Him purifies himself, just as He is pure" (1 John 3:3).

A TRUTH-LOVING LOOK

or adulterating the word of God, but by the manifestation of truth commending ourselves to every man's conscience in the sight of God. (4:2*b*)

Jesus Christ is truth incarnate; He Himself declared: "I am . . . the truth" (John 14:6; cf. John 1:14, 17; Rev. 19:11). When people look to Him for salvation, they fall in love with the truth; the lost will perish eternally "because they did not receive the love of the truth so as to be saved" (2 Thess. 2:10). Therefore being saved means loving the truth.

From his conversion, along with his hidden life of sin and shame, Paul also renounced any feeling of shame because of the offense of the gospel that might make him guilty of **adulterating the word of God** (cf. Phil. 1:20). **Adulterating** is from *doloō*, a word used in extrabiblical Greek to speak of corrupting gold or wine with inferior ingredients (Richard C. Trench, *Synonyms of the New Testament* [Reprint; Grand Rapids: Eerdmans, 1983], 230). Paul's message was the plain, pure, un-mixed truth of the gospel.

The same could not be said, however, for the false apostles. They were busy **adulterating** the Word of God for their own purposes. In 2 Corinthians 2:17 Paul denounced them as being guilty of "peddling the word of God." They were con men, cheats, charlatans, and frauds, guilty of the same deception of which they falsely accused Paul. No doubt they accused him of tampering with the truth by not preaching the Mosaic Law. They probably also insisted that Paul's simplistic message denied the hidden, secret things of God, that therefore he was guilty of failing to preach the whole counsel of God. Sadly, many today level the same charges at those who proclaim the sufficiency of Scripture. The idea that the Bible alone—apart from psychology, mysticism, or supposed supernatural experiences—contains everything needed to live a joyous, fulfilled, God-honoring life is derided as quaintly naïve and overly simplistic. Even sadder is the reality that many Christians "will not endure sound doctrine; but wanting to have their ears tickled, they . . . accumulate for themselves teachers in accordance to their own desires, and . . . turn away their ears from the truth and . . . turn aside to myths" (2 Tim. 4:3–4). The siren song of sophisticated false teaching lures many to make shipwreck of their faith.

A sure mark of a growing Christian is love for biblical **truth.** When there is an open, clear **manifestation** of the truth of Scripture, no matter what public scorn it brings, there is the source for spiritual power and impact. But when preachers, ashamed of the gospel, proclaim human wisdom deceitfully in the name of divine truth, their work is impotent. Thus, the faithful preacher's world is the realm of biblical truth. His task is to proclaim the clear, pure doctrine that is the foundation of the faith. All believers should love the truth; they should "like newborn babies, long for the pure milk of the word, so that by it [they] may grow in respect to salvation" (1 Peter 2:2; cf. 1 Tim. 4:6).

Paul's plain, straightforward preaching of the gospel had the effect of **commending** him **to every man's conscience.** All people, even those who have not heard the gospel, have an innate (though limited) knowledge of God's law. The preaching of the gospel activates the **conscience,** which bears witness to the truth of the message even in those who reject it. That is true because "the word of God is living and active and sharper than any two-edged sword, and piercing as far as the division of soul and spirit, of both joints and marrow, and able to judge the thoughts and intentions of the heart" (Heb. 4:12).

As with everything else in his life, Paul preached the truth **in the sight of God.** In 1 Corinthians 4:3–4 he wrote, "But to me it is a very small thing that I may be examined by you, or by any human court; in fact, I do not even examine myself. For I am conscious of nothing against myself, yet I am not by this acquitted; but the one who examines me is the Lord." He sought God's approval, not man's, knowing that He is the One to whom every preacher (and every believer) is ultimately accountable.

The measure of a believer's spiritual maturity is his or her loyalty to the truth (cf. Ps. 119:97–106; 113, 119, 127, 161–162, 174). Throughout its history, those who have had the greatest impact in the life of the church have been those most committed to the truth. And those who love it will find it in Jesus (Eph. 4:21).

A PRIVILEGED LOOK

And even if our gospel is veiled, it is veiled to those who are perishing, in whose case the god of this world has blinded the minds of the unbelieving so that they might not see the light of the gospel of the glory of Christ, who is the image of God. (4:3–4)

Not everyone has the privilege of looking into the face of Jesus, "for the gate is small and the way is narrow that leads to life, and there are few who find it" (Matt. 7:14). Only those who have had the veil of spiritual blindness removed in Christ (cf. 2 Cor. 3:14) can look into His face.

As noted above, one of the criticisms the false apostles leveled against Paul was that his evangelistic methodology was defective. His approach, which he defined in 1 Corinthians 2:2, was simple and straight-forward: "For I determined to know nothing among you except Jesus Christ, and Him crucified." He frankly admitted, "My message and my preaching were not in persuasive words of wisdom, but in demonstration of the Spirit and of power" (1 Cor. 2:4). His preaching was a plain, bold, direct presentation of sin, repentance, and faith. Because of that, the false apostles accused him of being offensive and ineffective. His preaching was alienating people; it was "to Jews a stumbling block and to Gentiles foolishness" (1 Cor. 1:23). He needed a better marketing plan to over-come consumer resistance.

That kind of thinking is prevalent in today's church. Contempo-rary critics argue for a subtler and less offensive approach to presenting the gospel. Preaching sin, repentance, judgment, and hell is out; "user-friendly" churches are in. Worship services give way to entertainment designed to make nonbelievers feel comfortable and not threatened. The thinking is that they will then be open to considering Christ.

Underlying much of modern evangelism is the heretical idea that anyone can and will respond to the gospel if it is presented in an ingenious enough way. That view sees unbelievers as consumers, for whom the gospel must be cleverly packaged in order to make the sale. Roy Clements writes perceptively of this trend:

> A preacher . . . is a herald, and a herald is precisely a one-way commu-nicator; he does not dialogue, he announces a message he has received. But if our communication experts are correct, announce-ments do not change anybody. Where is the flaw in their reasoning? . . . It lies in the theology. For people who argue like this are assuming that Christian preaching is analogous to a marketing exercise. You have your product: the gospel. You have your consumers: the congregation. And the preacher is the salesman. It is his job to overcome consumer resistance and persuade people to buy.

> According to Paul, there is one very simple but overwhelming reason why that analogy is not a good one. The preacher does not overcome consumer resistance. He cannot. Consumer resistance is far too large for any preacher to overcome. All the preacher does, Paul says, is to expose that resistance in its formidable impenetrability. If our gospel is veiled, it is veiled to those who are perishing. The god of this age has blinded their minds and "they cannot see the light of the gospel of the glory of Christ." . . . The preacher does not save anybody. He is an instru-ment whereby people who are being saved become aware of the fact.

> Evangelism has to be proclamation because preaching is a sacrament of the divine sovereignty. (*The Strength of Weakness* [Grand Rapids: Baker, 1995], 75–76)

Salvation is never the result of human persuasion; it is a sovereign act of God. In John 6:44 Jesus declared, "No one can come to Me unless the Father who sent Me draws him." Acts 11:18 affirms that "God has granted to the Gentiles also the repentance that leads to life." Lydia was saved when "the Lord opened her heart to respond to the things spoken by Paul" (Acts 16:14). Paul counseled Timothy,

> The Lord's bond-servant must not be quarrelsome, but be kind to all, able to teach, patient when wronged, with gentleness correcting those who are in opposition, if perhaps God may grant them repentance leading to the knowledge of the truth, and they may come to their senses and escape from the snare of the devil, having been held captive by him to do his will. (2 Tim. 2:24–26)

The apostle reminded Titus that "[God] saved us, not on the basis of deeds which we have done in righteousness, but according to His mercy, by the washing of regeneration and renewing by the Holy Spirit" (Titus 3:5).

The issue is not the skill of the one proclaiming the message, the packaging of the message, or the technique used in proclaiming it. The issue is the condition of the hearer. Jesus illustrated that principle in the parable of the sower. The same message (the seed) is proclaimed by the same individual (the sower); the only variable is the condition of the four soils. What is essential for messengers of the gospel is not cleverness but clarity. Only God can open the sin-blinded eyes of those who are "dead in [their] trespasses and sins" (Eph. 2:1; cf. v. 5; Matt. 8:22; Eph. 4:18).

To those who criticized his preaching as irrelevant, offensive, and ineffective Paul replied, **Even if our gospel is veiled, it is veiled to those who are perishing.** Fallen, dead in their sins, and spiritually blind, those who reject the gospel message are headed for eternal doom (cf. 2 Cor. 2:15; 3:14; Luke 13:3, 5; Rom. 2:12; 1 Cor. 1:18; 2 Thess. 2:9–11). Therefore "a natural man does not accept the things of the Spirit of God, for they are foolishness to him; and he cannot understand them, because they are spiritually appraised" (1 Cor. 2:14). The issue is not contriving nonthreatening church services or developing better marketing skill in pitching the gospel. The issue is that those who reject the gospel message do so because "[they love] the darkness rather than the Light, for their deeds [are] evil" (John 3:19).

In addition to their own love of sin, unbelievers reject the gospel because **the god of this world has blinded the minds of the unbelieving.** The **unbelieving** are the same ones described in verse 3 as those who are perishing; the two terms are synonyms. Despite the claims of some, there can be no such thing as an "unbelieving Christian," since the unbelieving are the perishing. *Aiōn* (**world**) is better translated "age" (as it is in Matt. 12:32; 13:39, 40, 49; 24:3; 28:20; Luke 16:8; 18:30; 20:34; 1 Cor. 1:20; 2:6, 7, 8; 3:18; Gal. 1:4; Eph. 1:21; Col. 1:26; Titus 2:12; Heb. 6:5, etc.). The **god of this world** or age is Satan, (John 12:31; 14:30; 16:11; Eph. 2:2; 2 Tim. 2:26; 1 John 5:19), who controls the ideologies, opinions, hopes, aims, goals, and viewpoints current in the world (cf. 2 Cor. 10:3–5). He is behind the world's systems of philosophy, psychology, education, sociology, ethics, and economics. But perhaps his greatest influence is in the realm of false religion. Satan, of course, is not a **god** but a created being. He is called a **god** because his deluded followers serve him as if he were one. Satan is the archetype of all the false gods in all the false religions he has spawned.

It is that massive and pervasive influence over society by which Satan deludes the unregenerate **so that they might not see the light of the gospel.** Except in rare cases, Satan and his demons do not directly indwell individuals. They do not need to. Satan has created a system that panders to the depravity of unbelievers and drives them deeper into darkness. In addition to being dead in their trespasses and sins (Eph. 2:1), veiled from the truth (2 Cor. 3:15), haters of light and lovers of darkness (John 3:19–20), unbelievers walk "according to the course of this world, according to the prince of the power of the air, of the spirit that is now working in the sons of disobedience . . . [living] in the lusts of [the] flesh, indulging the desires of the flesh and of the mind, and [are] by nature children of wrath" (Eph. 2:2–3). They are "of [their] father the devil, and [they] want to do the desires of [their] father" (John 8:44). All the evil of the human heart—crime, hatred, bitterness, anger, injustice, immorality, and conflict between nations and individuals—is pandered to by Satan's agenda. The world system he has created inflames the evil desires of fallen people, causing them to be willfully blind and love their darkness.

Minds translates *noēma,* which refers to the ability to reason or think. Unregenerate people cannot think properly about spiritual truth (1 Cor. 2:14) because they have a "depraved mind" (Rom. 1:28; 1 Tim. 6:5; 2 Tim. 3:8). No matter how slick the presentation is, it will not persuade a depraved mind to respond favorably to the gospel. Only God can turn on the light in the human heart (cf. 2 Cor. 4:6; Luke 24:45; Acts 26:18) so that it can respond in saving faith to **the gospel of the glory of Christ.** God's **glory** is revealed in Jesus Christ, because He **is the image of God**

(John 1:14; Col. 1:19; 2:9; Heb. 1:3). The privilege of seeing God's **glory** revealed in Christ is granted only to those to whom God in His mercy grants spiritual sight.

A HUMBLING LOOK

For we do not preach ourselves but Christ Jesus as Lord, and ourselves as your bond-servants for Jesus' sake. (4:5)

The immeasurable privilege of proclaiming the glorious gospel of Jesus Christ might lead some to become proud and boastful. In fact, one of the slanderous accusations the false apostles made against Paul was that he preached with selfish motives. He was in the ministry, they claimed, for his own self-exaltation, self-promotion, self-aggrandizement, power, prestige, and prominence. Nothing could have been further from the truth. By declaring, **We do not preach ourselves,** Paul distinguished himself from the false apostles, who did, in fact, preach themselves. Later in this epistle he wrote, "For we are not bold to class or compare ourselves with some of those who commend themselves"—the false apostles, who foolishly "measure[d] themselves by themselves and compare[d] themselves with themselves," demonstrating that "they [were] without understanding" (10:12). Thus Paul's disclaimer was both a denial of the false apostles' charge and an indictment of them.

Far from being arrogant, proud, and self-assured, Paul ministered in Corinth "in weakness and in fear and in much trembling" (1 Cor. 2:3). Instead of boasting of his own abilities and successes, he wrote, "On my own behalf I will not boast, except in regard to my weaknesses. . . . I will rather boast about my weaknesses, so that the power of Christ may dwell in me" (2 Cor. 12:5, 9). Paul's vision of the glory of Christ dominated his life, and his love for Him consumed the apostle.

Instead of promoting his own agenda, Paul proclaimed **Christ Jesus as Lord.** He preached Him as the humble (Phil. 2:8) crucified Savior (1 Cor. 2:2), who died to save His people from their sins (Matt. 1:21; John 1:29; Acts 5:31; 13:38; 1 John 2:2; 3:5; Rev. 1:5). But he also preached Him as the sovereign Lord, who demands submission, allegiance, and obedience (Rom. 10:9; 1 Cor. 12:3; Phil. 2:10–11). (I discuss the vital lordship of Christ in my books *The Gospel According to Jesus* and *The Gospel According to the Apostles* referred to earlier in this chapter.)

The heart of new covenant preaching is communicating the truth about Jesus Christ, since "faith comes from hearing, and hearing by the word of [lit., "about," or "concerning"] Christ" (Rom. 10:17). True preaching about Christ includes the truth that He is both Savior and

Lord. Its goal is to get people to understand who Jesus is, why He came, and what He accomplished. God, in His sovereign grace, then uses that truth to bring salvation to the human heart.

Unlike the proud, boastful false apostles, Paul mentioned himself only to express his humility. The apostle frequently declared himself to be a **bond-servant** of Jesus Christ (e.g., Rom. 1:1; Gal. 1:10; Phil. 1:1; Titus 1:1) who served the church **for Jesus' sake.** A true look into the face of Jesus is the most humbling experience possible. Those who love Christ and are devoted to serving Him will be self-effacing, not self-exalting. They will also humbly serve God's people. Conversely, those who are proud are not looking into the face of Jesus. Their primary concern is with themselves, not the welfare of God's people.

A SOVEREIGNLY GRANTED LOOK

For God, who said, "Light shall shine out of darkness," is the One who has shone in our hearts to give the Light of the knowledge of the glory of God in the face of Christ. (4:6)

Redemption is as much a sovereign work of God as creation; in fact, Paul used the analogy of creation to describe salvation when he wrote, "If anyone is in Christ, he is a new creature; the old things passed away; behold, new things have come" (2 Cor. 5:17). Here he also uses an analogy for salvation drawn from the creation of the physical world, noting that the same **God, who said, "Light shall shine out of darkness"** (cf. Gen. 1:3) **is the One who has shone in our hearts.** The same God who turned on the light physically turns on the light spiritually—and does both without using any evolutionary process.

Spiritual darkness envelopes the unredeemed until God shines the light of the gospel in their hearts; He alone can dispel the darkness of sin and ignorance. But at salvation God "qualified us to share in the inheritance of the saints in Light. For He rescued us from the domain of darkness, and transferred us to the kingdom of His beloved Son" (Col. 1:12–13). Jesus declared in John 8:12, "I am the Light of the world; he who follows Me will not walk in the darkness, but will have the Light of life" (cf. John 9:5; 12:46). At salvation sinners receive **the Light of the knowledge of the glory of God in the face of Christ.** When God sovereignly shines that **Light** into sin-darkened hearts through the preaching of the gospel (Rom. 10:13–15), it brings true knowledge of who Christ is; that He is God incarnate, and that the **glory of God** shines perfectly **in** His **face.**

In this rich passage Paul has revealed that the essence of the Christian life involves "fixing our eyes on Jesus, the author and perfecter of faith" (Heb. 12:2). Looking to Him begins the Christian life (justification), is the basis for living the Christian life (sanctification), and will be believers' occupation throughout eternity (glorification).

Priceless Treasure in Clay Pots (2 Corinthians 4:7–15)

10

But we have this treasure in earthen vessels, so that the surpassing greatness of the power will be of God and not from ourselves; we are afflicted in every way, but not crushed; perplexed, but not despairing; persecuted, but not forsaken; struck down, but not destroyed; always carrying about in the body the dying of Jesus, so that the life of Jesus also may be manifested in our body. For we who live are constantly being delivered over to death for Jesus' sake, so that the life of Jesus also may be manifested in our mortal flesh. So death works in us, but life in you. But having the same spirit of faith, according to what is written, "I believed, therefore I spoke," we also believe, therefore we also speak, knowing that He who raised the Lord Jesus will raise us also with Jesus and will present us with you. For all things are for your sakes, so that the grace which is spreading to more and more people may cause the giving of thanks to abound to the glory of God. (4:7–15)

The old adage that you cannot judge the value of something by the packaging it comes in is certainly true of Christians. Like valuable treasure buried in dirt (cf. Matt. 13:44), or a precious pearl hidden in an ugly oyster (cf. Matt. 13:46), the human container does not reflect the value of the gospel treasure it holds. The amazing contrast between "the glory of God in the face of Christ" (2 Cor. 4:6) and the feeble, imperfect, homely containers in which it is carried is the heart of this passage.

Paul communicated that truth not simply by principle but by example. Like much of 2 Corinthians, which presents profound insights into Paul's life, this passage is biographical, not didactic. It presents Paul not as a teacher communicating information but as a life to emulate. The apostle's life demonstrated what it genuinely means to walk with God. Thus, he could exhort the Corinthians, "Be imitators of me, just as I also am of Christ" (1 Cor. 11:1).

As he penned this epistle, Paul was under furious attack in Corinth. False apostles had infiltrated the church there, assaulting Paul so as to create an environment for purveying legalistic heresy. To gain a hearing for their demonic lies, they first had to destroy Paul's apostolic and spiritual credibility in the eyes of the Corinthian church. To that end, they launched an all-out blitz on the apostle's character and ministry. Their attack was merciless, relentless, and petty. So low did the false apostles sink that they even resorted to ridiculing Paul's personal appearance, declaring contemptuously that "his personal presence is unimpressive and his speech contemptible" (2 Cor. 10:10). Paul, according to them, was not a very imposing figure; he lacked good looks, charm, and oratorical skills. He may even have had a repulsive eye condition that marred his appearance (cf. Gal. 4:13–15). The reason so many rejected Paul's message, the false apostles claimed, was that he was an unimpressive, common, run-of-the-mill man.

Those hurtful, hateful attacks, moving people's loyalty from divine truth to satanic lies, demanded a response from Paul. He was not interested in defending himself for his own sake but for the sake of the gospel. Paul knew that if the false teachers could discredit him, they could replace him as the authoritative teachers at Corinth. They would then be free to deceive the Corinthians with their false teaching.

The false teachers' attacks on him put Paul between a rock and a hard place. If he defended himself against their slander, which he had to do to hold the church to the truth (written and incarnate), he risked looking proud. And, in truth, no one was more acutely aware of his shortcomings than Paul himself. In fact, he was constantly amazed that he was in the ministry at all. In his first inspired letter to the Corinthians Paul confessed, "I am the least of the apostles, and not fit to be called an apostle, because I persecuted the church of God" (1 Cor. 15:9). To Timothy he wrote, "I thank Christ Jesus our Lord, who has strengthened me, because He considered me faithful, putting me into service, even though I was formerly a blasphemer and a persecutor and a violent aggressor. Yet I was shown mercy because I acted ignorantly in unbelief" (1 Tim. 1:12–13).

How then was Paul to extricate himself from this dilemma? How was he to defend himself and the gospel he preached without seeming proud? Rather than deny the false apostles' allegations that he was weak and imperfect, he embraced them. The apostle declared that the priceless truth of the gospel was held in a humble container. In fact, his weaknesses, far from being reasons to reject him, were among his most convincing apostolic credentials. To express this, he used the analogy of a precious treasure kept in a clay pot.

Like all preachers (and all believers), Paul's imperfections stood out in stark relief against the shining glory of the gospel. But if God could not use imperfect people, there would be no one in the ministry. Since there are no sinless people, God must choose His ministers from the fallen, weak, imperfect human race.

Even the noblest saints were far from perfect. Fearing for his life, Abraham, the father of the faithful, twice pretended his wife Sarah was his sister (Gen. 12:13; 20:2). Moses, the human deliverer of Israel from Egypt, had a fiery temper (Ex. 2:11–12) and was, by his own admission, a completely inadequate speaker (Ex. 4:10). David, a man after God's own heart (1 Sam. 13:14) and the sweet psalmist of Israel (2 Sam. 23:1), was guilty of adultery and murder (2 Sam. 11). Elijah boldly confronted hundreds of false prophets in the name of the God of Israel, and then, in doubt and fear, ran for his life from Jezebel (1 Kings 19:1–3). The noble prophet Isaiah confessed to being a man of unclean lips (Isa. 6:5). Peter, the leader of the Twelve, openly confessed that he was "a sinful man" (Luke 5:8) and proved it by vehemently and repeatedly denying the Lord (Matt. 26:69–74). The apostle John, the apostle of love, was also a "son of thunder," who jealously sought to curtail the ministry of someone who was not part of his group (Mark 3:17; Luke 9:49). Later, he indignantly wanted to call down fire from heaven to incinerate a Samaritan village that had rejected Jesus (Luke 9:54).

Paul was merely another in a long line of clay pots that God has successfully used. The genuineness of his apostleship in spite of his humanity is evident not from his human abilities, skills, or achievements, but from his spiritual character. This passage unfolds seven spiritual characteristics that marked Paul as a very useful clay pot. He was humble, invincible, sacrificial, fruitful, faithful, hopeful, and worshipful.

HUMBLE

But we have this treasure in earthen vessels, so that the surpassing greatness of the power will be of God and not from ourselves; (4:7)

But introduces a contrast with verse 6, which describes the immense and incalculable glory of the eternal God revealed in the incarnate Christ. That priceless divine treasure is contained in a lowly human container—a humbling perspective every preacher and believer must have. Paul's humble view of himself was at the heart of what made him so usable. Later in this epistle he wrote, "For we are not bold to class or compare ourselves with some of those who commend themselves" (2 Cor. 10:12). He refused to evaluate himself based on the false apostles' shallow, external criteria; he was not interested in comparing himself with those who "measure themselves by themselves and compare themselves with themselves" (10:12). He would not "boast beyond . . . measure" (10:13), because "he who boasts is to boast in the Lord" (10:17) and, "It is not he who commends himself that is approved, but he whom the Lord commends" (10:18).

The **treasure** in view here is the same as the "ministry" in 4:1. Both terms describe the glorious gospel message that the eternal God came into the world in the person of Jesus Christ, and died on the cross and rose again to provide forgiveness of sin and eternal life for all who repent and believe. The **treasure** is of incalculable worth, because "in [Christ] are hidden all the treasures of wisdom and knowledge. . . . For in Him all the fullness of Deity dwells in bodily form" (Col. 2:3, 9). The gospel message reveals the most profound truths the world has ever known, which produce the most powerful eternal effects. Through the gospel people are freed from the power of sin and death (Rom. 8:2; Heb. 2:14), released from condemnation (Rom. 8:1), transformed into the image of Jesus Christ (Rom. 8:29; 2 Cor. 3:18), and given eternal joy, peace, and satisfaction.

Yet, amazingly, that priceless gospel treasure is contained in simple **earthen vessels.** *Ostrakinos* (**earthen**) refers to baked clay. The **vessels** Paul describes here were just common pots: cheap, breakable, easily replaceable, and virtually valueless. Occasionally they were used to hide valuables, such as gold, silver, and jewelry. The pots containing such valuable items would often be buried in the ground. In fact, the man in Jesus' parable who found the treasure hidden in a field (Matt. 13:44) might have discovered it when his plow broke a buried pot. Clay pots were also used to store valuable documents; the Dead Sea Scrolls were discovered stored in clay pots in a cave near Qumran.

But **earthen vessels** were most frequently used for ignoble, everyday purposes. In ancient times, human waste and garbage were stored and transported in clay pots. They were "vessels . . . of earthenware . . . to dishonor" (2 Tim. 2:20); that is, they were used for dishonorable, distasteful, unmentionable tasks. Such clay pots had no intrinsic value; their only worth came from the valuables they contained or the service they performed.

Far from disputing the false apostles' disparaging assessment of him, Paul embraced it and turned it into an affirmation of his authenticity. The apostle acknowledged his human limitations and weaknesses, even describing himself as the "foremost" of sinners (1 Tim. 1:15). But like a cheap, fragile, ordinary clay pot used to hide valuable treasure, Paul carried the priceless treasure of the glorious new covenant gospel. Therefore he could boldly affirm, "I consider myself not in the least inferior to the most eminent apostles" (2 Cor. 11:5). In the next verse he declared, "Even if I am unskilled in speech, yet I am not so in knowledge." Though he lacked the polished oratorical skills so highly prized by the Greeks, Paul was not at all lacking in spiritual knowledge.

God delights in using humble, common people, those who are overlooked by society. He places in such clay pots the incalculable treasure of the gospel. In his first inspired letter to the Corinthians, Paul reminded them of that truth:

> For consider your calling, brethren, that there were not many wise according to the flesh, not many mighty, not many noble; but God has chosen the foolish things of the world to shame the wise, and God has chosen the weak things of the world to shame the things which are strong, and the base things of the world and the despised God has chosen, the things that are not, so that He may nullify the things that are, so that no man may boast before God. (1 Cor. 1:26–29)

Earlier he asked rhetorically, "Where is the wise man? Where is the scribe? Where is the debater of this age? Has not God made foolish the wisdom of the world?" (1 Cor. 1:20). By using common clay pots, God gets the glory, "so that, just as it is written, 'Let him who boasts, boast in the Lord'" (1 Cor. 1:31). The prerequisite for spiritual usefulness is to be humble, to see one's self for what one really is, and acknowledge that all the glory for one's accomplishments belongs to God, who placed the treasure in us. His own trials had taught Paul the lesson that God's glory and strength were best manifest in his weakness. Because God said to him, "My grace is sufficient for you, for power is perfected in weakness" (2 Cor. 12:9), Paul could joyously affirm, "Therefore I am well content with weaknesses, with insults, with distresses, with persecutions, with difficulties, for Christ's sake; for when I am weak, then I am strong" (12:10).

The world is filled with people too enamored with their own cleverness, importance, and ability to be used by God. But when God chose the men through whom He would give His Word to mankind, He did not choose the learned scholars of Alexandria, the distinguished philosophers of Athens, the eloquent orators of Rome, or the self-righteous religious leaders of Israel. He passed them all by in favor of simple Galilean fishermen like Peter, John, James, and Andrew, despised traitors like Matthew the tax collector, and obscure men like Philip, Mark, and Nathanael (see John MacArthur, *Twelve Ordinary Men* [Nashville: Word Publishing, 2002]). Even the educated people He chose, such as Luke the physician and Paul, the rabbinic scholar, were humble, unimposing people. To those common, **earthen vessels** God entrusted the priceless treasure of the gospel.

God chooses humble people to proclaim the gospel message **so that the surpassing greatness of the power will be of** Him. He alone reveals "the Light of the knowledge of the glory of God in the face of Christ" (4:6). By using frail, fallible people, God makes it clear that the power lies not in the human messenger but in the divine message. God's power transcends the limitations of the clay pot. And it is precisely those limitations that allow Christians to experience the greatest demonstration of God's power.

INVINCIBLE

we are afflicted in every way, but not crushed; perplexed, but not despairing; persecuted, but not forsaken; struck down, but not destroyed; (4:8–9)

Paul's humility and weakness did not cripple or destroy him but instead strengthened him. Paradoxically, he found encouragement in his frailty, because then the power of God flowed unhindered through him. Far from being a liability to his ministry, an honest assessment of his spiritual limitations was his greatest asset.

Paul was a mercilessly battered clay pot, whose many enemies sought to shatter him completely. In 1:5 he wrote that "the sufferings of Christ are ours in abundance." In verses 8 and 9 he added, "We were burdened excessively, beyond our strength, so that we despaired even of life; indeed, we had the sentence of death within ourselves so that we would not trust in ourselves, but in God who raises the dead." He endured "afflictions . . . hardships . . . distresses . . . beatings . . . imprisonments . . . tumults . . . labors . . . sleeplessness . . . hunger" (6:4–5), and knew what it was to be "hungry and thirsty . . . poorly clothed . . . roughly treated, and . . . homeless" (1 Cor. 4:11). In addition to all the physical suffering Paul endured (cf. 1 Cor. 11:23–27), he constantly carried the heavy burden of "concern for all the churches" (11:28). Yet despite all his suffering, there was an aura of confidence about this noble servant of God, because though he lacked strength, the power of God flowed through him.

Paul's humanly unimposing persona posed an unanswerable question for his opponents: How could they explain the undeniable impact of his life? Since he did not have the power in himself to accomplish what he had accomplished, the power must have come from God. And if Paul ministered in the power of God, he was a true servant of heaven, and his opponents' accusations against him were false. Paul's impact despite his lack of human giftedness was a powerful rebuttal to the false allegations leveled against him.

By a series of four contrasts, the apostle demonstrated that his inabilities did not cripple his ability to minister. First, he was **afflicted in every way, but not crushed. Afflicted** is from the verb *thlibō* and refers to being under pressure. As noted above, Paul was under constant physical and spiritual pressure—so much so that he wrote earlier in this epistle, "We were burdened excessively, beyond our strength, so that we despaired even of life; indeed, we had the sentence of death within ourselves" (2 Cor. 1:8–9). But despite that pressure, Paul was **not crushed. Crushed** is from the verb *stenochōreō*, which refers to being confined to a narrow, tight place. The pressure he faced could not keep Paul's ministry bottled up.

Second, Paul was **perplexed, but not despairing.** The Greek text contains a play on words; the participles translated **perplexed** and **despairing** are from the verbs *aporeō* and *exaporeō*, respectively. Paul was at a loss but not at a total loss. He was at his wit's end, but there was still a way out; he was at the brink of defeat but not defeated.

Third, the apostle was **persecuted, but not forsaken. Persecuted** is from *diōkō,* which means "to pursue," or "to hunt." Paul's many enemies stalked him day in and day out (cf. Acts 9:23–24, 28–29; 14:5–6, 19; 20:3; 23:12). But despite that, Paul was **not forsaken,** deserted, or abandoned. His Lord never left him to face an impossible difficulty on his own.

Finally, Paul was **struck down, but not destroyed. Struck down** is from *kataballō* and means "to strike down," as with a weapon, or "to throw down," as in a wrestling match. **Destroyed** is from *apollumi,* which could also be translated "ruined," "lost," or even "killed." In modern boxing terms, Paul may have been knocked down, but he was not knocked out. He triumphed not by escaping adversity but by successfully enduring it.

No one could withstand such an onslaught in his own strength and still maintain his joy and peace, let alone do the work of the ministry. The power of God made Paul fearless and formidable. Nothing his enemies could do would destroy him. Even killing him would only usher him into the Lord's presence (Phil. 1:21). God's sustaining power enabled this otherwise weak man to triumph over his difficulties and his enemies (cf. 2 Cor. 2:14).

SACRIFICIAL

always carrying about in the body the dying of Jesus, so that the life of Jesus also may be manifested in our body. For we who live are constantly being delivered over to death for Jesus' sake, so that the life of Jesus also may be manifested in our mortal flesh. (4:10–11)

In verse 10 Paul summarizes and interprets the paradoxes in verses 8 and 9: They amounted to **carrying about in the body the dying of Jesus, so that the life of Jesus also may be manifested in** his **body.** The word **always** indicates the unrelieved nature of Paul's suffering; as he wrote in 1 Corinthians 15:31, "I die daily" (cf. Rom. 8:36). Suffering was a way of life for him.

The truth that Paul was continually **carrying about in** his **body the dying of Jesus** was a powerful rebuttal to the allegations of the false apostles. They argued that Paul suffered because God was chastening him for his secret life of sin. But in reality Paul suffered at the hands of evil men because of his identification with Jesus Christ. Those who hate the Lord persecute His people. Therefore Paul's trials, far from being a sign of God's displeasure, were actually a badge of honor (cf. 2 Cor. 1:5; Gal. 6:17; Phil. 3:10; Col. 1:24).

Suffering for the cause of Christ should not surprise any Christian, since Jesus Himself predicted it:

> Behold, I send you out as sheep in the midst of wolves; so be shrewd as serpents and innocent as doves. But beware of men, for they will hand you over to the courts and scourge you in their synagogues; and you will even be brought before governors and kings for My sake, as a testimony to them and to the Gentiles. But when they hand you over, do not worry about how or what you are to say; for it will be given you in that hour what you are to say. For it is not you who speak, but it is the Spirit of your Father who speaks in you. Brother will betray brother to death, and a father his child; and children will rise up against parents and cause them to be put to death. You will be hated by all because of My name, but it is the one who has endured to the end who will be saved. But whenever they persecute you in one city, flee to the next; for truly I say to you, you will not finish going through the cities of Israel until the Son of Man comes. A disciple is not above his teacher, nor a slave above his master. (Matt. 10:16–24; cf. John 15:18–21)

Dying does not translate *thanatos*, Paul's usual word for death, but *nekrōsis*. *Thanatos* speaks of death as a fact or an event, while *nekrōsis* describes the process of dying. As noted above, Paul constantly faced death, which led him to write, "I die daily" (1 Cor. 15:31). He knew well what it was to "deny himself, and take up his cross daily and follow [Christ]" (Luke 9:23).

But, paradoxically, Paul manifested **the dying of Jesus, so that the life of Jesus** would **also be manifested in** his **body.** As he wrote to the Galatians, "I have been crucified with Christ; and it is no longer I who live, but Christ lives in me; and the life which I now live in the flesh I live by faith in the Son of God, who loved me and gave Himself up for me" (Gal. 2:20). The apostle's courageous, faithful, patient enduring of suffering manifested the power of the living Christ in his life. And, as noted above, there was no explanation for the impact of Paul's ministry except that God's power flowed through him.

Paul reiterated in verse 11 that he simultaneously experienced the dying and life of Jesus in his life and expanded it to include all believers. **We who live** denotes the redeemed, those in whom the life of Christ dwells (cf. 2 Cor. 13:5; John 14:20; Eph. 3:17; Col. 1:27). They, like Paul, **are constantly being delivered over to death for Jesus' sake.** The world hates them and threatens them with physical death because of their association with Christ (cf. Matt. 24:9). **Delivered over** is from *paradidōmi*, the same verb used to describe Jesus being delivered over for crucifixion (Matt. 17:22; 20:18–19; 26:2; 27:26; Acts 3:13; Rom. 4:25; 8:32). But the purpose of believers' dying daily is, as it was for Paul, **so that the life of Jesus also may be manifested in** their **mortal flesh** (their physical bodies). Believers' suffering is a purposeful sacrifice that results in the power of God being unleashed in their lives.

FRUITFUL

So death works in us, but life in you. (4:12)

This latest in a series of paradoxical statements summarizes the fruitful results of Paul's sacrificial service. The phrase **death works in us** refers back to the reality of verses 10 and 11 that Paul faced death every day. He literally looked death in the face regularly so he could bring the message of eternal **life** to the Corinthians; he was even willing to die physically so that they could live spiritually.

Paul's suffering was not for himself but for the building up of the church. He reminded the Philippians, "Even if I am being poured out as a drink offering upon the sacrifice and service of your faith, I rejoice and share my joy with you all" (Phil. 2:17). To the Colossians he wrote, "I rejoice in my sufferings for your sake, and in my flesh I do my share on behalf of His body, which is the church, in filling up what is lacking in

Christ's afflictions" (Col. 1:24). He wrote to Timothy, "For this reason I endure all things for the sake of those who are chosen, so that they also may obtain the salvation which is in Christ Jesus and with it eternal glory" (2 Tim. 2:10). It was Paul's joyous privilege to suffer in bringing the gospel to others, who then became the fruit of his courageous endurance. Philip E. Hughes writes,

> It is the unconquerable life of the risen Jesus within that enables His servants willingly and perpetually to be handed over to death for His sake, in order that the same life of Christ may be kindled in the hearts of others, enabling them to win others. This is the chain of faith . . . unbroken through the ages. (*The Second Epistle to the Corinthians*, The New International Commentary on the New Testament [Grand Rapids: Eerdmans, 1992], 145)

The hostility Paul faced from unbelievers was not because of poor technique on his part in proclaiming the gospel. On the contrary, it was proof that his fruitful ministry was drawing satanic opposition.

FAITHFUL

But having the same spirit of faith, according to what is written, "I believed, therefore I spoke," we also believe, therefore we also speak, (4:13)

Paul's desire for fruitfulness did not mean that he would compromise the gospel message. He would remain true to his convictions and preach what he knew to be true.

The apostle declared that he had **the same spirit** or attitude **of faith**—in other words, he believed in the same thing—as **what is written.** That is, he agreed with the psalmist who wrote, **I believed, therefore I spoke** (Ps. 116:10). That was Paul's response to the critics of his bold preaching. His unwavering faith compelled him to preach (cf. Rom. 1:15; 1 Cor. 9:16); it was impossible for him to believe the gospel truth but not long to proclaim it. Those who lack conviction in their preaching do so because they lack conviction in their hearts. Because they have weak confidence in the truth of God, they seek the comfort, prestige, and popularity that come from muting the message. True belief impels strong, consistent, unwavering testimony to the truth. On trial for his faith before the Diet of Worms, Martin Luther defiantly declared,

> Unless I can be instructed and convinced with evidence from the Holy Scriptures or with open, clear, and distinct grounds and reasoning— and my conscience is captive to the Word of God—then I cannot and

will not recant, because it is neither safe nor wise to act against conscience. Here I stand. I can do no other. God help me! Amen. (James M. Kittelson, *Luther the Reformer* [Minneapolis: Augsburg, 1986] 161)

Those who genuinely **believe** the truth cannot help but **speak** that truth.

HOPEFUL

knowing that He who raised the Lord Jesus will raise us also with Jesus and will present us with you. (4:14)

Because the gospel provides the most glorious and important reality, the hope of resurrection for all who believe, Paul was bold and fearless in preaching it. In doing so, the apostle willingly put his life on the line **knowing that He who raised the Lord Jesus** (God the Father; cf. 1:9; Acts 2:24, 32; 3:15; 4:10; 5:30; 10:40; 13:30, 33, 37; Rom. 8:11; 10:9; 1 Cor. 6:14; 15:15; Gal. 1:1; Col. 2:12; 1 Peter 1:21) would **raise** him **also with Jesus.** Death held no terror for him, for he knew that the "sufferings of this present time are not worthy to be compared with the glory that is to be revealed to us" (Rom. 8:18). As he awaited execution he could write to Timothy,

For I am already being poured out as a drink offering, and the time of my departure has come. I have fought the good fight, I have finished the course, I have kept the faith; in the future there is laid up for me the crown of righteousness, which the Lord, the righteous Judge, will award to me on that day; and not only to me, but also to all who have loved His appearing. (2 Tim. 4:6–8)

Paul was confident that God would **present** both himself and the Corinthians holy and blameless in His sight. In 2 Corinthians 11:2 he wrote, "For I am jealous for you with a godly jealousy; for I betrothed you to one husband, so that to Christ I might present you as a pure virgin" (cf. Eph. 5:27; Jude 24). Paul willingly risked his life not only because of his own hope of heaven but also for those who would hear and believe.

WORSHIPFUL

For all things are for your sakes, so that the grace which is spreading to more and more people may cause the giving of thanks to abound to the glory of God. (4:15)

Paul's declaration that he did **all things for** the Corinthians' **sakes** reveals his selflessness. But his ultimate goal was that God be glorified by the saving **grace** that was **spreading to more and more people** through the evangelistic efforts of both himself, as well as the Corinthian believers. The result was that **the giving of thanks** would **abound to the glory of God** as the redeemed praised Him for the blessing of salvation.

Clearly, Paul's goal was never his own comfort, reputation, or popularity. Nor was it ultimately the salvation of others. The final goal of Paul's selfless, sacrificial service was that more voices would be added to the hallelujah chorus of praise and worship to God. The Lord's servants bathe their hearts and souls in the light of God's glory reflected in the face of Jesus Christ. They then selflessly reflect that majestic glory to others so that they can be saved and worship God. In the words of Daniel 12:3, "Those who have insight will shine brightly like the brightness of the expanse of heaven, and those who lead the many to righteousness, like the stars forever and ever."

God's astounding plan is to use common clay pots to carry the priceless treasure of the glorious gospel to needy sinners. As they humbly, faithfully serve Him, His power flows through them to others. The final result is that more and more people will worship and glorify God, crying out, "To Him who sits on the throne, and to the Lamb, be blessing and honor and glory and dominion forever and ever" (Rev. 5:13).

Secrets to Endurance (2 Corinthians 4:16–18)

11

Therefore we do not lose heart, but though our outer man is decaying, yet our inner man is being renewed day by day. For momentary, light affliction is producing for us an eternal weight of glory far beyond all comparison, while we look not at the things which are seen, but at the things which are not seen; for the things which are seen are temporal, but the things which are not seen are eternal. (4:16–18)

Life for Christians in this fallen world is a mixture of joy and sorrow, of blessing and suffering, of triumph and tragedy. For all people, fulfilling relationships, pleasant times, and exhilarating experiences are mitigated by the reality that "man is born for trouble, as sparks fly upward" (Job 5:7). Even Christians are not exempt from normal human trouble. Jesus warned, "In the world you have tribulation" (John 16:33). Paul and Barnabas instructed young believers, "Through many tribulations we must enter the kingdom of God" (Acts 14:22). Paul reminded Timothy, "All who desire to live godly in Christ Jesus will be persecuted" (2 Tim. 3:12). James wrote, "Consider it all joy, my brethren, when you encounter various trials" (James 1:2). Disappointment, discontent, pain, grief, loss, disasters of various kinds, unexpected turns, and persecution will mark life's course.

Those who are able to cope successfully with life's difficulties are those who learn how to endure. This passage reveals the means for facing life like Paul did, of being "afflicted in every way, but not crushed; perplexed, but not despairing; persecuted, but not forsaken; struck down, but not destroyed" (2 Cor. 4:8–9). Those who learn the strength of endurance will experience the paradox of being on the edge of death every moment, yet at the height of life, of "always carrying about in the body the dying of Jesus, so that the life of Jesus also may be manifested in our body. For we who live are constantly being delivered over to death for Jesus' sake, so that the life of Jesus also may be manifested in our mortal flesh" (4:10–11). They will be able to exult with David, "The steps of a man are established by the Lord, and He delights in his way. When he falls, he will not be hurled headlong, because the Lord is the One who holds his hand" (Ps. 37:23–24). They will be noted for their "perseverance and faith in the midst of all [their] persecutions and afflictions which [they] endure" (2 Thess. 1:4). They will be "strong in the grace that is in Christ Jesus" (2 Tim. 2:1), able to "suffer hardship . . . as . . . good soldier[s] of Christ Jesus" (2 Tim. 2:3; cf. 4:5).

The apostle Paul understood how to endure the most threatening difficulties of life. And because his suffering was so severe, Scripture has provided him as the best example from which to learn endurance. It is hard to imagine anyone suffering more constant and serious hostility than Paul suffered, so his response can take us as far as we could go in being persecuted—and far beyond where most of us ever will go.

From his conversion on, Paul was a target for opposition and persecution. After his dramatic transformation on the road to Damascus (Acts 9:1–19), Paul "immediately . . . began to proclaim Jesus in the synagogues, saying, 'He is the Son of God'" (Acts 9:20). And he "kept increasing in strength and confounding the Jews who lived at Damascus by proving that this Jesus is the Christ" (Acts 9:22). As a result, "the Jews plotted together to do away with him, but their plot became known to Saul. They were also watching the gates day and night so that they might put him to death; but his disciples took him by night and let him down through an opening in the wall, lowering him in a large basket" (9:23–25). In Pisidian Antioch "when the Jews saw the crowds, they were filled with jealousy and began contradicting the things spoken by Paul, and were blaspheming" (13:45). They then "incited the devout women of prominence and the leading men of the city, and instigated a persecution against Paul and Barnabas, and drove them out of their district" (13:50). In Iconium "the Jews who disbelieved stirred up the minds of the Gentiles and embittered them against the brethren" (14:2). As a result, "the people of the city were divided; and some sided with the Jews, and some with the apostles. And when an attempt was made by both the Gentiles and the Jews with their rulers, to mistreat and to stone them, they became aware of it and fled to the cities of Lycaonia, Lystra and Derbe, and the surrounding region" (14:4–6). In Lystra "Jews came from Antioch and Iconium, and having won over the crowds, they stoned Paul and dragged him out of the city, supposing him to be dead. But while the disciples stood around him, he got up and entered the city" (14:19–20). In Philippi he was beaten and imprisoned (16:16–24). In Thessalonica his preaching infuriated the Jews, and the ensuing uproar forced the apostle to leave the city for Berea (17:5–10). "But when the Jews of Thessalonica found out that the word of God had been proclaimed by Paul in Berea also, they came there as well, agitating and stirring up the crowds" (17:13). In Corinth "Paul began . . . solemnly testifying to the Jews that Jesus was the Christ. But when they resisted and blasphemed, he shook out his garments and said to them, 'Your blood be on your own heads! I am clean. From now on I will go to the Gentiles'" (18:5–6). Later the frustrated Jews hauled Paul before the Roman proconsul Gallio, who summarily dismissed their charges against the apostle (18:12–16). In Ephesus Paul's fearless preaching brought him into conflict with the craftsmen who profited from the worship of the goddess Artemis. Seeing their trade threatened by the increasing number of converts to Christ Paul was influencing, they provoked a riot by the goddess's frenzied followers (19:23ff.). On his way back to Palestine, Paul was forced to change his travel plans because of a plot by the Jews to take his life (20:3). In Jerusalem, Paul was recognized in the temple by Jews from Asia Minor. Their false allegations against him stirred up the crowd, and it was only the arrival of a detachment of Roman soldiers that saved Paul from being beaten to death by the angry mob (21:27–32). Even after he was in Roman custody, the Jews still sought to kill Paul. More than forty of them formed a plot to take his life, a plot that was thwarted when Paul's nephew discovered it and reported it to the Roman commander (23:12–22). After languishing in Roman custody for two years, Paul exercised his right as a Roman citizen to appeal to Caesar. The ensuing voyage to Rome ended in a shipwreck after a harrowing two-week-long storm at sea (Acts 27). Though released from his first Roman imprisonment, Paul was eventually rearrested. In that last imprisonment the apostle was forsaken by his friends. He wrote sadly to Timothy, "You are aware of the fact that all who are in Asia turned away from me, among whom are Phygelus and Hermogenes. . . . At my first defense no one supported me, but all deserted me; may it not be counted against them" (2 Tim. 1:15; 4:16).

But despite the relentlessness of those hardships, Paul endured triumphantly and declared at the end of his life, "I have fought the good fight, I have finished the course, I have kept the faith; in the future there is laid up for me the crown of righteousness, which the Lord, the righteous Judge, will award to me on that day" (2 Tim. 4:7–8). He endured to the end of the race; he never went AWOL in the midst of the battle; he remained faithful to his dying breath. And so did his Lord, causing Paul to write out of his own experience

> Who will separate us from the love of Christ? Will tribulation, or distress, or persecution, or famine, or nakedness, or peril, or sword? Just as it is written, "For Your sake we are being put to death all day long; we were considered as sheep to be slaughtered." But in all these things we overwhelmingly conquer through Him who loved us. For I am convinced that neither death, nor life, nor angels, nor principalities, nor things present, nor things to come, nor powers, nor height, nor depth, nor any other created thing, will be able to separate us from the love of God, which is in Christ Jesus our Lord. (Rom. 8:35–39)

All Christians can learn from Paul's example how to endure the loneliness, disappointment, pain, and persecution they face. It was his vision of God's glory revealed in the face of Jesus Christ (see the discussion of 3:18–4:6 in chapter 9 of this volume) that radically changed Paul's perspective on life—including his sufferings. That vision is the foundation for living a triumphant life; because of the astounding realities of all that was his in Christ and the new covenant, Paul could **not lose heart.** No amount of trouble could make him neglect his calling, privileges, or duty. Based on the reality of God's glory revealed in Jesus Christ and God's mighty care in his life, Paul gives three heavenly reasons for earthly endurance in verses 16–18; three principles that enabled him **not to lose heart.** He exhorts believers to value spiritual strength over physical strength, value the future over the present, and value eternal realities over temporal realities.

VALUE SPIRITUAL STRENGTH OVER PHYSICAL STRENGTH

Therefore we do not lose heart, but though our outer man is decaying, yet our inner man is being renewed day by day. (4:16)

The phrase **but though** could be translated "even if," "even when," or "since." It introduces a condition assumed to be true and establishes the first reason Paul endured suffering and did **not lose heart.** He could endure anything in the physical realm because he was far more concerned about the spiritual realm. **Outer man** is, like "earthen vessels" (4:7), and "mortal flesh" (4:11), a reference to the physical body, the perishable part of man. From birth to death that body is constantly **decaying**—a process graphically depicted by Solomon in Ecclesiastes 12:1–7:

> Remember also your Creator in the days of your youth, before the evil days come and the years draw near when you will say, "I have no delight in them"; before the sun and the light, the moon and the stars are darkened, and clouds return after the rain; in the day that the watchmen of the house [the arms and hands] tremble, and mighty men [the legs] stoop, the grinding ones [the teeth] stand idle because they are few, and those who look through windows [the eyes] grow dim; and the doors on the street are shut as the sound of the grinding mill is low, and one will arise at the sound of the bird [sleeplessness], and all the daughters of song will sing softly [hearing loss]. Furthermore, men are afraid of a high place and of terrors on the road [because their brittle bones are easily broken]; the almond tree blossoms [the hair turns white], the grasshopper drags himself along [lack of mobility], and the caperberry is ineffective. For man goes to his eternal home while mourners go about in the street. Remember Him before the silver cord [possibly the spinal cord] is broken and the golden bowl [possibly the brain] is crushed, the pitcher by the well is shattered and the wheel at the cistern [possibly the heart and circulatory system] is crushed; then the dust will return to the earth as it was, and the spirit will return to God who gave it [death—the ultimate end of the aging process].

But Paul's **outer man** was **decaying** not only because of the normal aging process but also because of the abnormally arduous life he led. The apostle was old before his time, worn out in the cause of Christ. Nor was it merely hunger, sleeplessness, and illness that took its toll on Paul; it was the battering his body took at the hands of his enemies. Not without reason did Paul write to the Galatians, "I bear on my body the brand-marks of Jesus" (Gal. 6:17). His body bore the scars of beatings (Acts 16:22; 21:30–32), whippings (2 Cor. 11:24), and even a stoning (Acts 14:19; 2 Cor. 11:25), as well as imprisonments (Acts 16:24).

But in direct correlation to the dying of Paul's **outer man** was the growth and maturing of his **inner man.** The **inner man** is the heart, the soul that lives forever. It is in salvation reborn, newly created (2 Cor. 5:17), becoming the new self (Eph. 4:24; Col. 3:10), constantly being **renewed** by sanctifying grace. Paul prayed for the Ephesians that God would continue this renewing in them "according to the riches of His glory" and defined that sanctifying, renewing work as being "strengthened with power through His Spirit in the inner man" (Eph. 3:16). As that takes place, the truths of Ephesians 3:17–19 become reality:

So that Christ may dwell in your hearts through faith; and that you, being rooted and grounded in love, may be able to comprehend with all the saints what is the breadth and length and height and depth, and to know the love of Christ which surpasses knowledge, that you may be filled up to all the fullness of God.

The seemingly paradoxical truth is that when believers are physically weak and at the end of their own resources, they are in the place where they can be made spiritually strong: "Therefore," Paul wrote, "I am well content with weaknesses, with insults, with distresses, with persecutions, with difficulties, for Christ's sake; for when I am weak, then I am strong" (2 Cor. 12:10). Isaiah echoed that same truth:

> Do you not know? Have you not heard? The Everlasting God, the Lord, the Creator of the ends of the earth does not become weary or tired. His understanding is inscrutable. He gives strength to the weary, and to him who lacks might He increases power. Though youths grow weary and tired, and vigorous young men stumble badly, yet those who wait for the Lord will gain new strength; they will mount up with wings like eagles, they will run and not get tired, they will walk and not become weary. (Isa 40:28–31)

Life's trials, troubles, and difficulties serve only to build inner strength, because they drive believers to humbly, prayerfully, hopefully depend on God. Because of what he experienced of God's power in his suffering, Paul could say, "I can do all things through Him who strengthens me" (Phil. 4:13). At the end of his life, bereft of human comfort and support, Paul declared, "The Lord stood with me and strengthened me" (2 Tim. 4:17). Peter added, "After you have suffered for a little while, the God of all grace, who called you to His eternal glory in Christ, will Himself perfect, confirm, strengthen and establish you" (1 Peter 5:10). Suffering energizes spiritual growth.

The decaying **outer man** will perish, but all believers will one day receive a new, imperishable body (2 Cor. 5:1–5; Rom. 8:22–23; 1 Cor. 15:42–44, 49). Recognizing that motivates believers to value the **inner man** over the **outer man,** and that produces spiritual endurance.

VALUE THE FUTURE OVER THE PRESENT

For momentary, light affliction is producing for us an eternal weight of glory far beyond all comparison, (4:17)

Not only did Paul's physical suffering make him spiritually strong, it also enriched his eternal reward. The apostle towered over his enemies and his troubles; rather than harming him, they actually secured for him a greater heavenly reward.

Like Paul, suffering and persecuted believers must view earth through heaven's eyes. When weighed in the balance with believers' eternal reward in heaven, earthly pain amounts to little. Paul expressed the proper perspective on suffering by describing it as **momentary, light affliction.** Though Paul's **affliction** was constant and intense, he viewed it as **momentary** and **light** (easy to bear; insignificant) in view of eternity. He knew that his life was "just a vapor that appears for a little while and then vanishes away" (James 4:14), after which "man goes to his eternal home" (Eccl. 12:5). To the Romans he wrote, "We suffer with Him so that we may also be glorified with Him. For I consider that the sufferings of this present time are not worthy to be compared with the glory that is to be revealed to us" (Rom. 8:17–18). Peter also wrote of the relationship between suffering and eternal glory. After describing believers' heavenly inheritance in 1 Peter 1:3–5 he wrote,

> In this you greatly rejoice, even though now for a little while, if necessary, you have been distressed by various trials, so that the proof of your faith, being more precious than gold which is perishable, even though tested by fire, may be found to result in praise and glory and honor at the revelation of Jesus Christ. (vv. 6–7)

The trials, troubles, and difficulties of life have a positive effect, because they are **producing for us an eternal weight of glory.** Weighed in the balance with the suffering of this life, that **weight of glory** tips the scales heavily in favor of eternal reward. There is a direct correlation between suffering in this life and **glory** (capacity to praise and glorify God) in the next. The greatest glory ever given was that given to Jesus for enduring the greatest suffering ever endured. Because "He humbled Himself by becoming obedient to the point of death, even death on a cross . . . God highly exalted Him, and bestowed on Him the name which is above every name" (Phil. 2:8–9). Jesus confirmed that principle in an incident recorded in Matthew 20:20–23:

> Then the mother of the sons of Zebedee came to Jesus with her sons, bowing down and making a request of Him. And He said to her, "What do you wish?" She said to Him, "Command that in Your kingdom these two sons of mine may sit one on Your right and one on Your left." But Jesus answered, "You do not know what you are asking. Are you able to drink the cup that I am about to drink?" They said to Him, "We are able." He said to them, "My cup you shall drink; but to sit on My right and on

My left, this is not Mine to give, but it is for those for whom it has been prepared by My Father."

In response to their selfish request for the places of prominence in the kingdom, Jesus pointed out that those places are for those who drink the cup of suffering—a reference to His death on the cross (Matt. 26:39). Thus the greater glory in the kingdom is reserved for those who suffer the most in this life. "To the degree that you share the sufferings of Christ," wrote Peter, "keep on rejoicing, so that also at the revelation of His glory you may rejoice with exultation" (1 Peter 4:13).

In fact, the **eternal weight of glory** believers will experience is so much greater than the suffering of this life that Paul described it as **beyond all comparison.** The Greek text literally reads *huperbolē* (from which the English word *hyperbole* derives) *eis huperbolē,* forming a double expression for strongest emphasis. The phrase means, "out of all proportion." The **weight of glory** awaiting believers exceeds all limits; it is beyond the possibility of overstatement or exaggeration. Paul also used the word *huperbolē* in 2 Corinthians 1:8 to describe the intensity of his sufferings. Though he suffered more in comparison to others on earth, he would be glorified beyond all proportion or comparison in heaven. (In Hebrew, the word "glory" comes from the same root as a word meaning "heavy," perhaps influencing Paul's choice of words here.)

It should be noted that the only suffering that produces the **eternal weight of glory** is suffering for the sake of Christ, or that honors Him. Whether suffering comes from believers' faithful, loyal, committed testimony about Jesus Christ, or the patient enduring of life's normal trials, such as disease, divorce, poverty, and loneliness, if endured with a humble, grateful, God-honoring attitude, it will add to the **eternal weight of glory.** On the other hand, suffering the consequences of sin does not contribute to our heavenly blessing and could remove some of the reward already gained (2 John 8). Peter wrote, "For what credit is there if, when you sin and are harshly treated, you endure it with patience? But if when you do what is right and suffer for it you patiently endure it, this finds favor with God" (1 Peter 2:20), and

> If you are reviled for the name of Christ, you are blessed, because the Spirit of glory and of God rests on you. Make sure that none of you suffers as a murderer, or thief, or evildoer, or a troublesome meddler; but if anyone suffers as a Christian, he is not to be ashamed, but is to glorify God in this name. (1 Peter 4:14–16)

Through his present tears Paul never lost sight of the future glory that awaited him in heaven.

VALUE THE ETERNAL OVER THE TEMPORAL

while we look not at the things which are seen, but at the things which are not seen; for the things which are seen are temporal, but the things which are not seen are eternal. (4:18)

Recognizing that "the form of this world is passing away" (1 Cor. 7:31; cf. 1 John 2:17), Paul kept his focus on eternity. He stressed the importance of having a heavenly perspective when he reminded the Corinthians in verse 14 of this chapter, "He who raised the Lord Jesus will raise us also with Jesus and will present us with you." In 1 Corinthians 2:9 he wrote, "Things which eye has not seen and ear has not heard, and which have not entered the heart of man, all that God has prepared for those who love Him." He called the Philippians to focus on the reality that "our citizenship is in heaven, from which also we eagerly wait for a Savior, the Lord Jesus Christ; who will transform the body of our humble state into conformity with the body of His glory, by the exertion of the power that He has even to subject all things to Himself" (Phil. 3:20–21). He exhorted the Colossians, "Set your mind on the things above, not on the things that are on earth" (Col. 3:2).

But such a focus on eternal, heavenly realities is not automatic; it requires effort on believers' part; it only happens, Paul wrote, **while we look.** Endurance comes as long as believers look in the right direction, that is **not at the things which are seen, but at the things which are not seen; for,** Paul explains, **the things which are seen are temporal, but the things which are not seen are eternal.** *Proskairos* (**temporal**) refers to things that are temporary, that do not last, that are destined to perish one day, that belong to time. In short, *proskairos* encompasses everything that is not eternal—all the material world's temporal ideas, values, standards, and achievements.

The allurements of the passing world system were of no interest to Paul. He was not interested in amassing a fortune, having a palatial estate, or a prominent career. That attitude made him seem, by worldly standards, a colossal failure. After all, Paul was a highly educated Hellenistic Jew, a student of the most prominent rabbi of his day, Gamaliel (Acts 22:3; cf. 5:34), possibly even a member of the Sanhedrin (Acts 26:10). He might have risen to the pinnacle of Jewish society (cf. Gal. 1:14). Yet he gladly rejected all that to become, as his enemies disdainfully put it, "a ringleader of the sect of the Nazarenes" (Acts 24:5). Such a worldly evaluation of him was of scant concern to the apostle, because he recognized that "the world is passing away, and also its lusts; but the one who does the will of God lives forever" (1 John 2:17).

When Paul called for believers to focus on the **things** that are

eternal he had in mind the triune God and the souls of men. (The other eternal beings are the holy and fallen angels [demons], but they are not in view here.) His devotion to God can be seen in his many outbursts of praise to Him (e.g., Rom. 11:33–36; 16:27; Gal. 1:5; Eph. 3:21; Phil. 4:20; 1 Tim. 1:17; 6:16; 2 Tim. 4:18). His unswerving loyalty to Christ caused him to "prefer rather to be absent from the body and to be at home with the Lord" (2 Cor. 5:8; cf. Phil 1:23). The highest goal of his life was be a follower of Jesus Christ (1 Cor. 11:1). And Paul lived in submission to the Spirit's leading (cf. Acts 16:6–7), ministered in the Spirit's power (1 Thess. 1:5), and manifested the fruit of the Spirit (cf. Gal. 5:22–23).

Paul was also zealous for the souls of men, so much so that he exclaimed, "I am telling the truth in Christ, I am not lying, my conscience testifies with me in the Holy Spirit, that I have great sorrow and unceasing grief in my heart. For I could wish that I myself were accursed, separated from Christ for the sake of my brethren, my kinsmen according to the flesh, who are Israelites" (Rom. 9:1–4). His passion for men's everlasting souls was the reason he was willing to "endure all things for the sake of those who are chosen, so that they also may obtain the salvation which is in Christ Jesus and with it eternal glory" (2 Tim. 2:10). That passion eventually cost Paul his life.

Paul was the supreme example of one who understood the secret of enduring no matter how difficult the trial or painful the circumstances. Those who, like Paul, cultivate spiritual strength in their inner person, do not let the present blind them to the future, and set their hearts on eternal, not temporal, realities will be able to exult with the apostle, "We are afflicted in every way, but not crushed; perplexed, but not despairing; persecuted, but not forsaken; struck down, but not destroyed" (2 Cor. 4:8–9).

Facing Death Confidently (2 Corinthians 5:1–8)

12

For we know that if the earthly tent which is our house is torn down, we have a building from God, a house not made with hands, eternal in the heavens. For indeed in this house we groan, longing to be clothed with our dwelling from heaven, inasmuch as we, having put it on, will not be found naked. For indeed while we are in this tent, we groan, being burdened, because we do not want to be unclothed but to be clothed, so that what is mortal will be swallowed up by life. Now He who prepared us for this very purpose is God, who gave to us the Spirit as a pledge. Therefore, being always of good courage, and knowing that while we are at home in the body we are absent from the Lord—for we walk by faith, not by sight—we are of good courage, I say, and prefer rather to be absent from the body and to be at home with the Lord. (5:1–8)

As he penned this letter, Paul was facing death on a daily basis. Hostility swirled around him, animosity was constant, and so was the reality and threat of opposition and terminal persecution. Both unbelieving Jews and Gentiles sought to take his life, viewing him as a danger to their religion (cf. Acts 13:50; 18:13), their economic prosperity (cf. Acts

19:23–27), and even to their political stability (cf. Acts 17:6). The apostle's sense of imminent death comes through repeatedly in this epistle:

> For we do not want you to be unaware, brethren, of our affliction which came to us in Asia, that we were burdened excessively, beyond our strength, so that we despaired even of life; indeed, we had the sentence of death within ourselves so that we would not trust in ourselves, but in God who raises the dead; who delivered us from so great a peril of death, and will deliver us, He on whom we have set our hope. (2 Cor. 1:8–10)

> But we have this treasure in earthen vessels, so that the surpassing greatness of the power will be of God and not from ourselves; we are afflicted in every way, but not crushed; perplexed, but not despairing; persecuted, but not forsaken; struck down, but not destroyed; always carrying about in the body the dying of Jesus, so that the life of Jesus also may be manifested in our body. For we who live are constantly being delivered over to death for Jesus' sake, so that the life of Jesus also may be manifested in our mortal flesh. So death works in us, but life in you. (4:7–12)

He described his life as "dying yet behold, we live; punished yet not put to death" (6:9), and "often in danger of death" (11:23). How did he face the reality that he, like a soldier in the front lines, constantly lived on the brink of death?

Some might have expected Paul to tone down his fearless heralding of the gospel, since it was that preaching that enraged his enemies and thus jeopardized his life. Being less confrontive would have mitigated the threat he faced. But the more the hostility and persecution escalated, the bolder Paul became. He never wavered in courageously proclaiming the truth. Because he faced death confidently, even gladly, that triumphant perspective caused him to write, "[I] prefer rather to be absent from the body and to be at home with the Lord" (5:8), and "For to me, to live is Christ and to die is gain. . . ." "I am hard-pressed from both directions, having the desire to depart and be with Christ, for that is very much better" (Phil. 1:21, 23). And because he did not fear death, Paul did not fear persecution, pain, or suffering; he was able always to be "of good courage" (2 Cor. 5:6, 8).

This passage builds on the truths Paul revealed in 4:16–18, when he wrote that no matter how difficult his circumstances were, he "[did] not lose heart," because "though [his] outer man [was] decaying, yet [his] inner man [was] being renewed day by day." He understood that "momentary, light affliction is producing for us an eternal weight of glory far beyond all comparison, while we look not at the things which are seen, but at the things which are not seen; for the things which are seen are temporal, but the things which are not seen are eternal" (4:16–18). He gladly suffered in this world for a far greater reward in the world to come.

For all, death comes like an utterly unsympathetic landlord waving an eviction notice. But that eviction merely releases believers from a wretched earthly neighborhood to an infinitely grand and glorious dwelling in a heavenly neighborhood. For the believer, then, the sorrows, disappointments, and suffering of this life are worse than death. Death releases believers from the relatively dilapidated slum in which they now live and ushers them into a room in the house of the eternal Father in the heavenly city.

Knowing that, Christians should not fear death. They should long "to depart and be with Christ, for that is very much better" (Phil. 1:23). That does not mean, of course, that they are to be foolishly reckless or careless with their lives; their bodies belong to God (1 Cor. 6:19–20). But an obsessive concern for one's physical well-being or a morbid fear of death is inconsistent with a Christian perspective. Believers should long for heaven like a prisoner longs for freedom, like a sick man longs for health, like a hungry man longs for food, like a thirsty man longs for a drink, like a poor man longs for a payday, and like a soldier longs for peace. Hope and courage in facing death is the last opportunity for Christians to exhibit their faith in God, to prove their hope of heaven is genuine and to adorn their confidence in the promises of God.

From this passage four motives for facing death confidently emerge: The next body is the best, the next life is perfect, the next existence fulfills God's purpose, and the next dwelling is with the Lord.

The Next Body Is the Best

For we know that if the earthly tent which is our house is torn down, we have a building from God, a house not made with hands, eternal in the heavens. (5:1)

The "eternal weight of glory" Paul described in 4:17 includes a new body. That truth was of great comfort to the apostle, whose physical body had been so mercilessly battered by the effects of the Fall, personal sin, hardships, illness, the rigors of life, and persecution that he longed for his incorruptible, immortal resurrection body.

Paul's confident assertion **for we know** indicates that believers' glorified bodies are not a remote possibility or a vague wish. They are a fixed reality, a settled fact based on the promise of God (Rom. 8:18, 23; 1 Cor. 15:35–49; Phil. 3:21), not philosophical speculation or mystical fantasy.

Paul wrote **if** instead of "when" because, though he was ready to die, he did not see his death as inevitable. He viewed the return of Jesus Christ as imminent and believed it was possible for him to live until the Lord returned. That was his deepest desire, as his use of the plural pronoun "we" in passages describing the Rapture indicates. In 1 Corinthians 15:51 he wrote, "Behold, I tell you a mystery; we will not all sleep, but we will all be changed." To the Thessalonians he wrote,

> For this we say to you by the word of the Lord, that we who are alive and remain until the coming of the Lord, will not precede those who have fallen asleep. For the Lord Himself will descend from heaven with a shout, with the voice of the archangel and with the trumpet of God, and the dead in Christ will rise first. Then we who are alive and remain will be caught up together with them in the clouds to meet the Lord in the air, and so we shall always be with the Lord. (1 Thess. 4:15–17)

If he could not live until the Rapture, Paul preferred "to be absent from the body and to be at home with the Lord" (2 Cor. 5:8). He expressed that same truth to the Philippians when he wrote of his "desire to depart and be with Christ, for that is very much better" (Phil. 1:23). Remaining on in the flesh was only his third choice.

The phrase **if the earthly tent which is our house is torn down** refers metaphorically to death (cf. Isa. 38:12). As a tentmaker himself (Acts 18:3), Paul chose to use the analogy of an **earthly tent** (the physical body) to describe the soul's temporary **house** in this world (cf. 2 Peter 1:13–14). Speaking of the incarnation of Christ, the apostle John used the verb *skēnoō,* (lit., "to live in a tent") to depict the eternal God coming into the world and taking a human body (John 1:14). A **tent** is an apt metaphor for the human body, which is a temporary home for the eternal souls of those whose real home is in heaven (Phil. 3:20) and who are aliens and strangers in this world (Gen. 47:9; 1 Chron. 29:15; Ps. 119:19; Heb. 11:13; 1 Peter 1:1, 17; 2:11). Just as the tabernacle of Israel's wanderings in the wilderness was replaced with a permanent building when Israel entered the Promised Land, so the temporary **tent** in which believers now dwell will be replaced one day in heaven with an eternal, imperishable body (1 Cor. 15:42, 53–54).

After death dismantles believers' **earthly tent,** they **have a building from God, a house not made with hands, eternal in the heavens.** A **building** suggests something on a solid foundation that is fixed, secure, and permanent. Since it replaced his **earthly tent** (his physical body), the **building from God** Paul referred to must be his glorified body, which he would receive after "He who raised the Lord Jesus ... raise[d him] also with Jesus" (2 Cor. 4:14).

In Romans, written shortly after 2 Corinthians, Paul expressed the same longing for his glorified resurrection body:

> For I consider that the sufferings of this present time are not worthy to be compared with the glory that is to be revealed to us. For the anxious longing of the creation waits eagerly for the revealing of the sons of God. For the creation was subjected to futility, not willingly, but because of Him who subjected it, in hope that the creation itself also will be set free from its slavery to corruption into the freedom of the glory of the children of God. For we know that the whole creation groans and suffers the pains of childbirth together until now. And not only this, but also we ourselves, having the first fruits of the Spirit, even we ourselves groan within ourselves, waiting eagerly for our adoption as sons, the redemption of our body. For in hope we have been saved, but hope that is seen is not hope; for who hopes for what he already sees? (Rom. 8:18–24)

The entire created universe, subjected to futility by the Fall, will one day "be set free from its slavery to corruption" (v. 21). In that glorious and longed-for day, writes Paul, believers will experience "the redemption of our body" (v. 23).

Paul longed for his glorified body not primarily because it would be free of physical weakness, blemishes, and defects, but because it would be free of sin. The tent of the body is sin's home, causing Paul to lament, "I am of flesh, sold into bondage to sin" (Rom. 7:14); "sin ... dwells in me" (Rom. 7:17, 20); "evil is present in me" (Rom. 7:21); and "Wretched man that I am! Who will set me free from the body of this death?" (Rom. 7:24). The apostle longed to serve, worship, and praise God in absolute purity, freed from the restrictions of his fallen, sinful flesh. That is the best feature of resurrection reality.

Paul further described the glorified, resurrection body as a **house not made with hands.** It is not a procreated, physical body. Referring to Jesus' words in John 2:19, the false witnesses at His trial said, "We heard Him say, 'I will destroy this temple made with hands, and in three days I will build another made without hands'" (Mark 14:58). They misconstrued those words as a reference to Herod's temple, but in reality Jesus "was speaking of the temple of His body" (John 2:21)—that is, His resurrection body. Paul used the same phrase in Colossians 2:11 when he wrote, "you were also circumcised with a circumcision made without hands, in the removal of the body of the flesh by the circumcision of Christ." But perhaps the most definitive use of the phrase **not made with hands** is in Hebrews 9:11: "But when Christ appeared as a high priest of the good things to come, He entered through the greater and more perfect tabernacle, not made with hands, that is to say, not of this creation." That verse equates **not made with hands** with "not of this creation." It therefore refers to what is spiritual, transcendent, and eternal, not to what is earthly, physical, and temporal.

Paul gave the most detailed description of believers' resurrection body in 1 Corinthians 15:36–49. He wrote that section of his epistle in reply to those who asked, "How are the dead raised? And with what kind of body do they come?" (v. 35). Paul answered that question in four ways.

First, he gave an illustration from nature in verses 36–38:

> You fool! That which you sow does not come to life unless it dies; and that which you sow, you do not sow the body which is to be, but a bare grain, perhaps of wheat or of something else. But God gives it a body just as He wished, and to each of the seeds a body of its own.

There is no way to extrapolate from the plain, simple, ugly appearance of a seed the magnificent glory of the flower, tree, or plant that will grow out of its death. So also the glory of believers' immortal, resurrection bodies cannot be imagined from our perishing, physical bodies.

Second, Paul gave a series of comparisons in verses 39–42*a*:

> All flesh is not the same flesh, but there is one flesh of men, and another flesh of beasts, and another flesh of birds, and another of fish. There are also heavenly bodies and earthly bodies, but the glory of the heavenly is one, and the glory of the earthly is another. There is one glory of the sun, and another glory of the moon, and another glory of the stars; for star differs from star in glory. So also is the resurrection of the dead.

Just as the bodies of men, beasts, birds, fish, heavenly bodies, and earthly bodies differ from each other, so also will the resurrection body differ radically from the physical body.

Third, Paul listed a series of contrasts in verses 42*b*–44:

> It is sown a perishable body, it is raised an imperishable body; it is sown in dishonor, it is raised in glory; it is sown in weakness, it is raised in power; it is sown a natural body, it is raised a spiritual body. If there is a natural body, there is also a spiritual body.

The physical body is perishable, sinful, and weak. In contrast, the resurrection body is imperishable, free of sin, and powerful.

Finally, Paul gave the prototype of believers' resurrection bodies in verses 45–49:

> So also it is written, "The first man, Adam, became a living soul." The last Adam became a life-giving spirit. However, the spiritual is not first, but the natural; then the spiritual. The first man is from the earth, earthy; the second man is from heaven. As is the earthy, so also are those who are earthy; and as is the heavenly, so also are those who are heavenly. Just

as we have borne the image of the earthy, we will also bear the image of the heavenly.

Just as they have physical bodies like Adam's, so believers will one day have glorified bodies like Christ's. To the Philippians Paul wrote, "For our citizenship is in heaven, from which also we eagerly wait for a Savior, the Lord Jesus Christ; who will transform the body of our humble state into conformity with the body of His glory, by the exertion of the power that He has even to subject all things to Himself" (Phil. 3:20–21). The apostle John wrote, "Beloved, now we are children of God, and it has not appeared as yet what we will be. We know that when He appears, we will be like Him, because we will see Him just as He is" (1 John 3:2).

THE NEXT LIFE IS PERFECT

For indeed in this house we groan, longing to be clothed with our dwelling from heaven, inasmuch as we, having put it on, will not be found naked. For indeed while we are in this tent, we groan, being burdened, because we do not want to be unclothed but to be clothed, so that what is mortal will be swallowed up by life. (5:2–4)

The twice-repeated phrase **for indeed** expressed Paul's intense longing for heaven and the certainty that he would one day enter its glory. But in the meantime, for all believers, **in this house we groan, longing to be clothed with our dwelling from heaven.** Those who love the Lord Jesus yearn for the next life "when this perishable will have put on the imperishable, and this mortal will have put on immortality" (1 Cor. 15:54). Paul was weary of the frustrations, disappointments, limitations, weaknesses, and sins of this present life and longed "for the revealing of the sons of God" (Rom. 8:19). The apostle passionately longed to be **clothed with** his **dwelling from heaven.** Paul's mixed metaphor (putting on a building as if it were clothing) refers to his resurrection body and the perfections of eternal life, which would replace forever the debilitating, sin-caused corruptions of life in this world and set him free from his fallen humanness.

The phrase **inasmuch as we** (v. 3) carries the same thought along and means that since verse 2 is true, and he will put on the new body, he will **not be found naked.** To be **naked,** then, is to be only a soul without a resurrection body. The apostle's hope of a future glorified body was in sharp contrast to the philosophical dualism that permeated Greek culture. That philosophy taught that matter is evil and spirit is good. Therefore the ultimate goal for its adherents was to be freed from their bodies and to become disembodied spirits. William Barclay writes,

> Greek and Roman thinkers despised the body. "The body," they said, "is a tomb." Plotinus could say that he was ashamed that he had a body. Epictetus said of himself, "Thou art a poor soul burdened with a corpse." Seneca wrote, "I am a higher being and born for higher things than to be the slave of my body which I look upon as only a shackle put upon my freedom. . . . In so detestable a habitation dwells the free soul." Even Jewish thought sometimes had this idea. "For the corruptible body presses down upon the soul and the earthly tabernacle weighs down the mind that muses on many things." (*Wisdom* 9:15).

> With Paul there is a difference. He is not looking for a Nirvana with the peace of extinction; he is not looking for absorption in the divine; he is not looking for the freedom of a disembodied spirit; he is waiting for the day when God will give him a new body, a spiritual body, in which he will still be able, even in the heavenly places, to serve and adore God. (*The Letters to the Corinthians*, rev. ed. [Louisville: Westminster, 1975], 204–5)

Philosophical dualism posed a dangerous threat to the early church. Paul warned Timothy about Hymenaeus and Philetus, two false teachers at Ephesus who taught that the resurrection had already passed. They likely argued that believers' identification with Christ's death and resurrection was the only resurrection there is and denied the future resurrection of the body. The Corinthians had been so influenced by that dualistic philosophy that Paul had to write an entire chapter in 1 Corinthians defending bodily resurrection (1 Cor. 15). Even after Paul addressed the issue in 1 Corinthians, it apparently still remained an influence.

The pagan Greeks may have felt that their souls needed to be freed from their bodies before they could enter the highest state of bliss, but not Paul. Therefore he reminded the Corinthians that when his earthly tent was dismantled by death he would not exist forever as a **naked** disembodied spirit. He was not looking for release from his body but for the perfections of his resurrection body. So passionate was his longing that Paul's desire was to experience the Rapture, when living believers' physical bodies will be instantly transformed into their glorified bodies (1 Cor. 15:51–52). He knew that if he died before the Rapture, he would have to wait until then for his glorified body (1 Thess. 4:16). The saints in heaven are awaiting their resurrection bodies, which is why the writer of Hebrews refers to them as "the spirits of the righteous made perfect" (Heb. 12:23).

Repeating the phrase **for indeed** to emphasize his point, Paul reiterated the truth that believers, **while** they **are in this tent, groan, being burdened.** Paul repeated this fact in Romans 8:23: "We ourselves, having the first fruits of the Spirit, even we ourselves groan within ourselves, waiting eagerly for our adoption as sons, the redemption of our body." It is the crushing burden of sin and affliction believers experience in their physical bodies that makes them yearn for their spiritual bodies. Repeating his disdain for soul nakedness, Paul emphasized again that he did **not want to be unclothed** as a disembodied spirit, **but to be clothed** with his glorified body. Then, **what is mortal will be swallowed up by** the fullness and perfections of eternal **life,** and believers will be like their risen Lord. Like John, they "know that when He appears, [they] will be like Him, because [they] will see Him just as He is" (1 John 3:2).

Summarizing Paul's point, Augustine, the great theologian of the early church, wrote

> We are burdened with this corruptible body; but knowing that the cause of this burdensomeness is not the nature and substance of the body, but its corruption, we do not desire to be deprived of the body, but to be clothed with its immortality. . . . If Adam had not sinned, he would not have been divested of his body, but would have been clothed upon (superinvested) with immortality and incorruption, that his mortal (body) might have been absorbed by life; that is, that he might have passed from his natural body to the spiritual body. (Cited in Philip E. Hughes, *The Second Epistle to the Corinthians,* The New International Commentary on the New Testament [Grand Rapids: Eerdmans, 1992], 171.)

THE NEXT EXISTENCE FULFILLS GOD'S PURPOSE

Now He who prepared us for this very purpose is God, who gave to us the Spirit as a pledge. (5:5)

What is yet future for believers was **prepared** by **God** in the past and unfolds according to His plan and will. In eternity past, God sovereignly chose believers for salvation; in time, He redeemed them; in the future, He will give them their glorified, resurrection bodies. The phrase **for this very purpose** emphatically states that believers obtain their glorified bodies in fulfillment of God's sovereign plan from all eternity, bound up in His elective decree. In Romans 8:28–30 Paul wrote the familiar words,

> And we know that God causes all things to work together for good to those who love God, to those who are called according to His purpose.

> For those whom He foreknew, He also predestined to become con-
> formed to the image of His Son, so that He would be the firstborn
> among many brethren; and these whom He predestined, He also
> called; and these whom He called, He also justified; and these whom
> He justified, He also glorified.

God's ultimate purpose in salvation is not justification but glorification,
when believers "become conformed to the image of His Son" (v. 29). And
being transformed into Christ's image includes receiving a glorified body
like His (1 Cor. 15:49). Jesus swept through the fulfillment of the eternal
decree from calling to glorification when He said,

> All that the Father gives Me will come to Me, and the one who comes
> to Me I will certainly not cast out. For I have come down from heaven,
> not to do My own will, but the will of Him who sent Me. This is the will
> of Him who sent Me, that of all that He has given Me I lose nothing, but
> raise it up on the last day. For this is the will of My Father, that everyone
> who beholds the Son and believes in Him will have eternal life, and I
> Myself will raise him up on the last day. (John 6:37–40)

So God's glorious purpose for believers stretches from eternity to
eternity. It was planned in eternity past and will be fulfilled in eternity
future; time is but a fleeting moment in the middle. No matter what level
of spiritual maturity they attain or how effectively they serve God, the
divine purpose will only be fulfilled in a glorified body.

Further reinforcing the apostle's confidence in facing death was
the knowledge that God **gave to us the Spirit as a pledge** (down payment; first installment; guarantee; cf. 2 Cor. 1:22; Eph. 1:14). The indwelling Holy Spirit (Rom. 5:5; 8:9; 1 Cor. 6:19–20) is God's promise that His
ultimate purpose for believers will be fulfilled. "For I am confident of this
very thing," Paul wrote to the Philippians, "that He who began a good
work in you will perfect it until the day of Christ Jesus" (Phil. 1:6). Nothing can interrupt that process, as Paul emphatically declared in Romans
8:35–39:

> Who will separate us from the love of Christ? Will tribulation, or distress,
> or persecution, or famine, or nakedness, or peril, or sword? Just as it is
> written, "For Your sake we are being put to death all day long; we were
> considered as sheep to be slaughtered." But in all these things we over-
> whelmingly conquer through Him who loved us. For I am convinced
> that neither death, nor life, nor angels, nor principalities, nor things
> present, nor things to come, nor powers, nor height, nor depth, nor any
> other created thing, will be able to separate us from the love of God,
> which is in Christ Jesus our Lord.

The indwelling Holy Spirit is God's guarantee that believers are His possession and that He will redeem them to the praise of His glory. For that reason it is ludicrous to believe that Christians can lose their salvation. Nothing can interrupt the plan God set in motion in eternity past (election) and has pledged Himself to carry through until eternity future (glorification). To argue otherwise is to assume that God is incapable of achieving His purposes and thus to diminish His glory.

THE NEXT DWELLING IS WITH THE LORD

Therefore, being always of good courage, and knowing that while we are at home in the body we are absent from the Lord—for we walk by faith, not by sight—we are of good courage, I say, and prefer rather to be absent from the body and to be at home with the Lord. (5:6–8)

In verses 6–8 Paul reached the pinnacle of heavenly anticipation. He looked forward to his new, glorified body, the perfection of heaven, and the eternal fulfillment of God's plan. But beyond all of that was the wonderful reality that death would usher him into the presence of the Lord. **Therefore** points back to the foundational truths Paul expressed in verses 1–5. On the basis of those truths, Paul was **always of good courage** in the face of death. His **courage** was not a temporary feeling or a passing emotion; it was a constant state of mind. He faced death cheerfully, with complete confidence. It was not that he did not love the people in his life, but he loved the Lord more. Life for Paul was a race to finish, a battle to win, a stewardship to discharge. Once the race was over, the battle won, and the stewardship discharged, Paul saw no reason to cling to this life. The only reason for him to remain on earth was to serve God, and he stated his readiness to leave when that service was complete:

> For I am already being poured out as a drink offering, and the time of my departure has come. I have fought the good fight, I have finished the course, I have kept the faith; in the future there is laid up for me the crown of righteousness, which the Lord, the righteous Judge, will award to me on that day; and not only to me, but also to all who have loved His appearing. (2 Tim. 4:6–8)

The reality of life in this world for believers, however, is **that while we are at home in the body** (living in the flesh) **we are absent from the Lord.** Believers communicate with the Lord through prayer and study of the Word and have communion with Him through the indwelling Holy Spirit. Yet there is still a sense in which they are separated from God and long for that separation to end. Psalm 42:1–2 expresses that desire: "As the deer pants for the water brooks, so my soul pants for You, O God. My soul thirsts for God, for the living God; when shall I come and appear before God?" "Whom have I in heaven but You?" the psalmist asked rhetorically. "And besides You, I desire nothing on earth" (Ps. 73:25). Paul longed for the day when he would "always be with the Lord" (1 Thess. 4:17). That sense of separation caused Abraham to look for "the city . . . whose architect and builder is God" (Heb. 11:10) and the Old Testament saints to acknowledge "that they were strangers and exiles on the earth" (Heb. 11:13). It is only in heaven that believers will have intimate, unbroken fellowship with God (cf. Rev. 21:3–4, 22–23; 22:3–4).

The parenthetical statement in verse 7 that **we walk by faith, not by sight** explains how believers can have fellowship with and serve the invisible God in this life. Such **faith** is not a wishful fantasy or a vague superstition but a strong confidence grounded in the truth of Scripture. It is "the assurance of things hoped for, the conviction of things not seen" (Heb. 11:1).

Then Paul concludes the passage with the triumphant declaration, **we are of good courage, I say, and prefer rather to be absent from the body and to be at home with the Lord.** He repeats the truth from verse 6 that he was always positive toward the future despite the constantly looming reality of death. To **prefer rather to be absent from the body and to be at home with the Lord** is to understand the brief, temporary time on earth only as an alien's and stranger's experience and heaven as our true and permanent home.

The reality of death faces every believer who dies before the Lord raptures the church. Those who look forward to receiving their glorified bodies, to the perfections of life in heaven, to the fulfillment of God's purpose for them, and to living forever in His presence will be able to say triumphantly with Paul, "O death, where is your victory? O death, where is your sting?" (1 Cor. 15:55).

The Noblest Ambition
(2 Corinthians 5:9–10)

13

Therefore also we have as our ambition, whether at home or absent, to be pleasing to Him. For we must all appear before the judgment seat of Christ, so that each one may be recompensed for his deeds in the body, according to what he has done, whether good or bad. (5:9–10)

Ambition has always had a bad reputation. The noble Puritan writer Thomas Brooks wrote, "Ambition is a gilded misery, a secret poison, a hidden plague, the engineer of deceit, the mother of hypocrisy, the parent of envy, the original of vices, the moth of holiness, the blinder of hearts, turning medicines into maladies and remedies into diseases. High seats are never but uneasy, and crowns are always stuffed with thorns" (cited in John Blanchard, *Truth for Life* [Welwyn: Evangelical Press, 1986], 179). Blind ambition causes people to compromise their convictions, violate their beliefs, and sacrifice their character. Ambition is often associated with words like "unscrupulous," "self-centered," "proud," "driven," "insensitive," and "ruthless." Those negative modifiers reflect the carnage inflicted on family, friends, and principles abandoned in the wake of onrushing ambition. Ambition drives people to seek wealth, prestige, power, social prominence, popular acclaim, and dominance over others.

The English word "ambition" derives from the Latin word *ambitio,* which comes from a verb that literally means, "to go around." The word was used by the Romans to refer to politicians who went around canvasing for votes to get themselves elected. It was used to describe those with no convictions, who sought promotion at any cost, doing anything to achieve selfish ends. Thus, to describe someone as ambitious was to comment on his or her character in a decidedly negative way. Expressing that negative connotation of ambition, Stephen Neill said, "I am inclined to think that ambition in any ordinary sense of the term is nearly always sinful in ordinary men. I am certain that in the Christian it is always sinful, and that it is most inexcusable of all in the ordained minister" (cited in J. Oswald Sanders, *Spiritual Leadership,* rev. ed. [Chicago: Moody, 1980], 14).

It could be argued that ambition is the chief sin for which Jesus Christ died:

> Because we children of Adam want to become great,
> He became small.
> Because we will not stoop,
> He humbled Himself.
> Because we want to rule,
> He came to serve. (Sanders, 16)

The Bible condemns sinful ambition. Speaking through the prophet Jeremiah, God said, "But you, are you seeking great things for yourself? Do not seek them" (Jer. 45:5).

Despite the word's normally negative connotation, Paul wrote, **also we have as our ambition.** There is a type of ambition that is legitimate; the Bible forbids selfish ambition, not ambition to please the Lord. Paul did not use the term in a negative sense but in the positive sense of loving what is noble or honorable. In fact, *philotimeomai* (**have as our ambition**) is a compound word from *philos* ("love") and *timē* ("honor"). It was that type of noble ambition that characterized Paul.

Paul used *philotimeomai* two other times in his writings (the only other times it appears in the New Testament). In Romans 15:20 he wrote, "I aspired [from *philotimeomai*] to preach the gospel, not where Christ was already named, so that I would not build on another man's foundation"; while in 1 Thessalonians 4:11 he exhorted the Thessalonians, "Make it your ambition to lead a quiet life and attend to your own business and work with your hands, just as we commanded you." Though Paul used different Greek words, the same point is made in 1 Timothy 3:1: "If any man aspires [from *oregō*] to the office of overseer, it is a fine work he desires [from *epithumeō*] to do."

There is a central place in the Christian life for noble ambition, for a passion for what is excellent and honorable. From this passage three aspects of Paul's ambition emerge: He had sanctified ambition for the highest goal, with the widest devotion, and from the deepest motive.

PAUL HAD AMBITION FOR THE HIGHEST GOAL

to be pleasing to Him. (9c)

The noblest and highest ambition to which anyone can aspire is **to be pleasing** to **God.** Paul used the adjective *euarestos* (**pleasing**) frequently in his writings. In Romans 12:1–2 and 14:18 he used it to speak of behavior that is acceptable to God. He urged the Ephesians to try "to learn what is pleasing to the Lord" (Eph. 5:10). He described the Philippians' financial support of him as being "well-pleasing to God" (Phil. 4:18). In Colossians 3:20 he noted that children's obedience to their parents "is well-pleasing to the Lord." *Euarestos* also appears in Titus 2:9, where it describes slaves who are pleasing to their masters. Godly ambition seeks to please the Lord in all aspects of life (Col. 1:10).

Nowhere is the focus of Paul's ambition more clearly articulated than in 1 Corinthians 4:3–5:

> But to me it is a very small thing that I may be examined by you, or by any human court; in fact, I do not even examine myself. For I am conscious of nothing against myself, yet I am not by this acquitted; but the one who examines me is the Lord. Therefore do not go on passing judgment before the time, but wait until the Lord comes who will both bring to light the things hidden in the darkness and disclose the motives of men's hearts; and then each man's praise will come to him from God.

One of the many problems besetting the Corinthian church was that of judging others unrighteously. Its various factions (cf. 1 Cor. 1:12; 3:4) constantly sat in condemnation on each other. As noted in previous chapters of this volume, even Paul was under relentless, merciless assault from some demonic self-styled false apostles at Corinth. Those false teachers attacked his apostolic credentials, his ministry methods, his character, and even the gospel message he preached.

Unperturbed by the savage onslaught against him, Paul responded, "But to me it is a very small thing that I may be examined by you, or by any human court" (1 Cor. 4:3). Their opinion of him was not important to him, because he did not seek to please men, but God. Paul viewed himself as a servant and steward of God (1 Cor. 4:1; cf. 9:17; Eph. 3:2; Col. 1:25; Titus 1:7) and therefore accountable to Him. The apostle was not concerned with earthly, biased evaluations of him (whether positive or negative); no human court, whether an official tribunal or the unofficial court of human opinion, could render the ultimate verdict on him.

Going beyond that, Paul wrote, "In fact, I do not even examine myself" (1 Cor. 4:3). He was wise enough to know that he was biased in his own favor and thus lacked objectivity. Though he was "conscious of nothing against [himself]" (v. 4; cf. 2 Cor. 1:12), Paul understood that "the heart is more deceitful than all else and is desperately sick; who can understand it?" (Jer. 17:9). Therefore he applied to himself the warning he expressed in 1 Corinthians 10:12: "Let him who thinks he stands take heed that he does not fall."

Paul's was not a brash, defiant, self-righteous attitude that refused to submit to scrutiny or judgment. Nor was he arguing that believers should not confront other believers who continue in sin (cf. 1 Cor. 5:12; 6:1–5). He was not talking about a sin issue, for he wrote that he was "conscious of nothing against [himself]" (1 Cor. 4:4). The apostle's point was that neither he nor the Corinthians were able to judge him properly; that judgment was reserved for a higher court, "because the one who examines [him] is the Lord" (v. 4).

Paul concluded his point by exhorting the Corinthians, "Therefore do not go on passing judgment before the time" (v. 5). The ultimate and accurate verdict on anyone's life and ministry will be rendered by the Lord, who when He returns "will both bring to light the things hidden in the darkness and disclose the motives of men's hearts; and then each man's praise will come to him from God" (v. 5). In light of that reality believers should "walk in a manner worthy of the Lord, to please Him in all respects" (Col. 1:10; cf. 1 Thess. 4:1). At the end of his life, Paul believed he had some measure of fulfillment of his spiritual ambition (2 Tim. 4:7–8).

PAUL WAS AMBITIOUS WITH THE WIDEST DEVOTION

whether at home or absent, (9*b*)

Paul's devotion to his noble ambition knew no limits, as the all-encompassing phrase **whether at home or absent** indicates. That phrase connects Paul's thought with the previous passage (cf. 5:6, 8), as does the phrase "therefore also" that begins verse 9. As noted in the discussion of 5:1–8 in chapter 12 of this volume, Paul constantly lived on the brink of death. Describing that ever-present threat, the apostle wrote poignantly,

> We are afflicted in every way, but not crushed; perplexed, but not despairing; persecuted, but not forsaken; struck down, but not destroyed; always carrying about in the body the dying of Jesus, so that

the life of Jesus also may be manifested in our body. For we who live are constantly being delivered over to death for Jesus' sake, so that the life of Jesus also may be manifested in our mortal flesh. So death works in us, but life in you. (2 Cor. 4:8–12; cf. 6:9)

Because he constantly stared death in the face, Paul longed, as he wrote in 2 Corinthians 5:1, to leave his "earthly tent" (his physical body) and receive his "building from God, a house not made with hands, eternal in the heavens" (his resurrection body). Paul's first choice was to live until the Rapture, when that transformation would take place. If that was not God's will for him (as in fact it was not), Paul's second choice was "to be absent from the body and to be at home with the Lord" (5:8). His third choice was "to remain on in the flesh" (Phil. 1:24).

In 2 Corinthians 5:6 Paul spoke of being at **home** in the body and **absent** from the Lord; in verse 8 he spoke of being **absent** from the body and at **home** with the Lord. Paul's ambition to please God, imperfectly on earth or perfectly in heaven, remained unchanged. Expressing that same breadth of devotion he affirmed, "For not one of us lives for himself, and not one dies for himself; for if we live, we live for the Lord, or if we die, we die for the Lord; therefore whether we live or die, we are the Lord's" (Rom. 14:7–8).

Some might assume that Paul's longing for heaven implied an indifference to his earthly body; that he espoused an antinomian view that it does not matter what one does with the sinful, physical body. Such a view would have been in harmony with the prevailing Greek philosophical dualism of his day (see the discussion in chapter 12 of this volume) that held the body to be the worthless and inconsequential prison of the soul. But Paul knew that he could serve God in his physical body in a way that would produce an eternal reward. Thus, his longing for heaven and his resurrection body made him even more careful about how he lived in this world. In 1 Corinthians 9:27 he wrote, "I beat my body and make it my slave, so that, after I have preached to others, I myself will not be disqualified" (NIV). He admonished the Romans, "Present your bodies a living and holy sacrifice, acceptable to God, which is your spiritual service of worship" (Rom. 12:1). Paul's ambition to please God in this life or the life to come demonstrates the broad scope of his devotion to the Lord.

Paul Was Driven by the Deepest Motive

For we must all appear before the judgment seat of Christ, so that each one may be recompensed for his deeds in the body, according to what he has done, whether good or bad. (5:10)

Driving Paul's noble ambition was the knowledge that there would be a penetrating uncovering of the depths of his heart by the Lord Himself. That will take place in the future when believers **must all appear before the judgment seat of Christ.** The strong terms **must** and **all** stress the inevitability and comprehensiveness of this event. That knowledge produced in Paul strong motivation to please God in this life.

Phaneroō (**appear**) means, "to make manifest," "to make clear," "to make visible," or "to reveal." Commenting on the meaning of *phaneroō*, Philip E. Hughes writes, "To be made manifest means not just to appear, but to be laid bare, stripped of every outward façade of respectability, and openly revealed in the full and true reality of one's character" (*The Second Epistle to the Corinthians*, The New International Commentary on the New Testament [Grand Rapids: Eerdmans, 1992], 180). Some have argued that believers' secret motives and heart attitudes will be made manifest to the holy angels; there is, however, no biblical support for such speculation. Others hold that the disclosure of which Paul writes will be to other believers, a view also without biblical support. Believers will be too preoccupied with the unveiling of their own deeds to pay attention to the revealing of others'. Nor do believers' hearts need to be made manifest to the omniscient God, who already knows every detail of their lives.

In that day, the full truth about their lives, character, and deeds will be made clear to each believer. Each will discover the real verdict on his or her ministry, service, and motives. All hypocrisy and pretense will be stripped away; all temporal matters with no eternal significance will vanish like wood, hay, and stubble, and only what is to be rewarded as eternally valuable will be left. First Samuel 16:7 declares that "God sees not as man sees, for man looks at the outward appearance, but the Lord looks at the heart." "There is no creature hidden from His sight," the writer of Hebrews adds, "but all things are open and laid bare to the eyes of Him with whom we have to do" (Heb. 4:13). The true assessment of the work God has done in and through believers will be disclosed on that day.

Believers will not be judged for sin at the judgment seat of Christ. Every sin of every believer was judged at the Cross, when God "made Him who knew no sin to be sin on our behalf, so that we might become the righteousness of God in Him" (2 Cor. 5:21). At the cross "Christ redeemed us from the curse of the Law, having become a curse for us" (Gal. 3:13). As our substitute, "He Himself bore our sins in His body on the cross, so that we might die to sin and live to righteousness" (1 Peter 2:24); "He, having offered one sacrifice for sins for all time, sat down at the right hand of God" (Heb. 10:12; cf. Eph. 1:7; 4:32; 1 John 2:1–2). Because of His atoning sacrifice on our behalf, "There is now no condemnation for those who are in Christ Jesus. . . . Who is the one who condemns? Christ Jesus is He who died, yes, rather who was raised, who is at the right hand of God, who also intercedes for us" (Rom. 8:1, 34). But though salvation is not by works, works are the inevitable result of true salvation. Philip Hughes comments,

> It is worth remembering that a passage like this shows that, so far from there being discord, there is an essential agreement between the teaching of Paul and that of James on the subject of faith and works. The justification of the sinner, it is true, is by faith in Christ and not by works of his own; but the hidden root of faith must bring forth the visible fruit of good works. This fruit is expected by Christ, for it brings glory to the Father and is evidence to the world of the dynamic reality of divine grace. And it is especially in the bearing of *much* fruit that the Father is glorified (Jn. 15:8). (*The Second Epistle to the Corinthians*, 183. Italics in original.)

Judgment seat translates *bēma*, which, in its simplest definition, describes a place reached by steps, or a platform. The Septuagint (the Greek translation of the Old Testament) uses it that way in Nehemiah 8:4. In Greek culture *bēma* referred to the elevated platform on which victorious athletes received their crowns, much like the medal stand in the modern Olympic games. In the New Testament it was used of the judgment seats of Pilate (Matt. 27:19; John 19:13), Herod (Acts 12:21), and Festus (Acts 25:6, 10, 17). There was also a *bēma* at Corinth, where unbelieving Jews unsuccessfully accused Paul before the Roman proconsul Gallio (Acts 18:12, 16, 17). A person was brought before a *bēma* to have his or her deeds examined, in a judicial sense for indictment or exoneration, or for the purpose of recognizing and rewarding some achievement. Writing to the Romans of this same event, Paul described it as "the judgment seat [*bēma*] of God" (Rom. 14:10). God the Father is the ultimate Judge, but He has "given all judgment to the Son" (John 5:22). Paul Barnett notes,

> A parallel passage—"we shall all stand before the judgment seat of God" (Rom. 14:10)—implies an identity of function of Christ and God; God judges and Christ judges. The NT often refers to Christ as God's appointed judge, appropriate to his role as Son of Man, as in Dan. 7:13, 14, 26–27 (e.g., John 5:22, 27; 9:39; Matt. 25:31–32; Acts 10:42; 17:31; cf. Rev. 20:11–15). (*The Second Epistle to the Corinthians*, The New International Commentary on the New Testament [Grand Rapids: Eerdmans, 1997], 275 n. 45)

The phrase **each one** stresses the personal nature of believers' judgment; it is an individual, not a collective, judgment. Its purpose, as noted above, is not judicial; it is that every believer **may be recompensed for his deeds in the body. Recompensed** translates a form of the verb *komizō*, which means, "to receive back what is due"—whether punishment for a criminal, or reward for one to be honored. When believers stand before the Lord Jesus Christ they will **be recompensed for** the **deeds** they have done **in the body** (cf. Rev. 22:12). Therefore, they cannot disregard their bodies, or treat them with contempt in some antinomian or dualistic fashion. Instead, they are to "present [their] bodies a living and holy sacrifice, acceptable to God, which is [their] spiritual service of worship" (Rom. 12:1). Things done in the body do have potential eternal value (cf. Matt. 6:19–21).

The use of the word **bad** does not indicate that believers' judgment is a judgment on sin, since all their sin has already been judged in Christ. The contrast between **good** and **bad** is not one between moral good and moral evil. **Bad** does not translate *kakos* or *ponēros*, the words for moral evil, but *phaulos,* which means "worthless," or "useless." Richard C. Trench writes that *phaulos* "contemplates evil under another aspect, not so much that either of active or passive malignity, but that rather of its good-for-nothingness, the impossibility of any true gain coming forth from it" (*Synonyms of the New Testament* [Reprint; Grand Rapids: Eerdmans, 1983], 317). *Phaulos* describes those mundane things that inherently are neither of eternal value nor sinful, such as taking a walk, going shopping, taking a drive in the country, pursuing an advanced degree, moving up the corporate ladder, painting pictures, or writing poetry. Those morally neutral things will be judged when believers stand before the judgment seat of Christ. If they were done with a motive to glorify God, they will be considered **good.** If they were pursued for selfish interests, they will be considered **bad.**

The clearest definition of the difference between **good** and **bad** (worthless) things is in 1 Corinthians 3:11–15:

> For no man can lay a foundation other than the one which is laid, which is Jesus Christ. Now if any man builds on the foundation with gold, silver, precious stones, wood, hay, straw, each man's work will become evident; for the day will show it because it is to be revealed with fire, and the fire itself will test the quality of each man's work. If any man's work which he has built on it remains, he will receive a reward. If any man's work is burned up, he will suffer loss; but he himself will be saved, yet so as through fire.

The only foundation of the Christian life is the Lord Jesus Christ (cf. 1 Peter 2:6–8), but believers must build on that foundation, as Peter exhorted:

> But also for this very reason, giving all diligence, add to your faith

virtue, to virtue knowledge, to knowledge self-control, to self-control

perseverance, to perseverance godliness, to godliness brotherly kindness, and to brotherly kindness love. For if these things are yours and
abound, you will be neither barren nor unfruitful in the knowledge of
our Lord Jesus Christ. For he who lacks these things is shortsighted,
even to blindness, and has forgotten that he was cleansed from his old
sins. Therefore, brethren, be even more diligent to make your call and
election sure, for if you do these things you will never stumble. (2 Peter
1:5–10 NKJV)

Believers build for eternity not with "wood, hay, or straw," but with "gold,
silver, [and] precious stones." The latter are valuable, permanent, and
indestructible and will survive the fire of judgment; the former, though
not evil, are worthless and combustible. They illustrate things with no
lasting, eternal value. The fire, symbolizing judgment, will consume them
in that day when "each man's work will become evident." Believers will
only be rewarded for deeds with motives that please and glorify the
Lord. Paul's longing for heaven did not cause him to act irresponsibly or
unfaithfully here on earth; it did just the opposite.

A Ministry of Integrity
(2 Corinthians 5:11–17)

14

Therefore, knowing the fear of the Lord, we persuade men, but we are made manifest to God; and I hope that we are made manifest also in your consciences. We are not again commending ourselves to you but are giving you an occasion to be proud of us, so that you will have an answer for those who take pride in appearance and not in heart. For if we are beside ourselves, it is for God; if we are of sound mind, it is for you. For the love of Christ controls us, having concluded this, that one died for all, therefore all died; and He died for all, so that they who live might no longer live for themselves, but for Him who died and rose again on their behalf. Therefore from now on we recognize no one according to the flesh; even though we have known Christ according to the flesh, yet now we know Him in this way no longer. Therefore if anyone is in Christ, he is a new creature; the old things passed away; behold, new things have come. (5:11–17)

Though there is variety in leadership styles, several common qualities are indispensable, especially for effective spiritual leaders.

First, leaders who make an impact are focused. They have a clearly defined mission, which they pursue with unrelenting clarity of purpose.

Second, leaders who have an impact are internally motivated. They do not usually depend on favorable external factors to achieve.

Third, leaders who impact are courageous. They are usually so dedicated to their tasks and goals that they refuse to back down in the face of adversity or be stopped by hindrances or obstacles.

Fourth, leaders who succeed are knowledgeable. They understand what they need to know, are sure of what they believe, and are eager to learn more.

Fifth, leaders who make an impact are strong. They have the strength to endure the arduous, difficult labor that achievement demands.

Sixth, for leaders to have an impact they need to be optimistic, to believe the best about their plans and their people.

Seventh, leaders who ennoble others are enthusiastic and persuasive. They generate a contagious excitement about their visions and ministries that enables them to enlist the eager support of others.

Eighth, effective leaders are willing to take risks. They put everything on the line for what they believe must be done.

Ninth, leaders who have an impact are skilled communicators. They can articulate their visions, ideas, and plans effectively so as to motivate those with them.

Tenth, leaders who impact are imaginative. They are usually not content with maintaining the status quo but pursue greater things.

Finally, impactful leaders tend to be independent, strong enough to stand and survive on their own.

Tying all those essential qualities together is consistency or integrity. Without it, the rest of the above-mentioned leadership qualities add up to nothing more than superficiality. Integrity solidifies and unites all the other qualities; it is the glue that holds all attitudes and actions together.

Integrity (from the Latin word *integer,* "entire") may be defined as the condition or quality of being undivided. It describes those who adhere to their ethical or moral standards without hypocrisy or duplicity. People with integrity lead lives that are one with their stated convictions; they "practice what they preach." They are honest, sincere, and incorruptible. In biblical terms, those with integrity are "above reproach"—a quality that is to characterize all believers (Phil. 2:15; 1 Tim. 5:7), but especially elders (1 Tim. 3:2; Titus 1:6–7).

The Bible stresses the value of integrity by condemning hypocrisy. Jesus repeatedly denounced the religious leaders of His day as hypocrites (Matt. 6:2, 5, 16; 15:7; 22:18; Luke 12:1, 56; 13:15). Matthew 23 records His blistering malediction on the scribes and Pharisees for their lack of integrity, because "they say things and do not do them" (v. 3). After a series of curses, each introduced by the phrase "woe to you" (vv. 13–16,

23, 25, 27, 29), and after repeatedly denouncing them as hypocrites, Jesus concluded with a stern rebuke: "You serpents, you brood of vipers, how will you escape the sentence of hell?" (v. 33).

In Romans 12:9 Paul commanded that "love be without hypocrisy," and he did not hesitate to condemn Peter and Barnabas when they lapsed into hypocrisy (Gal. 2:11–13). He warned in 1 Timothy 4:2 about "the hypocrisy of liars" (lit., "hypocritical lie-speakers") who would deceive many. James noted that godly, biblical wisdom is "without hypocrisy" (James 3:17) and that God gives blessing (1:5–8) and grace (4:8) to those whose lives are not duplicitous ("double-minded"); Peter also taught that hypocrisy has no place in believers' lives (1 Peter 2:1).

Scripture also affirms the importance of integrity, both by precept and example. Despite the terrible suffering he endured, Job maintained his integrity. In Job 2:3, "The Lord said to Satan, 'Have you considered My servant Job? For there is no one like him on the earth, a blameless and upright man fearing God and turning away from evil. And he still holds fast his integrity, although you incited Me against him to ruin him without cause.'" Though foolish, his wife's advice to him nonetheless affirmed Job's integrity: "Do you still hold fast your integrity? Curse God and die!" (2:9). Though they falsely accused him of harboring unrepentant sin, Job's would-be counselors acknowledged his claim to integrity. In 4:6 Eliphaz said, "Is not your fear of God your confidence, and the integrity of your ways your hope?" Job never gave in to the accusations of his carping critics but steadfastly maintained his integrity: "Far be it from me that I should declare you right; till I die I will not put away my integrity from me" (27:5); "Let Him weigh me with accurate scales, and let God know my integrity" (31:6).

Like Job, David was also a man of integrity, as God Himself affirmed:

> Now it came about when Solomon had finished building the house of the Lord, and the king's house, and all that Solomon desired to do, that the Lord appeared to Solomon a second time, as He had appeared to him at Gibeon. The Lord said to him, "I have heard your prayer and your supplication, which you have made before Me; I have consecrated this house which you have built by putting My name there forever, and My eyes and My heart will be there perpetually. As for you, if you will walk before Me as your father David walked, in integrity of heart and uprightness, doing according to all that I have commanded you and will keep My statutes and My ordinances, then I will establish the throne of your kingdom over Israel forever, just as I promised to your father David, saying, 'You shall not lack a man on the throne of Israel.'" (1 Kings 9:1–5)

In Psalm 78:72 the psalmist declared, "So [David] shepherded them according to the integrity of his heart."

David repeatedly testified to his integrity in the Psalms: "Vindicate me, O Lord, according to my righteousness and my integrity that is in me" (7:8); "Let integrity and uprightness preserve me, for I wait for You" (25:21). "Vindicate me, O Lord, for I have walked in my integrity" (26:1); "But as for me, I shall walk in my integrity" (26:11); "As for me, You uphold me in my integrity" (41:12); "I will walk within my house in the integrity of my heart" (101:2).

Scripture also describes the blessings of integrity: "O Lord, who may abide in Your tent? Who may dwell on Your holy hill? He who walks with integrity, and works righteousness, and speaks truth in his heart" (Ps. 15:1–2); "He stores up sound wisdom for the upright; He is a shield to those who walk in integrity" (Prov. 2:7); "He who walks in integrity walks securely, but he who perverts his ways will be found out" (Prov. 10:9); "The integrity of the upright will guide them, but the falseness of the treacherous will destroy them" (Prov. 11:3); "Better is a poor man who walks in his integrity than he who is perverse in speech and is a fool" (Prov. 19:1); "A righteous man who walks in his integrity—how blessed are his sons after him" (Prov. 20:7); "Better is the poor who walks in his integrity than he who is crooked though he be rich" (Prov. 28:6).

Since integrity is essential to spiritual life and leadership, obviously it must be protected. In 1 Corinthians 9:24–27 Paul described the intense self-discipline he practiced to avoid being disqualified from the ministry by sin:

> Do you not know that those who run in a race all run, but only one receives the prize? Run in such a way that you may win. Everyone who competes in the games exercises self-control in all things. They then do it to receive a perishable wreath, but we an imperishable. Therefore I run in such a way, as not without aim; I box in such a way, as not beating the air; but I discipline my body and make it my slave, so that, after I have preached to others, I myself will not be disqualified.

True spiritual leadership belongs to those whose lives are pure, blameless, and above reproach (1 Tim. 3:2; Titus 1:6–7; cf. Ps. 101:6).

But leaders must also protect their integrity against the false accusations that could destroy it. It is this second aspect of guarding integrity that prompted Paul to write. He knew the importance not only of guarding his life against sin but also of guarding his reputation against lies. As has been noted in previous chapters of this volume, the theme of this epistle is Paul's defense of his integrity (cf. 2 Cor. 1:12–13; 2:17; 3:5; 4:2, 5; 5:9–10; 6:3–4, 11; 7:2; 8:20–21; 10:7; 11:5–6, 30; 12:11–12; 13:5–6). The apostle's credibility was under attack from false teachers who had infiltrated the church at Corinth (cf. 6:8). Before they could get a hearing for their lies, they first had to tear down Paul's credibility in the minds of the people. Though their accusations were false, they were nonetheless dangerous; if the Corinthians believed the allegations, confidence in the Word of God through Paul would be destroyed.

Sadly, the false teacher's slanderous lies had convinced many in the Corinthian assembly that Paul was not a man of integrity. His usefulness as an authoritative messenger of divine truth hung in the balance. It was that danger that motivated Paul to defend himself for the sake of the truth and the God of truth.

But Paul faced a dilemma. If he did not defend himself, the Corinthians might abandon him in favor of the false teachers. Yet if he did defend himself, he left himself open to the charge that he was pridefully commending himself. To refute the false accusation that he was guilty of self-commendation, Paul was forced to give a defense of himself.

The key to understanding this passage lies in the meaning of the verb *peithō* (**persuade**). Some commentators believe that it refers to persuading people of the truth of the gospel, as it does in Acts 17:4; 18:4; 19:8, 26; 26:28; and 28:23–24. But the gospel is not the issue in 2 Corinthians; this is not primarily an evangelistic epistle. Paul was not trying to persuade the Corinthian believers of the truth of the gospel, but rather of the truth of his integrity. Therefore, *peithō* could be better rendered "seek the favor of," as it is in Galatians 1:10. Paul sought a favorable judgment from the Corinthians on his integrity.

Though the Corinthians may have questioned it, Paul's true spiritual condition was already **made manifest to God;** his sincerity, honesty, and genuineness were perfectly evident to Him. Paul's bold declaration manifests the absence of the Holy Spirit convicting him of sin through an accusing conscience and was convincing proof of his integrity (cf. 2 Cor. 1:12; Acts 23:1; 24:16; 2 Tim. 1:3).

It was Paul's **hope that** his integrity would be **made manifest also in** the Corinthians' **consciences,** as it was in his. As he wrote earlier, he had "renounced the things hidden because of shame, not walking in craftiness or adulterating the word of God, but by the manifestation of truth commending [himself] to every man's conscience in the sight of God" (2 Cor. 4:2). The choice the Corinthians faced was simple: Were they going to listen to the testimony of their consciences or to the lies of Paul's critics? Their consciences were well informed; they knew of his godly life and impeccable moral character because he had ministered daily among them for at least eighteen months (Acts 18:11). That firsthand observation should have left no doubts regarding Paul's integrity.

As he defended his integrity against the vicious liars who were attacking him, Paul gave six motives for his defense: reverence for the Lord, concern for the church, devotion to the truth, gratitude to the Savior, desire for righteousness, and burden for the lost.

REVERENCE FOR THE LORD

Therefore, knowing the fear of the Lord (5:11*a*)

To **fear** God is to have reverence, awe, and respect for Him resulting in worship, adoration, and service (cf. 7:1; Job 28:28; Pss. 19:9; 22:23;
111:10; Prov. 1:7; 8:13; 9:10). Acts 9:31 records that "the church throughout
all Judea and Galilee and Samaria enjoyed peace, being built up; and
going on in the fear of the Lord and in the comfort of the Holy Spirit, it
continued to increase." Thus, the "fear of the Lord" does not refer to dread
or terror, since that type of fear would not result in "peace" and "comfort."
Paul was deeply disturbed that someone might think he misrepresented the Lord whom he intensely loved and reverently served. He
was appalled to be viewed by some as dishonoring the name of Jesus
Christ (cf. Rom. 2:24). It was unacceptable that people would think him
to be living a life that was the opposite of what he lived for—to glorify
God (1 Cor. 10:31; cf. Rom. 12:1). Nor could he remain silent while he was
falsely accused of dishonoring Him, for such slander would render his
ministry useless and unfruitful. Therefore he was obligated to defend his
integrity, though he did so with humble reluctance (cf. 2 Cor. 10:12–18).

CONCERN FOR THE CHURCH

**We are not again commending ourselves to you but are giving
you an occasion to be proud of us, so that you will have an
answer for those who take pride in appearance and not in heart.**
(5:12)

Not only did Paul defend himself for God's sake but also for the
church's sake. He knew that the false accusations against him, if left
unchallenged, could devastate the church. If enough of the Corinthians
believed the false teachers' lies about him, the congregation could split
into pro-Paul and anti-Paul factions. The church's unity, which was so precious to the apostle (12:20; Eph. 4:3, 13; Col. 3:14; cf. John 17:20–23),
would be shattered; nothing will split a church faster than attacks on the
reputation of its leaders.
The assaults on Paul's integrity threatened not only to split the
church but also to stunt its spiritual growth. He was the channel through
which God's revelation came to them, and if the Corinthians lost their
trust in him, that apostolic source would be rejected. Worse, it would be

replaced by the demon doctrines of the false teachers. The result would be devastating evangelistically.

Paul repeated the disclaimer he had made earlier in this epistle (2 Cor. 3:1), reminding the Corinthians, **We are not again commending ourselves to you.** He was well aware that "It is not he who commends himself that is approved, but he whom the Lord commends" (10:18). And, as he reminded them in 12:11, "Actually I should have been commended by you." He was not trying to vindicate himself for his sake, but for theirs. Paul's repeated declarations that he was not commending himself suggests, as noted earlier, that he had been accused of doing just that. The false apostles wrongly accused Paul of blowing his own horn, of boosting his own ego, of advancing his own selfish agenda. They were doing so in his absence and likely did so during his sorrowful or painful visit to Corinth (2:1).

Actually, Paul was the last person to boast about himself. In 1 Corinthians 4:4 he wrote, "For I am conscious of nothing against myself, yet I am not by this acquitted; but the one who examines me is the Lord." Twice he reminded the Corinthians, "Let him who boasts, boast in the Lord" (1 Cor. 1:31; 2 Cor. 10:17). The only boasting he did was about his weakness (11:30; 12:9–10). He would not even take credit for what he had accomplished in his ministry; in his first epistle to the Corinthians he wrote, "If I preach the gospel, I have nothing to boast of, for I am under compulsion; for woe is me if I do not preach the gospel" (1 Cor. 9:16).

Further clarifying his motives, Paul wrote that he intended this defense of his integrity to give the Corinthians **an occasion to be proud** of him in the right sense, **so that** they would **have an answer for those** false apostles **who take pride in appearance and not in heart.** Rather than commend himself to his enemies, Paul wisely chose instead to arm his friends to defend him. He knew that replying directly to his enemies was pointless; they would twist his words to fit their own evil purposes (cf. Prov. 26:4; 29:9). Therefore it was more effective for him to equip his supporters at Corinth so that they would **have an answer for** his detractors (Prov. 27:2). By so doing Paul also gave them **an occasion** or opportunity **to be proud of** him. *Kauchēma* (**proud**) can refer to improper, sinful boasting (Rom. 4:2; 1 Cor. 5:6), but here it refers to their confidence in his spiritual integrity (cf. 2 Cor. 1:14; 9:3; Gal. 6:4; Phil. 1:26; 2:16; Heb. 3:6).

Turning the tables on his accusers, Paul denounced them as **those who take pride in appearance and not in heart.** Because their outward religious **appearance** did not match the corruption that was in their **hearts** they, not Paul, were the hypocrites lacking integrity. They were like those whom Jesus denounced as "whitewashed tombs which on the outside appear beautiful, but inside they are full of dead men's bones and all uncleanness ... [who] outwardly appear righteous to men, but inwardly . . . are full of hypocrisy and lawlessness" (Matt. 23:27–28), and those whom Paul exposed as "desir[ing] to make a good showing in the flesh" (Gal. 6:12).

There was no dichotomy, however, between what Paul appeared to be on the outside and what he really was on the inside. That truth was evident not only to God, but also to the Corinthians' consciences as they responded to what they knew to be true of the apostle.

DEVOTION TO THE TRUTH

For if we are beside ourselves, it is for God; if we are of sound mind, it is for you. (5:13)

One of the false teachers' scurrilous charges against Paul was that he was a fool, bereft of a sound and sober mind (cf. 11:1, 16–17; 12:6, 11; 1 Cor. 4:10). *Existēmi,* the root of the verb translated **we are beside ourselves,** is used in Mark 3:21 to describe Jesus' relatives' mistaken belief that He had "lost His senses." The verb literally means "to stand outside of oneself," or "to be beside oneself" in the sense of being "out of one's mind." Such was Paul's passionate devotion to the truth that his enemies deemed him fanatical to the point of being imbalanced mentally. Incredibly, instead of being rejected outright, those false and outrageous allegations generated a debate in the Corinthian church with those who insisted that he was **of sound mind.** That term means to be sane, sensible, and in control of one's faculties.

The world often looks unfavorably on people who are dogmatic and zealous about the truth, like John the Baptist, who denounced the hypocritical Jewish religious leaders in no uncertain terms: "When he saw many of the Pharisees and Sadducees coming for baptism, he said to them, 'You brood of vipers, who warned you to flee from the wrath to come?'" (Matt. 3:7). As a result, in predictable fashion, they derided him, claiming, "He has a demon!" (Matt. 11:18).

Not surprisingly, those same hypocrites blasphemously accused the Lord Jesus Christ, truth incarnate (John 1:14, 17; 14:6; Rev. 3:7; 19:11), of having lost touch with reality. In Matthew 11:19 Jesus referred to their scornful denunciation of him as "a drunkard," under the control of alcohol. As they had John the Baptist, they accused Jesus of being demon possessed, asking Him mockingly, "Do we not say rightly that You are a Samaritan and have a demon?" (John 8:48; cf. 7:20; 8:52; 10:20). But taking their evil reviling a step further, they demeaned Him as being possessed by Satan himself, insisting, "This man casts out demons only by

Beelzebul the ruler of the demons" (Matt. 12:24; cf. 10:25). They thereby committed the most wicked act of sacrilege conceivable, the unpardonable sin of blasphemy against the Holy Spirit (Matt. 12:31–32).

This was not the only time that Paul's commitment to the truth had caused some to question his sanity. After he gave the dramatic testimony of his conversion and a powerful, straightforward presentation of the gospel before King Agrippa, the Roman governor Festus "said in a loud voice, 'Paul, you are out of your mind! Your great learning is driving you mad'" (Acts 26:24). But Paul was not insane, as his calm, dignified reply demonstrated: "I am not out of my mind, most excellent Festus, but I utter words of sober truth" (v. 25).

If Paul was zealous **it** was **for God.** He was a steward (1 Cor. 4:1; 9:17; Eph. 3:2; Col. 1:25), entrusted with the precious truth of God's Word and ambitious to glorify Him. He could not preach that truth without passion and conviction, because he understood that God is honored when His Word is so proclaimed. Even if Paul were out of control, as his enemies claimed, it was because of his desire that God's truth be heard, believed, and exalted (cf. Eph. 6:19; Col. 4:3; 2 Thess. 3:1).

On the other hand, if he was **of sound mind,** thinking sensibly, **it** was **for** the Corinthians' sake. Whether people thought him **beside** himself or **of sound mind** was of no consequence to him (cf. 1 Cor. 4:1–5). The issue for Paul was that God be honored by the truth proclaimed, so he faithfully did that. But for the Corinthians' sake he was at the same time gentle, humble, and patient (2 Cor. 10:1; 2 Tim. 4:2).

GRATITUDE TO THE SAVIOR

For the love of Christ controls us, having concluded this, that one died for all, therefore all died; (5:14)

While Paul's love for his Lord certainly compelled him, the phrase **the love of Christ** is best seen in this context as Christ's love for Paul—a love most clearly seen in His sacrificial death, which is the subsequent theme. It was that magnanimous, free, unmerited **love** that controlled, drove, and motivated Paul to defend himself. Since Christ loved him savingly, he wanted to be certain that nothing hindered his ability to serve Him.

Paul never lost his sense of wonder at Christ's love, as he expressed so monumentally in Romans 8:35–39:

> Who will separate us from the love of Christ? Will tribulation, or distress, or persecution, or famine, or nakedness, or peril, or sword? Just as it is written, "For Your sake we are being put to death all day long; we were

considered as sheep to be slaughtered." But in all these things we overwhelmingly conquer through Him who loved us. For I am convinced
that neither death, nor life, nor angels, nor principalities, nor things
present, nor things to come, nor powers, nor height, nor depth, nor any
other created thing, will be able to separate us from the love of God,
which is in Christ Jesus our Lord.

He expressed the sacrificial aspect of Christ's love in the familiar words
of Galatians 2:20, "I have been crucified with Christ; and it is no longer I
who live, but Christ lives in me; and the life which I now live in the flesh I
live by faith in the Son of God, who loved me and gave Himself up for
me." To the Ephesians he wrote that "the love of Christ . . . surpasses
knowledge" (Eph. 3:19; cf. 5:25). Christ's incomprehensible, unbreakable,
unconditional love overwhelmed Paul.

More than that, it controlled him. *Sunechō* (**controls**) describes
pressure that produces action. The magnitude of Christ's love for believers like Paul compelled him to serve Him wholeheartedly, as an act of
grateful worship. If he were to be discredited and his ministry lost, he
would lose that opportunity to express his gratitude to Christ through his
ministry. That threat was a key factor that constrained the apostle to
defend his integrity.

Christ's love controlled Paul because he had **concluded** in a
deep and profound way the reality of his identification with Christ. His
confidence was **that one died for all, therefore all died.** Under the
old covenant the deaths of countless thousands of sacrificial animals
could not provide full and complete pardon for sin, "for it is impossible
for the blood of bulls and goats to take away sins" (Heb. 10:4). There
never was any efficacy in the death of an animal. All such deaths incessantly testified to the old covenant's futility as a means of salvation. But
in sharp contrast Jesus Christ, "by one offering . . . has perfected for all
time those who are sanctified" (Heb. 10:14; cf. 9:14, 28; 10:10, 12, 19; 13:12;
Rom. 3:24–25; 5:9; Eph. 1:7; 1 Peter 1:18–19; 1 John 1:7; Rev. 1:5).

The preposition *huper* (**for**) could be translated "in behalf of," or
"for the benefit of," but the best rendering seems to be "in the place of." It
introduces the essential and irreplaceable truth of the substitutionary
atonement; that is, that Christ died in the place of **all** who put their faith
in Him. By His death He "redeemed us from the curse of the Law, having
become a curse for us" (Gal. 3:13) because God "made Him who knew
no sin to be sin on our behalf, so that we might become the righteousness of God in Him" (2 Cor. 5:21).

In the Old Testament, Isaiah prophesied that Messiah would die
as a substitute for sinners:

Surely our griefs He Himself bore,
And our sorrows He carried;
Yet we ourselves esteemed Him stricken,
Smitten of God, and afflicted.
But He was pierced through for our transgressions,
He was crushed for our iniquities;
The chastening for our well-being fell upon Him,
And by His scourging we are healed.
All of us like sheep have gone astray,
Each of us has turned to his own way;
But the Lord has caused the iniquity of us all
To fall on Him. . . .

As a result of the anguish of His soul,
He will see it and be satisfied;
By His knowledge the Righteous One, My Servant, will justify the many,
As He will bear their iniquities.
Therefore, I will allot Him a portion with the great,
And He will divide the booty with the strong;
Because He poured out Himself to death,
And was numbered with the transgressors;
Yet He Himself bore the sin of many,
And interceded for the transgressors. (Isa. 53:4–6, 11–12)

The concept of substitution, prophesied in the Old Testament, is elucidated in the New Testament. In one of the richest, most profound theological passages in all of Scripture the apostle Paul wrote,

For while we were still helpless, at the right time Christ died for the ungodly. For one will hardly die for a righteous man; though perhaps for the good man someone would dare even to die. But God demonstrates His own love toward us, in that while we were yet sinners, Christ died for us. Much more then, having now been justified by His blood, we shall be saved from the wrath of God through Him. For if while we were enemies we were reconciled to God through the death of His Son, much more, having been reconciled, we shall be saved by His life. (Rom. 5:6–10; cf. John 6:51; 2 Cor. 5:21; Eph. 5:2; 1 Thess. 5:9–10; 1 Tim. 2:5–6; Titus 2:14; Heb. 2:9; 1 Peter 2:24; 3:18)

The substitutionary atonement of the Lord Jesus Christ is the heart of Christian theology (see the discussion of 5:21 in chapter 16 of this volume). All people are sinners (Rom. 3:23), for whom God's justice demands the death penalty (Rom. 6:23). But Christ's death fully satisfied God's justice and propitiated His wrath (Rom. 3:22, 25–26; Heb. 2:17; 1 John

2:2; 4:10) for all those who put their faith in Him (Rom. 3:28, 30; 4:5; 5:1; Gal. 2:16; 3:8, 11, 24).

It is crucial to understand the identity of the **all** for whom Christ died. The phrase **one died for all,** if it stood alone, could imply that Christ died for every person who ever lived. But Paul clarified his meaning by adding the phrase **therefore all died.** He did not say, "all were dead," which would have described every sinner who ever lived, since all are dead in sin (Eph. 2:1). He was not talking about a condition, however, but an event—believers' union with Christ in His death. Together, the two phrases define the **all** for whom Christ died as the **all** who **died** in Him (cf. Rom. 6:1–4) through faith in Him (Rom. 3:24–26). Just as all who are in Adam (the whole race) became sinners because of his sin, so also all who are in Christ (those who believe savingly) become righteous because of His death (Rom. 5:19; 1 Cor. 15:21–22).

God is the "Savior of all men" (1 Tim. 4:10) in a physical and temporal sense in that He does not give sinners the death they deserve when they sin the first time and many times after. God's patience and salvation from immediate death and hell show He is a Savior by nature. Consequently, all the unsaved benefit from common grace. God "causes His sun to rise on the evil and the good, and sends rain on the righteous and the unrighteous" (Matt. 5:45). He shows compassionate love for all men (cf. Jer. 48:35–37; Matt. 23:37; Mark 10:21; Luke 19:41–44), takes no pleasure in their death (Ezek. 18:30–32; 33:11), and offers them the gospel (Matt. 11:28–30; 22:2–14; Rev. 22:17; cf. Isa. 55:1–2). But though God "is the Savior of all men" temporally and physically, He is "especially [the Savior] of believers" eternally and spiritually (1 Tim. 4:10); the atonement is only substitutionary for those who by grace through faith died in Christ. If Christ died as a substitute for the whole human race, then every person who ever lived would be saved, because their sins would be paid for and divine justice satisfied. But that clearly is not the case, since most people will reject God's salvation and be sent by Him to pay for their sins for eternity in hell (Matt. 25:41, 46; 2 Thess. 1:9; Rev. 14:9–11; 20:11–15; cf. Matt. 7:13–14; Luke 13:23–24).

Paul was overwhelmed with gratitude that the eternal, holy God sent His Son to die as a substitute to pay the penalty for his sins. That marvelous truth left him no room for self-congratulation, as if he had contributed something to his salvation. But Christ's death did not merely put him in a position to be saved; it procured his salvation. From that reality flows reconciliation, justification, forgiveness of sin, peace with God, and deliverance from wrath and judgment. Paul desired above all else to live for the One who sovereignly and graciously redeemed him through His blood. Therefore the apostle defended his ministry, so as not to lose the opportunity to show his gratitude through his service.

DESIRE FOR RIGHTEOUSNESS

and He died for all, so that they who live might no longer live for themselves, but for Him who died and rose again on their behalf. (5:15)

This point is inextricably linked to the previous one. The reason Christ **died for all** who died in Him was **so that they who live might no longer live for themselves, but for Him who died and rose again on their behalf.** The marvelous miracle of salvation includes not only believers' union with Christ in His death, but also in His resurrection:

> Therefore we have been buried with Him through baptism into death, so that as Christ was raised from the dead through the glory of the Father, so we too might walk in newness of life. For if we have become united with Him in the likeness of His death, certainly we shall also be in the likeness of His resurrection.... Now if we have died with Christ, we believe that we shall also live with Him.... For the death that He died, He died to sin once for all; but the life that He lives, He lives to God. Even so consider yourselves to be dead to sin, but alive to God in Christ Jesus. (Rom. 6:4–5, 8, 10–11)

> For through the Law I died to the Law, so that I might live to God. I have been crucified with Christ; and it is no longer I who live, but Christ lives in me; and the life which I now live in the flesh I live by faith in the Son of God, who loved me and gave Himself up for me. (Gal. 2:19–20)

> For you have died and your life is hidden with Christ in God. (Col. 3:3)

Thus, in Christ believers experience not only death to sin but also resurrection to righteousness. As a result, they are **no longer** to **live for themselves, but for Him who died and rose again on their behalf** (cf. Eph. 2:10; Titus 2:14; 1 Peter 2:24).

Like all true Christians, Paul lived for Jesus Christ. In his farewell address to the Ephesian elders, he affirmed, "I do not consider my life of any account as dear to myself, so that I may finish my course and the ministry which I received from the Lord Jesus, to testify solemnly of the gospel of the grace of God" (Acts 20:24). He reminded the Romans, "For if we live, we live for the Lord, or if we die, we die for the Lord; therefore whether we live or die, we are the Lord's" (Rom. 14:8). Contrasting himself to the proud, boastful false teachers troubling the Galatians, Paul declared, "But may it never be that I would boast, except in the cross of our Lord Jesus Christ, through which the world has been crucified to me, and I to the world" (Gal. 6:14). To the Philippians he wrote, "For to me, to live is Christ and to die is gain" (Phil. 1:21), and "I press on toward the goal for the prize of the upward call of God in Christ Jesus" (Phil. 3:14). The Lord Jesus Christ was the apostle's very life (Col. 3:4).

To be viewed as one who dishonored Christ would devastate Paul, for the most important thing in his life was to live for Him. Paul also defended his integrity so that he could continue to be a model of what it means to live for Christ. In 1 Corinthians 11:1 he urged the Corinthians, "Be imitators of me, just as I also am of Christ" (cf. 1 Cor. 4:1; 1 Thess. 1:6). If he allowed his integrity to be destroyed by lies, the Corinthians would not follow him, but the false apostles instead. Such a situation was intolerable to Paul and prompted his vigorous defense of his integrity.

Burden for the Lost

Therefore from now on we recognize no one according to the flesh; even though we have known Christ according to the flesh, yet now we know Him in this way no longer. Therefore if anyone is in Christ, he is a new creature; the old things passed away; behold, new things have come. (5:16–17)

The overarching reason Paul defended his integrity, the one that incorporated all the rest, was so that he could continue to reach the lost. He passionately longed to see people come to saving faith in Christ. In the pagan cultural center of Athens, for example, Paul found that "his spirit was being provoked within him as he was observing the city full of idols" (Acts 17:16). To the Romans he wrote, "I do not want you to be unaware, brethren, that often I have planned to come to you (and have been prevented so far) so that I may obtain some fruit among you also, even as among the rest of the Gentiles" (Rom. 1:13). In his first inspired letter to them, Paul made it clear to the Corinthians that his mission was "to preach the gospel" (1 Cor. 1:17); in fact, as he wrote later in that epistle, "I am under compulsion; for woe is me if I do not preach the gospel" (1 Cor. 9:16).

But perhaps the most poignant glimpse of Paul's burden for the lost comes in a shocking statement in his letter to the Romans:

> I am telling the truth in Christ, I am not lying, my conscience testifies with me in the Holy Spirit, that I have great sorrow and unceasing grief in my heart. For I could wish that I myself were accursed, separated from Christ for the sake of my brethren, my kinsmen according to the flesh. (Rom. 9:1–3)

So intense was the apostle's desire to see his lost fellow Israelites saved that he was willing to forfeit, were that possible, his own salvation to bring that about. Not surprisingly, his constant "desire and . . . prayer to God for them [was] for their salvation" (Rom. 10:1). Paul's burden for the lost moved him to defend his integrity, lest he lose his credibility and with it his ability to effectively preach the gospel.

These two verses define when Paul's burden for the lost began. The conjunction *hōste* (**therefore**) points back to verses 14 and 15, which describe salvation. After his conversion, the way Paul viewed people changed radically. From then on, he did not **recognize** (*oida;* lit. "know," or "perceive") anyone **according to the flesh;** he no longer evaluated people based on external, worldly standards, as the false teachers did (cf. 2 Cor. 5:12; Gal. 6:12). The proud Pharisee, who once scorned Gentiles, and even those Jews outside of his group (cf. John 7:49), now looked beyond mere outward appearances. His prejudice and hatred gave way to a love for all, including "Greek and Jew, circumcised and uncircumcised, barbarian, Scythian, slave and freeman" (Col. 3:11).

Not only did Paul's view of people change but also his view of **Christ.** He had once **known** Him **according to the flesh;** he had made a human assessment of Him, concluding that He was merely a man. Worse, he had decided Jesus was a false messiah; a heretic and a rebel against Judaism; one worthy of death. As a result, Paul dedicated his life to persecuting His followers. As he later confessed,

> So then, I thought to myself that I had to do many things hostile to the name of Jesus of Nazareth. And this is just what I did in Jerusalem; not only did I lock up many of the saints in prisons, having received authority from the chief priests, but also when they were being put to death I cast my vote against them. And as I punished them often in all the synagogues, I tried to force them to blaspheme; and being furiously enraged at them, I kept pursuing them even to foreign cities. (Acts 26:9–11)

Yet after his conversion Paul knew **Him in this way no longer.** The assessment of Paul the apostle was radically different than that of Saul the Pharisee. No longer did he view Jesus as an itinerant Galilean rabbi and self-appointed messianic impostor who was the enemy of Judaism. Instead, he saw Him for who He really is, God incarnate, the Savior, the Lord of heaven, the true Messiah who alone fulfills all Old Testament promises and provides forgiveness for sin. The transformation in Paul's view took place in one blinding moment when he met the risen Lord on the road to Damascus. And when his assessment of Jesus changed, so did his assessment of everyone else. He knew that the same profound change that took place in his life would take place in the lives of all those who put their faith in Christ.

Therefore, in a conclusion also deriving from verse 15, Paul wrote, **if anyone is in Christ, he is a new creature.** God's grace and mercy are wide enough to encompass anyone, even the most vile, wicked sinner—even the foremost of sinners (1 Tim. 1:15–16). But God is only "the justifier of the one who has faith in Jesus" (Rom. 3:26; cf. Gal. 3:26). His substitutionary death becomes their death, and His resurrection life their life.

The familiar Pauline expression **in Christ** succinctly and profoundly summarizes all the rich blessings of salvation (cf. Rom. 8:1; 16:3, 7; 1 Cor. 1:30; Gal. 3:28; Eph. 1:1; Phil. 1:1; 4:21; Col. 1:2, 28; Philem. 23). Everyone who is **in Christ** becomes **a new creature** (cf. Gal. 6:15). *Kainos* (**new**) means new in quality, not just in sequence; believers' "old self was crucified with Him" (Rom. 6:6); they have therefore laid "aside the old self . . . and put on the new self" (Eph. 4:22, 24; Col. 3:9–10).

The transformation wrought by the new birth is not only an instantaneous miracle but also a lifelong process of sanctification. For those so transformed, everything changes; **the old things** have **passed away.** Old values, ideas, plans, loves, desires, and beliefs vanish, replaced by the **new things** that accompany salvation. The perfect tense of the verb *ginomai* (**have come**) indicates a past act with continuing results in the present. God plants new desires, loves, inclinations, and truths in the redeemed, so that they live in the midst of the old creation with a new creation perspective (cf. Gal. 6:14). That perspective, as it is nourished and developed, helps believers gain victory in the battle against sin and conforms them to the image of Jesus Christ.

So Paul defended his integrity in order to preach with boldness, knowing that he was trusted. In addition, his reverence and gratitude to the Savior who had done so much for him, his deep concern for the church, passionate devotion to the truth, desire for righteousness, and longing to see the lost come to the Savior compelled him to maintain his integrity. Because he did so, he could confidently challenge the Corinthians, "Therefore do not go on passing judgment before the time, but wait until the Lord comes who will both bring to light the things hidden in the darkness and disclose the motives of men's hearts; and then each man's praise will come to him from God" (1 Cor. 4:5).

The Ministry of Reconciliation (2 Corinthians 5:18–20)

15

Now all these things are from God, who reconciled us to Himself through Christ and gave us the ministry of reconciliation, namely, that God was in Christ reconciling the world to Himself, not counting their trespasses against them, and He has committed to us the word of reconciliation. Therefore, we are ambassadors for Christ, as though God were making an appeal through us; we beg you on behalf of Christ, be reconciled to God. (5:18–20)

Today's church is confronted by a seemingly endless variety of ministry methods, strategies, and styles. Some argue that the church should agitate for social and political change to force cultural morality (moralism), or even help usher in the kingdom (postmillennialism). Others insist the church's message should be inoffensive, upbeat, and affirming, to create a positive atmosphere in which nonbelievers can feel welcome and not threatened (pragmatism). Still others believe their church's primary task is to defend its theological distinctives (denominationalism).

But there is no confusion in Scripture about what the church's mission is to be—evangelism. This definitive passage clearly articulates the heart and soul of the church's responsibility as it represents Jesus

Christ in the world. God has called all believers, especially pastors, to proclaim the message of reconciliation—a term which appears in some form five times in these three verses.

The glorious good news of the gospel is that the sin-devastated relationship between lost sinners and the holy God can be restored. That at first glance seems impossible. God's perfect, infinite, righteous justice demands the punishment of all who violate His law. Standing before the bar of His justice are helpless, guilty sinners, unable either to satisfy God or to change their condition. But through God's plan of reconciliation all the hostility, animosity, and alienation separating the Holy One and sinners vanishes, and those who were once His enemies become His friends. The high calling and noble privilege of preaching this message of reconciliation is the most important duty in the world, since it deals with eternal destinations.

The gospel of reconciliation was the heart of Paul's preaching. To the Romans he wrote, "So, for my part, I am eager to preach the gospel to you also who are in Rome. For I am not ashamed of the gospel, for it is the power of God for salvation to everyone who believes, to the Jew first and also to the Greek" (Rom. 1:15–16). Paul also expressed the burning desire of his heart to preach the message of reconciliation in his first inspired letter to the Corinthians:

> For Christ did not send me to baptize, but to preach the gospel, not in cleverness of speech, so that the cross of Christ would not be made void. . . . But we preach Christ crucified, to Jews a stumbling block and to Gentiles foolishness. . . . My message and my preaching were not in persuasive words of wisdom, but in demonstration of the Spirit and of power. (1 Cor. 1:17, 23; 2:4)

In Ephesians 3:8 he expressed the wonder that to him, "the very least of all saints, this grace was given, to preach to the Gentiles the unfathomable riches of Christ." Paul never lost his focus on the simple, straightforward message that sinners can be reconciled to God through the cross of Christ (cf. 1 Cor. 2:2).

In this, the most theological section of this epistle, Paul gives a comprehensive statement of how God has made this reconciliation possible. The text reveals that reconciliation is by the will of God, by the act of forgiveness, and by the obedience of faith. (The next chapter of this volume, covering 5:21, will show that reconciliation is effected by means of substitution.)

RECONCILIATION IS BY THE WILL OF GOD

Now all these things are from God, who reconciled us to Himself through Christ and gave us the ministry of reconciliation, (5:18)

The phrase **all these things** points back to the immediately preceding section of this epistle, which described the total transformation taking place at conversion (vv. 14–17). In that passage Paul described believers' death and resurrection in Christ as being transformed into new creatures. **All these things,** that is, those related to the transformation, come **from God** (cf. 1 Cor. 8:6; 11:12; James 1:17); sinners cannot be reconciled to Him on their own terms. Unregenerate people have no ability to appease God's anger against sin, satisfy His holy justice, or conform to His standard of righteousness. They are guilty of fatally violating God's law and face eternal banishment from His presence. The deadly, deceptive premise of all false religion is that sinners, based on their own moral and religious efforts and achievements, can reconcile themselves to God. But God alone designed the way of reconciliation, and only He can initiate the reconciliation of sinners; that **God . . . reconciled us to Himself** is precisely the good news of the gospel.

God so loved the world that He made the way of reconciliation. He desired to reconcile sinners to Himself—to make them His children. Such a desire is not foreign to God's holy character but consistent with it. One of the glorious realities of God's person is that He is a Savior by nature.

From before the foundation of the world, God freely and apart from outside influence determined to save sinners in order to eternally display the glory of His grace. He chose those He would rescue from His own wrath on sin and wrote their names in the Book of Life. He is no reluctant Savior; in fact, Scripture frequently gives Him that title (Ps. 106:21; Isa. 43:3, 11; 45:15, 21; 49:26; 60:16; 63:8; Hos. 13:4; Luke 1:47; 1 Tim. 1:1; 2:3; 4:10; Titus 1:3, 4; 2:10, 13; 3:4, 6; Jude 25).

From Genesis 3:8–9 where God said, "Where are you?" He has been seeking to save sinners. Ezekiel 34:16 says, "I will seek the lost, bring back the scattered, bind up the broken and strengthen the sick." He Himself is the eager reconciler, as Paul wrote to the Romans:

> Much more then, having now been justified by His blood, we shall be saved from the wrath of God through Him. For if while we were enemies we were reconciled to God through the death of His Son, much more, having been reconciled, we shall be saved by His life. And not only this, but we also exult in God through our Lord Jesus Christ, through whom we have now received the reconciliation. (Rom. 5:9–11)

It is to God's plan through Jesus Christ that we owe the gratitude for our reconciliation.

Both the verb *katallassō* (**reconciled**) and the noun *katallagē* (**reconciliation**) appear in the New Testament only in Paul's writings. The terms always portray God as the reconciler and sinners as the ones reconciled, since it was human sin that ruptured the relationship between God and man (cf. Isa. 59:2). In Romans 5:11 Paul declares, "We also exult in God through our Lord Jesus Christ, through whom we have now received the reconciliation." To the Ephesians Paul wrote,

> But now in Christ Jesus you who formerly were far off have been brought near by the blood of Christ. For He Himself is our peace, who made both groups into one and broke down the barrier of the dividing wall, by abolishing in His flesh the enmity, which is the Law of commandments contained in ordinances, so that in Himself He might make the two into one new man, thus establishing peace, and might reconcile them both in one body to God through the cross, by it having put to death the enmity. (Eph. 2:13–16)

Colossians 1:20–22 affirms that God chose

> through [Christ] to reconcile all things to Himself, having made peace through the blood of His cross; through Him, I say, whether things on earth or things in heaven. And although you were formerly alienated and hostile in mind, engaged in evil deeds, yet He has now reconciled you in His fleshly body through death, in order to present you before Him holy and blameless and beyond reproach.

Thus, reconciliation is not something man does but what he receives; it is not what he accomplishes but what he embraces. Reconciliation does not happen when man decides to stop rejecting God but when God decides to stop rejecting man. It is a divine provision by which God's holy displeasure against alienated sinners is appeased, His hostility against them removed, and a harmonious relationship between Him and them established. Reconciliation occurs because God was graciously willing to design a way to have all the sins of those who are His removed from them "as far as the east is from the west" (Ps. 103:12), "cast all their sins into the depths of the sea" (Mic. 7:19), and "cast all [their] sins behind [His] back" (Isa. 38:17).

In the most magnanimous expression of sacrificial love the universe will ever know, God reconciled believers to Himself **through Christ;** that is, at His expense. God the Son's perfect sacrifice is the only one that could satisfy the demands of God the Father's holy justice. Jesus Christ is the only Mediator between God and man (1 Tim. 2:5; cf. Heb. 8:6; 9:15; 12:24), and "there is salvation in no one else; for there is no other name under heaven that has been given among men by which we must be saved" (Acts 4:12). God, for His own purpose and by His own will, designed the sacrificial death of His Son to reconcile believers to Himself:

> But now in Christ Jesus you who formerly were far off have been brought near by the blood of Christ. For He Himself is our peace, who made both groups into one and broke down the barrier of the dividing wall, by abolishing in His flesh the enmity, which is the Law of commandments contained in ordinances, so that in Himself He might make the two into one new man, thus establishing peace, and might reconcile them both in one body to God through the cross, by it having put to death the enmity. (Eph. 2:13–16)

"[Christ] has now reconciled [them] in His fleshly body through death," making them "holy and blameless and beyond reproach" in the sight of God (Col. 1:22). "Now once at the consummation of the ages [Jesus Christ] has been manifested to put away sin by the sacrifice of Himself" (Heb. 9:26); "He, having offered one sacrifice for sins for all time, sat down at the right hand of God" (Heb. 10:12). His sacrifice propitiated God's holy wrath (Rom. 3:25; Heb. 2:17; 1 John 2:2; 4:10), making reconciliation possible.

It is to all reconciled people that God gives **the ministry of reconciliation.** This is equal to the Great Commission (Matt. 28:19–20) and all calls to proclaim the gospel. *Diakonia* (**ministry**) denotes humble service, such as serving meals (cf. Luke 10:40; Acts 6:1). But though the messengers may be humble (see the discussion of 4:7 in chapter 10 of this volume), the message they proclaim to the lost world is the most exalted one ever proclaimed.

RECONCILIATION IS BY THE ACT OF FORGIVENESS

namely, that God was in Christ reconciling the world to Himself, not counting their trespasses against them, and He has committed to us the word of reconciliation. (5:19)

The phrase *hōs hoti* (**namely**) introduces Paul's explanation of how **God was in Christ reconciling the world to Himself.** The phrase **in Christ,** along with the phrase "through Christ" in verse 18, identifies the Son of God as the agent of reconciling. The phrase **in Christ** identifies the way that agency operates—by union between the believer and the Savior. All who are **in Christ** become "ambassadors for Christ" (v. 20).

The phrase **reconciling the world** must not be understood as teaching universalism, the false doctrine that all people will be saved. If God has reconciled the world, universalists simplistically argue, then the barrier between God and man has been removed for all, and everyone will be saved.

Scripture does teach that there is a sense in which Christ died for the whole world. John the Baptist declared of Him, "Behold, the Lamb of God who takes away the sin of the world!" (John 1:29). In the familiar words of John 3:16, "For God so loved the world, that He gave His only begotten Son, that whoever believes in Him shall not perish, but have eternal life." The Bible twice calls Jesus Christ "the Savior of the world" (John 4:42; 1 John 4:14). Jesus declared in John 6:51, "I am the living bread that came down out of heaven; if anyone eats of this bread, he will live forever; and the bread also which I will give for the life of the world is My flesh." First Timothy 2:6 says that He "gave Himself as a ransom for all;" Hebrews 2:9 says that "by the grace of God He might taste death for everyone"; and 1 John 2:2 says that "He Himself is the propitiation for our sins; and not for ours only, but also for those of the whole world."

Those passages cannot mean that Christ actually paid the penalty for everyone's sins, because the Bible teaches that most people will suffer eternal punishment in hell (Matt. 25:41, 46; 2 Thess. 1:9; Rev. 14:9–11; 20:11–15; cf. Ezek. 18:4, 20; Matt. 7:13–14; Luke 13:23–24; John 8:24), and few will be saved (Matt. 7:13–14). If Christ paid the penalty for everyone's sins, how could God sentence people to hell for sins that Christ bore the punishment for? And if He did not pay for the sins of those who are eternally lost, then in what sense was **God . . . in Christ reconciling the world to Himself?**

The answer to that apparent dilemma is that the universal language (e.g., "world," "all," "everyone") in the above-mentioned passages must be understood as referring to mankind in general. Christ did not die for all men without exception, but for all men without distinction. **World,** in this context, indicates the sphere in which reconciliation takes place; it denotes the class of beings with whom God seeks reconciliation—people from every national, racial, and ethnic group.

Christ's death *does* have infinite and unlimited value, because He is the infinite Son of God. His sacrifice is sufficient to pay the penalty for the sins of as many or as few as God saves. Because the intrinsic merit of Christ's death is unlimited, the offer of salvation is legitimately unlimited as well. Therefore the general call to salvation goes out to all men (Isa. 45:22; 55:1; Matt. 11:28; 22:14; Rev. 22:17); "God is now declaring to men that all people everywhere should repent" (Acts 17:30); and believers can call every person in the world to come to Christ (Matt. 28:19; Luke

24:47; Acts 1:8). But though the gospel is freely offered to all, Christ's death actually expiated only the sins of those who would believe.

God has determined from all eternity those who would believe in the Lord Jesus Christ; "He chose [them] in Him before the foundation of the world" (Eph. 1:4), and their names have "been written from the foundation of the world in the book of life of the Lamb who has been slain" (Rev. 13:8; cf. 17:8; 21:27). God designed the atonement of Jesus Christ to be efficacious only for those people and actually pay the penalty for their sins alone. For that reason, Scripture also presents a narrow perspective of the beneficiaries of Christ's death. In John 10:11 Jesus declared, "I am the good shepherd; the good shepherd lays down His life for the sheep," while in verse 15 He added, "I lay down My life for the sheep." In His high-priestly prayer Jesus said, "I ask on their behalf; I do not ask on behalf of the world, but of those whom You have given Me; for they are Yours" (John 17:9). God "did not spare His own Son, but delivered Him over for us all . . . God's elect . . . those whom He [justifies]" (Rom. 8:32–33). "Husbands, love your wives," Paul admonished, "just as Christ also loved the church and gave Himself up for her" (Eph. 5:25).

It is helpful in this context to insert part of my exposition of 1 Timothy 4:10 from another volume in this commentary series. That verse reads, "For it is for this we labor and strive, because we have fixed our hope on the living God, who is the Savior of all men, especially of believers." Commenting on that text I wrote,

> In what sense God **is the Savior of all men, especially of believers** has been much disputed. Some, wanting to eliminate the scriptural teaching of an eternal hell, argue that Paul here teaches universalism, that all men will be saved. That view violates the basic hermeneutical principle known as *analogia Scriptura.* According to that principle, the Bible never contradicts itself. It will never teach something in one passage that violates what it teaches elsewhere.
>
> The Bible clearly teaches that those who reject God will be sentenced to hell (Rev. 20:11–15). Matthew 25:41 and 46 state that the duration of that punishment will be eternal. Second Thessalonians 1:8–9 says that those who do not know God and refuse to obey the gospel will suffer eternal punishment away from God's presence. Jesus repeatedly spoke of the danger of hell (Matt. 8:12; 13:41–42, 49–50; 22:13; 24:51; 25:30; Luke 13:28). He solemnly warned those who rejected Him that they would die in their sins (John 8:24). Universalism is undeniably contrary to Scripture, since the same words in the original that describe hell as eternal also describe God and heaven as eternal.
>
> A second view might be dubbed the potential/actual view. According to this view, Christ is potentially the Savior of all men, but actually only

of those who believe. It is true that Christ's death was powerful enough to have redeemed the whole human race and to satisfy the justice of God and remove the barrier between God and all men. Therefore, all can be called to salvation and justly damned if they refuse that call. By means of Christ's death, God made provision for the sins of the world (cf. the discussion of 1 Tim. 2:6 in chapter 6 of this volume).

That such is not the teaching of this verse, however, is revealed by the use of the adverb *malista* (**especially**), which must mean that all men will enjoy to some extent the same kind of salvation as **believers** enjoy. The adverb is not adversative or contrastive, it cannot be saying that **all men** are saved in one sense, but believers in another. The difference is one of degree, not kind.

It seems best to understand this verse to be teaching that God is really the Savior of all men, who actually does save them—but only in the temporal sense, while believers He saves in the eternal sense. In both cases, He is their Savior and there is a saving that He does on their behalf. In this life, all men experience to some degree the protecting, delivering, sustaining power of God. Believers will experience that to the fullest degree for time and for all eternity.

The word **Savior** is not always in Scripture limited to salvation from sin. In the Septuagint, the Greek translation of the Old Testament, *sotēr* (**Savior**) is sometimes used in the lesser sense of "deliverer" (cf. Judg. 3:9; 2 Kings 13:5; Neh. 9:27). Words in the same word group occasionally have that sense in the New Testament as well (cf. Luke 1:71; Acts 7:25; 27:34; Phil. 1:19; Heb. 11:7). A related word, *sōzō* ("to save") is used in the Gospels to refer to physical healing (Matt. 9:21–22; Mark 5:23; Luke 8:36, 50; John 11:12; cf. Acts 4:9). God **is the Savior of all men** in that He withholds the death and judgment all sinners should receive because of sin (cf. Ezek. 18:4, 32; Rom. 6:23). The reality that God delivers men from instant damnation and does "good and [gives them] rains from heaven and fruitful seasons, satisfying [their] hearts with food and gladness" (Acts 14:17) shows He is the Savior of all. He graciously gives "to all people life and breath and all things" (Acts 17:25), and "causes His sun to rise on the evil and the good, and sends rain on the righteous and the unrighteous" (Matt. 5:45). He gives common grace to all men. Unbelievers experience God's goodness and mercy in that they are not instantly killed for their sin. Nor does He give them constant pain and permanent deprivation. They experience His temporal blessings in this life.

That principle is illustrated in Isaiah 63:8–10:

> For He said, "Surely, they are My people, sons who will not deal falsely." So He became their Savior. In all their affliction He was afflicted, and the angel of His presence saved them; in His love

and in His mercy He redeemed them, and He lifted them and carried them all the days of old. But they rebelled and grieved His Holy Spirit; therefore He turned Himself to become their enemy, He fought against them.

Verse 8 says God became Israel's Savior. He brought the nation out of Egypt, and cared for them. He provided food, water, and deliverance from their enemies. That He was not the Savior in a spiritual sense of every Israelite is clear from verse 10, which says He became their enemy and fought against them. That passage is analogous to Paul's thought in 4:10. God **is the Savior of all men** in the temporal sense, and **especially of believers** in the spiritual sense that they are delivered from sin's penalty forever! (The MacArthur New Testament Commentary: *1 Timothy* [Chicago: Moody, 1995], 167–69)

The phrase **not counting their trespasses against them** reveals the means of reconciliation—the forgiveness of sins. Only by having the guilt of sin forgiven can sinners be reconciled to God, since it is sin that separates them eternally from Him. Isaiah wrote, "Your iniquities have made a separation between you and your God, and your sins have hidden His face from you so that He does not hear" (Isa. 59:2). "You and your sins must separate," warned Charles Spurgeon, "or you and your God will never come together" ("Rightly Dividing the Word of Truth," in *The Metropolitan Tabernacle Pulpit*, vol. 21 [Pasadena, Tex.: Pilgrim, 1980], 88).

Like the gracious king in the Lord's parable (Matt. 18:27), God freely forgives repentant and believing sinners, canceling their unpayable debt and reconciling them to Himself (1 Cor. 1:30; Phil. 1:11; 3:9; 2 Peter 1:1; cf. Isa. 61:10). Expressing the exhilaration of forgiveness David wrote, "How blessed is he whose transgression is forgiven, whose sin is covered! How blessed is the man to whom the Lord does not impute iniquity" (Ps. 32:1–2). In Romans 4:8 Paul echoed that glorious reality, writing, "Blessed is the man whose sin the Lord will not take into account." Earlier in that chapter he described God as "Him who justifies the ungodly" (v. 5; cf. Rom. 3:26), while he reminded the Colossians that God has "forgiven us all our transgressions" (Col. 2:13). Christ died in the place of believers, paying the penalty for their sin and bearing its guilt. Their sin is no longer charged to their account and never will be again (cf. Rom. 8:31–39). All debts have been fully paid by Christ's righteousness imputed to their account (cf. the discussion of 5:21 in chapter 16 of this volume).

To all those whom He has reconciled, God **has committed** (*tithēmi;* lit., "placed" or "set") **. . . the word of reconciliation.** Paul was so overwhelmed with the responsibility and privilege of preaching the message of reconciliation, which is the ministry of reconciliation mentioned in verse 18, that he clarified that truth here. *Logos* (**word**) is more than just a synonym for "message," as Philip E. Hughes explains:

> In Greek thought, *logos* indicates what is true and trustworthy as opposed to the term "myth" (*mythos*) which is descriptive of what is fictitious and spurious. Socrates, for example, declares that a particular story is "no fictitious myth but a true logos." Hence the term "logos" carries with it, like a kind of overtone, the implication of truth and genuineness, and is accordingly peculiarly appropriate as a synonym for the gospel, which is "the word of truth." (*The Second Epistle to the Corinthians*, The New International Commentary on the New Testament [Grand Rapids: Eerdmans, 1992], 207)

Scripture therefore describes the message of reconciliation as the word (*logos*) of the kingdom (Matt. 13:19), salvation (Acts 13:26), the gospel (Acts 15:7), the cross (1 Cor. 1:18), life (Phil. 2:16), and truth (Eph. 1:13; Col. 1:5). In a world of religious myths, Christians proclaim the truth about the only way that people can be reconciled to God and, thereby, escape hell and enjoy heaven forever.

RECONCILIATION IS BY THE OBEDIENCE OF FAITH

Therefore, we are ambassadors for Christ, as though God were making an appeal through us; we beg you on behalf of Christ, be reconciled to God. (5:20)

While it is true, as noted above, that God alone is the reconciler, reconciliation nevertheless does not happen apart from the sinner's faith. **Therefore,** Paul wrote, **we are ambassadors for Christ** (cf. Eph. 6:20). As in our day, being an ambassador in ancient times was an important and highly regarded duty. **Ambassadors** is a form of the verb *presbeuō*, which derives from *presbus* ("old man"). The term is an apt one, for ambassadors in ancient times were usually older, experienced men. An ambassador is both a messenger for and a representative of the one who sent him, and believers are messengers and representatives of the court of heaven. And just as an ambassador lives in a foreign land, so also do believers. Though citizens of heaven (Phil. 3:20), they represent their King in this world, where they live "as aliens and strangers" (1 Peter 2:11). They proclaim to the lost, perishing rebels of this fallen world the good news that they can be reconciled to the holy King of heaven:

> For "Whoever will call on the name of the Lord will be saved." How then will they call on Him in whom they have not believed? How will they

believe in Him whom they have not heard? And how will they hear without a preacher? How will they preach unless they are sent? Just as it is written, "How beautiful are the feet of those who bring good news of good things!" (Rom. 10:13–15)

Because believers are His ambassadors, it is **as though God,** the Savior Father, **were making an appeal** to the lost **through** them. **We beg** unbelievers also **on behalf of** the Savior Son, **Christ, to be reconciled to God.** This begging of people to be reconciled makes it clear that the sinner is never delivered from wrath and judgment to blessing and reward without personal response to the truth of the gospel through the means He has provided—faith. In John 6:47 Jesus said, "He who believes has eternal life" (cf. v. 40; 1:12; 3:16, 18, 36; 5:24; 1 John 5:13). God is "the justifier of the one who has faith in Jesus" (Rom. 3:26), because "a man is justified by faith apart from works of the Law" (Rom. 3:28, cf. v. 30). In a passage demonstrating that Abraham was justified by faith alone Paul wrote, "But to the one who does not work, but believes in Him who justifies the ungodly, his faith is credited as righteousness" (Rom. 4:5). It is those who have "been justified by faith" who "have peace with God" (Rom. 5:1). To the Galatians, under assault by legalistic heretics teaching salvation by works, Paul wrote

> Nevertheless knowing that a man is not justified by the works of the Law but through faith in Christ Jesus, even we have believed in Christ Jesus, so that we may be justified by faith in Christ and not by the works of the Law; since by the works of the Law no flesh will be justified. . . . Now that no one is justified by the Law before God is evident; for, "The righteous man shall live by faith." . . . Therefore the Law has become our tutor to lead us to Christ, so that we may be justified by faith. (Gal. 2:16; 3:11, 24)

Paul wrote to the Philippians that his hope of salvation in Christ was "not [based on] having a righteousness of [his] own derived from the Law, but that which is through faith in Christ, the righteousness which comes from God on the basis of faith" (Phil. 3:9).

The objective element of saving faith involves believing that Jesus is God (John 8:24), that God raised Him from the dead (Rom. 4:24; 10:9), that there is salvation in no one else (John 14:6; Acts 4:12), and confessing Him as Lord (Rom. 10:9). But there is an often-overlooked subjective element of saving faith, a humble attitude of mourning over sin, repentance, and pleading with God for mercy. James wrote, "Draw near to God and He will draw near to you. Cleanse your hands, you sinners; and purify your hearts, you double-minded. Be miserable and mourn and weep; let your laughter be turned into mourning and your joy to gloom. Humble yourselves in the presence of the Lord, and He will exalt you" (James 4:8–10; cf. Matt. 5:3–11).

Paul saw his mission, as Christ's ambassador as one, "to bring about the obedience of faith among all the Gentiles for His name's sake" (Rom. 1:5). The Lord Jesus Christ assigned that same mission to all believers when He commanded them, "Go therefore and make disciples of all the nations, baptizing them in the name of the Father and the Son and the Holy Spirit" (Matt. 28:19). There is therefore no higher calling, no greater privilege, no more urgent task than the ministry of reconciliation God has entrusted to all believers.

Fifteen Words of Hope
(2 Corinthians 5:21)

16

He made Him who knew no sin to be sin on our behalf, so that we might become the righteousness of God in Him. (5:21)

It began with one of history's earliest recorded instances of biological warfare. In 1347 a Mongol army besieging the Genoese trading post of Caffa in the Crimea (modern Ukraine) catapulted the bodies of bubonic plague victims over the town's walls. The terrified defenders fled to Italy, carrying with them the deadly plague bacteria (and the rats and fleas that spread them). Over the next three years the plague spread throughout Europe in the massive epidemic now known as the Black Death. Before the epidemic ran its course an estimated twenty million people—approximately one-third to one-half of Europe's population—perished. The coming centuries would see recurring outbreaks of the bubonic plague, which would remain a dangerous, unchecked killer until the development of antibiotics in the twentieth century.

Though the Black Death is the most infamous epidemic in history, it was not the only one. The influenza epidemic of 1918–19 killed an estimated thirty to fifty million people, and several million more died at about that same time in an outbreak of typhus in eastern Europe. Other infectious diseases, such as malaria, yellow fever, and in more recent times AIDS, have also claimed uncounted millions of victims.

But there is one plague that is more widespread and deadly than all others combined; it is, as the Puritan writer Ralph Venning called it, the "plague of plagues." It affects every person who ever lived—and is 100 percent fatal. Unlike other plagues, which cause only physical death, this plague causes spiritual and eternal death as well. It is the plague of sin.

Because Adam's fall plunged the entire human race into sin (Rom. 5:12–21), all people are sinners from birth. "Behold, I was brought forth in iniquity," lamented David, "and in sin my mother conceived me" (Ps. 51:5). In Psalm 58:3 he added, "The wicked are estranged from the womb; these who speak lies go astray from birth" (cf. Gen. 8:21; Isa. 48:8). Not only are all people sinners by nature, they are also sinners by action. To the Romans Paul wrote, "There is none righteous, not even one" (Rom. 3:10; cf. Pss. 14:1–3; 53:1–3). Later in that chapter he added, "For all have sinned and fall short of the glory of God" (Rom. 3:23); consequently, "there is no man who does not sin" (1 Kings 8:46), and no one can say, "I have cleansed my heart, I am pure from my sin" (Prov. 20:9).

The inevitable outcome for all those infected by the sin plague is death. Ezekiel 18:20 states plainly, "The person who sins will die" (cf. v. 4). Adam's tragic epitaph, "and he died" (Gen. 5:5) will be written for all his descendants (cf. vv. 8, 11, 14, 17, 20, 27, 31; 9:29). Nor is the prognosis any better in the spiritual realm. Sin produces two disastrous spiritual consequences: alienation from God in this life (Eph. 2:12; 4:18; Col. 1:21), and unrelenting punishment in hell in eternity (Matt. 25:41, 46; 2 Thess. 1:9; Rev. 14:9–11; 20:11–15).

But the good news of the gospel is that there is a cure for the sinner infected by the deadly sin epidemic. God, in His mercy and love, provided a remedy for sin—the sacrifice of His Son. The Lord Jesus Christ "released us from our sins by His blood" (Rev. 1:5), "for by one offering He has perfected for all time those who are sanctified" (Heb. 10:14). Those who experience "redemption through His blood, the forgiveness of [their] trespasses, according to the riches of His grace" (Eph. 1:7) are cured from sin's deadly spiritual effects. As a result, they have "passed out of death into life" (John 5:24; 1 John 3:14), and "are no longer strangers and aliens, but . . . are fellow citizens with the saints, and are of God's household" (Eph. 2:19).

How God made the cure possible is the theme of verses 18–20. In those three verses, Paul described the glorious truth of reconciliation—that the sin-severed relationship between holy God and unregenerate sinners can be restored "through" and "in" Christ. But reconciliation raises some profound questions. How can an absolutely and infinitely holy God be reconciled to sinners? How can His just and holy law, which demands the condemnation and punishment of all who violate it, be satisfied? How can those who deserve no mercy receive it? How can God uphold true righteousness and give grace? How can the demands of both justice and love be met? How can God be both "just and the justifier" (Rom. 3:26) of sinners?

As hard as those questions seem, one brief verse answers them all and resolves the seeming paradox of redemption. With a conciseness and brevity reflective of the Holy Spirit, this one brief sentence, only fifteen words in the Greek text, resolves the dilemma of reconciliation. This sentence reveals the essence of the atonement, expresses the heart of the gospel message, and articulates the most glorious truth in Scripture—how fallen man's sin-sundered relationship to God can be restored. Verse 21 is like a cache of rare jewels, each deserving of a careful, reverential examination under the magnifying glass of Scripture. It yields truths about the benefactor, the substitute, the beneficiaries, and the benefit.

The Benefactor

He made (5:21*a*)

The end of verse 20 reveals the antecedent of **He** to be God the Father, as seen in the previous chapter of this volume. Reconciliation is His plan, and it could not occur unless He initiated and applied it. Sinners cannot devise their own religious approach to God, because they are "dead in [their] trespasses and sins" (Eph. 2:1). The damning lie of false religion is that man can reconcile himself to God by his own efforts, but all attempts to do so are futile. Sinners' "righteous deeds are like a filthy garment; and all of [them] wither like a leaf, and [their] iniquities, like the wind, take [them] away" (Isa. 64:6). As a result, "There is none righteous, not even one" (Rom. 3:10).

Not even the "Israelites, to whom belongs the adoption as sons, and the glory and the covenants and the giving of the Law and the temple service and the promises, whose are the fathers, and from whom is the Christ according to the flesh" (Rom. 9:4–5) could devise a way to reconcile themselves to God by their own efforts. Romans 10:1–3, expressing Paul's deep concern for them, reflects that truth:

> Brethren, my heart's desire and my prayer to God for them is for their salvation. For I testify about them that they have a zeal for God, but not in accordance with knowledge. For not knowing about God's righteousness and seeking to establish their own, they did not subject themselves to the righteousness of God.

Despite their zeal for God, they had not achieved salvation, because they sought it through their own righteousness. The religion of human achievement, whether practiced by Jews or Gentiles, can never bring reconciliation with God. The only way reconciliation can take place is if God reached out to sinners; and He did by the sacrifice of His Son.

Jesus therefore did not go to the cross because fickle people turned on Him, though they did. He did not go to the cross because demon-deceived false religious leaders plotted His death, though they did. He did not go to the cross because Judas betrayed Him, though he did. He did not die because an angry, unruly mob intimidated a Roman governor into sentencing Him to crucifixion, though they did. Jesus went to the cross as the outworking of God's plan to reconcile sinners to Himself. In the first Christian sermon ever preached, Peter declared to the nation of Israel that Jesus was "delivered over [to death] by the predetermined plan and foreknowledge of God" (Acts 2:23; cf. 3:18; 13:27; Matt. 26:24; Luke 22:22; John 18:11; Heb. 10:5, 7).

Only God could design an atonement for sin that would satisfy the demands of His justice, propitiate His wrath, and be consistent with His love, grace, and mercy. Only God could conceive the plan in which the second person of the Trinity would, "being found in appearance as a man, [humble] Himself by becoming obedient to the point of death, even death on a cross" (Phil. 2:8). Only God knew what it would take to rescue sinners "from the domain of darkness, and [transfer them] to the kingdom of His beloved Son" (Col. 1:13), making them "qualified . . . to share in the inheritance of the saints in Light" (Col. 1:12). Only God knew how to make sinners deserving of hell acceptable in His sight and fit to spend eternity in His presence. Therefore, only God could author and execute the plan of redemption and reconcile sinners to Himself. That plan is so utterly beyond the comprehension of the unregenerate that it seems foolishness to them (1 Cor. 1:18, 23; 2:14). No religion of human design has anything like it.

Reconciliation flows out of God's love; it was because He "so loved the world, that He gave His only begotten Son, that whoever believes in Him shall not perish, but have eternal life" (John 3:16). "God demonstrates His own love toward us," wrote Paul, "in that while we were yet sinners, Christ died for us" (Rom. 5:8); though "we were enemies we were reconciled to God through the death of His Son" (Rom. 5:10). Because "God [is] rich in mercy, [and] because of His great love with which He loved us, even when we were dead in our transgressions, [He] made us alive together with Christ (Eph. 2:4–5).

It is this emphasis on a loving God reaching out to sinners that sets Christianity apart from the false religions of the world. The gods of those religions are sometimes depicted as cruel, angry, and hostile and hence to be feared and appeased—even by such appalling means as child sacrifice (cf. 2 Kings 16:3; 23:10; Jer. 32:35; Ezek. 16:21; 23:37). Others are viewed as apathetic and indifferent to the worshipers who grovel before them, like Baal, whose followers Elijah mockingly challenged, "Call out with a loud voice, for he is a god; either he is occupied or gone aside, or is on a journey, or perhaps he is asleep and needs to be awakened" (1 Kings 18:27). Their devotees are often driven to desperate measures to get their attention (cf. 1 Kings 18:28).

But Christianity proclaims the glorious, liberating truth that God is neither hostile nor indifferent but a loving Savior by nature. He does not need to be appeased (and indeed cannot be by any human means). Instead, He Himself has provided His own appeasement for justice and the means for sinners to become His beloved children through the sacrifice of His Son (Rom. 8:32; 1 John 4:10, 14), which fully propitiated His wrath. As a result, those who come to Him through faith are "justified as a gift by His grace through the redemption which is in Christ Jesus" (Rom. 3:24). Because Christ's sacrifice perfectly satisified the demands of God's righteousness and justice, God freely offers forgiveness and reconciliation: "Ho! Every one who thirsts, come to the waters; and you who have no money come, buy and eat. Come, buy wine and milk without money and without cost" (Isa. 55:1; cf. Rev. 22:17).

Reconciliation required the death of God's Son because "the wages of sin is death" (Rom 6:23) and therefore, "The person who sins will die" (Ezek. 18:20). The slaughter of countless millions of sacrificial animals under the Old Testament economy graphically illustrated that truth. Though unable to atone for sin, since "it is impossible for the blood of bulls and goats to take away sins" (Heb. 10:4), those sacrifices forcibly drove home the point that sin results in death, and death is required to satisfy the demands of God's law when it is violated. They also made the people who incessantly offered them long for the final substitute to whom the sacrifices pointed (cf. Isa. 53). And when in accordance with the Father's plan the final substitute came, He willingly laid down His life to bring the final satisfaction to God only pictured in the sacrificial ceremonies and ritual killings of animals (John 10:11, 18; Phil. 2:7–8).

THE SUBSTITUTE

Him who knew no sin to be sin (5:21*b*)

This designation points unmistakably to the only possible sacrifice for sin. It eliminates every human who ever lived, "for there is no man who does not sin" (1 Kings 8:46), since "all have sinned and fall short of the glory of God" (Rom. 3:23). Only one who **knew no sin** of his own could qualify to bear the full wrath of God against the sins of others. The perfect sacrifice for sin would have to be a human being, for only a man could die for other men. Yet he would also have to be God, for only God is sinless. That narrows the field to one, the God-man, Jesus Christ.

In the design of God, the second person of the Trinity became a man (Gal. 4:4–5). The Bible makes it clear that though He had a human mother, the Lord Jesus Christ did not have a human father. Joseph is never referred to as His father, because He was conceived by the Holy Spirit (Matt. 1:18, 20; Luke 1:35). As the God-man, He was the perfect One to be the sacrifice for sin (John 1:29; 1 Peter 1:19), fulfilling the Old Testament picture of the unblemished sacrificial lamb (Ex. 12:5; Ezek 46:13).

The impeccability (sinlessness) of Jesus Christ is universally affirmed in Scripture, by believers and unbelievers alike. In John 8:46 Jesus challenged His Jewish opponents, "Which one of you convicts Me of sin?" Before sentencing Him to death, Pilate repeatedly affirmed His innocence, declaring, "I find no guilt in this man" (Luke 23:4; cf. vv. 14, 22). The repentant thief on the cross said of Jesus, "This man has done nothing wrong" (Luke 23:41). Even the hardened, callous Roman centurion in charge of the execution detail admitted, "Certainly this man was innocent" (Luke 23:47).

The apostles, those who most closely observed Jesus' life during His earthly ministry, also testified to His sinlessness. Peter publicly proclaimed Him to be the "Holy and Righteous One" (Acts 3:14). In his first epistle he declared Jesus to be "unblemished and spotless" (1 Peter 1:19); one "who committed no sin" (2:22); and "just" (3:18). John also testified to His sinlessness, writing, "in Him there is no sin" (1 John 3:5). The inspired writer of Hebrews notes that "we do not have a high priest who cannot sympathize with our weaknesses, but One who has been tempted in all things as we are, yet without sin" (Heb. 4:15), because He is "holy, innocent, undefiled, separated from sinners and exalted above the heavens" (7:26).

But the most powerful testimony concerning Christ's sinlessness comes from God the Father. On two occasions He said of Christ, "This is My beloved Son, in whom I am well-pleased" (Matt. 3:17; 17:5). Jesus' unbroken fellowship with the Father also testifies to His sinlessness; in John 10:30 He said simply, "I and the Father are one" (cf. 14:9).

After presenting Jesus as the absolutely holy substitute for sinners, the text makes the remarkable statement that God made Him **to be sin.** That important phrase requires a careful understanding. It does not mean that Christ became a sinner; the above-mentioned verses establishing His utter sinlessness unequivocally rule out that possibility. As God in human flesh, He could not possibly have committed any sin or in any way violated God's law. It is equally unthinkable that God, whose "eyes are too pure to approve evil" (Hab. 1:13; cf. James 1:13), would make anyone a sinner, let alone His own Holy Son. He was the unblemished Lamb while on the cross, personally guilty of no evil.

Isaiah 53:4–6 describes the only sense in which Jesus could have been made sin:

> Surely our griefs He Himself bore,
> And our sorrows He carried;
> Yet we ourselves esteemed Him stricken,
> Smitten of God, and afflicted.
> But He was pierced through for our transgressions,
> He was crushed for our iniquities;
> The chastening for our well-being fell upon Him,
> And by His scourging we are healed.
> All of us like sheep have gone astray,
> Each of us has turned to his own way;
> But the Lord has caused the iniquity of us all
> To fall on Him.

Christ was not made a sinner, nor was He punished for any sin of His own. Instead, the Father treated Him as if He were a sinner by charging to His account the sins of everyone who would ever believe. All those sins were charged against Him as if He had personally committed them, and He was punished with the penalty for them on the cross, experiencing the full fury of God's wrath unleashed against them all. It was at that moment that "Jesus cried out with a loud voice, saying, . . . 'My God, My God, why have You forsaken Me?'" (Matt. 27:46). It is crucial, therefore, to understand that the only sense in which Jesus was made sin was by imputation. He was personally pure, yet officially culpable; personally holy, yet forensically guilty. But in dying on the cross Christ did not become evil like we are, nor do redeemed sinners become inherently as holy as He is. God credits believers' sin to Christ's account, and His righteousness to theirs.

In Galatians 3:10, 13 Paul further explained the necessity of believers' sins being imputed to Christ. In verse 10 he wrote that "as many as are of the works of the Law are under a curse; for it is written, 'Cursed is everyone who does not abide by all things written in the book of the law, to perform them.'" There is no way for sinners to reconcile themselves to God, because no one is able to "abide by all things written in the book of the law to perform them." Violating even one precept of the Law warrants eternal punishment in hell. Thus, the entire human race is cursed and unable to do anything to lift that curse. Therefore, the only reason believers can be reconciled to God is because "Christ redeemed us from the curse of the Law, having become a curse for us—for it is written, 'Cursed is everyone who hangs on a tree'" (v. 13). Were it not for the fact that "while we were still helpless, at the right time Christ died for the ungodly" (Rom. 5:6), no one could be reconciled to God.

THE BENEFICIARIES

on our behalf, (5:21*c*)

The antecedent of **our** is the phrase "ambassadors for Christ" in verse 20; those to whom the "word of reconciliation" was committed (v. 19), who have been reconciled to God (v. 18), and are new creatures in Christ (v. 17). Christ's substitutionary death was efficacious only for those who would believe (John 1:12; 3:16–18; Rom. 10:9–10); all those whom the Father gives Him and draws to Him (John 6:37, 44, 65). (For further information on this point, see the discussion of verse 14 in chapter 14 of this volume.) That God raised Jesus from the dead is proof that He accepted His sacrifice on behalf of His people (Rom. 4:25).

THE BENEFIT

so that we might become the righteousness of God in Him. (5:21*d*)

The phrase **so that** reflects a purpose clause in the Greek text. The benefit of God's imputing believers' sins to Christ and His righteousness to them is that they **become** righteous before Him. They are "found in Him, not having a righteousness of [their] own derived from the Law, but that which is through faith in Christ, the righteousness which comes from God on the basis of faith" (Phil. 3:9). The very **righteousness** God requires before He can accept the sinner is the very righteousness He provides.

Because Jesus paid the full penalty for believers' sin, God no longer holds it against them. In Psalm 32:1 David wrote, "How blessed is he whose transgression is forgiven, whose sin is covered!" In Psalm 130:3–4 the psalmist added, "If You, Lord, should mark iniquities, O Lord, who could stand? But there is forgiveness with You, that You may be feared." In metaphorical pictures of forgiveness, God is said to have removed believers' sins as far from them as the east is from the west (Ps. 103:12); cast their sins behind His back (Isa. 38:17); promised never to remember them (Isa. 43:25); hidden them from His sight behind a thick cloud (Isa. 44:22); and cast them into the depths of the sea (Mic. 7:19).

Believers experience the blessedness of forgiveness solely by faith in the complete redemption provided by Jesus Christ; "the righteousness of God [comes] through faith in Jesus Christ for all those who believe" (Rom. 3:22). They are "justified as a gift by His grace through the redemption which is in Christ Jesus" (Rom. 3:24); therefore, God is "the justifier of the one who has faith in Jesus" (Rom. 3:26). In Romans 3:28 Paul stated definitively, "For we maintain that a man is justified by faith apart from works of the Law" (cf. 4:5; 5:1; Gal. 2:16; 3:24).

When repentant sinners acknowledge their sin (Ps. 32:5), affirm Jesus as Lord (Rom. 10:9), and trust solely in His completed work on their behalf (Acts 4:12; 16:31), God credits His righteousness to their account. On the cross God treated Jesus as if He had lived our lives with all our sin, so that God could then treat us as if we lived Christ's life of pure holiness. Our iniquitous life was legally charged to Him on the cross, as if He had lived it, so that His righteous life could be credited to us, as if we lived it. That is the doctrine of justification by imputation—the high point of the gospel. That truth, expressed so concisely and powerfully in this text, is the only cure for the sin plague.

Honor and Dishonor—The Paradox of Ministry (2 Corinthians 6:1–10)

17

And working together with Him, we also urge you not to receive the grace of God in vain—for He says, "At the acceptable time I listened to you, and on the day of salvation I helped you." Behold, now is "the acceptable time," behold, now is "the day of salvation"—giving no cause for offense in anything, so that the ministry will not be discredited, but in everything commending ourselves as servants of God, in much endurance, in afflictions, in hardships, in distresses, in beatings, in imprisonments, in tumults, in labors, in sleeplessness, in hunger, in purity, in knowledge, in patience, in kindness, in the Holy Spirit, in genuine love, in the word of truth, in the power of God; by the weapons of righteousness for the right hand and the left, by glory and dishonor, by evil report and good report; regarded as deceivers and yet true; as unknown yet well-known, as dying yet behold, we live; as punished yet not put to death, as sorrowful yet always rejoicing, as poor yet making many rich, as having nothing yet possessing all things. (6:1–10)

It is an ironic truth that the preacher is often one of the most loved and respected of men, yet at the same time one of the most hated and despised in his community. To those who believe the gospel he preaches, he is a revered spiritual father, mentor, and teacher. He proclaims to them the divine truth, encourages them, gives them hope, and instructs them in applying God's Word. But to those who reject his message, his is the judgmental voice of conviction, irritation, and agitation. To them he is a troublemaker (cf. 1 Kings 18:17; Jer. 38:2–4; Amos 7:10; Luke 23:5; Acts 16:20; 24:5), disrupting the tranquility of their shameful lives and turning their sinful world upside down (Acts 17:6).

During His earthly ministry, the Lord Jesus Christ faced the extremes of being adored and despised. While some acclaimed Him as the Lord of heaven, the fulfiller of their hopes and dreams and the source of eternal forgiveness, happiness, peace, and joy, bowing before Him in worship, others despised Him as a demon-possessed charlatan, a threat to their power, a disturber of their peace, and an enemy of their religion. That rejection culminated in the cries of the people, "Away with Him, away with Him, crucify Him!" (John 19:15).

Since Jesus was treated in such diametrically opposite ways, His followers can expect no less. Affirming that expectation, in Matthew 10:24 our Lord reminded His followers that "a disciple is not above his teacher, nor a slave above his master." In His final teaching time with the Twelve before His death, He added,

> If the world hates you, you know that it has hated Me before it hated you. If you were of the world, the world would love its own; but because you are not of the world, but I chose you out of the world, because of this the world hates you. Remember the word that I said to you, "A slave is not greater than his master." If they persecuted Me, they will also persecute you; if they kept My word, they will keep yours also. (John 15:18–20)

As ambassadors (2 Cor. 5:20), believers bring the message of reconciliation to an alienated world. Those who hear that message will either embrace the truth of it and cherish the messengers or reject both the message and those who proclaim it. Thus, Christ's messengers "are a fragrance of Christ to God among those who are being saved and among those who are perishing; to the one an aroma from death to death, to the other an aroma from life to life" (2:15–16). Those who proclaim the true gospel with power and conviction cannot expect to be popular with everyone. To be honored and dishonored, respected and reviled, is their lot; to experience the most profound blessing and at the same time suffer the most severe disappointment comes usually to the most faithful and zealous evangels.

None is a better example than Paul, who was caught up in those conflicting realities when he penned this epistle. Despite their shortcomings, the Corinthians were a blessing to him. They had shared in Christian love (12:15); earlier in this epistle he wrote of "the love which [he had] especially for [them]" (2:4); later he added, "I do not speak to condemn you, for I have said before that you are in our hearts to die together and to live together" (7:3). His heart was filled with joy because many of them had believed the gospel. Yet the Corinthian congregation had also caused Paul much heartache. He had been savagely attacked by false teachers who had infiltrated their assembly. And a trip to Corinth had not gone well for Paul, turning into a painful, sorrowful visit (cf. 2:1). The apostle experienced the full range of emotions, from the heights of joy to the depths of sorrow, in his dealings with the Corinthians.

Nowhere is such tension between honor and dishonor, between joy and sorrow, better expressed than in this epistle and especially in this passage. The polarized responses to the ministry of Paul reveal his endurance, which is related to maintaining four perspectives: privilege, pleading, protection, and paradox.

PRIVILEGE

And working together with Him, (6:1*a*)

The noblest view of ministry is to see it as **working together** (from *sunergeō;* "to cooperate with someone") in partnership **with** God. Disappointment over the difficulties in the ministry begins with a failure to understand the high privilege to which God's servants are called. As noted in the discussion of 2:14–17 in chapter 5 of this volume, all who serve Christ should be consummately grateful for the privilege and be faithful to it—no matter how severe the difficulties. The NASB italicizes the phrase **with Him,** indicating it is not in the original Greek text. The translators were correct in supplying it, however, since God is the antecedent from 5:19 ("God ... has committed to us the word of reconciliation") and 20 ("we are ambassadors for Christ, as though God were making an appeal through us"). Amazingly, the God of glory condescends to work through believers to proclaim His gospel of reconciliation.

Despite the trials he faced, Paul never lost sight of that reality. Even if no one responded to his message, the high privilege of being God's coworker was enough to sustain him. Not surprisingly, then, Paul emphasized that truth throughout his epistles. In 1 Corinthians 3:9 he stated plainly, "We are God's fellow workers." Later in that letter he wrote, "There are varieties of effects, but the same God who works all things in all persons. ... But one and the same Spirit works all these things, distributing to each one individually just as He wills" (1 Cor. 12:6, 11), and, "But by the grace of God I am what I am, and His grace toward me did not prove vain; but I labored even more than all of them, yet not I, but the grace of God with me" (1 Cor. 15:10). Paul prayed that the Ephesians would understand "what is the surpassing greatness of His power toward us who believe. These are in accordance with the working of the strength of His might" (Eph. 1:19). Later he reminded them that he was "made a minister, according to the gift of God's grace which was given to [him] according to the working of His power" (Eph. 3:7), and prayed again, "Now to Him who is able to do exceeding abundantly beyond all that we ask or think, according to the power that works within us" (v. 20; cf. John 15:4–5). He reminded the Philippians that "it is God who is at work in you, both to will and to work for His good pleasure" (Phil. 2:13; cf. Heb. 13:20–21). To the Colossians he wrote, "For this purpose also I labor, striving according to His power, which mightily works within me" (Col. 1:29). Returning to Antioch after their first missionary journey, Paul and Barnabas "gathered the church together, [and] began to report all things that God had done with them and how He had opened a door of faith to the Gentiles" (Acts 14:27; cf. 15:4).

In Mark 4:26–29 Jesus told a parable illustrating the mystery and wonder of believers' ministering together with God:

> And He was saying, "The kingdom of God is like a man who casts seed upon the soil; and he goes to bed at night and gets up by day, and the seed sprouts and grows—how, he himself does not know. The soil produces crops by itself; first the blade, then the head, then the mature grain in the head. But when the crop permits, he immediately puts in the sickle, because the harvest has come."

Those who proclaim the gospel plant the seed, but only God can generate new spiritual life and growth. As Paul wrote in his first inspired letter to the Corinthians, "I planted, Apollos watered, but God was causing the growth. So then neither the one who plants nor the one who waters is anything, but God who causes the growth" (1 Cor. 3:6–7). It was the greatest of honors, yet no cause for pride.

That Paul was humble, yet never lost the sense of awe he felt at the great privilege granted him as a minister of the gospel, is clear from what he wrote to Timothy:

> I thank Christ Jesus our Lord, who has strengthened me, because He considered me faithful, putting me into service, even though I was formerly a blasphemer and a persecutor and a violent aggressor. Yet I was shown mercy because I acted ignorantly in unbelief; and the grace of our Lord was more than abundant, with the faith and love which are found in Christ Jesus. It is a trustworthy statement, deserving full acceptance, that Christ Jesus came into the world to save sinners, among

whom I am foremost of all. Yet for this reason I found mercy, so that in me as the foremost, Jesus Christ might demonstrate His perfect patience as an example for those who would believe in Him for eternal life. (1 Tim. 1:12–16)

Overwhelmed that God saved him and called him into the ministry though he was a wretched sinner, Paul closed his testimony with a doxology: "Now to the King eternal, immortal, invisible, the only God, be honor and glory forever and ever. Amen" (1 Tim. 1:17).

PLEADING

we also urge you not to receive the grace of God in vain—for He says, "At the acceptable time I listened to you, and on the day of salvation I helped you." Behold, now is "the acceptable time," behold, now is "the day of salvation"— (6:1b–2)

Paul's use of the verb *parakaloumen* (**urge;** "plead"; "beg") in the present tense reflects his constant, passionate concern for the Corinthians (cf. 2:8; 10:1; 1 Cor. 16:15–16). God's ambassadors are privileged pleaders, begging their hearers to respond to the truth.

Specifically, Paul was urging the Corinthians **not to receive the grace of God in vain;** not to turn away from the gracious opportunity to hear the gospel of forgiveness he had so faithfully preached to them. He had poured his life into the Corinthians during his long stay in their city (Acts 18:11), pleading with them for the gospel and teaching the new converts how to grow in grace. But events in Corinth caused the apostle to fear that his intense labor had been for nothing. The church was riddled with sin, as Paul's first inspired epistle to them reveals. False teachers, those wolves in sheep's clothing both Jesus (Matt. 7:15) and Paul warned of (Acts 20:29), were luring many in the assembly away from the truth. This passionate concern for the Corinthians was behind what he wrote later:

But I am afraid that, as the serpent deceived Eve by his craftiness, your minds will be led astray from the simplicity and purity of devotion to Christ. For if one comes and preaches another Jesus whom we have not preached, or you receive a different spirit which you have not received, or a different gospel which you have not accepted, you bear this beautifully. (2 Cor. 11:3–4)

Paul could not stand idly by and allow his diligent efforts to be undone. He could not permit his spiritual children (1 Cor. 4:15) to be deceived by a false gospel or led astray from the true path of sanctification. His duty before God, like that of all faithful ministers, was to exhort people **not to receive the grace of God in vain.** The apostle had given them **the grace of God,** as embodied in the truth of the gospel of grace, for their eternal benefit.

Paul was concerned first that the Corinthians not receive God's grace in regard to salvation **in vain.** As in any church, not everyone in the Corinthian assembly was redeemed. Some had intellectual knowledge of the gospel but did not have saving faith. That is why Paul challenged them, "Test yourselves to see if you are in the faith; examine yourselves! Or do you not recognize this about yourselves, that Jesus Christ is in you— unless indeed you fail the test?" (2 Cor. 13:5). Those in the congregation who were not regenerate were in grave danger of being deceived by the false teachers. To follow those preaching another Jesus, another Spirit, and another gospel would lead to a waste of their privilege and to spiritual ruin. Paul was similarly concerned about the Galatians:

> I am amazed that you are so quickly deserting Him who called you by the grace of Christ, for a different gospel; which is really not another; only there are some who are disturbing you and want to distort the gospel of Christ. But even if we, or an angel from heaven, should preach to you a gospel contrary to what we have preached to you, he is to be accursed! As we have said before, so I say again now, if any man is preaching to you a gospel contrary to what you received, he is to be accursed! (Gal. 1:6–9)

The Corinthians were also in danger of receiving God's grace in vain with regard to sanctification. The legalists sought to turn them away from living in the power of the Spirit to living in the strength of the flesh. Paul chided the Galatians, also under assault by legalism, "Are you so foolish? Having begun by the Spirit, are you now being perfected by the flesh?" (Gal. 3:3). Sanctification, like justification, is a work of God. It does not come from legalistically conforming to an external set of rules but from a Spirit-generated, heartfelt love for and obedience to the Lord Jesus Christ.

Some of the unsaved Corinthians were being led astray by a false gospel of salvation by works. Others were saved, but legalistic false teaching was stunting their spiritual growth. In either case, the grace of God to them that sent Paul with the gospel was in danger of being nullified.

The corrupting influence of the false teachers hindered evangelism. That made the Corinthians' defection all the more galling to Paul, for it was (and still is) the time for the ministry of reconciliation. To stress the urgency of this time, Paul quoted from Isaiah 49:8, where God declared, **"At the acceptable time I listened to you, and on the day of salvation I helped you."**

There is a time in God's grace when He may be sought by sinners. The Lord warned the pre-Flood world, "My Spirit shall not strive with man forever, because he also is flesh; nevertheless his days shall be one hundred and twenty years" (Gen. 6:3). Isaiah 55:6 commands, "Seek the Lord while He may be found; call upon Him while He is near." Hosea warned that apostate Israel "will go with their flocks and herds to seek the Lord, but they will not find Him; He has withdrawn from them" (Hos. 5:6).

Repeating **behold** and **now** to emphasize his point, Paul declared that **now is "the acceptable time," "the day of salvation"** when God will listen to repentant sinners. Now, when the fields are ripe for the harvest (John 4:35), is not the time to waste gospel opportunity, or to be feeble, vacillating, or deceived by false teachers. It is the time to hold fast to the truth and faithfully proclaim it. "We must work the works of Him who sent Me as long as it is day," Jesus admonished. "Night is coming when no one can work" (John 9:4).

Knowing the urgency of the times Paul, true to the urgency of his calling, passionately pleaded with the Corinthians not to let God's grace in their lives be in vain.

PROTECTION

giving no cause for offense in anything, so that the ministry will not be discredited, but in everything commending ourselves as servants of God, in much endurance, in afflictions, in hardships, in distresses, in beatings, in imprisonments, in tumults, in labors, in sleeplessness, in hunger, in purity, in knowledge, in patience, in kindness, in the Holy Spirit, in genuine love, in the word of truth, in the power of God; by the weapons of righteousness for the right hand and the left, (6:3–7)

Paul was a protective shepherd. He knew it was inevitable that some would reject the grace of God, and he wanted to make sure that it was not because he put a stumbling block in their path. He wanted no indictment of his life and ministry, such as the one God pronounced on Israel in Romans 2:24: "The name of God is blasphemed among the Gentiles because of you." Unbelievers are blinded by Satan (2 Cor. 4:4) and unable to understand the things of God (1 Cor. 2:14). Therefore Paul was careful to give **no cause for offense in anything, so that the ministry** would **not be discredited.** He determined never to allow any stain on his virtue that would undermine the integrity of his gospel (1 Cor. 9:27). The negative adjective *mēdemian* (**no**) is a strong term and could be translated "no, not at all." It is followed by another strong negative term, *mēdeni,* which means, "not anything." Those two terms leave no room at all for an **offense** (*proskopē;* "cause of stumbling"). Paul would avoid anything that would bring disgrace on Christ or cause someone to find fault with the truth and purity of the gospel. His own integrity was protection for his people.

That the church's evangelistic outreach not be hindered was Paul's constant concern as he expressed to Titus:

> But as for you, speak the things which are fitting for sound doctrine. Older men are to be temperate, dignified, sensible, sound in faith, in love, in perseverance. Older women likewise are to be reverent in their behavior, not malicious gossips nor enslaved to much wine, teaching what is good, so that they may encourage the young women to love their husbands, to love their children, to be sensible, pure, workers at home, kind, being subject to their own husbands, so that the word of God will not be dishonored. Likewise urge the young men to be sensible; in all things show yourself to be an example of good deeds, with purity in doctrine, dignified, sound in speech which is beyond reproach, so that the opponent will be put to shame, having nothing bad to say about us. Urge bondslaves to be subject to their own masters in everything, to be well-pleasing, not argumentative, not pilfering, but showing all good faith so that they will adorn the doctrine of God our Savior in every respect. (Titus 2:1–10)

Paul knew that the church's purity was essential if it was to effectively evangelize the island of Crete (where Titus was located). To that end it needed negatively to avoid dishonoring God's Word (v. 5) and thereby not give unbelievers any cause to speak ill of it (v. 8). Positively its members needed to adorn (make attractive) the message of truth with their lives (v. 10).

Paul not only sought negatively to avoid putting up barriers to faith in Christ, but positively to be **in everything commending** himself as a **servant of God.** A minister is not commended by his seminary degree, theology, popularity, personality, or success. His life is the only letter of commendation that matters; the only one that people will read.

Ultimately, what commends faithful servants of God is their **endurance.** *Hupomonē* (**endurance**) is one of the most magnificent New Testament virtues. No single English word can fully express its rich meaning, which encompasses bearing up under hard labor, surviving the shock of battle, and remaining steadfast in the face of death. The New Testament uses it in conjunction with several other words, such as "tribulation" (Rom. 5:3), "faith" (James 1:3), "hope" (1 Thess. 1:3), and "joy" (Col. 1:11). *Hupomonē* is also associated with the idea of future glory (Rom. 2:7; 8:25); thus, it does not describe the grim, stoic, weary acceptance of trials, but rather faith, hope, and joy in anticipation of future glory. The word might best be rendered "triumphant patience." Hebrews 11 commends God's Old Testament servants for their ability to endure hostility and remain faithful.

Endurance marked Paul's life. He endured faithfully to his death despite continual temptation, threats from his enemies, and trouble in the churches, continually serving God with all his strength and providing a protective influence on the church. Earlier in this epistle Paul expressed his triumphant, patient endurance of suffering:

> We are afflicted in every way, but not crushed; perplexed, but not despairing; persecuted, but not forsaken; struck down, but not destroyed; always carrying about in the body the dying of Jesus, so that the life of Jesus also may be manifested in our body. For we who live are constantly being delivered over to death for Jesus' sake, so that the life of Jesus also may be manifested in our mortal flesh. (2 Cor. 4:8–11)

His faith never wavered; his hope never diminished; his joy never abated. He never lost sight of the reality that "the sufferings of this present time are not worthy to be compared with the glory that is to be revealed to us" (Rom. 8:18; cf. 2 Cor. 4:16–18; Acts 20:24; Phil. 3:8).

The list that follows in 2 Corinthians 6:4–7 defines the various elements of endurance. Verses 4 and 5 discuss the negative aspects, verses 6 and 7 the positive. In emotionally charged words, Paul defines the ministry of reconciliation not as one in which we make demands on God, but one in which He makes demands on us. Ambassadors of Jesus Christ do not seek greater comfort and prosperity but greater endurance.

Both the negative and positive lists may be subdivided into three groups of three. The first three negative elements are internal results of external pressures. **Afflictions** translates *thlipsis*, which refers to spiritual, physical, or emotional suffering. Paul warned in Acts 14:22 that it is "through many tribulations [*thlipsis*] [that] we must enter the kingdom of God." He also used *thlipsis* in Acts 20:23 to describe the "afflictions" that awaited him in Jerusalem. **Hardships** is a general word for the difficulties that attend life in a fallen world (cf. 1 Cor. 7:26; 1 Thess. 3:7). It has the sense of inevitability (Matt. 18:7 renders it, "inevitable") and is sometimes translated "compulsion" (e.g., 1 Cor. 9:16; 2 Cor. 9:7; Philem. 14). *Stenochōria* (**distresses**) literally refers to being confined in a narrow space. It describes trials and difficulties from which there is no escape.

The second three elements are external threats. **Beatings** can refer to blows from fists (Luke 10:30), rods (Acts 16:22–23), or whips (Luke 12:48). Paul also was no stranger to **imprisonments** (2 Cor. 11:23 cf. Acts 16:24; 24:23–27; 28:16, 30; 2 Tim. 1:8, 16; 2:9) nor to the **tumults** (riots; civil disturbances; mob violence) that constantly attended his ministry (cf. Acts 13:45; 14:19; 17:5; 18:12–17; 19:29; 21:30; 22:22–23; 23:10).

The third group involves self-inflicted trials. *Kopos* (**labors**) refers to hard work to the point of exhaustion. Not only was Paul's ministry arduous, but he also worked with his hands to support himself and those who traveled with him (Acts 20:34; 1 Cor. 4:12; 1 Thess. 2:9; 2 Thess. 3:8). The result of that long, hard labor was often **sleeplessness** (cf. 2 Cor. 11:27), as Paul tirelessly ministered to the churches under his care (cf. Acts 20:31) and worked to support himself financially (2 Thess. 3:8). The demands of Paul's ministry, especially his frequent travels, often resulted in **hunger** (cf. 2 Cor. 11:27; 1 Cor. 4:11; Phil. 4:12). There were no restaurants at which to get meals. The few inns that existed in Paul's day were often little more than vermin-infested brothels. Yet the apostle gladly endured all the hardships of his ministry, summed up in these nine words, because he did "not consider [his] life of any account as dear to [himself], so that [he might] finish [his] course and the ministry which [he] received from the Lord Jesus, to testify solemnly of the gospel of the grace of God" (Acts 20:24).

Paul's remarkable **endurance** also manifested itself in nine positive qualities. **Purity** (*hagnotēs*) rightly heads the list. It is a comprehensive word encompassing purity of life, thought, and motive. Paul was above reproach, as all believers (Phil. 2:15; 1 Tim. 5:7), especially church leaders (1 Tim. 3:2; Titus 1:6–7), are to be. The apostle's **knowledge** of divine truth was unsurpassed, and he never wavered from a true understanding of sinful men, the strategies of Satan, false religious systems, God's redeeming love, and the principles of effective teaching, evangelism, and discipling. "Even if I am unskilled in speech," he said in reply to his critics, "yet I am not so in knowledge" (2 Cor. 11:6). A clear understanding of the truth that was never altered was the foundation of his endurance. *Makrothumia* (**patience**) refers particularly to tolerance for people (cf. Eph. 4:2; 2 Tim. 4:2). There were many, not least the Corinthians themselves, who sorely tested Paul's endurance. He constantly faced wicked, ignorant, sinful, weak, unruly, judgmental, critical, even mutinous people. But whether they caused him physical or emotional suffering, the apostle patiently loved, rebuked, instructed, encouraged, and comforted them.

Paul also modeled the essential virtue of **kindness,** which describes goodness in action. No matter how people treated him, Paul responded by doing useful deeds for them. He expressed his credo when he exhorted the Galatians, "Let us do good to all people, and especially to those who are of the household of the faith" (Gal. 6:10). It is **the Holy Spirit** who empowers endurance. Paul walked in the Spirit (Gal. 5:16), was filled with the Spirit (Acts 13:9), accessed the Father through the Spirit (Eph. 2:18), was called to (Acts 13:2) and gifted for ministry by Him (1 Cor. 12:7, 11), ministered in His power (Rom. 15:19), followed His leading (Acts 16:6–7), was taught by Him (1 Cor. 2:13), prayed in the Spirit (Eph. 6:18), and worshiped in the Spirit (Phil. 3:3). He did not grieve the Spirit (Eph. 4:30), or quench Him (1 Thess. 5:19). The Spirit also produced in him the **genuine** (without hypocrisy; Rom. 12:9) **love,** which He "poured out within our hearts" (Rom. 5:5; cf. Gal. 5:22). *Agapē* (**love**) is the self-sacrificial love of the will, not the senses or emotions. Paul's love was wide enough to encompass his friends, those in the churches he ministered to (cf. 2 Cor. 11:11; 12:15; 1 Cor. 16:24), and even his enemies (Matt. 5:44).

The **word of truth** is the Bible (2 Tim. 2:15; James 1:18). Specifically in this passage, Paul has in mind the gospel (Col. 1:5) message that God reconciles sinners to Himself through the substitutionary death of His Son. The apostle faithfully preached that message without wavering until the day of his death (2 Tim. 4:7–8). Believers must follow his example, for the Enemy viciously attacks the gospel. Satan knows that by sowing confusion over the doctrine of salvation he can reap a deadly harvest of damned souls. Paul preached the gospel **in the power of God,** not his own cleverness. The gospel "is the power of God for salvation to everyone who believes, to the Jew first and also to the Greek" (Rom. 1:16). In 1 Corinthians 1:18 he added, "The word of the cross is foolishness to those who are perishing, but to us who are being saved it is the power of God." Paul did not water down, redefine, or simplify the gospel. He did not shrink from proclaiming its difficult demands, or seek to avoid making sinners feel uncomfortable. He preached the gospel clearly and unambiguously "so that," as he wrote earlier to the Corinthians, "your faith would not rest on the wisdom of men, but on the power of God" (1 Cor. 2:5). Paul "fought the good fight" (2 Tim. 4:7) using **the weapons of righteousness for the right hand and the left.** He was fully armed to take on all adversaries of the truth. The apostle described the **weapons of righteousness** in detail in 2 corinthians 10:3–5:

> For though we walk in the flesh, we do not war according to the flesh, for the weapons of our warfare are not of the flesh, but divinely powerful for the destruction of fortresses. We are destroying speculations and every lofty thing raised up against the knowledge of God, and we are

taking every thought captive to the obedience of Christ.

He did not battle spiritual foes (Eph. 6:12) with the powerless weapons of human ideas, wisdom, and ingenuity, but with the invincible truth of the Word of God. (For a detailed exposition of 10:3–5, see chapter 25 of this volume.)

PARADOX

by glory and dishonor, by evil report and good report; regarded as deceivers and yet true; as unknown yet well-known, as dying yet behold, we live; as punished yet not put to death, as sorrowful yet always rejoicing, as poor yet making many rich, as having nothing yet possessing all things. (6:8–10)

As noted earlier in this chapter, those who proclaim the gospel are both loved and despised. In this section, Paul expounds the paradoxical character of the ministry in a series of contrasts. The faithful preacher experiences both **glory and dishonor;** he is praised and despised, exalted and maligned, flattered and criticized, cherished and vilified. Consequently, some will give an **evil report** about him, **and** others a **good report.** Those who are faithful to the truth cannot expect all people to speak well of them (cf. Luke 6:26), and Paul was no exception. Some told the truth about him, profoundly grateful for his impact in their lives. Others assaulted his character and slandered his name, seeking to discredit his ministry. The Corinthian church reflected this dichotomy; some were devoted followers of Paul (1 Cor. 1:12; 3:4), while others savagely attacked him and brought him sorrow (2 Cor. 2:1).

Faithful ambassadors of God can also expect to be **regarded as deceivers and yet true,** as was the Lord Jesus Christ. John 7:12 records that "there was much grumbling among the crowds concerning Him; some were saying, 'He is a good man'; others were saying, 'No, on the contrary, He leads the people astray.'" Likewise Paul was accused of being a false apostle (1 Cor. 9:2), when in reality he was "not in the least inferior to the most eminent apostles" (2 Cor. 11:5). Satan, the father of lies (John 8:44), seeks to destroy the reputation of anyone who becomes a force for the truth.

Further expounding the dichotomy of the ministry, Paul continued with the enigmatic statement that he was **unknown yet well-known.** In his early years, he was **well-known** to the Jewish elite (cf. Acts 26:4–5) as one "advancing in Judaism beyond many of [his] contemporaries" (Gal. 1:14), yet personally **unknown** to the believers (Gal. 1:22). But after his conversion, the situation was reversed. He became unknown to his former associates, in the sense that they wanted nothing more to do with him. And he eventually became **well-known** to the church as the beloved Apostle to the Gentiles. He was largely **unknown** to the unregenerate world but well-known by person, reputation, or ministry to all Christians.

Because he was always seemingly on the brink of death, Paul described himself **as dying yet behold, we live.** Earlier in this epistle he wrote of the threat of death that constantly hung over him:

> For we do not want you to be unaware, brethren, of our affliction which came to us in Asia, that we were burdened excessively, beyond our strength, so that we despaired even of life; indeed, we had the sentence of death within ourselves so that we would not trust in ourselves, but in God who raises the dead; who delivered us from so great a peril of death, and will deliver us, He on whom we have set our hope. And He will yet deliver us. (2 Cor. 1:8–10)

> Always carrying about in the body the dying of Jesus, so that the life of Jesus also may be manifested in our body. For we who live are constantly being delivered over to death for Jesus' sake, so that the life of Jesus also may be manifested in our mortal flesh. So death works in us, but life in you. (2 Cor. 4:10–12)

From the time of his conversion, Paul faced death threats from his Jewish countrymen (Acts 9:24, 29; 14:19; 20:3, 23:12; 25:3), who viewed him as a traitor to Judaism. But despite their plots, he continued to **live** under the Lord's protection (2 Tim. 4:17) until God determined it was time for him to die. Until then, Paul may have been **punished, yet** his enemies were **not** able to **put** him **to death** (cf. 2 Cor. 11:23–27).

Because of Paul's arduous, painful life, one would expect him to be **sorrowful** (cf. Rom. 9:2). His heart was broken over the lost, over disobedient, immature believers, and over the threats false teaching posed to the church. Not surprisingly, he was occasionally depressed (cf. 2 Cor. 7:5–6). **Yet** despite such sorrow, Paul was **always rejoicing.** He had a deep, unfailing joy because of God's grace, power, and goodness. Therefore he could write, "Rejoice in the Lord always; again I will say, rejoice!" (Phil. 4:4), and "Rejoice always" (1 Thess. 5:16), and frequently punctuated his letters with doxologies of praise. Life for Paul was a seeming paradox of unending sorrow mingled with continual joy.

Paul was undeniably **poor** in terms of this world's possessions. Some have speculated that his family disinherited him after he became a Christian. Certainly he had no large bank account to fall back on but had to rely on financial support from the churches (Phil. 4:16) and his own hard work (1 Thess. 2:9) to support himself. **Yet** he made those around him who believed his message eternally **rich** with an eternal inheritance (2 Cor. 8:9; Eph. 1:11; 3:8; Col. 1:12; cf. 1 Peter 1:4).

Making himself poor to make others rich bothered Paul not in the least. Though he appeared to have **nothing, yet** in reality he possessed all the eternal **things** that really matter (cf. Matt. 6:19–20; Luke 12:33). In 1 Corinthians 3:21–22 he wrote, "All things belong to you, whether Paul or Apollos or Cephas or the world or life or death or things present or things to come; all things belong to you." To the Romans he added, "He who did not spare His own Son, but delivered Him over for us all, how will He not also with Him freely give us all things?" (Rom. 8:32).

People burn out in ministry not because of overwork, but because of unmet expectations. But those who do not have unrealistic expectations will not become frustrated when they are not met. To have proper expectations in the ministry, one must view it from the proper perspective. Understanding the privilege of ministry, maintaining its passion, carefully protecting it, and expecting paradoxical reactions to it keep one's vision clear.

Accents of Love
(2 Corinthians 6:11–13; 7:2–4)

18

Our mouth has spoken freely to you, O Corinthians, our heart is opened wide. You are not restrained by us, but you are restrained in your own affections. Now in a like exchange—I speak as to children—open wide to us also. . . . Make room for us in your hearts; we wronged no one, we corrupted no one, we took advantage of no one. I do not speak to condemn you, for I have said before that you are in our hearts to die together and to live together. Great is my confidence in you; great is my boasting on your behalf. I am filled with comfort; I am overflowing with joy in all our affliction. (6:11–13; 7:2–4)

The most difficult, painful experience for a faithful minister is to be misrepresented, to be falsely accused, to have one's integrity unfairly attacked. Such assaults have the potential, by destroying people's trust and confidence in the minister, of devastating his ministry. Such slanderous attacks are hard to retrieve and correct, because those who make them are not interested in the truth. Nor are they motivated by virtue, love, or righteousness, but rather by hatred, revenge, bitterness, jealousy, and self-promotion. Purveyors of such falsehoods do not seek the unity and blessing of the church, the glory of the Lord, or the good of those they attack.

Throughout history, God's faithful servants have endured such slanderous false accusations. The whole early church was wrongly accused of atheism (because Christians rejected the Roman gods), cannibalism (based on a misunderstanding of the Lord's Supper), and immorality (based on a misunderstanding of the "holy kiss" [Rom. 16:16; 1 Cor. 16:20; 2 Cor. 13:12; 1 Thess. 5:26; 1 Peter 5:14]). The papal bull excommunicating Martin Luther said of him, "This Luther favors the Bohemians and the Turks, deplores the punishment of heretics, spurns the writings of the holy doctors, the decrees of the ecumenical councils, and the ordinances of the Roman pontiffs, and gives credence to the opinions of none save himself alone, which no heretic before ever presumed to do" (Roland H. Bainton, *Here I Stand* [Nashville: Abingdon, 1950], 148).

Charles Spurgeon's unwavering defense of biblical truth earned him many enemies. Speaking of the vicious attacks he endured, Spurgeon said, "Scarce a day rolls over my head in which the most villainous abuse, the most fearful slander is not uttered against me both privately and by the public press; every engine is employed to put down God's minister—every lie that man can invent is hurled at me" (cited in Iain Murray, *The Forgotten Spurgeon* [Edinburgh: Banner of Truth, 1986], 60).

But no one endured more vicious, relentless, and unjust attacks than the patriarch of ministerial pain, the apostle Paul. The kingdom of darkness—Satan, the demons, and ungodly people—constantly assaulted him. At Corinth, as noted in previous chapters of this volume, that assault came from false apostles, who attacked his character and spread lies about him. They sought power, money, prominence, and the opportunity to supplant the truth with their demon doctrines. To accomplish those goals, they first had to destroy trust in Paul's character and teachings by falsely accusing him of being a lying, self-serving hypocrite. The confidence of many of the Corinthians was affected, and they were doubting Paul.

Profoundly concerned, the apostle vigorously defended his integrity, not for his sake, but for the Corinthians'. He was the Lord's personally chosen channel through which divine truth flowed to them. To allow the false teachers' lies to go unchallenged would allow that flow of divine truth to be blocked. Worse, it would allow it to be replaced with false doctrine. Again, here, he reminded them of the integrity he had manifested during his long stay in their city (cf. Acts 18:11), in this text defending his love for them.

Heading the list of false accusations against Paul was the charge that he had no real affection for the Corinthians. The apostle, according to the false teachers, was abusive, manipulative, and dictatorial; he was merely using the Corinthians to further his own personal agenda. Therefore Paul repeatedly affirmed his love for the church. In 2 Corinthians 2:4 he wrote, "For out of much affliction and anguish of heart I wrote to you with many tears; not so that you would be made sorrowful, but that you might know the love which I have especially for you." In 11:11 he added, "Why? Because I do not love you? God knows I do!" while in 12:15 he asked them plaintively, "If I love you more, am I to be loved less?" He also twice referred to them as his "beloved" (7:1; 12:19).

Paul defined the character of his love for the Corinthians in connection with his actions toward them. In so doing, he provided a clear-cut description of love in action (cf. 1 Cor. 13:4–8). This discussion of love brackets the intervening section (2 Cor. 6:14–7:1; see chapter 19 of this volume) dealing with separating from unbelievers.

As he described the essence of what real love is like, Paul expressed ten accents or characteristics of love: honesty, affection, fellowship, purity, humility, forgiveness, loyalty, trust, pride, and joy.

HONESTY

Our mouth has spoken freely to you, O Corinthians, our heart is opened wide. (6:11)

Paul spoke **freely** (candidly, straightforwardly) to the **Corinthians** because love holds back nothing that would be profitable for its objects. The apostle reminded the Ephesian elders, "I did not shrink from declaring to you anything that was profitable, and teaching you publicly and from house to house. . . . I did not shrink from declaring to you the whole purpose of God" (Act 20:20, 27). Jesus declared that "the mouth speaks out of that which fills the heart" (Matt. 12:34), and Paul's love caused him to speak honestly about three things.

First, Paul spoke honestly about God. He was candid and truthful about God's Word and God's standards. Earlier in this letter he defended his truthfulness, reminding the Corinthians, "For we write nothing else to you than what you read and understand . . . by the manifestation of truth commending ourselves to every man's conscience in the sight of God." (2 Cor. 1:13; 4:2). In 4:13 he noted that he spoke the truth because he believed the truth, while in 13:8 he declared, "For we can do nothing against the truth, but only for the truth."

Second, Paul spoke honestly about sin. Some argue that it is unloving to confront people about their sin, but Scripture affirms that truth and love are inseparably linked (Eph. 4:15). Paul lovingly, truthfully presented the gospel to the Corinthians, fully expounding the realities of sin and righteousness. He preached Christ crucified and all that that implied. He also confronted sin and called for their repentance, and in this letter warned them that he would not spare disciplining them (cf. 2 Cor. 12:18–13:3). He even challenged them to test the genuineness of their faith (13:5). In 2:9 he explained his motive in writing the severe letter (2:4) that he sent them between 1 and 2 Corinthians:"For to this end also I wrote, so that I might put you to the test, whether you are obedient in all things" (cf. 7:8–10).

Finally, Paul spoke honestly about his affections toward the Corinthians. He loved them intensely, as the vocative expression, **O Corinthians** indicates. Paul's **heart** was **opened wide** (lit.,"enlarged" or "broadened") to them; he had been open, candid, and vulnerable (cf. 4:2). The expression also means that there was plenty of room in his heart for them; in 7:3 he told the Corinthians,"You are in our hearts" (cf. 3:2; Phil. 1:7). That Paul could have them in his heart after all the sorrow they had caused him proves his love was genuine (cf. 2 Cor. 12:14–15).

AFFECTION

You are not restrained by us, but you are restrained in your own affections. (6:12)

Restrained is from *stenochōreō,* which literally means,"to make narrow" or "to confine." Paul had not **restrained** the Corinthians; he had done nothing to cause any estrangement or hinder the relationship between them. On the contrary, they were self-**restrained in** their **own affections** toward him. A number of them had squeezed the apostle out of their lives and closed their hearts to him. They had believed lies about Paul and turned away from him to follow false teachers. As a result, they had left their affection for him.

The Corinthians' rejection hurt Paul deeply. Yet despite that, he never lost his affection for them, because genuine love "bears all things" and "endures all things" (1 Cor. 13:7). That does not mean, of course, that Paul tolerated their sin and error. He disciplined and corrected them when necessary, but that reflected his true affection for them. Love and discipline are inseparable even with the Lord; "for those whom the Lord loves He disciplines, and He scourges every son whom He receives" (Heb. 12:6).

FELLOWSHIP

Now in a like exchange—I speak as to children—open wide to us also. . . . Make room for us in your hearts; (6:13; 7:2*a*)

Few things in life are more painful then unrequited love, because love longs for a response. Paul's plaintive words express the penetrating sadness he felt over the Corinthians' failure to return his love. Though they broke his heart, Paul's love for the Corinthians would not allow him to abandon them. Instead, he pleaded with them, using the phrase **in a like exchange;** literally, "in an exchange that is exact." Paul begged them to love him as he loved them—sacrificially, consistently, and permanently. He could **speak** to them **as to children** because they were his spiritual children (1 Cor. 4:14–15; cf. Gal. 4:19; 1 Tim. 1:2, 18; 2 Tim. 1:2; 2:1; Titus 1:4; Philem. 10), which made their rejection of him all the more painful.

Here is a tender, almost melancholy scene. The noble apostle did not hesitate to plead for the love of the most troubled of his churches. He was not too proud to open his heart and let them see that he was hurting. Even the discussion of separation that follows (2 Cor. 6:14–7:1) reveals Paul's longing for the Corinthians to break away from the false teachers and return to him.

Then he reached out to them again, pleading, **Make room for us in your hearts.** The translators rightly added the phrase **in your hearts,** which does not appear in the Greek text, because it fits the context (cf. v. 3; 6:11, 13). Having reminded them that his heart was wide open to them, Paul begged the Corinthians to open wide their hearts and **make room** for him. The apostle knew that as long as they clung to their sinful associations with his enemies, their love relationship with him could not be restored. That made it all the more urgent for the Corinthians to follow his instructions in 6:14–7:1 and sever all ties with the false teachers.

PURITY

we wronged no one, we corrupted no one, (7:2b)

Paul's claim is especially appropriate in light of his exhortation to separate from unbelievers in 6:14–7:1. Despite the false charges leveled against him (cf. 4:2), Paul had **wronged no one. Wronged** is from *adikeō*, which means "to treat unjustly," or "to injure." Those who made this charge may have had in mind Paul's turning the incestuous man over to Satan (1 Cor. 5:5). But the apostle did not mistreat him but rather dealt properly with his sin.

Actually, it was the Corinthians who had **wronged** Paul; he had neither harmed nor **corrupted** any of them. *Phtheirō* (**corrupted**) refers to moral corruption, as its use in 1 Corinthians 15:33 ("Bad company corrupts good morals") indicates. Again, it was not Paul, but his opponents who were guilty of ruining the Corinthians' morals (cf. 2 Cor. 11:3). Paul's love for the Corinthians expressed itself both in his own purity, and in his concern for theirs. He would never directly or indirectly, either by his teaching or his example, encourage any kind of immoral conduct.

HUMILITY

we took advantage of no one. (*7:2c*)

Love necessarily involves humility, for only humble people can love others unselfishly. Proud people, who love themselves, cannot love others. *Pleonekteō* (**we took advantage of**) refers to defrauding others by selfishly using them for gain. Specifically, it conveys the idea of manipulating people for financial gain, as its use in 12:17–18 indicates:

> Certainly I have not taken advantage of you through any of those whom I have sent to you, have I? I urged Titus to go, and I sent the brother with him. Titus did not take any advantage of you, did he? Did we not conduct ourselves in the same spirit and walk in the same steps?

Neither Paul nor anyone associated with him took advantage of the Corinthians financially, despite the repeated accusations by the false teachers.

In fact, the opposite was true. Rather than using the Corinthians for personal gain, Paul humbly, sacrificially endured suffering and hardship for them. "For we who live are constantly being delivered over to death for Jesus' sake," he wrote earlier in this epistle, "so that the life of Jesus also may be manifested in our mortal flesh. So death works in us, but life in you" (4:11–12). Paul's love for the Corinthian believers was so great that he was willing to risk his life for them (cf. John 15:13). His humble, self-effacing, sacrificial love did "not seek its own" (1 Cor. 13:5); it did not "merely look out for [its] own personal interests, but also for the interests of others" (Phil. 2:4).

FORGIVENESS

I do not speak to condemn you, (*7:3a*)

Paul did not want the Corinthians to interpret his strong defense of his integrity in verse 2 (or elsewhere) as an attack on them. *Katakrisis* (**condemn**) refers to passing final judgment. In its only other New Testament appearance, it refers to the Law's work of condemning sinners

(3:9). Paul was not passing a final verdict on them; he was not giving up on them. He was not angry; he was not consigning them to final judgment. He did not want to sever his relationship with them, but restore it. Therefore he rebuked their sin and rebellion and called for them to repent and reaffirm their loyalty to him. The apostle knew the truth that Solomon expressed: "Faithful are the wounds of a friend" (Prov. 27:6). Paul was a noble example of genuine biblical love, which "does not take into account a wrong suffered" (1 Cor. 13:5), "because love covers a multitude of sins" (1 Peter 4:8).

LOYALTY

for I have said before that you are in our hearts to die together and to live together. (7:3*b*)

Paul's declaration, **You are in our hearts** repeats his thought from 6:11. The phrase **to die together and to live together** reflects Paul's undying loyalty to the Corinthians. Colin G. Kruse explains:

> In the papyri the expression "to live together and to die together" is found where mutual friendship and loyalty are extolled. The idea is that those involved have a friendship that will be sustained throughout life and will keep them together even if death is involved (cf. Mk. 14:31). In his affirmation of friendship Paul reverses the order, i.e., not to live and die, but to die and live together, and this reflects a fundamental Christian outlook. (*The Second Epistle of Paul to the Corinthians*, The Tyndale New Testament Commentaries [Grand Rapids: Eerdmans, 1995], 142)

Further, that relationship will transcend death and last forever in the glory of heavenly life. Paul's love was loyal to the death, like that of Ruth, who said to Naomi,

> Do not urge me to leave you or turn back from following you; for where you go, I will go, and where you lodge, I will lodge. Your people shall be my people, and your God, my God. Where you die, I will die, and there I will be buried. Thus may the Lord do to me, and worse, if anything but death parts you and me. (Ruth 1:16–17)

TRUST

Great is my confidence in you; (7:4*a*)

At first glance, this is an astonishing, even shocking, statement. The Corinthian church was the most trouble-plagued of any New Testament church. Yet Paul was open and bold, freely speaking (*parrēsia* [**confidence**] can also be translated "freedom of speech") of the work of the Lord in that assembly. Certainly, then, Paul's **great** trust and **confidence** in the Corinthians was not based on their track record. In fact, their performance called for cautious scrutiny, not open trust. But true love, though not naïve, "believes all things, [and] hopes all things" (1 Cor. 13:7). It is extremely reluctant to believe anything but the best about its objects.

That does not, of course, reflect the modern myth that positive thoughts make good things happen. Paul's hope was not that his positive attitude would change the Corinthians. True biblical love does not make good things happen, but believes and hopes for them.

Therefore, despite their unfaithfulness, disloyalty, and sin, Paul maintained his **confidence** in the Corinthians—not because of them, but because he knew that God would complete the saving work He had begun in them (cf. Phil. 1:6).

PRAISE

great is my boasting on your behalf. (7:4*b*)

That Paul would engage in **boasting on behalf** of a church filled with immaturity, disloyalty, doubt, and disaffection is amazing. Though *kauchēsis* (**boasting**) can have the negative connotation of pride (e.g., Rom. 3:27; James 4:16), it more often has the positive connotation of praise, as it does here (cf. 2 Cor. 7:14; 8:24; 11:10, 17; Rom. 15:17; 1 Cor. 15:31). Proper boasting is that which is done in the Lord (2 Cor. 10:17; 1 Cor. 1:31), and Paul's boast of praise was of what the Lord was doing in the Corinthian church. He boasted to Titus, as 2 Corinthians 7:14 records: "For if in anything I have boasted to him about you, I was not put to shame; but as we spoke all things to you in truth, so also our boasting before Titus proved to be the truth." Paul also boasted about the Corinthians to other churches: "Therefore openly before the churches, show them the proof of your love and of our reason for boasting about you" (8:24). Paul was eager to praise the Lord for them despite all their shortcomings. This is evidence of the genuineness of his love.

Joy

I am filled with comfort; I am overflowing with joy in all our affliction. (7:4c)

Even more surprising than Paul's trust in and praise for the Corinthians was that they brought him joy. Despite all the problems they caused him, Paul used a perfect passive indicative verb to say that he had been and still was **filled with comfort.** No amount of **affliction** could stem the **overflowing joy** he felt. Not only Paul, but also Titus experienced joy because of the Corinthians (7:13).

These ten accents of genuine love are reflections of God's love for believers. He loves them enough to be honest and has a deep affection for them so that He is grieved when sin disrupts their fellowship with Him. God's love also causes Him to desire His people's purity (Titus 2:14). Because of that, the Lord Jesus Christ "humbled Himself by becoming obedient to the point of death, even death on a cross" (Phil. 2:8) so that believers' sins could be forgiven. His love also ensures God's eternal loyalty to His people (Heb. 13:5) and causes Him to entrust them with the gospel (1 Thess. 2:4). And God loves His people, takes pride in them, and rejoices over them (cf. Ps. 149:4; Zeph. 3:17). Taking Paul as their model, believers are to love others the way God loves them.

Separating from Unbelievers
(2 Corinthians 6:14–7:1)

19

Do not be bound together with unbelievers; for what partnership have righteousness and lawlessness, or what fellowship has light with darkness? Or what harmony has Christ with Belial, or what has a believer in common with an unbeliever? Or what agreement has the temple of God with idols? For we are the temple of the living God; just as God said, "I will dwell in them and walk among them; and I will be their God, and they shall be My people. Therefore, come out from their midst and be separate," says the Lord. "And do not touch what is unclean; and I will welcome you. And I will be a father to you, and you shall be sons and daughters to Me," says the Lord Almighty. Therefore, having these promises, beloved, let us cleanse ourselves from all defilement of flesh and spirit, perfecting holiness in the fear of God. (6:14–7:1)

Saving faith in the Lord Jesus Christ produces a radical transformation of every aspect of a person's being. Christians are "new creature[s]," for whom "the old things [have] passed away; behold, new things have come" (5:17). They have been "born again" (John 3:3, 7; 1 Peter 1:3, 23); "rescued . . . from the domain of darkness, and transferred . . . to the kingdom of His beloved Son" (Col. 1:13); and have turned "from darkness to light and from the dominion of Satan to God" (Acts 26:18).

Believers and unbelievers inhabit two opposing worlds. Christians are in Christ's kingdom, which is characterized by righteousness, light, and eternal life. Unbelievers are in Satan's kingdom, characterized by lawlessness, darkness, and spiritual death. The saved and the unsaved have different affections, beliefs, principles, motives, goals, attitudes, and hopes. In short, they view life from opposing perspectives.

Consequently, relationships between believers and unbelievers are at best limited to the temporal and external. They may enjoy family ties, work at the same job, share in business relationships, live in the same community, experience the same hobbies and pastimes, and even agree on certain political and social issues. But on the spiritual level, believers and unbelievers live in two completely different worlds.

It should be obvious that believers cannot live in both worlds. The apostle John clearly indicated that when he wrote, "Do not love the world nor the things in the world. If anyone loves the world, the love of the Father is not in him. For all that is in the world, the lust of the flesh and the lust of the eyes and the boastful pride of life, is not from the Father, but is from the world" (1 John 2:15–16). James expressed in forceful language that same reality: "You adulteresses, do you not know that friendship with the world is hostility toward God? Therefore whoever wishes to be a friend of the world makes himself an enemy of God" (James 4:4), while Paul exhorted believers, "Do not be conformed to this world" (Rom. 12:2).

The Corinthians had struggled greatly to make a clean break from the idolatrous and immoral lifestyle of their past. Despite having professed faith in Christ and become part of the church, some in the congregation were still clinging to elements of their pagan religion. And though they, like the Thessalonians, had "turned to God from idols to serve a living and true God" (1 Thess. 1:9), still they failed to make a clean break with their idolatrous past. The lure of their former paganism, which permeated every aspect of life in Corinth, had proven hard to shake, as Paul's first epistle to them makes evident.

Making matters worse, the false teachers who had come to the church brought with them a quasi-Christian syncretism of gospel truth, Jewish legalism, and pagan mysticism. They were eager to stay connected to the Corinthians' former behavior, to make themselves more popular and, thereby, more prosperous. Thus Paul gave this mandate to separate.

The familiar command to separate in this passage is frequently both misunderstood and violated. The separation demanded here does not refer to refusing association with those who do not follow a certain set of rules for living the Christian life, as many legalistic Christians have advocated. It does not mean refusing to cooperate with those who teach the truth but do not agree with all the distinctives of one's own theology or ministry style. Nor does separation mean retreating completely from the world into monasticism. And separating from unbelievers does not, as some at Corinth imagined, mean divorcing an unbelieving spouse (1 Cor. 7:12–13). Biblical separation certainly does not cancel the church's responsibility to "go into all the world and preach the gospel to all creation" (Mark 16:15).

The Corinthians would have understood Paul's call for separation in the context of what he had already written to them. In 1 Corinthians 9:19–21 he wrote,

> For though I am free from all men, I have made myself a slave to all, so that I may win more. To the Jews I became as a Jew, so that I might win Jews; to those who are under the Law, as under the Law though not being myself under the Law, so that I might win those who are under the Law; to those who are without law, as without law, though not being without the law of God but under the law of Christ, so that I might win those who are without law.

Nor was the apostle's command "not to associate with immoral people" (1 Cor. 5:9) a charge to avoid unbelievers; as he explained, "I did not at all mean with the immoral people of this world, or with the covetous and swindlers, or with idolaters, for then you would have to go out of the world" (v. 10). To do that would be to shirk the responsibility Jesus gave the church in the Great Commission (Matt. 28:19–20) and to ignore the example He set by being "a friend of tax collectors and sinners" (Luke 7:34; cf. Matt. 9:10–11). "Actually," Paul explained, "I wrote to you not to associate with any so-called brother if he is an immoral person, or covetous, or an idolater, or a reviler, or a drunkard, or a swindler—not even to eat with such a one" (v. 11). He did not want them to socially separate from non-Christians, but from unrepentant professing Christians in the church. Since there was no way to separate the religious from the secular in pagan cultures, believers would inevitably be in some places and at some events that contained elements of idolatry.

In 1 Corinthians Paul wrote two passages that define the limits of Christian freedom in such cases (1 Cor. 8; 10:23–33). Both passages are important for this discussion because they assume that believers will be involved with unbelievers in pagan religious settings. In 1 Corinthians 8:10 Paul cautioned the mature believers, "If someone sees you, who have knowledge, dining in an idol's temple, will not his conscience, if he is weak, be strengthened to eat things sacrificed to idols?" Knowing an idol was nothing anyway (v. 4), some of the stronger believers saw no harm in eating a social meal on the grounds of an idol temple with no thought of worshiping the idol. The apostle did not forbid such socializing with unbelievers. Instead, he warned those who did so against causing weaker brothers newly delivered from idolatry (who might be tempted to follow their example) to be exposed to the old ways and plunge back into sin.

Controversy also raged in Corinth about eating meat that had been offered to idols. The temple priests could not eat all of the meat brought for sacrifice, and so they sold the excess in the meat market. Since the gods represented by the idols did not really exist (1 Cor. 8:4), there was no harm in believers eating meat offered to them. Once again, however, Paul cautioned the strong believers against causing the weak ones just emerging from idol worship to be offended by such liberty:

> If one of the unbelievers invites you and you want to go, eat anything that is set before you without asking questions for conscience' sake. But if anyone says to you, "This is meat sacrificed to idols," do not eat it, for the sake of the one who informed you, and for conscience' sake. (1 Cor. 10:27–28)

As did his earlier discussion of eating a meal at an idol temple, this passage assumes that Christians would socialize with their pagan friends and families. Paul did not restrict such contact but encouraged those who did it to prevent weaker believers from being led into sin or violating their consciences, which are so necessary to holiness.

So what did the Holy Spirit intend by His command **not** to **be bound together with unbelievers? Bound together** translates a participial form of the verb *heterozugeō,* which means, "to be unequally yoked." Paul drew his analogy from Deuteronomy 22:10, where the Mosaic Law commanded the Israelites, "You shall not plow with an ox and a donkey together." Those two animals do not have the same nature, gait, or strength. Therefore it would be impossible for such a mismatched pair to plow together effectively. Nothing in the context would lead to the idea that he is referring to earthly issues of human endeavors. In Paul's analogy, believers and unbelievers are two different breeds and cannot work together in the spiritual realm. He called for separation in matters of the work of God, since such cooperation for spiritual benefit is impossible. The false teachers were eager to blend the people of God with the pagan worshipers, because that hinders the gospel. That is what this text forbids.

To infiltrate churches under the guise of tolerance and cooperation is one of Satan's most cunning ploys. He does not want to fight the church as much as join it. When he comes against the church, it grows stronger; when he joins with the church, it grows weaker. Undiscerning believers who join in a common spiritual cause with unbiblical forms of

Christianity or other false religions open the door wide to satanic infiltration and forfeit the blessing of God. Further, embracing those heretical systems falsely reassures their followers that all is well between them and God, when actually they are headed for eternal damnation.

To compromise by alliances with false religion was a constant and severe temptation for the struggling church in Corinth. Their city was an especially wicked one, even by the loose moral standards of that day. In fact, Corinth was so infamous for its debauchery that the Greek verb "to Corinthianize" came to mean "to go to bed with a prostitute." Idolatry permeated every aspect of the city's culture and social life, leading Paul to warn the Corinthian believers, "Do not be idolaters. . . . Flee from idolatry" (1 Cor. 10:7, 14). Because "the things which the Gentiles sacrifice, they sacrifice to demons and not to God," Paul wrote, "I do not want you to become sharers in demons. You cannot drink the cup of the Lord and the cup of demons; you cannot partake of the table of the Lord and the table of demons" (1 Cor. 10:20–21).

An important element of the idol worship at Corinth involved ritual prostitution. The temple of Aphrodite, located on Corinth's acropolis, was home to one thousand priestesses, who were little more than "religious" prostitutes. Every evening they would descend into the city to ply their trade. Paul's stern warning against sexual immorality in 1 Corinthians 6:15 may also have had them in mind: "Do you not know that your bodies are members of Christ? Shall I then take away the members of Christ and make them members of a prostitute? May it never be!" Just as he had in regard to idolatry (1 Cor. 10:7, 14), Paul commanded the Corinthians to "flee immorality" (1 Cor. 6:18; cf. 2 Tim. 2:22; 1 Peter 2:11).

Having given the command not to be bound together with unbelievers in any religious event, enterprise, or activity, Paul supported it by giving five reasons for following that mandate. To be bound together with unbelievers in any spiritual effort is irrational, sacrilegious, disobedient, unprofitable, and ungrateful.

IRRATIONAL

for what partnership have righteousness and lawlessness, or what fellowship has light with darkness? Or what harmony has Christ with Belial, or what has a believer in common with an unbeliever? (6:14b–15)

For believers to join with unbelievers in a common spiritual effort makes no sense. To demonstrate that reality, Paul makes four rhetorical common-sense contrasts, each in the form of a question that assumes a negative answer.

What partnership have righteousness and lawlessness? (6:14*b*)

Metochē (**partnership**) appears only here in the New Testament and is a synonym for the word *koinonia* (**fellowship**), which appears in the next question. A related word is used to speak of Peter's partners in the fishing business (Luke 5:7), of believers' sharing in a heavenly calling (Heb. 3:1), and of their union with Christ (Heb. 3:14). It thus describes being involved in a relationship of common life and effort.

Obviously, **righteousness** and **lawlessness** are opposites. **Righteousness** is obedience to the law of God; **lawlessness** is rebellion against His holy law. **Righteousness** characterizes believers (Rom. 4:7; Eph. 2:10; Titus 2:14; Heb. 8:12; 10:17), because Christ's righteousness has been imputed to them (2 Cor. 5:21; cf. Rom. 5:19; 1 Cor. 1:30; Phil. 3:9) and because they are born of God and therefore possess a new nature, which is made righteous (Rom. 6:19). Unbelievers, on the other hand, are characterized by **lawlessness,** since that is the nature of unredeemed sinners. The apostle John made the difference unmistakably clear:

> Everyone who practices sin also practices lawlessness; and sin is lawlessness. You know that He appeared in order to take away sins; and in Him there is no sin. No one who abides in Him sins; no one who sins has seen Him or knows Him. Little children, make sure no one deceives you; the one who practices righteousness is righteous, just as He is righteous; the one who practices sin is of the devil; for the devil has sinned from the beginning. The Son of God appeared for this purpose, to destroy the works of the devil. No one who is born of God practices sin, because His seed abides in him; and he cannot sin, because he is born of God. By this the children of God and the children of the devil are obvious: anyone who does not practice righteousness is not of God, nor the one who does not love his brother. (1 John 3:4–10)

Anomia (**lawlessness**) characterizes all the unregenerate, since all rebel against God's law, though not always visibly, and some are more lawless than others. Jesus strongly rebuked the scribes and Pharisees, who were noted for their external righteousness and observance of the Law: "Woe to you, scribes and Pharisees, hypocrites! For you are like whitewashed tombs which on the outside appear beautiful, but inside they are full of dead men's bones and all uncleanness. So you, too, outwardly appear righteous to men, but inwardly you are full of hypocrisy and lawlessness" (Matt. 23:27–28).

Ultimately, those who are lawless face eternal punishment in hell. In one of the most sobering passages in Scripture, Jesus warned of what His judgmental response to such people will be: "Then I will declare to them, 'I never knew you; depart from Me, you who practice lawlessness'" (Matt. 7:23). In Matthew 13:41–42 He again described the terrifying fate that awaits those who refuse to repent of their lawlessness: "The Son of Man will send forth His angels, and they will gather out of His kingdom all stumbling blocks, and those who commit lawlessness, and will throw them into the furnace of fire; in that place there will be weeping and gnashing of teeth." Because they refuse to believe in Jesus as "God and Savior" (Titus 2:13; 2 Peter 1:1), they will "die in [their] sins" (John 8:24).

The righteous and the rebellious cannot partner in any common spiritual enterprise because of this absolute contrast between them. They are as separated as sin is from virtue.

QUESTION 2

What fellowship has light with darkness? (6:14c)

It is self-evident that **light** and **darkness** are mutually exclusive; thus, this contrast is a common biblical metaphor (cf. Isa. 5:20; John 1:5; 3:19; 8:12; 12:35, 46; Acts 26:18; Rom. 13:12; Eph. 5:8, 11; Col. 1:12–14; 1 Thess. 5:5; 1 Peter 2:9; 1 John 1:5; 2:8–9). Intellectually, **light** refers to truth, **darkness** to error; morally **light** refers to holiness, **darkness** to evil. Those who are righteous in Christ walk in the light (John 8:12; 12:35; Eph. 5:8; 1 John 1:7); those who are unrighteous are part of Satan's kingdom of darkness (Luke 22:53; Eph. 6:12; Col. 1:13). The ultimate destination of the righteous is the eternal light of heaven (Col. 1:12; 1 Peter 2:9; Rev. 22:5), that of the unrighteous the eternal darkness of hell (Matt. 8:12; 22:13; 25:30; 2 Peter 2:17). To expect the children of **light** to work together with the children of **darkness** is as foolish as to expect it to be both light and dark in the same place at the same time.

QUESTION 3

What harmony has Christ with Belial? (6:15a)

The first two rhetorical questions focused on the radically different natures possessed by believers (righteousness, light), and unbelievers (lawlessness, darkness). Paul's third rhetorical question showing mutual exclusivity deals with the leaders of the respective kingdoms. Obviously, there is a fundamental and eternal antagonism between **Christ,** the ruler of the kingdom of light and righteousness, and **Belial** (an ancient name for Satan), the ruler of the kingdom of darkness and lawlessness. **Belial** (*Beliar* in the Greek text) is used only here in the New Testament. The Hebrew phrase "sons of Belial" (the NKJV translates this phrase "corrupt" or perverted" men, while it is translated "worthless men" in the NASB; e.g., Deut. 13:13 [13:14 in the Hebrew text]; Judg. 19:22; 1 Sam. 2:12; 2 Chron. 13:7) appears more than a dozen times in the Old Testament. The term "Belial" is found in the Dead Sea Scrolls in reference to Satan. The title is a fitting one for him, because he is the utterly and supremely worthless one. To assume that Christ and Satan could cooperate in any common spiritual effort is utterly absurd.

Since **harmony** (*sumphōnēsis* ["to agree with"], from which the English word *symphony* derives) between Christ and Satan is impossible, so also is cooperation in spiritual matters between his children and God's. Believers, who "do all to the glory of God" (1 Cor. 10:31), cannot join forces with the sons of disobedience, who walk "according to the prince of the power of the air" (Eph. 2:2). The children of God have nothing in common with the children of the devil (John 8:44; 1 John 3:10).

QUESTION 4

What has a believer in common with an unbeliever? (6:15*b*)

This question sums up the first three, reinforcing the obvious truth that a **believer** has no **common** spiritual ground **with an unbeliever.** Faith has nothing in common with unbelief; the faithful and the faithless are committed to mutually exclusive ideologies and energized by opposing powers. As God asked in His maxim to wayward Israel, "Can two walk together, unless they are agreed? (Amos 3:3 NKJV).

SACRILEGIOUS

Or what agreement has the temple of God with idols? For we are the temple of the living God; just as God said, "I will dwell in them and walk among them; and I will be their God, and they shall be My people." (6:16)

Paul's fifth rhetorical question introduces a second reason for believers not to be bound together with unbelievers. All false religion is in the final analysis "doctrines of demons" (1 Tim. 4:1; cf. Deut. 32:17; Rev. 9:20) and is virulently hostile to the true God. There can be no **agreement** between **the temple of God** and **idols.** Christianity is incompatible with every form of false religion.

The Old Testament graphically depicts the disastrous consequences of attempting to mingle idolatry with the worship of the true God. It is instructive to read 2 Kings 21:1–9, which describes the reign of Manasseh, the most wicked of Judah's kings:

> Manasseh was twelve years old when he became king, and he reigned fifty-five years in Jerusalem; and his mother's name was Hephzibah. He did evil in the sight of the Lord, according to the abominations of the nations whom the Lord dispossessed before the sons of Israel. For he rebuilt the high places which Hezekiah his father had destroyed; and he erected altars for Baal and made an Asherah, as Ahab king of Israel had done, and worshiped all the host of heaven and served them. He built altars in the house of the Lord, of which the Lord had said, "In Jerusalem I will put My name." For he built altars for all the host of heaven in the two courts of the house of the Lord. He made his son pass through the fire, practiced witchcraft and used divination, and dealt with mediums and spiritists. He did much evil in the sight of the Lord provoking Him to anger. Then he set the carved image of Asherah that he had made, in the house of which the Lord said to David and to his son Solomon, "In this house and in Jerusalem, which I have chosen from all the tribes of Israel, I will put My name forever. And I will not make the feet of Israel wander anymore from the land which I gave their fathers, if only they will observe to do according to all that I have commanded them, and according to all the law that My servant Moses commanded them." But they did not listen, and Manasseh seduced them to do evil more than the nations whom the Lord destroyed before the sons of Israel.

The phrase "abominations of the nations" refers to the idolatry Manasseh brought back into Judah. Specifically, "he rebuilt the high places which Hezekiah his father had destroyed; and he erected altars for Baal and made an Asherah, as Ahab king of Israel had done, and worshiped all the host of heaven and served them." Even worse, Manasseh "built altars in the house of the Lord, of which the Lord had said, 'In Jerusalem I will put My name.' For he built altars for all the host of heaven in the two courts of the house of the Lord." And if that were not bad enough, he put an idol in the temple itself: "Then he set the carved image of Asherah that he had made, in the house of which the Lord said to David and to his son Solomon, 'In this house and in Jerusalem, which I have chosen from all the tribes of Israel, I will put My name forever.'" That blasphemous insult to God provoked His devastating judgment on the nation:

> Now the Lord spoke through His servants the prophets, saying, "Because Manasseh king of Judah has done these abominations, having done wickedly more than all the Amorites did who were before him, and has also made Judah sin with his idols; therefore thus says the Lord, the God of Israel, 'Behold, I am bringing such calamity on Jerusalem and Judah, that whoever hears of it, both his ears shall tingle. I will stretch over Jerusalem the line of Samaria and the plummet of the house of Ahab, and I will wipe Jerusalem as one wipes a dish, wiping it and turning it upside down. I will abandon the remnant of My inheritance and deliver them into the hand of their enemies, and they shall become as plunder and spoil to all their enemies; because they have done evil in My sight, and have been provoking Me to anger since the day their fathers came from Egypt, even to this day.'" (vv. 10–15)

First Samuel 4 and 5 record another incident that illustrates the incompatibility of the true God with idols. Israel was at war with the Philistines and lost four thousand men in one skirmish (4:1–2). Dismayed by the Lord's failure to help them in battle (which was due to their sin and apostasy), the Israelites sent to Shiloh for the ark of the covenant, the visible representation of God's presence (4:3–5). Thinking themselves now to be invincible, they fought the Philistines again—this time losing 30,000 men and the ark: "So the Philistines fought and Israel was defeated, and every man fled to his tent; and the slaughter was very great, for there fell of Israel thirty thousand foot soldiers. And the ark of God was taken; and the two sons of Eli, Hophni and Phinehas, died" (4:10–11).

The triumphant Philistines brought the ark to the temple of their god Dagon in Ashdod (5:1–2). The next morning, much to their surprise, they discovered that the idol of Dagon had prostrated itself before the ark (5:3). They put the idol back in its place, only to have the same thing happen the next day—this time with Dagon's head and hands cut off. The message was clear: The true God tolerates no rivals. He will not share billing with false gods.

Ezekiel chapter 8 further illustrates that reality. In verse 3 the Lord took Ezekiel (who was actually in Babylon) by means of a vision to the temple in Jerusalem, "to the entrance of the north gate of the inner court, where the seat of the idol of jealousy, which provokes to jealousy, was located," alongside "the glory of the God of Israel" (v. 4). Such a situation was intolerable to God, who declared in verse 6, "Son of man, do you see what they are doing, the great abominations which the house of Israel are committing here, so that I would be far from My sanctuary?" Rather than share His own sanctuary with pagan idols, God chose to abandon it.

But that idol was not the only thing provoking God to abandon His temple. At the end of verse 6 He told Ezekiel, "You will see still greater abominations," which verses 7–10 describe:

> Then He brought me to the entrance of the court, and when I looked, behold, a hole in the wall. He said to me, "Son of man, now dig through the wall." So I dug through the wall, and behold, an entrance. And He said to me, "Go in and see the wicked abominations that they are committing here." So I entered and looked, and behold, every form of creeping things and beasts and detestable things, with all the idols of the house of Israel, were carved on the wall all around.

Shockingly, the apostate Israelites had carved idolatrous graffiti on the walls of the temple. And in what they supposed was a secret place, seventy elders of Israel were conducting idolatrous worship in front of that graffiti (vv. 11–12).

Even that appalling scene did not fully express the depths to which apostate Israel had plunged. In his vision, the Lord "brought [Ezekiel] to the entrance of the gate of the Lord's house which was toward the north; and behold, women were sitting there weeping for Tammuz" (v. 14). Committing blasphemy in the temple along with the women, "at the entrance to the temple of the Lord, between the porch and the altar, were about twenty-five men with their backs to the temple of the Lord and their faces toward the east; and they were prostrating themselves eastward toward the sun" (v. 16). Like the women weeping for the false god Tammuz, these men were engaged in idolatrous worship in the very temple of the true God. God's reaction, recorded in verse 18, was to promise judgment: "Therefore, I indeed shall deal in wrath. My eye will have no pity nor shall I spare; and though they cry in My ears with a loud voice, yet I shall not listen to them." In 586 B.C. the Babylonians made their third and last invasion, destroying Jerusalem and taking captives. With that judgment, God did just as He had promised, using the Babylonians as a divine weapon to destroy the corrupted, profaned temple.

Today believers, both individually (1 Cor. 6:19) and collectively (1 Cor. 3:16–17; Eph. 2:22), **are the temple of the living God.** The phrase **the living God,** appearing more than two dozen times in Scripture (e.g., 2 Cor. 3:3; Rom. 9:26; 1 Thess. 1:9; 1 Tim. 3:15; 4:10), contrasts Him with the dead idols of false religion. The authoritative phrase **just as God said** introduces a statement confirming that believers are God's temple. In that statement, a mosaic of several Old Testament passages (cf. Lev. 26:11–12; Jer. 24:7; Ezek. 37:27), God promised, **"I will dwell in them and walk among them; and I will be their God, and they shall be My people."** As the temple of God, the people of His covenant, His precious possession, and His dwelling place, believers cannot join forces with false religion. To be so unequally yoked for the purpose of serving God has always been unacceptable and blasphemous.

DISOBEDIENT

"Therefore, come out from their midst and be separate," says the Lord. "And do not touch what is unclean"; (6:17*a*)

To be bound together with unbelievers is not only foolish and irreverent, but it also disobeys God's explicit command, expressed in the two imperative verbs translated **come out** and **be separate. Therefore** links the command in this verse with the principle expressed in verse 16. As those personally indwelt by the living God, believers are to avoid any joint spiritual effort with unbelievers. As the temple of the living God, they must not be linked for the cause of the advancement of divine truth with any form of false religion.

The thought in this verse hearkens back to Isaiah 52, where God commanded His people, "Depart, depart, go out from there, touch nothing unclean; go out of the midst of her, purify yourselves, you who carry the vessels of the Lord" (v. 11; cf. Rev 18:4). Christians, like Israel at the time of her salvation (vv. Isa. 52:7–10), must make a clean break with all false religion to avoid its contaminating influence (cf. 2 Tim. 2:16–17). Paul repeated this principle in Ephesians 5:5–11:

> For this you know with certainty, that no immoral or impure person or covetous man, who is an idolater, has an inheritance in the kingdom of Christ and God. Let no one deceive you with empty words, for because of these things the wrath of God comes upon the sons of disobedience. Therefore do not be partakers with them; for you were formerly darkness, but now you are light in the Lord; walk as children of Light (for the fruit of the Light consists in all goodness and righteousness and truth), trying to learn what is pleasing to the Lord. Do not participate in the unfruitful deeds of darkness, but instead even expose them.

The "children of Light" must "not be partakers" with the "sons of disobedience." They must be concerned with "pleasing . . . the Lord," not sinful men. To that end, they must "not participate in the unfruitful deeds of darkness, but instead even expose them." The church's goal is not to make unbelievers feel comfortable and nonthreatened. On the contrary, it is to make them feel uncomfortable with their sins and threatened by God's judgment and the terrors of hell that they face.

It has always been God's will for His people to be distinct from unbelievers. In Leviticus 20:24, 26 God said to Israel, "I am the Lord your

God, who has separated you from the peoples. . . . Thus you are to be holy to Me, for I the Lord am holy; and I have set you apart from the peoples to be Mine." In the New Testament Peter reiterated that principle, exhorting believers, "As obedient children, do not be conformed to the former lusts which were yours in your ignorance, but like the Holy One who called you, be holy yourselves also in all your behavior; because it is written, 'You shall be holy, for I am holy'" (1 Peter 1:14–16).

Strengthening the point that failing to separate from unbelievers is disobedience is the third command in this verse, **Do not touch what is unclean. Touch** is from *haptō* and refers to a harmful touch, as in 1 John 5:18. Believers are not to be involved with **unclean,** false teaching. They are to "save [those trapped in false religions], snatching them out of the fire . . . hating even the garment polluted by the flesh" (Jude 23). But the church cannot worship, evangelize, or minister with those who pervert or reject the truth of the Word of God.

UNPROFITABLE

"and I will welcome you. And I will be a father to you, and you shall be sons and daughters to Me," says the Lord Almighty. (6:17b–18)

Failing to separate from unbelievers is foolish, because such disobedience cuts believers off from the blessings of an intimate relationship with God. He promises those who heed His command to separate from unbelievers (v. 17) that He will **welcome** them. *Eisdechomai* (**welcome**), used only here in the New Testament, means "to receive," or "to admit into one's favor." In the Septuagint (the Greek translation of the Old Testament) rendering of Ezekiel 20:34, *eisdechomai* is used to speak of God's gathering Israel to Himself out of the nations. The idea is that those who separate from unbelievers will find God's arms open wide to receive them.

They will also enjoy the full range of blessings bestowed by their heavenly **father** on His **sons and daughters.** Paul probably had in mind 2 Samuel 7:14, where God promised David that he would bless his son Solomon: "I will be a father to him and he will be a son to Me." God blesses His obedient children, as He did Solomon. But in the last part of the verse God warned, "When he [Solomon] commits iniquity, I will correct him with the rod of men and the strokes of the sons of men." The writer of Hebrews also affirmed God's discipline of His children: "For those whom the Lord loves He disciplines, and He scourges every son whom He receives" (Heb. 12:6). As always, obedience brings blessing; disobedience brings chastening.

Sadly, Solomon forfeited the promised blessing by making compromising alliances with unbelievers. First Kings 11:1–11 tells the tragic story of his downfall. Solomon

> loved many foreign women along with the daughter of Pharaoh: Moabite, Ammonite, Edomite, Sidonian, and Hittite women, from the nations concerning which the Lord had said to the sons of Israel, "You shall not associate with them, neither shall they associate with you, for they will surely turn your heart away after their gods." Solomon held fast to these in love." (vv. 1–2)

Just as the Lord had predicted, "when Solomon was old, his wives turned his heart away after other gods" (v. 4). As a result, "his heart was not wholly devoted to the Lord his God, as the heart of David his father had been" (v. 4). Despite Solomon's wisdom and understanding of the truth, his compromising alliances with unbelievers proved his undoing. The allurement of idolatry proved too much, and he

> went after Ashtoreth the goddess of the Sidonians and after Milcom the detestable idol of the Ammonites. Solomon did what was evil in the sight of the Lord, and did not follow the Lord fully, as David his father had done. Then Solomon built a high place for Chemosh the detestable idol of Moab, on the mountain which is east of Jerusalem, and for Molech the detestable idol of the sons of Ammon. Thus also he did for all his foreign wives, who burned incense and sacrificed to their gods. (vv. 5–8)

Because of his disobedience,

> the Lord was angry with Solomon because his heart was turned away from the Lord, the God of Israel, who had appeared to him twice, and had commanded him concerning this thing, that he should not go after other gods; but he did not observe what the Lord had commanded. So the Lord said to Solomon, "Because you have done this, and you have not kept My covenant and My statutes, which I have commanded you, I will surely tear the kingdom from you, and will give it to your servant." (vv. 9–11)

The devastating result of Solomon's compromise with unbelievers was the division of his kingdom.

Any alliance with the unsaved is disobedience that defiles and therefore interrupts believers' communion with their Father, forfeiting His blessing.

UNGRATEFUL

Therefore, having these promises, beloved, let us cleanse ourselves from all defilement of flesh and spirit, perfecting holiness in the fear of God. (7:1)

Having God's **promises** provides powerful motivation for believers to separate from unbelievers. Paul's use of the word **therefore** is a call for action based on what he has previously written (cf. Rom. 12:1–2; 2 Peter 1:3–8). The apostle moves beyond the commands of 2 Corinthians 6:14, 17 and appeals to God's **promises** enumerated in 6:16–18. Those **promises** should elicit love, gratitude, and thankfulness for His overwhelming generosity. In fact, one of the things that characterizes unrepentant sinners is ingratitude (Luke 6:35; Rom. 1:21; 2 Tim. 3:2)

The endearing term **beloved** (cf. 2 Cor. 12:19; Rom. 1:7; 12:19; 1 Cor. 10:14; Col. 3:12; 1 Thess. 1:4; 2 Thess. 2:13) defines who God's promises apply to. Only His **beloved** children, accepted by Him because of their union with His beloved Son (Eph. 1:6; Col. 1:13), receive God's promises.

Paul defined the appropriate act of gratitude in both negative and positive terms. Negatively, believers must **cleanse** themselves **from all defilement of flesh and spirit** (cf. Isa. 1:16; James 1:21). The reflexive pronoun *heatous* (**ourselves**) indicates that though the cleansing work is God's (cf. Acts 15:9; Eph. 5:26; Titus 3:5), it does not happen apart from believers' effort (cf. Phil. 2:12–13). *Molusmos* (**defilement**) appears only here in the New Testament. In all three of its uses in the Septuagint, however, it refers to religious defilement. Paul calls believers not only to cleanse themselves from sin and immorality but especially, in this context, from all associations with false religion. That complete cleansing is to be both **of flesh and spirit;** that is, both inward and outward. False teaching defiles the whole person by pandering to sinful human appetites and corrupting the mind. Therefore, believers must avoid both the fleshly sins and the pollution of the mind that false religion brings.

Positively, cleansing oneself from false religion involves **perfecting holiness in the fear of God.** Perfecting is from *epiteleo*, which means, "to finish," "to complete," or "to fulfill." Believers are to pursue the goal of **holiness** (Lev. 20:26; Matt. 5:48; 1 Peter 1:16) by separating from all the lies and deceptions that would defile them, encouraged by the hope that the goal will someday be achieved (Phil. 1:6; 1 Peter 5:10; 1 John 3:2). Motivating believers' pursuit of holiness is the reverential **fear of God,** which is foundational to godly living (Job 28:28; Pss. 19:9; 34:11; 111:10; Prov. 1:7; 8:13; 9:10; 15:33; 16:6; 23:17; Acts 9:31).

The church must confront the world to fulfill the Great Commission given to us by our Lord (Matt. 28:19–20). Yet we must not compromise with false religion to do so. To disobey God's explicit command to separate from unbelievers is foolish, blasphemous, ungrateful, and forfeits God's blessing.

Comforting the Sorrowful Pastor (2 Corinthians 7:5–16)

20

For even when we came into Macedonia our flesh had no rest, but we were afflicted on every side: conflicts without, fears within. But God, who comforts the depressed, comforted us by the coming of Titus; and not only by his coming, but also by the comfort with which he was comforted in you, as he reported to us your longing, your mourning, your zeal for me; so that I rejoiced even more. For though I caused you sorrow by my letter, I do not regret it; though I did regret it—for I see that that letter caused you sorrow, though only for a while—I now rejoice, not that you were made sorrowful, but that you were made sorrowful to the point of repentance; for you were made sorrowful according to the will of God, so that you might not suffer loss in anything through us. For the sorrow that is according to the will of God produces a repentance without regret, leading to salvation, but the sorrow of the world produces death. For behold what earnestness this very thing, this godly sorrow, has produced in you: what vindication of yourselves, what indignation, what fear, what longing, what zeal, what avenging of wrong! In everything

NOTE: Second Corinthians 7:2–4 is covered in chapter 18.

you demonstrated yourselves to be innocent in the matter. So although I wrote to you, it was not for the sake of the offender nor for the sake of the one offended, but that your earnestness on our behalf might be made known to you in the sight of God. For this reason we have been comforted. And besides our comfort, we rejoiced even much more for the joy of Titus, because his spirit has been refreshed by you all. For if in anything I have boasted to him about you, I was not put to shame; but as we spoke all things to you in truth, so also our boasting before Titus proved to be the truth. His affection abounds all the more toward you, as he remembers the obedience of you all, how you received him with fear and trembling. I rejoice that in everything I have confidence in you. (7:5–16)

There are few things in life more painful than broken relationships. Shattered marriages, wayward children, and disrupted friendships produce intense suffering and deep sorrow. When those broken relationships involve fellow believers, the pain is even more severe. Watching believers suffer the consequences of their sinful conduct compounds the grief from the breaking of the relationship.

Though richly rewarding in many ways, the ministry is arduous. To properly interpret the Word of God, understand theology, edify believers, and refute those in error requires diligent, hard labor. Proving to be an example to the flock, developing and training leaders, admonishing the unruly, encouraging the fainthearted, and helping the weak (1 Thess. 5:14) all take their toll. But the most painful aspect of ministry involves difficult relationships between the sheep and the shepherds. All pastors know the hurt that comes when those in whom they have invested the most return the least.

As he penned this epistle, Paul nursed a broken heart over the church he loved and served. He was under severe external pressure, experiencing afflictions (1:4, 6, 8) and suffering (1:5, 7) to the point that he "despaired even of life" (1:8), "had the sentence of death within [himself]" (1:9), and needed to be "delivered . . . from so great a peril of death" (1:10). In 4:8–12 he described himself as

> afflicted in every way, but not crushed; perplexed, but not despairing; persecuted, but not forsaken; struck down, but not destroyed; always carrying about in the body the dying of Jesus, so that the life of Jesus also may be manifested in our body. For we who live are constantly being delivered over to death for Jesus' sake, so that the life of Jesus also may be manifested in our mortal flesh. So death works in us, but life in you.

In 6:4–10 Paul again spoke of the suffering he endured:

> In everything commending ourselves as servants of God, in much endurance, in afflictions, in hardships, in distresses, in beatings, in imprisonments, in tumults, in labors, in sleeplessness, in hunger, in purity, in knowledge, in patience, in kindness, in the Holy Spirit, in genuine love, in the word of truth, in the power of God; by the weapons of righteousness for the right hand and the left, by glory and dishonor, by evil report and good report; regarded as deceivers and yet true; as unknown yet well-known, as dying yet behold, we live; as punished yet not put to death, as sorrowful yet always rejoicing, as poor yet making many rich, as having nothing yet possessing all things.

Chapter 11 records perhaps the most well-known description of the apostle's trials:

> Are they servants of Christ?—I speak as if insane—I more so; in far more labors, in far more imprisonments, beaten times without number, often in danger of death. Five times I received from the Jews thirty-nine lashes. Three times I was beaten with rods, once I was stoned, three times I was shipwrecked, a night and a day I have spent in the deep. I have been on frequent journeys, in dangers from rivers, dangers from robbers, dangers from my countrymen, dangers from the Gentiles, dangers in the city, dangers in the wilderness, dangers on the sea, dangers among false brethren; I have been in labor and hardship, through many sleepless nights, in hunger and thirst, often without food, in cold and exposure. (11:23–27)

In short, Paul's life was fraught with "weaknesses . . . insults . . . distresses . . . persecutions [and] difficulties" (12:10).

But what really broke Paul's heart was not what the world did to him but what the church did to him. In 11:28, after listing the trials he had endured, Paul wrote, "Apart from [of a completely different nature] such external things, there is the daily pressure on me of concern for all the churches." And none caused him more trouble than the church in Corinth. The church in which he had invested nearly two years of his life had repaid him with disloyalty. They had allowed false teachers to come into their assembly and attack Paul's character and ministry. Even worse, some of the Corinthians believed their lies and joined in a mutiny against him. One of them had apparently verbally assaulted and abused Paul (cf. 2:5–8, 10) during the apostle's painful, sorrowful visit to Corinth. That the majority in the church had not defended him from those attacks wounded Paul deeply. The visit was so discouraging that he did not want to return to Corinth and expose himself to more pain (2:1). As a result of the visit, he had written a sternly worded letter, rebuking the Corinthians for their disaffection, disloyalty, and lack of love toward him. Writing that letter was extremely painful for Paul, as he noted in 2:4: "For out of much affliction and anguish of heart I wrote to you with many tears."

Paul sent the letter to Corinth with Titus, his beloved son in the faith (Titus 1:4), who was also to bring the Corinthians' response back to him. The apostle left Ephesus (where he had written the severe letter) and went to Troas (a seaport on the west coast of Asia Minor), where he hoped to rendezvous with Titus. But Paul was so anxious about the situation in Corinth that he could not minister in Troas (2 Cor. 2:13), even though the Lord opened a door for him there (2:12). Restless, unable to wait any longer, the apostle set off for Macedonia, anxious to meet Titus sooner and find out the Corinthians' response to the severe letter (2:13).

At that point (2:13) the narrative broke off, and Paul entered into a prolonged digression about his ministry (2:14–7:4). Here, in 7:5, the apostle returned to the events that followed the sending of the severe letter. **When** he **came into Macedonia** from Troas in search of Titus, his **flesh had no rest** (cf. 2:13). Nothing changed; he had no relief from his concern over the situation at Corinth. In fact, he had new concerns. What if the severe letter had made things worse? Was the breach with the Corinthians now irreparable? How would they treat Titus? Corinth, as Paul well knew, could be a hostile environment for a lonely preacher; would the church leave Titus to fend for himself? Lack of relief from the heavy burden of grief and concern Paul bore sapped the joy of his ministry. His experience reflected the truth of Proverbs 13:12, "Hope deferred makes the heart sick."

Instead of the relief he hoped for, Paul found himself **afflicted on every side.** He described that affliction first as **conflicts without.** *Machē* (**conflicts**) literally means, "fights," or "strife" and appears to be the source of the word *machaira* ("sword"). It describes serious quarrels (2 Tim. 2:23), disputes (Titus 3:9), and conflicts (James 4:1). It likely refers to those in Macedonia who wanted to get rid of Paul. They would have remembered him as the troublemaker who sparked a riot in Philippi, was miraculously released from jail by an earthquake, and then humiliated the city's magistrates by demanding a public apology for being wrongfully imprisoned (Acts 16:16–40). Certainly, they would not have welcomed Paul back into their territory but would have applied great pressure on him to leave.

As he anxiously awaited Titus, Paul was also beset by **fears within.** *Phobos* (**fears**), the source of the English word *phobia*, describes Paul's intense anxiety over the situation in the church at Corinth. The external and internal pressures he faced troubled him to the point that he became **depressed.** *Tapeinos* (**depressed**) refers to those who are downcast, downhearted, and down-and-out, whose very condition elicits compassion (cf. Rom. 12:16). But those are precisely the people whom God comforts. In contrast to the cruel gods of paganism, God is by nature a comforter; He is the "God of all comfort" (2 Cor. 1:3; cf. Isa. 49:13; 2 Thess. 2:16).

The narrative does not end with Paul being depressed. **God, who comforts the depressed, comforted** him **by the coming of Titus.** This is, therefore, a passage about joy, not depression. In fact, comfort is mentioned six times in these verses and joy or rejoicing five times. In this section God comforts the anxious, grieving pastor and restores his joy.

The **coming of Titus** brought the joy to Paul's heart. The apostle rejoiced that he was safe and in the renewal of their fellowship. However, it was not only Titus's presence that comforted Paul but also the report that he brought about the situation at Corinth. There were still unresolved problems (which Paul addressed in chapters 10–13). But the majority of the Corinthian believers had repented and reaffirmed their loyalty to the apostle and the truth he taught, which brought him immense relief.

This very personal section offers profound insights into restoring broken relationships. It lists seven indicators of a genuine desire for real restoration: loyalty, repentance, purity, spirituality, unity, obedience, and trust. And though the context is the relationship between a pastor and his people, these principles are vital for restoring any broken relationship.

LOYALTY

and not only by his coming, but also by the comfort with which he was comforted in you, as he reported to us your longing, your mourning, your zeal for me; so that I rejoiced even more. (7:7)

As noted above, Titus's return comforted Paul. But the apostle was **not only** comforted **by his coming, but also by the comfort with which he was comforted** by the Corinthians. Titus shared Paul's concern over the Corinthians' defection and no doubt viewed his mission to Corinth with some anxiety, not knowing what to expect. But the Corinthians had brought him comfort and joy by their repentant attitude. They had responded properly to the severe letter.

Specifically, Titus reported three characteristics of the Corinthians' response that revealed their loyalty to Paul: **longing, mourning,** and **zeal.** Together they define loyalty—a word that is fast disappearing from the contemporary vocabulary. In a postmodern society where self-centered narcissism reigns supreme, loyalty is seen not as an asset but as a liability. But loyalty is the most desirable virtue in any human relationship. On the other hand, disloyalty devastates a relationship.

The Corinthians' response to the severe letter was not one of grudging acceptance of Paul's apostolic authority. Instead, it was one of **longing** and yearning to see him and have their relationship with him restored. Paul wrote the severe letter "out of much affliction and anguish of heart . . . with many tears" (2:4). Realizing that their sin had caused him pain and sorrow, the Corinthians responded by **mourning.** They grieved over the breach in their relationship with Paul and deeply regretted their disloyalty to him. They also expressed **zeal,** both to restore their relationship with the apostle and to defend him from further attacks. **Zeal** is a combination of two equally strong emotions: love and hate. It produces a strong love that hates anything that would harm its object. The Lord Jesus Christ expressed both aspects of zeal when He cleansed the temple; it was His passionate love for His Father's house that caused Him to hate the terrible iniquity that desecrated it (John 2:13–17; cf. Ps. 69:9). The Corinthians' loyalty to Paul encouraged the apostle so much that he **rejoiced even more** than he did at Titus's return.

REPENTANCE

For though I caused you sorrow by my letter, I do not regret it; though I did regret it—for I see that that letter caused you sorrow, though only for a while—I now rejoice, not that you were made sorrowful, but that you were made sorrowful to the point of repentance; for you were made sorrowful according to the will of God, so that you might not suffer loss in anything through us. For the sorrow that is according to the will of God produces a repentance without regret, leading to salvation, but the sorrow of the world produces death. (7:8–10)

The Corinthians not only responded correctly to Paul but also to God. They reaffirmed their loyalty to the apostle and acknowledged their disloyalty to him as a sin against God. That recognition is essential to restoring broken relationships.

Paul knew that he had **caused** the Corinthians **sorrow by** the strongly confrontational **letter** he had sent them (2:4). And, as his parenthetical statement **I do not regret it; though I did regret it** reveals, he did experience temporary remorse over writing that letter. While he anxiously waited for Titus to return with the Corinthians' response, the apostle worried that the letter might have only made things worse. **That letter** had in fact **caused** them **sorrow, though only for a while.** The

Greek text reads "for an hour," a metaphor for a brief period of time. The pleasure of sin is brief while the sorrow it produces lasts; the sorrow of repentance is brief, while the joy it produces lasts.

Sometimes confronting sin requires going beyond what love and compassion might be comfortable with. But it is necessary to do so, because sin is a deadly killer. Paul was not an abusive, harsh disciplinarian but a reluctant one, and he took no joy in causing even temporary sorrow to the Corinthians. He was like a father who has mixed feelings about disciplining a beloved child. But what motivated him to write the severe letter was his love for them and the truth, and his fear of the consequences of their sin. Despite his temporary regret, Paul knew that rebuking the Corinthians' sin had to be done.

There are times in the ministry when strong, confrontational words are necessary. Sin crouches at the door; false teachers are everywhere, and Satan constantly seeks to destroy the work of God. The faithful pastor must not shrink from calling his people to obedience to Scripture. That obedience presupposes true repentance, which can only come about when there is sorrow over sin. Therefore, Paul could **rejoice, not that** the Corinthians **were made sorrowful, but that** they **were made sorrowful to the point of repentance.** His regret vanished when he saw the results of the sorrow.

The Corinthians' remorse was not the sorrow of self-pity, of getting caught, of despair, bitterness, wounded pride, or manipulative remorse. Their sorrow led to **repentance** (*metanoia;* a change of heart and life; a turning from sin to holiness), which produced genuine change. They were not defensive; they did not view themselves as victims or seek to justify their sinful behavior. Their sorrow was **according to the will of God;** it was the healing, transforming sorrow for sin that God intended for them to feel, because it produces repentance.

The Corinthians' repentance comforted Paul; he was relieved **that they might not suffer** the **loss** of **anything** available **through** him and his ministry companions. There were many blessings God could pour out on the Corinthians through his ministry. Had they remained alienated from him, they would have forfeited those blessings. The phrase **suffer loss** also appears in 1 Corinthians 3:15, where it refers to the future judgment of believers' works. The loss of blessings from Paul's ministry would have resulted in the Corinthians accumulating valueless "wood, hay, [and] straw," fit only to be burned (1 Cor. 3:12). Paul's selfless love made him anxious not only that the Corinthians might experience God's chastening and lose their present blessings, but also that they might forfeit their future rewards (cf. 2 John 8). His concern was not for his loss, but theirs.

No one who truly repents will ever regret it or the sorrow that led to it, because **the sorrow that is according to the will of God produces a repentance without regret.** The Corinthians' **repentance** marked them as genuine believers, in the sphere of **salvation.** It involved turning from sin to God (1 Thess. 1:9). True biblical repentance is not psychological, emotional human remorse, seeking merely to relieve stress and improve one's circumstances. Though it inevitably produces the fruit of a changed life (cf. Matt. 3:8; Luke 3:8; Acts 26:20), it is not behavioral, but spiritual. The **sorrow of the world**—remorse, wounded pride, self-pity, unfulfilled hopes—has no healing power, no transforming, saving, or redeeming capability. It **produces** guilt, shame, resentment, anguish, despair, depression, hopelessness, even, as in the case of Judas (Matt. 27:3–5), **death.**

This passage is incompatible with the teaching that repentance is not necessary for salvation. The progression it reveals is obvious: confrontation of sin leads to sorrow, which leads to repentance, which leads to salvation. Nor will this passage allow repentance to be defined as merely changing one's mind about who Jesus is. The text inextricably connects repentance with sorrow over sin. Repentance is not, of course, a meritorious human work that earns salvation. Like every aspect of salvation, repentance is a gracious work of God in the human heart (Acts 5:31; 11:18; 2 Tim. 2:25). (For a discussion of the necessity of repentance for salvation, see John MacArthur, *The Gospel According to Jesus,* rev. ed. [Grand Rapids: Zondervan, 1994], and *The Gospel According to the Apostles* [Nashville: Word, 2000.)

PURITY

For behold what earnestness this very thing, this godly sorrow, has produced in you: what vindication of yourselves, what indignation, what fear, what longing, what zeal, what avenging of wrong! In everything you demonstrated yourselves to be innocent in the matter. (7:11)

To Paul's great relief and joy, the Corinthians **demonstrated** themselves **to be innocent in the matter.** *Hagnos* (**innocent**) has the idea of "pure" (11:2; Phil. 4:8; Titus 2:5; James 3:17; 1 John 3:3), "free from sin" (1 Tim. 5:22), and "chaste" (1 Peter 3:2). The Corinthians demonstrated the genuineness of their repentance by their purity. When John the Baptist called for his hearers to "bear fruit in keeping with repentance" (Matt. 3:8), he was calling them to holiness of life.

This verse lists seven characteristics of the purity true repentance produces and it provides the clearest definition of repentance anywhere in Scripture. Paul introduced those characteristics with the exclamatory phrase **for behold,** which indicated his overwhelming exhilaration. The apostle was excited by Titus's report of the improved situation at Corinth. The repeated use of the comparative **what** before each element underscores the intense emotion Paul felt.

First, the Corinthians' **godly sorrow** produced an **earnestness** or eagerness for righteousness on their part. It ended their indifference toward Paul and their complacency about their sin. They were eager to make things right, to make restitution, to restore their broken relationship with the apostle.

Second, the Corinthians' genuine repentance manifested itself in a desire for **vindication.** *Apologia* (**vindication**), the source of the English word *apologetics,* literally means, "a speech in defense." It describes Paul's defense of himself before the mob at Jerusalem (Acts 22:1; cf. 25:16), his defense of his rights as an apostle (1 Cor. 9:3), his defense of the gospel (Phil. 1:7, 16), and his defense before the Roman authorities (2 Tim. 4:16). The Corinthians had a strong desire to clear their name, remove the stigma of their sin, rid themselves of their guilt, and prove themselves trustworthy. Therefore, they made sure that all who had known of their sin now knew of their repentance.

Third, their repentance resulted in **indignation.** *Aganaktēsis* (**indignation**) appears only here in the New Testament. It is related to the verb *aganakteō,* which means, "to be indignant," or "to be angry" (Matt. 20:24; 21:15; 26:8; Mark 10:14, 41; 14:4; Luke 13:14). The Corinthians were outraged over their sin; they were angry that they had brought shame on themselves, offended Paul, and sinned against God. They now hated the sin they had formerly cherished (cf. Rom. 6:21).

Fourth, the Corinthians' **fear** proved the genuineness of their repentance. They had a reverential fear and awe of God as the One who chastens and judges. Their brash, bold sinning had turned into a solicitous concern that they no longer disobey and dishonor Him.

Fifth, the Corinthians' repentance resulted in a **longing** or yearning to see their relationship to Paul restored.

Sixth, the Corinthians experienced a renewed **zeal** for holiness (cf. the discussion of **zeal** in v. 7 earlier in this chapter).

Seventh, the Corinthians' **avenging of wrong** evidenced the reality of their repentance. Truly repentant people have a strong desire to see justice done and to make restitution for the wrongs they have committed (cf. 2 Cor. 2:6–7). Instead of protecting themselves, they accept the consequences of their sins.

Repentance had brought purity to the sinning saints in the Corinthian assembly, and every aspect of their lives reflected it.

SPIRITUALITY

So although I wrote to you, it was not for the sake of the offender nor for the sake of the one offended, but that your earnestness on our behalf might be made known to you in the sight of God. (7:12)

Because of the Corinthians' immaturity and sinfulness, they were "fleshly . . . walking like mere men" (1 Cor. 3:3). Consequently, they had lost touch with how they truly felt about Paul. Therefore, one of the apostle's goals was to strip away their sinful, fleshly attitudes and reveal to the Corinthians their real attitude toward him.

Paul led up to his point by first eliminating other potential reasons for writing. That roundabout approach served to heighten the dramatic impact of his words. When he **wrote** the severe letter, **it was not for the sake of the offender.** He did not write primarily to condemn the man who had caused him so much grief during his painful visit to Corinth (2 Cor. 2:1). Nor was his main concern **for** himself as **the one offended;** he was not seeking personal vengeance. The most important reason Paul wrote the severe letter was **that** the Corinthians' **earnestness on** his **behalf might be made known to** them **in the sight of God.**

Sin's deceitfulness had caused them to lose sight of their **earnestness** (eagerness), loyalty, and love for Paul and the truth he preached. They had been so deceived that their outward attitude toward the apostle was inconsistent with how they really felt about him. His letter peeled back the layers of deceit that had encrusted their hearts and **made known** to them their true feelings for him. It restored their spiritual sight and enabled them to see Paul as the trusted servant of God they had always known him to be.

UNITY

For this reason we have been comforted. And besides our comfort, we rejoiced even much more for the joy of Titus, because his spirit has been refreshed by you all. (7:13)

The Corinthians' repentance, purity, and renewed loyalty to Paul were **reason** enough for him to **have been comforted.** But **besides** his own **comfort,** Paul rejoiced **even much more for the joy of Titus** over the Corinthians' repentance and obedience. **Because** of their repentance Titus's **spirit** had **been refreshed.** As noted in 2:6, the Corinthians had demonstrated their allegiance to Paul by uniting to discipline the individual who had attacked him. Their unity was especially comforting to both Paul and Titus (cf. Ps. 133:1; John 17:21; Eph. 4:3, 13; Phil. 2:2), since unity was at a premium in the Corinthian assembly. Their many factions (cf. 1 Cor. 1:10–13; 3:3–4; 11:18–19) resulted in the most chaotic church in the New Testament. But now they had come together, seeking to restore their relationship to Paul and hold to his teaching.

Anapauō (**refreshed**) refers here to temporary relief as opposed to a permanent peace (cf. Matt. 26:45; Mark 6:31; 14:41; Luke 12:19; Rev. 6:11). Though he was overjoyed at what had transpired in Corinth, Paul was wise enough to realize that pockets of dissent still existed. In fact, he addressed those dissenters later in this epistle. But for the moment, there was a truce involving the majority of the Corinthians.

As noted above, a mark of genuine repentance is a desire to make restitution for the harm sin has caused. The repentant Corinthians went to the others who had turned against Paul and encouraged them to repent. The movement spread until it encompassed the majority of the church, producing a unity in the congregation that comforted Paul and Titus.

OBEDIENCE

For if in anything I have boasted to him about you, I was not put to shame; but as we spoke all things to you in truth, so also our boasting before Titus proved to be the truth. His affection abounds all the more toward you, as he remembers the obedience of you all, how you received him with fear and trembling. (7:14–15)

As a result of their repentance, many of the Corinthians who had rebelled against Paul now submitted to him (cf. Heb. 13:17). He had been confident that they were genuine believers and would repent when confronted with their sin. Therefore, he had hopefully **boasted** to Titus before sending him to Corinth that the Corinthians would respond obediently. Paul, in a sense, staked his reputation as a man of discernment on the outcome, and he **was not put to shame.** Just as the apostle **spoke all things** to the Corinthians **in truth** (cf. 2 Cor. 2:17; 4:2; 6:7), **so also** his **boasting before Titus proved to be the truth.** His truthfulness and discernment were vindicated by the Corinthians' obedient response. Paul rejoiced in seeing his conviction vindicated because it meant his integrity, and thus his usefulness to them as a servant of God, remained intact.

The Corinthians' reception of Paul's representative, Titus, **with fear and trembling** (cf. 1 Cor. 2:3; Eph. 6:5; Phil. 2:12) was further evidence of their **obedience.** Their obedience had calmed Titus's fears and caused him to develop a strong affection for the Corinthian church. It also allowed both Titus and Paul to "keep watch over [their] souls . . . with joy and not with grief" (Heb. 13:17).

Their willing obedience to the Word of God proved the genuineness of the Corinthians' repentance. When people are truly repentant, they submit to the commands of Scripture without reluctance, caveat, or qualification. To have a congregation of such obedient people brings great joy to their leaders.

TRUST

I rejoice that in everything I have confidence in you. (7:16)

Paul's reaffirmation of his trust in the Corinthians brought closure to the issue. **Confidence** is from *tharreō,* which means, "to be courageous," "to be bold," or "to dare." Paul had the courage to entrust himself to the Corinthians again and dare to believe they would not fail him.

The apostle's newly restored confidence is a fitting climax to the first section (chaps. 1–7) of this epistle. The Corinthians' repentance encouraged Paul to share with them a project that was dear to his heart, the collection for the needy believers in the Jerusalem church (chaps. 8–9). It also gave him the boldness to confront the last remaining pockets of resistance to his apostolic authority (chaps. 10–13).

A Biblical Model for Giving (2 Corinthians 8:1–8)

21

Now, brethren, we wish to make known to you the grace of God which has been given in the churches of Macedonia, that in a great ordeal of affliction their abundance of joy and their deep poverty overflowed in the wealth of their liberality. For I testify that according to their ability, and beyond their ability, they gave of their own accord, begging us with much urging for the favor of participation in the support of the saints, and this, not as we had expected, but they first gave themselves to the Lord and to us by the will of God. So we urged Titus that as he had previously made a beginning, so he would also complete in you this gracious work as well. But just as you abound in everything, in faith and utterance and knowledge and in all earnestness and in the love we inspired in you, see that you abound in this gracious work also. I am not speaking this as a command, but as proving through the earnestness of others the sincerity of your love also. (8:1–8)

How people view money is an effective barometer of their spirituality. Money is neither good nor bad in itself; corrupt people can put it to evil uses, while good people can put it to righteous uses. Though it is morally neutral, what people do with their money reflects their internal morality. In the words of Jesus, "Where your treasure is, there your heart will be also" (Luke 12:34).

The Bible does not forbid the possession of money; in fact, it teaches that "God [gives the] power to make wealth" (Deut. 8:18) and "richly supplies us with all things to enjoy" (1 Tim. 6:17). Because of His blessing, many godly men in Scripture, such as Job (Job 1:3), Abraham (Gen. 13:2), Isaac (Gen. 26:12–13), Jacob (Gen. 30:43), Boaz (Ruth 2:1), and Solomon (1 Kings 10:23), were extremely wealthy. God promised His people that their obedience to Him would result in material as well as spiritual blessings (Deut. 15:4–6; 26:15; 28:11).

But while the Bible does not forbid possessing money, it does forbid loving it, warning that "the love of money is a root of all sorts of evil, and some by longing for it have wandered away from the faith and pierced themselves with many griefs" (1 Tim. 6:10). Later in that chapter, Paul exhorted Timothy to "instruct those who are rich in this present world not to be conceited or to fix their hope on the uncertainty of riches" (v. 17). To love money is to have an unhealthy affection for it and be driven to pursue it. Such a pursuit is the height of folly. "Do not weary yourself to gain wealth," the book of Proverbs counsels. "Cease from your consideration of it. When you set your eyes on it, it is gone. For wealth certainly makes itself wings like an eagle that flies toward the heavens" (Prov. 23:4–5). Though he was one of the wealthiest men who ever lived, Solomon was wise enough to know that "he who loves money will not be satisfied with money, nor he who loves abundance with its income" (Eccl. 5:10).

Achan's love of money brought disaster to himself, his family, and his nation (Josh. 7:1–25). Balaam's love of money caused him to foolishly attempt to curse God's chosen people (Num. 22–24), which resulted in his death (Num. 31:8). Delilah's love of money led her to betray Samson (Judg. 16:4–6), which ultimately led to the death of thousands (Judg. 16:27–30). Judas's love of money caused him to betray the Lord Jesus Christ (Matt. 26:14–16) and damn himself to eternal torment in hell (Matt. 26:24; Acts 1:25). Ananias's and Sapphira's love of money led them to hypocritically lie about their giving (Acts 5:1–2), resulting in God's execution of them (Acts 5:5, 10).

Loving money makes people forget God (Deut. 8:11–14; Prov. 30:9), trust in their riches rather than Him (Job 31:24–28; Ps. 52:7; Prov. 11:28), be deceived (Mark 4:19), compromise convictions, be proud (Deut. 8:14), steal from God (Mal. 3:8), and ignore the needs of others (1 John 3:17; cf. Prov. 3:27). Love of money causes people to pursue it illegitimately by stealing (whether directly [Ex. 20:15; Eph. 4:28] or by fraud [Ps. 37:21; Hos. 12:7; Amos 8:5; Mic. 6:11]), usury (Ex. 22:25; Lev. 25:36–37; Neh. 5:7, 10; Ps. 15:5; Prov. 28:8), and gambling, which foolishly trusts in chance rather than in the providence of God.

The Bible lists several acceptable ways to acquire money, including gifts (Acts 20:35; Phil. 4:16), investments (Matt. 25:27), saving (Prov. 21:20; 30:25), wise planning (Prov. 27:23–24), and, primarily, work (Ex. 20:9; Prov. 6:6–8; 14:23; 24:30–34; 28:19; Eph. 4:28; 2 Thess. 3:10; 1 Tim. 5:8).

Those who violate biblical principles in regard to money may find that they do not have enough of it. People in that situation need to consider whether they actually need more money, or merely want more. They should also recognize that their limited resources may be God's way of revealing that their priorities are wrong. Misuse of the resources God has given in the past—especially the abuse of credit (cf. Prov. 6:1–5; 11:15; 17:18; 20:16; 22:7)—may lead to a lack of resources in the present. People may also lack money because of stinginess (Luke 6:38; Prov. 11:24), impulsiveness or hastiness; Prov. 21:5), lack of discipline (Prov. 10:4; 13:18), laziness (Prov. 14:23; 19:15; 20:13; 24:30–34), indulgence (Prov. 21:17; 23:21), and craftiness (Prov. 28:19).

The Bible also gives guidelines on how to spend money. It is to be used to provide for the needs of one's household (1 Tim. 5:8), pay debts (Rom. 13:8), and save for the future (Prov. 21:20; 30:25). Having met those basic obligations, believers are ready to give money to further the kingdom.

Though many view giving as merely another obligation, it is in reality a priceless privilege, because it is the pipeline which brings God's promised blessings to His people. In Luke 6:38 Jesus promised, "Give, and it will be given to you. They will pour into your lap a good measure—pressed down, shaken together, and running over. For by your standard of measure it will be measured to you in return." Paul added, "He who sows sparingly will also reap sparingly, and he who sows bountifully will also reap bountifully" (2 Cor. 9:6). Significantly, the only direct quote from Jesus' earthly ministry recorded outside of the Gospels addresses the issue of giving: "In everything I showed you that by working hard in this manner you must help the weak and remember the words of the Lord Jesus, that He Himself said, 'It is more blessed to give than to receive'" (Acts 20:35).

Generous giving to God results in greater giving from God; it is impossible to outgive Him. The promises associated with giving should stimulate believers to be sacrificially generous givers. Sadly, the powerful lure of the world's advertising, slick appeals from purportedly Christian ministries, self-indulgence, and lack of faith all hinder believers from experiencing the full blessing of giving.

The early believers experienced no such hindrances. They freely gave in two general ways. First, they gave to support those who were responsible for leading and serving the church. In his first inspired epistle to the Corinthians Paul reminded them,

Or do only Barnabas and I not have a right to refrain from working? Who at any time serves as a soldier at his own expense? Who plants a vineyard and does not eat the fruit of it? Or who tends a flock and does not use the milk of the flock? I am not speaking these things according to human judgment, am I? Or does not the Law also say these things? For it is written in the Law of Moses, "You shall not muzzle the ox while he is threshing." God is not concerned about oxen, is He? Or is He speaking altogether for our sake? Yes, for our sake it was written, because the plowman ought to plow in hope, and the thresher to thresh in hope of sharing the crops. If we sowed spiritual things in you, is it too much if we reap material things from you? If others share the right over you, do we not more? Nevertheless, we did not use this right, but we endure all things so that we will cause no hindrance to the gospel of Christ. Do you not know that those who perform sacred services eat the food of the temple, and those who attend regularly to the altar have their share from the altar? So also the Lord directed those who proclaim the gospel to get their living from the gospel. (1 Cor. 9:6–14)

To Timothy he wrote: "The elders who rule well are to be considered worthy of double honor, especially those who work hard at preaching and teaching" (1 Tim. 5:17).

Second, the early church gave to meet the needs of the poor. Most of its members were from the lower classes (cf. 1 Cor. 1:26), and many were unable to meet their own financial needs. As Paul penned chapters 8 and 9 of this epistle, he had in mind this second aspect of giving. He did not write about the poor in the Corinthian assembly; the Corinthians were apparently faithful in caring for them. Nor was the apostle's focus on giving to the poor in general. He was concerned specifically about the many needy saints in the Jerusalem church.

From its birth on the Day of Pentecost, the Jerusalem church had had to cope with the extreme poverty of many of its members. There were three main reasons for that situation.

First, the Jerusalem church consisted largely of pilgrims. Many, if not most, of the first converts were visiting Jerusalem to celebrate the Day of Pentecost, when the church was born. They were Hellenistic Jews, who lived in the Gentile lands to which the Jewish people had been scattered in the Diaspora. Acts 2:9–11 describes them as "Parthians and Medes and Elamites, and residents of Mesopotamia, Judea and Cappadocia, Pontus and Asia, Phrygia and Pamphylia, Egypt and the districts of Libya around Cyrene, and visitors from Rome, both Jews and proselytes, Cretans and Arabs." On that Day of Pentecost, three thousand people were added to the church (Acts 2:41). Soon afterward, the number of men in the church reached five thousand (Acts 4:4), not counting the women. Since there were no churches or Christians anywhere else in the world, the converted pilgrims remained in Jerusalem. Only there could they sit under the apostles' teaching and find fellowship with other believers. Most of them were not wealthy and could not afford to stay indefinitely in Jerusalem's inns, nor would they wish to, given the condition of the typical inn. And many of those staying with Jewish relatives were alienated from family after becoming Christians and had to leave. They would have had no option but to move in with the Jewish believers who lived in Jerusalem. Many of them were also poor, so housing thousands of converted pilgrims would have been a great hardship for them.

Another reason for the Jerusalem church's poverty was persecution. New converts lost their jobs or businesses and were ostracized by their families and friends. Just as Jesus had predicted, they became the outcasts of Jewish society (John 16:2).

A third reason for the Jerusalem church's poverty was the generally poor economic climate of the region. The Romans extracted all they could from their conquered territories, seizing their resources and imposing a heavy burden of taxation. The result was rampant poverty in Israel. Adding to the region's economic woes was the worldwide famine predicted in Acts 11:27–29.

The Jerusalem church made a noble effort to meet the needs of its poor members. Acts 2:44–45 records that "all those who had believed were together and had all things in common; and they began selling their property and possessions and were sharing them with all, as anyone might have need," while Acts 4:32 adds, "The congregation of those who believed were of one heart and soul; and not one of them claimed that anything belonging to him was his own, but all things were common property to them." Because of their selfless dedication to meeting one another's needs, in the early days of the church "there was not a needy person among them" (Acts 4:34). But eventually, as the needs grew and persecution mounted (cf. Acts 8:1), the Jerusalem church was overwhelmed with needs and undersupplied with money.

Paul recognized their need and determined to take up a collection for the Jerusalem church from the churches of Asia Minor and Europe (Rom. 15:25–27). He also sought by doing that to strengthen the spiritual bond between those largely Gentile congregations and the Jewish church in Jerusalem. The apostle knew that the love offering would help ease the suspicion, bitterness, and hostility with which Jews and Gentiles generally regarded each other. It would tangibly express the spiritual reality that through His death, Jesus Christ "broke down the barrier of the dividing wall" between Jews and Gentiles, making them one (Eph. 2:14).

Paul first wrote to the Corinthians about this collection at the end of his first inspired letter to them (1 Cor. 16:1–4). But he had asked them to participate earlier, during his ministry in Corinth. Their rebellion against Paul had temporarily halted the collection, and since the relationship was restored, Paul instructed them to pick up where they left off. Paul had Titus encourage the Corinthians to begin the collection when he brought the severe letter to Corinth (2 Cor. 8:6).

In chapter 8, Paul listed several motives for giving. The first, because giving is the behavior of devout Christians (8:1–8), derives from the example of the Macedonian churches (Philippi, Thessalonica, Berea). This passage reveals that giving is motivated by God's grace, transcends difficult circumstances, is with joy, not hindered by poverty, generous, proportionate, sacrificial, voluntary, a privilege, an act of worship, in submission to pastors, in concert with other Christian virtues, and evidence of love.

GIVING IS MOTIVATED BY GOD'S GRACE

Now, brethren, we wish to make known to you the grace of God which has been given in the churches of Macedonia, (8:1)

The particle *de* (**now**) marks Paul's transition to a new subject. Since the apostle's relationship with his beloved **brethren** at Corinth had been restored (7:5–16), he could now discuss with them the issue of giving. He began by calling their attention to **the grace of God which has been given in the churches of Macedonia,** whom he would use as an example of giving. The Roman province of **Macedonia,** the ancient kingdom of Alexander the Great, was located in the northern part of modern Greece. As noted above, the three **churches of Macedonia** Paul had in mind were Philippi, Thessalonica, and Berea. **Macedonia** was an abysmally poor region, ravaged by wars and plundered by the Romans. But despite its deep poverty, the Macedonian believers were amazingly generous (cf. 11:9; Phil. 2:25; 4:15, 18).

The Corinthians were apparently unaware of the magnitude of the Macedonians' generosity, prompting Paul to **make** it **known** to them. Their giving was not motivated primarily by philanthropy or human kindness, but by the **grace of God** at work in their hearts. One of the effects of saving, transforming, sanctifying **grace** is a longing to give generously and sacrificially to those in need, especially other believers.

The Macedonians did not give like worldly rich people often do, mere tokens of their riches, without sacrifice. Nor did they give like selfish Christians, whose love for temporal things matches their love for eternal things. Giving for them is a battle, because they are still holding on to the temporal. The Macedonians gave magnanimously and abundantly, consistent with Christ's command to "seek first His kingdom and His righteousness, and all these things will be added to you" (Matt. 6:33). But Paul shuts out all thought of human merit by noting that they did so because they were prompted by God's grace (cf. Eph. 2:10).

GIVING TRANSCENDS DIFFICULT CIRCUMSTANCES

that in a great ordeal of affliction (8:2*a*)

Paul's strong language vividly depicts the Macedonians' desperate situation. *Polus* (**great**) means "much," or "many" and indicates the extreme nature of their **ordeal.** *Dokimē* (**ordeal**) refers to a test or a trial (cf. 2:9 and the use of the related verb *dokimazō* in 1 Cor. 3:13; 1 Peter 1:7). *Thlipsis* (**affliction**) literally refers to pressure, as in crushing grapes. Figuratively, it describes the spiritual pressure the Macedonians endured from their poverty and persecution.

Scripture repeatedly describes the suffering endured by the Macedonian churches. After Paul and Silas initially preached the gospel in Thessalonica

> the Jews, becoming jealous and taking along some wicked men from the market place, formed a mob and set the city in an uproar; and attacking the house of Jason, they were seeking to bring them out to the people. When they did not find them, they began dragging Jason and some brethren before the city authorities, shouting, "These men who have upset the world have come here also; and Jason has welcomed them, and they all act contrary to the decrees of Caesar, saying that there is another king, Jesus." They stirred up the crowd and the city authorities who heard these things. (Acts 17:5–8)

Paul also referred to persecution in his epistles to the Macedonian churches:

> You also became imitators of us and of the Lord, having received the word in much tribulation with the joy of the Holy Spirit. (1 Thess. 1:6)

> For you, brethren, became imitators of the churches of God in Christ Jesus that are in Judea, for you also endured the same sufferings at the hands of your own countrymen, even as they did from the Jews, who both killed the Lord Jesus and the prophets, and drove us out. (1 Thess. 2:14–15)

Therefore, we ourselves speak proudly of you among the churches of God for your perseverance and faith in the midst of all your persecutions and afflictions which you endure. (2 Thess. 1:4)

For to you it has been granted for Christ's sake, not only to believe in Him, but also to suffer for His sake. (Phil. 1:29)

But the Macedonians rose above their trying circumstances. They did not allow their situation to have a negative effect on their giving. In the midst of their trials, they put the needs of others, whom they had never met, ahead of their own. Though their poverty may have limited the amount they could give, it did not diminish their love. Devout Christians give no matter what the situation, because even the worst circumstances cannot hinder their devotion to Jesus Christ.

GIVING IS WITH JOY

their abundance of joy (8:2b)

Perisseia (**abundance**) means "a surplus," or "an overflow." Paul used it to describe God's saving grace that He pours out on believers through Jesus Christ (Rom. 5:17). The Macedonians did not give grudgingly, reluctantly, out of a sense of duty, or under duress. Nor were they motivated by fear of divine punishment or of Paul's displeasure. They gave gladly, freely, joyfully, knowing that "God loves a cheerful giver" (2 Cor. 9:7).

The Macedonians' joy transcended their pain, sorrow, and suffering. "You also became imitators of us and of the Lord," Paul wrote to the Thessalonians, "having received the word in much tribulation with the joy of the Holy Spirit" (1 Thess. 1:6; cf. Acts 5:41). Their giving reflected that reality, as they joyfully divested themselves of what little they possessed. They rejoiced at laying up treasures in heaven (Matt. 6:20; 19:21; Luke 12:33), knowing that the greater blessing is to the giver, not the receiver (Acts 20:35), and that God will give back in greater measure (Luke 6:38).

GIVING IS NOT HINDERED BY POVERTY

and their deep poverty (8:2c)

To express how little the Macedonians actually had, Paul described their impoverishment in strong language. **Deep** translates the phrase *kata bathos* (lit., "according to the depth"). The corresponding English expression would be "extremely deep"; or in the vernacular, "the pits" or "rock bottom." High taxes, slavery, low economic status, and persecution had all reduced the Macedonian believers to abject **poverty.** *Ptōcheia* (**poverty**) describes those with almost nothing, forced to beg to survive. Paul used it in 8:9 to describe Christ's poverty when He "emptied Himself, taking the form of a bond-servant, and being made in the likeness of men" (Phil. 2:7). A related word, *ptōchos,* is used to describe the blind and the lame (Luke 14:13, 21), a destitute widow (Mark 12:42), and Lazarus the beggar (Luke 16:20).

The Macedonians' confidence that God would supply all their needs (Ps. 37:25; Phil. 4:19) freed them to give generously. Devout Christians do not wait until they have more money; they give despite their poverty, like the poor widow of Luke 21:1–4. Jesus said in Luke 16:10, "He who is faithful in a very little thing is faithful also in much; and he who is unrighteous in a very little thing is unrighteous also in much." Giving is not a matter of how much one possesses but is an expression of an unselfish and loving heart. The Macedonians' refusal to allow their poverty to stifle their generosity made them models of Christian giving.

GIVING IS GENEROUS

overflowed in the wealth of their liberality. (8:2*d*)

Paul now explicitly stated what has been implied throughout the passage, piling up words to express the profound generosity of the Macedonians. **Overflowed** translates *perissueō,* the verb form of the noun translated "abundance" earlier in verse 2. Scripture uses it to describe the surplus goods of the rich (Mark 12:44), an abundance of material possessions (Luke 12:15), God's saving grace that abounds to sinners (Rom. 5:15; Eph. 1:7–8), the abundant hope produced by the Holy Spirit (Rom. 15:13), the abundant comfort that believers have in Christ (2 Cor. 1:5), and God's abundant grace toward believers (2 Cor. 9:8). Though it can refer to material riches (e.g., Matt. 13:22; 1 Tim. 6:17; James 5:2; Rev. 18:17), *ploutos* (**wealth**) is more commonly used in the New Testament to speak of spiritual riches (e.g., Eph. 1:7, 18; 2:7; 3:8, 16; Phil. 4:19; Col. 1:27; 2:2; Heb. 11:26), as it is here.

Though they were not rich in material possessions, the Macedonians did possess a **wealth of liberality.** *Haplotēs* (**liberality**) can also be translated "simplicity" (2 Cor. 11:3) or "sincerity" (Eph. 6:5; Col. 3:22). It is the opposite of duplicity, or being double-minded. Double-minded people find their ability to give crippled, because their concern for themselves and temporal matters conflicts with their concern for others and the kingdom of God. But the Macedonians were rich in single-mindedness, and gave with no thought of themselves or this world. Their selfless generosity was a practical application of Paul's command, "Do nothing from selfishness or empty conceit, but with humility of mind regard one another as more important than yourselves; do not merely look out for your own personal interests, but also for the interests of others" (Phil. 2:3–4).

GIVING IS PROPORTIONATE

For I testify that according to their ability, (8:3*a*)

Paul's use of *martureō* (**I testify**) reveals his firsthand experience of the Macedonians' generosity (cf. Phil. 4:15–18). They gave in proportion to what they had, **according to their ability.** *Dunamis* (**ability**) literally means "power," or "strength," and here refers to the Macedonians' capacity or means (cf. its use in Matt. 25:15) to give.

The Bible sets no fixed amount or percentage for giving (see the discussion of tithing below). Instead, giving is to be "according to what a person has, not according to what he does not have" (2 Cor. 8:12), as "[each person] may prosper" (1 Cor. 16:2). Any fixed amount or percentage would prove sacrificial for some but inconsequential for others. And, as the next aspect of the Macedonians' giving reveals, giving is to be sacrificial.

GIVING IS SACRIFICIAL

and beyond their ability, (8:3*b*)

The Macedonians gave according to what they had but in proportions that were sacrificial. Their giving was **beyond** what could reasonably be expected of such a poor congregation. Life was difficult for them; as noted in verse 2, they faced extreme poverty and persecution. Yet despite their desperate circumstances, they joyfully gave with no regard for themselves, compelled by the needs of the poor saints in Jerusalem (cf. Heb. 13:16). They believed God's promise to supply all their needs (Phil. 4:19) and refused to worry about them (Matt. 6:25–34), gladly placing themselves in deeper dependence on Him. Like David, who would not give the Lord something that cost him nothing (1 Chron. 21:24), and the poor widow, who gave all she had (Mark 12:42–44), the Macedonians gave with selfless abandon.

GIVING IS VOLUNTARY

they gave of their own accord, (8:3c)

The Macedonians' giving was on their own initiative; it was self-motivated and spontaneous. *Authairetos* (**of their own accord**) refers to one who chooses his own course of action. In its only other New Testament appearance, Paul used it to speak of Titus's choice to visit Corinth (8:17). The Macedonians were not coerced, manipulated, or intimidated, but gave freely.

It is possible that Paul, aware of their deep poverty, had not even asked them to contribute to the poor saints in Jerusalem. It is evident from 8:10 and 9:2 that about a year had passed since he first told the Corinthians about that collection. When Paul told the Macedonians about the zeal of the believers in Achaia (where Corinth was located) to contribute, the Macedonians were moved to give (9:2). Events had now come full circle. The Corinthians' zeal had initially prompted the Macedonians to give, and now Paul held them up as an example of sacrificial giving for the lagging Corinthians to imitate.

Despite the claims of those who advocate mandatory tithing, Christian giving is entirely voluntary. Paul did not require a fixed amount or percentage from either the Macedonians or the Corinthians, nor does any other New Testament writer. The argument for tithing is based on a misunderstanding of the Old Testament. Its proponents argue that tithing not only was commanded in the Mosaic Law but also existed before it. Therefore, they maintain, tithing transcends the Law and is a universal divine standard for giving.

But that seemingly convincing argument is seriously flawed. First, it is faulty reasoning to assume that an ordinance is permanent merely because it existed before the Law was given. The Sabbath predates the Law (Ex. 16:23–29), yet the New Testament abrogates its mandatory observance (Rom. 14:5–6; Gal. 4:10–11; Col. 2:16). Animal sacrifices also existed before the Law (Gen. 4:2–4; 8:20; 22:13; Ex. 10:25), yet were done away with by the final sacrifice of Jesus Christ (Heb. 10:1–18).

While tithing is mentioned in the pre-Mosaic period, it was not the same as that later commanded by the Mosaic Law. In all periods of history, there has been both voluntary and required giving. The tithes given by Abraham (Gen. 14:20) and Jacob (Gen. 28:22), like all offerings in the period before Moses, were voluntary; there is no indication that God commanded them to give. Nor did Abraham give a tenth of everything he owned, but rather a tenth of the spoils he had taken in battle (Heb. 7:4). There is no record that either man gave a tithe again; their tithings were one-time events.

That required giving existed in this period is evident from the story of Joseph. At his recommendation, Pharaoh levied a 20 percent tax on the people of Egypt during the seven years of abundance. That food was stored up against the seven lean years that were to follow (Gen. 41:34; 47:24). From this earliest period of human history an important principle emerges: Freewill giving is to the Lord; required giving is to the government.

The period from Moses to Jesus, when the Law was in force, also saw freewill and required giving. According to Leviticus 27:30–32 the tithe, or tenth part, belonged to the Lord. In contrast to the tithes given by Abraham and Jacob, this tithe was required giving (since it already belonged to the Lord; cf. Mal. 3:8), not a voluntary offering. Numbers 18:21 and 24 reveal that the tithe was given to support the Levites in their priestly service to the Lord. Since Israel was a theocracy, the Levites, especially in the days before the monarchy, constituted Israel's government. The tithe was therefore a form of taxation. In addition, the Israelites had to pay a second tithe to fund the religious festivals (Deut. 12:10–11, 17–18). A third tithe, due every third year, went to support the poor (Deut. 14:28–29). Thus, required giving, or taxation, during the Mosaic era amounted to at least 23-and-a-third percent, and perhaps as much as 25 percent when various other required offerings are taken into account (cf. Lev. 19:9–10; Neh. 10:32–33).

Voluntary or freewill offerings were also given during this period. During the building of the tabernacle, for example, "The Lord spoke to Moses, saying, 'Tell the sons of Israel to raise a contribution for Me; from every man whose heart moves him you shall raise My contribution'" (Ex. 25:1–2). In contrast to the required giving, this offering was strictly voluntary. It was to be collected "from every man whose heart move[d] him [to give]." Similarly, the people of Israel later gave freely to provide the resources to build the temple (1 Chron. 29:1–9).

Like the pre-Mosaic era and the era of the Law, the New Testament also depicts both freewill and required giving. It teaches, both by precept and example, that taxes (required giving) are to be paid to governments. In addition to the taxes they paid to support the theocracy, the Israelites also had to pay taxes to their Roman overlords—a heavy burden that they deeply resented. But instead of instigating a tax revolt, the Lord Jesus Christ paid His taxes:

> When they came to Capernaum, those who collected the two-drachma tax came to Peter and said, "Does your teacher not pay the two-drachma tax?" He said, "Yes." And when he came into the house, Jesus spoke to him first, saying, "What do you think, Simon? From whom do the kings of the earth collect customs or poll-tax, from their sons or from strangers?" When Peter said, "From strangers," Jesus said to him, "Then

the sons are exempt. However, so that we do not offend them, go to the sea and throw in a hook, and take the first fish that comes up; and when you open its mouth, you will find a coin. Take that and give it to them for you and Me." (Matt. 17:24–27)

Though as God's Son He was exempt from the temple tax, Jesus nonetheless paid it. Nor did He criticize the Pharisees for paying their tithes (Matt. 23:23), but rather for ignoring the more important aspects of the Mosaic Law. Jesus also taught that taxes were to be paid even to the hated Romans:

Then the Pharisees went and plotted together how they might trap Him in what He said. And they sent their disciples to Him, along with the Herodians, saying, "Teacher, we know that You are truthful and teach the way of God in truth, and defer to no one; for You are not partial to any. Tell us then, what do You think? Is it lawful to give a poll-tax to Caesar, or not?" But Jesus perceived their malice, and said, "Why are you testing Me, you hypocrites? Show Me the coin used for the poll-tax." And they brought Him a denarius. And He said to them, "Whose likeness and inscription is this?" They said to Him, "Caesar's." Then He said to them, "Then render to Caesar the things that are Caesar's; and to God the things that are God's." (Matt. 22:15–21)

To pay taxes is to "render to Caesar the things that are Caesar's," and is not optional. Even though governments today are secular, not theocracies, they are still established by God (Rom. 13:1), and the taxes they impose are to be paid (Rom. 13:6–7).

The New Testament also speaks of freewill giving; as noted above, the Macedonians and Corinthians were not compelled to give. The amount a believer gives is personally determined: "Each one must do just as he has purposed in his heart, not grudgingly or under compulsion" (2 Cor. 9:7; cf. the example of Zaccheus [Luke 19:8]). Believers are not to base their giving on the Old Testament principle of tithing but on the example of the Lord Jesus Christ, who "though He was rich, yet for [their sakes] He became poor, so that [they] through His poverty might become rich" (2 Cor. 8:9). (For a further discussion of tithing, see John MacArthur, *Whose Money Is It, Anyway?* [Nashville: Word, 2000].)

GIVING IS A PRIVILEGE, NOT AN OBLIGATION

begging us with much urging for the favor of participation in the support of the saints, (8:4)

Paul once again stressed that he in no way pressured the Macedonians to give. Instead they asked, even begged, to participate. *Deomai* (**begging**) is a strong word, meaning "to implore," or "to plead." It is used in Luke 5:12 of a leper who implored Jesus to heal him, in Luke 9:38 of a father's desperate plea for Jesus to cast a demon out of his son, and in 2 Corinthians 5:20 begging sinners to be reconciled to God. The phrase **with much urging** could be translated "most insistently" and further testifies to the intensity of the Macedonians' desire to contribute.

The privilege the Macedonians sought so eagerly was **the favor of participation in the support of the saints. Favor** translates *charis*, which is commonly translated "grace." They literally begged for the blessing of helping to meet the needs of believers they had never met. They did so not out of a sense of obligation but out of the generosity of their transformed hearts.

Giving Is an Act of Worship

and this, not as we had expected, but they first gave themselves to the Lord (8:5*a*)

And this introduces the next feature of the Macedonians' giving. Their response was more than Paul **expected.** He had hoped for an offering, which they did freely give, **but they first gave themselves to the Lord. First** (*prōtos*) has the meaning here not of first in time, but of first in priority (it is so used in Mark 6:21; Luke 19:47; Acts 13:50; 16:12; 17:4; 25:2; 28:7, 17). The Macedonians' first priority was to give themselves wholeheartedly to the Lord, and giving financially to the church followed.

The supreme act of worship is not giving money, attending church, or singing hymns, but giving oneself. In Romans 12:1–2 Paul wrote,

> Therefore I urge you, brethren, by the mercies of God, to present your bodies a living and holy sacrifice, acceptable to God, which is your spiritual service of worship. And do not be conformed to this world, but be transformed by the renewing of your mind, so that you may prove what the will of God is, that which is good and acceptable and perfect.

As "a holy priesthood," believers are "to offer up spiritual sacrifices acceptable to God through Jesus Christ" (1 Peter 2:5), the most important of which is themselves. Only when it is from a devout life, given to Christ wholly, does financial giving become an acceptable act of worship.

GIVING IS IN SUBMISSION TO PASTORS

and to us by the will of God. So we urged Titus that as he had previously made a beginning, so he would also complete in you this gracious work as well. (8:5*b*–6)

Having given themselves to the Lord, the Macedonians also gave themselves to Paul, Titus, and Timothy. In fact, it was their devotion to the Lord that led them to submit to the leadership of their pastors. It is **the will of God** that Christians obey those over them in the Lord. Hebrews 13:17 instructs believers, "Obey your leaders and submit to them, for they keep watch over your souls as those who will give an account. Let them do this with joy and not with grief, for this would be unprofitable for you," while Peter exhorted his readers to "be subject to [their] elders" (1 Peter 5:5; cf. 1 Thess. 5:12–13).

Confident that the Corinthians would follow the example of the Macedonians and submit to their pastors' direction, Paul **urged Titus that as he had previously made a beginning, so he would also complete in** the Corinthians **this gracious work** of giving **as well.** As noted above, Titus had **made a beginning** of the work of collecting the Corinthians' offering about a year earlier (2 Cor. 9:2). He had recently returned to Corinth bringing the severe letter, and Paul had **urged** him to help the Corinthians complete their giving. So Paul through his letters (cf. 1 Cor. 16:2) and Titus through his visits had both informed the Corinthians about what they expected them to do.

GIVING IS IN CONCERT WITH OTHER CHRISTIAN VIRTUES

But just as you abound in everything, in faith and utterance and knowledge and in all earnestness and in the love we inspired in you, see that you abound in this gracious work also. (8:7)

Giving does not take place in a vacuum, isolated from other Christian virtues. It must not be done contrary to what is in the heart, for that would be hypocrisy.

Paul's affirmation to the Corinthians, **you abound in everything** (cf. 1 Cor. 1:4–7), was an encouraging compliment to those vacillating believers. They abounded in saving, securing, sanctifying **faith,** having a strong trust in and reliance on the Lord. *Logos* (**utterance**) refers here not to speech, but to doctrine, the "word [*logos*] of truth" (2 Cor. 6:7; cf. Col. 1:5; 2 Tim. 2:15; James 1:18). **Knowledge** is the ability to apply doctrine to the issues of life. **Earnestness** (*spoudē*) means "eagerness," "energy," or "spiritual passion" (cf. 2 Cor. 7:11–12). **Love** (*agapē*) is the noble love of self-sacrifice Paul had **inspired** in the Corinthians through his example, teaching, and preaching.

Because of the spiritual virtues they possessed, Paul exhorted the Corinthians, **See that you abound in this gracious work also.** God's grace had produced those virtues in them, and the apostle wanted it to flow out through their giving.

Giving Is Proof of Love

I am not speaking this as a command, but as proving through the earnestness of others the sincerity of your love also. (8:8)

As he concluded his discussion of exemplary giving, Paul reminded the Corinthians that he was **not speaking** by way of **command.** That emphasizes yet again the fundamental principle that giving to the church is voluntary, freewill giving. Had Paul prescribed an amount or a fixed percentage, the Corinthians' giving would have been in obedience to a **command.**

Instead, Paul challenged the Corinthians to prove **through the earnestness of others the sincerity of** their **love also.** The others to whom he referred were the Macedonians; the apostle urged the Corinthians to follow their example and prove the **sincerity of** their **love also.** The true test of love is not feelings, but actions: "If someone says, 'I love God,' and hates his brother, he is a liar; for the one who does not love his brother whom he has seen, cannot love God whom he has not seen. And this commandment we have from Him, that the one who loves God should love his brother also" (1 John 4:20–21).

The voluntary, generous, sacrificial giving modeled by the Macedonians was an example not only for the Corinthians but also for all believers. It is the path to experiencing God's rich blessing in time and eternity.

The Poverty That Made Us Rich (2 Corinthians 8:9) 22

For you know the grace of our Lord Jesus Christ, that though He was rich, yet for your sake He became poor, so that you through His poverty might become rich. (8:9)

The story is told of a Persian monarch who reigned in opulence and splendor, living amid the wealth and comfort of the royal palace. Yet his concern for the common people frequently drove him to dress as a poor man, leave the palace, and mingle with the lowliest of his subjects.

One day he visited a fireman, whose job was to heat the water in the bathhouse. Dressed in tattered clothes, the shah descended a long flight of steps down to the tiny cellar where the fireman sat on a pile of ashes, tending the fire. The ruler sat beside him, and the two men began to talk. At lunchtime, the fireman shared his humble meal of coarse bread and water with his guest. Eventually, the shah left, but he returned again and again, his heart filled with sympathy for the lonely man. The fireman opened his heart to his kind, compassionate friend, who gave him wise counsel.

Finally, the shah could not bear to keep up the pretense any longer and decided to reveal his true identity to his friend. He then asked the poor fireman to name a gift he could give him. To his surprise, the man said nothing, but merely sat looking at him with love and wonder. Thinking he had not understood him, the shah offered to make the fireman rich, elevate him to the nobility, or make him ruler over a city. But he replied, "Yes, my lord, I understood you. But leaving your palace to sit here with me, partake of my humble food, and listen to the troubles of my heart—even you could give me no more precious gift than that. You may have given rich gifts to others, but to me you gave yourself. I only ask that you never withdraw your friendship from me."

That parable illustrates the incarnation of the Lord Jesus Christ, heaven's King who left His glorious throne to become the friend of sinners. As the writer of the hymn, "Thou Didst Leave Thy Throne," eloquently expressed it,

> Thou didst leave Thy throne
> And Thy kingly crown
> When Thou camest to earth for me;
> But in Bethlehem's home
> Was there found no room
> For Thy holy nativity.
>
> Heaven's arches rang
> When the angels sang,
> Proclaiming Thy royal degree;
> But of lowly birth
> Didst Thou come to earth,
> And in greatest humility.

Tucked away in this very practical, pragmatic section of the discussion of giving is a profound doctrinal treasure. Like 5:21, this verse is a Christological gem of incalculable value, a many-faceted diamond that far outshines all the other jewels around it. The wonder of this verse is captivating. Its vast scope, profundity, and impact transcend the simplicity of the twenty-one Greek words that comprise it. Its truth is not couched in technical theological language; its words are not complex or confusing. And though its message may be grasped in one reading, the truth it contains may not be fully comprehended throughout eternity. It describes Christ's descent from riches to poverty so that believers might ascend from poverty to riches.

As noted in the previous chapter of this volume, the theme of chapters 8 and 9 of 2 Corinthians is Christian giving. In this section, Paul discussed the offering he was collecting for the poor saints in Jerusalem. To stimulate the Corinthians' giving, he pointed out the example of the Macedonians, who gave generously and sacrificially despite their deep poverty (8:1–8).

But as the apostle thought about the reality that love manifests itself in sacrificial giving, his mind was irresistibly drawn to the greatest example of such love and sacrifice the world has ever known—the Lord Jesus Christ. Unlike the rich of this world, who rarely if ever impoverish themselves by their giving, He, the worthy One, became poor to make unworthy ones rich.

For links this verse to verse 8, where Paul wrote, "I am not speaking this as a command, but as proving through the earnestness of others the sincerity of your love also." The apostle did not need to command the Corinthians to give because they knew **the grace of our Lord Jesus Christ.** They may have been unaware of the Macedonians' giving, but they knew that Christ came down from heaven and gave His life as a sacrifice for sinners. That magnanimous gift eclipses all others as the example for all Christians to follow.

The apostle used the term **grace** to refer to Christ's giving because His self-giving was motivated by unmerited, spontaneous kindness to undeserving sinners stemming from pure and uninfluenced love. That act of the Savior defines grace giving at its purest level.

Paul refers to Him using the full name of the Incarnate God, the **Lord Jesus Christ.** That rich title encompasses the fullness of His person and work. **Lord** is the name above every name that was given Him by the Father because He accomplished the work of redemption (Phil. 2:9); **Jesus** depicts Him as the Savior of His people (Matt. 1:21); **Christ** describes Him as the anointed Messiah and King (Matt. 27:11; John 18:37).

The many facets of truth contained in this verse may be categorized under three headings: the riches of Christ, the poverty of Christ, and the gift of Christ.

THE RICHES OF CHRIST

that though He was rich, (8:9a)

Though as God Jesus owns everything in heaven and on earth (Ex. 19:5; Deut. 10:14; Job 41:11; Pss. 24:1; 50:12; 1 Cor. 10:26), His riches do not consist primarily of what is material. The riches in view here are those of Christ's supernatural glory, His position as God the Son, and His eternal attributes. The eternity of Jesus Christ is the most crucial truth in all of Christology, and therefore the most crucial truth of the gospel as well. If He is not eternal, He must have had a beginning, and would therefore be a created being. The eternality of Christ offers clear, powerful, and irrefutable proof of His deity, for it is an attribute only God possesses.

Despite the false claims of heretics throughout history, the Bible teaches that Jesus Christ is not merely preexistent to human history, but eternal. He does not depend on anything outside of Himself for His existence, nor was there ever a time when the second person of the Trinity came into being. Jesus is not an emanation, demigod, Michael the archangel, a spirit created by God, or an exalted man; He is the Creator (John 1:3, 10; Col. 1:16; Heb. 1:2), not a creature.

In a prophecy predicting His birthplace, Micah 5:2 says of Him, "But as for you, Bethlehem Ephrathah, too little to be among the clans of Judah, from you One will go forth for Me to be ruler in Israel. His goings forth are from long ago, from the days of eternity." Isaiah 9:6 describes Jesus as the "Eternal Father" of His people. John's gospel opens with the truth that "in the beginning [of creation; cf. Gen. 1:1] was the Word, and the Word was with God, and the Word was God." Jesus Christ existed from all eternity, because when the universe was created and time began, He already existed. In John 8:58 Jesus declared His eternal existence to the unbelieving Jews: "Truly, truly, I say to you, before Abraham was born, I am." Had He merely been claiming to have preexisted, He would have said, "I was," instead of, "I am." In John 17:5 He prayed, "Now, Father, glorify Me together with Yourself, with the glory which I had with You before the world was."

As the eternal second person of the Trinity, Jesus is as **rich** as God the Father. To the Colossians Paul wrote, "For in Him [Jesus] all the fullness of Deity dwells in bodily form" (Col. 2:9), and "[Jesus] is the radiance of [God's] glory and the exact representation of His nature" (Heb. 1:3). Arguments for Christ's eternity and deity are inseparable. Since the Scriptures reveal Him to be eternal, and only God can be eternal, Jesus must be God. Therefore, He owns the universe and everything in it, possesses all power and authority (Matt. 28:18), and is to be glorified and honored (John 5:23; Phil. 2:9–11). The eminent nineteenth-century theologian Charles Hodge wrote,

> All divine names and titles are applied to Him. He is called God, the mighty God, the great God, God over all; Jehovah; Lord; the Lord of lords and the King of kings. All divine attributes are ascribed to Him. He is declared to be omnipresent, omniscient, almighty, and immutable, the same yesterday, to-day, and forever. He is set forth as the creator and upholder and ruler of the universe. All things were created by Him and for Him; and by Him all things consist. He is the object of worship to all intelligent creatures, even the highest; all the angels (i.e., all creatures between man and God) are commanded to prostrate themselves before Him. He is the object of all the religious sentiments; of reverence, love, faith, and devotion. To Him men and angels are responsible for their character and conduct. He required that men

should honour Him as they honoured the Father; that they should exercise the same faith in Him that they do in God. He declares that He and the Father are one; that those who had seen Him had seen the Father also. He calls all men unto Him; promises to forgive their sins; to send them the Holy Spirit; to give them rest and peace; to raise them up at the last day; and to give them eternal life. God is not more, and cannot promise more, or do more than Christ is said to be, to promise, and to do. He has, therefore, been the Christian's God from the beginning, in all ages and in all places. (*Systematic Theology,* [Reprint; Grand Rapids: Eerdmans, 1979], 2:382)

THE POVERTY OF CHRIST

yet for your sake He became poor, (8:9*b*)

Though Jesus possessed all the riches of God from all eternity, yet for believers' **sake He became poor.** Some have understood that statement as a reference to Christ's financial poverty during His earthly life. Augustine challenged his readers to imitate Christ's virtues, including poverty, citing this verse as proof of Christ's poverty (*Of Holy Virginity,* para. 28). In his sermon, *On the Words of the Gospel, Luke 14:16, "A Certain Man Made a Great Supper," Etc.* Augustine said, "Let the beggars come, for He inviteth them, 'who, though He was rich, for our sakes became poor, that we beggars through His poverty might be enriched'" (para. 8). John Calvin, commenting on this verse, wrote

> We see what destitution and lack of all things awaited Him right from His mother's womb and we hear what He Himself says, "The foxes have holes and the birds of the heaven have nests; but the Son of Man hath not where to lay His head" (Luke 9:58). Thus He sanctified poverty in His own person, so that believers should no longer shrink from it, and by His poverty He has enriched us so that we should not find it hard to take from our abundance what we may expend on behalf of our brethren. (*The Second Epistle of Paul the Apostle to the Corinthians and the Epistles to Timothy, Titus, and Philemon* [Reprint; Grand Rapids: Eerdmans, 1973], 111)

Many connect this alleged reference to Jesus' poverty with the gospel, as if eliciting sympathy for Jesus' poverty has some redemptive value.

But this verse is not a commentary on Jesus' economic status or the material circumstances of His life. Fred B. Craddock notes, "The gospel can no more be equated with the financial poverty of Jesus than it can be equated with the pain he endured on the cross" ("The Poverty of Christ," *Interpretation* 22 [Apr. 1968], 162). The Lord's true impoverishment did not consist in the lowly circumstances in which He lived but in the reality that "although He existed in the form of God, [He] did not regard equality with God a thing to be grasped, but emptied Himself, taking the form of a bond-servant, and being made in the likeness of men" (Phil. 2:6–7).

In reality, Jesus did not live His life in abject poverty:

> As far as Jesus' experience is concerned, it is true that Luke highlights the lowly circumstances of his birth, but this is not an indication of the poverty of the holy family, but rather of the overcrowded conditions in Bethlehem at the time of the census (Lk. 2:7). The offering that Mary made for her purification was that permitted to those who could not afford a lamb (Lk. 2:24; cf. Lv. 12:6–8), and this indicates the family were not well off. Jesus was known as "the carpenter, the son of Mary" (Mk. 6:3), and as a craftsman he would not be numbered among the abject poor. During his Galilean ministry he did remind a would-be disciple that "Foxes have holes, and birds of the air have nests; but the Son of man has nowhere to lay his head" (Lk. 9:58). However, this must not be taken to mean that as an itinerant preacher Jesus was continually in dire economic circumstances. The indications are that the costs of Jesus' itinerant ministry and the support for his followers were provided by a number of well-off sympathizers who had been the recipients of his healing ministry (Lk. 8:1–3). In addition it was a custom among the Jews to provide hospitality for travelling preachers (cf. Mt. 10:9–13) and Jesus enjoyed such hospitality at a number of homes, and especially at that of Mary and Martha (Lk. 10:38–42; Jn. 12:1–3.). On the evidence, then, Jesus was no poorer than most first-century Palestinian Jews, and better off than some (e.g., those reduced to beggary). Indeed Jesus and his band of disciples had sufficient money to be able to provide help for those worse off than themselves (cf. Jn. 12:3–6; 13:27–29). (Colin Kruse, *The Second Epistle of Paul to the Corinthians,* The Tyndale New Testament Commentaries [Grand Rapids: Eerdmans, 1995], 154)

The Lord did not make believers spiritually rich by becoming economically poor. Paul used the terms "rich" and "poor" in this verse in a spiritual sense, as he did when he described himself as "poor yet making many rich" (2 Cor. 6:10).

The Lord Jesus Christ **became poor** in His incarnation, when He was "born of a woman" (Gal. 4:4); "in the likeness of sinful flesh" (Rom. 8:3); "a descendant of David according to the flesh" (Rom. 1:3); and "made . . . for a little while lower than the angels" (Heb. 2:7, 9). He left heaven's glory (John 17:5) and laid aside the free use of His divine prerogatives. In the most profound theological description of the Incarnation in Scripture Paul wrote that,

> although [Jesus] existed in the form of God, [He] did not regard equality with God a thing to be grasped, but emptied Himself, taking the form of a bond-servant, and being made in the likeness of men. Being found in appearance as a man, He humbled Himself by becoming obedient to the point of death, even death on a cross. Therefore also God highly exalted Him, and bestowed on Him the name which is above every name, so that at the name of Jesus every knee will bow, of those who are in heaven and on earth and under the earth, and that every tongue will confess that Jesus Christ is Lord, to the glory of God the Father. (Phil. 2:6–11)

Though He existed eternally "in the form of God," possessing all the riches of deity, Jesus "emptied Himself," becoming poor by "taking the form of a bond-servant, and being made in the likeness of men." He suffered human weaknesses and limitations, becoming hungry (Matt. 4:2; 21:18), thirsty (John 4:7; 19:28), and tired (Mark 4:38; John 4:6). In addition, He was "tempted in all things as we are, yet without sin" (Heb. 4:15). So completely did Jesus identify with His people as their faithful high priest that "He humbled Himself by becoming obedient to the point of death."

Ephesians 4:8–10 gives another view of Christ' impoverishing Himself in the Incarnation:

> Therefore it says, "When He ascended on high, He led captive a host of captives, and He gave gifts to men." (Now this expression, "He ascended," what does it mean except that He also had descended into the lower parts of the earth? He who descended is Himself also He who ascended far above all the heavens, so that He might fill all things.)

Paul's quote from Psalm 68:18, "When He ascended on high, He led captive a host of captives, and He gave gifts to men," describes Christ's triumphant return to heaven after His victory over the forces of hell on Calvary. Through His sacrificial death, He freed sinners who had been captives to sin and Satan. After His ascension, He dispensed the spoils won by His death and resurrection and "gave gifts to men." But Christ's triumph on Calvary was only possible because He had first "descended into the lower parts of the earth." He left the glory of heaven and entered a world of suffering and death. Jesus' descent reached its deepest point when He went between His death and resurrection to the prison where the most wicked of the fallen angels are incarcerated. There He proclaimed to them His triumph over the forces of hell (cf. Col. 2:15; 1 Peter 3:18–19).

In the incarnation of Christ, the eternal God **became poor** by taking on human flesh and humbling Himself even to the point of death on the cross. By doing so, He defeated the powers of hell, accomplished the work of redemption God assigned Him, and gave His people the priceless riches of salvation.

THE GIFT OF CHRIST

so that you through His poverty might become rich. (8:9c)

The purpose of Christ's condescension was that **through His poverty** poor sinners **might become rich.** He did not make them materially rich but gave them all the blessings of salvation—forgiveness, joy, peace, eternal life, light, and glory. Peter described those riches as "an inheritance which is imperishable and undefiled and will not fade away, reserved in heaven for [believers]" (1 Peter 1:4).

Sinners desperately need the riches of Christ because they are spiritually destitute. They are the "poor in spirit" (Matt. 5:3), beggars with nothing to commend themselves. But through salvation, believers are made "heirs of God and fellow heirs with Christ" (Rom. 8:17), sharing His riches because they are made "partakers of the divine nature" (2 Peter 1:4). The ultimate goal of their salvation is to be made like Him (1 John 3:2), to reflect His glory in heaven, "so that in the ages to come He might show the surpassing riches of His grace in kindness toward us in Christ Jesus" (Eph. 2:7).

This was not the first time Paul described their riches in Christ to the Corinthians. In 1 Corinthians 1:4–5 he wrote, "I thank my God always concerning you for the grace of God which was given you in Christ Jesus, that in everything you were enriched in Him," while in 3:22 he added, "Whether Paul or Apollos or Cephas or the world or life or death or things present or things to come; all things belong to you."

The glorious truth that Christians have been "blessed . . . with every spiritual blessing in the heavenly places in Christ" (Eph. 1:3) through His self-emptying, self-sacrificial love should elicit gratitude from them. More than that, however, it should also motivate them to give freely, sacrificially, and generously to others. They must follow the example of the Lord Jesus Christ, who became poor to make others rich. How can Christians receive all the riches Christ impoverished Himself to give them, yet be unwilling to meet the needs of others? James wrote, "If a brother or sister is without clothing and in need of daily food, and one of you says to them, 'Go in peace, be warmed and be filled,' and yet you do not give them what is necessary for their body, what use is that?" (James 2:15–16). The apostle John added, "Whoever has the world's goods, and sees his brother in need and closes his heart against him, how does the love of God abide in him?" (1 John 3:17).

Some may view Paul's inclusion of this verse, with its profound theological truth, in the context of giving as incongruous. But that loses sight of the fact that theological truth does not exist in isolation from everyday life, as Fred B. Craddock notes:

> There is nothing mundane and outside the concern and responsibility of the Christian. There are not two worlds; there is but one. Money for the relief of the poor is as "spiritual" as prayer. . . . The offering for the saints in Judea was for Paul a definite implication of the Incarnation. It is no surprise that the discussion of the one should bring to mind the other. The offering, in fact, provided an occasion for teaching the meaning of Christology, and Christology informed and elicited the offering. ("The Poverty of Christ," *Interpretation* 22 [Apr. 1968] 169)

The seemingly mundane issue of the offering was in reality connected to the central truth of Christianity, namely, that Christ's voluntary poverty makes the spiritually destitute rich.

Stewardship with Integrity
(2 Corinthians 8:10–9:5)

23

I give my opinion in this matter, for this is to your advantage, who were the first to begin a year ago not only to do this, but also to desire to do it. But now finish doing it also, so that just as there was the readiness to desire it, so there may be also the completion of it by your ability. For if the readiness is present, it is acceptable according to what a person has, not according to what he does not have. For this is not for the ease of others and for your affliction, but by way of equality—at this present time your abundance being a supply for their need, so that their abundance also may become a supply for your need, that there may be equality; as it is written, "He who gathered much did not have too much, and he who gathered little had no lack." But thanks be to God who puts the same earnestness on your behalf in the heart of Titus. For he not only accepted our appeal, but being himself very earnest, he has gone to you of his own accord. We have sent along with him the brother whose fame in the things of the gospel has spread through all the churches; and not only this, but he has also been appointed by the churches to travel with us in this gracious work, which is being administered by us for the glory of the Lord Himself, and to show our readiness, taking precaution so

that no one will discredit us in our administration of this generous gift; for we have regard for what is honorable, not only in the sight of the Lord, but also in the sight of men. We have sent with them our brother, whom we have often tested and found diligent in many things, but now even more diligent because of his great confidence in you. As for Titus, he is my partner and fellow worker among you; as for our brethren, they are messengers of the churches, a glory to Christ. Therefore openly before the churches, show them the proof of your love and of our reason for boasting about you. For it is superfluous for me to write to you about this ministry to the saints; for I know your readiness, of which I boast about you to the Macedonians, namely, that Achaia has been prepared since last year, and your zeal has stirred up most of them. But I have sent the brethren, in order that our boasting about you may not be made empty in this case, so that, as I was saying, you may be prepared; otherwise if any Macedonians come with me and find you unprepared, we—not to speak of you—will be put to shame by this confidence. So I thought it necessary to urge the brethren that they would go on ahead to you and arrange beforehand your previously promised bountiful gift, so that the same would be ready as a bountiful gift and not affected by covetousness. (8:10–9:5)

There are few topics in the church more sensitive than that of money. Any mention of giving, contributions, or fund-raising campaigns is sure to be perceived by some as inappropriate, intrusive, even offensive. Critics accuse church leaders of constantly appealing for money, and often of mishandling what they receive

Unfortunately, there is some truth to those accusations. Many leaders do seem to be preoccupied with raising money. Some are sincere but misguided individuals, who in their zeal (or desperation) resort to questionable fund-raising techniques. But some are outright hucksters, willfully, cynically, and unethically bilking even the poor and desperate to pad their own pockets and build their own empires. As a result of their aggressive, high-pressure tactics and slick campaigns, millions of dollars are siphoned off in schemes that do not advance God's kingdom.

In the face of those abuses, some might think it wise to avoid the issue altogether. This cannot be the right solution. Every church and each believer must understand the divine will with regard to money, its use by believers and in the church. Giving in particular is a significant element in God's design for the Christian life. Giving advances His kingdom, glorifies His name, meets the needs of others, and lays up treasure in heaven, bringing God's blessing in this life and the next. It must be a regular feature of worship as the church comes together on the Lord's Day.

Christians are to be careful stewards of the resources God has entrusted to them. They must be wise about earning, saving, investing, and spending money. And just as they are careful in those areas, so they must also be in how they give their money. This passage is a rich contribution to Scripture's teaching about the privilege of giving. On the surface, the text appears to be nothing more than some passing notes about an event that took place two thousand years ago. Yet it contains timeless and practical principles that define stewardship for all believers. Through these verses, stewardship with integrity is defined as calling for giving that is voluntary, faithfulness to complete the project, amounts that are proportionate to what one has, giving that balances resources in the body of Christ, is in submission to pastoral leadership, is handled with accountability, is an expression of love, sets an example, and overcomes the sin of covetousness.

STEWARDSHIP WITH INTEGRITY CALLS FOR GIVING THAT IS VOLUNTARY

I give my opinion in this matter, for this is to your advantage, who were the first to begin a year ago not only to do this, but also to desire to do it. (8:10)

Giving does not involve a fixed amount or percentage but is entirely voluntary. (For a discussion of tithing, see chapter 21 of this volume.) Paul did not pressure or even expect the Macedonians to give a specific percent but rather commended them because "they gave of their own accord" (8:3). Nor did he issue a command to the Corinthians in this text but instead gave them his **opinion in this matter** of giving.

It was, the apostle knew, to the Corinthians' **advantage** to give sacrificially and generously. In 9:6 he wrote, "He who sows sparingly will also reap sparingly, and he who sows bountifully will also reap bountifully." Jesus expressed the same principle in Luke 6:38: "Give, and it will be given to you. They will pour into your lap a good measure—pressed down, shaken together, and running over. For by your standard of measure it will be measured to you in return." When believers give generously, God will bless them generously in return. Convinced of that truth, the Corinthians gave such a large offering that Paul referred to it as a "generous gift" (2 Cor. 8:20), capable of "fully supplying the needs of the saints" (9:12).

Stewardship programs with integrity do not pressure people to give. All too often, manipulative leaders coerce people into parting with their money—under wrong motivation from fear or selfishness. Any kind of compulsory giving to the Lord is not the biblical way. Stewardship with integrity involves people giving not from outward coercion, but from inward devotion.

Rather than demand a specific amount from the Corinthians, Paul motivated them by reminding them that they **were the first to begin** to give **a year ago.** The phrase **a year ago** could also be translated "last year," allowing for more than twelve months to have passed. They were **not only** the first to begin to give, **but also** the first **to desire to do it,** which again reveals that they gave freely, not under compulsion.

The chronology of Paul's dealings with the Corinthians concerning the collection for the Jerusalem church may be reconstructed as follows. After founding the Corinthian church on his second missionary journey (Acts 18:1–10), Paul ministered there for about twenty months (Acts 18:11, 18). He then left Corinth and went to Ephesus, from where he wrote a corrective letter to the Corinthians (1 Cor. 5:9), probably carried to Corinth by Titus. By that time, Paul had formulated his plan for the offering to give to the poor Christians in Jerusalem, and Titus told the Corinthians about it. The church responded positively but had some questions, which Paul answered in 1 Corinthians (16:1–4). After false teachers arrived in Corinth and led a rebellion against Paul, the Corinthians temporarily halted their giving. Paul dealt sternly with this rebellion in his third letter, known as the severe letter (2 Cor. 2:3–4), which he wrote between 1 and 2 Corinthians. The apostle received the encouraging news from Titus (who had carried the severe letter to Corinth) that most of the Corinthians had repented of their disaffection toward him. Therefore when he wrote 2 Corinthians, his fourth letter to them, Paul urged them to resume collecting the offering (chaps. 8, 9). He did so in keeping with the principle noted in 1 Corinthians 16:2, that all their giving was to be voluntary, i.e., "as [each person] may prosper."

STEWARDSHIP WITH INTEGRITY CALLS FOR
FAITHFULNESS TO COMPLETE THE COMMITMENT

But now finish doing it also, so that just as there was the readiness to desire it, so there may be also the completion of it (8:11*a*)

One of the most vexing aspects of the ministry is dealing with those who make a good beginning but never finish what they start. It is not easy to carry things through to completion; it takes discipline, devotion, and faithfulness. There are many who start, even make promises to give, but fail to complete that promise. All the Corinthians' good intentions would have meant little had they failed to complete the collection, so Paul urged them to **finish doing it.** Their **readiness to desire** to give was meaningless apart from **the completion of** the project. The apostle was concerned that, though they were willing, they might fail to perform. At the end of 1 Corinthians (16:2) Paul instructed the Corinthians, "On the first day of every week each one of you is to put aside and save, as he may prosper, so that no collections be made when I come." The giving was to be done in a systematic, orderly, routine manner on the Lord's Day; Paul did not want hasty collections to be taken only when he arrived.

As noted above, the Corinthians' giving was not halted by apathy or selfishness, but by the rebellion against Paul incited by the false apostles. One of their most devious lies about him was that he was in the ministry for the money; that he was "walking in craftiness" (2 Cor. 4:2). But unlike the false apostles, Paul was not guilty of "peddling the word of God" (2:17). Nevertheless, the false accusations against him had raised doubts about his integrity among the Corinthians, effectively halting the collection. Nothing cripples people's willingness to give as much as a loss of confidence in their leaders. But since the relationship between the apostle and the Corinthians had been restored, it was time for them to complete what they had started.

STEWARDSHIP WITH INTEGRITY CALLS FOR AMOUNTS THAT ARE PROPORTIONATE TO WHAT ONE HAS

by your ability. For if the readiness is present, it is acceptable according to what a person has, not according to what he does not have. (8:11b–12)

Though Paul expected the Corinthians to give generously, he did not expect them to give beyond their means. The Greek phrase translated **by your ability** literally reads, "out of what you have." As the apostle wrote in his first inspired letter to them, "Each one of you is to put aside and save, as he may prosper" (1 Cor. 16:2). Even the exemplary giving of the Macedonians was "according to their ability, and beyond their ability" (2 Cor. 8:3); that is, they gave out of what they had, but in sacrificial amounts, using money needed for the basic necessities of life. But **if the readiness** (*prothumia;* "willingness"; "eagerness"; "zeal") to give sacrificially with unique generosity **is present, it is acceptable** to God for believers to give beyond what would be expected. But God expects giving **according to what a person has, not according to what he does not have.** Believers should not, however, borrow to give. Going into debt to give with no ability to repay is foolish.

When believers are moved to give beyond their ability, and make sacrifices to increase their ability to give, they are following the example of the poor widow, of whom Jesus said, "Truly I say to you, this poor widow put in more than all the contributors to the treasury; for they all put in out of their surplus, but she, out of her poverty, put in all she owned, all she had to live on" (Mark 12:43–44).

Some of the Corinthians may have been using their lack of resources as an excuse not to give. It is true that those who, like the poor widow, have minimal resources can only give a little, while those with more substantial resources can give larger amounts. But with God the amount is not the issue but the attitude of the heart. He expects believers to give in proportion to their resources, not more, but also not less. Any ministry that attempts to pressure people to give beyond their resources is operating outside the bounds of biblical stewardship. So also are those who fail to give in proportion to their resources.

STEWARDSHIP WITH INTEGRITY CALLS FOR
GIVING THAT BALANCES RESOURCES IN THE BODY OF CHRIST

For this is not for the ease of others and for your affliction, but by way of equality—at this present time your abundance being a supply for their need, so that their abundance also may become a supply for your need, that there may be equality; as it is written, "He who gathered much did not have too much, and he who gathered little had no lack." (8:13–15)

Some of the Corinthians may also have been reluctant to give because of the charge of favoritism leveled against Paul by the false apostles. They accused him of being prejudiced in favor of the predominantly Jewish church at Jerusalem, since he also was Jewish. Thus, according to the anti-Paul faction, the apostle's goal in collecting the offering was to prejudicially enrich his countrymen at the expense of the Corinthians' deprivation.

Anticipating that objection, Paul assured the Corinthians that the collection was **not for the ease of others.** His goal was not to raise the Jerusalem saints' comfort level by causing the Corinthians **affliction** and hardship. He was not out to make the rich poor and the poor rich. Instead, his goal was to oppose favoritism and instead to bring about some **equality**—not economic egalitarianism in a Marxist or socialist sense, but a balancing of resources. Paul wanted those with more than they needed to help those who had less than they needed. Such an attitude is the mark of a genuine believer. "Whoever has the world's goods,"

John wrote, "and sees his brother in need and closes his heart against him, how does the love of God abide in him?" (1 John 3:17). John rightly questions the salvation of such a person.

Paul expressed this same principle to Timothy, telling him to "instruct those who are rich in this present world not to be conceited or to fix their hope on the uncertainty of riches, but on God, who richly supplies us with all things to enjoy. Instruct them to do good, to be rich in good works, to be generous and ready to share" (1 Tim. 6:17–18). There is nothing wrong with being rich if God so blesses. But the rich are not to be conceited or to trust in their riches. Instead, they are "to be generous and ready to share." There was nothing wrong with the Corinthians having more than the Jerusalem believers. But it would have been wrong for them to be unwilling to share. Christians are not isolated individuals but members of one body (Rom. 12:5). Therefore, they are responsible to meet one another's needs.

That does not mean, of course, that the church is to support those who choose not to work. The Bible does not approve of indolence. In fact, Paul declared forcefully regarding those who refuse to work, "If anyone is not willing to work, then he is not to eat, either" (2 Thess. 3:10). The church's responsibility is not to indulge laziness but to meet the basic needs of those unable to provide for themselves.

Though **at** the **present time** the Corinthians' **abundance** was **a supply for** the Jerusalem saints' **need,** that might not always be the case. The fortunes of life could change, and the time might come when persecution or disaster could impoverish the Corinthians. Should that happen, the Jerusalem saints' **abundance** would then **become a supply for** the Corinthians' **need.**

Paul illustrated his point with a quote from the Old Testament. He introduced it with the familiar phrase **as it is written,** the common New Testament way of introducing an Old Testament quote (cf. 2 Cor. 9:9; Mark 1:2; 7:6; Luke 2:23; 3:4; John 6:31; 12:14–15; Acts 7:42; 15:15; Rom. 1:17; 2:24; 3:4, 10; 4:17; 8:36; 9:13, 33; 10:15; 11:8, 26; 15:3, 9, 21; 1 Cor. 1:31; 2:9; 10:7). The quote, **"He who gathered much did not have too much, and he who gathered little had no lack"** comes from the account of Israel's wilderness wanderings. In response to the people's grumbling (Ex. 16:2–3), the Lord promised to send them bread from heaven (Ex. 16:4). When they gathered the manna, "some gathered much and some little" (Ex. 16:17). Yet "he who had gathered much had no excess, and he who had gathered little had no lack" (Ex. 16:18). Apparently, they shared what they gathered, so each person and family had enough to eat. So it is in the body of Christ; those who have an abundance share with those who are in need, so that everyone has enough.

STEWARDSHIP WITH INTEGRITY CALLS FOR
SUBMISSION TO PASTORAL LEADERSHIP

But thanks be to God who puts the same earnestness on your behalf in the heart of Titus. For he not only accepted our appeal, but being himself very earnest, he has gone to you of his own accord. (8:16–17)

Paul here anticipated and answered another potential objection to the offering, namely, that the project was his alone. But it was not just Paul's passion; **God** had put **the same earnestness** for the project **in the heart of Titus. Titus,** who knew them so well and loved them so dearly (cf. 7:15), was also wholeheartedly committed to the relief effort for the Jerusalem saints. That God had so united the hearts of Paul and Titus further confirmed that the collection was His will. Nor could the anti-Paul faction accuse Titus of having a Jewish bias, since he was a Gentile.

Lest any should think that Paul coerced Titus into being involved with the program, the apostle noted that **he not only accepted our appeal, but being himself very earnest, he has gone to you of his own accord.** Paul did ask Titus to participate, and he **accepted** the apostle's appeal. But so **earnest** was Titus's support for the project that he went to Corinth **of his own accord.** His voluntary participation along with Paul was further evidence of the unanimity between the two.

Forceful, strong-willed leaders can often ram through their projects. But biblically sound stewardship programs will be led by a plurality of godly men. The church's finances are to be overseen by wise, theologically sound, spiritually mature men who agree to seek the mind of God.

STEWARDSHIP WITH INTEGRITY
CALLS FOR ACCOUNTABILITY

We have sent along with him the brother whose fame in the things of the gospel has spread through all the churches; and not only this, but he has also been appointed by the churches to travel with us in this gracious work, which is being administered by us for the glory of the Lord Himself, and to show our readiness, taking precaution so that no one will discredit us in our administration of this generous gift; for we have regard for what is honorable, not only in the sight of the Lord, but also in the sight of men. We have sent with them our brother, whom we have often tested and found diligent in many things, but now even more dili-

gent because of his great confidence in you. As for Titus, he is my partner and fellow worker among you; as for our brethren, they are messengers of the churches, a glory to Christ. (8:18–23)

Not only was Titus, whom the Corinthians knew well and highly respected, involved in the collection, but so also was an unnamed **brother whose fame in the things of the gospel** had **spread through all the churches.** Paul had **sent** him **along with** Titus to Corinth to help with the collection. The inclusion of this highly regarded individual signaled Paul's intention to handle matters with absolute honesty and integrity. It further deflected any possible criticism that he might misuse the money.

Some have speculated that the unnamed **brother** was Tychicus, others that he was Trophimus or Luke. But since his name is not given, such speculation is futile. The Corinthians would certainly recognize him, if for no other reason than that he would arrive with Titus. The implication of Paul's words, however, is that they already knew him as a distinguished preacher of the gospel. Paul did not choose him to help with the collection because of his business acumen, but because of his spiritual maturity, unimpeachable character, and reputation for integrity. The involvement of another godly leader with the collection further enhanced the project's credibility. It was also in keeping with the New Testament pattern of entrusting money to the spiritual leadership of the church (cf. Acts 4:37).

Not only had Paul and Titus chosen the unnamed brother to help oversee the collection, **but he** had **also been appointed by the churches to travel with** them **in** that **gracious work.** He was not just another of the apostle's protégés who would be under his thumb. His appointment by the **churches** protected Paul and Titus from any false accusation that they were in collusion to mishandle the money. The reason for the apostle's concern was not that he and Titus could not be trusted, but rather that Paul's enemies at Corinth could not be trusted. They could not be allowed to make an accusation that would further confuse the already unsettled Corinthians.

The collection was **being administered by** Paul and his companions **for the glory of the Lord Himself.** They wanted to be absolutely certain that no reproach fell on the name of Christ. The unnamed preacher would act as an objective, outside auditor, ensuring that no valid criticism about the handling of the money could be made. They also wanted **to show** their **readiness** to help the poor, something Paul had always been eager to do (cf. Gal. 2:10).

So, anticipating his enemies' attacks on his credibility, Paul took the **precaution** of involving the godly preacher who would accompany Titus **so that no one** would **discredit** him **in** his **administration of** the

Corinthians' **generous gift.** It was a wise safeguard, since his enemies at Corinth had accused him of being in the ministry for money. Defending his rights and privileges as an apostle, Paul wrote in 1 Corinthians 9:3–15,

> My defense to those who examine me is this: Do we not have a right to eat and drink? Do we not have a right to take along a believing wife, even as the rest of the apostles and the brothers of the Lord and Cephas? Or do only Barnabas and I not have a right to refrain from working? Who at any time serves as a soldier at his own expense? Who plants a vineyard and does not eat the fruit of it? Or who tends a flock and does not use the milk of the flock? I am not speaking these things according to human judgment, am I? Or does not the Law also say these things? For it is written in the Law of Moses, "You shall not muzzle the ox while he is threshing." God is not concerned about oxen, is He? Or is He speaking altogether for our sake? Yes, for our sake it was written, because the plowman ought to plow in hope, and the thresher to thresh in hope of sharing the crops. If we sowed spiritual things in you, is it too much if we reap material things from you? If others share the right over you, do we not more? Nevertheless, we did not use this right, but we endure all things so that we will cause no hindrance to the gospel of Christ. Do you not know that those who perform sacred services eat the food of the temple, and those who attend regularly to the altar have their share from the altar? So also the Lord directed those who proclaim the gospel to get their living from the gospel. But I have used none of these things. And I am not writing these things so that it will be done so in my case; for it would be better for me to die than have any man make my boast an empty one.

Though Paul had every right to receive support from the Corinthians, he did not take it. He wanted to avoid lending credence to the false accusation that he was in the ministry for the money.

Later in 2 Corinthians he wrote,

> Or did I commit a sin in humbling myself so that you might be exalted, because I preached the gospel of God to you without charge? I robbed other churches by taking wages from them to serve you; and when I was present with you and was in need, I was not a burden to anyone; for when the brethren came from Macedonia they fully supplied my need, and in everything I kept myself from being a burden to you, and will continue to do so. (11:7–9; cf. 12:14–18)

Paul's caution was all the more justified because he expected the Corinthians' gift to be a large one. *Hadrotēs* (**generous gift**), which appears only here in the New Testament, refers to an abundance. It would have been a tempting target had Paul really been the embezzler his enemies falsely accused him of being.

Paul had **regard for what is honorable, not only in the sight of the Lord** (cf. the discussion of v. 19 above), **but also in the sight of men.** Some might wonder why Paul should care what men thought, as long as he acted appropriately **in the sight of the Lord.** He was no man pleaser (cf. 1 Cor. 9:22; Gal. 1:10; 1 Thess. 2:4). But neither was he unconcerned about what men thought; after all, they were the ones he was trying to reach with the gospel. He could not allow his enemies to make any false accusations that might discredit and bring suspicion on him before the watching world and hinder his preaching of the gospel (cf. Prov. 3:4; Rom. 12:17; 14:16; 1 Cor. 9:22; 10:32–33).

Further underscoring his concern to handle the collection with integrity, Paul **sent with** Titus and the unnamed preacher another unnamed **brother.** Once again, it is futile to speculate about his identity; like the famous preacher mentioned above, the Corinthians knew and respected him. Though he is not named, he is highly commended; Paul described him as one **whom we have often tested** (from *dokimazō;* to approve after testing) **and found diligent in many things.** His diligence or zeal was enhanced **because of his great confidence in** the Corinthians. He had heard of their repentance and renewed loyalty to Paul, which made him all the more eager to be involved.

Then Paul summarized the members of what amounted to his financial committee, reemphasizing their noble, unimpeachable character. **Titus** was not only Paul's **partner** (*koinōnos*) in ministry, but also a **fellow worker** (*sunergos;* cf. Rom. 16:3, 9, 21; Phil. 2:25; Col. 4:11; Philem. 1, 24) **among** the Corinthians. And **as for** the two unnamed **brethren, they** were **messengers** (lit., "apostles") **of the churches.** That phrase, occurring only here in the New Testament, designates them as officially authorized representatives of the churches. They were not apostles of Christ, as were the Twelve and Paul. They were not eyewitnesses of the risen Lord, chosen and commissioned by Him, either directly (Mark 3:13–19; Acts 9:15) or through those whom He had previously commissioned (Acts 1:21–22). These two faithful brothers were sent by the churches to help with the collection. Showing the high caliber of men to which the early church entrusted money, Paul called the three **a glory to Christ.** There could be no higher commendation, and those who lived to bring **glory to Christ** would not bring shame to His name and His church.

Stewardship with Integrity Calls for
Giving That Is an Expression of Love

Therefore openly before the churches, show them the proof of your love and of our reason for boasting about you. (8:24)

Paul had instructed the Corinthians about the importance and procedure of making their contribution. He had taken every reasonable precaution to avoid any appearance of impropriety. Now it was time for the Corinthians to give **openly before the churches** (lit., "before the face of the churches") so that all would clearly see their generosity. By so doing, they would **show them the proof of** their **love;** as Jesus said, "A new commandment I give to you, that you love one another, even as I have loved you, that you also love one another. By this all men will know that you are My disciples, if you have love for one another" (John 13:34–35). A loving church is a generous church, and the Corinthians' generous love would validate Paul's **boasting about** the work of Christ in them.

STEWARDSHIP WITH INTEGRITY CALLS FOR
GIVING THAT SETS AN EXAMPLE

For it is superfluous for me to write to you about this ministry to the saints; for I know your readiness, of which I boast about you to the Macedonians, namely, that Achaia has been prepared since last year, and your zeal has stirred up most of them. But I have sent the brethren, in order that our boasting about you may not be made empty in this case, so that, as I was saying, you may be prepared; otherwise if any Macedonians come with me and find you unprepared, we—not to speak of you—will be put to shame by this confidence. (9:1–4)

The chapter break here in the text is unfortunate, for these verses continue the thought expressed at the end of chapter 8. So confident was Paul in the Corinthians that he felt it was **superfluous for** him **to write to** them **about** the **ministry** (offering) **to the saints** in Jerusalem. He knew of their **readiness,** of the eagerness and zeal of their original response. That prompted the apostle to **boast about** them **to the Macedonians, namely, that Achaia** (the province in which Corinth was located) had **been prepared since** the previous **year.** In fact, as noted in chapter 21 of this volume, it was the example of the Corinthians' original **zeal** that **stirred up most of** the Macedonians to contribute so sacrificially to the project.

But as noted above, the rebellion against Paul incited by the false teachers had apparently halted their giving. He therefore **sent the brethren** (Titus and the two unnamed brothers) **in order that** his **boasting about** them **may not be made empty in this case;** in other words, **so that** they would have the offering **prepared.** Paul was concerned that if **any Macedonians** came **with** him to Corinth (as in fact some did; cf. Acts 20:2–4), they might **find** them **unprepared.** Should that happen, both Paul and the Corinthians would **be put to shame by** his false **confidence** that they had the offering ready. To forestall such embarrassment, the apostle called upon the Corinthians to finish what they had started. As their example had originally prompted the Macedonians to give, so the completion of their giving would also set an example. God desires giving that is not marginal, but exemplary.

STEWARDSHIP WITH INTEGRITY CALLS FOR
GIVING THAT HAS OVERCOME THE SIN OF COVETOUSNESS

So I thought it necessary to urge the brethren that they would go on ahead to you and arrange beforehand your previously promised bountiful gift, so that the same would be ready as a bountiful gift and not affected by covetousness. (9:5)

For the reasons noted above, Paul **thought it necessary to urge the brethren** (Titus and the two unnamed brothers) **that they would go on ahead to** Corinth **and arrange beforehand** the Corinthians' **previously promised bountiful gift.** Evidently, they had promised a specific, large amount, and Paul wanted to make certain they had it ready when he arrived.

Then Paul warned of the one sin that could keep the Corinthians from meeting their commitment: **covetousness**—the sin that is the greatest hindrance to giving. Since the Corinthians knew that the collection for the Jerusalem saints was God's work, and that it was being done in God's way, and since they had previously committed to be involved in it, to fail to keep that commitment was sinful covetousness.

Few sins are as ugly as covetousness; few sins manifest selfishness and pride so graphically as grasping for more at the expense of others. Covetousness is built into the very fabric of depraved human nature. "For from within, out of the heart of men," declared Jesus, "proceed . . . deeds of coveting" (Mark 7:21–22). Sinners covet because they have "a heart trained in greed" (2 Peter 2:14). Covetousness (greed) is idolatry (Eph. 5:5; Col. 3:5), and those who habitually practice it will not inherit the kingdom of God (1 Cor. 6:10; Eph. 5:5). Covetousness or greed characterizes a depraved mind (Rom. 1:28–29), leads people to oppress others (Mic. 2:2), and spurn the Lord (Ps. 10:3). Christians are "not to associate with any so-called brother if he is . . . covetous" (1 Cor. 5:11).

Stewardship with integrity, then, is marked by voluntary, faithful giving, proportionate to what one has, in submission to godly pastors who silence the critics by handling the money faithfully. It is motivated by exemplary love for God and others, and is completely free from selfish greed and covetousness. All giving must be measured by those noble standards.

The Path to Prosperity

(2 Corinthians 9:6–15)

24

Now this I say, he who sows sparingly will also reap sparingly, and he who sows bountifully will also reap bountifully. Each one must do just as he has purposed in his heart, not grudgingly or under compulsion, for God loves a cheerful giver. And God is able to make all grace abound to you, so that always having all sufficiency in everything, you may have an abundance for every good deed; as it is written, "He scattered abroad, he gave to the poor, his righteousness endures forever." Now He who supplies seed to the sower and bread for food will supply and multiply your seed for sowing and increase the harvest of your righteousness; you will be enriched in everything for all liberality, which through us is producing thanksgiving to God. For the ministry of this service is not only fully supplying the needs of the saints, but is also overflowing through many thanksgivings to God. Because of the proof given by this ministry, they will glorify God for your obedience to your confession of the gospel of Christ and for the liberality of your contribution to them and to all, while they also, by prayer on your behalf, yearn for you because of the surpassing grace of God in you. Thanks be to God for His indescribable gift! (9:6–15)

To the three American "unalienable Rights" of "Life, Liberty, and the pursuit of Happiness" proclaimed in the Declaration of Independence our society would add a fourth: the right to the pursuit of prosperity. The headlong pursuit of wealth is the consuming passion of the age. Self-styled financial gurus churn out a bewildering plethora of books, infomercials and other TV programs, Web sites, newsletters, and magazines. Some offer sound advice; most promote dubious get-rich-quick schemes. But they all claim to have the road map to the modern-day El Dorado—the mythical city of gold the Spanish Conquistadors so eagerly sought. People today pursue their own El Dorados with the ruthless single-mindedness that characterized the Conquistadors—and often just as unsuccessfully.

Sadly, the church has fallen prey to the world's relentless pursuit of materialism. Some Christians view wealth as a sign of God's blessing, and thus consider financial success to be an essential qualification for church leaders.

The most outrageous example of materialism in the name of Christianity is, unquestionably, the heretical Word Faith movement, or Health and Wealth Gospel. Its proponents unabashedly proclaim that God's will is for all believers to be rich. If they claim riches by faith and speak positively of them, that verbal confession itself creates the wealth. Word Faith teachers insist that God is obligated to deliver the goods believers request. They are so bold as to replace the sovereign God of Scripture (cf. Ps. 103:19; 1 Tim. 6:15) with the sovereignty of the believer who wields creative power to make himself healthy and wealthy by his own faith. God becomes a utilitarian genie who grants believers' every desire. (For a critique of the Word Faith movement, see John MacArthur, *Charismatic Chaos* [Grand Rapids: Zondervan, 1992]; D. R. McConnell, *A Different Gospel* [Peabody, Mass.: Hendrickson, 1988].)

But believers cannot, in spite of what Word Faith deceivers shamelessly proclaim, create their own reality for their own indulgence. Such a self-centered, prideful desire does not ever characterize genuine believers. It is true that some godly men, such as Job and Abraham, were very wealthy. Yet Paul described himself as "both hungry and thirsty, . . . poorly clothed, . . . roughly treated, and . . . homeless" (1 Cor. 4:11), while Jesus said of Himself, "The foxes have holes and the birds of the air have nests, but the Son of Man has nowhere to lay His head" (Luke 9:58). The church has always consisted of both rich (cf. Matt. 27:57; Acts 4:36–37; 8:27; 10:1–2; 16:14–15; 17:4; 1 Tim. 6:17) and poor (cf. Acts 6:1; 1 Cor. 1:26; 2 Cor. 8:2) people, because according to His own sovereign purposes "the Lord makes poor and rich; He brings low, He also exalts" (1 Sam. 2:7).

Rich or poor, however, the Bible warns against "the deceitfulness of riches" (Mark 4:19), and exhorts, "Do not weary yourself to gain wealth, cease from your consideration of it. When you set your eyes on it, it is gone. For wealth certainly makes itself wings like an eagle that flies toward the heavens" (Prov. 23:4–5). In Matthew 6:24 Jesus declared, "You cannot serve God and wealth," while in Luke 12:15 He warned, "Beware, and be on your guard against every form of greed." Greed characterizes unbelievers (Ps. 10:3; Rom. 1:29; 1 Cor. 6:10; Eph. 5:3), especially false teachers (1 Tim. 6:5; Titus 1:11; 2 Peter 2:1–3, 14–15; Jude 11), and is a form of idolatry (Eph. 5:5; Col. 3:5). In sharp contrast to the materialism promoted by prosperity teachers, Jesus commanded, "Do not store up for yourselves treasures on earth, where moth and rust destroy, and where thieves break in and steal. But store up for yourselves treasures in heaven, where neither moth nor rust destroys, and where thieves do not break in or steal" (Matt. 6:19–20).

God has a very different plan for financial soundness than that of worldly or pseudo-Christian materialism. Instead of trying to speak wealth into existence, God's plan involves hard work, wise investment, and careful saving. But in contrast to man-centered self-indulgence, the means for prosperity is not greedy accumulation—but the opposite, generous giving:

> Honor the Lord from your wealth and from the first of all your produce; so your barns will be filled with plenty and your vats will overflow with new wine. (Prov. 3:9–10)

> There is one who scatters, and yet increases all the more, and there is one who withholds what is justly due, and yet it results only in want. The generous man will be prosperous, and he who waters will himself be watered. (Prov. 11:24–25)

> One who is gracious to a poor man lends to the Lord, and He will repay him for his good deed. (Prov. 19:17)

> He who gives to the poor will never want. (Prov. 28:27)

> "Bring the whole tithe into the storehouse, so that there may be food in My house, and test Me now in this," says the Lord of hosts, "if I will not open for you the windows of heaven and pour out for you a blessing until it overflows." (Mal. 3:10)

> "Give, and it will be given to you. They will pour into your lap a good measure—pressed down, shaken together, and running over. For by your standard of measure it will be measured to you in return." (Luke 6:38)

The point of those verses is clear: The more one gives, the more God gives back in return.

In this passage Paul expressed that principle using familiar agricultural imagery: **Now this I say, he who sows sparingly will also reap sparingly, and he who sows bountifully will also reap bountifully.** Every farmer recognizes that the size of the harvest is directly proportionate to the amount of seed sown. The farmer who **sows** seed **sparingly** will **reap** a meager harvest; the one **who sows bountifully will . . . reap** a great harvest. In the spiritual realm, the principle is that giving to God results in blessing from God; **bountifully** translates *eulogia,* which literally means "blessing." Generous givers will reap generous blessings from God, while those who hold back selfishly fearing loss will forfeit gain.

In chapters 8 and 9, Paul sought to motivate the Corinthians to complete their giving for the needy members of the Jerusalem church. First, he reminded them of the example set by the Macedonians (8:1–9), then he gave them a direct exhortation (8:10–9:5), and in this section he pointed out the potential benefits. God graciously promises a harvest in accord with what believers sow. The appeal is not, of course, to self-interest. The promise is not that God will reward generous givers so they can consume it on their own desires. The real purpose of God's gracious rewarding of believers will become evident as the passage unfolds.

To motivate the Corinthians to give, Paul gave a fivefold description of the harvest that would result: love from God, generosity from God, glory to God, friends from God, and likeness to God.

LOVE FROM GOD

Each one must do just as he has purposed in his heart, not grudgingly or under compulsion, for God loves a cheerful giver. (9:7)

It is hard to imagine a more precious promise than to be the personal object of God's love. All the world's acclaim, honor, and rewards given to all philanthropists put together does not come close to this privilege of being loved by God. Yet that is what He promises the **cheerful giver.** God loves the world in a general sense (John 3:16), but He has a deeper, more wonderful love for His own (John 13:1; 1 John 4:16), and a special love for **each one** of His who gives cheerfully.

Cheerful giving comes from inside, from the heart, rather than from external coercion. It begins by giving **just as** one **has purposed in his heart.** Once again, Paul stressed the truth that Christian giving is strictly voluntary (see the discussion of 8:3 in chapter 21 of this volume).

But though it is not forced, neither is it casual, careless, or a mere after-thought. *Proaireō* (**purposed**), used only here in the New Testament, has the idea of predetermination. Though there is spontaneous joy in giving, it is still to be planned and systematic (1 Cor. 16:2), not impulsive and sporadic. Nor is giving to be done **grudgingly.** *Lupē* (**grudgingly**) liter-ally means, "sorrow," "grief," or "pain." Giving is not to be done with an atti-tude of remorse, regret, or reluctance, of mourning over parting with what is given. And, as noted above, it is not to be **under compulsion** from any legalistic external pressure.

The giving that God approves of comes from **a cheerful giver. Cheerful** translates *hilaros,* from which the English word *hilarious* derives. Happy, joyous givers, who are joyous in view of the privilege of giving, are the special objects of God's love.

GENEROSITY FROM GOD

And God is able to make all grace abound to you, so that always having all sufficiency in everything, you may have an abundance for every good deed; as it is written, "He scattered abroad, he gave to the poor, his righteousness endures forever." Now He who supplies seed to the sower and bread for food will supply and multiply your seed for sowing and increase the harvest of your righteousness; you will be enriched in everything for all lib-erality, (9:8–11*a*)

While it is possible to give without loving, it is not possible to love without giving. God gives His Son to all believers, but as previously noted, He blesses in a unique way generous, cheerful givers. In fact, He blesses such believers on such a grand, immense, staggering scale that it beggars language to express it. Trying to convey the magnanimity of God's gen-erosity, Paul resorted to hyperbole, using a form of the word *pas* (**all**) five times in verse 8. God's gracious giving has no limits; it is off the scale.

Since giving naturally seems to result in having less, not more, it takes faith to believe that giving will open up God's blessing. Christians must believe that what God has promised to do He **is able** to do. *Dunateō* (**is able**) literally means "has power." God's power is great (Deut. 4:37; 9:29; Neh. 1:10; Pss. 66:3; 79:11; Jer. 32:17; Nah. 1:3; Rev. 11:17) and is exhibited in creation, providence, miracles, salvation, the resurrections of Jesus Christ and believers, and in the eternal destruction of the wicked in hell. Not surprisingly, then, Paul expressed his concern "that [the Corinthians'] faith would not rest on the wisdom of men, but on the power of God" (1 Cor. 2:5).

Human wisdom teaches that prosperity comes from grasping for wealth, not from giving it away. But faith trusts in God's promise to bless the giver and in His ability to keep His promises, knowing that He is able to "do exceeding abundantly beyond all that [believers] ask or think" (Eph. 3:20), guard and preserve them (2 Tim. 1:12; Heb. 7:25; Jude 24), help them when they are tempted (Heb. 2:18), and raise them from the dead (Heb. 11:19). Believers, like Abraham, must be "fully assured that what God [has] promised, He [is] able also to perform" (Rom. 4:21).

God gives back magnanimously so as to **make all grace abound** to Christians who give generously. He gives so freely and abundantly that His children will **always** have **all sufficiency in everything.** In this context, that refers primarily to material resources, because the harvest must be of the same nature as the seed. Having sown material wealth by their giving, believers will reap an abundant harvest of material blessing in return. God graciously replenishes what they give so that they lack nothing; He will continuously provide the generous giver with the means of further expressing that generosity.

To the Cynic and Stoic philosophers of Paul's day *autarkeia* (**sufficiency**) meant independence from people and circumstances. They viewed such independence as essential to true happiness. But the believer's sufficiency does not come from independence from circumstances but rather from dependence on God. As Paul wrote to the Philippians, "My God will supply all your needs according to His riches in glory in Christ Jesus" (Phil. 4:19).

The reason God gives back to those who give is not, as prosperity teachers falsely imply and exemplify, so people can consume it on their own desires with bigger cars, homes, and jewels. God supplies them so they will have **an abundance for every good deed.** The Lord will fully supply cheerful givers with what they need to use for what is good work to the honor of the Lord. He constantly replenishes what they expend so the cycle of giving and ministering to others can continue. Generous givers are the people whose lives are most full of righteous deeds.

Lest anyone think this was some radical new social welfare plan he had concocted, Paul cited Psalm 112:9 to show this has always been God's plan. The phrase **as it is written** is the standard New Testament way of introducing an Old Testament quote (Mark 1:2; 7:6; Luke 2:23; 3:4; John 6:31; 12:14–15; Acts 7:42; 15:15; Rom. 1:17; 2:24; 3:4, 10; 4:17; 8:36; 9:13, 33; 10:15; 11:8, 26; 15:3, 9, 21; 1 Cor. 1:31; 2:9; 10:7). Because the generous giver **scatter[s] abroad** and gives **to the poor, his righteousness endures forever.** God will replenish and reward him both in time and eternity.

Deuteronomy 15:10–11 also illustrates this point. In verse 10 God declared through Moses, "You shall generously give to [the poor man], and your heart shall not be grieved when you give to him, because for this thing the Lord your God will bless you in all your work and in all your undertakings." Those who were generous to the needy received God's material blessings. But the purpose was not so that they could be like the rich fool in Jesus' parable, who said, "This is what I will do: I will tear down my barns and build larger ones, and there I will store all my grain and my goods. And I will say to my soul, 'Soul, you have many goods laid up for many years to come; take your ease, eat, drink and be merry'" (Luke 12:18–19). Verse 11 reveals the purpose of God's blessing. Moses reminded his hearers that "the poor will never cease to be in the land; therefore I command you, saying, 'You shall freely open your hand to your brother, to your needy and poor in your land.'" God's constant resupply allowed them to continually give to meet the needs of others.

Paul reinforced his point with a third Old Testament quote, this one from Isaiah 55:10. That generous giving will impoverish no one is evident since **He who supplies seed to the sower and bread for food will supply and multiply** their **seed for sowing.** God is the One **who supplies seed to the sower** because He created all the earth's vegetation (Gen. 1:11–12). Thus He provides the grain that provides **bread for food.** The same God who provides seed for the harvest in the natural world will **multiply** generous givers' **seed for sowing.** They sow the seed and then reap the harvest, which in turn provides more seed for sowing in an ever-expanding cycle. The ultimate harvest of generous giving is not only eternal reward, but also temporal blessing in this life for those who "sow with a view to righteousness, [and] reap in accordance with kindness" (Hos. 10:12). They **will be enriched in everything,** equipping them **for all liberality** in their giving.

GLORY TO GOD

which through us is producing thanksgiving to God. For the ministry of this service is not only fully supplying the needs of the saints, but is also overflowing through many thanksgivings to God. Because of the proof given by this ministry, they will glorify God for your obedience to your confession of the gospel of Christ and for the liberality of your contribution to them and to all (9:11b–13)

The noblest goal of any human endeavor is that God be glorified (cf. 1 Cor. 10:31). The Corinthians' generous liberality was already, **through** Paul, Titus, and the others involved in collecting the offering, **producing thanksgiving to God** from the people benefited. When the

Jerusalem saints received the Corinthians' gift, they too would praise and exalt God for motivating the Corinthians to this generosity.

The human race is like a thankless child, and God is deeply grieved and offended by those who do "not honor Him as God or give thanks" (Rom. 1:21). On the other hand, giving thanks brings glory to Him (2 Cor. 4:15). In verse 12 Paul described the Corinthians' **ministry** of giving with the word *leitourgia* (**service**), which refers to priestly service (cf. Luke 1:23). The collection was not primarily a social program but a spiritual service to God.

So generous did Paul expect the Corinthians' offering to be that he anticipated it would be capable of **fully supplying the needs of the saints.** The word translated **fully supplying** consists of the verb *plēroō* with two prepositions added to it for emphasis. The apostle again stressed the large size of the Corinthians' gift, which he had earlier referred to as a "generous gift" (8:20). That suggests that the Corinthians were relatively well-off financially. Corinth was an important commercial city, and persecution evidently had not affected the church there as it had the impoverished Macedonian churches. The Corinthians' generosity would meet needs, but more importantly, it would **also** result in **many thanksgivings to God** when the poor believers in Jerusalem praised God for the Corinthians' gift.

That gift would also give evidence of the genuineness of the Corinthians' salvation. **Because of the proof given by** the **ministry** (the Corinthians' gift), people would **glorify God for** that church's **obedience to** their **confession of the gospel of Christ.** Jewish believers in the early church were often suspicious of Gentile converts. Many in the Jerusalem church were appalled at the news that Peter had preached the gospel to Gentiles (Acts 11:1–3), and it was only with difficulty that they were persuaded to accept them as brothers in Christ (Acts 11:4–18). It must have been especially difficult for them to believe that the Corinthians' faith was genuine. The city's reputation for immorality was widespread in the Roman world, and the chaotic condition of the Corinthian church would have done little to allay Jewish believers' suspicions.

But the Corinthians' sacrificial giving tangibly demonstrated love for their fellow believers, that mark of genuineness (1 John 2:10; 3:17–18; 4:20–21). It proved they were "doers of the word, and not merely hearers who delude themselves" (James 1:22; cf. Eph. 2:10). The Corinthians' **obedience** proved the genuineness of their **confession of the gospel of Christ.** Their good works did not save them but gave evidence that they possessed a living faith, not a dead faith that is unable to save (James 2:14–26). **All** who heard of **the liberality of** the Corinthians' **contribution** would give "thanks . . . to the glory of God" (2 Cor. 4:15).

FRIENDS FROM GOD

while they also, by prayer on your behalf, yearn for you because of the surpassing grace of God in you. (9:14)

Some may think that poor believers have nothing to offer rich ones, but that is not the case. The prayers of the poor are the reward of the rich, and the believers in Jerusalem would repay the Corinthians' generosity by offering **prayer on** their **behalf.** And not only the Jerusalem saints, but also other believers would hear of the Corinthians' genuine faith and pray for them. Real unity in the church is founded on sound doctrine and mutual prayer. The Corinthians' gift would enlarge the circle of friends who were committed to praying for them; as Jesus said in the parable of the unjust manager (Luke 16:1–13), they would make "friends for [themselves] by means of the wealth of unrighteousness, so that when it fail[ed], they [would] receive [them] into the eternal dwellings" (v. 9).

Not only would their fellow believers pray for the Corinthians, they would also **yearn** for a deeper, more intimate fellowship with them. That desire would be stimulated when they saw **the surpassing grace of God in** the Corinthians. Other believers would long both to pray for and to have fellowship with those in whom God's grace was working so mightily.

LIKENESS TO GOD

Thanks be to God for His indescribable gift! (9:15)

This simple concluding benediction is one of the richest statements in Scripture. God's **indescribable gift** is, of course, His Son—the most magnanimous, glorious, wonderful gift ever given, the gift that inspires all other gifts.

> For a child will be born to us, a son will be given to us; and the government will rest on His shoulders; and His name will be called Wonderful Counselor, Mighty God, Eternal Father, Prince of Peace. (Isa. 9:6)

> "For God so loved the world, that He gave His only begotten Son, that whoever believes in Him shall not perish, but have eternal life. For God did not send the Son into the world to judge the world, but that the world might be saved through Him." (John 3:16–17)

> He who did not spare His own Son, but delivered Him over for us all, how will He not also with Him freely give us all things? (Rom. 8:32)

> But when the fullness of the time came, God sent forth His Son, born of a woman, born under the Law. (Gal. 4:4)

> By this the love of God was manifested in us, that God has sent His only begotten Son into the world so that we might live through Him. In this is love, not that we loved God, but that He loved us and sent His Son to be the propitiation for our sins. (1 John 4:9–10)

God's gift of the Lord Jesus Christ is the basis for Christian giving. Jesus was the "grain of wheat [that] falls into the earth and dies, . . . but if it dies, it bears much fruit" (John 12:24). God, as it were, planted Him as a seed and reaped a harvest of redeemed people. Believers are called to "be imitators of God, as beloved children" (Eph. 5:1), and they are never more like Him than when they give.

Subsequent history reveals how the Corinthians responded to Paul's plea in chapters 8 and 9 regarding the offering. Sometime after writing 2 Corinthians, Paul visited Corinth as he had planned (2 Cor. 12:14; 13:1–2). He remained there about three months (Acts 20:1–3), during which time he penned Romans. In that letter, Paul revealed that the Corinthians had responded positively concerning the collection:

> Now, I am going to Jerusalem serving the saints. For Macedonia and Achaia have been pleased to make a contribution for the poor among the saints in Jerusalem. Yes, they were pleased to do so, and they are indebted to them. For if the Gentiles have shared in their spiritual things, they are indebted to minister to them also in material things. (Rom. 15:25–27)

Not only had they contributed, but "they were pleased to do so"; they were joyful, happy, cheerful givers. They were on the path to true prosperity.

Winning the Spiritual War (2 Corinthians 10:1–6)

25

Now I, Paul, myself urge you by the meekness and gentleness of Christ—I who am meek when face to face with you, but bold toward you when absent! I ask that when I am present I need not be bold with the confidence with which I propose to be courageous against some, who regard us as if we walked according to the flesh. For though we walk in the flesh, we do not war according to the flesh, for the weapons of our warfare are not of the flesh, but divinely powerful for the destruction of fortresses. We are destroying speculations and every lofty thing raised up against the knowledge of God, and we are taking every thought captive to the obedience of Christ, and we are ready to punish all disobedience, whenever your obedience is complete. (10:1–6)

As the word **now** indicates, this passage begins a new section of this epistle. (For a refutation of the view that chaps. 10–13 were originally a separate letter, see the introduction.) The first section (chaps. 1–7) focused on matters related to Paul's restored relationship with the Corinthian church. In light of that restored relationship, the apostle felt it was appropriate to discuss the Corinthians' participation in the offering for the Jerusalem church (chaps. 8, 9). In those first two sections Paul's words were generally gentle, gracious, and conciliatory. But in this final section (chaps. 10–13) his tone abruptly changes, and his language becomes strong, authoritative, and confrontational. To understand why, it is necessary to review the situation of the Corinthian church when Paul wrote this epistle.

After founding the congregation and building it up for about twenty months (Acts 18:1–18), Paul left to minister elsewhere. Following his departure, word reached him that serious problems had arisen in the Corinthian assembly, motivating him to write a (noncanonical) letter to correct them (1 Cor. 5:9). Reports of further difficulties (1 Cor. 1:11), as well as some questions about which the Corinthians wrote him (cf. 1 Cor. 7:1), prompted Paul to write a second letter (1 Corinthians) to them. Soon, however, an even greater problem arose. Self-styled false apostles invaded the Corinthian church, vigorously assaulting Paul's ministry, apostolic credentials, and character. They sought to destroy his reputation and set themselves up as the authoritative teachers, so the Corinthians would believe their damning lies. Paul responded to the threat with a sternly worded letter, known as the severe letter (2 Cor. 2:3–4), which brought about the repentance of the majority in the Corinthian assembly. (The severe letter, like the letter Paul refers to in 1 Corinthians 5:9, was not included in Scripture, and the letters have never been found. They are known to have been written only by the apostle's references to them.)

But even though he acknowledged the repentance in the church, Paul was wise enough to know that the false teachers were still a force to be reckoned with. The general repentance of the congregation had likely only driven their poisonous stream underground. There some bided their time, hoping to rekindle the rebellion against Paul. In the meantime, they surely conducted more subtle warfare against him. To stamp out the last traces of the rebellion, the apostle launched a search-and-destroy mission to root out the remaining pockets of resistance at Corinth. His attack was two-pronged. The preliminary bombardment, as it were, came in the last four chapters of this epistle; the final assault came when Paul visited Corinth a couple of months later (2 Cor. 12:14; 13:1). The last section of this epistle, then, is addressed to the recalcitrant minority; namely, the false apostles and their remaining deluded followers.

Fittingly, Paul began this section with a warfare analogy, which he frequently used to depict the Christian life. For example, defending his right to financial support, Paul reminded the Corinthians, "Who at any time serves as a soldier at his own expense?" (1 Cor. 9:7). He also exhorted Timothy, "Suffer hardship with me, as a good soldier of Christ Jesus. No soldier in active service entangles himself in the affairs of everyday life, so that he may please the one who enlisted him as a soldier" (2 Tim.

2:3–4; cf. Phil. 2:25; Philem. 2). He told him to "fight the good fight of faith" (1 Tim. 6:12; cf. 1 Tim. 1:18).

Facing his own imminent death, he wrote triumphantly, "I have fought the good fight, I have finished the course, I have kept the faith" (2 Tim. 4:7). He urged all believers to put on their spiritual armor so they can effectively fight the forces of darkness (Eph. 6:10–18; cf. Rom. 13:12; 1 Thess. 5:8). From his conversion on the Damascus Road until his death, Paul's life was a constant struggle. He battled the forces of the kingdom of darkness, both demonic (Eph. 6:12; cf. Acts 26:16–18) and human (cf. Acts 9:23–24; 13:6–12, 45, 50; 14:2–5, 19; 17:5–9, 13; 18:12–17; 19:23–41; 20:3, 19; 1 Thess. 2:14–16; 1 Tim. 1:20; 2 Tim. 4:14–15). He contended with false brethren (2 Cor. 11:26; Gal. 2:4) and false apostles (2 Cor. 11:13), those savage wolves that threatened God's flock (Acts 20:29; cf. Matt. 7:15). He fought as well against the aberrant philosophies of the world (Col. 2:8; cf. Acts 17:18). Paul never fought, however, for his own honor; his goal was always to defend the truth of the gospel and the glory of his Lord. When he did reluctantly defend himself in this epistle, it was only to preserve his credibility as the apostle of Jesus Christ sent to declare the truth of the gospel of God. The issue was critical enough to overcome the reluctance of his characteristic humility and motivate him to this self-defense.

As the battle begins against the forces of wickedness at Corinth, Paul appears in his soldier's uniform to set the example for all to follow. He reveals four traits of a soldier who can triumph in the spiritual war: He is compassionate, courageous, competent, and calculating.

HE IS COMPASSIONATE

Now I, Paul, myself urge you by the meekness and gentleness of Christ—I who am meek when face to face with you, but bold toward you when absent! (10:1)

As noted above, the word **now** marks Paul's transition to the final section of this epistle. But before beginning his assault on the false apostles and their followers, the apostle expressed his unwillingness to engage in combat. Good soldiers take no pleasure in using deadly force and do so only with great reluctance. Surveying the carnage at the battle of Fredericksburg, Robert E. Lee said soberly, "It is well that war is so terrible —we should grow too fond of it" (James M. McPherson, *Battle Cry of Freedom,* The Oxford History of the United States [New York: Oxford Univ., 1988], 572). A noble warrior's power is constrained by his compassion and exercised only when there is no other option. That is the spirit in which Paul introduced this forceful section of his epistle.

That does not mean, of course, that Paul doubted or downplayed the authority delegated to him directly by the sovereign Lord. In fact, he boldly asserted it by beginning, **I, Paul, myself.** Unlike the false apostles, Paul did not depend on any human source for his authority; as he sarcastically asked the Corinthians earlier in this letter, "Are we beginning to commend ourselves again? Or do we need, as some, letters of commendation to you or from you?" (3:1). His words manifested divine authority, and so would his power, if necessary, when he visited Corinth (cf. 13:1–3).

But before wielding his apostolic might, Paul first manifested his compassion. He **urge[d]** the insubordinate minority **by the meekness and gentleness of Christ** to end their rebellion and be reconciled to the truth. Instead of seeking personal vengeance on his enemies, Paul showed them the same patience that the Lord Jesus Christ had shown him (1 Tim. 1:16). *Prautēs* (**meekness**) is usually translated "gentleness" in the New Testament. It refers to the humble and gentle attitude that results in the patient endurance of offenses. *Prautēs* marks those free of anger, hatred, bitterness, and a desire for revenge. The word denotes not weakness, but power under control. *Epieikeia* (**gentleness**) is translated "kindness" in its only other New Testament appearance (Acts 24:4). When applied to those in authority, it means "leniency" and describes those who graciously refuse to insist on the full measure of their legal rights.

Of course, no one more perfectly manifested the attitude expressed in those two words than did **Christ;** no one had greater power or controlled it better. Peter set forth Christ's gentleness and power under control as an example for believers to follow:

> For this finds favor, if for the sake of conscience toward God a person bears up under sorrows when suffering unjustly. For what credit is there if, when you sin and are harshly treated, you endure it with patience? But if when you do what is right and suffer for it you patiently endure it, this finds favor with God. For you have been called for this purpose, since Christ also suffered for you, leaving you an example for you to follow in His steps, who committed no sin, nor was any deceit found in His mouth; and while being reviled, He did not revile in return; while suffering, He uttered no threats, but kept entrusting Himself to Him who judges righteously. (1 Peter 2:19–23)

Matthew 12:20 says of Christ's gentleness with the suffering, "A battered reed He will not break off, and a smoldering wick He will not put out." He gently said to the woman taken in adultery, "'Woman, where are they? Did no one condemn you?' She said, 'No one, Lord.' And Jesus said, 'I do not condemn you either. Go. From now on sin no more'" (John 8:10– 11). He prayed for those who crucified Him, "saying, 'Father, forgive them; for they do not know what they are doing'" (Luke 23:34). He even concluded His scathing malediction against the Jewish religious leaders with the tender, compassionate cry, "Jerusalem, Jerusalem, who kills the prophets and stones those who are sent to her! How often I wanted to gather your children together, the way a hen gathers her chicks under her wings, and you were unwilling" (Matt. 23:37).

Paul knew that Christ's character sets the standard for all His soldiers to follow, since He commanded them, "Take My yoke upon you and learn from Me, for I am gentle and humble in heart" (Matt. 11:29). The apostle sought to imitate the Lord by patiently holding his power in check. Despite his being mistreated by some in the assembly, the apostle viewed using his rod against them only as a last resort (cf. 1 Cor. 4:21).

Perversely, Paul's enemies put a negative spin on his compassion, scornfully condemning it as cowardly weakness. They slanderously accused him of being **meek when face to face with** them, **but bold toward** them **when absent!** *Tapeinos* (**meek**) is used elsewhere in the New Testament as a positive virtue, but Paul's opponents meant it in a derogatory sense. When confronted **face to face,** his adversaries insinuated Paul was a weakling; in today's terminology, he was a wimp. But put him a safe distance away, they sneered, and he would act as fierce as a lion.

It is true that Paul was humble. In 1 Corinthians 2:3 he wrote that he had been "with [them] in weakness and in fear and in much trembling." But the false apostles took Paul's genuine humility, his lack of confidence in himself apart from God's power, and twisted it into cringing weakness. They were not completely unlike those in Israel, who expecting the Messiah to come in power and annihilate their enemies, rejected Jesus when He proved to be "gentle and humble in heart" (Matt. 11:29; cf. Isa. 53; Zech. 9:9).

The allegation that Paul was bold when absent but weak when present was a clever contrivance. Any way Paul answered could be twisted. If he reaffirmed his strength in his letters, or defended his meekness in their presence, he would seemingly confirm one of the false allegations. Therefore, to answer his opponents' charges, Paul shows in the closing section of this epistle how his life and words weld strength to weakness, proving that one can be a bold warrior for the truth, while at the same time compassionate.

He Is Courageous

I ask that when I am present I need not be bold with the confidence with which I propose to be courageous against some, who regard us as if we walked according to the flesh. (10:2)

Those who mistook Paul for a weakling were drastically mistaken. When all attempts at compassion were exhausted, Paul would fight fiercely to preserve his integrity for the sake of the truth. The biblical record of his courageous life speaks for itself. He faced hostile mobs, beatings, imprisonments, riots, shipwrecks, and plots on his life (11:23–33). Paul fearlessly proclaimed the gospel before the Jewish Sanhedrin (Acts 23), Roman governors (Acts 24, 25), King Herod Agrippa (Acts 26), even the emperor (Acts 25:11; 27:24). He also confronted those who proclaimed false doctrine (cf. Acts 15:2). Nor did he shrink even from publicly rebuking Peter, the leader of the Twelve (Gal. 2:11–14).

Because of his compassionate desire to spare the rebels, Paul called on them to repent. If they did, **when** he was **present** with them he would **not** need to **be bold with the confidence** he had in his authority. The aorist infinitive form of *tharrheō* (**bold**) is ingressive, meaning, "to become courageous." The apostle pleaded with them not to force him to display the confrontive courage of which he was capable. **Courageous** translates a synonym, *tolmaō*, which has the connotation of being daring, of acting without fear regardless of the threats or consequences. When it came to defending the truth, Paul was absolutely fearless. He would not back away from a fight with those who threatened the church; as he wrote earlier to the Corinthians, "I will come to you soon, if the Lord wills, and I shall find out, not the words of those who are arrogant but their power" (1 Cor. 4:19). Near the end of this epistle he wrote, "For this reason I am writing these things while absent, so that when present I need not use severity, in accordance with the authority which the Lord gave me for building up and not for tearing down" (2 Cor. 13:10).

The apostle would wage his war, if neccessary, **against some, who regard us as if we walked according to the flesh.** The false teachers and their followers slanderously accused Paul of living **according to the flesh,** that is, of being controlled by the sinful desires of unredeemed humanness arising in a corrupt heart. He was, according to them, motivated by evil self-interest, the lustful pursuit of money, and illicit desires.

Throughout this epistle, Paul defended himself against those scurrilous charges, which were at the heart of the conspiracy against him. In 2 Corinthians 1:12 he wrote, "For our proud confidence is this: the testimony of our conscience, that in holiness and godly sincerity, not in fleshly wisdom but in the grace of God, we have conducted ourselves in the world, and especially toward you." Unlike the false apostles, Paul handled the Word accurately: "For we are not like many, peddling the word of God, but as from sincerity, but as from God, we speak in Christ in the sight of God" (2:17). Nor did he have a secret life of sin, having "renounced the things hidden because of shame, not walking in craftiness or adulterating the word of God, but by the manifestation of truth commending [himself] to every man's conscience in the sight of God" (4:2). "Make room for us in your hearts," he begged the Corinthians. "We wronged no one, we corrupted no one, we took advantage of no one" (7:2). He had given the rebels fair warning. If they did not repent it would mean war—a war Paul was fully equipped to win.

HE IS COMPETENT

For though we walk in the flesh, we do not war according to the flesh, for the weapons of our warfare are not of the flesh, but divinely powerful for the destruction of fortresses. We are destroying speculations and every lofty thing raised up against the knowledge of God, and we are taking every thought captive to the obedience of Christ, (10:3–5)

The battlefields of history are strewn with the wreckage of courageous, but ill-equipped, soldiers. At the famous battle of the Little Big Horn, George Armstrong Custer recklessly led his men against a much larger force of Sioux and Cheyenne warriors. In the ensuing battle his regiment was destroyed, and he and all 210 men under his immediate command killed. When the Nazi blitzkrieg rolled into Poland, a brigade of Polish cavalry gallantly, but foolishly, charged a formation of German tanks. The troopers' lances and swords were no match for the panzers' cannons and machine guns, and they were all slaughtered.

In addition to being compassionate and courageous, the Christian soldier must also be properly armed for the struggle. If any of his adversaries imagined that Paul was not a competent soldier, they were in for a rude awakening. The apostle gave his opponents fair warning that he was armed with the "the weapons of righteousness" (6:7) and ready for battle. His statement, **For though we walk in the flesh, we do not war according to the flesh** is a play on words. In verse 2 the false teachers had accused Paul of walking in the flesh in a moral sense—of being corrupt and immoral, driven by lust, greed, and pride. Playing off his opponents' moral use of the term, Paul affirmed that he did **walk in the flesh** in the physical sense; that is, he was a man. He denied the false charge that he was corrupt (cf. 1:12) but acknowledged the reality of his humanity. Though he was an apostle of Jesus Christ, he bore that authority in a frail human body. He was, as he wrote in 4:7, nothing but a clay pot, living in a transitory "earthly tent" (5:1), with an "outer man" that was "decaying" (4:16).

But though Paul walked in the flesh in the physical sense, he did **not war according to the flesh.** He was a man, but he did not go to battle using human weapons. *Strateuomai* (**war**) means "to engage in battle," or "to serve as a soldier." All believers are soldiers in the spiritual war against the kingdom of darkness; there are no exemptions or deferrals. They fight for the truth of Scripture, the honor and glory of the Lord Jesus Christ, the salvation of sinners, and the virtue of the saints. In Ephesians 6:12 Paul defined the battle as a "struggle . . . not against flesh and blood, but against the rulers, against the powers, against the world forces of this darkness, against the spiritual forces of wickedness in the heavenly places." These demonic powers are behind the evil world system.

A spiritual war, however, cannot be successfully fought with fleshly weapons. Therefore, the weapons in Paul's arsenal were not those of human ingenuity, human ideology, or human methodology. Human reason, wisdom, plans, strategies, organizations, skill, eloquence, marketing, religious showmanship, philosophical or psychological speculation, ritualism, pragmatism, or mysticism are all ineffective weapons against the forces of the kingdom of darkness, the "powers . . . world forces of this darkness . . . [and] spiritual forces of wickedness in the heavenly places" (Eph. 6:12). They cannot rescue sinners from the "domain of darkness" (Col. 1:13) or transform believers into Christ's likeness. Such weapons gain only superficial, temporary, and deceptive victories at best.

To successfully fight the spiritual war requires weapons from the heavenly arsenal. Only those **divinely powerful** weapons are suited **for the destruction of** the enemies' **fortresses.** That term would convey to the New Testament reader the thought of a formidable stronghold. Corinth, like most major cities in Greece, had an acropolis. Located on a mountain near the city, the acropolis was a fortified place into which the inhabitants could retreat when attacked. *Ochurōma* (**fortresses**) was also used in extrabiblical Greek to refer to a prison. People under siege in a fortress were imprisoned there by the attacking forces. The word was also used to refer to a tomb.

Fleshly weapons cannot successfully assault the formidable strongholds in which sinners have entrenched themselves. Such impotent weapons cannot bring about the **destruction** of those **fortresses,** which Paul defined specifically as **speculations** (*logismos*), a general word referring to any and all human or demonic thoughts, opinions, reasonings, philosophies, theories, psychologies, perspectives, viewpoints, and religions. The **fortresses** in view here are not demons, but ideologies. The notion that spiritual warfare involves direct confrontation with demons is foreign to Scripture. Christians who verbally confront demons waste energy and demonstrate ignorance of the real war. We are not called to convert demons, but sinners. The battle is rather with the false ideologies men and demons propagate so that the world believes them. Doomed souls are inside their fortresses of ideas, which become their prisons and eventually their tombs—unless they are delivered from them by belief in the truth.

Paul further defined sinners' strongholds of ideas as **every lofty thing**—that is, any unbiblical system of thought exalted as truth—that is **raised up against the knowledge of God.** There is the key. Spiritual warfare is not a battle with demons. It is a battle for the minds of people who are captive to lies that are exalted in opposition to Scripture. In 1 Corinthians 3:20, he called them the useless reasonings of the worldly wise —all the anti-biblical ideologies, false religions, and pseudo gospels spawned by Satan. Paul knew those fortresses well, having lived his entire life before his conversion in one of them. He was a zealous follower of the Judaism of his day, which had turned from its Old Testament roots and become a ritualistic system of works-righteousness. In Philippians 3:4–6 he described the stronghold in which his confidence had rested:

> Although I myself might have confidence even in the flesh. If anyone else has a mind to put confidence in the flesh, I far more: circumcised the eighth day, of the nation of Israel, of the tribe of Benjamin, a Hebrew of Hebrews; as to the Law, a Pharisee; as to zeal, a persecutor of the church; as to the righteousness which is in the Law, found blameless.

To the Galatians he wrote, "I was advancing in Judaism beyond many of my contemporaries among my countrymen, being more extremely zealous for my ancestral traditions" (Gal. 1:14). That zeal caused him "to do many things hostile to the name of Jesus of Nazareth" (Act 26:9). Paul "used to persecute the church of God beyond measure and tried to destroy it" (Gal. 1:13; cf. Acts 8:1, 3; 9:1–2, 13–14, 21; 22:4–5; 1 Cor. 15:9; Phil. 3:6; 1 Tim. 1:13). But on the Damascus Road, his vaunted fortress crumbled under God's power, and he was led captive to the Lord Jesus Christ.

Like Paul, before salvation, all unbelievers have a fortress in which they attempt to hide from the true knowledge of God. Those fortresses take endless forms in philosophy, psychology, world religions, cults, apostate forms of Christianity, or evolutionary naturalism—a predominant fortress in Western culture today. Naturalism, as its name implies, is the belief that nature is ultimate reality. James Sire defines it with the following propositions:

1. Matter exists eternally and is all there is. God does not exist.
2. The cosmos exists as a uniformity of natural cause and effect in a closed system.
3. Human beings are complex "machines"; personality is an interrelation of chemical and physical properties we do not yet fully understand.
4. Death is the extinction of personality and individuality.
5. History is a linear stream of events linked by cause and effect but without an overarching purpose.
6. Ethics is related only to human beings.
(See chapter 4, "The Silence of Finite Space: Naturalism," in *The Universe Next Door,* second edition [Downers Grove, Ill: InterVarsity, 1988], 61–83)

Naturalism attempts to fortify itself against God by altogether shutting Him out of public life, social policy, the courts, and eliminating all biblical influence in morality and ethics. This and all the other deceptive and deadly ideologies must be destroyed and the incarcerated sinners rescued.

The objective of our warfare is to change how people think—**taking every thought** they have and making it no longer captive to a damning ideology, but **captive to the obedience of Christ.** To do so, the proper weapon is necessary. To assault and throw down the fortresses of false religions, opinions, beliefs, and philosophies, only one weapon will suffice: the truth. That is so obvious that Paul does not mention it. Only one thing exposes and corrects lies—the truth. Thus, the only offensive weapon in the Christian soldier's armor is "the sword of the Spirit, which is the word of God" (Eph. 6:17). Spiritual warfare is an ideological conflict, fought in the mind by assaulting the proud fortresses of ideas that sinners erect against the truth. *Aichmalōtizō* (**taking captive**) literally means, "to take captive with a spear." Using God's truth, believers smash enemy fortresses to the ground, march the prisoners out, and bring them into subjection (**obedience**) to the Lord Jesus Christ. They rescue sinners from the domain of darkness, "snatching them out of the fire" (Jude 23). After being taken prisoner by Jesus Christ on the Damascus Road, Paul immediately asked, "What shall I do, Lord?" (Acts 22:10). The rebellion of his sinful, proud heart was ended; the walls of his fortress crashed down in ruin, and the Lord Jesus Christ conquered his heart. Such is the experience of all the redeemed; the term **the obedience of Christ** is a synonym for salvation (cf. Acts 6:7; Rom. 1:5; 15:18; 16:26; Heb. 5:9).

The key to being successful in spiritual warfare is becoming proficient at wielding the sword of the Word of God against the lies people believe. It is impossible to fight error without knowing the truth. Just as soldiers train constantly in the use of their weapons, so also must Christian soldiers constantly study the Scriptures. Only the power of God's truth can smash the lies of satanic false systems; to those "who are being saved it is the power of God" (1 Cor. 1:18). The gospel "is the power of God for salvation to everyone who believes" (Rom. 1:16; cf. 2 Cor. 6:7; Heb. 4:12). Paul exhorted his protégés Timothy and Titus to "preach the word; be ready in season and out of season; reprove, rebuke, exhort, with great patience and instruction. . . . Speak the things which are fitting for sound doctrine" (2 Tim. 4:2; Titus 2:1). Only then would they be able to heed his exhortation, "Suffer hardship with me, as a good soldier of Christ Jesus" (2 Tim. 2:3).

He Is Calculating

and we are ready to punish all disobedience, whenever your obedience is complete. (10:6)

The competent soldier understands the crucial importance of timing. Rather than fire blindly and risk killing friendly troops, he waits until the enemy is clearly in sight. Paul had the courage and the competence **to punish all disobedience** at Corinth. He would not allow the purveyors of error to destroy the church. But he also had the discipline to wait until the church's **obedience** was **complete.** Paul would not unleash his formidable apostolic power on anyone until each had taken his stand. That way, it would be clear who accepted the truth and who rejected it. Paul would be compassionate to the former, but the latter would find him to be a courageous and highly competent opponent.

It is not a question of whether Christians will fight the spiritual war for the truth against lies; the battle is unavoidable. But those who are successful in the conflict will imitate Paul's compassion, courage, competence, and caution.

How to Recognize a Man of God
(2 Corinthians 10:7–18)

26

You are looking at things as they are outwardly. If anyone is confident in himself that he is Christ's, let him consider this again within himself, that just as he is Christ's, so also are we. For even if I boast somewhat further about our authority, which the Lord gave for building you up and not for destroying you, I will not be put to shame, for I do not wish to seem as if I would terrify you by my letters. For they say, "His letters are weighty and strong, but his personal presence is unimpressive and his speech contemptible." Let such a person consider this, that what we are in word by letters when absent, such persons we are also in deed when present. For we are not bold to class or compare ourselves with some of those who commend themselves; but when they measure themselves by themselves and compare themselves with themselves, they are without understanding. But we will not boast beyond our measure, but within the measure of the sphere which God apportioned to us as a measure, to reach even as far as you. For we are not overextending ourselves, as if we did not reach to you, for we were the first to come even as far as you in the gospel of Christ; not boasting beyond our measure, that is, in other men's labors, but with the hope that as your faith grows, we

will be, within our sphere, enlarged even more by you, so as to preach the gospel even to the regions beyond you, and not to boast in what has been accomplished in the sphere of another. But he who boasts is to boast in the Lord. For it is not he who commends himself that is approved, but he whom the Lord commends. (10:7–18)

Ever since he deceived Eve in the Garden of Eden, Satan has assaulted God's truth with lies. He and the purveyors of his demon doctrines have lured multitudes onto the broad path that leads to eternal destruction. The leaders of God's people must therefore vigilantly guard those entrusted to their care from those who would lead them astray. Throughout redemptive history, God's watchmen have sounded the alarm, alerting God's people to the ever-present danger posed by satanic false teachers. Moses cautioned Israel,

> If a prophet or a dreamer of dreams arises among you and gives you a sign or a wonder, and the sign or the wonder comes true, concerning which he spoke to you, saying, "Let us go after other gods (whom you have not known) and let us serve them," you shall not listen to the words of that prophet or that dreamer of dreams; for the Lord your God is testing you to find out if you love the Lord your God with all your heart and with all your soul. (Deut. 13:1–3; cf. 18:20)

The Old Testament prophets took up his alarm:

> The prophets prophesied by Baal and walked after things that did not profit. (Jer. 2:8)

> The prophets prophesy falsely, and the priests rule on their own authority; and My people love it so! (Jer. 5:31)

> Then the Lord said to me, "The prophets are prophesying falsehood in My name. I have neither sent them nor commanded them nor spoken to them; they are prophesying to you a false vision, divination, futility and the deception of their own minds." (Jer. 14:14)

> "Behold, I am against those who have prophesied false dreams," declares the Lord, "and related them and led My people astray by their falsehoods and reckless boasting; yet I did not send them or command them, nor do they furnish this people the slightest benefit," declares the Lord. (Jer. 23:32)

> Thus says the Lord of hosts, the God of Israel, concerning Ahab the son of Kolaiah and concerning Zedekiah the son of Maaseiah, who are

prophesying to you falsely in My name, "Behold, I will deliver them into the hand of Nebuchadnezzar king of Babylon, and he will slay them before your eyes." (Jer. 29:21)

Your prophets have seen for you false and foolish visions; and they have not exposed your iniquity so as to restore you from captivity, but they have seen for you false and misleading oracles. (Lam. 2:14)

O Israel, your prophets have been like foxes among ruins. You have not gone up into the breaches, nor did you build the wall around the house of Israel to stand in the battle on the day of the Lord. They see falsehood and lying divination who are saying, "The Lord declares," when the Lord has not sent them; yet they hope for the fulfillment of their word. . . . along with the prophets of Israel who prophesy to Jerusalem, and who see visions of peace for her when there is no peace, declares the Lord God. (Ezek. 13:4–6, 16)

There is a conspiracy of her prophets in her midst like a roaring lion tearing the prey. They have devoured lives; they have taken treasure and precious things; they have made many widows in the midst of her. . . . Her prophets have smeared whitewash for them, seeing false visions and divining lies for them, saying, "Thus says the Lord God," when the Lord has not spoken. (Ezek. 22:25, 28)

Thus says the Lord concerning the prophets who lead my people astray; when they have something to bite with their teeth, they cry, "Peace," but against him who puts nothing in their mouths they declare holy war. Therefore it will be night for you—without vision, and darkness for you—without divination. The sun will go down on the prophets, and the day will become dark over them. The seers will be ashamed and the diviners will be embarrassed. Indeed, they will all cover their mouths because there is no answer from God. (Mic. 3:5–7)

The Lord Jesus Christ solemnly warned,

Beware of the false prophets, who come to you in sheep's clothing, but inwardly are ravenous wolves. (Matt. 7:15; cf. Zech. 13:4)

See to it that no one misleads you. For many will come in My name, saying, "I am the Christ," and will mislead many. . . . Many false prophets will arise and will mislead many. . . . For false Christs and false prophets will arise and will show great signs and wonders, so as to mislead, if possible, even the elect. (Matt. 24:4–5, 11, 24)

Following the Lord's lead, the apostles also cautioned believers to beware of false teachers:

I know that after my departure savage wolves will come in among you, not sparing the flock. (Acts 20:29)

Now I urge you, brethren, keep your eye on those who cause dissensions and hindrances contrary to the teaching which you learned, and turn away from them. For such men are slaves, not of our Lord Christ but of their own appetites; and by their smooth and flattering speech they deceive the hearts of the unsuspecting. (Rom. 16:17–18)

I am amazed that you are so quickly deserting Him who called you by the grace of Christ, for a different gospel; which is really not another; only there are some who are disturbing you and want to distort the gospel of Christ. But even if we, or an angel from heaven, should preach to you a gospel contrary to what we have preached to you, he is to be accursed! As we have said before, so I say again now, if any man is preaching to you a gospel contrary to what you received, he is to be accursed! (Gal. 1:6–9)

For many walk, of whom I often told you, and now tell you even weeping, that they are enemies of the cross of Christ, whose end is destruction, whose god is their appetite, and whose glory is in their shame, who set their minds on earthly things. (Phil. 3:18–19)

But the Spirit explicitly says that in later times some will fall away from the faith, paying attention to deceitful spirits and doctrines of demons. (1 Tim. 4:1)

Evil men and impostors will proceed from bad to worse, deceiving and being deceived. (2 Tim. 3:13)

But false prophets also arose among the people, just as there will also be false teachers among you, who will secretly introduce destructive heresies, even denying the Master who bought them, bringing swift destruction upon themselves. (2 Peter 2:1)

Know this first of all, that in the last days mockers will come with their mocking, following after their own lusts. (2 Peter 3:3)

Children, it is the last hour; and just as you heard that antichrist is coming, even now many antichrists have appeared; from this we know that it is the last hour. (1 John 2:18)

Beloved, do not believe every spirit, but test the spirits to see whether they are from God, because many false prophets have gone out into the world. (1 John 4:1)

For many deceivers have gone out into the world, those who do not acknowledge Jesus Christ as coming in the flesh. This is the deceiver and the antichrist. (2 John 7)

No church has ever been exempt from the Enemy's attack on the truth, and the assembly at Corinth certainly was no exception. Satan's emissaries, claiming to be apostles of Christ, had arrived in Corinth, seeking to lead the church "astray from the simplicity and purity of devotion to Christ" (2 Cor. 11:3). They knew that to do that they had to destroy Paul's credibility in the eyes of the Corinthians. Their savage attacks on the apostle did lead many in the Corinthian church to mutiny against him. He then took drastic action, writing a severely worded letter (2:3–4) that brought most of the congregation to repentance. The apostle was wise enough to realize, however, that the rebellion had not been totally put down; the false teachers were still there, waiting to seize the initiative again when the opportunity presented itself. Therefore, he wrote this epistle to defend himself against their attacks.

Paul did not specify the exact nature of the damning heresy which the false apostles concocted to seduce the Corinthians. In a sense, its identity really does not matter. Satan and his demons do not care what people believe, as long as they do not believe the truth. However several characteristics of the false teachers and the heresy designed to seduce the Corinthians can be gleaned from this epistle.

First, the false teachers came from outside the church (11:4; cf. 10:14—Paul had been the first to preach the gospel in Corinth). Little was known of their background, and the grandiose claims they made about themselves, their qualifications, and their authority, therefore, could not be verified. As the saying goes, all experts are from out of town.

Second, they claimed superior apostolic authority to Paul. In 11:5 he alluded to those claims, sarcastically referring to them as "the most eminent apostles." They attempted to support their claims with phony letters of commendation, supposedly from the Jerusalem church (3:1; cf. Acts 15:24).

Third, they were Jews (2 Cor. 11:22) who claimed to truly represent the religion of the Messiah. They sought to impose Jewish customs on the Gentiles in the Corinthian assembly. In reality, however, they were guilty of preaching "another Jesus" and "a different gospel" (11:4).

Fourth, they mingled elements of mysticism with Jewish legalism. They claimed to have a secret, higher knowledge, which in reality amounted to nothing but empty "speculations . . . raised up against the knowledge of God" (10:5).

Fifth, they adopted the popular sophistry and rhetoric so highly prized in Greek culture. Accordingly, they scorned Paul as being "unskilled in speech" (11:6).

Sixth, they were libertines, promoting an antinomian ideology that bore the evil fruit of "impurity, immorality and sensuality" (12:21) among the Corinthians.

Finally, like all false teachers, they were in the ministry for money. They mocked Paul's teaching as worthless, since he did not charge for it. Contrasting his humility with their greed, Paul wrote to the Corinthians, "Or did I commit a sin in humbling myself so that you might be exalted, because I preached the gospel of God to you without charge? I robbed other churches by taking wages from them to serve you" (11:7–8).

In chapters 1–9, Paul poured out his heart to the repentant majority, pleading for their continued trust and loyalty. In chapters 10–13 he turned his attention to the false teachers, directly refuting their attacks on him. The last four chapters of this letter form a powerful defense of Paul's apostleship, and 10:7–18 is a vital core of that defense. In this passage, Paul exhorted the Corinthians to make a sound judgment based on clear evidence. The translators of the *New American Standard Bible* understand Paul's opening statement in verse 7, **You are looking at things as they are outwardly,** as a statement of fact. But *blepete* (**you are looking**) could be either an indicative or an imperative verb. It seems best to take it as an imperative (as it unquestionably is every other time Paul used it in this form), and translate the sentence (as several English versions do) as a command. Paul commanded the Corinthians to look at what was obvious; to consider the facts and evidence that was right in front of them. If they did, the obvious conclusion was that Paul was a true apostle (cf. 1 Cor. 9:1–2), and his adversaries were the deceivers.

The best way to avoid being taken in by a counterfeit is to study what is genuine. Thus Paul defended his authenticity in these verses by giving the marks of a true man of God. In our day, when Christianity is awash in a flood of deceitful false teachers, Paul provides desperately needed instruction in discernment. Believers must be able to pick out the voice of the Good Shepherd and His genuine undershepherds amidst the howls of Satan's wolves (John 10:27). A true man of God can be recognized by his relationship to Jesus Christ, his impact on the church, his compassion for people, his disdain for fleshly methods, his integrity, and his humility.

A TRUE MAN OF GOD IS
KNOWN BY HIS RELATIONSHIP TO JESUS CHRIST

If anyone is confident in himself that he is Christ's, let him consider this again within himself, that just as he is Christ's, so also are we. (10:7b)

As noted above, the false apostles asserted that they were emissaries of Jesus Christ. They made arrogant claims of being personally commissioned by Him, having superior knowledge of Him, and wielding greater authority from Him. Paul's use of the singular **if anyone** may indicate that he was singling out the ringleader of the false apostles, who likely was the most vociferous in making such claims. The Greek text indicates a condition assumed to be true; Paul did not have a hypothetical situation in mind, but a real one. The false apostles were actually making these claims.

But such confidence was misplaced; anyone who had it was merely **confident in himself.** The false apostles' claims to represent Christ were without objective evidence to back them up. They had no track record of sinners converted, churches founded, and saints built up. There was nothing but the empty boast.

By claiming to be **Christ's** the false apostles were undoubtedly claiming more than just that they were Christians. They asserted that they had a unique devotion to Jesus, such as that claimed by the members of the "Christ party" (see 1 Cor. 1:12). They also meant that they were the true apostles of Christ. They likely also claimed a transcendent, higher knowledge of Him.

While claiming inflated credentials for themselves, the false apostles completely denied Paul's authenticity. He was, according to them, a deceiver, hiding a secret life of shameful sin, a man who preached lies for money. As such, he could hardly even be considered a Christian, let alone have the true message from God that they allegedly possessed, or still less be an apostle. Their lies were designed to discredit Paul so they could replace him as the authoritative teachers at Corinth.

At this point Paul did not deny their claim; he would do that later in his argument (2 Cor. 11:13–15). Here he merely noted that he, too, had a valid claim to belong to Jesus Christ. The apostle challenged the one who would reject his apostleship to **consider this again within himself, that just as he is Christ's, so also are we.** Since it was only a claim on the part of the false teacher, he should know that Paul could make the same claim. The issue could not be decided on the subjective basis of personal convictions, either Paul's or the false apostles'. For that reason Paul, as noted above, called on the Corinthians to examine the objective evidence. The facts of his life, conversion, and ministry were matters of public knowledge in the churches. His traveling companions and Ananias could verify the amazing story of his dramatic conversion on the Damascus Road. Barnabas, Silas, Luke, Timothy, and Paul's other ministry partners could testify to his fearless preaching of the gospel in city after city, to the converts he won, and the churches he founded and built up. In contrast to the false apostles, Paul's convictions were backed up by impressive, undeniable evidence (cf. 12:12).

True men of God have an intimate walk with Christ that is clearly seen in their lives. False teachers may give the outward appearance of orthodoxy but as Jesus said, "You will know them by their fruits. Grapes are not gathered from thorn bushes nor figs from thistles, are they? (Matt. 7:16; cf. v. 20). Despite their claims, false teachers' aberrant doctrine will inevitably manifest itself in their sinful behavior and in the sinful lives of their followers.

A True Man of God Is Known by His Impact on the Church

For even if I boast somewhat further about our authority, which the Lord gave for building you up and not for destroying you, I will not be put to shame, (10:8)

Though reluctant to **boast** any **further about** his **authority,** Paul did so because the circumstances compelled him to do so. Because of his unimpeachable life and impeccable apostolic credentials, he would **not be put to shame** in his boasting. He would never go too far and make empty boasts like the false apostles, because the Lord gave him his authority. Paul's claims were limited only by his humility.

Unlike the abusive, destructive false apostles, Paul used his authority **for building** the Corinthians **up and not for destroying** them. A true man of God will inevitably have a positive impact on the church as he edifies, strengthens, and matures it. Paul had preached the gospel with power, seen many come to saving faith in Christ, established churches throughout much of the Greco-Roman world, trained leaders, and perfected the saints. His ministry as a true apostle had undeniably resulted in the spiritual progress and strength of the church (12:19; Eph. 4:11–12).

On the other hand, false teachers invariably bring discord, disunity, destruction, and even death to the church. Their confusing, divisive influence is at cross-purposes with the Head of the church, who promised to build it (Matt. 16:18). Paul had them in mind when he warned, "If any man destroys the temple of God, God will destroy him, for the temple of God is holy, and that is what you are" (1 Cor. 3:17). Paul wielded his apostolic authority (cf. 1 Cor. 3:10:5–6) to build the church, not to destroy it.

A TRUE MAN OF GOD IS
KNOWN BY HIS COMPASSION FOR PEOPLE

for I do not wish to seem as if I would terrify you by my letters. (10:9)

False teachers tend to be self-centered, grasping, and abusive. People usually mean nothing to them, except as means to their own selfish ends. They are often overbearing, self-absorbed, and callous to the needs of others.

The false apostles perversely tried to assign to Paul the very evils they themselves were both familiar with and guilty of. They charged that he was an abusive leader, who tried to intimidate the Corinthians into submission. The false apostles no doubt pointed to the severe letter (2:3–4) as a prime example of Paul's purported abusive treatment of them. Paul replied to those false allegations by assuring the Corinthians, **I do not wish to seem as if I would terrify you by my letters.** He was not trying to **terrify** the Corinthians into obeying him. His goal was to bring them to repentance, so they would experience all the blessings that accompany salvation. He had been firm because the situation demanded it, and most of the Corinthians had responded positively to his correction (cf. 7:8–10).

Paul was a reluctant disciplinarian, as his agonizing over the severe letter reveals:

> But I call God as witness to my soul, that to spare you I came no more to Corinth. Not that we lord it over your faith, but are workers with you for your joy; for in your faith you are standing firm. But I determined this for my own sake, that I would not come to you in sorrow again. For if I cause you sorrow, who then makes me glad but the one whom I made sorrowful? This is the very thing I wrote you, so that when I came, I would not have sorrow from those who ought to make me rejoice; having confidence in you all that my joy would be the joy of you all. For out of much affliction and anguish of heart I wrote to you with many tears; not so that you would be made sorrowful, but that you might know the love which I have especially for you. (1:23–2:4)

In 7:3 he added, "I do not speak to condemn you, for I have said before that you are in our hearts to die together and to live together." The apostle much preferred the spirit of love and gentleness to the rod of correction (cf. 1 Cor. 4:21). "You are our letter," he wrote earlier in this epistle, "written in our hearts, known and read by all men; being manifested that you are a letter of Christ, cared for by us, written not with ink but with the Spirit of the living God, not on tablets of stone but on tablets of human hearts"

(2 Cor. 3:2–3). In 7:2 he begged the Corinthians,"Make room for us in your hearts; we wronged no one, we corrupted no one, we took advantage of no one," while in 11:11 and 12:15 he freely declared his love for them.

True men of God are marked by compassion. They care for their people with "the affection of Christ Jesus" (Phil. 1:8). But nothing is more characteristic of a false teacher than indifference or malice toward people. The difference between the two is the contrast between the good shepherd, who lays down His life for the sheep, and the hireling, who is not concerned about the flock (cf. John 10:11–13).

A TRUE MAN OF GOD IS
KNOWN BY HIS DISDAIN FOR FLESHLY METHODS

For they say, "His letters are weighty and strong, but his personal presence is unimpressive and his speech contemptible." (10:10)

That the apostle's **letters** were **weighty and strong** was obvious to all who read them. There was no denying the power of his inspired pen, the clarity, rationality, and spirituality of his writings. They resonated with fervor and conviction of the truth. To maintain otherwise would have been absurd, and the false apostles did not try to deny the obvious.

But after conceding the powerful impact of Paul's writings, the false apostles derided **his personal presence** as **unimpressive and his speech** as **contemptible.** Though they were certainly not impressed with Paul's physical appearance, what the false apostles really meant by **his personal presence** was his persona, aura, or demeanor. According to them, he lacked the kind of charisma and personal charm that commanded respect and loyalty. They no doubt reinforced that claim by depicting Paul's departure from Corinth after the sorrowful visit (2:1) as an ignominious retreat. The apostle, they sneered, was a sniveling, cowering wimp who crawled out of town after being offended. In their mind, that demonstrated that he lacked the power of a great leader.

The false teachers intended by this cutting criticism to portray themselves as strong, decisive leaders and Paul as weak and wishy-washy. They claimed he was reluctant to deal with issues that they faced head-on. Such criticism reveals their unacceptable model of spiritual leadership, one of dominant dictatorship. "You know that the rulers of the Gentiles lord it over them," Jesus declared of such leaders, "and their great men exercise authority over them" (Matt. 20:25). But that domineering view of leadership is the antithesis of the biblical view, which sees the leader as a servant:

> It is not this way among you, but whoever wishes to become great among you shall be your servant, and whoever wishes to be first among you shall be your slave; just as the Son of Man did not come to be served, but to serve, and to give His life a ransom for many. (Matt. 20:26–28)

Not content with ridiculing Paul's personal presence, the false apostles condemned **his speech** as being **contemptible.** By that they meant that he lacked the polished oratorical and rhetorical skills so highly prized in Greek culture. It is true that the apostle repudiated eloquent sophistry, though surely capable of it, preferring instead to preach the gospel in simplicity and power. In 1 Corinthians 2:1–5 he explained,

> And when I came to you, brethren, I did not come with superiority of speech or of wisdom, proclaiming to you the testimony of God. For I determined to know nothing among you except Jesus Christ, and Him crucified. I was with you in weakness and in fear and in much trembling, and my message and my preaching were not in persuasive words of wisdom, but in demonstration of the Spirit and of power, so that your faith would not rest on the wisdom of men, but on the power of God.

The false apostles, on the other hand, used their polished oratory and slick manipulative skills to sway and seduce victims for their own prestige and power. The true man of God, however, refuses to use fleshly methods. Instead, he preaches the Word of God clearly and powerfully, so that people's "faith [will] not rest on the wisdom of men, but on the power of God" (1 Cor. 2:5).

A True Man of God Is Known by His Integrity

Let such a person consider this, that what we are in word by letters when absent, such persons we are also in deed when present. (10:11)

Paul challenged any **person** who would accuse him of inconsistency to **consider this, that what we are in word by letters when absent, such persons we are also in deed when present.** Later in this epistle Paul warned the rebels in Corinth not to underestimate his ability and willingness to deal sternly with them.

I have previously said when present the second time, and though now

> absent I say in advance to those who have sinned in the past and to all the rest as well, that if I come again I will not spare anyone, since you
>
> are seeking for proof of the Christ who speaks in me, and who is not weak toward you, but mighty in you. (13:2–3)

The apostle's life was totally consistent; he was the same person **in deed when present** as he was in the **letters** he wrote **when absent.** He was no hypocrite; his integrity was unimpeachable.

Paul's life and ministry bore the stamp of divine approval. To the Thessalonians he wrote, "But just as we have been approved by God to be entrusted with the gospel, so we speak, not as pleasing men, but God who examines our hearts" (1 Thess. 2:4). But in contrast to true men of God, false teachers are often quite different in private from the public image they project. The numerous scandals that have rocked their ministries over the years bear sad testimony to that reality.

A TRUE MAN OF GOD IS
KNOWN BY HIS HUMILITY

For we are not bold to class or compare ourselves with some of those who commend themselves; but when they measure themselves by themselves and compare themselves with themselves, they are without understanding. But we will not boast beyond our measure, but within the measure of the sphere which God apportioned to us as a measure, to reach even as far as you. For we are not overextending ourselves, as if we did not reach to you, for we were the first to come even as far as you in the gospel of Christ; not boasting beyond our measure, that is, in other men's labors, but with the hope that as your faith grows, we will be, within our sphere, enlarged even more by you, so as to preach the gospel even to the regions beyond you, and not to boast in what has been accomplished in the sphere of another. But he who boasts is to boast in the Lord. For it is not he who commends himself that is approved, but he whom the Lord commends. (10:12–18)

There is no more noble Christian virtue than humility, the genuine conviction that one is utterly and completely unworthy of the goodness, mercy, and grace of God. The Bible paints a rich and diverse portrait of humility. Humble people recognize their spiritual bankruptcy (Matt. 5:3), refuse to think more highly of themselves than they should (Rom. 12:3), fall before their great and glorious God in lowliness and submission (Isa. 6:5; Luke 5:8), are eager to give God all the credit for everything good in their lives (1 Cor. 15:10), truly worship Him (Ps. 95:6; 1 Cor. 14:25), are convinced that no task is beneath them (John 13:3–15), and recognize that they are not yet what they should be (Phil. 3:12–14). Humble people are unwilling to boast, brag, or promote themselves (2 Cor. 11:30; cf. Gal. 6:14), in fact, they are somewhat embarrassed by commendation (Prov. 27:2). They do not hide their sins and shortcomings, or view themselves as superior to others (1 Tim. 1:15), they are willing to serve (Matt. 23:11), and are content to submit all their plans to the Lord's will (Ps. 37:5; Prov. 16:3). Paul summed up the attitude of a humble person when he wrote, "Not that we are adequate in ourselves to consider anything as coming from ourselves, but our adequacy is from God" (2 Cor. 3:5).

Nothing more clearly marks a man of God than the attitude of humility that characterized the Lord Jesus Christ (Matt. 11:29; cf. 5:3; 18:4; Acts 20:19). No one except the Lord had a more profound impact on the church than Paul. Yet he described himself as a clay pot, such as those used for the most menial household tasks (2 Cor. 4:7), a wretched man (Rom. 7:24), the very least of all saints (Eph. 3:8), the least of the apostles (1 Cor. 15:9), and the foremost of sinners (1 Tim. 1:15). That humility, contrasted with the blatant pride of the false apostles (cf. Jer. 23:32; Dan. 11:36; Luke 18:11–12; 2 Peter 2:18; Jude 16; 2 Thess. 2:3–4; Rev. 13:5–6), should have been conclusive proof to the Corinthians of Paul's apostleship.

But, unfortunately, many of them still did not get the point. Therefore Paul closed this section describing the marks of a true man of God with an extensive discussion of humility in verses 12–18. In a passage full of irony and sarcasm, Paul deflated the pompous claims of the false apostles, and offered his humility as proof of his genuineness. Verses 12–18 unfold five characteristics of a humble messenger whom God has changed and called.

A HUMBLE MESSENGER OF GOD IS
UNWILLING TO COMPARE HIMSELF WITH OTHERS

For we are not bold to class or compare ourselves with some of those who commend themselves; but when they measure themselves by themselves and compare themselves with themselves, they are without understanding. (10:12)

The Pharisee who proudly and arrogantly prayed, "God, I thank You that I am not like other people: swindlers, unjust, adulterers, or even like this tax collector" (Luke 18:11) typified the attitude of false teachers.

In their zeal to elevate themselves, they will tear down anyone who gets in their way. The proud, vain false apostles at Corinth sought to make themselves appear superior by attacking Paul.

But Paul refused to play their childish game of ego-building self-congratulation. He would not defend himself using their criteria. Instead, he wrote, **We are not bold to class or compare ourselves with some of those who commend themselves.** The phrase **we are not bold** has the sense of "I do not dare." The apostle had no intention of replying to **those who commend themselves** by commending himself; he would not dishonor God by stooping to their level (cf. Prov. 26:5).

The false apostles' standard of comparison was subjective, based on such superficial, external factors as personality, charisma, and oratorical skills. They invented their own personal standards for greatness, met them, and then proudly proclaimed their superiority. But those who **measure themselves by themselves and compare themselves with themselves . . . are without understanding;** they are foolish and irrational. The self-centered and self-satisfied are always self-deceived.

In contrast, Paul measured himself against a divine standard. Earlier he wrote to the Corinthians, "To me it is a very small thing that I may be examined by you, or by any human court; in fact, I do not even examine myself. For I am conscious of nothing against myself, yet I am not by this acquitted; but the one who examines me is the Lord" (1 Cor. 4:3–4). When Paul listed his apostolic credentials, he listed the things he had suffered (11:22–33), and his weakness (11:30; 12:5, 9; Acts 20:19). Humble people are keenly aware of how far short they fall of the perfect standard, the Lord Jesus Christ (1 Cor. 11:1).

A HUMBLE MESSENGER OF GOD IS
WILLING TO MINISTER WITHIN LIMITS

But we will not boast beyond our measure, but within the measure of the sphere which God apportioned to us as a measure, to reach even as far as you. (10:13)

False teachers tend to be megalomaniacs, who become enraged at those who would limit their grandiose designs. They continually seek to widen their influence and gain greater prestige, fame, and wealth. To that end, they often overstate or even falsify their qualifications and gifts. The false apostles presented the Corinthians with a rather amazing resumé. They claimed greater power, erudition, oratorical skills, and influence than Paul. They then used those phony credentials to gain influence in the Corinthian assembly.

But Paul refused to **boast** beyond **his measure;** he would **not** say anything about himself or his ministry that was not true. He refused to trade lies and exaggerations with the false apostles; his assessment of his ministry was honest and accurate. In contrast to their ambitious pretensions, he was content to remain **within the measure of the sphere which God apportioned to** him. To use the analogy of a race, Paul stayed in his lane. He had a sovereignly granted field of service, which he described in Romans 1:5: "We have received grace and apostleship to bring about the obedience of faith among all the Gentiles for His name's sake" (cf. Rom. 15:18; Acts 22:21; 26:15–18). He did not chafe under his God-ordained limits; he did not want to have a bigger or more important ministry than God intended for him. Paul was perfectly content with the sphere of ministry God had marked out for him. He focused on excellence rather than success; on the quality of his ministry rather than its size; on the depth of his ministry rather than its breadth.

Even Jesus ministered within strictly defined limits set by the Father. His ministry was limited by the Father's will (John 5:30; 6:38), timing (John 2:4; 7:30; 8:20), people (the "lost sheep of the house of Israel" [Matt. 15:24]), message ("the gospel of the kingdom" [Matt. 4:23; 9:35; Luke 4:18]), and priorities (the twelve apostles, not the wealthy and influential).

The false apostles' claims that Paul had overstepped his bounds were without foundation, since God had ordained his sphere of ministry **to reach even as far as** Corinth. For the Corinthians to argue otherwise was to saw off the very branch on which they were sitting. Paul was their spiritual father (1 Cor. 4:15), and their church owed its existence to his ministry. To deny Paul's legitimacy as an apostle was to deny the legitimacy of their salvation and their church.

A HUMBLE MESSENGER OF GOD IS
UNWILLING TO TAKE CREDIT FOR OTHERS' LABORS

For we are not overextending ourselves, as if we did not reach to you, for we were the first to come even as far as you in the gospel of Christ; not boasting beyond our measure, that is, in other men's labors, but with the hope that as your faith grows, we will be, within our sphere, enlarged even more by you, so as to preach the gospel even to the regions beyond you, and not to boast in what has been accomplished in the sphere of another. (10:14–16)

Paul was not guilty of **overextending** himself when he claimed that his sphere of ministry reached to Corinth. As noted above, he was **the first to come** to them with **the gospel of Christ.** He was **not boasting beyond** his **measure,** because of the indisputable fact that he had founded the Corinthian church (1 Cor. 3:6, 10; 4:15). He had not intruded on the false apostles' territory; it was the other way around. They were the interlopers, not Paul.

The false apostles invented a fanciful litany of their supposed achievements. Unlike Paul, they were not hesitant to boast **in other men's labors.** Having no legitimate accomplishments of their own, they were eager to take credit for those of others. But in reality, they had made no contribution to the Corinthians' spiritual growth, because they were not true servants of God. By preaching a false gospel and another Jesus (2 Cor. 11:3–4), they were interfering with the work Paul had accomplished. They were nothing but parasites, sucking the spiritual life out of the church in contrast to the true apostle, who edified it (cf. Eph. 2:20).

Paul's plan and **hope** was **that as** the Corinthians' **faith** grew, he would **be, within** his **sphere, enlarged even more by** them. His goal was, with their assistance, **to preach the gospel even to the regions beyond** Corinth. That was not possible at the time, however, because of the Corinthians' sin, immaturity, and rebellion. It would have to wait until they completely rejected the false apostles and returned to sound doctrine and holy living.

Paul was never one to rest on his laurels. His restless spirit drove him ever onward to preach the gospel where it had never been proclaimed. In Acts 19:21 he expressed his desire to preach the gospel in Rome, but he did not mean to stop there. He planned, with the Roman believers' aid, to reach Spain (Rom. 15:24, 28). When the Corinthians became strong enough in their faith, the apostle wanted them to launch him to the next mission field. But no matter where he went, Paul always wanted to stay within the sphere of ministry God had sovereignly designed for him. He humbly refused to follow in the footsteps of other men of God and take credit for their labors.

A HUMBLE MESSENGER OF GOD IS
WILLING TO SEEK ONLY THE LORD'S GLORY

But he who boasts is to boast in the Lord. (10:17)

This essential truth, found throughout Scripture, is a stinging rebuke to all self-glorying false teachers. In Psalm 20:7 David wrote, "Some boast in chariots and some in horses, but we will boast in the name of the Lord, our God," while in Psalm 34:2 he added, "My soul shall make its boast in the Lord; the humble shall hear it and rejoice." Through the prophet Jeremiah God declared,

> Thus says the Lord, "Let not a wise man boast of his wisdom, and let not the mighty man boast of his might, let not a rich man boast of his riches; but let him who boasts boast of this, that he understands and knows Me, that I am the Lord who exercises lovingkindness, justice and righteousness on earth; for I delight in these things," declares the Lord. (Jer. 9:23–24)

Paul had the above passage in mind when he wrote this verse, and also when he wrote earlier to the Corinthians, "Just as it is written, 'Let him who boasts, boast in the Lord'" (1 Cor. 1:31). To the Romans he wrote, "Therefore in Christ Jesus I have found reason for boasting in things pertaining to God. For I will not presume to speak of anything except what Christ has accomplished through me, resulting in the obedience of the Gentiles by word and deed" (Rom. 15:17–18). He vowed in Galatians 6:14, "But may it never be that I would boast, except in the cross of our Lord Jesus Christ, through which the world has been crucified to me, and I to the world."

After Martin Luther's death, his friends found a scrap of paper in his pocket on which the great Reformer had written, "We are all beggars." Humble men of God realize that they have nothing to boast about. If they preach the gospel, it is because God's Word is a fire in their bones (Jer. 20:9) and they are compelled to preach (1 Cor. 9:16). They serve the church only because Christ puts them into service (1 Tim. 1:12), and any success they have is attributable solely to the grace of God at work in them (1 Cor. 15:10). They cry out with the psalmist, "Not to us, O Lord, not to us, but to Your name give glory" (Ps. 115:1).

A HUMBLE MESSENGER OF GOD IS
UNWILLING TO PURSUE ANYTHING BUT ETERNAL GLORY

For it is not he who commends himself that is approved, but he whom the Lord commends. (10:18)

False teachers are totally focused on the here and now, as they pursue fame, accolades, notoriety, prestige, wealth, and power. But true servants of Christ look toward their heavenly reward (Matt. 5:12; Luke 6:23; Col. 3:24; Heb. 11:26). They understand that worldly self-commendation is meaningless, **for it is not he who commends himself that is approved.** They are not men pleasers; whether the world condemns or commends them is of no particular significance in the long run. What matters is **whom the Lord commends;** to whom He says, "Well done, good and faithful slave. . . . Enter into the joy of your master" (Matt. 25:21). That is the only evaluation that counts, as Paul wrote in his earlier inspired letter to the Corinthians:

> But to me it is a very small thing that I may be examined by you, or by any human court; in fact, I do not even examine myself. For I am conscious of nothing against myself, yet I am not by this acquitted; but the one who examines me is the Lord. Therefore do not go on passing judgment before the time, but wait until the Lord comes who will both bring to light the things hidden in the darkness and disclose the motives of men's hearts; and then each man's praise will come to him from God. (1 Cor. 4:3–5)

The church today faces the same challenge that it always has, to sort out the true preachers from the false deceivers. The sad story of the Corinthian church's gullibility has been repeated throughout history, as undiscerning believers have fallen for the lies of false teachers. As a result, churches, educational institutions, and denominations throughout the world have abandoned biblical truth. The Corinthians should have been able to tell the difference between true and false spiritual leaders, and so should today's church. True men of God are not showmen; they do not intimidate people; they do not seek to promote themselves; they value truth enough not to tolerate error; they seek to imitate the meekness of Jesus Christ; they have a high view of Scripture and preach the pure, unadulterated gospel; they are content to minister within the sphere in which God has placed them; they lead lives consistent with their teaching; they do not take credit for others' work; and they seek God's eternal glory, not temporal acclaim. The man "who in this way serves Christ is acceptable to God and approved by men" (Rom. 14:18).

Christian Loyalty (2 Corinthians 11:1–6)

27

I wish that you would bear with me in a little foolishness; but indeed you are bearing with me. For I am jealous for you with a godly jealousy; for I betrothed you to one husband, so that to Christ I might present you as a pure virgin. But I am afraid that, as the serpent deceived Eve by his craftiness, your minds will be led astray from the simplicity and purity of devotion to Christ. For if one comes and preaches another Jesus whom we have not preached, or you receive a different spirit which you have not received, or a different gospel which you have not accepted, you bear this beautifully. For I consider myself not in the least inferior to the most eminent apostles. But even if I am unskilled in speech, yet I am not so in knowledge; in fact, in every way we have made this evident to you in all things. (11:1–6)

Perhaps the most repugnant word in any language is its word for traitor. There are few people more despicable than those who betray their family, their friends, their cause, or their nation. In fact, the names of such infamous traitors as Benedict Arnold, Vidkun Quisling (who collaborated with the Germans occupying Norway during World War 2) and the ultimate betrayer, Judas Iscariot, have become synonymous with the term "traitor." In contrast, among the most treasured words in any language are loyalty and its synonyms—faithfulness, allegiance, fidelity, and devotion.

The Bible emphasizes the importance of loyalty. "Many a man proclaims his own loyalty," Solomon wrote, "but who can find a trustworthy man?" (Prov. 20:6). Not all those who proclaim loyalty demonstrate it, but the one "who pursues righteousness and loyalty finds life, righteousness and honor" (Prov. 21:21). Those in authority, Solomon added, must also display loyalty: "Loyalty and truth preserve the king, and he upholds his throne by righteousness" (Prov. 20:28).

But of far greater significance than loyalty to any human person or cause is loyalty to God, which may be defined as loving Him with all one's heart, soul, mind, and strength (Deut. 6:5; Mark 12:30). Such loyalty does not come cheaply or easily. In Matthew 10:34–38 Jesus described the price allegiance to Him might exact:

> Do not think that I came to bring peace on the earth; I did not come to bring peace, but a sword. For I came to set a man against his father, and a daughter against her mother, and a daughter-in-law against her mother-in-law; and a man's enemies will be the members of his household. He who loves father or mother more than Me is not worthy of Me; and he who loves son or daughter more than Me is not worthy of Me. And he who does not take his cross and follow after Me is not worthy of Me.

Loyalty to Jesus can be a sword that severs family ties or even costs people their lives—a truth attested to by the countless thousands of martyrs who preferred death to disloyalty.

Scripture repeatedly emphasizes the importance of loyalty to God. David exhorted Solomon to "serve [God] with a loyal heart and with a willing mind" (1 Chron. 28:9 NKJV) and prayed, "Give my son Solomon a loyal heart to keep Your commandments and Your testimonies and Your statutes" (1 Chron. 29:19 NKJV). At the dedication of the temple Solomon exhorted Israel, "Let your heart therefore be loyal to the Lord our God, to walk in His statutes and keep His commandments, as at this day" (1 Kings 8:61 NKJV). It was said of some Old Testament kings, such as Hezekiah (Isa. 38:3) and Asa (1 Kings 15:14), that their hearts were "loyal" (NKJV), or "wholly devoted" (NASB) to the Lord. Others, such as Abijam (1 Kings 15:1–3) and Amaziah (2 Chron. 25:1–2), were not loyal to Him. Tragically, in later life Solomon himself became disloyal to God: "For it was so, when Solomon was old, that his wives turned his heart after other gods; and his heart was not loyal to the Lord his God, as was the heart of his father David" (1 Kings 11:4 NKJV). His tragic defection shows that despite the best intentions, loyalty can be lost.

Sadly, following the example of her unfaithful rulers, Israel failed to remain loyal to the Lord. "What shall I do with you, O Ephraim? What shall I do with you, O Judah?" God lamented through the prophet Hosea, "For your loyalty is like a morning cloud and like the dew which goes away early" (Hos. 6:4). Calling Israel back to their allegiance to Him, God declared, "For I delight in loyalty rather than sacrifice, and in the knowledge of God rather than burnt offerings" (Hos. 6:6).

Like Israel, the church has often proven unfaithful to the Lord. Paul confronted Peter's disloyalty (Gal. 2:11–13), and rebuked the Galatians for their betrayal of the gospel of grace (Gal. 3:3). Peter and Jude warned of deceptive false teachers, who would lead many astray from the truth (2 Peter 2:1–3, 10–22; Jude 4–16). James warned those who are not completely loyal to God not to expect anything from Him (James 1:5–8). And five of the seven churches to whom John addressed Revelation (Rev. 2–3) were disloyal to the Lord Jesus Christ.

None of the New Testament writers were more concerned about loyalty than Paul, and nowhere was he more concerned about disloyalty than at Corinth. Deceived by the seductive lies of some self-appointed demonic false apostles, many of the Corinthians had openly rebelled against Paul. The apostle had dealt with that mutiny in a sternly worded letter (2 Cor. 2:1–4). As a result, most of the Corinthians had repented and reaffirmed their loyalty to him (7:6–11). Paul knew, however, that the rebellion had not been completely put down but merely driven underground. Therefore, he addressed the repentant majority in the Corinthian assembly in chapters 1–9, urging their continued loyalty to him. Then in chapters 10–13 he dealt firmly and directly with the false apostles and their unrepentant followers, defending himself against their vicious attacks on his character and ministry.

Paul found defending himself distasteful, and he abhorred self-commendation (2 Cor. 10:12, 13, 17, 18; cf. Prov. 27:2). Yet he could not permit the false teachers to destroy his reputation and undermine his teaching. They had exalted and promoted themselves (2 Cor. 10:12), and the Corinthians were impressed. If Paul did not defend himself, they would be cut off from him as the source of the divine truth and at the mercy of the false teachers. His defense was not for his sake but for theirs, as he explained in 12:19: "All this time you have been thinking that we are defending ourselves to you. Actually, it is in the sight of God that we have been speaking in Christ; and all for your upbuilding, beloved." So as distasteful as it was to him, Paul had to defend his integrity—not for pride, self-exaltation, or his ego, but because the gospel was at stake.

Beginning in chapter 11, Paul confronted the false apostles. Reluctantly, he compared himself to them so the Corinthians could distinguish a true messenger of God from false ones. As he began to confront the false apostles, Paul revealed that his motive for doing so was to call the Corinthians back to loyalty. He began by expressing his **wish that** they **would bear with** him in his defense of himself, which the apostle referred to as **a little foolishness.** He was about to answer fools as their folly deserved (Prov. 26:5). In reality, he would have preferred not to write this section, but the Corinthians' folly left him no choice. The apostle softened his blow by acknowledging that they were **indeed . . . bearing with** him, an affirmation of their positive response to his prior correction of them (2 Cor. 2:1–4; 7:6–11; 1 Corinthians). Paul asked for the same favorable response as he defended himself against the false teachers' attacks and the Corinthians' own foolish disloyalty.

In verses 2 through 6, Paul issued a four-count indictment of the Corinthians' disloyalty, each one introduced by the Greek conjunction *gar* ("for"). Paul expressed his concern about their disloyalty to God, Christ, the gospel, and the truth.

DISLOYALTY TO GOD

For I am jealous for you with a godly jealousy; (11:2a)

The thought of the Corinthians' being seduced into error by the false apostles was heartbreaking to Paul. Thus, what may have seemed to the Corinthians to be boasting on his part was actually extreme concern, prompted by **godly jealousy** (literally, "the jealousy of God"). Paul's jealousy on God's behalf manifested itself in righteous indignation at the possibility of the Corinthians' defection.

God's jealousy for His holy name and for His people is a major Old Testament theme. In Exodus 20:5 God said, "I, the Lord your God, am a jealous God." Exodus 34:14 reveals that one of God's names is "Jealous." Deuteronomy 4:24 describes the Lord as "a consuming fire, a jealous God" (cf. Deut. 5:9; 6:15; Josh. 24:19; Nah. 1:2), while Deuteronomy 32:16 and 21 reveal that His holy jealousy is provoked when His people worship idols (cf. Ps. 78:58; 1 Cor. 10:22). In Ezekiel 39:25 God declares, "I shall be jealous for My holy name."

Like David, who wrote in Psalm 69:9, "Zeal for [God's] house has consumed me, and the reproaches of those who reproach [Him] have fallen on me" (cf. John 2:17), Paul felt pain when God was dishonored. That pain produced a "daily pressure on [him] of concern for all the churches" (2 Cor. 11:28), particularly for those believers who were weak and led into sin (11:29). He was especially concerned that the Corinthians offer God the loyal, loving obedience in which He rejoices and of which He is worthy (cf. Deut. 6:5; 10:12; 11:1, 13, 22; 19:9; 30:16; Josh. 22:5; 23:11; Ps. 31:23; Matt. 22:37).

DISLOYALTY TO CHRIST

for I betrothed you to one husband, so that to Christ I might present you as a pure virgin. But I am afraid that, as the serpent deceived Eve by his craftiness, your minds will be led astray from the simplicity and purity of devotion to Christ. (11:2*b*–3)

Paul expressed his concern over the Corinthians' disloyalty to Christ by using the analogy of betrothal and marriage. As is the case today, the main elements of a Jewish wedding were the betrothal (engagement) and the actual ceremony. The betrothal period usually lasted about a year (though sometimes couples were betrothed as young children). The betrothed couple, though not allowed to consummate the union physically, was legally regarded as husband and wife; the betrothal could be broken only by death or divorce, and unfaithfulness during that time was considered adultery (cf. Matt. 1:18–19). The betrothal period culminated in the ceremony, marking the completion of the covenant.

During the betrothal period, it was the father's responsibility to ensure that his daughter remained faithful to her pledged husband. He would then present her to him at the wedding ceremony as a pure virgin.

When Paul preached the gospel to them, he **betrothed** the Corinthians **to one husband.** At salvation, they pledged their loyalty to Christ, and Paul wanted to make sure they remained faithful. As their spiritual father (1 Cor. 4:15), Paul was determined to **present** them **as a pure virgin to Christ.** Having been engaged to Him at salvation, the Corinthians (like all church-age believers) will be presented to Christ at the Rapture (cf. John 14:1–3) and have their marriage supper during the millennial kingdom (Rev. 19:7–9). Paul's overriding concern was that the church remain pure for her Bridegroom (cf. Eph. 5:25–27).

The phrase **I am afraid** expresses the heart of Paul's concern, both in this passage and in the entire epistle. His defense of his integrity and his ministry, his appeals for the Corinthians' loyalty, and his confrontation of the false teachers all were motivated by fear. The apostle's concern was justified, because the Corinthians had demonstrated an alarming susceptibility to being seduced, welcoming those who preached another Jesus and a different gospel (2 Cor. 11:4).

It is every pastor's fear that some of his sheep might go astray. As noted above, it was Paul's zeal for their purity that caused the "daily pressure on [him] of concern for all the churches" (11:28). A heartbreaking theme throughout history is the disloyalty of many who claimed to be followers of Jesus Christ. Countless churches that name the name of Christ have been seduced by "deceitful spirits" teaching "doctrines of demons" (1 Tim. 4:1) and become disloyal to Him.

Satan's deception of God's people began in the Garden of Eden when **the serpent** (Satan; Rev. 12:9; 20:2) **deceived Eve.** She did not intend to rebel against God, but as Paul wrote to Timothy, "the woman being deceived, fell into transgression" (1 Tim. 2:13). Eve thought that the information she received from Satan was correct and acted on it. In Genesis 3:1 Satan began by asking her, "Indeed, has God said, 'You shall not eat from any tree of the garden'?" God had, as Satan knew, clearly said just that. His question was intended to cast doubt on God's command. Having planted the seed of doubt in Eve's mind, Satan then proceeded to openly deny the truth of God's word, brazenly declaring to her, "You surely will not die!" (3:4). Finally, he offered a lie in its place: "For God knows that in the day you eat from it your eyes will be opened, and you will be like God, knowing good and evil" (3:5). Eve wanted God's best, so Satan's counsel seemed perfect. After all, what could be better than being like God? Having thus been thoroughly deceived, Eve ate the forbidden fruit, as did Adam—even though he was not deceived (1 Tim. 2:14). The catastrophic result was that the human race was plunged into sin (Rom. 5:12–19; 1 Cor. 15:21–22). Ever since Satan deceived Eve, false teachers, following his pattern, have portrayed the truth as error and then offered error as the truth.

Paul feared that Satan's emissaries, using the same **craftiness** (cf. 2 Cor. 11:13–15) by which their evil master deceived Eve, would lead the Corinthians' **minds** (the Greek word could also be translated "thoughts") **astray,** thus corrupting or ruining them (the Greek term also has those connotations). Lack of discernment is a major problem for the church (cf. Eph. 4:14), because the spiritual battle is an ideological one (see the discussion of 10:3–5 in chapter 25 of this volume). The church's willingness to tolerate error in the name of unity, coupled with a lack of biblical and doctrinal knowledge, has crippled its ability to discern. As a result, it is too often easy prey for the ravenous, savage wolves of whom both Jesus and Paul warned (Matt. 7:15; Acts 20:29), who wound it and sap its power and testimony.

The essence of the Christian life is **simplicity and purity of devotion to Christ.** To the Philippians Paul wrote, "For to me, to live is Christ and to die is gain" (Phil. 1:21; cf. Gal. 2:20; Col. 3:4). To not love Him supremely as Savior and Lord is an act of disloyalty. The danger false teachers pose is that they shift the focus off Jesus Christ and onto rituals, ceremonies, good works, miracles, emotional experiences, psychology, entertainment, political and social causes, and anything else that will distract people.

Loyalty to the Lord Jesus Christ is nonnegotiable in the Christian life—so much so that Scripture declares, "If anyone does not love the Lord, he is to be accursed" (1 Cor. 16:22).

DISLOYALTY TO THE GOSPEL

For if one comes and preaches another Jesus whom we have not preached, or you receive a different spirit which you have not received, or a different gospel which you have not accepted, you bear this beautifully. (11:4)

If could be better translated "since," because Paul was not writing about a hypothetical situation. False teachers had already come to Corinth. Though God had not sent them (cf. Jer. 23:21), the Corinthians had welcomed them and given them a platform from which to proclaim their false gospel. As noted in chapter 26 of this volume, Paul did not dignify the false teachers' heresy by giving a detailed explication of it. But here he summarized it under three general headings.

First, the false apostles preached **another Jesus,** not the true Lord Jesus Christ **whom** Paul **preached.** An aberrant Christology has always been a hallmark of false religions and cults. Instead of viewing Him as the eternal second person of the Trinity, who became a man and died as an atoning sacrifice for sin, they see Him as a prophet, guru, avatar, social or political revolutionary, Michael the archangel, a spirit child of God, an emanation from God—anything but the true God in flesh. Although the false apostles outwardly identified with Jesus, the Jesus they preached was not the Jesus of Scripture.

Second, the false apostles came in the power of **a different spirit,** a demonic spirit, not the Holy Spirit whom the Corinthians had **received** at salvation. All false teaching ultimately derives from Satan and his demon hosts, whom Paul described as "deceitful spirits" (1 Tim. 4:1), and John called "the spirit of error" (1 John 4:6; cf. 4:1).

The logical consequence of proclaiming a different Jesus in the power of a different spirit was that the false apostles preached **a different gospel.** They did not preach the true gospel that the Corinthians had **accepted** when Paul first preached it to them. As previously noted, Paul did not define this false gospel. It undoubtedly denied that salvation is by grace through faith alone, and it added human works. Incredibly, instead of rejecting this damning heresy, the Corinthians bore it **beautifully;** they tolerated it, thus justifying Paul's fear for their purity.

DISLOYALTY TO THE TRUTH

For I consider myself not in the least inferior to the most eminent apostles. But even if I am unskilled in speech, yet I am not so in knowledge; in fact, in every way we have made this evident to you in all things. (11:5–6)

Paul's hesitancy to boast (cf. 10:12) caused him to make the minimalistic and sarcastic claim that he was **not in the least inferior to the most eminent apostles** (lit., the "extra-special" or "super" apostles). He was not acknowledging them as his equals, since they were false apostles (11:12–15) and he was a true one (cf. 4:7–15; 6:4–10; 11:21–33; 12:12). But for the sake of argument, he called on the Corinthians to at least grant the obvious reality that he was **not in the least inferior to** the "super apostles," as they viewed themselves so superfluously.

Some commentators argue that the phrase **most eminent apostles** refers here and in 12:11 to the Twelve. But though it is true that Paul was fully equal to the Twelve (12:12; cf. Gal. 2:6–9), several considerations make it unlikely that he had them in mind here. First, Paul would not have referred to the Twelve with a sarcastic term like "super apostles." Second, the false apostles clearly are in view in 11:4, since Paul would never have accused the Twelve of preaching another Jesus or a different gospel. To abruptly shift to a discussion of the Twelve in verse 5 would be confusing and make no sense. Thus the context argues that the same group is in view in verses 4 and 5. Third, Paul admits in verse 6 to being unskilled in speech compared to the self-proclaimed "super apostles." But that would not be true if he were comparing himself to the Twelve, who were "uneducated and untrained men" (Acts 4:13). Finally, Paul would not have implied that he had spiritual knowledge that the Twelve lacked (2 Cor. 11:6).

As noted in the discussion of 10:10 in chapter 26 of this volume, the false apostles scorned Paul for being **unskilled in speech.** *Idiōtēs* (**unskilled**) has a contemptuous ring to it, reflecting the false apostles' view that Paul was a crude, amateurish, unrefined speaker. The apostle acknowledged that he was not interested in the rhetorical and oratorical skills that so impressed the Greeks, because he was not concerned with technique, but with the truth. He was not interested in theatrics or in manipulating his audience. Therefore, his message was the gospel, clear and simple. Paul knew that human eloquence draws people to the preacher, not to the cross; faithful preaching, on the other hand, results not in people admiring the preacher but the Christ he proclaims. The gospel itself is "the power of God for salvation" (Rom. 1:16) and does not need any human embellishing.

In his first inspired epistle to the Corinthians, Paul revealed his philosophy of preaching:

> For Christ did not send me to baptize, but to preach the gospel, not in cleverness of speech, so that the cross of Christ would not be made void. For the word of the cross is foolishness to those who are perishing, but to us who are being saved it is the power of God. For it is written, "I will destroy the wisdom of the wise, and the cleverness of the

clever I will set aside." Where is the wise man? Where is the scribe? Where is the debater of this age? Has not God made foolish the wisdom of the world? For since in the wisdom of God the world through its wisdom did not come to know God, God was well-pleased through the foolishness of the message preached to save those who believe. For indeed Jews ask for signs and Greeks search for wisdom; but we preach Christ crucified, to Jews a stumbling block and to Gentiles foolishness, but to those who are the called, both Jews and Greeks, Christ the power of God and the wisdom of God. Because the foolishness of God is wiser than men, and the weakness of God is stronger than men. . . . And when I came to you, brethren, I did not come with superiority of speech or of wisdom, proclaiming to you the testimony of God. For I determined to know nothing among you except Jesus Christ, and Him crucified. I was with you in weakness and in fear and in much trembling, and my message and my preaching were not in persuasive words of wisdom, but in demonstration of the Spirit and of power, so that your faith would not rest on the wisdom of men, but on the power of God. (1 Cor. 1:17–25; 2:1–5)

Nonetheless, Paul was not an ineffective speaker; on the contrary, he spoke with tremendous power and impact. But he was not interested in flowery oratory or being culturally relevant. He disdained theatrics, artificiality, and clever manipulative tricks as "persuasive words of [human] wisdom." His goal was to preach the gospel of Christ lucidly and convictingly, using all his mind and heart by the power of God, so that his hearers' "faith would not rest on the wisdom of men, but on the power of God."

Although his communication skills might have been deficient by the false apostles' standards, Paul was **not** lacking **in knowledge.** The false apostles claimed to have a secret knowledge not available to the uninitiated. But Paul was a "[steward] of the mysteries of God" (1 Cor. 4:1), with "insight into the mystery of Christ" (Eph. 3:4). He described that true spiritual knowledge in 1 Corinthians 2:6–16:

Yet we do speak wisdom among those who are mature; a wisdom, however, not of this age nor of the rulers of this age, who are passing away; but we speak God's wisdom in a mystery, the hidden wisdom which God predestined before the ages to our glory; the wisdom which none of the rulers of this age has understood; for if they had understood it they would not have crucified the Lord of glory; but just as it is written, "Things which eye has not seen and ear has not heard, and which have not entered the heart of man, all that God has prepared for those who love Him." For to us God revealed them through the Spirit; for the Spirit searches all things, even the depths of God. For who among men knows the thoughts of a man except the spirit of the man which is in him?

Even so the thoughts of God no one knows except the Spirit of God. Now we have received, not the spirit of the world, but the Spirit who is from God, so that we may know the things freely given to us by God, which things we also speak, not in words taught by human wisdom, but in those taught by the Spirit, combining spiritual thoughts with spiritual words. But a natural man does not accept the things of the Spirit of God, for they are foolishness to him; and he cannot understand them, because they are spiritually appraised. But he who is spiritual appraises all things, yet he himself is appraised by no one. For who has known the mind of the Lord, that he will instruct Him? But we have the mind of Christ.

Paul preached "God's wisdom in a mystery, the hidden wisdom which God predestined before the ages to our glory; the wisdom which none of the rulers of this age has understood." It was a knowledge that "God revealed . . . through the Spirit . . . not in words taught by human wisdom, but in those taught by the Spirit."

Paul did not keep his knowledge secret, but **in every way** he **made** it **evident to** the Corinthians **in all things.** As he had in Ephesus, Paul "did not shrink from declaring to [them] the whole purpose of God" (Acts 20:27). He had proclaimed to the Corinthians the "true knowledge of God's mystery, that is, Christ Himself" (Col. 2:2; cf. 1:27; 4:3; Eph. 3:4).

Yet despite the solid doctrinal foundation Paul had given them, the Corinthians were in grave danger of being seduced. The risk of wandering from the truth and becoming confused and disloyal is a constant threat to the church of Jesus Christ. Paul forcefully rebuked the Galatian churches, expressing his amazement that they were "so quickly deserting Him who called [them] by the grace of Christ, for a different gospel" (Gal. 1:6). Five of the seven churches John addressed Revelation to, churches founded under Paul's influence, had defected. That tragic pattern has been repeated throughout the church's history. Therefore, absolute loyalty to God, Jesus Christ, the gospel, and biblical truth are nonnegotiable principles for everyone who names the name of Christ.

Distinguishing Marks of True and False Apostles 28
(2 Corinthians 11:7–15, 20)

Or did I commit a sin in humbling myself so that you might be exalted, because I preached the gospel of God to you without charge? I robbed other churches by taking wages from them to serve you; and when I was present with you and was in need, I was not a burden to anyone; for when the brethren came from Macedonia they fully supplied my need, and in everything I kept myself from being a burden to you, and will continue to do so. As the truth of Christ is in me, this boasting of mine will not be stopped in the regions of Achaia. Why? Because I do not love you? God knows I do! But what I am doing I will continue to do, so that I may cut off opportunity from those who desire an opportunity to be regarded just as we are in the matter about which they are boasting. For such men are false apostles, deceitful workers, disguising themselves as apostles of Christ. No wonder, for even Satan disguises himself as an angel of light. Therefore it is not surprising if his servants also disguise themselves as servants of righteousness, whose end will be according to their deeds. . . . For you tolerate it if anyone enslaves you, anyone devours you, anyone takes advantage of you, anyone exalts himself, anyone hits you in the face. (11:7–15, 20)

The famous quote attributed to the circus promoter P. T. Barnum, "There's a sucker born every minute," aptly sums up a major result of the Fall. Thus, one of the most pervasive effects of total depravity is gullibility. Even today, in the most highly educated society in history, people remain amazingly gullible. Deceitful swindlers take in thousands with phony investment schemes, fake charities, bogus health claims, and a myriad of other scams. They ensnare their victims through a variety of means, including ads, telemarketing, and the latest high-tech twist, spam e-mail.

But far more dangerous than the petty plots of human hucksters are the deadly schemes of Satan. The former cost people their money; the latter cost them their eternal souls (cf. Matt. 16:26). Satan's deceptions succeed because people are born into this world easily deceivable and highly temptable. The unregenerate are "alienated from the life of God" (Eph. 4:18 NKJV; cf. 2:12; Gal. 4:8; Col. 1:21) and, not knowing Him (1 Thess. 4:5; cf. Eph. 2:12; 2 Thess. 1:8), are cut off from the source of truth (cf. 2 Cor. 4:4; Rom. 1:18; 2:8). Further, they are under the sway of the "prince of the power of the air . . . the spirit that is now working in the sons of disobedience" (Eph. 2:2; cf. 6:12; John 8:44; 12:31; 1 John 5:19), leaving them vulnerable to the lies and deception promoted by deceitful spirits (1 Tim. 4:1; cf. 1 Kings 22:22–23; 2 Thess. 2:9) and evil men (2 Tim. 3:13).

The deceptive schemes of demons and depraved people permeate every aspect of human society. Morality, sociology, education, politics, science, the arts, and, especially, religion are thoroughly infused with the deceptive falsehoods spawned by the "father of lies" (John 8:44). Having turned their backs on God and the truth (Rom. 1:18–32), the unregenerate cannot help but fall victim to Satan's plots (2 Tim. 2:26), as orchestrated by his minions (Eph. 6:12), since they belong to his kingdom (Col. 1:13). They are beguiled and seduced from the beginning to the end of their lives (Eph. 2:2–3).

But infinitely more tragic than the gullibility of the unregenerate world is the gullibility of the church. The church is the "the pillar and support of the truth" (1 Tim. 3:15), the possessor of "the word of truth, the gospel" (Col. 1:5) found in God's Word, the Bible, which is truth (John 17:17; cf. Pss. 12:6; 19:7; 119:151). Its Head is the Lord Jesus Christ, who is "the way, and the truth, and the life" (John 14:6; cf. John 1:17; Eph. 4:21), and it has "the mind of Christ" (1 Cor. 2:16). Therefore it is inexcusable for believers to fall victim to the "the schemes of the devil" (Eph. 6:11; cf. 2 Cor. 2:11) and "be children, tossed here and there by waves and carried about by every wind of doctrine, by the trickery of men, by craftiness in deceitful scheming" (Eph. 4:14; cf. 1 Cor. 14:20). (I discuss the danger of the church's lack of discernment in my book *Reckless Faith: When the Church Loses Its Will to Discern* [Wheaton, Ill: Crossway, 1994].)

Those who do not understand the truth are incapable of discerning error. The absence of discernment is a logical consequence of ignorance of Scripture, because discernment involves the application of biblical knowledge. Ignorance of doctrine results in spiritual immaturity, which leads to a lack of discernment and opens the door wide to Satan's deceptive schemes.

Throughout its history, the most damaging assaults on the church have not come from atheism, skepticism, humanism, or persecution. The church has been ravaged when undiscerning Christians have been seduced by what appears to be divine truth but is not. The people who pose the biggest threat to the church are not those who openly attack it. Of far greater danger are those who claim to represent God and to teach the truth of Scripture, but in reality are deceivers (cf. Matt. 7:15–23; Gal. 1:6–9; 2 Thess. 2:1–3; 1 Tim. 4:1–2; Titus 1:10–16; 2 Peter 2:1–3; Jude 4–16).

In his farewell address to the elders of the church at Ephesus, Paul warned of the twin dangers of false teachers and gullible believers. The apostle had built a solid foundation during his three years of ministry in the Ephesian church (Acts 20:31); he "did not shrink from declaring to [them] the whole purpose of God" (v. 27). But in spite of that, Paul knew they were still vulnerable. Therefore he commanded the elders,

> Be on guard for yourselves and for all the flock, among which the Holy Spirit has made you overseers, to shepherd the church of God which He purchased with His own blood. I know that after my departure savage wolves will come in among you, not sparing the flock; and from among your own selves men will arise, speaking perverse things, to draw away the disciples after them. Therefore be on the alert. (Acts 20:28–31)

Knowing that the church would be attacked, Paul pointed its leaders to the only source of protection: "And now I commend you to God and to the word of His grace, which is able to build you up and to give you the inheritance among all those who are sanctified" (v. 32). The only way to avoid being deceived is to be discerning, and the only way to be discerning is to understand and apply Scripture.

Sadly, lack of discernment had created havoc in the Corinthian church. False teachers were seeking to seduce the Corinthians and lead them "astray from the simplicity and purity of devotion to Christ" (2 Cor. 11:3). As a vigilant shepherd, Paul warned his flock of the danger they posed; in fact, this entire epistle is an antidote to their poisonous lies. In chapters 10–13 in particular, Paul directly confronted the false teachers.

This passage presents in stark terms the contrast between Paul, who lovingly, humbly proclaimed the truth, and the false teachers, who deceptively abused the Corinthians. The specific point at issue was money, always a prime motivation for false teachers (Rom. 16:18; 1 Tim. 6:5; Titus 1:11; 2 Peter 2:3, 14; Jude 11; cf. 1 Tim. 3:3; Titus 1:7; 1 Peter 5:3). The greedy false apostles took money from the Corinthians; Paul did not.

As he approached the distasteful task of making the comparison between himself and the false apostles, Paul listed three marks of a true apostle (humility, truth, and love) and three corresponding marks of a false apostle (pride, deception, and abuse). The same criteria may be used today to distinguish true men of God from false teachers.

Marks of a True Apostle

Or did I commit a sin in humbling myself so that you might be exalted, because I preached the gospel of God to you without charge? I robbed other churches by taking wages from them to serve you; and when I was present with you and was in need, I was not a burden to anyone; for when the brethren came from Macedonia they fully supplied my need, and in everything I kept myself from being a burden to you, and will continue to do so. As the truth of Christ is in me, this boasting of mine will not be stopped in the regions of Achaia. Why? Because I do not love you? God knows I do! (11:7–11)

As he reluctantly sat for a self-portrait, Paul painted a threefold picture of a genuine man of God.

HUMILITY

Or did I commit a sin in humbling myself so that you might be exalted, because I preached the gospel of God to you without charge? I robbed other churches by taking wages from them to serve you; and when I was present with you and was in need, I was not a burden to anyone; for when the brethren came from Macedonia they fully supplied my need, and in everything I kept myself from being a burden to you, and will continue to do so. (11:7–9)

Paul began his comparison with a question containing sarcasm and irony. Did the Corinthians really think him guilty of **a sin ... because** he **preached the gospel of God to** them **without charge?** The implication of the apostle's question is that they were as much as calling his humility a sin. **Or** points back to Paul's acknowledgement in verse 6 that he was "unskilled in speech." The apostle was referring to the false teachers' disdainful charge that his "speech [was] contemptible" (10:10). They scorned Paul as a rank amateur, who lacked the polished communication skills on which they prided themselves and, Paul says caustically, "Is this a sin?"

It was Paul's "amateur status" that raised the issue he alluded to in verse 7. The false apostles put a perverse spin on Paul's humble refusal to accept money from the Corinthians. In Greek culture, a skilled orator was considered a professional, one who made his living from the fees he charged. By ministering free of charge, they maintained, the apostle labeled himself an amateur who lacked their credentials and hence was not qualified to be heard by the Corinthians. Further, they insinuated, how could what Paul had to say be of any value if he did not charge for it? He himself had set the price tag on his teaching: He would not take any money for it because it was worthless. Amazingly, many of the Corinthians fell for that outrageous lie.

The Corinthians' gullibility on this issue was inexcusable. In his first inspired letter to them, Paul had explained at length why he did not take any money from them:

> My defense to those who examine me is this: Do we not have a right to eat and drink? Do we not have a right to take along a believing wife, even as the rest of the apostles and the brothers of the Lord and Cephas? Or do only Barnabas and I not have a right to refrain from working? Who at any time serves as a soldier at his own expense? Who plants a vineyard and does not eat the fruit of it? Or who tends a flock and does not use the milk of the flock? I am not speaking these things according to human judgment, am I? Or does not the Law also say these things? For it is written in the Law of Moses, "You shall not muzzle the ox while he is threshing." God is not concerned about oxen, is He? Or is He speaking altogether for our sake? Yes, for our sake it was written, because the plowman ought to plow in hope, and the thresher to thresh in hope of sharing the crops. If we sowed spiritual things in you, is it too much if we reap material things from you? If others share the right over you, do we not more? Nevertheless, we did not use this right, but we endure all things so that we will cause no hindrance to the gospel of Christ. Do you not know that those who perform sacred services eat the food of the temple, and those who attend regularly to the altar have their share from the altar? So also the Lord directed those who proclaim the gospel to get their living from the gospel. But I have used none of these things. And I am not writing these things so that it will be done so in my case; for it would be better for me to die than have any man make my boast an empty one. For if I preach the gospel, I have nothing to boast of, for I am under compulsion; for woe is me if I do not preach the gospel. For if I do this voluntarily, I have a reward;

> but if against my will, I have a stewardship entrusted to me. What then is my reward? That, when I preach the gospel, I may offer the gospel without charge, so as not to make full use of my right in the gospel. (1 Cor. 9:3–18; cf. Matt. 10:10)

Though he had every right to "reap material things" from the Corinthians, he chose to forgo that privilege. Since it was all so new, and all the other traveling teachers required money, he wanted to make sure that he would "cause no hindrance to the gospel of Christ." It was Paul's practice not to be supported by new churches he founded, for two important reasons. First, he wanted to distance himself from deceivers, who were in the ministry for money. Second, he worked to provide an example to the new believers, as he explained to the Thessalonians:

> Nor did we eat anyone's bread without paying for it, but with labor and hardship we kept working night and day so that we would not be a burden to any of you; not because we do not have the right to this, but in order to offer ourselves as a model for you, so that you would follow our example. (2 Thess. 3:8–9; cf. Acts 18:3; 20:34; 1 Cor. 4:12; 1 Thess. 2:9)

Though Paul did not take money from churches while he was establishing them, he did accept support from those churches after he left. They were thus able to share in his church-planting ministry (see the discussion of v. 9 below).

Paul's purpose **in humbling** himself was **that** the Corinthians **might be exalted.** The gospel elevated the Corinthians from darkness to light (Acts 26:18; Col. 1:13; Eph. 5:8; 1 Thess. 5:5; 1 Peter 2:9); from sin to righteousness (Rom. 6:18; 1 Peter 2:24); from Satan's domain to Christ's kingdom (Col. 1:13; cf. Acts 26:18); and from death to life (John 5:24; 1 John 3:14). Paul's free preaching of the gospel had elevated them from damnation to glory; where was the sin in that?

Rather than accept payment from them, Paul **robbed other churches by taking wages from them to serve** the Corinthians. *Sulaō* (**robbed**) is a strong term, generally used in a military context to speak of pillaging, or of stripping a dead soldier of his armor (Colin G. Kruse, *The Second Epistle of Paul to the Corinthians,* The Tyndale New Testament Commentaries [Grand Rapids: Eerdmans, 1995], 187). **Wages** translates *opsōnion,* which is used in Luke 3:14 to speak of soldiers' pay or rations (cf. its similar use in 1 Cor. 9:7).

Obviously, Paul was speaking metaphorically and with irony; he did not actually rob or defraud any church. But the gifts he received from poor churches made them still poorer, and Paul's humility made that seem to him as if he were plundering them. Specifically, the apostle had in mind the impoverished **churches** of Macedonia (Philippi, Berea, and Thessalonica). They not only contributed to the offering for the Jerusalem church (2 Cor. 8:1–5; Rom. 15:26) but also supported Paul's ministry on more than one occasion (Phil. 4:10, 14–18; cf. 1 Thess. 3:6 with Acts 18:5).

Even **when** Paul **was present with** them **and was in need,** he **was not a burden to anyone.** He had plied his trade as a tentmaker (or leather-worker) while in Corinth (Acts 18:3). However, either business became slack or the demands of his ministry curtailed the amount of time he had to work. In either case, Paul was for a time in a dire situation, lacking the basic necessities of life. Yet even then he refused to be a **burden** (the Greek verb literally means "to grow numb," and hence to be a dead weight) to the Corinthians. Eventually, Silas and Timothy arrived with the Macedonian churches' gifts, alleviating Paul's needs and allowing him to devote himself full-time to ministry (Acts 18:5). Just as Paul had **kept** himself **from being a burden to** the Corinthians in the past, so he would **continue to do so** on his upcoming visit (2 Cor. 12:14).

Unlike the proud, lying apostles, who would not dream of lowering themselves to do manual labor, Paul humbled himself to the place of a common worker. True men of God are "free from the love of money" (1 Tim. 3:3) and seek nothing but the opportunity to faithfully carry out their ministry.

TRUTH

As the truth of Christ is in me, this boasting of mine will not be stopped in the regions of Achaia. (11:10)

Paul could justly affirm that **the truth of Christ** was **in** him. He not only proclaimed the truth but also lived it out in absolute integrity. To do otherwise would be hypocrisy, which Paul abhorred (cf. 4:2; Rom. 12:9).

Earlier in this epistle he reminded the Corinthians, "For we are not like many, peddling the word of God, but as from sincerity, but as from God, we speak in Christ in the sight of God" (2 Cor. 2:17). He had "renounced the things hidden because of shame, [and was] not walking in craftiness or adulterating the word of God, but by the manifestation of truth commending [himself] to every man's conscience in the sight of God" (4:2). Paul ministered at all times "in purity, in knowledge, in patience, in kindness, in the Holy Spirit, in genuine love, in the word of truth" (6:6–7) and therefore could claim, "we spoke all things to you in truth" (7:14).

Paul's **boasting** would **not be stopped** because he was not going to change his policy. He would continue to minister free of charge, both at Corinth and throughout the surrounding **regions of Achaia.** That there were other churches in that province is clear from Paul's references to "all the saints who are throughout Achaia" (1:1), and to Phoebe, a member of the church at the nearby port city of Cenchrea (Rom. 16:1). That Paul included the surrounding region suggests that the false apostles' influence was not confined to Corinth.

Paul was a man of impeccable integrity, completely faithful to his convictions, which were based on God's revelation. He typifies all true men of God who demonstrate selfless humility, and whose lives reflect an unwavering devotion to the truth that they proclaim.

LOVE

Why? Because I do not love you? God knows I do! (11:11)

Another insidious charge leveled by the false apostles concerned Paul's humble refusal to take money from the Corinthians. That he did not do so, they argued, showed that he did not really love the Corinthians and wanted no strings to bind him to them.

Paul replied to that false allegation by asking the Corinthians the rhetorical question, **Why** did I not take money from you? **Because I do not love you?** That they could seriously entertain the notion that Paul did not love them was absurd in light of his repeated actions and affirmations (cf. 2:4; 12:15; 1 Cor. 4:21; 16:24). That those to whom he had sacrificially ministered (cf. 2 Cor. 1:6; 2:4; 4:8–15), asking nothing in return, could see that as proof that he did not love them shows the power of satanic deception.

Since the Corinthians doubted him, Paul appealed to the highest court, emphatically declaring, **God knows I do!** Philip E. Hughes writes,

> There were no depths to which these intruders were unwilling to descend in order to alienate the Apostle from his dearly loved children in the gospel. Hence Paul's question here: "Wherefore? Because I love you not?" and his protestation: "God knoweth!" It is a real cry from the heart. Words and explanations and justifications are out of place when the relationship of love involved is that between a father and his children. Before God both he and they need no persuasion that this accusation is a cruel and damnable falsehood. No man on earth had a warmer and more devoted heart than the Apostle Paul. Love was the impulse of his whole life and ministry as Christ's Apostle. And so he leaves this shocking and monstrous insinuation that he has no love for them to the judgment of God, who knows and will vindicate the truth. And in doing so he also leaves it to their consciences. (*The Second*

Epistle to the Corinthians, The New International Commentary on the New Testament [Grand Rapids: Eerdmans, 1992], 390)

That God knows their hearts is the ultimate refuge and comfort for believers when they are falsely accused (cf. 11:31; 12:2–3). Because he ministered in the sight of God (2:17; 4:2; 8:21; 12:19), Paul could appeal to Him with a clear conscience (1:12).

MARKS OF A FALSE APOSTLE

But what I am doing I will continue to do, so that I may cut off opportunity from those who desire an opportunity to be regarded just as we are in the matter about which they are boasting. For such men are false apostles, deceitful workers, disguising themselves as apostles of Christ. No wonder, for even Satan disguises himself as an angel of light. Therefore it is not surprising if his servants also disguise themselves as servants of righteousness, whose end will be according to their deeds. . . . For you tolerate it if anyone enslaves you, anyone devours you, anyone takes advantage of you, anyone exalts himself, anyone hits you in the face. (11:12–15, 20)

Just as Paul's humility, truth, and love paint a portrait of a true man of God, so the false apostles' pride, deception, and abuse typify false teachers.

PRIDE

But what I am doing I will continue to do, so that I may cut off opportunity from those who desire an opportunity to be regarded just as we are in the matter about which they are boasting. (11:12)

The false apostles' pride most clearly manifested itself in their greed. Though they desperately wanted to be seen as Paul's equals, Paul's refusal to take money from the Corinthians posed a major problem for them. Since they did take money from the Corinthians, they were caught on the horns of a dilemma. To continue to do so left them in an awkward and embarrassing position in comparison to Paul. On the other hand, for them to refuse to be paid was unthinkable, because they were in it for the money.

But despite the pressure from the false apostles, **what** Paul was **doing** he would **continue to do;** he would not give an **opportunity** to them **to be regarded just as** he was **in the matter about which they** were **boasting.** He would not help them out of their dilemma by changing his policy and taking money from the Corinthians. The contrast between his selflessness and the false apostles' greed should have made it clear to the Corinthians who was the genuine man of God. Paul was never a burden to them (v. 9), in contrast to the parasitic false apostles.

DECEPTION

For such men are false apostles, deceitful workers, disguising themselves as apostles of Christ. No wonder, for even Satan disguises himself as an angel of light. Therefore it is not surprising if his servants also disguise themselves as servants of righteousness, whose end will be according to their deeds. (11:13–15)

These three verses form the heart of this section. Paul denounced the false apostles in strong, forceful language because the truth was at stake. Unlike many today, Paul was not willing to sacrifice truth for unity. Throughout this epistle, he had alluded to the false apostles, referring to them obliquely as the "many" who were guilty of "peddling the word of God" (2:17); as "some, who regard us as if we walked according to the flesh" (10:2); as "those who commend themselves" (10:12); as those who preach "another Jesus" and "a different gospel" (11:4); and, sarcastically, as "the most eminent apostles" (11:5). But now the time had come to bluntly and directly expose them.

The measure of a person's love for the truth is how that person responds when confronted by it. Those who most loudly proclaim the virtue of tolerance are often those with the most to lose if confronted by the truth. And when the truth is brought to bear on them, they frequently retaliate with fury. But when the honor of God and Christ, and the truth of the gospel and Scripture were at stake, Paul was not one to equivocate. Demonstrating what many with shallow convictions would see as a shocking lack of tolerance, Paul exposed the deceiving teachers as Satan's servants (v. 15), masquerading as true men of God.

Paul probably coined the term *pseudapostolos* (**false apostles**), which appears nowhere else in the New Testament (cf. Rev. 2:2). Such deceivers have plagued God's people throughout redemptive history. The Lord through Jeremiah warned of deceitful false prophets: "The prophets are prophesying falsehood in My name. I have neither sent them nor commanded them nor spoken to them; they are prophesying to you a false vision, divination, futility and the deception of their own minds" (Jer. 14:14; cf. 23:14, 26). In the Sermon on the Mount Jesus warned, "Beware of the false prophets, who come to you in sheep's clothing, but inwardly are ravenous wolves" (Matt. 7:15). In the Olivet discourse, the Lord noted that they would be especially active in the end times: "For false Christs and false prophets will arise and will show great signs and wonders, so as to mislead, if possible, even the elect" (Matt. 24:24; cf. 1 Tim. 4:1; 2 Tim. 3:13). The Jerusalem Council cautioned against false teachers claiming to have been sent by the Jerusalem church: "We have heard that some of our number to whom we gave no instruction have disturbed you with their words, unsettling your souls" (Acts 15:24). "Beloved, do not believe every spirit," John warned, "but test the spirits to see whether they are from God, because many false prophets have gone out into the world" (1 John 4:1).

The **deceitful workers** plied their trade by **disguising themselves as apostles of Christ** to deceive the gullible and undiscerning. Though they brashly posed as equals to Paul and the Twelve, the false apostles were in reality **deceitful workers,** Satan's **servants** who would **disguise themselves as servants of righteousness.** The Bible reveals that deceit is a hallmark of false teachers. Paul warned the Romans that "such men are slaves, not of our Lord Christ but of their own appetites; and by their smooth and flattering speech they deceive the hearts of the unsuspecting" (Rom. 16:18). He wrote to Timothy that "evil men and impostors will proceed from bad to worse, deceiving and being deceived" (2 Tim. 3:13). To Titus he wrote, "For there are many rebellious men, empty talkers and deceivers, especially those of the circumcision" (Titus 1:10). Because of the ever-present danger they pose, the New Testament warns believers not to be taken in by them (Matt. 24:4; Gal. 6:7; Eph. 5:6; Col. 2:4, 8; 2 Thess. 2:3; 1 John 4:1).

It is **no wonder** that false teachers masquerade as God's servants **for even Satan,** the ruler of the domain of darkness (Luke 22:53; Eph. 6:12; Col. 1:13), **disguises himself as an angel of light.** It is in that guise that he appears to the church, not the pitchfork, horns, and pointed tail of mythology. Satan is most effective in the church when he comes not as an open enemy, but as a false friend; not when he persecutes the church, but when he joins it; not when he attacks the pulpit, but when he stands in it.

But neither Satan nor his servants will get away with their charade forever. John records that Satan will be bound at the start of the Millennium:

> Then I saw an angel coming down from heaven, holding the key of the abyss and a great chain in his hand. And he laid hold of the dragon, the serpent of old, who is the devil and Satan, and bound him for a thou-

> sand years; and he threw him into the abyss, and shut it and sealed it over him, so that he would not deceive the nations any longer, until the thousand years were completed; after these things he must be released for a short time. (Rev. 20:1–3)

Satan's ultimate fate will be eternal punishment in the lake of fire: "And the devil who deceived them was thrown into the lake of fire and brimstone, where the beast and the false prophet are also; and they will be tormented day and night forever and ever" (Rev. 20:10).

The Bible reveals that an equally fearful judgment awaits all false teachers. In Matthew 7:21–23 the Lord Jesus Christ solemnly warned,

> Not everyone who says to Me, "Lord, Lord," will enter the kingdom of heaven, but he who does the will of My Father who is in heaven will enter. Many will say to Me on that day, "Lord, Lord, did we not prophesy in Your name, and in Your name cast out demons, and in Your name perform many miracles?" And then I will declare to them, "I never knew you; depart from Me, you who practice lawlessness."

The destiny of false teachers **will be according to their deeds.**

ABUSE

For you tolerate it if anyone enslaves you, anyone devours you, anyone takes advantage of you, anyone exalts himself, anyone hits you in the face. (11:20)

This was a sad verse for Paul to write, for it reveals how seriously the Corinthians were seduced. They even willingly tolerated harsh treatment from the false apostles. **Enslaves** translates *katadouloō*, a verb that in its only other New Testament appearance refers to the Judaizers' enslavement of the Galatians (Gal. 2:4). The false works-righteousness system propagated by the lying teachers had robbed the Corinthians of their freedom in Christ. The Greek word translated **devours** pictures the false apostles preying on the Corinthians like predatory animals. It could be a reference to their demands for money (it is so used in Mark 12:40 and Luke 20:47 to describe the greedy Pharisees' seizing of widows' houses). The Corinthians stood by while the false teachers took **advantage** of them (cf. 2 Cor. 12:16) and **exalted** themselves in their pride and arrogance. Their mistreatment of the Corinthians was, in short, a slap **in the face,** which was (and is) a symbol of extreme disrespect (cf. 1 Kings 22:24; Lam. 3:30; Luke 22:64; John 18:22; Acts 23:2).

Three valuable principles may be distilled from Paul's contrast of himself with the false apostles:

First, believers must not be taken in by smooth, clever, seemingly spiritual oratory. Such speech may mask satanic lies and deception. Many false teachers use biblical terms but invest them with a radically different meaning.

Second, believers must go beyond a teacher's words and examine his life. Religion is big business to false teachers, but those consumed with accumulating wealth and power are not true servants of Jesus Christ (Matt. 6:24).

Finally, believers must avoid the temptation to make tolerance a virtue. D. A. Carson notes

> The appeal to limitless toleration . . . presupposes the greatest evil is to hold a strong conviction that certain things are true and their contraries are false. . . . But if we hold that God has revealed himself to men, supremely in the person of his Son, but also in the words and propositions of Scripture, then . . . we have no right to treat as optional anything God has said. (*From Triumphalism to Maturity* [Grand Rapids: Baker, 1984], 101)

Toleration is the supreme virtue only to those who lack strong convictions.

To discern the true from the false spiritual leaders is vital to the health of the church. To fail to exercise discernment is to open wide the door to the sheepfold and allow Satan's savage wolves to ravage God's flock.

Humble Boasting
(2 Corinthians 11:16–21)

29

Again I say, let no one think me foolish; but if you do, receive me even as foolish, so that I also may boast a little. What I am saying, I am not saying as the Lord would, but as in foolishness, in this confidence of boasting. Since many boast according to the flesh, I will boast also. For you, being so wise, tolerate the foolish gladly. For you tolerate it if anyone enslaves you, anyone devours you, anyone takes advantage of you, anyone exalts himself, anyone hits you in the face. To my shame I must say that we have been weak by comparison. But in whatever respect anyone else is bold—I speak in foolishness—I am just as bold myself. (11:16–21)

Humility is the noblest Christian virtue. It is the only appropriate response to a proper understanding of the glory of God and a genuine sense of His majesty. Humility results in a deep desire to worship God, honor Him, and seek His glory.

But as John Piper notes,

> Humility is not a popular trait in the modern world. It's not touted on the talk shows or celebrated in valedictory speeches or commended in diversity seminars or listed with corporate core values. And if you go

to the massive self-help section of your sprawling mall bookstore, you won't find many titles celebrating humility.

The basic reason for this is not hard to find: humility can only survive in the presence of God. When God goes, humility goes. In fact you might say that humility follows God like a shadow. We can expect to find humility applauded in our society about as often as we find God applauded.

In my local newspaper recently a guest editorial captured the atmosphere of our time that asphyxiates humility:

> *There are some who naively cling to the nostalgic memory of God. The average churchgoer takes a few hours out of the week to experience the sacred. . . . But the rest of the time, he is immersed in a society that no longer acknowledges God as an omniscient and omnipotent force to be loved and worshiped. …Today we are too sophisticated for God. We can stand on our own; we are prepared and ready to choose and define our own existence.*

In this atmosphere humility cannot survive. It disappears with God. When God is neglected, the runner-up god takes his place, namely man. And that, by definition, is the opposite of humility, namely, the haughty spirit called pride. So the atmosphere we breathe is hostile to humility. (*Future Grace* [Sisters, Ore.; Multnomah, 1995], 85–86. Italics in original.)

All sin is an affront to God and represents a turning away from Him. For example, covetousness involves turning away from God and His provision to seek satisfaction in material things. Lust involves turning away from God's design for sex to seek pleasure in illicit relationships. Anger involves turning away from God's justice and retribution to seek one's own vengeance. Impatience involves turning away from God's sovereignty to seek control over one's own life. Fear involves turning away from God's power to succumb to the dread of other powers. But pride is the ultimate idolatry, and therefore the most heinous sin, because it involves replacing God-centeredness with self-centeredness.

Scripture emphasizes the importance of humility by commanding it, extolling its blessings, and offering examples of humble people. In an Old Testament summary of godly living, the prophet Micah wrote, "He has told you, O man, what is good; and what does the Lord require of you but to do justice, to love kindness, and to walk humbly with your God?" (Mic. 6:8). "Do nothing from selfishness or empty conceit," Paul commanded the Philippians, "but with humility of mind regard one another as more important than yourselves" (Phil. 2:3). To the Colossians he wrote, "As those who have been chosen of God, holy and beloved, put on a heart of compassion, kindness, humility, gentleness and patience" (Col. 3:12).

The humble experience rich blessings. God hears them when they pray (Ps. 10:17; cf. 9:12); they enjoy His presence (Isa. 57:15; cf. 66:2); He will deliver them from trouble (Job 22:29); they are the objects of His concern (Ps. 138:6); He will lead and teach them (Ps. 25:9); they will experience His grace (James 4:6; 1 Peter 5:5); they will have wisdom (Prov. 11:2); and they will lead long and prosperous lives (Prov. 22:4). The humble will, paradoxically, be the most exalted and honored people (Prov. 15:33; 18:12; 29:23; Matt. 23:12; Luke 14:11; 18:14; James 4:10), the greatest in God's kingdom (Matt. 18:4; cf. 20:26–28). Included among their number are Abraham (Gen. 18:27); Jacob (Gen. 32:10); Job (Job 40:4); Moses (Num. 12:3); Gideon (Judg. 6:15); Manasseh (2 Chron. 33:12); Josiah (2 Chron. 34:27); Daniel (Dan. 10:12); Paul (Acts 20:19); and, supremely, the Lord Jesus Christ (Matt. 11:29; Phil. 2:8).

On the other hand, pride is the first sin, the one committed by Satan (Isa. 14:14; 1 Tim. 3:6). Scripture repeatedly warns against it (Prov. 21:4; cf. 1 Sam. 2:3; Ps. 75:5; Rom. 12:16; James 4:16; 1 John 2:16). God hates pride (Prov. 6:16–17; cf. Ps. 5:5) and expects His people to hate it (Prov. 8:13). Pride is expressed in boasting (1 Sam. 2:3; 2 Chron. 25:19); in persecution of the righteous by the wicked (Ps. 10:2); in evil speech (Ps. 31:18); in the lives of the wicked (Hab. 2:4; Rom. 1:30), especially false teachers (1 Tim. 6:3–4), and will be especially prevalent in the last days (2 Tim. 3:1–2).

The evil fruit of pride includes dishonor (Prov. 11:2); destruction (Prov. 16:18; 18:12); being opposed by God (James 4:6); being humbled by God (Prov. 29:23; cf. Ps. 18:27; 2 Sam. 22:28; Dan. 4:37); being defiled (Mark 7:21–23); and strife (Prov. 13:10; 28:25). Pride also keeps people from seeking (Ps. 10:4) and knowing God (Ps. 138:6). But most serious of all, pride results in God's judgment. Proverbs 16:5 warns, "Everyone who is proud in heart is an abomination to the Lord; assuredly, he will not be unpunished." Isaiah also foresaw the judgment of proud evildoers:

> The proud look of man will be abased and the loftiness of man will be humbled, and the Lord alone will be exalted in that day. For the Lord of hosts will have a day of reckoning against everyone who is proud and lofty and against everyone who is lifted up, that he may be abased. (Isa. 2:11–12)

Malachi 4:1 adds, "'For behold, the day is coming, burning like a furnace; and all the arrogant and every evildoer will be chaff; and the day that is coming will set them ablaze,' says the Lord of hosts, 'so that it will leave them neither root nor branch.'" "The Lord preserves the faithful," wrote David, "and fully recompenses the proud doer" (Ps. 31:23), while in Psalm 94:2 the psalmist prayed, "Rise up, O Judge of the earth, render recompense to the proud." Scripture deplores the pride both of individuals, such as Hezekiah (2 Chron. 32:25); Nebuchadnezzar (Dan. 4:30; 5:20); and Belshazzar (Dan. 5:22–23); and of nations, such as Moab (Isa. 16:6); Edom (Obad. 3); Babylon (Jer. 50:29, 32); and, tragically, Israel (Isa. 28:1; Jer. 13:9; Hos. 5:5).

No one was more convinced of the importance of humility than Paul. In fact, apart from the Lord Jesus Christ, no New Testament man appears more humble than he. Paul sought to follow Christ's example of humility (Matt. 11:29), as he did all aspects of His life (1 Cor. 11:1; cf. Eph. 5:1–2; Phil. 2:5) so that others could in turn follow his pattern (1 Cor. 4:16; 11:1; Phil. 3:17; 1 Thess. 1:6; 2 Thess. 3:9).

Because of his humility, Paul found the idea of boasting abhorrent. Yet that is exactly what he was compelled to do in writing this epistle. As noted in previous chapters of this volume, Paul's apostolic credentials were under massive assault from false apostles at Corinth. They had slanderously accused him of being a wicked, lying charlatan, and were seeking to destroy his credibility and replace him as the authoritative teachers of the Corinthian congregation. Alarmingly, many of the Corinthians had bought into the deceivers' lies about Paul. He had to take action, not for the sake of his ego, but for the sake of the gospel. He could not allow the false teachers to cut off the Corinthians' access to the divine truth he proclaimed.

The disinformation they spread about Paul included their assessment that he was too ordinary and unspectacular a man to be a genuine apostle. To counter those lies, he was forced to present his apostolic credentials, something he preferred not to have to do because they should be obvious. Paul was more comfortable discussing his weaknesses than his accomplishments (2 Cor. 4:7; 12:5, 9–10; cf. 1 Cor. 15:10; 1 Tim. 1:15–16), even though what he said about himself was true (cf. 2 Cor. 10:13–14).

The true measure of a person's humility is the ability to boast when necessary and yet remain humble. It is easy to be humble in failure —far more difficult to be humble in the midst of great success. Paul had been eminently privileged by the Lord, and his ministry had obviously been monumentally successful; the challenge was for him to say what was true and necessary, yet remain humble. When he presented his apostolic credentials in 11:22–12:13, he did just that.

But before he did so, Paul expressed one final time his reluctance to boast. He was doing so under protest, and only because the Corinthians' naïve acceptance of the false apostles' lies made it necessary. In this prologue to his defense of his apostleship, Paul gave two reasons why boasting is unprofitable: It is foolish, and it is fleshly.

BOASTING IS FOOLISH

Again I say, let no one think me foolish; but if you do, receive me even as foolish, so that I also may boast a little. What I am saying, I am not saying as the Lord would, but as in foolishness, in this confidence of boasting. (11:16–17)

The term **again** pointed the Corinthians back to Paul's earlier discussion of boasting in 11:1. He had digressed to discuss the issue of financial remuneration and to expose the false apostles as agents of Satan in disguise (vv. 2–15).

Before reluctantly launching his defense, which he regarded as foolishness, Paul distanced himself from the true fools. He did not want anyone to **think** him **foolish** like the false teachers; he was not habitually given to commending himself like they were. But if any of the Corinthians really did think him to be a fool, Paul asked that they grant him the same privilege that they did the false apostles and **receive** him **even as foolish.** The false apostles boasted incessantly; Paul would **boast** only **a little.** The apostle was no fool; he was merely answering fools as their folly deserved (Prov. 26:5) to protect the Corinthians from spiritual disaster. And it was their folly in being seduced by the false apostles that had necessitated Paul's boasting (2 Cor. 12:11).

Verses 17 and 18 form a parenthesis and provide another important disclaimer. Paul acknowledged that **what** he was **saying,** he was **not saying as the Lord would.** He was not, as some have foolishly asserted, denying that what he wrote in this passage was inspired Scripture (cf. 2 Peter 3:15–16). What he meant was that he was not following anything his Lord had done, because Jesus never boasted. That made it hard for him to do so, because the supreme goal of his life was to be like Christ (cf. 2 Cor. 11:1; Rom. 14:8; Phil. 1:21; 3:14).

Summarizing Paul's intent in this verse, Albert McShane writes,

> We must not conclude from this verse that here we have a part of Scripture which is not inspired. [Paul] had the Lord's permission to write as he does, but he owns that this is not the usual way His servants are expected to speak of themselves. Had any other course been hopeful of success, this one would never have been taken. The wiseacres at Corinth had fed too long at the table of fools to relish the normal diet of saints, so he is compelled to set before them what they can digest, even though he himself regards it as unpalatable. (*What the Bible*

Teaches: II Corinthians [Kilmarnock, Scotland: John Ritchie Ltd., 1986], 384)

What Paul said was accurate, and he said it without pride or self-commendation. Nevertheless, it rankled him that enemies of the truth had forced him into the **foolishness of** self-confident **boasting.**

Boasting Is Fleshly

Since many boast according to the flesh, I will boast also. For you, being so wise, tolerate the foolish gladly. For you tolerate it if anyone enslaves you, anyone devours you, anyone takes advantage of you, anyone exalts himself, anyone hits you in the face. To my shame I must say that we have been weak by comparison. But in whatever respect anyone else is bold—I speak in foolishness—I am just as bold myself. (11:18–21)

The **many** who **boast[ed] according to the flesh** (cf. 1 Cor. 3:21; 5:6; Gal. 6:13) were, of course, the false apostles. Their boasting was worldly, vain, and empty, based on their human accomplishments, as Paul's had been before his conversion (cf. Gal. 1:14; Phil. 3:4–6). The false apostles could not boast of what God had done through them, since they were the enemies of God. They were hucksters, guilty of "peddling the word of God" (2 Cor. 2:17); proclaimers of "another Jesus," and "a different gospel" (11:4); "false apostles, deceitful workers, disguising themselves as apostles of Christ" (11:13). As such, they could only boast of their personal achievements, which were motivated by their corrupt desires and prompted by their father, Satan (cf. John 8:44). To counter their false claims, Paul was forced to **boast also.**

In verses 19–21 Paul issued his final disclaimers before beginning his boasting in verse 22. He employed the most scathing language to be found anywhere in this epistle, using sarcasm to shock the Corinthians out of their complacent acceptance of the false apostles. Sarcasm is saying the opposite of what is true for effect. It is the strongest, most cutting way to use language, and hence the most effective way for Paul to get his point across. The apostle, as it were, verbally slapped the Corinthians to bring them to their senses.

This was not the first time Paul had been forced to resort to sarcasm in dealing with the Corinthians. In 1 Corinthians 4:8–10 he used it to deflate their arrogant pride:

> You are already filled, you have already become rich, you have become kings without us; and indeed, I wish that you had become kings so that

we also might reign with you. For, I think, God has exhibited us apostles
last of all, as men condemned to death; because we have become a
spectacle to the world, both to angels and to men. We are fools for
Christ's sake, but you are prudent in Christ; we are weak, but you are
strong; you are distinguished, but we are without honor.

"Is it so, that there is not among you one wise man who will be able to
decide between his brethren?" he chided them in 1 Corinthians 6:5. Later
in that epistle he added, "If anyone supposes that he knows anything, he
has not yet known as he ought to know" (1 Cor. 8:2).

Paul began by needling the Corinthians for **being "wise"**
enough to **tolerate the foolish** false apostles **gladly.** He sarcastically
pointed out that the Corinthians willingly listened to those who en-
slaved, exploited, entrapped, dominated, and humiliated them. That
being the case, they could surely bear with him.

Paul also used the Greek verb translated **enslaves** in Galatians
2:4 to describe the Judaizers' entrapment of the Galatians in their false
legalistic system. The false apostles had similarly ensnared many of the
Corinthians in the heretical teaching they espoused. Paul surely had in
mind the abusive control the false apostles exercised over them, enslaving the Corinthians to themselves—something neither he (2 Cor. 1:24)
nor any true servant of God would do (Matt. 20:25–26; 23:8–10; 1 Peter
5:3). In either case, they had robbed the Corinthians of their freedom in
Christ (cf. Matt. 11:28–30; John 8:32, 36; Rom. 8:2; 1 Cor. 9:19; Gal. 2:4; 5:1; 1
Peter 2:16).

The false teachers had **devour[ed]** the Corinthians in the sense
of plundering them financially (the same Greek word appears in Mark
12:40; cf. Ps. 14:4). Unlike Paul, who refused to be a burden to the
Corinthians (2 Cor. 12:14), the false apostles were "slaves, not of our Lord
Christ but of their own appetites" (Rom. 16:18).

The Corinthians had also been taken **advantage** of or entrapped by the false apostles. They had been caught like a fish on a hook
(cf. Luke 5:5, where the same Greek verb is translated "caught") or like an
animal in a trap.

The false teachers also elevated themselves in stark contrast to
Paul, who followed Christ's example of meekness and gentleness in his
dealings with the Corinthians (2 Cor. 10:1). Paul used the same verb
translated **exalts himself** in 10:5 to describe "speculations and every
lofty thing raised up against the knowledge of God." The false apostles
were obsessed with their own importance.

To strike someone **in the face** is the ultimate insult (cf. 1 Kings
22:24; Lam. 3:30; Mark 14:65; Acts 23:2). Shockingly, the Corinthians tolerated even the most extreme humiliation by the false apostles. They may

have physically struck some of the Corinthians to intimidate them, or the expression may be metaphorical. Either way, they allowed themselves to be humiliated. The false apostles' abusive treatment of the Corinthians makes it clear that they were not true men of God (the term "not pugnacious" [1 Tim. 3:3; Titus 1:7] literally means "not a striker").

Paul's sarcasm reached its peak when he wrote in verse 21, **To my shame I must say that** if the false apostles' behavior is the standard, **we have been weak by comparison.** Actually, his "weakness" in not enslaving, exploiting, entrapping, dominating, and humiliating the Corinthians proved to be the strength and proof of his genuineness as an apostle and the evidence of his love for them.

The last sentence in this passage, **But in whatever respect anyone else is bold . . . I am just as bold myself,** marks the transition to Paul's defense of his apostleship that begins in verse 22. Just as the false apostles had been **bold** in attacking him, so Paul would be **bold** in defending himself. He would write unhesitatingly, confidently, in the hope that the Corinthians would turn from the false apostles to the true one. His parenthetical phrase **I speak in foolishness** evidences the sarcasm of this section.

Throughout the church's history, God's people have suffered at the hands of abusive false leaders. Philip E. Hughes writes,

> As we look back over nineteen centuries of the history of the Christian Church, we cannot help being struck by the manner in which for most of the time so many of its adherents seem to have been content lamely to tolerate the impositions and extortions of ecclesiastical despots whose lives are a contradiction of the meekness and gentleness of Christ and whose concern has been less for the souls of the perishing than for the buttressing of their own reputation in the eyes of the world. The Reformation of the sixteenth century was a breaking away from this dark spirit of tyranny and the recovery, through returning to the pure doctrine of the New Testament, of that liberty in the gospel which is the birthright of every Christian man. (*The Second Epistle to the Corinthians,* The New International Commentary on the New Testament [Grand Rapids: Eerdmans, 1992], 401)

If they are to heed Paul's exhortation, "It was for freedom that Christ set us free; therefore keep standing firm and do not be subject again to a yoke of slavery" (Gal. 5:1), believers must reject those despotic false teachers who seek to enslave them. His passionate desire to see his beloved Corinthian congregation free from the scourge of the abusive false apostles motivated Paul's detailed defense of his apostleship, which begins in the next section of this epistle.

Apostolic Credentials
(2 Corinthians 11:22–12:4)

30

Are they Hebrews? So am I. Are they Israelites? So am I. Are they descendants of Abraham? So am I. Are they servants of Christ?—I speak as if insane—I more so; in far more labors, in far more imprisonments, beaten times without number, often in danger of death. Five times I received from the Jews thirty-nine lashes. Three times I was beaten with rods, once I was stoned, three times I was shipwrecked, a night and a day I have spent in the deep. I have been on frequent journeys, in dangers from rivers, dangers from robbers, dangers from my countrymen, dangers from the Gentiles, dangers in the city, dangers in the wilderness, dangers on the sea, dangers among false brethren; I have been in labor and hardship, through many sleepless nights, in hunger and thirst, often without food, in cold and exposure. Apart from such external things, there is the daily pressure on me of concern for all the churches. Who is weak without my being weak? Who is led into sin without my intense concern? If I have to boast, I will boast of what pertains to my weakness. The God and Father of the Lord Jesus, He who is blessed forever, knows that I am not lying. In Damascus the ethnarch under Aretas the king was guarding the city of the Damascenes in order to seize me, and I

was let down in a basket through a window in the wall, and so escaped his hands. Boasting is necessary, though it is not profitable; but I will go on to visions and revelations of the Lord. I know a man in Christ who fourteen years ago—whether in the body I do not know, or out of the body I do not know, God knows—such a man was caught up to the third heaven. And I know how such a man—whether in the body or apart from the body I do not know, God knows—was caught up into Paradise and heard inexpressible words, which a man is not permitted to speak. (11:22–12:4)

Paul at last, albeit still reluctantly, presents his apostolic credentials to the Corinthians, defending himself against the lies of those who denied his authenticity. Apart from the biographical insights it provides into the life of Paul, this section might seem to have little practical relevance for today. Such is not the case, however. Satan's tactics for assaulting the leaders of God's people have not changed. And the issue of Paul's apostolic authenticity is still vital today; he is an authoritative source of divine truth through all his writings, whatever may be the theme. And all Scripture is profitable (2 Tim. 3:16). This section also gives insight into how the noblest of Christians handled the extreme adversity he faced.

Though the Corinthians' naïve acceptance of the false teachers' lies forced Paul to defend himself, his humility made him reluctant to argue his case. Because of that, he gave the long series of often sarcastic disclaimers (10:12–11:21), making clear his distaste for the boasting he had been forced into. Paul regarded it as foolish and fleshly and not in keeping with the example of the Lord Jesus Christ. Nevertheless, the apostle knew that it was necessary, both to protect the Corinthians, who otherwise would be deceived—cut off from the divine truth he proclaimed —and to honor the truth.

Beginning in verse 23 Paul presented four apostolic credentials that set him apart from the false apostles: his experience of suffering, his experience of sympathy, his experience of submission, and his experience of the supernatural. They demonstrate powerfully that Paul was a genuine apostle of Christ, and that his opponents were not. But before demonstrating his superiority to them, Paul replied first to yet another one of their slanderous lies in verse 22. He showed that he was in no way inferior to the false apostles in regard to his Jewishness.

To each of the three questions he posed, Paul replied simply and powerfully, **So am I.** The term **Hebrews** defines the Jewish people ethnically and linguistically. Some scholars believe the name derives from a Hebrew verb meaning "to cross over" and refers to their origins beyond the Euphrates River (cf. Josh. 24:2). More likely, it derives from Eber (Gen.

11:15–17) and refers to his descendants. The title was first given to Abraham (Gen. 14:13) and was later used to describe the Jewish people, both by foreigners (e.g., Gen. 39:14, 17; 41:12; Ex. 1:16; 2:6; 1 Sam. 4:6, 9; 13:19; 14:11; 29:3) and by themselves (e.g., Gen. 40:15; Ex. 1:19; 2:7; 5:3; 1 Sam. 13:3; Jer. 34:14; Jon. 1:9).

In Paul's day the term **Hebrews** also distinguished the Palestinian Jews, whose native language was Hebrew or Aramaic, from the Hellenistic, Greek-speaking Jews of the Diaspora (cf. Acts 6:1). The false apostles may have questioned Paul's authenticity by arguing that he was not a Palestinian Jew like themselves and the Twelve, but a Hellenized Jew. But though Paul was born in Tarsus, a city in Asia Minor, he was nonetheless a "Hebrew of Hebrews" (Phil. 3:5); that is, he preserved his family's traditional Jewish heritage. Like most educated men of his day Paul spoke Greek (Acts 21:37). But that does not mean that he was a Hellenized Jew; in fact, the Bible implies that Hebrew or Aramaic, not Greek, was his native language (cf. Acts 21:40; 26:14). Further, although he was born in Tarsus, Paul evidently came to Jerusalem as a young child, was raised there, and studied there under Gamaliel (Acts 22:3; 26:4).

The term **Israelites** (Ex. 35:29; 1 Sam. 2:14; 14:21; 29:1; 2 Kings 3:24; Neh. 11:3; Rom. 9:4) views the Jewish people in terms of their descent from Jacob (Israel); in fact, the Old Testament refers to them as the "sons of Israel" more than six hundred times. It also expresses their theocratic identity as God's chosen people (Amos 3:2; cf. Ex. 19:5–6; Rom. 9:4–5).

Like the false apostles, Paul was also one of the **descendants of Abraham.** He was heir to all the covenant privileges and blessings that God promised to Abraham (Gen. 12:1–3).

This was not the only time Paul had to defend his Jewish heritage. To the Galatian churches he wrote, "For you have heard of my former manner of life in Judaism, how I used to persecute the church of God beyond measure and tried to destroy it; and I was advancing in Judaism beyond many of my contemporaries among my countrymen, being more extremely zealous for my ancestral traditions" (Gal. 1:13–14). In Philippians 3:4–6 the apostle also delineated his impressive qualifications:

> If anyone else has a mind to put confidence in the flesh, I far more: circumcised the eighth day, of the nation of Israel, of the tribe of Benjamin, a Hebrew of Hebrews; as to the Law, a Pharisee; as to zeal, a persecutor of the church; as to the righteousness which is in the Law, found blameless.

Having established that in every way—socially, religiously, culturally, linguistically, and covenantally—he was not at all inferior to the false apostles, Paul presented credentials that actually proved he was superior to them.

HIS EXPERIENCE OF SUFFERING

Are they servants of Christ?—I speak as if insane—I more so; in far more labors, in far more imprisonments, beaten times without number, often in danger of death. Five times I received from the Jews thirty-nine lashes. Three times I was beaten with rods, once I was stoned, three times I was shipwrecked, a night and a day I have spent in the deep. I have been on frequent journeys, in dangers from rivers, dangers from robbers, dangers from my countrymen, dangers from the Gentiles, dangers in the city, dangers in the wilderness, dangers on the sea, dangers among false brethren; I have been in labor and hardship, through many sleepless nights, in hunger and thirst, often without food, in cold and exposure. (11:23–27)

Paul might have defended himself by appealing to his impressive accomplishments and privileges. He could have pointed to his training under the famous rabbi Gamaliel, his association with the Jerusalem elite (cf. Acts 22:5), or his obvious zeal for Judaism that manifested itself in his persecution of the church (Acts 8:1–3; 1 Cor. 15:9; Gal. 1:13; Phil. 3:6). Paul might also have pointed to all God had done through him after his conversion, to the cities he had preached in, the converts he had made, and the churches he had planted. Instead, he gave very different credentials that, though unimpressive by the world's standards, marked him as a true man of God.

To call the false apostles **servants of Christ** even for the sake of argument was repulsive to Paul, so he hastened to add the disclaimer, **I speak as if insane. Insane** translates a form of the verb *paraphroneō*, which literally means, "to be beside oneself," or "to be out of one's mind." It is a stronger word than *aphrosunē*, which the apostle used earlier to describe his foolishness in boasting (11:1, 17, 21). If boasting was to Paul the act of a fool, suggesting that the false apostles were servants of Christ was the raving of a madman. The phrase also expresses Paul's view of his boasting. The whole discussion was insanity, but the Corinthians' lack of discernment made it necessary.

The phrase **I more so** marks the beginning of Paul's demonstration of his superiority over the false apostles. The first credential he presented, his suffering, seems a little unusual. Paul's detailed list of the things he had endured makes him sound more like someone who needed help from the Lord rather than an empowered and commissioned apostle of Jesus Christ. How could the fact that he antagonized so many people and put himself into so many difficulties possibly be evidence of his apostleship?

But suffering was exactly what Jesus predicted that His apostles would experience. Before sending the Twelve out on a preaching tour, Jesus warned them,

> Behold, I send you out as sheep in the midst of wolves; so be shrewd as serpents and innocent as doves. But beware of men, for they will hand you over to the courts and scourge you in their synagogues; and you will even be brought before governors and kings for My sake, as a testimony to them and to the Gentiles. But when they hand you over, do not worry about how or what you are to say; for it will be given you in that hour what you are to say. For it is not you who speak, but it is the Spirit of your Father who speaks in you. Brother will betray brother to death, and a father his child; and children will rise up against parents and cause them to be put to death. You will be hated by all because of My name, but it is the one who has endured to the end who will be saved. But whenever they persecute you in one city, flee to the next; for truly I say to you, you will not finish going through the cities of Israel until the Son of Man comes. A disciple is not above his teacher, nor a slave above his master. It is enough for the disciple that he become like his teacher, and the slave like his master. If they have called the head of the house Beelzebul, how much more will they malign the members of his household! (Matt. 10:16–25; cf. 21:33–39; 22:2–6; John 15:18–21; 16:1–4, 33)

In what was in effect their ordination sermon, Jesus warned the apostles that they would face a hostile environment, like "sheep in the midst of wolves." Therefore, they could expect the suffering that He delineated: arrests, beatings, betrayals, hatred, persecution, and slander. Shining the light of the gospel into the kingdom of darkness inevitably generates a hostile reaction.

To that general promise to the apostles of suffering, the Lord added a specific one to Paul. Speaking to Ananias, the Lord said of Paul, "He is a chosen instrument of Mine, to bear My name before the Gentiles and kings and the sons of Israel; for I will show him how much he must suffer for My name's sake" (Acts 9:15–16). Paul's life exemplified the truth of 2 Timothy 3:12: "Indeed, all who desire to live godly in Christ Jesus will be persecuted." The false apostles had their letters of commendation (2 Cor. 3:1), but Paul had "on [his] body the brand-marks of Jesus" (Gal. 6:17). The first credential he listed was suffering, because that is what Jesus said would characterize His apostles. False teachers, on the other hand, frequently seek a life of ease and comfort. And since they are part of his kingdom, Satan does not attack them.

This is the fourth and most detailed description in this epistle of Paul's suffering (cf. 2 Cor. 1:4–10; 4:7–12; 6:4–10). Though it gives more details of Paul's trials than Luke lists in Acts, it is by no means exhaustive; the apostle's humility caused him to say only what was necessary to make his point.

Kopos (**labors**) describes working to the point of sweat and exhaustion. It is translated "toil" in 1 Corinthians 15:58, and Paul also used it in an earlier list of his sufferings (6:5). The related verb describes the hard work put in by Peter and his fellow fishermen (Luke 5:5), Jesus' exhaustion after a long journey (John 4:6), those who worked hard in the Roman church (Rom. 16:6, 12), Paul's efforts in the ministry that surpassed all others (1 Cor. 15:10), the hardworking leaders of the Thessalonian church (1 Thess. 5:12), and the elders who "work hard at preaching and teaching" (1 Tim. 5:17). In addition to his intense effort in the ministry, Paul labored at his trade to support himself (cf. Acts 20:34–35; 1 Cor. 4:12; 1 Thess. 2:9).

Of Paul's **imprisonments** recorded in Acts (at Philippi [16:23–24], Jerusalem [22:24–29; 23:10, 18], Caesarea [23:35; 24:27], and Rome [28:16–31]) and his second Roman imprisonment (2 Tim. 1:8), only the one at Philippi had taken place as Paul penned this passage. How many other times he was imprisoned is unknown; the church father Clement of Rome, writing at the close of the first century, said Paul was imprisoned seven times.

Along with being imprisoned, Paul had been **beaten times without number.** So numerous were those official and unofficial beatings that the apostle could not even count them all. As will be seen when he delineates some of them in verses 23–24, they came at the hands of both his own countrymen and the Gentiles.

Paul lived constantly **in danger of death,** knowing that every day could be his last. As he wrote in 1 Corinthians 15:31, "I affirm, brethren, by the boasting in you which I have in Christ Jesus our Lord, I die daily." Almost from the moment of his conversion, Paul's enemies plotted to kill him (Acts 9:23, 29; 14:3–5; 17:4–5; 21:30–32; 23:12–21). Riots erupted when he preached (Acts 19:23–41); mobs formed to hunt him down (Acts 17:5–9); rulers sought his life (he describes one such incident in 2 Cor. 11:32–33). Yet he never wavered in his commitment or compromised the message he preached.

Paul next delineated two examples of the beatings he mentioned in verse 23. **Five times** he **received from the Jews thirty-nine lashes.** This particular punishment was prescribed by the Mosaic Law:

> If there is a dispute between men and they go to court, and the judges decide their case, and they justify the righteous and condemn the wicked, then it shall be if the wicked man deserves to be beaten, the

judge shall then make him lie down and be beaten in his presence with the number of stripes according to his guilt. He may beat him forty times but no more, so that he does not beat him with many more stripes than these and your brother is not degraded in your eyes. (Deut. 25:1–3)

The Jews of Paul's day, in their legalistic zeal for the external observance of the Law, limited the number of blows to **thirty-nine** lest they inadvertently miscount and give more than forty. Just as Jesus had warned (Matt. 10:17; 23:34), the unbelieving Jews beat the messengers He sent to them (cf. Acts 5:40).

Paul also experienced corporal punishment from the Romans, at whose hands he was **three times . . . beaten with rods.** That punishment was the equivalent of the Jews' thirty-nine lashes. The only such incident Luke recorded in Acts took place in Philippi (Acts 16:22–23, 37; cf. 1 Thess. 2:2). Paul proudly bore the scars from his beatings at the hands of the Jews and the Romans as the "brand-marks of Jesus" (Gal. 6:17).

The apostle was **stoned,** dragged out of the city, and left for dead at Lystra (Acts 14:19). That incident was an act of mob violence, not a formal, judicial stoning (Lev. 24:14–16, 23; Num. 15:35–36; Josh. 7:24–25), because the Romans did not grant the Jews the right of capital punishment (John 18:31).

Three times Paul's numerous sea voyages (Acts records nine before the writing of 2 Corinthians: 9:30; 11:25–26; 13:4, 13; 14:25–26; 16:11; 17:14–15; 18:18, 21–22; there were probably at least that many more after Paul wrote this epistle) ended with him being **shipwrecked.** That does not include the apostle's shipwreck on his voyage to Rome (Acts 27), which had not yet occurred. After one of those shipwrecks, Paul **spent a night and a day . . . in the deep** clinging to a piece of wreckage until he was rescued.

Paul next described some of the **dangers** he encountered on his **frequent journeys**—both the countless shorter trips that made up his three main missionary journeys and the many other trips he took. Fording the many **rivers** that crossed his path put Paul in constant danger of drowning, since bridges were few and floods were frequent. Another threat to travelers were the **robbers** that haunted the roads. The road from Perga to Pisidian Antioch (Acts 13:14), for example, crossed dangerous rivers and wound through the Taurus Mountains, which were infamous for the bandits who holed up in them. Paul may well have had that journey in mind when he penned this section.

Paul faced constant hostility from his **countrymen** almost from the moment of his conversion. While some of the Jews believed the gospel he preached and were saved, most rejected it and reacted violently against Paul (cf. Acts 9:23, 29; 13:6–8, 45; 14:2, 19; 17:5, 13; 18:6, 12–16; 19:9; 20:3, 19; 21:27–32; 23:12–22; 25:2–3; 28:23–28). Having rejected Jesus as the Messiah, they hated the gospel and sought to silence Paul's powerful proclamation of it.

Paul also faced hostility from **the Gentiles,** most notably at Philippi (Acts 16:16–40) and Ephesus (Acts 19:23–41; 1 Cor. 15:32).

Not only did Paul face danger from different people but also in different locations. He faced **dangers** in virtually every city he visited, including Damascus (Acts 9:20, 23), Jerusalem (Acts 9:29; 21:27–32; 23:12–22), Pisidian Antioch (Acts 13:14, 45), Iconium (Acts 14:1–2), Lystra (Acts 14:19), Philippi (Acts 16:16–40), Thessalonica (Acts 17:5–8), Berea (17:13), Corinth (18:1, 6, 12–16), and Ephesus (Acts 19:1, 9, 23–41; 1 Cor. 15:32). Nor was he safe outside the cities, for he also faced **dangers in the wilderness.** Paul did not always take the well-traveled roads; sometimes need drove him to journey through the backcountry. When he did so, he faced exposure to the elements, to extremes of cold and heat, to the torrential rain, dangerous lightning, and flash floods associated with thunderstorms, and to the blizzards that threatened travelers through the mountains in winter. He also faced the menace of wild animals, including bears (cf. 2 Kings 2:24), lions (cf. Judg. 14:5; 1 Kings 13:24; 20:36; 2 Kings 17:25), and venomous snakes (cf. Acts 28:3–5). Finally, as noted above, travel **on the sea** posed the ever-present danger of shipwreck.

But the most insidious danger of all were the **false brethren,** who posed as believers and then tried to destroy Paul's ministry. The false apostles at Corinth were prime examples of such treacherous pseudo-brethren, as were the Judaizers (Gal. 2:4). Because of the danger posed by false believers, Paul warned the elders of the Ephesian church, "From among your own selves men will arise, speaking perverse things, to draw away the disciples after them" (Acts 20:30).

In 2 Corinthians 11:27 Paul turned from the dangers that constantly threatened him to the **labor and hardship** that was also the normal routine of his life (Acts 20:34–35; 1 Cor. 4:12; 1 Thess. 2:9; 2 Thess. 3:8). Earning a living to support himself and sometimes his fellow missionaries (Acts 20:34) often meant working **through many sleepless nights.** After spending his days preaching the gospel and teaching and discipling new believers, Paul would often work all night (cf. 1 Thess. 2:9; 2 Thess. 3:8) at his trade (Acts 18:3) to provide life's necessities.

In spite of Paul's diligent, hard work, the demands of his ministry (cf. Acts 20:7, 11, 31; 1 Thess. 3:10; 2 Tim. 1:3) sometimes made it difficult for him to earn enough to sustain himself. As a result, he experienced **hunger and thirst** (cf. 1 Cor. 4:11), was **often without food** (cf. 2 Cor. 11:9), and faced **cold and exposure** (cf. 2 Tim. 4:13).

Paul's suffering set him apart from the money- and comfort-seeking false apostles and marked him as a true apostle of the Lord Jesus Christ. It also validated the security of his salvation, as he testifies in Romans 8:38–39: "For I am convinced that neither death, nor life, nor angels, nor principalities, nor things present, nor things to come, nor powers, nor height, nor depth, nor any other created thing, will be able to separate us from the love of God, which is in Christ Jesus our Lord."

His Experience of Sympathy

Apart from such external things, there is the daily pressure on me of concern for all the churches. Who is weak without my being weak? Who is led into sin without my intense concern? (11:28–29)

Like all false apostles, these manipulated and abused the Corinthians for their own selfish ends. Paul, on the other hand, was deeply concerned for their well-being, as he was for all the churches. The phrase **apart from such external things** could be better rendered "apart from the things not mentioned." In other words, Paul could have listed far more external hardships had his humility permitted him to do so. All of them, however, paled into insignificance in comparison to the internal, **daily pressure** he felt **of concern for all the churches.**

Paul felt deeply the pain of the church's weakness and suffering. To the Galatians he wrote, "My children, with whom I am again in labor until Christ is formed in you" (Gal. 4:19). He expressed his love and concern for the Thessalonians using the metaphor of a mother's tender care for her children: "But we proved to be gentle among you, as a nursing mother tenderly cares for her own children" (1 Thess. 2:7). Later in that chapter he added,

> But we, brethren, having been taken away from you for a short while— in person, not in spirit—were all the more eager with great desire to see your face. For we wanted to come to you—I, Paul, more than once— and yet Satan hindered us. For who is our hope or joy or crown of exultation? Is it not even you, in the presence of our Lord Jesus at His coming? For you are our glory and joy. (vv. 17–20)

Paul devoted his life to the saints. He agonized over them, prayed for them, and exhorted them. He was greatly burdened by their moral, spiritual, and doctrinal needs. The constant **pressure** that burden exerted on him assaulted his peace, joy, and satisfaction.

Paul further expressed his passionate concern for the churches by asking two rhetorical questions. The first, **Who is weak without my being weak?** expressed his empathy (cf. 1 Cor. 12:26) with the pain and suffering of weak, immature believers (1 Thess. 5:14; cf. Rom. 14:1; 15:1; 1 Cor. 9:22). Selfish, prideful false teachers do not care about people's struggles. Far from helping the weak, they are oppressive and ruthlessly take advantage of them (Jer. 23:2; Ezek. 34:2–6; Zech. 11:16; Matt. 23:2–4; Luke 20:47).

Paul was also concerned about the "unruly" (1 Thess. 5:14), as his second rhetorical question, **Who is led into sin without my intense concern?** reveals. **Intense concern** translates a form of the verb *puroō*, which literally means, "to set on fire," or "to inflame." Paul burned with righteous indignation when God's people were led into sin, as did Jesus, who solemnly warned, "Whoever causes one of these little ones who believe in Me to stumble, it would be better for him to have a heavy millstone hung around his neck, and to be drowned in the depth of the sea" (Matt. 18:6). Love is not the enemy of moral indignation but its partner. Holy indignation toward those who lead believers into sin is an expression of the purest kind of love.

His Experience of Submission

If I have to boast, I will boast of what pertains to my weakness. The God and Father of the Lord Jesus, He who is blessed forever, knows that I am not lying. In Damascus the ethnarch under Aretas the king was guarding the city of the Damascenes in order to seize me, and I was let down in a basket through a window in the wall, and so escaped his hands. (11:30–33)

To the Greeks and Romans, a leader was someone with an attractive, overpowering presence, one who could dominate a situation through the sheer force of his personality. Thus, the Corinthians might have expected Paul to defend his apostleship by showing his ability to take charge of any situation. Surprisingly, Paul gave an embarrassing illustration of his weakness instead. He told the story of how he fled from Damascus in the dead of night (Acts 9:25) to avoid those who sought his life. As always, **if** he had **to boast,** Paul would **boast** only **of what pertains to** his **weakness** (cf. 2 Cor. 1:8; 3:5; 4:7–12; 5:1; 6:4–10; 7:5; 12:7–10; 13:4).

That Paul would introduce the seemingly mundane story of his escape with the forceful declaration, **The God and Father of the Lord Jesus, He who is blessed forever, knows that I am not lying** seems strange. One would have expected such a vehement declaration of Paul's veracity to lead directly into the dramatic story of his trip to heaven (12:2ff.). That he used the declaration here emphasizes the significance of this event to him.

The Old Testament identifies God as the God of Abraham, Isaac, and Jacob (Ex. 3:6, 15, 16; 4:5; Matt. 22:32; Acts 3:13). The New Testament, however, identifies Him as the **Father of the Lord Jesus** (2 Cor. 1:3; Rom. 15:6; Eph. 1:3; 1 Peter 1:3; cf. John 20:17; Eph. 1:17). No one can truly worship God who does not believe that He shares His very essence and nature with His Son Jesus Christ, and that Jesus is God manifest in the flesh. God, **who is blessed forever** (cf. Dan. 2:20; Mark 14:61; Rom. 1:25; 9:5; 1 Tim. 1:11), would affirm that Paul was committed to the honor and reverence of God, in whose presence and under whose blessing he lived. The apostle was not about to lie in his testimony of God's deliverance in his life.

The escape Paul recounted took place after his Damascus Road conversion, when he returned to **Damascus** after spending three years in Nabatean Arabia (Gal. 1:17–18). Enraged by Paul's bold, fearless preaching of Jesus as the Messiah, the unbelieving Jews in Damascus plotted to take his life (Acts 9:23–24). As would happen throughout Paul's ministry, they enlisted the aid of the Gentiles (cf. Acts 13:50; 14:2; 17:13; 18:12–16). It is not known for certain whether Damascus was under Nabatean rule or Roman rule at this time. If the former, the **ethnarch** was the governor of the city under **Aretas the king;** if the latter, he was the leader of Damascus's Nabatean community, who had been appointed by **Aretas.** In either case, he cooperated with the Jews in their attempt to kill Paul, **guarding the city of the Damascenes in order to seize** him. The **ethnarch's** willingness to help the Jews suggests Paul's ministry during his three years in Arabia had aroused the Nabateans' hostility.

With the aid of fellow Christians (Acts 9:25), who **let** him **down in a basket through a window in the** city's **wall** (cf. Josh. 2:15), Paul **escaped** from Damascus and fled to Jerusalem (Acts 9:26). That many years later he used this event to illustrate his humility reveals how embarrassing this undignified experience was for him. D. A. Carson writes, "This toast of high rabbinic circles, this educated and sincere Pharisee, this man who had access to the highest officials in Jerusalem, slunk out of Damascus like a criminal, lowered like a catch of dead fish in a basket whose smelly cargo he had displaced" (*From Triumphalism to Maturity* [Grand Rapids: Baker, 1984], 127–28).

Lest anyone (including himself) should think too highly of Paul, this incident graphically illustrates the truth of his weakness apart from God's power. This story puts into perspective the amazing vision Paul was about to relate. The man who ascended into the third heaven was the same one who ignominiously descended from the Damascus city wall in a basket.

HIS EXPERIENCE OF THE SUPERNATURAL

Boasting is necessary, though it is not profitable; but I will go on to visions and revelations of the Lord. I know a man in Christ who fourteen years ago—whether in the body I do not know, or out of the body I do not know, God knows—such a man was caught up to the third heaven. And I know how such a man—whether in the body or apart from the body I do not know, God knows—was caught up into Paradise and heard inexpressible words, which a man is not permitted to speak. (12:1–4)

At first glance, the story of Paul's vision seems out of place in a section dealing with his suffering and weakness. But the Greeks believed that those who truly represented the gods would experience mystical visions, which some tried to induce through drunken orgies. Undoubtedly, then, the false apostles claimed visions and revelations of their own. The Corinthians, swept away by their phony claims, groveled before those lying braggarts. Thus, it was necessary for Paul (reluctantly) to relate his own genuine vision.

Before describing his supernatural vision, Paul added yet another disclaimer to the many he had already written (especially in 10:13–11:21), indicating once again how extremely distasteful he found even this boasting he had been forced into. He recognized that such **boasting** was **necessary,** but stressed that **it** was **not profitable.** Even **visions and revelations,** including the astounding one he was about to relate, were not helpful to talk about. They did not benefit the church (or else Paul surely would have told of this vision many times before), because they are not verifiable nor can they be repeated, and they could lead to pride (cf. 12:7). What is profitable is Scripture, which "is inspired by God and profitable for teaching, for reproof, for correction, for training in righteousness" (2 Tim. 3:16). Thus, Paul commended the Ephesian elders not to visions and extrabiblical revelations, but "to the word of His grace, which [was] able to build [them] up and to give [them] the inheritance among all those who are sanctified" (Acts 20:32). The Bible is complete and does not need to be supplemented by any further revelations, except that of the Lord Jesus Christ at His second coming (1 Cor. 1:7; 1 Peter 1:7, 13; 4:13).

Paul had received many visions in his life, six of which are recorded in Acts (9:3–12; 16:9–10; 18:9–10; 22:17–21; 23:11; 27:23–24). He had also received the gospel he preached by revelation (Gal. 1:11–12). But the vision he was about to describe was the most amazing and remarkable of them all. With characteristic humility, he related it in the third person, writing, **I know a man in Christ.** Obviously, Paul was that man, as verse 7 indicates.

The vision took place **fourteen years** before the writing of 2 Corinthians, which was in late A.D. 55 or early A.D. 56, putting it sometime between Paul's return to Tarsus from Jerusalem (Acts 9:30) and his commissioning by the Holy Spirit (Acts 13:1–3). Little is known about that period of Paul's life except that during it he ministered in Syria and Cilicia (Gal. 1:21). God may have granted him this personal experience to steel him against the suffering he would experience on his missionary journeys. Having been given a glimpse of the heaven that awaited him, he could face the most relentless and severe suffering that dogged every day of his life. Now, after fourteen years of silence, Paul was apparently relating the vision for the first time.

Exactly what was the reality of the experience was unclear even to Paul, as the twice-repeated phrase **whether in the body I do not know, or out of the body I do not know** emphasizes. He did not know **whether** his body and soul were **caught up to the third heaven** or whether his soul temporarily went **out of** his **body. Caught up** translates *harpazō*, the same verb used of the Rapture in 1 Thessalonians 4:17. Paul was suddenly snatched up into the **third heaven** which, transcending the first (earth's atmosphere; Deut. 11:11; 1 Kings 8:35; Isa. 55:10) and second (interplanetary and interstellar space; Gen. 15:5; Ps. 8:3; Isa. 13:10) heavens, is the abode of God (1 Kings 8:30; Ps. 33:13–14; Matt. 6:9). The parallelism of the two phrases demands that **Paradise** be equated with **heaven** (see Luke 23:43; cf. Rev. 2:7, which says the Tree of Life is in Paradise with Rev. 22:2, 14, 19, which place it in heaven). The Persian word from which the Greek word translated **Paradise** derives means "walled garden." The greatest honor a Persian king could bestow on one of his subjects was to grant him the right to walk with the king in the royal garden in intimate companionship.

Unlike modern charlatans, who claim trips to heaven and visions of God, Paul gave no sensational, detailed description of what he saw or experienced in heaven but mentioned only what he heard. And even that consisted of **inexpressible words, which a man is not permitted to speak.** What he heard was in a language unlike anything on earth. Though the apostle understood what was said, there were no words in human language to convey what he heard, nor would he have been **permitted to speak** about it even if that were possible. The veil between earth and heaven remains in place. What God wants known about heaven is revealed in the Bible; as for the rest, "The secret things belong to the Lord our God" (Deut. 29:29).

The true measure of a man of God does not lie in his claims of visions and experiences with God, or the force of his personality, the size of his ministry, his educational degrees, or any other human criteria. A true man of God is marked by how much he has suffered in the war against the kingdom of darkness, how concerned he is for people, how humble he is, and how accurately he handles the supernatural revelation found in God's Word (2 Tim. 2:15). Like Paul, such men patiently endure the suffering and humiliation of this life, knowing that such "momentary, light affliction is producing . . . an eternal weight of glory far beyond all comparison" (2 Cor. 4:17).

How God Uses Suffering
(2 Corinthians 12:5–10)

31

On behalf of such a man will I boast; but on my own behalf I will not boast, except in regard to my weaknesses. For if I do wish to boast I will not be foolish, for I will be speaking the truth; but I refrain from this, so that no one will credit me with more than he sees in me or hears from me. Because of the surpassing greatness of the revelations, for this reason, to keep me from exalting myself, there was given me a thorn in the flesh, a messenger of Satan to torment me—to keep me from exalting myself! Concerning this I implored the Lord three times that it might leave me. And He has said to me, "My grace is sufficient for you, for power is perfected in weakness." Most gladly, therefore, I will rather boast about my weaknesses, so that the power of Christ may dwell in me. Therefore I am well content with weaknesses, with insults, with distresses, with persecutions, with difficulties, for Christ's sake; for when I am weak, then I am strong. (12:5–10)

The question of why bad things happen to seemingly good people is an issue that troubles many. Disease, crime, hunger, poverty, accidents, and natural disasters seem to strike without rhyme or reason, affecting both the seemingly innocent and the guilty alike.

But the Bible teaches that bad things happen to all people because all are fallen sinners who live in a fallen world. No one is inherently good: "There is none righteous, not even one" (Rom. 3:10). Because of that reality, suffering is universal. According to Job 5:7, "Man is born for trouble, as sparks fly upward." Jesus declared, "In the world you have tribulation" (John 16:33), while Paul reminded Christians that it is "through many tribulations [that] we must enter the kingdom of God" (Acts 14:22), because "all who desire to live godly in Christ Jesus will be persecuted" (2 Tim. 3:12).

Even God's most noble servants are not immune to suffering. Jonathan Edwards was probably the greatest theologian America has ever known. For more than twenty years he faithfully labored as the pastor of a church in Northampton, Massachusetts. His preaching had a profound impact on the widespread eighteenth-century revival known as the Great Awakening. Incredibly, after more than two decades of faithful ministry, the congregation voted Edwards out of his church. They did so not because of any moral blemish or doctrinal deviation on his part, but because he insisted that only those who had made a public confession of faith be permitted to join the church and partake in the Lord's Supper.

Like Jonathan Edwards, Paul experienced the deepest pain in life—being rejected by those whom he cared for and ministered to. The apostle loved the Corinthians; he had brought the gospel to them, nurtured them, taught them, and poured his life into them. That many of them had abandoned him in favor of the false apostles hurt Paul deeply. He was, in fact, experiencing the severest pain of his life. He was so troubled that while anxiously awaiting Titus's report about the situation in Corinth, Paul uncharacteristically did not fully take advantage of an open door for ministry at Troas (2 Cor. 2:12–13).

As he noted in 11:22–27, Paul was no stranger to physical suffering. Yet far more painful was his burden of concern for the churches (11:28–29). He empathized with believers' weaknesses and burned with righteous indignation when they were led into sin.

How Paul handled suffering provides a model for all believers. No text in Scripture more powerfully unfolds God's purposes in believers' pain than does this passage. It is a gem of rare beauty, forged in the fiery heat of chapters 10–13, perhaps the most emotionally charged passage Paul ever penned. From the crucible of Paul's suffering emerge five reasons that God allows suffering in believers' lives: to reveal their spiritual condition, to humble them, to draw them to Himself, to display His grace, and to perfect His power.

GOD USES SUFFERING TO
REVEAL BELIEVERS' SPIRITUAL CONDITION

On behalf of such a man will I boast; but on my own behalf I will not boast, except in regard to my weaknesses. For if I do wish to boast I will not be foolish, for I will be speaking the truth; but I refrain from this, so that no one will credit me with more than he sees in me or hears from me. (12:5–6)

Trouble is the truest test of a person's spiritual character. When adversity strikes, the superficial veneer of peace and happiness is stripped away, revealing what is really in the heart. The Lord brought intense suffering into Paul's life in part to reveal his integrity for all to see and to establish his credibility.

As in verses 2–4, Paul humbly referred to himself in the third person, writing, **On behalf of such a man will I boast.** Speaking of himself like that also emphasized his passivity in his vision. He did nothing to make it happen; it was something God sovereignly chose to grant, not a reflection of any merit on Paul's part. He was just an ordinary man and would not boast **on** his **own behalf** as if he in any way merited the vision God had given him.

What Paul would boast about were his **weaknesses,** for they provided compelling proof of his apostleship. How else could his immense impact be explained, except that God's power was at work in him? As his enemies were quick to point out, Paul's "personal presence [was] unimpressive and his speech contemptible" (10:10). But what they failed to understand was that, paradoxically, Paul was strongest when he was weakest (12:10).

Paul's **boast** was **not . . . foolish,** for unlike the false apostles and their specious claims, he was **speaking the truth;** his vision really happened, and to deny that would be false humility. Nonetheless, he wisely decided to **refrain from** resting his case for his apostleship on his vision. The problem was that it was not repeatable, verifiable, or even fully comprehensible. Using it to prove his apostleship would open the door for charlatans to claim authority to speak for God based on their own alleged mystical experiences. Besides, the vision did not draw him closer to God; in fact, it was actually a source of temptation to pride (12:7).

Paul was concerned **that no one** should **credit** him **with more than he** saw **in** him **or** heard **from** him. The true measure of a man of God is not his alleged mystical experiences but his godly life and his faithfulness to the Word of God. The most startling, spectacular vision or supernatural revelation is not as significant as the least righteous act.

God plunged Paul into the deepest sorrow and the severest pain to reveal most clearly that he was a genuine man of God. True spiritual power, authority, and integrity do not come from visions and revelations but from godly humility (cf. 4:7; Col. 2:18–19).

GOD USES SUFFERING TO
MAKE BELIEVERS HUMBLE

Because of the surpassing greatness of the revelations, for this reason, to keep me from exalting myself, there was given me a thorn in the flesh, a messenger of Satan to torment me—to keep me from exalting myself! (12:7)

The evidence of Paul's success in ministry was the power of the gospel to transform lives that led to the churches he founded and built up. They were a monument to his faithfulness and to God's power working through him. To see any of those churches being led astray by false teachers was a painful, humbling experience for Paul, yet one that he needed. Twice in verse 7 he emphasized that God allowed his **thorn in the flesh to keep** him **from exalting** himself. Though he was the noblest Christian of all, Paul was not impervious to the normal struggles of life. Certainly, **because of the surpassing greatness of the revelations** he had experienced (Acts records six visions apart from the one related in this passage; he also received the gospel he preached by revelation [Gal. 1:11–12; cf. Eph. 3:3]), pride was a constant temptation. Therefore, to keep him humble, Paul was **given . . . a thorn in the flesh, a messenger of Satan to torment** him.

The identity of that **thorn in the flesh** has been much debated. Paul did not describe it in detail, indicating that the Corinthians knew what it was. Most commentators assume it was a physical ailment, such as migraines, ophthalmia, malaria, epilepsy, gallstones, gout, rheumatism, an intestinal disorder, or even a speech impediment. That such a wide range of possibilities has been put forth indicates a lack of specific support in Scripture for any of them. (Even if Paul's words in Gal. 6:11, "See with what large letters I am writing to you with my own hand," indicate an eye problem, there is nothing in that verse that connects it with the apostle's thorn in the flesh.) *Skolops* (**thorn**) could be better translated "stake," graphically indicating the intensity of the suffering it caused Paul; it was not a small thorn but a large stake.

The apostle acknowledged that the **thorn in the flesh** ultimately **was given** to him from God. (See Job 1 and 2, where God permitted Satan to afflict Job for His own purposes; cf. Gen. 50:20.) The phrase **in**

the flesh could also be rendered "for" or "because of the flesh." **Flesh** should be understood here not in a physical sense, but in a moral sense as a reference to Paul's unredeemed humanness (cf. Rom. 6:19; 7:5, 18, 25; 8:4–9). The Lord allowed Paul's intense suffering to impale his otherwise proud flesh; to humble the one who had so many revelations.

It is best to understand Paul's **thorn** as a demonic **messenger of Satan** sent **to torment** him by using the deceivers to seduce the Corinthians into a rebellion against him. At least four lines of evidence support that interpretation. First, in the overwhelming majority of its uses in the New Testament (including every other occurrence in Paul's writings), *angelos* (**messenger**) refers to angels. An angel sent from Satan would, of course, be a demon. Second, the verb translated **torment** always refers to harsh treatment from someone (Matt. 26:67; Mark 14:65; 1 Cor. 4:11; 1 Peter 2:20). Third, the Old Testament sometimes refers metaphorically to opponents as thorns (e.g., Num. 33:55; Josh. 23:13; Judg. 2:3; Ezek. 28:24). Finally, the verb translated "leave" in verse 8 is always used in the New Testament to speak of someone departing. Likely, then, the demonic **messenger** was tormenting Paul by being the indwelling spirit in the leading false apostle (cf. 2 Cor. 11:13–15; 1 Tim. 4:1). Again, this is consistent with Paul's testimony that his severest suffering came from his concern for the church (11:28–29).

Satan's assault on Paul did not take place outside of God's will. God is sovereign over all of His creation and will use even the forces of the kingdom of darkness to accomplish His righteous purposes (cf. Num. 22:2–24:25; 1 Kings 22:19–23; Luke 22:31–32). Paul was critical to God's redemptive plan, and He would keep him humble by whatever means necessary, including using a demon. If this seems unusual, remember the accounts of Job (Job 1:6–12; 2:1–7) and Peter (Luke 22:31). In both cases God allowed Satan to bring devastating suffering on His saints to achieve their greater usefulness. This is a good reminder of the foolishness of those who try to tell Satan and demons what to do and where to go. If we could command demons, we might thwart the purposes of God with our faulty assumptions.

GOD USES SUFFERING TO
DRAW BELIEVERS TO HIMSELF

Concerning this I implored the Lord three times that it might leave me. (12:8)

Faced with this demonic work in Corinth that brought him intense pain, Paul went for help to the "Father of mercies and God of all comfort, who comforts us in all our affliction" (1:3–4). He did not seek a quick fix to his problem through some technique devised by human wisdom. Nor did he attempt to bind Satan or cast out the demons assaulting the Corinthian church. Paul followed the example of the Lord Jesus Christ, who, in His time of intense suffering in Gethsemane, also appealed three times to God to deliver Him (Matt. 26:36–44). Paul drew near to God in the intensity of his pain. That is the most blessed place a believer can be, though we usually do not feel as compelled to be near Him if we are not suffering.

Implored translates a form of the verb *parakaleō*, which is frequently used in the Gospels by those appealing to Jesus for healing (Matt. 8:5; 14:36; Mark 1:40; 5:23; 6:56; 7:32; 8:22; Luke 7:4; 8:41). Paul was a model of persistence in prayer (cf. Gen. 18:23–32; Matt. 15:22–28; Luke 11:5–10; 18:1; Col. 4:12) as he pleaded with **the Lord three times that** the thorn **might leave** him. Though God did not remove Paul's pain, that does not mean that He did not answer Paul's prayer; the answer was simply different from what the apostle had asked for.

GOD USES SUFFERING TO
DISPLAY HIS GRACE

And He has said to me, "My grace is sufficient for you," (12:9*a*)

Paul's three requests for relief resulted in the same answer from the Lord. Each time He did not answer by removing Paul's pain, because, as noted above, that pain was spiritually productive. It revealed Paul's true character, kept him humble, and drew him intimately in prayer to God. The Lord granted Paul relief not by removing his suffering but by giving him **grace sufficient** to endure it.

The magnificent, rich term *charis* (**grace**) appears 155 times in the New Testament. **Grace** describes God's undeserved favor to mankind. It is a dynamic force, totally transforming believers' lives, beginning at salvation (Acts 15:11; 18:27; Rom. 3:24; Eph. 1:7; 2:5, 8; 2 Tim. 1:9; Titus 2:11; 3:7) and continuing through sanctification (2 Peter 3:18) to glorification (Eph. 2:7). Grace sets the Christian faith apart from all other religions. God is gracious, benevolent, and kind, in contrast to the gods of false religions, who are at best indifferent and need constantly to be cajoled and appeased.

The Bible teaches that believers "have all received . . . grace upon grace" through the Lord Jesus Christ (John 1:16), since "grace and truth were realized through" Him (John 1:17) and He, as God incarnate, is "full of grace and truth" (John 1:14). Thus, Luke, writing of the early Christians, said that "abundant grace was upon them all" (Acts 4:33); Paul wrote of the "grace in which we stand" (Rom. 5:2); James spoke of grace that is greater than sin's power (James 4:6; cf. Rom. 5:20); and Peter described the "manifold [multifaceted] grace of God" (1 Peter 4:10). No wonder Paul called it the "surpassing grace of God in [believers]" (2 Cor. 9:14), and was confident that "God is able to make all grace abound to [believers], so that always having all sufficiency in everything, [they] may have an abundance for every good deed" (2 Cor. 9:8).

Sadly, many evangelical churches today deny in practice the sufficiency of God's grace for all of life's problems, supplementing it with the humanistic theories of psychology. The idea that the grace of God is sufficient for even the most serious issues believers may face is derided as antiquated, simplistic, and naïve, like putting a Band-Aid on a broken leg. It is suggested by so-called Christian psychologists that divine grace may be sufficient for solving shallow problems, but deeper issues require therapy.

That raises some troubling questions. If God's Word does not have the answers to all of life's problems, how can it be perfect, able to totally transform the soul (Ps. 19:7–11)? Was Paul mistaken when he wrote under divine inspiration, "All Scripture is inspired by God and profitable for teaching, for reproof, for correction, for training in righteousness; so that the man of God may be adequate, equipped for *every* good work" (2 Tim. 3:16–17; italics added)? Why does the "wisdom from above" (James 3:17) need to be supplemented by the foolishness of human wisdom (1 Cor. 1:20–21; 2:5; 3:19)? If believers are complete in Christ (Col. 2:10) and have been granted in Him "*everything* pertaining to life and godliness" (2 Peter 1:3; italics added), what more do they need? When Paul said, "I can do *all* things through Him who strengthens me" (Phil. 4:13; italics added), did he have in mind only superficial, minor issues? Was he mistaken when he wrote, "Not that we are adequate in ourselves to consider anything as coming from ourselves, but our adequacy is from God" (2 Cor. 3:5)? Does God, who "knows the secrets of the heart" (Ps. 44:21), need the insights of humanistic psychology in order to fully understand people's problems? Is "the word of God" really "living and active and sharper than any two-edged sword . . . piercing as far as the division of soul and spirit, of both joints and marrow, and able to judge the thoughts and intentions of the heart" (Heb. 4:12)? If it is an essential tool for removing the barriers to sanctification, how were God's people sanctified before the advent of psychology in the nineteenth and twentieth centuries? What a tragic delusion for God's people to imagine that the answers to life's problems lie outside of His all-sufficient and unbounded grace. (I discuss the sufficiency of God's grace at length in my book, *Our Sufficiency in Christ* [Dallas: Word, 1991].)

When God declared to Paul in answer to his prayer, **"My grace is sufficient for you,"** He affirmed the total sufficiency of His grace for every need in life—to believe the gospel; to understand and apply the Word to all the issues of life; to overcome sin and temptation; to endure suffering, disappointment, and pain; to obey God; to serve Him effectively; and to worship Him. God's grace was sufficient for the deepest pain Paul (or any other believer) could ever experience.

The comforting truth is that "no temptation has overtaken [believers] but such as is common to man; and God is faithful, who will not allow [them] to be tempted beyond what [they] are able, but with the temptation will provide the way of escape also, so that [they] will be able to endure it" (1 Cor. 10:13). The way of escape is the way of endurance in grace. The writer of Hebrews urged suffering believers to "draw near with confidence to the throne of grace, so that [they] may receive mercy and find grace to help in time of need" (Heb. 4:16). Deuteronomy 33:26 reminds believers, "There is none like the God of Jeshurun, who rides the heavens to your help, and through the skies in His majesty." God's promise of His strengthening presence to Joshua, "Be strong and courageous! Do not tremble or be dismayed, for the Lord your God is with you wherever you go" (Josh. 1:9) applies to all believers, as does His promise to Israel:

> But now, thus says the Lord, your Creator, O Jacob, and He who formed you, O Israel, "Do not fear, for I have redeemed you; I have called you by name; you are Mine! When you pass through the waters, I will be with you; and through the rivers, they will not overflow you. When you walk through the fire, you will not be scorched, nor will the flame burn you." (Isa. 43:1–2)

If God's grace was "more than abundant" to save Paul (1 Tim. 1:14), it was certainly sufficient to strengthen him in any subsequent trial he faced.

The following anecdote from my book *Our Sufficiency in Christ* illustrates the sufficiency of God's grace:

> The story is told of Charles Haddon Spurgeon, who was riding home one evening after a heavy day's work, feeling weary and depressed, when the verse came to mind, "My grace is sufficient for you."
>
> In his mind he immediately compared himself to a little fish in the Thames River, apprehensive lest drinking so many pints of water in the river each day he might drink the Thames dry. Then Father Thames says to him, "Drink away, little fish. My stream is sufficient for you."
>
> Next he thought of a little mouse in the granaries of Egypt, afraid lest its daily nibbles exhaust the supplies and cause it to starve to death.

Then Joseph comes along and says, "Cheer up, little mouse. My granaries are sufficient for you."

Then he thought of a man climbing some high mountain to reach its lofty summit and dreading lest his breathing there might exhaust all the oxygen in the atmosphere. The Creator booms His voice out of heaven, saying, "Breathe away, oh man, and fill your lungs. My atmosphere is sufficient for you!" (pp. 256–57)

God Uses Suffering to Perfect His Power

"for power is perfected in weakness." Most gladly, therefore, I will rather boast about my weaknesses, so that the power of Christ may dwell in me. Therefore I am well content with weaknesses, with insults, with distresses, with persecutions, with difficulties, for Christ's sake; for when I am weak, then I am strong. (12:9b–10)

God not only wanted to display His grace in Paul's life, but also His power; He not only wanted the apostle to be humble, but also strong. Because **"power is perfected in weakness,"** it was necessary for the fires of affliction to burn away the dross of pride and self-confidence. Paul had lost all ability, humanly speaking, to deal with the situation at Corinth. He had visited there, sent others there, and written the Corinthians letters. But he could not completely fix the situation. He was at the point when he had to trust totally in God's will and power.

It is when believers are out of answers, confidence, and strength, with nowhere else to turn but to God that they are in a position to be most effective. No one in the kingdom of God is too weak to experience God's power, but many are too confident in their own strength. Physical suffering, mental anguish, disappointment, unfulfillment, and failure squeeze the impurities out of believers' lives, making them pure channels through which God's power can flow.

Though his circumstances had not changed, Paul could still exclaim, **Most gladly, therefore, I will rather boast about my weaknesses, so that the power of Christ may dwell in me.** In 1 Corinthians 1:27 he reminded the Corinthians that "God has chosen the foolish things of the world to shame the wise, and God has chosen the weak things of the world to shame the things which are strong." The apostle himself had ministered among the Corinthians "in weakness and in fear and in much trembling" (1 Cor. 2:3). Paul's weakness was not self-induced or artificial; it was not a superficial psychological self-esteem game he played with himself. It was real and God-given. He did not love the pain caused by the false apostles, knowing it was satanic in origin. Yet he embraced it as the means by which God released His power through him.

Verse 10 summarizes the truth of this passage. *Eudokeō* (**well content**) could be translated, "pleased," or "delighted." He was thrilled with the **weaknesses, insults, distresses, persecutions,** and **difficulties** he endured **for Christ's sake,** not because he was a masochist, but because **when** he was **weak, then** he was **strong.**

Having a proper perspective on trouble, trials, and suffering is the cornerstone of Christian living. Focusing all one's efforts on removing difficulties is not the answer. Believers need to embrace the trials God allows them to undergo, knowing that those trials reveal their character, humble them, draw them closer to God, and allow Him to display His grace and power in their lives. They should heed the counsel of James to "Consider it all joy, my brethren, when you encounter various trials, knowing that the testing of your faith produces endurance. And let endurance have its perfect result, so that you may be perfect and complete, lacking in nothing" (James 1:2–4).

Apostolic Uniqueness (2 Corinthians 12:11–12)

32

I have become foolish; you yourselves compelled me. Actually I should have been commended by you, for in no respect was I inferior to the most eminent apostles, even though I am a nobody. The signs of a true apostle were performed among you with all perseverance, by signs and wonders and miracles. (12:11–12)

One of the most disturbing phenomena in contemporary Christianity is the Charismatic Movement. Through its television networks, televangelists, healing services, and best-selling authors, the movement is one of the most visible fabrications of Christianity to the watching world. A number of emphases characterize it, most notably experientialism and belief in continuing revelation, healing, fainting, and speaking in tongues. But at its core is the belief that the apostolic era was not unique but rather is normative for the church in all ages. As a corollary to that, some even try to convince people that there are apostles today, thus denying their uniqueness as well. Some even claim more power and impact on the world than the apostles of Jesus Christ themselves.

But confusion over the unique role of the apostles is nothing new. The early church had to contend with those who falsely claimed to be apostles. The Lord Jesus Christ commended the church at Ephesus because they "put to the test those who call[ed] themselves apostles, and they [were] not, and . . . found them to be false" (Rev. 2:2). Like the church at Ephesus, the Corinthian church had been infiltrated by false apostles (2 Cor. 11:13). Lacking the discernment displayed by the Ephesian church, however, many of the Corinthians had embraced those lying deceivers. As a result, the Corinthian church was in turmoil, with some of its members believing the false teachers' attacks on Paul's apostleship.

That such attacks occurred is not surprising. Satan, the father of lies (John 8:44) and inveterate Enemy of God's truth (Mark 4:15; Luke 22:3; John 13:27; Acts 5:3; 2 Cor. 4:4; 1 Thess. 2:18; Rev. 20:3, 8, 10), has always opposed God's messengers and message. One of the tactics he uses is to attack the credibility of God's spokesmen (cf. Zech. 3:1; Luke 22:31) so that people will not believe their message. Because of Paul's important role in God's redemptive plan, no one except for the Lord Jesus Christ Himself has been more systematically assaulted by Satan.

Though he reluctantly defended himself to the Corinthians, Paul found doing so distasteful, repeatedly describing it as **foolish** (cf. 2 Cor. 11:1, 16, 17, 21, 12:6). He fully agreed with Solomon's wise counsel, "Let another praise you, and not your own mouth; a stranger, and not your own lips" (Prov. 27:2). Yet it was the Corinthians themselves who **compelled** him to boast, their silence forcing him to speak. Paul knew that the issue was critically important; the Corinthians' continued faithfulness to Jesus Christ was at stake (11:3).

But instead of having to defend himself to them Paul **should have been commended by** the Corinthians. There was no excuse for their confusion. They should have risen to his defense; after all, he was their spiritual father (1 Cor. 4:15; cf. 9:2), the one who brought the gospel to Corinth (Acts 18:1–8; 1 Cor. 3:6, 10; 15:1; 2 Cor. 10:14). The false apostles had their deceptive letters of commendation, but the Corinthians themselves were Paul's letter of commendation (3:2). What made their failure to defend him all the more inexcusable was that the Corinthians knew that the allegations against Paul were false. They had observed his life during his ministry among them (Acts 18:11) and knew that he was above reproach. To be silent when aspersions are cast on the lives and ministries of godly men is to share in the guilt of their detractors.

The truth is that Paul was **in no respect . . . inferior to the most eminent apostles.** As noted in the discussion of 11:5 in chapter 27 of this volume, the phrase **the most eminent apostles** (or "super apostles") is a sarcastic reference to the false apostles. Most likely, that was how they billed themselves. In reality, even though Paul's characteristic humility caused him to describe himself as a **nobody** (cf. 4:7; 1 Cor. 15:9), he was superior to them, since he alone was a true apostle.

Though he was humble and reluctant to boast, the Corinthians' naïve acceptance of the false apostles' claims left Paul no choice. Beginning in chapter 10, he directly confronted the false apostles, concluding that confrontation in 11:22ff. with a presentation of his apostolic credentials. In 12:12, Paul presented irrefutable proof that he was a genuine apostle that, in a broader sense, also establishes the uniqueness of the apostles. He showed that apostles possessed unique qualifications and powers.

UNIQUE QUALIFICATIONS

The signs of a true apostle were performed among you (12:12a)

The apostles had a one-of-a-kind, non-repeatable, and nontransferable role in the history of the church. To fail to understand that role is to have an incomplete understanding of the history of redemption. **Apostle** translates the Greek word *apostolos* (from the verb *apostellō;* "to send"), which appears eighty times in the New Testament. The term, which means, "messenger," "delegate," or "ambassador," is primarily used in the New Testament to designate fourteen men—the Twelve (Matt. 10:2), Matthias (Acts 1:26), and Paul (1 Cor. 9:1). Its Aramaic (the language Jesus probably spoke) equivalent is *šālîah*, a term which

> has become important for NT exegesis. Rab. Judaism in the time of Jesus clearly recognized the function of the representative or proxy derived from the old Sem. law concerning messengers. It is expressed briefly in the principle found in the Mishnah, "A man's agent (*šālîah*) is like himself" (Ber. 5:5 *et al.*). Hence the messenger becomes the proxy of the one who has given him the commission (cf. 1 Sam. 25:40f.; 2 Sam. 10:4, 6). Irrespective of the personality of the messenger or of the one who commissioned him, irrespective even of the commission, the expression *šālîah* means a person acting with full authority for another. (E. von Eicken, H. Lindner, "Apostle," in Colin Brown, ed., *The New International Dictionary of New Testament Theology* (Grand Rapids: Zondervan, 1975), 1:127–28)

Therefore Jesus could say to the Twelve, "Truly, truly, I say to you, he who receives whomever I send receives Me; and he who receives Me receives Him who sent Me" (John 13:20; cf. Heb. 3:1).

In addition to the Twelve and Paul, the New Testament names several other individuals as "messengers [apostles] of the churches" (2 Cor. 8:23). In that passage, the phrase refers to the two unnamed brothers who assisted Titus with the collection at Corinth. Barnabas (Acts 14:4, 14), Andronicus, Junius, and others (Rom. 16:7), James, the Lord's brother

(Gal. 1:19), and Epaphroditus (Phil. 2:25) were also apostles of the churches. Unlike the Twelve and Paul, they were not personally commissioned by Jesus Christ. Instead, they were chosen by the churches to serve as their officially authorized representatives.

The signs that were the benchmark of **a true apostle** of Jesus Christ **were performed** by Paul at Corinth. The passive voice of the verb translated **were performed** emphasizes that it was God's power working through Paul that enabled him to perform those **signs.** The apostles were conduits for divine power, not deceptive magicians. That they saw first-hand the **signs** Paul performed is another reason the Corinthians should have defended him (see the discussion of v. 11 above). In addition to the supernatural signs, wonders, and miracles, which will be discussed below, the Bible lists several other **signs,** or characteristics, of the apostles.

First, the apostles were sovereignly chosen by God for their ministry. The Lord told Ananias, "[Paul] is a chosen instrument of Mine, to bear My name before the Gentiles and kings and the sons of Israel" (Acts 9:15). Paul reflected on God's choice of him both to salvation and to apostolic service in Galatians 1:15: "God . . . set me apart even from my mother's womb and called me through His grace." In his first inspired letter to the Corinthians, Paul affirmed that he was "called as an apostle of Jesus Christ by the will of God" (1 Cor. 1:1; cf. Rom. 1:1; 2 Cor. 1:1; Eph. 1:1; Col. 1:1; 1 Tim. 1:1). He reminded Timothy, "For this I was appointed a preacher and an apostle (I am telling the truth, I am not lying) as a teacher of the Gentiles in faith and truth" (1 Tim. 2:7; cf. 2 Tim. 1:11). God also chose the other apostles (Acts 10:41; 1 Cor. 12:28).

Second, the apostles were personally appointed by the Lord Jesus Christ. Luke 6:13 records that "He called His disciples to Him and chose twelve of them, whom He also named as apostles." In John 15:16 He told the apostles, "You did not choose Me but I chose you, and appointed you that you would go and bear fruit, and that your fruit would remain." Jesus even sovereignly chose Judas, who betrayed Him: "Jesus answered them, 'Did I Myself not choose you, the twelve, and yet one of you is a devil?' Now He meant Judas the son of Simon Iscariot, for he, one of the twelve, was going to betray Him" (John 6:70–71). Paul spoke to the Ephesian elders of "the ministry which [he] received from the Lord Jesus, to testify solemnly of the gospel of the grace of God" (Acts 20:24). At his conversion on the Damascus Road Jesus said to Paul, "For this purpose I have appeared to you, to appoint you a minister and a witness not only to the things which you have seen, but also to the things in which I will appear to you" (Acts 26:16). To the Romans he wrote, "Through [Jesus Christ] we have received grace and apostleship to bring about the obedience of faith among all the Gentiles for His name's sake" (Rom. 1:5). As "an apostle [Paul was] not sent from men nor through the agency of man, but through Jesus Christ" (Gal. 1:1). To Timothy he added, "I thank Christ Jesus our Lord, who has strengthened me, because He considered me faithful, putting me into service" (1 Tim. 1:12). Christ's call of the apostles was the outworking of God's eternal choice.

Third, the apostles had to have been eyewitnesses of Christ's life, death, and resurrection. After Judas's defection and suicide,

> Peter stood up in the midst of the brethren (a gathering of about one hundred and twenty persons was there together), and said, "Brethren, the Scripture had to be fulfilled, which the Holy Spirit foretold by the mouth of David concerning Judas, who became a guide to those who arrested Jesus. For he was counted among us and received his share in this ministry." (Now this man acquired a field with the price of his wickedness, and falling headlong, he burst open in the middle and all his intestines gushed out. And it became known to all who were living in Jerusalem; so that in their own language that field was called Hakeldama, that is, Field of Blood.) "For it is written in the book of Psalms, 'Let his homestead be made desolate, and let no one dwell in it'; and, 'Let another man take his office.'" (Acts 1:15–20)

Judas's replacement had to meet very specific requirements:

> "Therefore it is necessary that of the men who have accompanied us all the time that the Lord Jesus went in and out among us—beginning with the baptism of John until the day that He was taken up from us— one of these must become a witness with us of His resurrection." So they put forward two men, Joseph called Barsabbas (who was also called Justus), and Matthias. And they prayed and said, "You, Lord, who know the hearts of all men, show which one of these two You have chosen to occupy this ministry and apostleship from which Judas turned aside to go to his own place." And they drew lots for them, and the lot fell to Matthias; and he was added to the eleven apostles. (vv. 21–26)

The candidates had to have accompanied Jesus and the other apostles through His entire earthly ministry, "beginning with the baptism of John until the day that He was taken up" in His ascension. The Lord sovereignly revealed His will through the drawing of lots and "Matthias . . . was added to the eleven apostles."

Peter told those gathered at the house of Cornelius that the apostles were "witnesses of all the things [Jesus] did both in the land of the Jews and in Jerusalem" (Acts 10:39). Specifically, the apostles were eyewitnesses of Jesus' resurrection: "God raised Him up on the third day and granted that He become visible, not to all the people, but to witnesses who were chosen beforehand by God, that is, to us who ate and drank with Him after He arose from the dead" (vv. 40–41).

Paul had not been one of Jesus' followers during His earthly ministry, yet he was no less an apostle. "Am I not an apostle?" he challenged the Corinthians; "Have I not seen Jesus our Lord?" (1 Cor. 9:1). Recounting the postresurrection appearances of Christ, Paul concluded, "Last of all, as it were to one untimely born, He appeared to me also" (1 Cor. 15:8). In addition to his initial vision on the Damascus Road, Acts records that Paul saw the resurrected Christ three other times (18:9–10; 22:17–21; 23:11).

Fourth, the apostles received the gospel by direct revelation from Jesus Christ, not from other men. The Lord taught the Twelve during His time on earth (e.g., Matt. 20:17–19; John 13–17), including the forty days between His resurrection and ascension (Acts 1:1–3). Paul, though he did not sit under Christ's teaching during the Lord's earthly ministry, nevertheless received the gospel directly from Him. In Galatians 1:11–12 he wrote, "For I would have you know, brethren, that the gospel which was preached by me is not according to man. For I neither received it from man, nor was I taught it, but I received it through a revelation of Jesus Christ." Writing to the Corinthians about the Lord's Supper Paul said,

> For I received from the Lord that which I also delivered to you, that the Lord Jesus in the night in which He was betrayed took bread; and when He had given thanks, He broke it and said, "This is My body, which is for you; do this in remembrance of Me." In the same way He took the cup also after supper, saying, "This cup is the new covenant in My blood; do this, as often as you drink it, in remembrance of Me." (1 Cor. 11:23–25)

He prefaced his synopsis of the gospel he had preached to the Corinthians by reminding them, "I delivered to you as of first importance what I also received" (1 Cor. 15:3). To the Ephesians Paul wrote, "By revelation there was made known to me the mystery, as I wrote before in brief. By referring to this, when you read you can understand my insight into the mystery of Christ" (Eph. 3:3–4). He also affirmed that the gospel, "which in other generations was not made known to the sons of men . . . has now been revealed to His holy apostles and prophets in the Spirit" (v. 5).

Fifth, the apostles were the foundation of the church. In Ephesians 2:20 Paul wrote that the church was "built on the foundation of the apostles and prophets, Christ Jesus Himself being the corner stone" (cf. Matt. 16:18). God gave apostles to the church "for the equipping of the saints for the work of service, to the building up of the body of Christ" (Eph. 4:12). From the earliest days of the church the believers "were continually devoting themselves to the apostles' teaching" (Acts 2:42). The apostles laid the doctrinal foundation of the church, which is codified in the New Testament. Those who followed them built on that foundation. Having been laid once and for all (Jude 3), the foundation does not need to be continuously laid today by self-proclaimed apostles. After giving the church the Word of God in the New Testament (2 Peter 1:19), the apostles passed from the scene, never to be replaced.

Sixth, the apostles were given unique ministry duties. Their first responsibility was to be discipled by the Lord. Mark 3:14 says that Jesus "appointed twelve, so that they would be with Him." They then were to be models of godliness for other believers to follow. Therefore Paul exhorted the Corinthians, "Be imitators of me, just as I also am of Christ" (1 Cor. 11:1; cf. 1 Cor. 4:16; 1 Thess. 1:6).

A second essential responsibility of the apostles was to preach the gospel. Mark 3:14 says that Jesus called the Twelve not only to disciple them, but also so He could "send them out to preach." Luke 9:2 records that "He sent [the Twelve] out to proclaim the kingdom of God and to perform healing." The apostles faithfully carried out Jesus' mandate. Acts 4:33 records that "with great power the apostles were giving testimony to the resurrection of the Lord Jesus." Peter told the Gentiles gathered in Cornelius's house that Jesus "ordered [the apostles] to preach to the people, and solemnly to testify that this is the One who has been appointed by God as Judge of the living and the dead" (Acts 10:42). Along with their responsibility to preach the gospel to unbelievers the apostles also taught believers. As noted above, their teaching was the foundation of the church. In 2 Peter 3:2 Peter exhorted his readers to "remember the words spoken beforehand by the holy prophets and the commandment of the Lord and Savior spoken by your apostles." Paul twice wrote of his call to be a "preacher and an apostle and a teacher" (2 Tim. 1:11; cf. 1 Tim. 2:7).

A third responsibility of the apostles, which will be examined in more detail later in this chapter, was to exercise their divine power in the realm of the supernatural. Jesus gave the Twelve "authority to cast out the demons" (Mark 3:15; cf. 6:7; Matt. 10:1, 8; Luke 9:1). Paul also had that authority, as he demonstrated by casting a demon out of the slave girl in Philippi (Acts 16:16–18; cf. 19:11–12). The apostles were also granted the power to heal the sick. In Luke 9:1 Jesus "called the twelve together, and gave them power and authority over all the demons and to heal diseases" (cf. Matt. 10:1; Mark 6:13; Acts 3:1–8; 9:34–41). Paul also demonstrated the apostolic sign of healing (Acts 14:8–10; 28:8).

Finally, the apostles collectively were given the task of writing the New Testament. It is true that not all of the apostles wrote New Testament books. Yet all of the New Testament was written either by an apostle (Paul, Peter, John, Matthew), or a close associate of the apostles (Mark, Luke, James, Jude). Jesus promised the apostles, "The Helper, the Holy Spirit, whom the Father will send in My name, He will teach you all things, and bring to your remembrance all that I said to you" (John 14:26;

cf. 16:13). As an apostle, Paul also wrote Scripture under divine inspiration, as he noted in 1 Corinthians 2:13: "Which things we also speak, not in words taught by human wisdom, but in those taught by the Spirit, combining spiritual thoughts with spiritual words."

Seventh, the twelve apostles were promised a unique place of honor in the future. In reply to Peter's question, "Behold, we have left everything and followed You; what then will there be for us?" (Matt. 19:27) Jesus promised the Twelve, "Truly I say to you, that you who have followed Me, in the regeneration [the millennial kingdom] when the Son of Man will sit on His glorious throne, you also shall sit upon twelve thrones, judging the twelve tribes of Israel" (v. 28). The twelve apostles, including Matthias as Judas's replacement, will fulfill a special role in the millennial kingdom, that of governing the twelve tribes of Israel.

The apostles will also receive special honor in the heavenly city. In his vision of the New Jerusalem, John saw that "the wall of the city had twelve foundation stones, and on them were the twelve names of the twelve apostles of the Lamb" (Rev. 21:14). Though Scripture does not give any details, Paul unquestionably will also be greatly honored both in the millennial kingdom and in the eternal state.

The stringent requirements for the apostolic office are such that only the Twelve and Paul qualified. Claims to apostleship made by others throughout the history of the church are therefore false.

Unique Power

by signs and wonders and miracles. (12:12c)

These words "do not describe three types of miracles but miracles in general considered from three aspects—their ability to authenticate the message ("signs"), evoke awe ("wonders"), and display divine power ("mighty deeds")" (Murray J. Harris, "2 Corinthians," in Frank E. Gaebelein, ed., *The Expositor's Bible Commentary* [Grand Rapids: Zondervan, 1976], 10:398). The supernatural **miracles** done by the apostles were **signs** pointing to them as genuine messengers of God. They were **wonders** that created amazement and astonishment, drawing the onlookers' attention to the message the apostles proclaimed.

That miracles are not normative for all periods of church history should be obvious from Paul's designation of them as the signs of an apostle. If they were commonplace, they could hardly have distinguished the apostles from ordinary believers. It was their rarity, as well as their unusual extent, that made them definitive signs of the apostles. Nor were miracles scattered haphazardly throughout redemptive history.

Scripture reveals a threefold purpose for signs, wonders, and miracles that confines them to specific periods.

First, miracles introduced successive eras of divine revelation. The miracles recorded in Scripture took place during three time periods: the time of Moses and Joshua, the time of Elijah and Elisha, and the ministry of Christ and the apostles. God attested the giving of the Law with some miracles at the time of Moses and Joshua. The miracles done by Elijah and Elisha symbolized the second great era of Old Testament revelation, the prophets (cf. Matt. 5:17; 7:12; 22:40). The miracles God performed through them authenticated them as prophets who spoke for Him (see the discussion below). Still, these periods had few miracles.

By far the greatest number of miracles in redemptive history occurred during the time of Christ and the apostles. The Incarnation of the second Person of the Trinity and the dawn of the day of redemption, as well as the revelation of the New Testament and of the church sparked an outpouring of miracles unequaled either before or since.

While all miracles are supernatural acts of God, not all supernatural acts of God are miracles. These signs, wonders, and miracles were supernatural acts done by God *through a human agent.* The reason for that lies in the second purpose of miracles: to authenticate the messengers of God. Miracles were designed to act as signs creating wonder that drew people to conclude that the message from those who performed them came from God. Thus, such expressions of God's power as creation, the Flood, and other acts of divine judgment are supernatural acts of God, but not signs and wonders. Signs and wonders are thus a subcategory of God's supernatural acts.

God granted Moses miraculous powers to prove to the Israelites that he was God's messenger (Ex. 4:1–9; cf. Acts 7:36). Elijah's ability to call down fire from heaven demonstrated that he was a man of God (2 Kings 1:10, 12; cf. 1 Kings 18:36–38), as did his restoration of the widow's dead son to life (1 Kings 17:17–24). In his sermon on the Day of Pentecost Peter declared, "Men of Israel, listen to these words: Jesus the Nazarene, a man attested to you by God with miracles and wonders and signs which God performed through Him in your midst, just as you yourselves know" (Acts 2:22; cf. Mark 6:2; Luke 19:37; John 3:2; 5:36; 7:31; 10:25, 38; 11:47; 12:37; 14:11; Acts 10:38). The apostles were authenticated in the same way as God's earlier spokesmen. Hebrews 2:3–4 warns,

> How will we escape if we neglect so great a salvation? After it was at the first spoken through the Lord, it was confirmed to us by those who heard, God also testifying with them, both by signs and wonders and by various miracles and by gifts of the Holy Spirit according to His own will.

Acts 2:43 records that "Everyone kept feeling a sense of awe; and many wonders and signs were taking place through the apostles" (cf. Acts 4:30; 5:12). Describing the ministry of Paul and Barnabas at Iconium, Luke noted that "the Lord . . . was testifying to the word of His grace, granting that signs and wonders be done by their hands" (Acts 14:3; cf. 15:12; 19:11). Paul reminded the Romans,

> Therefore in Christ Jesus I have found reason for boasting in things pertaining to God. For I will not presume to speak of anything except what Christ has accomplished through me, resulting in the obedience of the Gentiles by word and deed, in the power of signs and wonders, in the power of the Spirit; so that from Jerusalem and round about as far as Illyricum I have fully preached the gospel of Christ. (Rom. 15:17–19)

To the Thessalonians he wrote, "Our gospel did not come to you in word only, but also in power and in the Holy Spirit and with full conviction" (1 Thess. 1:5). Though Acts does not record any of the miracles Paul performed at Corinth, it is clear that he did. Otherwise, his claim, **The signs of a true apostle were performed among you . . . by signs and wonders and miracles,** would have made no sense.

Finally, God used miracles to reveal truth about Himself to those who observed them. God commanded Moses, "Say, therefore, to the sons of Israel, 'I am the Lord, and I will bring you out from under the burdens of the Egyptians, and I will deliver you from their bondage. I will also redeem you with an outstretched arm and with great judgments'" (Ex. 6:6–7). In Exodus 34:10

> God said, "Behold, I am going to make a covenant. Before all your people I will perform miracles which have not been produced in all the earth nor among any of the nations; and all the people among whom you live will see the working of the Lord, for it is a fearful thing that I am going to perform with you."

Nehemiah 9:10 says, "Then You performed signs and wonders against Pharaoh, against all his servants and all the people of his land; for You knew that they acted arrogantly toward them, and made a name for Yourself as it is this day." Psalm 135:9 reveals that God "sent signs and wonders into [the] midst [of] Egypt, upon Pharaoh and all his servants." Jeremiah wrote, "[God] set signs and wonders in the land of Egypt, and even to this day both in Israel and among mankind; and [He] . . . made a name for [Himself], as at this day" (Jer. 32:20).

The apostles held a unique, nontransferable, and highly privileged place in the history of the church. The apostolate was never intended to be a perpetual institution; in fact, there are clear indications in the New Testament the apostolic era was already drawing to a close. According to Acts 5:16, all the sick who came to the apostles were healed. However, by the end of Paul's life the situation had dramatically changed. His beloved son in the faith Timothy faced a recurring illness. But instead of healing him, Paul counseled him to treat the illness by drinking wine (1 Tim. 5:23). Nor was Paul able to heal another of his close companions, Trophimus, whom he had to leave sick at Miletus (2 Tim. 4:20).

The early days of the Jerusalem church were punctuated by signs and wonders (Acts 2:43; 5:12). Yet Acts records no miracles in that city after Stephen's martyrdom (cf. Acts 6:8). Some might argue that the apostles left the city, and thus were not present to perform miracles. Yet they remained in Jerusalem after the outbreak of the persecution associated with the death of Stephen (Acts 8:1). The supernatural invincibility afforded the apostles during the early years (cf. Acts 12:6–11) was also gradually withdrawn, and nearly all of the apostles were martyred. Finally, the writer of Hebrews spoke both of the apostles ("those who heard" the Lord) and of the signs and wonders they performed in the past tense (Heb. 2:3–4). Both the time of the apostles and the miracles associated with them were passing away.

Their qualifications and foundational role in God's plan for the church made the apostles unique. Having laid the solid doctrinal foundation for the church, they passed from the scene, never to be replaced. Apostles, signs, wonders, and miracles are not normative for the church today. What is normative is the Bible, which is complete (Jude 3; Rev. 22:18), stands forever (Isa. 40:8; Matt. 5:17–18; 24:35), and is "profitable for teaching, for reproof, for correction, for training in righteousness; so that the man of God may be adequate, equipped for every good work" (2 Tim. 3:16–17).

Concerns of a True Pastor
(2 Corinthians 12:12–19)

33

The signs of a true apostle were performed among you with all perseverance, by signs and wonders and miracles. For in what respect were you treated as inferior to the rest of the churches, except that I myself did not become a burden to you? Forgive me this wrong! Here for this third time I am ready to come to you, and I will not be a burden to you; for I do not seek what is yours, but you; for children are not responsible to save up for their parents, but parents for their children. I will most gladly spend and be expended for your souls. If I love you more, am I to be loved less? But be that as it may, I did not burden you myself; nevertheless, crafty fellow that I am, I took you in by deceit. Certainly I have not taken advantage of you through any of those whom I have sent to you, have I? I urged Titus to go, and I sent the brother with him. Titus did not take any advantage of you, did he? Did we not conduct ourselves in the same spirit and walk in the same steps? All this time you have been thinking that we are defending ourselves to you. Actually, it is in the sight of God that we have been speaking in Christ; and all for your upbuilding, beloved. (12:12–19)

The church today faces an identity crisis generated by being inundated with a vast amount of literature on pastoral ministry and church leadership, promoting a myriad of different approaches, styles, and techniques. Pastors face a bewildering number of choices as they seek the key to growing their own churches. They read books, attend seminars, follow programs promoted by church-growth gurus, and pattern their leadership style after successful pastors. But all too often, the programs, methods, and gimmicks fail to achieve spiritual results, cheating both pastors and congregations of the true blessings of God.

Based on the enormous volume of available material, pastoral ministry would seem to be very complicated indeed. In actuality, however, it is confoundingly simple. The principles and directions for successful ministry that are laid out in Scripture are sufficient to fully equip the man of God (2 Cor. 3:5–6; cf. 2 Tim. 3:16–17). Instead of studying demographics and marketing techniques, or searching for cultural hot buttons to push, the church needs to understand and obey biblical truth. Methods and trends come and go, and today's sensational new programs will be tomorrow's failed experiments. But the principles of godly truth and virtue that characterize an effective minister are timeless. Power and effectiveness in the ministry come from a heart that is right before God and passionately concerned about His plan and His people. (For a treatment of biblical principles of ministry, see John MacArthur, ed., *Rediscovering Pastoral Ministry* [Dallas: Word, 1995].)

Nowhere is there a better model of a godly spiritual leader than the apostle Paul. In this very personal section of the most pastoral of all his letters, Paul did not share a personal philosophy of ministry or delineate a methodology for church growth. Instead, he opened his heart, revealing his spiritual aspirations and motives. Paul's success in the ministry was the overflow of his godly life. He was a man who was focused on the right goals, driven by the right passions, and motivated by the right desires.

The backdrop of this section, as it is for the entire epistle, is the devastating assault on the Corinthian church by false apostles. As noted in previous chapters of this volume, they had savagely attacked Paul's credibility, forcing him to defend himself by presenting his apostolic credentials. This section continues Paul's sharp differentiation of himself from the false apostles, contrasting his correct view of the ministry with their wrong view. It does so by revealing five vital concerns of Paul's heart with regard to the world, himself, the ministry, the Lord, and the church. In all those areas, Paul's godly attitudes contrasted with the ungodly ones of the false apostles, who typify those of all false teachers.

First, concerning the world, false teachers are proud. They seek fame, popularity, and prestige, playing to the crowds and thrusting themselves into the limelight.

Second, concerning themselves, false teachers are selfish. Their own comfort and prosperity are their highest priorities.

Third, concerning the ministry, false teachers are deceptive. As did the false apostles at Corinth, they can weave a very sophisticated web of lies. Often, they are able to engage other people in their deceitful enterprises, lending them a façade of credibility.

Fourth, concerning God, false teachers are blasphemous and irreverent. They have no regard for His person, His truth, His Word, or His glory.

Finally, concerning the church, false teachers are destructive. They use people, abuse them, and lead them into sin and error.

This passage exposes Paul's concerns as a true man of God. In contrast to the five wrong attitudes noted above that mark false teachers, Paul and all true men of God are known by their concerns regarding the world (faithfulness), themselves (sacrifice), the ministry (honesty), the Lord (reverence), and the church (edification).

PAUL'S CONCERN WITH
REGARD TO THE WORLD: FAITHFULNESS

with all perseverance, (12:12b)

Unlike the false apostles, who sought wealth, fame, and power, Paul's goal was to be faithful to the Lord. Because he was determined to be loyal to God's will no matter what the cost, he performed the signs of an apostle (see chapter 32 of this volume) **with all perseverance.** Despite all the hostility, opposition, and persecution from the world he faced, Paul remained faithful.

Hupomonē (**perseverance**) literally means, "to remain under." Paul endured the pressure of worldly opposition throughout his ministry without abandoning his position. The apostle knew, as he wrote to the Romans, "that tribulation brings about perseverance" (Rom. 5:3). Earlier in this epistle he wrote, "But if we are afflicted, it is for your comfort and salvation; or if we are comforted, it is for your comfort, which is effective in the patient enduring [*hupomonē*] of the same sufferings which we also suffer" (2 Cor. 1:6). He commended himself as a servant of God "in much endurance" (6:4).

The Lord Jesus Christ predicted that His apostles would be persecuted. In John 15:18–21 He warned them,

> If the world hates you, you know that it has hated Me before it hated you. If you were of the world, the world would love its own; but because you are not of the world, but I chose you out of the world, because of

this the world hates you. Remember the word that I said to you, "A slave is not greater than his master." If they persecuted Me, they will also persecute you; if they kept My word, they will keep yours also. But all these things they will do to you for My name's sake, because they do not know the One who sent Me.

Later in that same Upper Room Discourse the Lord added,

They will make you outcasts from the synagogue, but an hour is coming for everyone who kills you to think that he is offering service to God. . . . These things I have spoken to you, so that in Me you may have peace. In the world you have tribulation, but take courage; I have overcome the world. (16:2, 33; cf. Matt. 10:14; Luke 9:5; John 21:18–19)

Like the Twelve, Paul ministered with joy under constant duress and relentless persecution. As he wrote in his first inspired letter to the Corinthians, "I affirm, brethren, by the boasting in you which I have in Christ Jesus our Lord, I die daily" (1 Cor. 15:31). He lived every day knowing it could be his last; the mob in the next town he preached in (cf. Acts 17:5–9; 19:23–41) might take his life, or one of the numerous Jewish plots against his life (Acts 20:19) might finally succeed. Not surprisingly, Paul's affliction was a constant theme in this epistle. He described it in detail in 1:3–9:

Blessed be the God and Father of our Lord Jesus Christ, the Father of mercies and God of all comfort, who comforts us in all our affliction so that we will be able to comfort those who are in any affliction with the comfort with which we ourselves are comforted by God. For just as the sufferings of Christ are ours in abundance, so also our comfort is abundant through Christ. But if we are afflicted, it is for your comfort and salvation; or if we are comforted, it is for your comfort, which is effective in the patient enduring of the same sufferings which we also suffer; and our hope for you is firmly grounded, knowing that as you are sharers of our sufferings, so also you are sharers of our comfort. For we do not want you to be unaware, brethren, of our affliction which came to us in Asia, that we were burdened excessively, beyond our strength, so that we despaired even of life; indeed, we had the sentence of death within ourselves so that we would not trust in ourselves, but in God who raises the dead. (cf. 4:7–12; 6:4–10; 7:5; 11:22–33; 12:7–10; Acts 9:16)

God's spokesmen have always faced opposition and hostility. He warned Jeremiah, "'Now, gird up your loins and arise, and speak to them all which I command you. Do not be dismayed before them, or I will dismay you before them. . . . They will fight against you, but they will not overcome you, for I am with you to deliver you,' declares the Lord" (Jer. 1:17, 19). He charged Ezekiel, "And you, son of man, neither fear them nor fear their words, though thistles and thorns are with you and you sit on scorpions; neither fear their words nor be dismayed at their presence, for they are a rebellious house" (Ezek. 2:6). John the Baptist was the greatest man who had lived up to his time (Matt. 11:11), yet he suffered imprisonment (Matt. 14:3) and martyrdom (Matt. 14:10).

The persecution that attends the preaching of the Word results from three causes. First, God may sovereignly bring it for His own purposes: to test His preachers' faithfulness, break their pride, humble them, and draw them closer to Himself. Earlier, Paul acknowledged God's purpose in permitting the messenger of Satan that afflicted him:

> Because of the surpassing greatness of the revelations, for this reason, to keep me from exalting myself, there was given me a thorn in the flesh, a messenger of Satan to torment me—to keep me from exalting myself! Concerning this I implored the Lord three times that it might leave me. And He has said to me, "My grace is sufficient for you, for power is perfected in weakness." Most gladly, therefore, I will rather boast about my weaknesses, so that the power of Christ may dwell in me. Therefore I am well content with weaknesses, with insults, with distresses, with persecutions, with difficulties, for Christ's sake; for when I am weak, then I am strong. (12:7–10)

Persecution also comes from the evil world system that is unalterably opposed to God, yet allowed by Him. Because the Word exposes and judges sin, those who proclaim it will inevitably face the world's hostility.

Satan, who is behind the world system, also persecutes God's messengers. He bitterly opposes the church and seeks to destroy it. His plan is first to strike down the shepherds, then to scatter the flock (cf. Zech. 13:7; Matt. 26:31).

On the other hand, false prophets do not face such opposition. Because they do not preach the truth, but deceitful, damning lies, the world welcomes them enthusiastically. They are, in fact, part of the world system. Nor do they face persecution from Satan; since they are his servants it would be counterproductive to attack them (cf. Matt. 12:26).

Because they proclaim God's Word and call sinners to repentance, the unbelieving world views true ministers of Jesus Christ as their enemies. They hate those who bear the message of truth and light, because they hate the Truth and the Light (John 3:20; cf. 15:18–19; 17:14; Matt. 10:22; 24:9; Luke 6:22; 1 John 3:13). It is essential, however, that preachers be hated solely for the cause of Christ, not any wrongdoing on their part; the preaching of the gospel must be the only offense they give.

Like Paul, they must be determined to give "no cause for offense in anything, so that the ministry will not be discredited" (2 Cor. 6:3; cf. 1:12; 8:20; 1 Cor. 9:12; 10:32–33).

Because the world has nothing of lasting value to offer them, God's servants seek an eternal reward. Jesus told His followers, "Blessed are you when people insult you and persecute you, and falsely say all kinds of evil against you because of Me. Rejoice and be glad, for your reward in heaven is great" (Matt. 5:11–12). In 1 Corinthians 3:8 Paul wrote, "Now he who plants and he who waters are one; but each will receive his own reward according to his own labor." At the end of his life Paul wrote triumphantly to Timothy, "In the future there is laid up for me the crown of righteousness, which the Lord, the righteous Judge, will award to me on that day; and not only to me, but also to all who have loved His appearing" (2 Tim. 4:8). The writer of Hebrews reminded his readers that "God . . . is a rewarder of those who seek Him" (Heb. 11:6).

False teachers work for earthly rewards; true preachers work faithfully for a heavenly reward. Paul was determined to remain loyal to his calling despite the hostility from the world, knowing that "momentary, light affliction is producing for us an eternal weight of glory far beyond all comparison" (2 Cor. 4:17; cf. Rom. 8:18; 1 Peter 4:13).

PAUL'S CONCERN WITH
REGARD TO HIMSELF: SACRIFICE

For in what respect were you treated as inferior to the rest of the churches, except that I myself did not become a burden to you? Forgive me this wrong! Here for this third time I am ready to come to you, and I will not be a burden to you; for I do not seek what is yours, but you; for children are not responsible to save up for their parents, but parents for their children. I will most gladly spend and be expended for your souls. If I love you more, am I to be loved less? But be that as it may, I did not burden you myself; (12:13–16a)

Micah 3:2–3, 5 graphically depicts false teachers as greedy, grasping, and self-centered:

> You who hate good and love evil,
> Who tear off their skin from them
> And their flesh from their bones,
> Who eat the flesh of my people,
> Strip off their skin from them,
> Break their bones

> And chop them up as for the pot
> And as meat in a kettle. . . .
> Thus says the Lord concerning the prophets
> Who lead my people astray;
> When they have something to bite with their teeth,
> They cry, "Peace,"
> But against him who puts nothing in their mouths
> They declare holy war.
> (cf. Ezek. 34:2–3; Zech. 11:16; Mark 12:38–40)

True men of God are the opposite; they are selfless and sacrificial. One of the many slanderous accusations the false apostles made against Paul was that his treatment of the Corinthians had been selfishly substandard. That allegation was false, as Paul's question, **In what respect were you treated as inferior to the rest of the churches?** reveals. As verse 12 indicates, Paul had ministered in the same way in Corinth that he had in other churches (cf. Rom. 15:19).

The only way the Corinthians were treated differently was that Paul **did not become a burden to** them; the only thing they did not get from him was a bill. Although he had a right to their support (1 Cor. 9:1–18), Paul chose not to accept it, preferring to distance himself from the money-loving false apostles. They, of course, took everything they could get from the Corinthians (cf. 2 Cor. 11:20) and hated Paul for making them look bad. To salvage their reputations, they attempted to put a negative spin on Paul's selflessness. They argued first that he refused to take money from the Corinthians because he knew his ministry was worthless. A second and more sinister allegation was that Paul did not want the Corinthians' money because he did not love them and thus did not want to be obligated to them. But as Paul has already shown, those allegations were completely false. In 11:7–9 he wrote,

> Did I commit a sin in humbling myself so that you might be exalted, because I preached the gospel of God to you without charge? I robbed other churches by taking wages from them to serve you; and when I was present with you and was in need, I was not a burden to anyone; for when the brethren came from Macedonia they fully supplied my need, and in everything I kept myself from being a burden to you, and will continue to do so. (cf. the discussion of this passage in chapter 28 of this volume)

Resorting again to sarcasm (cf. 11:19–21; 1 Cor. 4:8–10) to bring the Corinthians to their senses Paul exclaimed, **Forgive me this wrong!** The false apostles' claim that he had mistreated the Corinthians by not taking money from them was ludicrous. The only thing they had been deprived of was the burden of supporting Paul and his companions.

On Paul's first visit to Corinth he founded the church (Acts 18); his second was the painful disciplinary visit described in 2:1 (cf. 13:2). When he visited Corinth for the **third time** he would still refuse to **be a burden to** the church. Paul's selfless pastoral love for the Corinthians meant that he did **not seek what** was theirs, **but** them. He did not want their money; he wanted their hearts. He wanted their lives for the king- dom of God, and for them to live in righteous obedience to the Word for the glory of God.

Paul illustrated his point using the analogy of parents caring for their children, pointing out the axiomatic truth that **children are not responsible to save up for their parents, but parents for their chil- dren.** The Corinthians were, of course, Paul's spiritual children (1 Cor. 4:15), and he willingly sacrificed himself for them. He would, he wrote, **most gladly spend and be expended for** the spiritual well-being of their **souls.** The superlative form of the adjective *hēdeōs* (**most gladly**) expresses extreme elation. Paul was not reluctant or hesitant to sacrifice for the Corinthians; he was thrilled, or overjoyed, at being able to **spend and be expended for** them. **Spend** translates a form of the verb *dapanaō*, which means, "to spend freely." Mark 5:26 uses it in reference to a woman who had spent all her money on physicians, while in Luke 15:14 it describes the prodigal son's profligate spending. *Ekdapanaō* (**be expended**) appears only here in the New Testament. It is a strengthened form of *dapanaō* and means, "to be completely spent." Paul was willing to sacrifice himself for his people until he had nothing left to give. To the Philippians he wrote, "But even if I am being poured out as a drink offer- ing upon the sacrifice and service of your faith, I rejoice and share my joy with you all" (Phil. 2:17; cf. Col. 1:24). He followed the example of the Lord Jesus Christ, who said of Himself, "For even the Son of Man did not come to be served, but to serve, and to give His life a ransom for many" (Mark 10:45).

Sadly, the Corinthians responded inversely to Paul's self-sacrificial love for them, prompting the apostle's pathetic heart cry, **If I love you more, am I to be loved less?** The relationship was going backwards; the more affection he gave them, the less they returned (cf. 2 Cor. 6:11– 13). Paul had poured his life into the Corinthian church, joyously labor- ing and sacrificing for them. All he asked for in return was their love —and they were unwilling to give it.

Paul was saddened but undeterred by the Corinthians' disap- pointing response to his sacrificial love for them. **But be that as it may**—despite their unreturned love for him—Paul would still not be a **burden** to them. Their love may have diminished, but his would not.

Despite their diffidence, coldness, and disaffection, he would continue to love them sacrificially.

PAUL'S CONCERN WITH
REGARD TO THE MINISTRY: HONESTY

nevertheless, crafty fellow that I am, I took you in by deceit. Certainly I have not taken advantage of you through any of those whom I have sent to you, have I? I urged Titus to go, and I sent the brother with him. Titus did not take any advantage of you, did he? Did we not conduct ourselves in the same spirit and walk in the same steps? (12:16b–18)

If Paul was plotting to defraud the Corinthians, as the false apostles charged, the point of his plot was not immediately obvious. As noted in the previous point, he took nothing from them. The idea that he would run a scam that netted him nothing was absurd, and Paul rebuked the Corinthians once again for their naiveté, writing sarcastically, **Nevertheless, crafty fellow that I am, I took you in by deceit.** That was, no doubt, what the false apostles were saying about him. *Panourgos* (**crafty fellow**), used only here in the New Testament, literally means, "ready to do anything." It has the negative connotation of "unscrupulous," "tricky," or "deceptive." *Dolos* (**deceit**) refers literally to bait used to catch fish. Paul, so the false teachers claimed, was willing to do anything to hook the Corinthians with his devious scheme.

To get around the glaringly obvious difficulty that Paul had not taken any money from the Corinthians, the false apostles insisted that he had not yet sprung his trap. Paul had already described in detail the collection he was taking for the poor saints at Jerusalem (chaps. 8, 9). That, according to the false apostles, was the point of Paul's scheme; the money that was collected at Corinth would never reach Jerusalem. Instead, they claimed, it would go to line Paul's pockets. After all, that is what they would have done if they were in his place. The false apostles projected their own greedy attitude onto Paul and assumed that he was acting as they would have. They exemplified the truth that "to the pure, all things are pure; but to those who are defiled and unbelieving, nothing is pure, but both their mind and their conscience are defiled" (Titus 1:15).

To refute the false teachers' outrageous accusation, Paul reminded the Corinthians that he was not acting alone in taking the collection. Not only had he not personally defrauded the Corinthians, but he also had **not taken advantage of** them **through any of those whom** he had **sent to** Corinth. By impugning Paul's motives, the false apostles were also impugning those of his ministry partners who were also involved in the collection. If Paul had, as the false apostles insisted, planned to embezzle the collection, he could not have acted alone. There would have had to have been collusion between him and his ministry partners. That, of course, made the allegations even more far-fetched. **Titus,** whom the Corinthians knew well (cf. 8:23), was also involved in the collection (cf. 2 Cor. 8:6, 16). In addition, two unnamed brothers in Christ (8:18–19, 22) had assisted him. One of those two was "the brother whose fame in the things of the gospel [had] spread through all the churches" (8:18) and who had been "appointed by the churches to travel with [Paul and the others] in this gracious work [the collection]" (8:19); the other was a man who had been "often tested and found diligent in many things" (8:22). The idea that three such highly respected individuals would join Paul in a plot to defraud the Corinthians was completely absurd. But if they were not involved in any such plot, how could Paul have been? **Did we not conduct ourselves in the same spirit,** Paul demanded, **and walk in the same steps?** They had all acted with the same integrity and honesty toward the Corinthians, and they knew it.

Honesty is a nonnegotiable characteristic of a true man of God. To the Romans Paul wrote, "I am telling the truth in Christ, I am not lying, my conscience testifies with me in the Holy Spirit" (Rom. 9:1). Earlier in this epistle he testified, "The God and Father of the Lord Jesus, He who is blessed forever, knows that I am not lying" (2 Cor. 11:31). He assured the Galatians, "(Now in what I am writing to you, I assure you before God that I am not lying)" (Gal. 1:20). To Timothy he wrote, "For this I was appointed a preacher and an apostle (I am telling the truth, I am not lying) as a teacher of the Gentiles in faith and truth" (1 Tim. 2:7).

Paul's complete truthfulness led him to declare, "For our proud confidence is this: the testimony of our conscience, that in holiness and godly sincerity, not in fleshly wisdom but in the grace of God, we have conducted ourselves in the world, and especially toward you" (2 Cor. 1:12), and "We have renounced the things hidden because of shame, not walking in craftiness or adulterating the word of God, but by the manifestation of truth commending ourselves to every man's conscience in the sight of God" (4:2). The Corinthians knew that he had ministered among them without deceit.

PAUL'S CONCERN WITH
REGARD TO THE LORD: REVERENCE

All this time you have been thinking that we are defending ourselves to you. Actually, it is in the sight of God that we have been speaking in Christ; (12:19a)

Paul did not want the Corinthians to misinterpret his lengthy defense of his apostleship and integrity. He was not on trial before them, and they were not his judges. Still less was he making excuses for blemishes in his character and lapses in his conduct, as the false apostles insinuated.

Through **all this time** (i.e., through the entire epistle) they had **been thinking that** Paul was **defending** himself **to** them. **Actually,** Paul stood before a divine tribunal; **it** was **in the sight of God that** he had **been speaking in Christ** (cf. 2:17). God is the only audience the faithful preacher is concerned about. He had made that quite clear when he wrote in 1 Corinthians 4:3–5,

> But to me it is a very small thing that I may be examined by you, or by any human court; in fact, I do not even examine myself. For I am conscious of nothing against myself, yet I am not by this acquitted; but the one who examines me is the Lord. Therefore do not go on passing judgment before the time, but wait until the Lord comes who will both bring to light the things hidden in the darkness and disclose the motives of men's hearts; and then each man's praise will come to him from God.

Earlier in this epistle Paul affirmed, "For we must all appear before the judgment seat of Christ, so that each one may be recompensed for his deeds in the body, according to what he has done, whether good or bad" (2 Cor. 5:10). To Timothy he wrote, "I solemnly charge you in the presence of God and of Christ Jesus, who is to judge the living and the dead, and by His appearing and His kingdom: preach the word; be ready in season and out of season; reprove, rebuke, exhort, with great patience and instruction" (2 Tim. 4:1–2). Later in that same chapter Paul reminded Timothy, "In the future there is laid up for me the crown of righteousness, which the Lord, the righteous Judge, will award to me on that day; and not only to me, but also to all who have loved His appearing" (v. 8). Paul knew that God alone would render the final verdict on his life—and that verdict would be, "Well done, good and faithful slave.... Enter into the joy of your master" (Matt. 25:21).

PAUL'S CONCERN WITH
REGARD TO THE CHURCH: EDIFICATION

and all for your upbuilding, beloved (12:19b)

Paul's goal in everything he did in relation to the Corinthian church, both in ministering to them and defending himself, was their

upbuilding. That was also the goal of the Lord Jesus Christ, who promised, "I will build My church; and the gates of Hades will not overpower it" (Matt. 16:18).

The question naturally arises, since God was Paul's Judge, Why should he bother to defend himself? He did so because if he were discredited the Corinthians would not listen to him; if they did not listen to him, they would not hear the truth of the Word of God that he taught; if they did not hear the Word of God, they could not grow spiritually.

The tender term **beloved** reminded the Corinthians that though he was at times exasperated with them, Paul nevertheless loved them as his spiritual children. It was not his intent to use his apostolic authority to destroy them; God gave him that authority "for building [them] up and not for destroying [them]" (2 Cor. 10:8; cf. 13:10). The Corinthians were not Paul's judges, but they were his spiritual responsibility.

That reality marks the transition to the closing section of this epistle, which deals with the edification of the church and the sanctification of its members. The elements of a sanctified church will be the theme of the closing chapters of this volume.

The Pattern of Sanctification: Repentance (2 Corinthians 12:20–21)

34

For I am afraid that perhaps when I come I may find you to be not what I wish and may be found by you to be not what you wish; that perhaps there will be strife, jealousy, angry tempers, disputes, slanders, gossip, arrogance, disturbances; I am afraid that when I come again my God may humiliate me before you, and I may mourn over many of those who have sinned in the past and not repented of the impurity, immorality and sensuality which they have practiced. (12:20–21)

The role of the pastor today is at a crossroads. As the church grows increasingly worldly, so also does the pastor's job description. He is often viewed (either by himself or by his congregation) as a CEO, entertainer, fund-raiser, master of ceremonies, or psychologist.

None of those perspectives are in harmony with the biblical model of spiritual leadership. The primary function of a pastor or elder according to Scripture can be summed up in one word: edification. A pastor's main concern is the spiritual maturity of the believers under his care, as Paul made clear in Ephesians 4:11–13:

> And He gave some as apostles, and some as prophets, and some as evangelists, and some as pastors and teachers, for the equipping of the

saints for the work of service, to the building up of the body of Christ; until we all attain to the unity of the faith, and of the knowledge of the Son of God, to a mature man, to the measure of the stature which belongs to the fullness of Christ.

In its broadest, most significant sense, the pastor's role is to build the church by maturing the saints, helping them become more like Jesus Christ.

The biblical emphasis on spiritual maturity contrasts sharply with that of many churches. The issues of life in this world—illness, economic problems, marital and family struggles, and political and social matters—are their main concern. But the church's role is not to make its members more comfortable in a world in which they are "aliens and strangers" (1 Peter 2:11; cf. 1:1,17; 1 Chron. 29:15; Heb. 11:13), but to prepare them for their true home in heaven (Ps. 73:25; Matt. 6:20; 19:21; Luke 6:22–23; 12:21,33; 2 Cor. 4:18; 5:1–4,8; Phil. 3:20; Col. 1:5; 1 Peter 1:4).

Like any true man of God, the apostle Paul's passionate concern was the spiritual well-being of believers. His hopes, fears, desires, and expectations focused on their sanctification. He expressed that concern in two terms that bracket this section of his epistle: "upbuilding" (2 Cor. 12:19), and "building up" (13:10). In between, he described the process of sanctification. In verses 20 and 21, the apostle outlined the first step in accomplishing that objective: repentance.

Repentance is an essential element of the gospel, since no one can come to Jesus Christ apart from the complete change of heart, mind, and will that constitutes repentance. Repentance was at the heart of the gospel message proclaimed by John the Baptist (Matt. 3:2, 8), the Lord Jesus Christ (Matt. 4:17; Mark 1:15; Luke 13:3,5; 15:7,10), the Twelve (Mark 6:12; Acts 2:38; 3:19; 11:18), and the apostle Paul (Acts 17:30; 20:21; 2 Cor. 7:9–11; 2 Tim. 2:25). It is central to the Great Commission that Christ gave to the church (Luke 24:47).

Despite its critical importance, however, repentance is a needlessly misunderstood and controversial topic in contemporary Christianity. Some would strip repentance of any connection with sin, defining it as merely a change of mind about who Christ is. They see it as merely a synonym for faith that does not involve turning from sin. Writes one advocate of that view, "Repentance means to change one's mind; it does not mean to change one's life" (Thomas L. Constable, "The Gospel Message," in Donald K. Campbell, ed., *Walvoord: A Tribute* [Chicago: Moody, 1982],207).

But Scripture knows nothing of a repentance that does not involve turning from sin. In the Old Testament Isaiah cried out, "Let the wicked forsake his way and the unrighteous man his thoughts; and let him return to the Lord, and He will have compassion on him, and to our God, for He will abundantly pardon" (Isa. 55:7). In Luke 5:32 the Lord also connected repentance and sin, declaring, "I have not come to call the righteous but sinners to repentance." As noted above, Jesus declared in Luke's account of the Great Commission that "repentance *for forgiveness of sins* would be proclaimed in His name to all the nations, beginning from Jerusalem" (Luke 24:47; italics added). Paul told King Agrippa that the message he proclaimed was "that [people] should repent and turn to God, performing deeds appropriate to repentance" (Acts 26:20; cf. Matt. 3:8). Scripture characterizes unbelievers as those who will "not repent of their deeds" (Rev. 16:11; cf. 9:20–21). (I define repentance at length in my books *The Gospel According to Jesus*, rev. ed. [Grand Rapids: Zondervan, 1994], and *The Gospel According to the Apostles* [Nashville: Word, 2000].)

Repentance is the necessary first step in the sanctification process, because sin inhibits spiritual growth. Sin is anything that displeases God, and nothing that displeases Him can contribute to the process of sanctification. Like faith, repentance is not a one-time act at conversion but is characteristic of living the Christian life (cf. 1 John 1:9). Therefore, dealing with sinning Christians is an essential aspect of the pastor's role. His deep concern must be to call them to repentance.

To motivate the Corinthians to repent, the apostle pointed out two damaging consequences of impenitence: the problems it caused for them and the pain it caused for him.

THE PROBLEMS CAUSED BY THE CORINTHIANS' UNREPENTANT SIN

For I am afraid that perhaps when I come I may find you to be not what I wish and may be found by you to be not what you wish; that perhaps there will be strife, jealousy, angry tempers, disputes, slanders, gossip, arrogance, disturbances; ... the impurity, immorality and sensuality which they have practiced. (12:20, 21b)

Paul's fears concerning the Corinthians' sins were well founded, given their history. He had dealt extensively with sin in their congregation in 1 Corinthians and in the severe letter (2:3–4), and had even made a visit to Corinth to confront their sin and rebellion in person (2:1). With good reason, then, he was **afraid that perhaps when** he visited them for the third time (12:14; 13:1) there would still be unrepentant sin in their assembly. The apostle knew that there was great potential for that, even though the majority of the congregation had repented (cf. 7:6–11), and he had expressed his confidence in them (7:16). Sin and error die hard, and the false teachers were still around, spouting their deadly heresy. As Paul well knew, theological error inevitably leads to sin in practice.

Afraid translates a form of the verb *phobeō*, from which the English word *phobia* derives. It refers to an intense, deep-seated anxiety, fear, or misgiving, and expresses Paul's great concern over the situation at Corinth. As he wrote in 11:29, "Who is led into sin without my intense concern?" Nothing is more painful for the faithful pastor than unrepentant sin among his flock.

Paul's use of the term **perhaps** shows his restraint and tenderness. Rather than making a complete denunciation of the Corinthians, the apostle merely expressed his concern and misgivings. When he arrived in Corinth, he would determine their spiritual condition and take the appropriate action. In the meantime, he wrote this epistle to begin the process of rooting out the noxious weeds of unrepentant sin in the church.

Specifically, Paul feared first of all that he might **find** the Corinthians **to be not what** he would **wish** them to be. His **wish,** of course, was for them to be growing in grace, becoming more like Jesus Christ, and repenting of their sin; his fear was that their spiritual growth would be hindered by unrepentant sin. Should that prove to be the case, the Corinthians would find Paul **to be not what** they would **wish.** Instead of loving affirmation, he would bring stern discipline. As he asked them pointedly in 1 Corinthians 4:21, "What do you desire? Shall I come to you with a rod, or with love and a spirit of gentleness?" The choice was theirs. If they repented of their sin, he would arrive in love and gentleness. If they did not, he would come with the rod of discipline.

So that the Corinthians would be forewarned, Paul listed some of the sins that could cause such a troublesome and tragic meeting. As are his other lists of sins, (e.g., Rom. 1:28–31; 1 Cor. 6:9–10; Gal. 5:19–21; Col. 3:8–9), this one is not exhaustive but is typical of the sins with which the Corinthians struggled. The sins on it may be divided into two broad categories.

The first group involves sins of personal conflict that destroy the church's unity, which Paul wanted preserved at all costs (Eph. 4:3, 13; cf. John 17:21; 1 Cor. 1:10). They were typical of the divisive, selfish, pagan behavior of Corinthian society and were exacerbated by the destructive influence of the false apostles. That such sins existed in the Corinthian church is evident from the fact that all of them were also addressed in 1 Corinthians.

Eris (**strife**) describes the contention, conflict, and quarrels that result from enmity and dissension. According to Romans 1:29, it characterizes unbelievers, and Paul warned the Roman Christians to avoid it (Rom. 13:13). Galatians 5:20 includes it as one of the deeds of the flesh, while in Philippians 1:15 it characterizes those who preached Christ from selfish motives. The apostle also warned of the **strife** caused by false teachers (1 Tim. 6:4) and false teaching (Titus 3:9). Paul had already cautioned the Corinthians against this sin in 1 Corinthians 1:11 ("quarrels") and 3:3.

Zēlos can have the positive connotation of godly zeal (2 Cor. 7:7, 11; 9:2; 11:2; John 2:17), but here it has the negative one of **jealousy,** the grasping, protective, self-centeredness that causes people to be suspicious of others as potential rivals. In the New Testament it marked, among others, the high priest and the Sadducees (Acts 5:17) and the unbelieving Jews at Pisidian Antioch (Acts 13:45). Paul warned the Romans to avoid it (Rom. 13:13) and listed it among the deeds of the flesh (Gal. 5:20). James warned his readers that **jealousy** was a hallmark of earthly, demonic wisdom (James 3:14, 16). It, too, had crept into the Corinthian church (1 Cor. 3:3).

Angry tempers translates *thumos,* which means, "rage" or "violent anger," the anger that flares up in an instant. It marked the synagogue congregation at Nazareth that became enraged at Jesus' teaching (Luke 4:28), the pagan crowd that rioted at Ephesus (Acts 19:28), and Satan's rage (Rev. 12:12). It, too, is one of the deeds of the flesh (Gal. 5:20), and hence believers are to avoid it (Eph. 4:31; Col. 3:8). Though the word does not appear in 1 Corinthians, the Corinthians certainly exhibited **angry tempers** toward each other (cf. 1 Cor. 6:1ff.).

Eritheia (**disputes**) describes ambitious rivalries, factious attitudes, divisiveness, and partisanship. Paul used it of those who were "selfishly ambitious" (Rom. 2:8) and of those who preached Christ from "selfish ambition" (Phil. 1:17). *Eritheia* is also one of the deeds of the flesh and characterizes earthly, demonic wisdom (James 3:14, 16). It is the opposite of "humility of mind" (Phil. 2:3). Once again, although the word does not appear in 1 Corinthians, the concept does (cf. 1 Cor. 1:11ff.; 3:4ff.; 11:19).

Slanders translates the onomatopoeic word *katalalia* ("insults," "evil reports"), which appears only here and in 1 Peter 2:1. The related verb *katalaleō* is translated "speak against" in James 4:11. Using a different Greek word, Paul had warned the Corinthians not to associate with a "reviler" (1 Cor. 5:11; cf. 6:10). In contrast to **gossip,** which is quiet, subtle, behind-the-back defamation (the Greek verb rendered **gossip** means, "to whisper"), slander is open, public vilification. Both stem from **arrogance** (cf. 1 Cor. 4:6, 18, 19; 5:2; 8:1) and result in **disturbances.** The net result was the divisions that plagued the Corinthian church (1 Cor. 11:18).

In verse 21 Paul turned to three sins that destroy the church's purity. All three refer to sexual immorality, which was rife in the idolatrous pagan culture of Corinth—so much so that in Greek the verb "to Corinthianize" meant, "to go to bed with a prostitute" (cf. R. C. H. Lenski, *The Interpretation of the Acts of the Apostles* [Minneapolis: Augsburg, 1961], 744).

Akatharsia (**impurity**) is frequently associated in the New Testament with sexual sin. In Romans 1:24 Paul wrote of unregenerate mankind, "God gave them over in the lusts of their hearts to impurity, so that their bodies would be dishonored among them." Galatians 5:19 lists **impurity** as one of the deeds of the flesh, while in Ephesians 4:19 it characterizes the unregenerate who "having become callous, have given themselves over to sensuality for the practice of every kind of impurity." "Impurity . . . must not even be named among [believers]" (Eph. 5:3); they are to "consider the members of [their] earthly bod[ies] as dead to . . . impurity" (Col. 3:5), because "God has not called us for the purpose of impurity, but in sanctification" (1 Thess. 4:7).

Immorality translates *porneia,* the source of the English word *pornography.* Sometimes translated "fornication," *porneia* refers to any sexual act outside of marriage. Paul wrote in 1 Thessalonians 4:3, "For this is the will of God, your sanctification; that is, that you abstain from sexual immorality" (cf. Eph. 5:3; Col. 3:5). **Immorality** was an integral part of pagan religion (cf. Acts 15:20, 29; 21:25). In 1 Corinthians 5:1 Paul expressed his shock and dismay that the foolish Corinthians had proudly tolerated it in their assembly: "It is actually reported that there is immorality among you, and immorality of such a kind as does not exist even among the Gentiles, that someone has his father's wife." He told them plainly that "the body is not for immorality, but for the Lord" (1 Cor. 6:13) and warned them, "Flee immorality. Every other sin that a man commits is outside the body, but the immoral man sins against his own body" (1 Cor. 6:18).

Aselgeia (**sensuality**) describes public, unrestrained, flagrant, sexual sin. The King James Version translates it, "lasciviousness," or "wantonness"; other versions render it "licentiousness" In Romans 13:13 Paul associated it with such public sins as "carousing," "drunkenness," and "sexual promiscuity"; while Peter linked it to "lusts, drunkenness, carousing, drinking parties and abominable idolatries" (1 Peter 4:3). **Sensuality** is also one of the deeds of the flesh (Gal. 5:19), and characterizes the behavior of the unregenerate (Eph. 4:19), particularly false teachers (2 Peter 2:2, 18; Jude 4). Peter also used it to describe the unspeakably evil homosexual vice of the men of Sodom, who tried to rape angels (2 Peter 2:7).

Paul's great fear for the Corinthians was that, influenced by the false teachers, they would fall back into the sins **which they** had previously **practiced.** Like any pastor worthy of the title, Paul's passionate concern for his people was that they lead holy lives. That painful concern for their sanctification prompted him to call for their repentance.

THE PAIN CAUSED BY THE
CORINTHIANS' UNREPENTANT SIN

I am afraid that when I come again my God may humiliate me before you, and I may mourn over many of those who have sinned in the past and not repented (12:21*a*)

No pastor, of course, realistically expects his people to be sinless. Yet when they do sin, his heart yearns for them to repent and be restored to fellowship with God and other believers (cf. Gal. 6:1). To that end, he prays for them, exhorts them, and calls them to repentance.

Paul was **afraid that when** he came to Corinth he would find that **many of those who** had **sinned in the past** had **not repented.** The perfect tense participle *proēmartēkotōn* (**those who have sinned in the past**) refers to those whose sin began in the past and continues in the present. In other words, it describes those who were continuing in sin and refusing to repent. Should Paul find that in the Corinthian assembly, it would affect him in two ways.

First, it would deeply **humiliate** him. His credibility was at stake, for, as he wrote earlier in this epistle, the Corinthians were his "letter . . . known and read by all men" (2 Cor. 3:2). To have the Corinthian church, which Paul had pastored for nearly two years, marked by unrepentant sin would cause him shame. It would also give ammunition to those critics who attacked his authenticity. Paul had learned the valuable lesson of the importance of humility (12:7–10). But to be humbled by God was one thing; to be humiliated by the Corinthians' failure to repent was something else. Unrepentant sin in his congregation is heartbreaking, distressing, and discouraging for a pastor. It crushes him, saps his strength, and may, if unchecked, drive him out of his church, if not out of the ministry altogether. Understandably, then, Paul was anxious about what he would find when he arrived in Corinth.

Second, the unrepentant sin in the Corinthian congregation was a source of great sorrow to Paul. He did not write that he would be angry with those who refused to repent, but rather that he would **mourn over** them. *Pentheō* (**mourn**) refers to lamenting stemming from a deep-seated sorrow or grief, not to mere superficial sadness. Paul was so sick at heart over the situation at Corinth that he became depressed (7:6). Now he dreaded the sorrow he would experience if he again found unrepentant sinners in the Corinthian church. The apostle did not want to experience sorrow like that which he had experienced on his last visit to Corinth (2:1).

The faithful pastor's concern for the repentance of his people mirrors that of the Lord of the church. In the letters to the seven churches (Rev. 2, 3), the Lord Jesus Christ repeatedly called for repentance and warned of the consequences of failing to repent. His message to the church at Ephesus was, "Therefore remember from where you have fallen, and repent and do the deeds you did at first; or else I am coming to you and will remove your lampstand out of its place—unless you repent" (Rev. 2:5). "Therefore repent;" He warned the church at Pergamum, "or else I am coming to you quickly, and I will make war against them with the sword of My mouth" (Rev. 2:16). He declared of the false prophetess Jezebel in the church at Thyatira, "I gave her time to repent, and she does not want to repent of her immorality. Behold, I will throw her on a bed of sickness, and those who commit adultery with her into great tribulation, unless they repent of her deeds" (Rev. 2:21–22). He exhorted the church at Sardis, "Remember what you have received and heard; and keep it, and repent. Therefore if you do not wake up, I will come like a thief, and you will not know at what hour I will come to you" (Rev. 3:3). The Lord reminded the Laodicean church, "Those whom I love, I reprove and discipline; therefore be zealous and repent" (Rev. 3:19). Thus, Jesus had to rebuke five of the seven churches for harboring unrepentant sin. Only the faithful churches in Smyrna and Philadelphia escaped His call to repentance—not because their members were not sinning, but because they were repenting.

Paul's call for repentance not only echoed that of the Lord Jesus Christ, but also of God the Father, to whom David confessed, "A broken and a contrite heart, O God, You will not despise (Ps. 51:17; cf. Isa. 57:15; 66:2). The promise to those who do repent is God's gracious and complete forgiveness (Prov. 28:13; 1 John 1:9). Those who fail to repent face discipline, which will be the subject of the next chapter in this volume.

The Pattern of Sanctification: Discipline
(2 Corinthians 13:1–2)

35

This is the third time I am coming to you. Every fact is to be confirmed by the testimony of two or three witnesses. I have previously said when present the second time, and though now absent I say in advance to those who have sinned in the past and to all the rest as well, that if I come again I will not spare anyone, (13:1–2)

Every year since 1790 the president of the United States, as required by the Constitution, has delivered the "State of the Union" message to Congress and the American people. In his message, the president outlines his concerns, goals, priorities, and agenda for the nation. As loyal citizens (Rom. 13:1–7; 1 Peter 2:17), Christians should be concerned about the state of their country. But as those whose "citizenship is in heaven" (Phil. 3:20; cf. Eph. 2:19), they should be far more concerned about the state of God's kingdom.

Indeed, the present state of the church is a cause for grave concern, prompting widespread calls for renewal. Seminars, conferences, and books offer suggestions for remaking the church so it can better market itself to contemporary society. Self-styled experts sound dire warnings that the church's very existence is threatened. If it is to survive, they insist, it must reinvent itself. It must become more culturally relevant and improve the packaging and promoting of its message. They argue that the church must do a better job of targeting people's felt needs, and it must reach them with more efficient forms of communication than it currently employs.

To that end, a number of innovations have been proposed to save the church from the oblivion that these self-appointed experts believe threatens it. Some suggest developing virtual churches on the Internet. These would, in effect, be technologically updated versions of the drive-in church, where people can worship without the exposure of interacting with others. Such "cyber churches" would also offer the convenience of allowing people to "worship" from the comfort of their own homes. And if the service did not meet their felt needs, they could simply close their Internet browser.

Some would replace traditional churches with more congenial, less confrontational forums, such as house churches. They believe the low level of control, lack of structure and authority, and absence of historical and theological traditions in such settings would make unbelievers feel more comfortable. If the traditional church structure is to be retained, significant changes need to be made. Preachers must be replaced by presenters, who use no notes and do not hide behind pulpits. Presumably, that will generate a more positive response from their hearers. Sermons are obsolete, because one-way communication is ineffective. Furthermore, excessive references to Scripture should be avoided, because they are distracting to the biblically illiterate. Systematic Bible exposition will also have to go, because most people attend church sporadically and find it irritating to miss messages in a series.

Frankly, the idea that the church might go out of existence unless it reinvents itself in the fashion recommended by the so-called experts is a brash and irresponsible, if not blasphemous, assertion. Will God's plan, formed in eternity past, to call out a people for Himself, redeem them, and bring them to eternal glory be thwarted if the church fails to reinvent itself to fit worldly expectations? Is the church, which Jesus Himself promised to build, and which He declared would not be overpowered even by the "gates of Hades" (Matt. 16:18), to be rendered ineffective by a lack of cultural sensitivity and marketing savvy? Having purchased the church with His own blood (Acts 20:28; 1 Peter 1:18–19), will the Lord Jesus Christ stand by and allow it to be relegated to the scrap heap of history by its own ineptness?

The theories of the modern church-growth experts raise the crucial question of who determines what the church is to be. Many of the suggested changes noted above are the result of surveys. The idea is that the church, like any business, should find out what its customers want and then give it to them. Only then can it hope to remain relevant. That may be good marketing strategy, but it overlooks the fact that the church is not a business selling a commodity. The church's priorities are not determined by surveys of unbelievers or marginal Christians, but by the truth of God's Word, which discloses the will of the Head of the church—the Lord Jesus Christ.

What the church desperately needs, therefore, is consistent, faithful, clear theological exposition of the mind of the Lord as revealed on the pages of Scripture. Only then will it be equipped to effectively counter the moral and spiritual crises of our time. The church must submit to the authority of Scripture. When it does so, the result will not merely be sound information, but holiness, which is the key to the church's blessing and impact in the world.

Even though Scripture is clear that holiness is central to the Lord's will for the life of the church, the most neglected principle of the church-growth movement is the confrontation, restoration, or discipline of those who sin. To intrude on people's privacy and hold them accountable for their behavior seems the height of folly, certain to alienate people and destroy the church. Confronting sin seems outdated in an age of moral relativism and ambiguity. People want the freedom to do what they want. Churches have become fellowships of independent members, with minimal accountability to God and still less to each other. The result is an entire generation of pastors and church members who have no experience of the church confronting sinning people and calling them to repentance or removal; thus, no serious, personal dealing with sin, so essential to the spiritual virtue of the saints.

The biggest problem facing the church is not cultural insensitivity, but insensitivity to sin. The disinterest in confronting sinning people in the church for the purpose of repentance and restoration, or exclusion if they do not repent, is the most visible symptom of the church's moral and spiritual decline. It is its most disastrous failure, for it signals a lack of concern for holiness—to say nothing of a lack of reverence for the Lord of the church and a shallow commitment to Scripture. Its failure to practice church discipline is the most glaring evidence of the church's worldliness and a major reason for its impotence.

Underscoring its importance, the very first instruction the Lord Jesus Christ gave regarding the church concerned church discipline:

> If your brother sins, go and show him his fault in private; if he listens to you, you have won your brother. But if he does not listen to you, take one or two more with you, so that by the mouth of two or three witnesses every fact may be confirmed. If he refuses to listen to them, tell it to the church; and if he refuses to listen even to the church, let him be to you as a Gentile and a tax collector. (Matt. 18:15–17)

The vision of the glorified Christ in Revelation 1:12–16 symbolizes the concern for the purity of His church that He expressed in Matthew 18. His white hair (v. 14), reminiscent of that of the Ancient of Days in Daniel's vision (Dan. 7:9), symbolizes His divine wisdom. His laserlike eyes (v. 14), searching the depths of His church, reveal Christ's omniscience. Those attributes equip Him to judge His church, a judgment depicted by His glowing, burnished bronze feet (v. 15).

Thus, church discipline is not optional but is a critical element of life in the church prescribed and practiced by the Lord of the church Himself. God takes discipline so seriously that He Himself took the lives of two prominent unrepentant sinners in the early church (Ananias and Sapphira; Acts 5:1–11).

The church in the grossly wicked city of Corinth faced a crisis. Most of its members had come to Christ out of paganism and idolatry and brought some of the immoral practices associated with their former lifestyle into the church. In 1 Corinthians Paul confronted a long litany of iniquities they were still engaging in. As if that were not enough, the false teachers who had invaded the Corinthian church were leading it astray into further sin. The apostle was deeply concerned, not for the church's cultural relevance, but for its holiness. He knew that if the Corinthians failed to lead godly lives, the church would dishonor her Lord and be spiritually ineffective. A church that tolerates sin undermines the gospel, which proclaims transformation in Christ resulting in living a life of obedient righteousness (cf. Rom. 6:16–18).

Paul had expressed his concern for the Corinthians' purity in 2 Corinthians 11:2, where he wrote, "I am jealous for you with a godly jealousy; for I betrothed you to one husband, so that to Christ I might present you as a pure virgin." Paul's concern mirrored that of the Lord of the church, who desires to "present to Himself the church in all her glory, having no spot or wrinkle or any such thing; but that she would be holy and blameless" (Eph. 5:27). The true church consists only of believers, and its primary objective is not to make unbelievers feel comfortable but to bring believers to spiritual maturity.

In this epistle, which reflects the intense concern of his heart, Paul's goal was to edify the Corinthians and redirect their hearts away from the poisonous lies of the false teachers. The concluding section (2 Cor. 12:19–13:10) focuses on several key elements of the sanctification process. Paul discussed the first of those, repentance, in 12:20–21 (see chapter 34 of this volume). In 13:1–2 he turned to the next logical step in the sanctification process, church discipline, which addresses the issue of what to do with those who sin and refuse to repent. He discussed the motive for church discipline and the method of church discipline.

THE MOTIVE FOR CHURCH DISCIPLINE

This is the third time I am coming to you. . . . I have previously said when present the second time, and though now absent I say in advance to those who have sinned in the past and to all the rest as well, that if I come again I will not spare anyone, (13:1*a*, 2)

The most important reason for church discipline lies in God's oft-repeated charge to His people, "Be holy, for I am holy" (Lev. 11:44; cf. v. 45; 19:2; 20:7, 26; Ex. 22:31; Num. 15:40; Deut. 6:17–18; 7:6; 1 Peter 1:15–16; 2:9–12). Church discipline is sometimes necessary to help believers "cleanse [themselves] from all defilement of flesh and spirit, perfecting holiness in the fear of God" (2 Cor. 7:1).

God Himself disciplines His people so they can share His holiness (Heb. 12:10). Job 5:17 notes, "Behold, how happy is the man whom God reproves, so do not despise the discipline of the Almighty." The psalmist declared, "Blessed is the man whom You chasten, O Lord" (Ps. 94:12). Paul reminded the Corinthians, "But when we are judged, we are disciplined by the Lord so that we will not be condemned along with the world" (1 Cor. 11:32). The writer of Hebrews urged his readers not to forget "the exhortation which is addressed to [them] as sons, 'My son, do not regard lightly the discipline of the Lord, nor faint when you are reproved by Him; for those whom the Lord loves He disciplines, and He scourges every son whom He receives'" (Heb. 12:5–6; cf. Prov. 3:11–12). The Lord Jesus Christ declared in Revelation 3:19, "Those whom I love, I reprove and discipline; therefore be zealous and repent."

As part of that process, God has given the church the responsibility of disciplining its sinning members. As noted above, the first instruction Jesus gave the church involved discipline (Matt. 18:15–17). That is such a basic element of the church's life that Paul was outraged when the Corinthians failed to practice it. He strongly rebuked them for failing to discipline one of their members, who was living in unrepentant immorality:

> It is actually reported that there is immorality among you, and immorality of such a kind as does not exist even among the Gentiles, that someone has his father's wife. You have become arrogant and have not mourned instead, so that the one who had done this deed would be removed from your midst. . . . Your boasting is not good. Do you not know that a little leaven leavens the whole lump of dough? Clean out the old leaven so that you may be a new lump, just as you are in fact unleavened. . . . I wrote you in my letter not to associate with immoral people; I did not at all mean with the immoral people of this world, or with the covetous and swindlers, or with idolaters, for then you would

have to go out of the world. But actually, I wrote to you not to associate with any so-called brother if he is an immoral person, or covetous, or an idolater, or a reviler, or a drunkard, or a swindler—not even to eat with such a one. For what have I to do with judging outsiders? Do you not judge those who are within the church? But those who are outside, God judges. Remove the wicked man from among yourselves. (1 Cor. 5:1–2, 6–7, 9–13)

Nor was the situation at Corinth unique; Paul expected all churches to practice discipline. To the Thessalonians he wrote,

Now we command you, brethren, in the name of our Lord Jesus Christ, that you keep away from every brother who leads an unruly life and not according to the tradition which you received from us. . . . If anyone does not obey our instruction in this letter, take special note of that person and do not associate with him, so that he will be put to shame. Yet do not regard him as an enemy, but admonish him as a brother. (2 Thess. 3:6, 14–15)

He exhorted Titus, overseeing the churches on the island of Crete, "Reject a factious man after a first and second warning, knowing that such a man is perverted and is sinning, being self-condemned" (Titus 3:10–11).

Besides the obvious one of obedience to Scripture, there are at least two other important reasons for practicing church discipline. First, it is necessary to maintain the purity of the church's fellowship and also shows that the church takes seriously what the Bible says about sin. A second reason, and goal of church discipline, is to bring sinning believers to repentance and restoration—to the place of God's blessing. Some denounce the practice of church discipline as an unloving intrusion into peoples' private lives. But in reality it is the strongest expression of love, because love seeks to protect its objects from what would harm them. And nothing is more damaging to believers than unrepentant sin, which forfeits God's blessing and brings His chastening.

Paul not only preached church discipline but also practiced it. He had already put one unrepentant sinner out of the Corinthian church (1 Cor. 5:3–5; cf. 1 Tim. 1:20) and now gave fair warning that he would discipline when he came again. Wanting to spare the Corinthians the pain of chastening, Paul had avoided confronting them. In 2 Corinthians 1:23 he reminded them, "I call God as witness to my soul, that to spare you I came no more to Corinth." He had warned the sinning members of the Corinthian assembly to repent **previously . . . when** he was **present** in Corinth for the **second time** (during the sorrowful visit; cf. 2:1). **And though** he was still **absent** from Corinth, he issued a warning **in advance** to all **those who** had **sinned in the past** (cf. 12:21) **and to all the rest** of the unrepentant sinners **as well** that when he came to them for **the third time** he would **not spare anyone.** *Pheidomai* (**spare**) is a strong word, used in classical Greek to speak of sparing someone's life on the battle-field. It conveyed the idea of having mercy on an enemy. Paul's declara-tion that he would not spare them was not an idle threat; those who refused to repent would get exactly what their sin called for.

The time for grace, mercy, and patience was over. There would be no more warnings; when he came again Paul would deal with the sin-ners at Corinth. If they failed to repent, they would find Paul not to their liking when he visited (12:20). As a faithful parent (1 Cor. 4:14–15), Paul could not leave his spiritual children in a state of disobedience; he had to discipline them and bring to the place of obedience and blessing. Their persistent failure to repent would bring action on his part.

For God's glory, the church's purity, and sinning believers' well-being, and gospel witness, Paul did not hesitate to confront sin in the churches under his care. As previously noted, he had already rebuked the Corinthians for their failure to discipline the man living in immorality (1 Cor. 5). In a sharply worded section of his letter to them, Paul chided the Galatians for tolerating false teachers, who brought both doctrinal error and sin into the church:

> I am amazed that you are so quickly deserting Him who called you by the grace of Christ, for a different gospel; which is really not another; only there are some who are disturbing you and want to distort the gospel of Christ. But even if we, or an angel from heaven, should preach to you a gospel contrary to what we have preached to you, he is to be accursed! As we have said before, so I say again now, if any man is preaching to you a gospel contrary to what you received, he is to be accursed! (Gal. 1:6–9)

Paul's willingness to confront sinners proved he was not a man pleaser: "For am I now seeking the favor of men, or of God? Or am I striving to please men? If I were still trying to please men, I would not be a bond-servant of Christ" (v. 10). In fact, Paul fearlessly confronted even the apos-tle Peter, the leader of the Twelve, and the greatest preacher and miracle worker of the early days of the church:

> But when Cephas came to Antioch, I opposed him to his face, because he stood condemned. For prior to the coming of certain men from James, he used to eat with the Gentiles; but when they came, he began to withdraw and hold himself aloof, fearing the party of the circumci-sion. The rest of the Jews joined him in hypocrisy, with the result that even Barnabas was carried away by their hypocrisy. But when I saw that they were not straightforward about the truth of the gospel, I said to Cephas in the presence of all, "If you, being a Jew, live like the

Gentiles and not like the Jews, how is it that you compel the Gentiles to live like Jews?" (Gal. 2:11–14)

He told the Thessalonians bluntly, "For even when we were with you, we used to give you this order: if anyone is not willing to work, then he is not to eat, either" (2 Thess. 3:10). Paul put Hymenaeus and Alexander out of the church in Ephesus (1 Tim. 1:20).

Paul was a compassionate man and ministered with meekness, gentleness, and humility (cf. 2 Cor. 10:1). He loved the Corinthians (12:15). But unlike many in the church today, Paul saw no conflict between love and discipline. Discipline is an expression of love, because it is those whom the Lord loves that He disciplines (Prov. 3:11–12). Paul was absolutely intolerant of sin, because he knew it would infect, sicken, weaken, and ultimately destroy the church. J. Carl Laney writes,

> The church today is suffering from an infection which has been allowed to fester. As an untreated boil oozes germ-infested pus and contaminates the whole body, so the church has been contaminated by sin and moral compromise. As an infection weakens the body by destroying its defense mechanisms so the church has been weakened by this ugly sore. The church has lost its power and effectiveness in serving as a vehicle for social, moral and spiritual change. This illness is due, at least in part, to a neglect of spiritual discipline. (*A Guide to Church Discipline* [Minneapolis: Bethany House, 1985], 12)

Unrepentant sin also robs individual believers of the joy of God's pleasure. "Behold, the Lord's hand is not so short that it cannot save; neither is His ear so dull that it cannot hear," wrote Isaiah. "But your iniquities have made a separation between you and your God, and your sins have hidden His face from you so that He does not hear" (Isa. 59:1–2). Paul loved the Corinthians too much to ignore the sin that ravaged the lives of individuals and destroyed the power and testimony of the church.

THE METHOD OF CHURCH DISCIPLINE

Every fact is to be confirmed by the testimony of two or three witnesses. (13:1*b*)

Church discipline is not a witch-hunt, where people's reputations are destroyed by flimsy, unsupported allegations. Because God is a God of justice (Isa. 30:18), He has designed a discipline process that is both thorough and fair. Paul's chastening of the unrepentant sinners at Corinth would be carried out in strict accordance with God's law, as his quote of Deuteronomy 19:15 assured the Corinthians. *Rhēma* (**fact**) can refer to the allegations in a judicial proceeding. Matthew's gospel uses it in relation to church discipline in 18:16, where Deuteronomy 19:15 is also quoted, and in 27:12–14, where it refers to the charges against Jesus at His trial before Pilate.

The Old Testament Law affirmed that no one could be convicted of a crime unless the accused person's guilt was **confirmed by the testimony of two or three witnesses.** In addition to Deuteronomy 19:15, which Paul quoted, Numbers 35:30 says, "If anyone kills a person, the murderer shall be put to death at the evidence of witnesses, but no person shall be put to death on the testimony of one witness." Deuteronomy 17:6 expounds on that principle: "On the evidence of two witnesses or three witnesses, he who is to die shall be put to death; he shall not be put to death on the evidence of one witness" (cf. John 8:17; Heb. 10:28).

That same requirement for multiple witnesses holds true in the process of church discipline. No one is to be put out of the church until a thorough four-step process has been completed. First, a person who knows of a sinning Christian is to reprove him in private (Matt. 18:15; Gal. 6:1). If he refuses to repent, the one who confronted him does so again, this time bringing one or two others along as witnesses (Matt. 18:16). If he still refuses to repent, the entire church becomes involved in calling him to repentance (Matt. 18:17). If he ignores the church's call to repent, he is to be put out of the church and treated as an unbeliever (Matt. 18:17). In 1 Timothy 5:19 Paul repeated the principle that multiple witnesses are required, this time in connection with allegations against church leaders: "Do not receive an accusation against an elder except on the basis of two or three witnesses." The sins that trigger the discipline process include serious doctrinal error (1 Tim. 1:18–20), sins that threaten church unity (Titus 3:10), and issues of purity (1 Cor. 5).

An undisciplined church is as shameful and tragic as an unruly child (Prov. 10:1, 5; 17:21, 25; 29:15). It brings reproach on the name of Jesus Christ and grief to the Great Shepherd and His undershepherds. If the church doesn't take sin seriously enough to take action against it, how can it expect the world to take the gospel of deliverance from sin seriously? If the church is to honor Jesus Christ and have a powerful testimony in the world, it must engage in confronting its sinning members. Only then can they be called back to holiness and progress toward spiritual maturity.

The Pattern of Sanctification: Authority
(2 Corinthians 13:3–4)

since you are seeking for proof of the Christ who speaks in me, and who is not weak toward you, but mighty in you. For indeed He was crucified because of weakness, yet He lives because of the power of God. For we also are weak in Him, yet we will live with Him because of the power of God directed toward you. (13:3–4)

Americans have always been a fiercely independent people. Having thrown off the rule of the British monarchy, the fledgling American republic agonized over how much power the Constitution should grant to the central government and how much the states should keep. The issue of states' rights was not completely resolved until the Civil War. The pioneers, frontiersmen, and cowboys who explored and settled the West were legendary for their self-reliance, independent spirit, and cavalier attitude toward authority. Perhaps the most blatant example of disdain for authority in recent American history was the counterculture movement of the 1960s.

Like so many other societal trends, a negative view of spiritual authority has made its way into the church. In their zeal to make the church more appealing to non-Christians, some have argued for a

449

decentralization of authority. They propose that authority be taken out of the hands of the pastors and elders and given to the congregation. They want an organizational structure that is more horizontal and less vertical.

Such proposals amount to a tragic mutiny against Scripture and the Lord of the church. The church is not a democracy, but a monarchy; believers are subjects of the kingdom of God the Father (cf. Mark 12:34; Luke 4:43; 6:20; John 3:3; Acts 1:3; 8:12; 19:8; 28:31; 1 Thess. 2:12) and the Lord Jesus Christ (cf. Matt. 13:41; 16:28; Col. 1:13; Eph. 5:5; 2 Tim. 4:1; 2 Peter 1:11). The only true authority in the church stems from its Head, Jesus Christ (Eph. 4:15; 5:23), and is delegated by Him to those who preach and teach His Word—namely, its pastors and elders. To argue for a decentralization of authority in the church, thus rejecting its God-ordained leaders, is to reject the authority of Christ, its Head.

Because it is based on the authoritative Word of God, true biblical preaching is also authoritative. The preacher's goal is not to make people feel good about themselves, still less to entertain them. He is to accurately present the truth of God's Word and call for obedience—for people to submit to Scripture's authority or to reject it. The same holds true for proclaiming the gospel to unbelievers. God does not share His message as an option to be considered, nor does He *suggest* that unbelievers repent; He *commands* "that all people everywhere should repent" (Acts 17:30; cf. Matt. 3:2; 4:17; Mark 6:12). Stripped of their authoritative element, sermons become weak counterfeits of true biblical preaching.

The Lord Jesus Christ set the example for all preachers to follow. At the conclusion of the Sermon on the Mount, "the crowds were amazed at His teaching; for He was teaching them as one having authority, and not as their scribes" (Matt. 7:28–29; cf. Mark 1:22, 27). Even His enemies acknowledged His authority, demanding of Him, "By what authority are You doing these things, or who gave You this authority to do these things?" (Mark 11:28). Jesus derived His authority during His earthly ministry from the Father, as the following exchange with His critics, recorded in John 7:14–18, reveals:

> But when it was now the midst of the feast Jesus went up into the temple, and began to teach. The Jews then were astonished, saying, "How has this man become learned, having never been educated?" So Jesus answered them and said, "My teaching is not Mine, but His who sent Me. If anyone is willing to do His will, he will know of the teaching, whether it is of God or whether I speak from Myself. He who speaks from himself seeks his own glory; but He who is seeking the glory of the One who sent Him, He is true, and there is no unrighteousness in Him."

In John 8:28 "Jesus said, 'When you lift up the Son of Man, then you will know that I am He, and I do nothing on My own initiative, but I speak these things as the Father taught Me'" (cf. vv. 38, 40). In John 12:49 He added, "For I did not speak on My own initiative, but the Father Himself who sent Me has given Me a commandment as to what to say and what to speak."

The New Testament preachers, following the Lord's example, also proclaimed God's Word with binding force. Jesus told His disciples that carrying out the Great Commission involves "teaching [people] to observe all that [He] commanded" (Matt. 28:20). Paul instructed Titus, "These things speak and exhort and reprove with all authority. Let no one disregard you" (Titus 2:15). He directed Timothy, "These things command and teach" (1 Tim. 4:11 NKJV). "Whoever speaks," wrote Peter, "is to speak, as it were, the utterances of God" (1 Peter 4:11).

The Lord of the church delegates the authority of Scripture to the leaders of the church. It is important to remember that their authority does not derive from the force of their personality, their communication skill, their personal charisma, their ordination, or their education. Nor does an ecclesiastical hierarchy, a denomination, or even a church grant their authority to them. Pastors and elders also do not derive their authority from any spiritual experiences they allegedly have had. The sole source of authority for all who teach and preach is the Word of God. What the church desperately needs, therefore, is not decentralized dialogue but careful, clear, authoritative exposition and proclamation of Scripture.

It should come as no surprise when surveys suggest that church-goers want less authority in their churches. Non-Christians and marginal believers balk at placing themselves under the binding demands of Scripture. Thus, those who authoritatively preach the Word with conviction and challenge their hearers to obey it are not popular with unbelievers and the disobedient. And such preaching, since it means one person telling others what is true and what to do, runs counter to the prevailing view of our culture, which holds that all people's views are equally valid. Authority is being undermined at every level of society for several reasons.

First and foremost, rebellion against God's authority is the very essence of sin. Therefore, rejecting authority comes natural to fallen mankind. Satan began the rebellion against God's authority, pridefully desiring to "make [himself] like the Most High" (Isa. 14:14; cf. Ezek. 28:12–16). Eve inaugurated rebellion on the human level (Gen. 3:6), and when Adam joined her in rebellion, the human race fell into sin (Rom. 5:12, 14, 1 Cor. 15:22). As a result, "even though [sinners] knew God, they did not honor Him as God" (Rom. 1:21). As their way of life, they refuse to obey His law and do His will.

Another contributing factor to the decline of authority is the absence of moral absolutes. Having rejected the objective divine standards revealed in Scripture, people are left with nothing but subjective opinions; morality is determined by popular consensus. Obviously, there can be no authority if there are no absolutes to enforce. Like Israel during the chaotic period of the judges, "Every man [does] what [is] right in his own eyes" (Judg. 17:6). To question anyone's opinion is intolerable.

The failure of parents to discipline their children has also undermined authority. An entire generation, having grown up without parental discipline, is now raising another generation of undisciplined children. The breakdown of the home due to sexual immorality, homosexuality, divorce, and working mothers has had a devastating impact on children. Having failed to learn discipline, virtue, and self-control in society's most basic unit, the family, they are ill prepared to accept authority in other settings. Rebellious children pose such a serious threat to every society's stability that under the Mosaic Law they could be put to death:

> If any man has a stubborn and rebellious son who will not obey his father or his mother, and when they chastise him, he will not even listen to them, then his father and mother shall seize him, and bring him out to the elders of his city at the gateway of his hometown. They shall say to the elders of his city, "This son of ours is stubborn and rebellious, he will not obey us, he is a glutton and a drunkard." Then all the men of his city shall stone him to death; so you shall remove the evil from your midst, and all Israel shall hear of it and fear. (Deut. 21:18–21; cf. Ex. 21:15, 17; Lev. 20:9; Prov. 30:17).

Finally, the overemphasis on personal rights engendered by humanism has eroded authority. Society is engulfed in a narcissistic sea of personal freedom that is hostile to anything or anyone that would limit that freedom. Commanding people is politically incorrect.

One of the many problems plaguing the Corinthian church was a rebellion, fomented by some false apostles, against Paul's apostolic authority. As has been noted in previous chapters of this volume, they knew that before they could replace him as the authoritative teachers at Corinth, they first had to undermine that authority. Therefore, they argued that Paul could not be a true apostle, because unlike them, he lacked apostolic authority. For example, they argued that he did not have the proper letters of commendation (cf. 2 Cor. 3:1–2) to authenticate his claim to be an apostle. But Paul was a true apostle and had authority granted him by the Lord Jesus Christ (10:8; 13:10). Thus, he spoke "in Christ in the sight of God" (2:17). He had no secret life of sin, having "renounced the things hidden because of shame, not walking in craftiness or adulterating the word of God, but by the manifestation of truth commending [himself] to every man's conscience in the sight of God" (4:2). Unlike false teachers (cf. Jer. 5:30–31), Paul did not preach on his own authority. He did "not preach [himself] but Christ Jesus as Lord, and [himself] as [the Corinthians'] bond-servant for Jesus' sake" (2 Cor. 4:5; cf. 1 Thess. 2:13). He always ministered "in purity, in knowledge, in patience, in kindness, in the Holy Spirit, in genuine love, in the word of truth, in the power of God; by the weapons of righteousness for the right hand and the left" (2 Cor. 6:6–7).

In this passage, Paul describes the assault on his authority and then reaffirms his privilege and duty to speak the truth of God commandingly.

THE ASSAULT ON PAUL'S AUTHORITY

since you are seeking for proof of the Christ who speaks in me, (13:3*a*)

The goal of every faithful preacher is to allow Christ to speak through him. That does not happen through an audible voice but through the proclamation of God's Word. A sure mark of a true man of God, therefore, is that he accurately handles the Word of God (2 Tim. 2:15).

Though Paul had preached the truth to the Corinthians, some, influenced by the false teachers, were questioning his apostolic authority. They were unimpressed with Paul's meekness and gentleness (2 Cor. 10:1), mistaking it for weakness. What they wanted was to see Paul display his power and crush his opponents. David E. Garland writes,

> Meekness and gentleness were not virtues in a Corinthian culture marked by pitched battles for social supremacy over others. Ruthlessly bludgeoning one's social rivals was the rule. The Corinthians therefore may have expected some miracle of power from Paul against adversaries who so boldly opposed him. They may have thought that an apostle would be a lot tougher, louder, bolder, and more fiery. He would unleash shafts of lightning, hailstones of wrath, and raging tempests to lay waste the opposition. Something along the order of what happened to Elymas, who was struck blind for trying to thwart Paul (Acts 13:11), would have provided convincing proof that Christ's power was indeed working in him. (*2 Corinthians*, The New American Commentary [Nashville: Broadman & Holman, 1999], 543)

The Corinthians were right in **seeking for proof** that **Christ** did, in fact, speak through those who claimed to be apostles (cf. Rev. 2:2); unfortunately, they were measuring them by the wrong standards. Since

Paul did not display the forceful personality traits that marked the proud, arrogant false apostles (cf. 2 Cor. 11:20–21; 12:13), which impressed many of the Corinthians, some demanded convincing proof of his apostleship.

In reality, Paul had already offered conclusive proof of his authenticity. In 12:12 he reminded the Corinthians, "The signs of a true apostle were performed among you with all perseverance, by signs and wonders and miracles" (see the discussion of this verse in chapter 32 of this volume). Further, for the Corinthians to doubt Paul's genuineness as an apostle was to doubt their own genuineness as Christians, since he was God's instrument in their salvation and in their sanctification. They would be, in effect, sawing off the branch they were sitting on. (See the discussion of 13:6 in chapter 37 of this volume.) Even worse, to challenge Paul's apostleship was to challenge the authority of the Lord Jesus Christ, who personally and supernaturally chose, commissioned, and sent him.

Paul was not the first of God's servants to have his authority challenged. Korah, Dathan, and Abiram "assembled together against Moses and Aaron, and said to them, 'You have gone far enough, for all the congregation are holy, every one of them, and the Lord is in their midst; so why do you exalt yourselves above the assembly of the Lord?'" (Num. 16:3). Even Moses' own sister and brother rebelled against his authority: "Miriam and Aaron spoke against Moses because of the Cushite woman whom he had married (for he had married a Cushite woman); and they said, 'Has the Lord indeed spoken only through Moses? Has He not spoken through us as well?'" (Num. 12:1–2). Numbers 20:3 records that "the people thus contended with Moses and spoke, saying, 'If only we had perished when our brothers perished before the Lord!'" Angrily, Moses replied to them, "Listen now, you rebels; shall we bring forth water for you out of this rock?" (v. 10). In John 2:18 "the Jews . . . said to [Jesus], 'What sign do You show us as Your authority for doing these things?'" (cf. 6:30; Matt. 12:38; 16:1; Mark 8:11; Luke 11:29). As He did when His other servants' authority was challenged, God worked powerfully through Paul to remove all doubt about his apostolic authority.

THE AFFIRMATION OF PAUL'S AUTHORITY

and who is not weak toward you, but mighty in you. For indeed He was crucified because of weakness, yet He lives because of the power of God. For we also are weak in Him, yet we will live with Him because of the power of God directed toward you. (13:3b–4)

If the Corinthians demanded further evidence of his apostolic authority, Paul would give it to them. But it would not be to their liking.

When he again visited Corinth, he would demonstrate his apostolic power and authority by not sparing anyone who refused to repent (13:2). If Paul did not find them to be what he wanted them to be; that is, repentant, they would also find him not to their liking. He would come bearing the authoritative rod of discipline instead of the spirit of love and gentleness (cf. 1 Cor. 4:21).

The Lord Jesus Christ was certainly **not weak toward** the Corinthians, since it was His **mighty** power working in them that both redeemed and was sanctifying them. As noted above, Paul was severely criticized by the false apostles for being weak. Though he bombarded the Corinthians from a safe distance with "weighty and strong" letters, "his personal presence," they declared contemptuously, "[was] unimpressive and his speech contemptible" (2 Cor. 10:10). He lacked the potent, charismatic personality and highly polished oratorical skills Greek culture expected in a great teacher.

In fact, Paul's weakness, humanly speaking, permeates this epistle. He began by discussing his afflictions (1:3–10). Later he spoke of the tears he shed over the harsh treatment he received during his sorrowful visit to Corinth (2:4). In 6:4–10, 11:23–33, and 12:7–10 Paul described his suffering and weakness and acknowledged being depressed (7:6). He also admitted to being with the Corinthians "in weakness and in fear and in much trembling" (1 Cor. 2:3). The apostle summarized his weakness by describing himself metaphorically as a lowly clay pot (2 Cor. 4:7).

Paul compares himself with Christ, who in His humanity took on weakness. In His incarnation Christ "emptied Himself, taking the form of a bond-servant, and being made in the likeness of men." (Phil. 2:7). He was not born into a wealthy family, nor was He raised in the court of an earthly ruler. Before beginning His public ministry, Jesus was a carpenter (Mark 6:3), as His father had been before Him (Matt. 13:55). He lived humbly during His earthly ministry, with no permanent place to stay (Matt. 8:20), and at His death He owned little more than the clothes on His back (Matt. 27:35; Mark 15:24; Luke 23:34; John 19:24). **Indeed He was crucified because of weakness;** "He humbled Himself by becoming obedient to the point of death, even death on a cross" (Phil. 2:8; cf. Acts 2:23; 4:10; 5:30). The crucifixion of Jesus Christ is the unmistakable and supreme evidence of His weakness. His human nature was so weak as to be fully susceptible to death.

But the story does not end with Christ's death. **He lives because of the power of God,** who raised Him from the dead (Rom. 1:4; 7:4; 8:34; 10:9; 1 Cor. 6:14; 15:4, 20; Gal. 1:1; Col. 2:12; 1 Peter 1:21). That was the triumphant message that the early Christian preachers boldly proclaimed (Acts 2:24, 32; 3:15, 26; 4:10; 5:30; 10:40; 13:30, 33, 37). Just as Christ's death showed His human weakness, so also did His resurrection demonstrate His divine power.

Paul, too, experienced the same juxtaposition of weakness and strength seen in Jesus Christ. He **also** was **weak in Him;** he ministered in fear and trembling, and suffered constant sorrow, pain, and disappointment. Yet Paul would **live with Him;** that is, he, like all believers, possessed resurrection life, being raised with Christ to eternal glory. As he explained to the Romans,

> Therefore we have been buried with Him through baptism into death, so that as Christ was raised from the dead through the glory of the Father, so we too might walk in newness of life. For if we have become united with Him in the likeness of His death, certainly we shall also be in the likeness of His resurrection, knowing this, that our old self was crucified with Him, in order that our body of sin might be done away with, so that we would no longer be slaves to sin; for he who has died is freed from sin. Now if we have died with Christ, we believe that we shall also live with Him, knowing that Christ, having been raised from the dead, is never to die again; death no longer is master over Him. For the death that He died, He died to sin once for all; but the life that He lives, He lives to God. Even so consider yourselves to be dead to sin, but alive to God in Christ Jesus. (Rom. 6:4–11)

Paul's weakness did not hinder God's power from flowing through him; on the contrary, it allowed God's power to operate freely in his life (2 Cor. 12:9–10).

Returning to his warning, Paul told the Corinthians that **the power of God** that raised him with Christ and gave him eternal life would be **directed toward** the Corinthians when he again visited Corinth. The apostle would come in the authority and divine power of Christ and deal firmly with those who persisted in their sinful rebellion. He would be like the Lord, who warned the church at Pergamum, "Therefore repent; or else I am coming to you quickly, and I will make war against them with the sword of My mouth" (Rev. 2:16). Philip E. Hughes writes,

> The Apostle discerns an analogy between the smaller, localized setting of his relations with the Corinthian church and the cosmic drama in which his Master Christ is the chief actor. The weakness of the cross at Christ's first advent is to be followed by the manifested power of His majestic authority as King of kings and Lord of lords at His second advent, when He will appear as the Judge of the whole world (cf. Rev. 19:11ff.) . . . . "The cross," writes Denney, "does *not* exhaust Christ's relation to sin; He passed from the cross to the throne, and when He comes again it is as Judge. . . . When Christ comes again *He* will not spare. The two things go together in Him: the infinite patience of the cross, the inexorable righteousness of the throne." So too Paul, who is one with his Master in the "weakness" of compassion and patience and long-

suffering, desiring the repentance of all, is one with Him also in the "power" of authority and judgment. If his former visit appeared to be marked by weakness, the defiant ones in Corinth will find that his impending visit is marked by power. (*The Second Epistle to the Corinthians,* The New International Commentary on the New Testament [Grand Rapids: Eerdmans, 1992], 479–80. Italics in original.)

When Paul returned to Corinth he would come in judgment on sin, just as the Lord Jesus Christ will return to earth in judgment. Then his authority would be seen.

If pastors and elders are to call the church to repentance and discipline those who refuse to repent, they must possess divine authority to do so. That authority rests in the Word of God, making it essential that it be preached and applied clearly, compellingly, and with conviction. As will be seen in the next chapter, those who persistently reject the authority of Scripture call into question the genuineness of their salvation.

The Pattern of Sanctification: Authenticity
(2 Corinthians 13:5–6)

37

Test yourselves to see if you are in the faith; examine yourselves! Or do you not recognize this about yourselves, that Jesus Christ is in you—unless indeed you fail the test? But I trust that you will realize that we ourselves do not fail the test. (13:5–6)

In the closing section of his epistle (12:20–13:10) Paul focuses on several issues of great importance in the life of the church. Like all true men of God, he longed for his people to become mature in Christ. Thus, the preceding chapters of this volume have discussed the vitally important issues of repentance, discipline, and biblical authority.

But that discussion presupposes that the people concerned are authentic Christians. Unfortunately, that is not the case in the church. In any congregation there will be "false brethren" (11:26; Gal. 2:4), tares among the wheat (Matt. 13:25–30, 36–42). At the heart, therefore, of the pastor's concern for the spiritual well-being of his people is that they be spiritually alive. If they are not, they obviously cannot truly repent, accept discipline, or submit to authority. Paul's goal for the Corinthians, as it was for all believers, was that they live at the highest level of spiritual maturity. But for them to grow in Christ, they first had to be in Him. Therefore Paul called them to examine themselves and determine their true spiritual condition.

To do so is critically important, since those who misjudge their spiritual state face eternal tragedy. They will hear from the Lord Jesus Christ the most chilling, horrifying, terrible words imaginable: "I never knew you; depart from Me, you who practice lawlessness" (Matt. 7:23). In one sense, the most dangerous place for an unconverted person to be is in the church. Hearing the truth but not responding to it brings greater accountability and severer judgment.

By way of challenging the Corinthians to do a spiritual inventory on their lives, Paul both called them to genuine faith and extolled its benefits.

THE CALL TO GENUINE FAITH

Test yourselves to see if you are in the faith; examine yourselves! (13:5a)

The Corinthians, prompted by the evil insinuations of the false apostles, had demanded proof of Paul's apostleship. He reluctantly defended himself, not for his own sake, but for the Lord's, and so the Corinthians would not be cut off from the truth he preached to them. But in this passage, he turned the tables on his accusers and challenged them to **test** and **examine** themselves. The Greek text places the pronouns before the verbs for emphasis and literally reads, "Yourselves test to see if you are in the faith; yourselves examine." Instead of arrogantly and foolishly challenging the genuineness of Paul's relationship to the Lord, the Corinthians needed to examine the genuineness of their own salvation. The familiar New Testament terms *peirazō* (**test**) and *dokimazō* (**examine**) are used here as synonyms. They convey the idea of putting something to the test to determine its genuineness. The test was **to see if** the Corinthians were **in the faith.** *Pistis* (**faith**) refers here not to the subjective element of belief but to the objective body of Christian truth —the Christian faith.

Paul's call for self-examination was not a new concept. Job cried out to God, "How many are my iniquities and sins? Make known to me my rebellion and my sin" (Job 13:23; cf. 31:4–6). In Psalm 17:3 David declared, "You have tried my heart. . . . You have tested me and You find nothing." "Examine me, O Lord, and try me;" he pleaded in Psalm 26:2. "Test my mind and my heart." In perhaps the most familiar Old Testament example of self-examination David prayed, "Search me, O God, and know my heart; try me and know my anxious thoughts; and see if there be any hurtful way in me, and lead me in the everlasting way" (Ps. 139:23–24). In Lamentations 3:40 Jeremiah exhorted his fellow Israelites, "Let us examine and probe our ways, and let us return to the Lord," while the Lord's challenge to Israel was, "Consider your ways!" (Hag. 1:5, 7). Describing the self-examination that is a prerequisite for participating in the Lord's Supper, Paul wrote, "A man must examine himself, and in so doing he is to eat of the bread and drink of the cup. . . . But if we judged ourselves rightly, we would not be judged" (1 Cor. 11:28, 31).

Like Paul, the writer of Hebrews understood well the danger of self-deception. Some of the people he addressed in his epistle were intellectually convinced of the truth of the gospel but uncommitted to Christ. He called them to examine the danger of that position in a series of warning passages, which show clearly the great risk of being in the church, but not in Christ.

The first of those warnings is in Hebrews 2:1–3:

> For this reason we must pay much closer attention to what we have heard, so that we do not drift away from it. For if the word spoken through angels proved unalterable, and every transgression and disobedience received a just penalty, how will we escape if we neglect so great a salvation? After it was at the first spoken through the Lord, it was confirmed to us by those who heard.

The phrase "for this reason" points the reader back to the majesty and glory of Jesus Christ expressed in chapter 1. He is revealed as the "heir of all things" (v. 2), the One who "made the world" (v. 2), "the radiance of [God's] glory and the exact representation of His nature" (v. 3), and the One who "upholds all things by the word of His power" (v. 3). After making "purification of sins" on the cross, Christ rose from the dead and ascended to "the right hand of the Majesty on high" (v. 3). Jesus Christ is superior to the angels (vv. 4–7), since He is God (v. 8), the supreme Ruler of the universe (v. 13), and will judge those who fail to come all the way to faith in Him.

The writer also noted a second reason not to reject the gospel, reminding his readers, "If the word spoken through angels [the Old Testament; cf. Acts 7:53; Gal. 3:19] proved unalterable, and every transgression and disobedience received a just penalty, how will we escape if we neglect so great a salvation?" (Heb. 2:2–3). The Law was given through Moses, but the gospel through Jesus Christ (John 1:17). If those who rejected the Old Testament Law did not escape punishment, how will those who reject the gospel?

Finally, the writer warned his readers that they were accountable because the gospel they had heard "was at the first spoken through the Lord," then "confirmed to [them] by those who heard [the apostles], God also testifying with them, both by signs and wonders and by various miracles and by gifts of the Holy Spirit according to His own will" (Heb. 2:3–4). They could not plead ignorance, having seen the gospel verified by supernatural signs.

Because of the majesty of Christ, the example of what happened to those who rejected the Old Testament Law, and the powerful, miracle-attested preaching of the apostles, those who reject the gospel are without excuse.

A second warning passage comes in Hebrews 3:6–4:2, 6–12:

> Christ was faithful as a Son over His house—whose house we are, if we hold fast our confidence and the boast of our hope firm until the end. Therefore, just as the Holy Spirit says, "Today if you hear His voice, do not harden your hearts as when they provoked Me, as in the day of trial in the wilderness, where your fathers tried Me by testing Me, and saw My works for forty years. Therefore I was angry with this generation, and said, 'They always go astray in their heart, and they did not know My ways'; as I swore in My wrath, 'They shall not enter My rest.'" Take care, brethren, that there not be in any one of you an evil, unbelieving heart that falls away from the living God. But encourage one another day after day, as long as it is still called "Today," so that none of you will be hardened by the deceitfulness of sin. For we have become partakers of Christ, if we hold fast the beginning of our assurance firm until the end, while it is said, "Today if you hear His voice, do not harden your hearts, as when they provoked Me." For who provoked Him when they had heard? Indeed, did not all those who came out of Egypt led by Moses? And with whom was He angry for forty years? Was it not with those who sinned, whose bodies fell in the wilderness? And to whom did He swear that they would not enter His rest, but to those who were disobedient? So we see that they were not able to enter because of unbelief. Therefore, let us fear if, while a promise remains of entering His rest, any one of you may seem to have come short of it. For indeed we have had good news preached to us, just as they also; but the word they heard did not profit them, because it was not united by faith in those who heard.... Therefore, since it remains for some to enter it, and those who formerly had good news preached to them failed to enter because of disobedience, He again fixes a certain day, "Today," saying through David after so long a time just as has been said before, "Today if you hear His voice, do not harden your hearts." For if Joshua had given them rest, He would not have spoken of another day after that. So there remains a Sabbath rest for the people of God. For the one who has entered His rest has himself also rested from his works, as God did from His. Therefore let us be diligent to enter that rest, so that no one will fall, through following the same example of disobedience. For the word of God is living and active and sharper than any two-edged sword, and piercing as far as the division of soul and spirit, of both joints and marrow, and able to judge the thoughts and intentions of the heart.

The writer reminded his largely Jewish audience of one of the most tragic events in their history. He quoted from Psalm 95, which describes Israel's unbelief and rebellion in the wilderness after God delivered them from Egypt. Even though they saw His miraculous works on their behalf, many still refused to believe. As a result, God sentenced the unbelieving rebels, who "always [went] astray in their heart, and ... did not know [His] ways," to die in the wilderness and never enter the Promised Land (cf. 1 Cor. 10:1–5). They symbolize those who come near but, because of their sin and unbelief, never enter into the final rest of salvation.

Based on their sobering example, the writer of Hebrews warned his readers, "Take care, brethren, that there not be in any one of you an evil, unbelieving heart that falls away from the living God. But encourage one another day after day, as long as it is still called 'Today,' so that none of you will be hardened by the deceitfulness of sin" (Heb. 3:12–13), and "Today if you hear His voice, do not harden your hearts, as when they provoked Me" (v. 15). His great "fear" was that "while a promise remains of entering His rest, any one of [his readers] may seem to have come short of it" (4:1). Those in the church "have had good news preached to [them], just as [the Israelites in the wilderness] also; but the word they heard did not profit them, because it was not united by faith in those who heard" (v. 2). Hearing the gospel but not coming to faith merely increases a person's condemnation. Those who are outwardly involved in the church but who through disobedience, love of sin, and unbelief fail to embrace Christ will not enter the eternal rest of heaven. The longer they are exposed to the gospel without committing themselves to it, the harder their hearts will become. "Therefore," the writer of Hebrews urged his readers, "let us be diligent to enter that rest, so that no one will fall, through following the same example of disobedience" (v. 11).

Perhaps the most familiar of the warning passages in Hebrews is found in 6:4–9:

> For in the case of those who have once been enlightened and have tasted of the heavenly gift and have been made partakers of the Holy Spirit, and have tasted the good word of God and the powers of the age to come, and then have fallen away, it is impossible to renew them again to repentance, since they again crucify to themselves the Son of God and put Him to open shame. For ground that drinks the rain which often falls on it and brings forth vegetation useful to those for whose sake it is also tilled, receives a blessing from God; but if it yields thorns and thistles, it is worthless and close to being cursed, and it ends up being burned. But, beloved, we are convinced of better things concerning you, and things that accompany salvation, though we are speaking in this way.

In 6:1 the writer addressed those who were sitting on the fence, who had becoming superficially involved in the church but had not come to faith in Christ. He exhorted them, "Therefore leaving the elementary teaching about the Christ, let us press on to maturity [salvation], not laying again a foundation of repentance from dead works and of faith toward God." They needed to move beyond the incomplete Old Testament teaching about the coming Messiah, repentance, and faith in God to embrace the fullness of the New Testament gospel of Jesus Christ.

Though they were not saved, they had experienced significant spiritual opportunity. They had been "enlightened" (understood the gospel intellectually), had "tasted of the heavenly gift" (experienced some of the nonsalvation benefits Christ brought; i.e., healing, deliverance from demons), been "made partakers of the Holy Spirit" (either through seeing His miraculous gifts operating in the church or experiencing His convicting of sin, which can be resisted; cf. Acts 7:51), and "tasted the good word of God and the powers of the age to come" (the miraculous gifts referred to in Heb. 2:4). It should be noted that none of those terms refer anywhere in Scripture to salvation.

These uncommitted people were in a disastrous position. If, after experiencing all of those spiritual benefits, they were to "[fall] away, it [would be] impossible to renew them again to repentance, since they again crucify to themselves the Son of God and put Him to open shame." Because they reject the gospel despite having a full understanding of it, such apostates are unredeemable; there is no further revelation to give them. They have rejected with full light.

Using a simple agricultural illustration in verses 7 and 8, the writer pointed out that there are ultimately only two kinds of people in the church. Similar to Jesus' parable of the sower (Matt. 13:18–23), they are represented by two different types of soil. When the rain, symbolizing the gospel, falls on the good soil (representing true believers), it "brings forth vegetation useful to those for whose sake it is also tilled, [and] receives a blessing from God" (Heb. 6:7). On the other hand, the worthless ground (representing those who hear and understand the gospel but reject it) "yields thorns and thistles, it is worthless and close to being cursed, and it ends up being burned" (v. 8).

Hebrews 10:26–31 reiterates the danger facing those who understand the gospel but remain uncommitted to Christ as Lord:

> For if we go on sinning willfully after receiving the knowledge of the truth, there no longer remains a sacrifice for sins, but a terrifying expectation of judgment and the fury of a fire which will consume the adversaries. Anyone who has set aside the Law of Moses dies without mercy on the testimony of two or three witnesses. How much severer punishment do you think he will deserve who has trampled under foot the

> Son of God, and has regarded as unclean the blood of the covenant by which he was sanctified, and has insulted the Spirit of grace? For we know Him who said, "Vengeance is Mine, I will repay." And again, "The Lord will judge His people." It is a terrifying thing to fall into the hands of the living God.

Those who refuse to repent and confess Jesus as Lord will die in their sins despite their knowledge of the gospel. There is no other Savior than Jesus Christ and no other sacrifice for sins. "There is salvation in no one else; for there is no other name under heaven that has been given among men by which we must be saved" (Acts 4:12).

Those who reject Christ face "a terrifying expectation of judgment and the fury of a fire which will consume the adversaries." The reference, taken from Isaiah 26:11, is to God's eternal destruction of His enemies in hell (cf. Matt. 5:22; 18:9; Mark 9:43; Rev. 19:20; 20:14–15; 21:8). If those who broke the Mosaic Law were put to death without mercy, the writer asks, "How much severer punishment do you think he will deserve who has trampled under foot the Son of God, and has regarded as unclean the blood of the covenant by which he was sanctified, and has insulted the Spirit of grace?" The sobering reality is that the greater people's exposure to the gospel, the more severe their punishment will be if they reject it. To allow them to continue unchallenged in their rejection of the gospel only increases their condemnation. The church, knowing "it is a terrifying thing to fall into the hands of the living God," must call them to repentance. It should be remembered by unbelievers that sitting under the preaching of the gospel is high-risk behavior, because rejection intensifies eternal punishment.

A final warning from the writer of Hebrews comes in 10:38–39: "But My righteous one shall live by faith; and if he shrinks back, My soul has no pleasure in him. But we are not of those who shrink back to destruction, but of those who have faith to the preserving of the soul." The righteous, who "live by faith," are the opposite of apostates, who are devoid of faith. Those who associate themselves outwardly with the church, give intellectual assent to the gospel, yet "shrink back" from a full commitment to Jesus Christ face the terrifying reality of "destruction"—eternal punishment in hell. But the righteous will experience the "preserving of [their] soul" for eternal bliss in heaven (cf. Col. 1:5; 1 Peter 1:4).

Before the storm of divine judgment bursts upon them, people need to examine the foundation of their spiritual life. Only what is built on the bedrock of true saving faith in Jesus Christ will survive (cf. Matt. 7:24–27).

THE BENEFITS OF GENUINE FAITH

Or do you not recognize this about yourselves, that Jesus Christ is in you—unless indeed you fail the test? But I trust that you will realize that we ourselves do not fail the test. (13:5b–6)

Paul confidently expected that when the Corinthians examined themselves they would **recognize** that **Jesus Christ** was in them. "Christ in you" (Col. 1:27) is the great truth of the gospel. "I have been crucified with Christ," wrote Paul to the Galatians, "and it is no longer I who live, but Christ lives in me; and the life which I now live in the flesh I live by faith in the Son of God, who loved me and gave Himself up for me" (Gal. 2:20). He dwells in the hearts of the redeemed (Eph. 3:17; cf. John 6:56; 14:20; 15:4–5; 17:23, 26; Col. 3:11; 1 John 3:24), and that reality is their hope of eternal glory (Col. 1:27; cf. Rom. 8:9–11). The transformed life that results (2 Cor. 5:17) offers recognizable proof of true salvation.

The New Testament affirmation that people can know that they have been saved directly contradicts the teaching of the Roman Catholic Church. Rome officially holds that "no one can know with the certainty of faith, which cannot be subject to error, that he has obtained the grace of God" (Chapter IX of the Decree Concerning Justification promulgated by the Council of Trent; as cited in John C. Olin, ed., *A Reformation Debate: John Calvin and Jacopo Sadoleto* [Reprint; Grand Rapids: Baker, 1976], 122). Canon 16 of the Canons Concerning Justification promulgated by the Council of Trent adds, "If anyone says that he will for certain, with an absolute and infallible certainty, have that great gift of perseverance even to the end, unless he shall have learned this by a special revelation, let him be anathema" (as cited in Olin, *A Reformation Debate,* 133). That denial of the assurance of salvation flies in the face not only of Paul's teaching in this passage, but also of the rest of the New Testament as well. Romans 8:16 declares, "The Spirit Himself testifies with our spirit that we are children of God," and the apostle John repeatedly assured his readers that they could know that they had eternal life:

> By this we know that we have come to know Him, if we keep His commandments. . . . We know that we have passed out of death into life, because we love the brethren. He who does not love abides in death. . . . These things I have written to you who believe in the name of the Son of God, so that you may know that you have eternal life. (1 John 2:3; 3:14; 5:13).

Paul's call for the Corinthians to examine themselves to see if they were truly saved would have been pointless if such knowledge were impossible to obtain. The apostle was confident that the majority of the Corinthians would find their faith genuine and experience the blessings of assurance discussed above. Those who did **fail the test** could also experience those blessings if they repented and exercised genuine faith in Christ.

But Paul, too, would benefit when the majority examined themselves and discovered their faith to be real. In fact, since they were the fruit of his ministry, it would prove that he was a genuine apostle. The Corinthians were caught on the horns of a dilemma, as D. A. Carson points out:

> If the Corinthians declare they have failed the test, then doubtless Paul will be humiliated (cf. 2 Cor. 12:21); but in that case the Corinthians are in no position to point the finger at anyone. If on the other hand, they feel they have passed the test, then since Paul did all the initial evangelization among them he is the last person they are in a position to condemn. (*From Triumphalism to Maturity* [Grand Rapids: Baker, 1984], 179)

If they doubted Paul's apostleship, they would have to doubt his message. But if they doubted his message, they would also have to doubt their own conversion. The most convincing proof of Paul's apostleship was the Corinthians' own transformed lives; if they were truly saved, then he had to be a true apostle. Paul knew the majority of the Corinthians were genuine believers and would therefore **realize that** he did **not fail the test.**

What are people to look for when they examine themselves? What are the marks of genuine saving faith? Popular answers might include praying a prayer, walking an aisle, having an emotional experience, being baptized, attending church, leading an outwardly moral life, feeling conviction for sin, or knowing the facts about Jesus. None of those, however, are authentic marks of saving faith. Scripture nowhere teaches that a mere profession of faith (Luke 8:13–14), baptism (Eph. 2:8–9), being part of the visible church (Matt. 13:25–30, 36–42), feeling conviction for sin (Matt. 27:3–5), or merely believing the facts of the gospel (John 8:31; James 2:19) saves anyone.

Even the demons believe (James 2:19), but that will not save them. Their knowledge of spiritual realities far surpasses that of any human. They are completely convinced of the truth of what they know. They are terrified of God's judgment (cf. Matt. 8:29) because of their overwhelming sense of guilt (cf. Luke 8:31; they know they deserve to be sent to the Abyss). They are deeply involved in the religious activities of the world (Deut. 32:17; 1 Cor. 10:20–21). They also acknowledge the total superiority of Jesus Christ (Mark 1:24). Yet despite all of that knowledge, the demons are utterly and eternally lost.

In the same way, people can have knowledge of spiritual things (Rom. 1:21), believe the truth (John 2:23–25), fear God's judgment (cf. Rev. 6:15–17 with 9:20–21), feel guilt (Acts 24:25; Felix's guilt made him afraid), desire to have eternal life (the rich young ruler desired salvation but did not get it; Matt. 19:16,22), be outwardly religious (like the scribes and Pharisees; Matt. 5:20), and affirm the superiority of Jesus Christ (the same crowd that hailed Him as the Messiah on Sunday of Passion Week [Matt. 21:9] screamed for His blood on Friday [Matt. 27:22–25]), yet die in their sins.

The following are some of the key marks of the faith that does save. (For a more complete discussion of the marks of true faith, see John MacArthur, *Saved Without a Doubt* [Wheaton, Ill: Victor, 1992]; Gardiner Spring, *The Distinguishing Marks of Christian Character* [Phillipsburg, N.J., Presb. & Ref., n.d.]; Matthew Mead, *The Almost Christian Discovered* [Reprint; Beaver Falls, Pa.; Soli Deo Gloria, n.d.]

First, genuine faith is marked by penitence. Jesus said in the Beatitudes, "Blessed are the poor in spirit, for theirs is the kingdom of heaven" (Matt. 5:3). True faith produces an overwhelming sense of sinfulness, which causes believers to mourn over their sin (v. 4), be humble (v. 5), and acknowledge and confess their transgressions. In one of his penitential psalms David wrote, "I acknowledged my sin to You, and my iniquity I did not hide; I said, 'I will confess my transgressions to the Lord'; and You forgave the guilt of my sin" (Ps. 32:5). It is those who confess their sins who obtain mercy and forgiveness (Prov. 28:13; cf. 2 Sam. 12:13; 24:10). The apostle John wrote,

> If we walk in the Light as He Himself is in the Light, we have fellowship with one another, and the blood of Jesus His Son cleanses us from all sin. If we say that we have no sin, we are deceiving ourselves and the truth is not in us. If we confess our sins, He is faithful and righteous to forgive us our sins and to cleanse us from all unrighteousness. If we say that we have not sinned, we make Him a liar and His word is not in us. (1 John 1:7–10)

Those who refuse to turn from their sin give evidence that they have not experienced the transformation that takes place at salvation. After his conversion, Paul expressed the saints' normal attitude toward their sins: "Wretched man that I am! Who will set me free from the body of this death?" (Rom. 7:24). True believers desire what is right and pure, while recognizing the powerful force of sin in their nature that is still at work because they are not yet glorified. They know that what is wrong in them is not lack of self-esteem, mistreatment by other people, or childhood trauma, but sin. They hate their fallenness, because it dishonors the God whom they love and serve. Arthur Pink notes,

> One of the surest tests to apply to the professed conversion is the heart's attitude towards sin. Where the principle of holiness has been planted, there will necessarily be a loathing of all that is unholy. If our hatred of evil be genuine, we are thankful when the Word reproves even the evil which we suspected not. (*Profiting from the Word* [Edinburgh: Banner of Truth, 1977], 13)

Second, genuine faith is marked by desire for righteousness. In Matthew 5:6 Jesus said that the redeemed are "those who hunger and thirst for righteousness." True believers are marked not only by an aversion to sin but also by an attraction to righteousness. Their righteousness is internal, not external like that of the scribes and Pharisees (cf. Matt. 5:20). External righteousness does not murder; internal righteousness does not hate (vv. 21–22). External righteousness does not commit sexual sin; internal righteousness does not lust (vv. 27–28). External righteousness cleverly avoids false vows while still deceiving others; internal righteousness does not lie (vv. 33–37). External righteousness limits its vengeance to that prescribed by the Law; internal righteousness does not retaliate at all (vv. 38–42). External righteousness loves its friends and hates its enemies; internal righteousness loves its friends and its enemies (vv. 43–47). External righteousness parades itself before men (Matt. 6:1); internal righteousness longs to be perfect like its heavenly Father is (5:48).

Those whose faith is genuine seek to abstain from wickedness (2 Tim. 2:19), while those with false faith "profess to know God, but by their deeds they deny Him, being detestable and disobedient and worthless for any good deed" (Titus 1:16). The apostle John declared that "everyone also who practices righteousness is born of Him" (1 John 2:29; cf. 3:5–7, 10). Genuine saving faith produces a deep longing to obey God from the heart.

Third, genuine faith is marked by submission to divine authority. Sinners are rebels against God; saints are His willing servants. Jesus made it clear that those who would be His disciples must submit unreservedly to Him no matter what the cost:

> Now large crowds were going along with Him; and He turned and said to them, "If anyone comes to Me, and does not hate his own father and mother and wife and children and brothers and sisters, yes, and even his own life, he cannot be My disciple. Whoever does not carry his own cross and come after Me cannot be My disciple. For which one of you, when he wants to build a tower, does not first sit down and calculate

> the cost to see if he has enough to complete it? Otherwise, when he has laid a foundation and is not able to finish, all who observe it begin to ridicule him, saying, 'This man began to build and was not able to finish.' Or what king, when he sets out to meet another king in battle, will not first sit down and consider whether he is strong enough with ten thousand men to encounter the one coming against him with twenty thousand? Or else, while the other is still far away, he sends a delegation and asks for terms of peace. So then, none of you can be My disciple who does not give up all his own possessions. Therefore, salt is good; but if even salt has become tasteless, with what will it be seasoned? It is useless either for the soil or for the manure pile; it is thrown out. He who has ears to hear, let him hear." (Luke 14:25–35)

The rich young ruler refused to submit to Christ's authority and turned his back on Him (Matt. 19:16–22). Though no one, of course, understands at salvation all that submission to God entails, those who desire forgiveness and heaven at any cost gladly submit to His will whatever that may unfold for them.

Fourth, genuine saving faith is marked by obedience. Jesus pointedly asked, "Why do you call Me, 'Lord, Lord,' and do not do what I say?" (Luke 6:46). "Not everyone who says to Me, 'Lord, Lord,' will enter the kingdom of heaven," He declared, "but he who does the will of My Father who is in heaven will enter" (Matt. 7:21; cf. vv. 22–27). To those who professed faith in Him Jesus said, "If you abide in My word, then you are truly disciples of Mine" (John 8:31). In the Upper Room Discourse Jesus taught His disciples,

> If you love Me, you will keep My commandments. . . . If anyone loves Me, he will keep My word; and My Father will love him, and We will come to him and make Our abode with him. He who does not love Me does not keep My words; and the word which you hear is not Mine, but the Father's who sent Me. (John 14:15, 23–24; cf. 15:10)

John echoed his Master's words many decades later when he wrote,

> By this we know that we have come to know Him, if we keep His commandments. The one who says, "I have come to know Him," and does not keep His commandments, is a liar, and the truth is not in him; but whoever keeps His word, in him the love of God has truly been perfected. . . . The one who keeps His commandments abides in Him, and He in him. We know by this that He abides in us, by the Spirit whom He has given us. . . . By this we know that we love the children of God, when we love God and observe His commandments. For this is the love of God, that we keep His commandments; and His commandments are not burdensome. (1 John 2:3–5; 3:24; 5:2–3)

Those whose faith is real will "prove [themselves] doers of the word, and not merely hearers who delude themselves" (James 1:22).

Finally, genuine saving faith is marked by love, both for God and for other people. It is a mark of the elect that they love God (Rom. 8:28). According to James 2:5, God has promised His kingdom to those who love Him (cf. 1 Cor. 2:9). Believers prove themselves to be children of God by their love for Him (1 John 5:2). In contrast, those with false faith "do not have the love of God in [themselves]" (John 5:42; cf. 8:42). Instead, they are in love with the world (James 4:4; 1 John 2:15–16).

Love for other believers also characterizes those whose faith is genuine. They have "passed out of death into life, because [they] love the brethren. He who does not love abides in death" (1 John 3:14). False faith, on the other hand, is marked by a lack of love:

> The one who says he is in the Light and yet hates his brother is in the darkness until now. The one who loves his brother abides in the Light and there is no cause for stumbling in him. But the one who hates his brother is in the darkness and walks in the darkness, and does not know where he is going because the darkness has blinded his eyes. (1 John 2:9–11)

A true spiritual inventory does not focus on external behavior or religious activities but on the internal attitudes of the heart. Jesus' words to the church at Sardis, "I know your deeds, that you have a name that you are alive, but you are dead" (Rev. 3:1), stand as a sobering warning to all who profess a faith they do not possess. No amount of resolve or outward religious involvement can transform the heart; it is only in Christ that people become new creatures (2 Cor. 5:17). In the words of the great hymn writer Isaac Watts,

> How helpless guilty nature lies, unconscious of its load;
> The heart unchanged can never rise to happiness and God.
> The will perverse, the passions blind in paths of ruin stray,
> Reason debased can never find the safe, the narrow way.

> Can aught beneath a power Divine the stubborn will subdue,
> 'Tis Thine, Almighty Savior, Thine, to form the heart anew.
> O change these wretched hearts of ours and give them life divine,
> Then shall our passions and our powers, Almighty Lord, be Thine.

The Pattern of Sanctification: Obedience and Integrity
38
(2 Corinthians 13:7–10)

Now we pray to God that you do no wrong; not that we ourselves may appear approved, but that you may do what is right, even though we may appear unapproved. For we can do nothing against the truth, but only for the truth. For we rejoice when we ourselves are weak but you are strong; this we also pray for, that you be made complete. For this reason I am writing these things while absent, so that when present I need not use severity, in accordance with the authority which the Lord gave me for building up and not for tearing down. (13:7–10)

The New Testament is rich with images and metaphors that depict the duties and responsibilities of pastors and elders. They are pictured as leaders (Heb. 13:17, 24), overseers (Acts 20:28; Phil. 1:1; 1 Tim. 3:1, 2; Titus 1:7), shepherds (Acts 20:28; 1 Peter 5:2), teachers (Acts 13:1; 1 Cor. 12:28; Eph. 4:11), warners (1 Thess. 4:6), servants (1 Cor. 3:5; Col. 1:7; 1 Tim. 4:6), stewards (Titus 1:7), comforters (2 Cor. 1:4), and examples (Phil. 3:17; 2 Thess. 3:7, 9; 1 Tim. 4:12; Titus 2:7; 1 Peter 5:3).

But the one image that pulls all of those functions together is that of parents. Like pastors, parents lead, oversee, shepherd, teach, warn, serve, have a stewardship for, comfort, and are examples to their children.

Pastors, in turn, are like parents to their spiritual family, the church (cf. 1 Cor. 4:14–15; 2 Cor. 12:14).

Both the maternal and paternal aspects of the parental metaphor for spiritual leadership are in view in 1 Thessalonians 2:7–12:

> But we proved to be gentle among you, as a nursing mother tenderly cares for her own children. Having so fond an affection for you, we were well-pleased to impart to you not only the gospel of God but also our own lives, because you had become very dear to us. For you recall, brethren, our labor and hardship, how working night and day so as not to be a burden to any of you, we proclaimed to you the gospel of God. You are witnesses, and so is God, how devoutly and uprightly and blamelessly we behaved toward you believers; just as you know how we were exhorting and encouraging and imploring each one of you as a father would his own children, so that you would walk in a manner worthy of the God who calls you into His own kingdom and glory.

Like a "nursing mother," pastors tenderly care for their people, are fondly affectionate toward them, and labor sacrificially for them. They also exhort, encourage, and implore them "as a father would his own children." The result is believers who "walk in a manner worthy of the God who calls [them] into His own kingdom and glory."

Such a loving balance of tender care and strong instruction marks every faithful pastor. A true man of God is not concerned with building his reputation, padding the size of his congregation, or any other selfish pursuit. As it was with Paul, his consuming passion is the nurturing of his spiritual children to maturity. The apostle expressed the depth of that concern when he wrote to the Galatians: "My children, with whom I am again in labor until Christ is formed in you" (Gal. 4:19).

As he closed his letter, Paul summarized the elements necessary for spiritual growth. If they are to become like Jesus Christ, believers must deal with their sin. Therefore, he discussed the vital issue of repentance in 2 Corinthians 12:20–21, expressing his concern that the Corinthians turn from their sin and pursue godliness. Believers who fail to repent need the church to encourage that repentance through the discipline process (13:1–2). Just as children cannot develop maturity apart from submission to parental authority and discipline, so believers must also submit to those in authority in the church (13:3–4). And since believers must be authentic children before they can go on to spiritual maturity, they must examine themselves to be sure they are truly saved (13:5–6).

In this passage, Paul concludes the main body of his letter by addressing two more essential elements of the sanctification process: obedience and integrity.

OBEDIENCE

Now we pray to God that you do no wrong; not that we ourselves may appear approved, but that you may do what is right, even though we may appear unapproved. For we can do nothing against the truth, but only for the truth. For we rejoice when we ourselves are weak but you are strong; (13:7–9a)

One of the pastor's most essential duties is to **pray** for his people, and Paul's letters reflect his constant intercession for the churches. He prayed that the Ephesians would "know what is the hope of [God's] calling, what are the riches of the glory of His inheritance in the saints, and what is the surpassing greatness of His power toward us who believe" (Eph. 1:18–19). The apostle asked that the Philippians' "love [would] abound still more and more in real knowledge and all discernment, so that [they would] approve the things that are excellent, [and] be sincere and blameless until the day of Christ" (Phil. 1:9–10). His request for the Colossians was that they might

> be filled with the knowledge of His will in all spiritual wisdom and understanding, . . . walk in a manner worthy of the Lord, . . . [and] please Him in all respects, bearing fruit in every good work and increasing in the knowledge of God; [and be] strengthened with all power, according to His glorious might, for the attaining of all steadfastness and patience." (Col. 1:9–11)

To the Thessalonians he wrote, "Night and day [we] keep praying most earnestly that we may see your face, and may complete what is lacking in your faith" (1 Thess. 3:10), while in his second epistle to them he added,

> To this end also we pray for you always, that our God will count you worthy of your calling, and fulfill every desire for goodness and the work of faith with power, so that the name of our Lord Jesus will be glorified in you, and you in Him, according to the grace of our God and the Lord Jesus Christ. (2 Thess. 1:11–12)

The apostle also prayed for individuals within the churches, such as Timothy (2 Tim. 1:3) and Philemon (Philem. 4).

Overshadowing this passage, as they have the entire epistle, are the false apostles who were influencing the Corinthian church. Many in the congregation had become enamored with them, and as a result, they were partially successful in undermining the church's loyalty to Paul. The false teachers had viciously attacked him, denying that he was a genuine apostle of Christ. They managed to beguile some of the Corinthians into "seeking for proof of the Christ who [spoke] in [Paul]" (2 Cor. 13:3). Such questioning of Paul's apostolic authority was sinful folly. He had ministered among the Corinthians for almost two years (cf. Acts 18:11, 18), performing the signs of an apostle (2 Cor. 12:12). They had seen ample proof of his genuineness in their own regeneration.

As Paul wrote this epistle to affirm his authenticity in the face of the false apostles' attacks, he was not jealously guarding his own reputation. But he was very aware that if the church turned away from him it would be turning away from Christ.

It would have been natural, humanly speaking, for Paul to have wanted to come to Corinth to convincingly display his power. After all, the false apostles and their followers had scorned and mocked him as a weakling and a coward (cf. 1 Cor. 2:3). To boldly assert his authority and put them in their place would have been gratifying. Paul was willing to display his apostolic power if necessary (though not, of course, to gain revenge on his enemies; cf. Rom. 12:19), as he had already made clear (2 Cor. 12:20; 13:2; cf. 1 Cor. 4:21). But his concern for the Corinthians did not necessarily require his pressure. Instead he could **pray to God that** they would **do no wrong . . . but that** they would **do what is right.** His prayer was that the Corinthians' obedience would make it unnecessary for him to come to wield his authority and discipline them, or if he came, they would have repented so there would be nothing to confront. Paul's deepest desire for the Corinthians, as it was for the Philippians, was that they would "be sincere and blameless until the day of Christ; having been filled with the fruit of righteousness" (Phil. 1:10–11). Like a loving father, he was more concerned with his children's obedience than his own reputation.

As noted above, it was essential that the Corinthians accept Paul as a true apostle. Rejecting him in favor of the false teachers would be rejecting the truth of the gospel for Satan's lies. Thus, it was crucial for Paul to be **approved** by the Corinthians for what he really was, an apostle of Jesus Christ. Yet in a remarkable display of selflessness, Paul's main goal was **not that** he himself might **appear approved.** As important as that was for the reasons already noted, Paul, ironically, would gladly **appear unapproved** if the Corinthians' obedience obviated the need for him to display his apostolic power. Their purity and obedience took precedence over how men viewed him. Let the false apostles and their deceived followers go on considering him disqualified as an apostle; as long as the majority were living in obedience to the truth, Paul was content. The apostle knew that since God was his Judge, it was unimportant what men thought of him (1 Cor. 4:3–4).

The extent of Paul's selflessness may be seen in Romans 9:1–3, perhaps the most shocking statement he ever penned: "I am telling the truth in Christ, I am not lying, my conscience testifies with me in the Holy Spirit, that I have great sorrow and unceasing grief in my heart. For I could wish that I myself were accursed, separated from Christ for the sake of my brethren, my kinsmen according to the flesh." So intense was Paul's concern for his unbelieving Jewish brethren that if it were possible, he would be willing to go to hell if that would allow them to go to heaven. The apostle's concern mirrored that of Moses, who made a similar plea regarding his fellow Israelites in Exodus 32:32: "But now, if You will, forgive their sin—and if not, please blot me out from Your book which You have written!"

As one who rejoiced in it (1 Cor. 13:6), sought to manifest it (2 Cor. 4:2), always spoke it (2 Cor. 7:14), and lived it with complete integrity (2 Cor. 11:10), Paul could **do nothing against the truth.** *Alētheia* (**truth**) refers here to the whole of God's revelation in Scripture (cf. 6:7; John 17:17; Col. 1:5; 2 Tim. 2:15; James 1:18). If the Corinthians were living in obedience to the truth, Paul could not and would not discipline them. On the other hand, he would not hesitate to act decisively **for the truth** if some of the Corinthians persisted in disobedience. Loving the truth means honoring it, and Paul would not hesitate to confront those who strayed from it. In 1 Corinthians 5:3–5 he had delivered to Satan the man having an affair with his father's wife. In Galatians 2:11–14 he publicly rebuked Peter for his hypocrisy, while in 1 Timothy 1:20 he put Hymenaeus and Alexander out of the church for their errors.

Paul's willingness to be perceived as weak as long as his children were strong (cf. 1 Cor. 4:9–13) prompted him to write, **We rejoice when we ourselves are weak but you are strong.** His concern was that the Corinthians be obedient and **strong** (cf. 1 Cor. 16:13; Eph. 6:10; 2 Tim. 2:1). Nor did he mind appearing **weak** in the eyes of the world, even though actually he ministered in the power of God (2 Cor. 4:7; 6:7; 13:4). He had learned that weakness was the path to power; it was his human weakness that allowed God's strength to flow through him. Earlier in this letter he wrote, "Most gladly, therefore, I will rather boast about my weaknesses, so that the power of Christ may dwell in me. Therefore I am well content with weaknesses, with insults, with distresses, with persecutions, with difficulties, for Christ's sake; for when I am weak, then I am strong" (12:9–10).

INTEGRITY

this we also pray for, that you be made complete. (13:9*b*)

This quality of integrity or completeness sums up the elements previously mentioned: repentance (12:20–21), confronting sin through church discipline (13:1–2), submission to authority (13:3–4), authenticity (13:5–6), and obedience (13:7–9a). *Katartisis* (**complete**), which appears only here in the New Testament, means, "adequate," "fully qualified," or "sufficient." The related verb *katartizō* (cf. v. 11) has the basic idea of putting things in order, or in their proper place, or restoring or fixing something that is broken. In Matthew 4:21 it speaks of James and John mending fishing nets. Paul used it in Galatians 6:1 to describe restoring a sinning believer to fellowship with God.

Perhaps the English word *integrity* best expresses the meaning of *katartisis* in this passage. A person with integrity is one whose thoughts, beliefs, words, and actions are all in perfect harmony. For the Christian, integrity involves having every area of life in submission to the truth of God's Word, with nothing inconsistent or out of sync. A person with integrity is not like Talkative in *Pilgrim's Progress,* who was described by those who knew him as a saint abroad but a devil at home.

Integrity can be illustrated by the process of baking bread. If one merely put water, flour, yeast, sugar, salt, and other ingredients in a pan and put it in the oven, what came out would not be bread. An absolutely essential step in the bread-making process is to mix the ingredients together. So also must all the different "ingredients" in the life of a believer be properly mixed together to produce integrity.

Since the perfect picture of integrity is the Lord Jesus Christ, "who knew no sin" (2 Cor. 5:21; cf. Isa. 53:9; Heb. 7:26; 1 Peter 2:22; 1 John 3:5), the goal of integrity is to be like Him. That was a frequent request of Paul's when he prayed for believers. In Colossians 1:28–29, the apostle summarized the goal of his ministry as "proclaim[ing Christ], admonishing every man and teaching every man with all wisdom, so that we may present every man complete in Christ. For this purpose also I labor, striving according to His power, which mightily works within me." To the Galatians he wrote, "My children, with whom I am again in labor until Christ is formed in you" (Gal. 4:19). He described Epaphras to the Colossians as "always laboring earnestly for you in his prayers, that you may stand perfect and fully assured in all the will of God" (Col. 4:12).

Psalm 15 aptly and succinctly summarizes integrity. David wrote,

O Lord, who may abide in Your tent?
Who may dwell on Your holy hill?
He who walks with integrity, and works righteousness,
And speaks truth in his heart.
He does not slander with his tongue,
Nor does evil to his neighbor,
Nor takes up a reproach against his friend;

> In whose eyes a reprobate is despised,
> But who honors those who fear the Lord;
> He swears to his own hurt and does not change;
> He does not put out his money at interest,
> Nor does he take a bribe against the innocent.
> He who does these things will never be shaken.

Integrity flows from the heart to encompass every aspect of life.

The noble Old Testament saint Daniel's name is virtually synonymous with integrity, conviction, and an uncompromising life. Neither the allurements of the fabulous wealth of Nebuchadnezzar's court, the temptation to give in to the Babylonians' demands so he could attain political power and influence, nor the threat of the fiery furnace or the lions' den could sway him. Daniel remained wholly devoted throughout his long life to the truth of God's Word. (For a further discussion of integrity, see my book *The Power of Integrity* [Wheaton, Ill: Crossway, 1997].)

In verse 10 Paul concludes the main body of his epistle with what is in effect a one-sentence summary of this treatise: **For this reason I am writing these things while absent, so that when present I need not use severity, in accordance with the authority which the Lord gave me for building up and not for tearing down.** His goal in **writing these things while absent** from Corinth was **so that when** he was **present** with them again on his upcoming visit (12:14; 13:1) he **need not use severity** in confronting them (cf. Titus 1:13 where the same Greek word translated **severity** appears). He much preferred to use **the** positive **authority which the Lord gave** him **for building up** the Corinthians (cf. Rom. 14:19) **and not** the negative **for tearing** them **down.**

Paul then gave a final warning. If the situation warranted—if some of the Corinthians persisted in their sin and defiance of the Word and will of the Lord—he would not hesitate to act. *Kathairesis* (**tearing down**) could also be translated "destruction," or "demolition." Paul used it in 10:8, where he also spoke of using his authority to edify the Corinthians, not to destroy them. He fervently hoped they would heed the rebukes in this letter so his third visit could be different from his second one, which was so sad and painful for him (2:1).

Did Paul succeed? Did the Corinthians heed his admonitions, repent, and turn away from the false teachers? Did they welcome Paul on his third visit? The apostle did, as he promised, visit Corinth again. Acts 20:2–3 records that he spent three months in Greece. Since verse 2 says that he came into Greece from Macedonia (the northern part of Greece; v. 1), and when he left he went back through Macedonia, "Greece" (v. 2) must refer to Achaia (the southern part of Greece). Since Corinth was located in Achaia, Paul undoubtedly spent most or all of that three-month period in that city. Though the New Testament offers no specific details of that visit, four lines of evidence suggest that the Corinthians responded positively to this letter and his visit to them was the joyful one Paul had hoped for.

First, Paul wrote Romans during this three-month stay in Corinth (cf. the references to Phoebe, Gaius, and Erastus—all of whom were associated with Corinth—in Romans 16). Nowhere in Romans did Paul express any concerns about his present situation. That implies that things were calm and peaceful while he was in Corinth.

Second, Paul wrote to the Romans about his plan to visit Spain via Rome (Rom. 15:24). If things were still chaotic in Corinth, it is unlikely that he would have had imminent plans to leave there.

Third, Romans 15:26–27 indicates that the Achaians (as noted above, Corinth was in Achaia) had responded to Paul's appeal regarding the collection for the Jerusalem church (2 Cor. 8, 9). The Corinthians would not likely have made that contribution (particularly by handing it over to Paul) if they still harbored doubts about whether he was a true apostle.

Finally, the inclusion of 2 Corinthians in the New Testament canon argues that the Corinthians responded favorably to the letter. Had it failed to achieve its purpose, it would not likely have been accepted by the church as Scripture.

This letter, in which Paul poured out his heart to the Corinthians, achieved its goal of reconciling them to him. Like the rest of Scripture, it will infallibly achieve what God designed it to achieve. As God declared through the prophet Isaiah,

> For as the rain and the snow come down from heaven,
> And do not return there without watering the earth
> And making it bear and sprout,
> And furnishing seed to the sower and bread to the eater;
> So shall My word be which goes forth from My mouth;
> It shall not return to Me empty,
> Without accomplishing what I desire,
> And without succeeding in the matter for which I sent it. (Isa. 55:10–11)

The Pattern of Sanctification: Perfection, Affection, and Benediction (2 Corinthians 13:11–14)

39

Finally, brethren, rejoice, be made complete, be comforted, be like-minded, live in peace; and the God of love and peace will be with you. Greet one another with a holy kiss. All the saints greet you. The grace of the Lord Jesus Christ, and the love of God, and the fellowship of the Holy Spirit, be with you all. (13:11–14)

In fighting the "the good fight of faith" (1 Tim. 6:12), Christians face three implacable foes: the world, the flesh, and the devil. The world is hostile to believers (as it was to their Lord; John 7:7), because though they were once part of it (Eph. 2:2), they are no longer. Jesus warned His followers, "Because you are not of the world, but I chose you out of the world, because of this the world hates you" (John 15:19; cf. 17:14; 1 John 3:13). Christians are not to love the world (1 John 2:15–16; cf. James 4:4) or be conformed to it (Rom. 12:2), but rather are to overcome it (1 John 5:4).

The flesh is man's unredeemed humanness. Unlike the external assaults from the world, it attacks people from the inside where they are weak (Matt. 26:41; Rom. 6:19). In light of that, Peter cautioned believers "to abstain from fleshly lusts which wage war against the soul" (1 Peter 2:11). The flesh is inherently evil (Rom. 7:18) and hostile to God (Rom. 8:7–8), and it produces unspeakably wicked deeds (Gal. 5:19–21). The redeemed "are not in the flesh but in the Spirit" (Rom. 8:9) and must not live as "men of flesh" (1 Cor. 3:1; cf. Rom. 8:12–13). To that end, they are to "make no provision for the flesh" (Rom. 13:14) and cleanse themselves from its defilements (2 Cor. 7:1).

Manipulating the world and the flesh to assault believers is the main operation of the devil, Satan. Once the most exalted of all created beings, the "anointed cherub who covers" (Ezek. 28:14; the reference is to Satan's privileged position as an angel guarding God's throne), he is now the epitome of evil. There is no truth in him, Jesus declared, but he is a liar by nature (John 8:44). In fact, he "disguises himself as an angel of light" (2 Cor. 11:14) to "[blind] the minds of the unbelieving so that they might not see the light of the gospel" (2 Cor. 4:4). Accuser (Rev. 12:10), tempter (1 Thess. 3:5), and hinderer (1 Thess. 2:18), Satan is indeed a formidable adversary, who threatens to devour believers if they are ignorant of his schemes (2 Cor. 2:11; Eph. 6:11). If they are to successfully resist him (James 4:7; 1 Peter 5:8–9), believers must "put on the full armor of God" (Eph. 6:11) and not give him an opening to attack them (Eph. 4:27).

Like all believers, the Corinthian church was under siege from those three formidable adversaries. The world system was exceptionally vile in Corinth, one of the most debauched cities of the ancient world. The city was so evil that in the Greek language "to Corinthianize" meant to go to bed with a prostitute. Unfortunately, much of the evil pervading the surrounding culture continued to find a foothold in the flesh of the Corinthians even after their salvation. As a result, they were falling victim to the sins that they had indulged in before they came to Christ. And the devil, who specializes in false religion, made his presence felt through the false apostles who deceived many of the Corinthians. As do all believers, they faced all three enemies.

As he drew this magnificent letter to a close, Paul gave a final summary of his concerns for the Corinthian church. He was not primarily concerned with their prosperity, success, health, comfort, self-esteem, or prestige. Instead, he listed three worthy goals that every pastor should have for his congregation: perfection, affection, and benediction. Along with repentance (2 Cor. 12:20–21), discipline (13:1–2), submission to authority (13:3–4), self-examination (13:5–6), obedience (13:7–9a), and integrity (13:9b), they form a strong defense against the world, the flesh, and the devil.

PERFECTION

Finally, brethren, rejoice, be made complete, be comforted, be like-minded, live in peace; and the God of love and peace will be with you. (13:11)

Finally introduces Paul's farewell remarks to his beloved **brethren** at Corinth (cf. 1:8; 8:1). The key to understanding this verse lies in the phrase **be made complete.** *Katartizō* (**be made complete**) is the verb form of the noun *katartisis,* (v. 9). It has the sense here not of adding something that is lacking, but of putting things in order, of adjusting things that are out of adjustment. It is used, for example, to speak of fishermen mending their nets (Matt. 4:21). Paul exhorted the Corinthians to mend their ways, to straighten themselves out, and restore harmony among themselves. Spiritual wholeness comes when the church, both collectively and individually, is in complete conformity to God's Word. To equip the saints to do so is the responsibility of the church's leaders (cf. Eph. 4:11–16).

As the imperative form of the verb *katartizō* indicates, believers are commanded to pursue integrity; it is not optional. As they grow in grace they must constantly reevaluate their priorities, get their behavior in line with Scripture, and be restored to spiritual wholeness. Theological errors need to be corrected; biblical knowledge needs to be increased; sin needs to be dealt with; violated relationships need to be restored; laziness, indifference, and apathy need to be turned into energetic, devoted service. In his first inspired letter to the Corinthians, Paul wrote, "Now I exhort you, brethren, by the name of our Lord Jesus Christ, that you all agree and that there be no divisions among you, but that you be made complete in the same mind and in the same judgment" (1 Cor. 1:10). To the Thessalonians he wrote, "We night and day keep praying most earnestly that we may see your face, and may complete what is lacking in your faith" (1 Thess. 3:10). Powerful evangelism is a by-product of spiritual integrity; it is the natural outflow of a church that is in holy harmony with God's will.

The Corinthians certainly needed to get things in order; to repent of their sin, reject the false teachers, and return to Paul, acknowledging him as the genuine apostle that he was and submitting to the truth of God he preached. To help them align themselves with God's truth, Paul gave them four final exhortations: four commands expressed by four imperative verbs.

The first is joy. Some translations (e.g., the KJV and NIV) render *chairete* (**rejoice**) "farewell" or "good-by," since the word was also used as a greeting (it is so used in Matt. 28:9) and a farewell. In that sense, it is similar to the Hebrew word *shalom,* which literally means "peace" but is also used for "hello," and "good-bye." Using *chairete* as a greeting was appropriate, because joy is essential in the life of the church.

Christians are to be characterized by joy. It is one of the fruits produced in their lives by the indwelling Holy Spirit (Gal. 5:22). Paul commanded the Philippians, "Rejoice in the Lord always; again I will say, rejoice!" (Phil. 4:4; cf. 2:18, 28; 3:1). In 1 Thessalonians 5:16 he wrote simply, "Rejoice always." Peter exhorted his readers to "keep on rejoicing" (1 Peter 4:13). Joy is part of the legacy the Lord Jesus Christ left His followers. "These things I have spoken to you," He told the apostles gathered in the Upper Room, "so that My joy may be in you, and that your joy may be made full" (John 15:11), and promised them, "I will see you again, and your heart will rejoice, and no one will take your joy away from you" (John 16:22). He asked the Father that His followers "may have [His] joy made full in themselves" (John 17:13). Scripture describes believers' joy as great (Luke 24:52; Acts 15:3), abundant (2 Cor. 8:2), overflowing (2 Cor. 7:4), animated (Luke 6:23), inexpressible (1 Peter 1:8), and full of awe (Ps. 2:11).

Christian joy is not a giddy, superficial happiness that can be devastated by illness, economic difficulties, broken relationships, or the countless other vicissitudes and disappointments of life. Instead, it flows from the deep, unshakable confidence that God is eternally in control of every aspect of life for the good of His beloved children—a confidence rooted in the knowledge of His Word. God's character, the saving work of Christ, the sanctifying work of the Holy Spirit, divine providence, spiritual blessings, the promise of future glory, answered prayer, and Christian fellowship all cause believers to rejoice.

The second exhortation is to submit. *Parakaleō* (**be comforted**) can refer to speaking authoritatively (cf. Luke 3:18; Acts 2:40; 20:1–2; Rom. 12:8; 1 Cor. 1:10; 4:16; 14:31; 1 Thess. 4:1; 2 Thess. 3:12; 2 Tim. 4:2; Titus 1:9; 2:15; 1 Peter 5:1, 12) and could probably be better translated here, "exhorted" or "admonished." Submission to authority was essential if the Corinthians were to get their church in order. That is why Paul told them in 1 Corinthians 4:14, "I do not write these things to shame you, but to admonish you as my beloved children."

The command to **be like-minded** reveals a third exhortation: Be committed to the truth. The Greek phrase translated **be like-minded** literally means, "think the same thing" or "have the same convictions and beliefs." The conformity Paul called for is the antithesis of a shallow, superficial truce based on the notion that doctrine is divisive and everyone's opinion is equally valid. Nor is it a pragmatic working agreement with those who are not committed to "contend[ing] earnestly for the faith which was once for all handed down to the saints" (Jude 3). Paul called for believers to have a common understanding of and conformity to the truth of God's Word.

Paul exhorted the Philippians, "Only conduct yourselves in a manner worthy of the gospel of Christ, so that whether I come and see you or remain absent, I will hear of you that you are standing firm in one spirit, with one mind striving together for the faith of the gospel" (Phil. 1:27). Conformity must flow from "the unity of the faith," which is based on a true "knowledge of the Son of God," and results in spiritual maturity "to the measure of the stature which belongs to the fullness of Christ" (Eph. 4:13). Paul taught that like-mindedness comes from a common understanding of Scripture:

> For whatever was written in earlier times was written for our instruction, so that through perseverance and the encouragement of the Scriptures we might have hope. Now may the God who gives perseverance and encouragement grant you to be of the same mind with one another according to Christ Jesus, so that with one accord you may with one voice glorify the God and Father of our Lord Jesus Christ. (Rom. 15:4–6)

When believers together heed what is written in the Scriptures, they will "be of the same mind with one another according to Christ Jesus" and will "with one accord" and "with one voice glorify the God and Father of our Lord Jesus Christ." Instead of downplaying the significance of doctrine, the church is called to be "the pillar and support of the truth" (1 Tim. 3:15).

It must be clearly understood that unlike the enforced conformity found in cults and false religions, the Bible does not call for mindless submission to some religious system or authority. Even the apostle Paul could "do nothing against the truth, but only for the truth" (2 Cor. 13:8). The church does not adhere to an arbitrary human standard but to the Word of the living God.

The final demand Paul made of the Corinthians is unity, which underlies the command that they **live in peace.** Peace and unity flow logically from a common understanding of and submission to the Word of God. Even so, believers must pursue peace (Rom. 14:19) and be diligent to preserve it (Eph. 4:3). On the other hand, those who teach false doctrine "to draw away the disciples after them" (Acts 20:30) will shatter the church's unity. But when believers' minds are firmly fixed on the truth, the church will experience unity and peace.

The wonderful promise that attends obedience to these exhortations is divine blessing by the presence of the **God of love and peace.** He is called the **God of love** only here in Scripture but is several times referred to as the "God of peace" (Rom. 15:33; 16:20; Phil. 4:9; 1 Thess. 5:23; Heb. 13:20). As such, He is the source of both for His obedient children. When the church pursues spiritual wholeness, it will experience the powerful and enriching presence of God.

On the other hand, churches that lack joy, submission, truth, and unity will find themselves lacking God's blessing. "Therefore remember from where you have fallen, and repent and do the deeds you did at first," declared the Lord of the church to the Ephesian church, "or else I am coming to you and will remove your lampstand out of its place—unless you repent" (Rev. 2:5). To have their light put out would be the opposite of having God in their midst. Jesus warned the church at Pergamum, "'Therefore repent; or else I am coming to you quickly, and I will make war against them with the sword of My mouth" (Rev. 2:16). Instead of peace, He would bring war. To the church at Sardis the Lord declared, "Remember what you have received and heard; and keep it, and repent. Therefore if you do not wake up, I will come like a thief, and you will not know at what hour I will come to you" (Rev. 3:3). Obviously, a thief does not bring peace, and neither does the Lord come to disobedient churches in peace. Finally, He warned the nauseatingly lukewarm church at Laodicea, "Because you are lukewarm, and neither hot nor cold, I will spit you out of My mouth" (Rev. 3:16). Rather than enjoying His blessed presence, they would be cast away from Him.

It is not, of course, only perfect churches that enjoy the blessings of God's presence. There are no perfect churches, because all are made up of imperfect sinners. But those who diligently pursue completeness will enjoy the rich reward of God's presence in **love and peace.**

AFFECTION

Greet one another with a holy kiss. All the saints greet you. (13:12–13)

A **kiss** was a common form of greeting in the ancient Near East (cf. 2 Sam. 15:5; 20:9; Matt. 26:48; Luke 7:45). It typically was a cheek-to-cheek embrace between members of the same sex. In the early church it was not a mere formality, like a handshake in Western culture today. The **holy kiss** took on a special significance as a physical expression of brotherly love and mutual affection between church members (Rom. 16:16; 1 Cor. 16:20; 1 Thess. 5:26). David E. Garland notes, "A *holy* kiss represents something more than a social custom. It is a sign of mutual fellowship among persons of mixed social background, nationality, race, and gender who are joined together as a new family in Christ" (*2 Corinthians*, The New American Commentary [Nashville: Broadman & Holman, 1999], 554. Italics in original.). That it was to be a **holy** kiss eliminates any suggestion of sexual impurity. Unfortunately, it gradually became a formal, institutionalized part of the church's liturgy, lost its true meaning, and eventually faded from the church altogether. Today, it seems to be making a welcome comeback in some churches.

The brotherly love that Jesus commanded believers to demonstrate (John 13:34–35) is to be shown on every level. It involves sacrificial service and ministry to one another and compassionate meeting of needs. But brotherly love also involves affection. The **holy kiss** is a physical manifestation of that affection; in fact, Peter called it a "kiss of love" (1 Peter 5:14). It was often done at the Lord's Table, where repentant sinners would be visibly restored to fellowship with a physical embrace. Paul wanted the Corinthians, rocked by conflict, division, and sin, to display their affection openly, because he knew it would help break down the barriers between them.

Though distance prevented them from giving the Corinthians a holy kiss, **all the saints** with Paul when he penned this epistle still wished to **greet** (send their love to) their Corinthian brethren. They would have been Macedonians since, as noted in the introduction to this volume, 2 Corinthians was written from Macedonia (probably Philippi). Brotherly love, then, is not to be confined to members of the same congregation; it is to be shared by all believers.

BENEDICTION

The grace of the Lord Jesus Christ, and the love of God, and the fellowship of the Holy Spirit, be with you all. (13:14)

To pronounce a benediction is to solemnly invoke a blessing, and Paul frequently did so in his epistles (e.g., Rom. 1:7; 16:20; 1 Cor. 1:3; 16:23; Gal. 1:3–4; 6:18; Eph. 1:2; 6:23–24; Phil. 1:2; 4:23; Col. 1:2; 1 Thess. 1:1; 5:28; 2 Thess. 1:2; 3:18; Philem. 3). No New Testament benediction, however, is as theologically rich and profound as this one. It is the only one that mentions all three persons of the Trinity. Two important features of this magnificent benediction call for closer examination.

First, as noted above, it is a Trinitarian benediction, reflecting a truth that is central to the Christian faith. Paul does not give here a formal, systematic exposition of the doctrine of the Trinity; this Trinitarian statement just flowed in natural and uninhibited fashion from him, as every blessing in the Christian life flows from the triune God.

Obviously, the doctrine of the Trinity is essential to the Christian faith. Those who deny it commit idolatry by worshiping a nonexistent false god, and thereby forfeit the possibility of salvation. While it does not contain a formal, precise theological declaration of the doctrine of the Trinity in one statement, Scripture nonetheless clearly and unmistakably teaches that the one true God has eternally existed in three co-equal and co-eternal persons. The biblical proof for the doctrine of the Trinity can be summarized in a simple syllogism: The Bible teaches there is only one

God. Yet it calls three persons God. Therefore, the three persons are the one God.

That there is only one God is the undeniable teaching of Scripture. God Himself declared in Deuteronomy 32:39, "See now that I, I am He, and there is no god besides Me." "You alone are God," exclaimed David (Ps. 86:10). Through the prophet Isaiah, God made it clear that there is not now, never was, and never will be any other god: "'You are My witnesses,' declares the Lord, 'and My servant whom I have chosen, in order that you may know and believe Me and understand that I am He. Before Me there was no God formed, and there will be none after Me'" (Isa. 43:10). To the Corinthians, surrounded by pagan idolatry, Paul wrote, "Therefore concerning the eating of things sacrificed to idols, we know that there is no such thing as an idol in the world, and that there is no God but one" (1 Cor. 8:4). (See also Deut. 4:35, 39; 6:4; 1 Sam. 2:2; 2 Sam. 7:22; 22:32; 1 Kings 8:23, 60; 2 Kings 19:15, 19; 2 Chron. 6:14; Neh. 9:6; Ps. 18:31; Isa. 37:16, 20; 44:6, 8; 45:5–6, 21; 46:9; Joel 2:27).

The Bible calls God the Father in such passages as 1 Corinthians 15:24; Galatians 1:1, 3; Ephesians 6:23; Philippians 1:2; and Jude 1, as few would dispute.

But despite the teachings of various demonic cults to the contrary, the Son is also called God. John opened his gospel with a powerful affirmation of Christ's deity: "In the beginning was the Word [Jesus Christ; v. 14], and the Word was with God, and the Word was God" (John 1:1). The former skeptic Thomas (John 20:25) cried out when he saw the resurrected Christ, "My Lord and my God!" (v. 28). Romans 9:5 describes Jesus as "God blessed forever," while Titus 2:13 and 2 Peter 1:1 refer to Him as "our God and Savior." God the Father calls the Son God in Hebrews 1:8, saying to Him, "Your throne, O God, is forever and ever, and the righteous scepter is the scepter of His kingdom."

The Holy Spirit is also called God. In Acts 5:3 Peter asked Ananias, "Why has Satan filled your heart to lie to the Holy Spirit?" But in the next verse he told him, "You have not lied to men but to God." Second Corinthians 3:18 refers to the Holy Spirit as "the Lord, the Spirit."

Thus, Scripture plainly teaches the profound, incomprehensible reality of the triune God (cf. Isa. 48:16; Matt. 28:19; Luke 3:21–22; 1 Cor. 12:4–6).

But this benediction is not only Trinitarian but also redemptive. It is in salvation that the Trinity is most clearly seen. The **love of God** the Father caused Him to plan redemption and choose those who would be saved (John 3:16; Rom. 5:8–10). It was through the **grace of the Lord Jesus Christ** in dying as a sacrifice for sins that salvation was effected for the redeemed (Rom. 5:6; 1 Cor. 15:3; 1 Peter 3:18; 1 John 2:2). As a result of salvation, believers are ushered into the **fellowship of the**

Holy Spirit, as He indwells them (Rom. 8:9, 11; 1 Cor. 6:19; Gal. 4:6) and places them into the body of Christ (1 Cor. 12:13).

Paul's benediction forms a fitting conclusion to this epistle, which despite all its stern rebuke of the Corinthians' folly and sin ends on a note of blessing. It was the apostle's desire that the Corinthians put themselves in a position to experience all the blessings that salvation brings. It was with that goal in mind that he defended his commission and his message, and that he rebuked, encouraged, and prayed for them. There can be no higher goal for any faithful pastor than that his people would know the full riches God grants them through redemption.

Bibliography

Barclay, William. *The Letters to the Corinthians.* Revised Edition. Louisville: Westminster, 1975.

Barnett, Paul. *The Second Epistle to the Corinthians.* The New International Commentary on the New Testament. Grand Rapids: Eerdmans, 1997.

Barrett, C. K. *The Second Epistle to the Corinthians.* Black's New Testament Commentary. Peabody, Mass.: Hendrickson, 1997.

Carson, Donald A. *From Triumphalism to Maturity.* Grand Rapids: Baker, 1984.

Craddock, Fred B. "The Poverty of Christ," *Interpretation* 22 (Apr. 1968), 158–70.

Garland, David E. *2 Corinthians.* The New American Commentary. Nashville: Broadman & Holman, 1999.

Guthrie, Donald. *New Testament Introduction.* Revised Edition. Downers Grove, Ill: InterVarsity, 1990.

Harris, Murray J. "2 Corinthians" in Frank E. Gabelein, ed. *The Expositor's Bible Commentary,* Vol. 10. Grand Rapids: Zondervan, 1976.

Hughes, Philip E. *The Second Epistle to the Corinthians.* The New International Commentary on the New Testament. Grand Rapids: Eerdmans, 1992.

Kistemaker, Simon J. *II Corinthians.* Grand Rapids: Baker, 1997.

Kruse, Colin G. *The Second Epistle of Paul to the Corinthians.* The Tyndale New Testament Commentaries. Grand Rapids: Eerdmans, 1995.

Lenski, R. C. H. *The Interpretation of St. Paul's First and Second Epistles to the Corinthians.* Minneapolis: Augsburg, 1963.

Martin, Ralph P. *2 Corinthians.* Word Biblical Commentary. Waco, Tex.: Word, 1986.

McShane, Albert. *What the Bible Teaches: II Corinthians.* Kilmarnock, Scotland: John Ritchie Ltd., 1986.

Pfeiffer, Charles F. and Howard F. Vos. *The Wycliffe Historical Geography of Bible Lands.* Chicago: Moody, 1967.

Robertson, A. T. *The Glory of the Ministry.* New York: Revell, 1911.

Tasker, R. V. G. *The Second Epistle of Paul to the Corinthians.* The Tyndale New Testament Commentaries. Grand Rapids: Eerdmans, 1975.

Trench, Richard C. *Synonyms of the New Testament.* Reprint. Grand Rapids: Eerdmans, 1983.

Indexes

Index of Greek Words

Index of Scripture

19:16–22	470	25:46	201, 203, 210	9:43	465
19:21	278	26:2	145	10:14	267
19:27	414	26:4	481	10:21	191
19:28	414	26:8	267	10:41	267
20:17–19	412	26:14–16	272	12:30–31	84
20:18–19	145	26:24	212	12:42–44	280
20:20–23	155–56	26:28	97–98	12:42	279
20:24	267	26:39	156	12:44	279
20:25	342	26:41	37	14:4	267
20:26–28	343	26:45	269	14:31	239
20:34	123	26:48	486	14:41	269
21:15	267	26:63–64	43	14:58	163
21:19	468	26:69–74	139	14:61	393
21:33–39	387	27:3–5	266, 467	15:24	455
22:2–6	387	27:11	289	15:34	19
22:13	203, 249	27:14	447		
22:18	182, 293	27:19	177	**Luke**	
22:32	393	27:22–25	468	1:5–6	110
22:40	414	27:26	145	1:35	214
23	182	27:35	455	1:47	199
23:2–4	391	27:46	12, 215	1:71	204
23:3	182	27:66	45	1:78	20
23:11	345	28:9	483	2:7	292
23:13–16	182	28:18	290	2:22	110
23:23	182, 283	28:19	202, 208	2:24	292
23:24	58	28:19–20	201, 245,	2:36	110
23:25	182		257	3:8	266
23:27	126, 182	28:20	132	4:17–21	110
23:27–28	187–88,			4:18	45, 347
	249	**Mark**		4:22	123
23:29	182	1:24	468	4:35	123
23:33	182–83	1:41	123	5:5	388
23:34	389	3:13–19	307	5:7	248
23:37	191	3:14	413	5:8	139, 344
24:3	132	3:15	413	5:12	284
24:4–5	335	4:15	408	5:21	288
24:9	145	4:19	272	6:13	410
24:13	13	4:26–29	222	6:23	349, 484
24:35	417	4:38	292–93	6:26	230
24:36	19	5:19	123	6:35	257
24:51	203	5:23	204	6:38	273, 278, 299
25:15	280	6:2	414	6:46	470
25:21	349	6:3	292, 455	7:13	123
25:27	273	6:7	413	7:34	245
25:30	203, 249	6:13	413	7:45	486
25:31–32	177	6:21	284	8:1–3	292
25:41	191, 201,	6:31	269	8:13	467
	203, 210	7:21–22	309	8:13–14	467

8:36	204	20:23	127	3:16–17	319
8:50	204	20:34	132	3:16–18	216
9:1	413	20:47	392	3:18	89, 207
9:2	413	21:1–4	279	3:19	131–32, 249
9:23	145	22:3	408	3:33	45
9:38	284	22:20	115	3:36	89, 207
9:49	139	22:22	212	4:6	292–93, 388
9:54	139	22:31	408	4:7	293
9:58	291–92	22:31–32	17, 23	4:35	226
10:30	228	22:53	249	4:42	202
10:38	292	23:4	214	5:17–18	19
10:40	201	23:5	220	5:22	177
12:1	182	23:14	214	5:23	290
12:8	484	23:22	214	5:24	207, 210
12:11	315	23:34	52	5:27	177
12:15	279	23:41	214	5:30	347
12:18–19	317	23:43	395	5:36	414
12:19	269	23:47	214	5:39	110
12:33	232, 278	24:25	110	5:46	110
12:34	272	24:44	44	6:5	15
12:48	228	24:45	132	6:6	15
12:56	182	24:47	202–3	6:7–9	15
13:3	131	24:52	484	6:27	45
13:5	131			6:30	454
13:14	267	**John**		6:37	216
13:15	182	1:1	19, 488	6:37–40	168
13:23–24	191, 201	1:3	290	6:38	347
13:28	293	1:5	249	6:40	207
14:13	279	1:10	290	6:44	131
14:16	291, 279	1:12	89, 207, 216	6:47	207
14:25–35	469–70	1:14	113, 128, 132,	6:51	191, 202
14:27	25		162, 188	6:56	466
15:11–32	50	1:17	188, 461	6:65	216
16:8	132	1:22	168	6:70–71	410
16:10	279	1:29	133, 202, 214	7:7	2, 481
16:20	279	2:4	347	7:12	230
17:3	59	2:13–17	264	7:14–18	455
18:9–14	99	2:18	454	7:20	188
18:11	345	2:19	163	7:30	347
18:11–12	345	2:21	163	7:31	414
18:11–14	112	2:23–25	467	7:36	123
18:13	88	3:2	414	7:37–39	116
18:21	112	3:3	115, 243	7:49	194
18:30	132	3:4–10	248	8:12	112–13, 249
19:8	283	3:5	89, 115	8:17	447
19:37	414	3:7	243	8:20	347
19:41–44	191	3:16	202, 207,	8:24	19, 202–3,
19:47	284		212, 313		207, 249

8:31	467	15:13	238	2:32	147, 455
8:44	132, 230,	15:18–20	25, 220	2:41	274
	250, 408, 481	15:18–21	144, 387,	2:42	412
8:46	214		421–22	2:43	415, 417
8:48	188	15:19	2, 481	2:44–45	275
8:52	188	15:26	120	3:1–8	413
8:58	19, 290	16:1–4	387	3:13	145, 393
9:4	226	16:7	120	3:14	214
9:39	177	16:8	115	3:15	147, 455
9:45	134	16:11	132	3:18	212, 214
10:10–11	342	16:13	413–14	3:26	455
10:11	203, 213	16:22	275, 484	4:4	274
10:16	82	16:24	57	4:9	204
10:18	213	16:33	120, 149, 398	4:10	147, 455
10:20	188	17:2	123	4:12	89, 123,
10:25	414	17:5	290, 292		200–201,
10:27	82, 337	17:9	203		207, 217, 465
10:30	19	17:13	57, 484	4:13	85
11:12	204	17:14	481	4:27	45
11:47	414	17:15	112	4:29	85
12:3–6	292	17:17	476	4:30	415
12:31	132	17:20–23	186	4:32	275
12:35	249	17:21	269	4:33	413
12:37	414	17:33	203	4:34	275
12:46	134, 249	18:11	212	4:36–37	312
13–17	412	18:31	389	4:37	305
13:1	313	18:37	289	5:1–2	272
13:3–5	345	19:13	177	5:1–11	442
13:20	409	19:15	220	5:3	408, 488
13:27	408	19:25	188	5:3–4	113
13:27–29	292	19:28	293	5:5	272
13:34–35	58, 308,	20:17	19, 393	5:10	272
	487	20:25	488	5:12	415, 417
14:6	89, 128,	20:28	19	5:16	417
	188, 207			5:30	147, 455
14:9	19, 123	**Acts**		5:31	133, 266
14:11	414	1:1–3	412	5:34	157
14:15	470	1:8	202–2	5:40	389
14:16	120, 123	1:15–20	411	5:41	15, 25, 278
14:16–17	116	1:19	214	6:1	201, 312, 385
14:20	145, 466	1:21–22	307	6:8	417
14:23–24	470	1:21–26	411	7:6	23
14:26	120, 413	1:25	272	7:25	204
14:28	19	1:26	409	7:36	414
14:30	132	2:20	37, 484	7:51	110, 464
15:4–5	222	2:22	214	7:53	461
15:10	470	2:23	212, 455	8:1	275
15:11	51, 484	2:24	147, 455	8:1–3	386

Index of Subjects

MOODY
Publishers™

From the Word to Life

Lift your study to new heights with the *complete* MacArthur New Testament Commentary series.

Respected Bible scholar and author John MacArthur opens up the wonder of the New Testament, offering verse-by-verse analysis, theological insights, and points of application. These works are sure to enrich your study of the Bible, and indeed your faith.

The MacArthur New Testament Commentary series includes:

Matthew 1–7
Matthew 8–15
Matthew 16–23
Matthew 24–28
Mark 1–8
Mark 9–16
Luke 1–5
Luke 6–10
Luke 11–17
Luke 18–24
John 1–11
John 12–21
Acts 1–12
Acts 13–28
Romans 1–8
Romans 9–16
First Corinthians
Second Corinthians
Galatians
Ephesians
Philippians
Colossians & Philemon
First & Second Thessalonians
First Timothy
Second Timothy
Titus
Hebrews
James
First Peter
Second Peter & Jude
First–Third John
Revelation 1–11
Revelation 12–22

www.MoodyPublishers.com | 1-800-678-6928